OUR AMERICAN SISTERS

OUR AMERICAN ♀ SISTERS

Women in American Life and Thought

Third Edition

Jean E. Friedman
University of Georgia

William G. Shade
Lehigh University

D. C. HEATH AND COMPANY
Lexington, Massachusetts Toronto

Preface

Gloria Steinem recently appeared at Lehigh University to commemorate that formerly all-male institution's first decade of coeducation. Thirteen hundred people attended and responded enthusiastically to her message. She recalled an earlier appearance in 1970, when one-third that number turned out to jeer. That visit, along with the developments of the late 1960s, led in part to the publication of the first edition of *Our American Sisters*. Putting together a decent anthology at that time meant searching for a few obscure articles or excerpting segments from books dedicated to other subjects. In the 1970s, however, women's history in the United States came of age. The problem today is in choosing from the wide range of excellent articles and books that have appeared since 1970.

This new edition represents a major revision of the second edition, which appeared in 1976 and which proved to be extremely successful. In this edition we have attempted to respond to suggestions from friends and colleagues who have used previous editions in their classes. Accordingly, the basic structure of the book has been retained, and the essays reflect our conception of women's history as expressed in the introduction. *Our American Sisters* continues to be a comprehensive anthology of writings on the history of American women that includes extensive material on the colonial era and the nineteenth century. We have tried to choose essays that combine a high scholarly standard with a high level of readability.

The content, however, has greatly changed. There are ten new essays which incorporate the most recent scholarship and broaden the scope of the book. These essays reflect a greater regional, ethnic, and social diversity among women. The introductions to each section have been rewritten, and up-to-date bibliographies have been added to guide interested students.

Dozens of people have helped us in this effort. To the list of those we have noted in early editions, we would like to add Ann Knight, our editor; Peter Filene, Sally Kohlstedt, and Glenda Riley, who read the manuscript; and Bebe Crosby Miles, Mary Jane Capozzoli, Mary Lou Shade, and Susan Hurd Cumings, who performed various indispensable tasks.

J.E.F.
W.G.S.

Contents

3 ৬ The Progressive Impulse

4 ৬ The Illusion of Equality

Introduction

Two decades ago one of the leading historians in the United States warned his colleagues that their traditional approaches to American history seriously perverted the subject. At the time, David Potter was referring to the way in which historians have ignored women and belittled their role in American history. Major generalizations about the American character have totally ignored women, and when historians have commented upon women, their views have been wildly inconsistent. In part this situation was a product of ignorance. Only a handful of relevant monographs existed in the 1960s, and the treatment of women in general studies was woefully inadequate. Few aspects of the history of women in America had drawn serious attention. As late as 1969 Gerda Lerner could write, "The striking fact about the historiography of women is the general neglect of the subject by historians."

By the mid-1970s the situation changed dramatically. The emergence of the movement for women's liberation in the 1960s heightened women's consciousness of their position in American society and led to demands for college courses that would enable women to regain their history. By 1975 approximately ninety colleges offered interdisciplinary majors in Women's Studies; of the over 4,000 courses on women, there were approximately 300 on the history of American women. At the same time, historians—many of whom were feminists—revealed a new concern for the subject. The number of texts and monographs has grown geometrically. Scholarly journals are increasingly open to studies concerning women. Rarely does an issue of the *American Quarterly*, *Journal of Social History*, or *Journal of Interdisciplinary History* fail to include at least one relevant article, and new journals such as *Feminist Studies*, *Women's Studies*, and *Signs* are devoted

1

entirely to the subject.* Conferences on the history of women have been sponsored across the country. The programs of the annual meetings of major historical organizations feature growing numbers of sessions on women. By almost any measure, the history of women is now attracting unparalleled interest.

The origins of this dramatic change in the historical treatment of women can be found in the shift in attitudes toward women in American society, in the rise of women's professional aspirations and their place in the history profession, and in a renewed interest in social history and historical sociology. Although all historians of women are not feminists—feminist history is not simply propaganda for the movement—the revival of interest in the history of women is intimately linked to the revival of feminism in the past decade.

Earlier in this century, the passage of the Nineteenth Amendment sparked a good deal of professional interest in the history of American women, and a number of major books on the subject appeared during the interwar period. Feminism was probably in better repute in the 1920s than at any time in American history. During that decade the birth rate fell precipitously, and increasing numbers of women entered graduate schools. The proportion of women earning M.A.'s and Ph.D.'s rose dramatically to a high point in 1930 and then declined slightly during the Great Depression. The number of women college professors grew, and women played a relatively more important role within the history profession than they do today. At the time that this generation of women was entering the history profession, several influential historians evidenced heightened interest in the role of women in history, as part of their rebellion against the legalistic and narrowly political focus of their predecessors.

The fascination of Progressive historians with social and economic aspects of history and their tendency to view American history in terms of the conflict between conservatives and reformers led at least two of the most important and widely read male historians of this era to study the role of women in American history. In 1922, Arthur Schlesinger, in *New Viewpoints in American History*, included an essay on women that protested "the pall of silence" cast over the subject. Later in the decade Charles and Mary Beard co-authored the extremely influential, *The Rise of American Civilization*, which devoted a large amount of

---

*In the past decade eleven historical journals have devoted entire issues to aspects of women's history: *American Jewish History* 70 (September 1980); *American Quarterly* 22 (Winter 1978); *Baptist History and Heritage* 12 (January 1977); *Current History* 70 (May 1976); *History of Education Quarterly* 15 (Spring 1974); *Journal of Presbyterian History* 52 (Summer 1974); *Journal of Urban History* 4 (May 1978); *Labor History* 17 (Winter 1976); *Teacher's College Record* 76 (February 1974); *Pacific Historical Review* 49 (May 1980); and *Utah Historical Quarterly* 46 (Spring 1978).

space to women, emphasizing their economic importance. During the interwar years men and women influenced by the Progressive school integrated discussions of women's roles into studies of social history and produced a number of classic monographs on women in America.

Although historians trained in the 1920s and 1930s maintained their concern for the history of women, by 1940 a reversal of earlier trends became apparent. The feminists, whose story Schlesinger thought "one of the noblest chapters in the history of American democracy," fell into increasing public disrepute. The birth rate rose dramatically as the post-World War II generation of women appeared dominated by what sociologist Jesse Bernard has called the "Motherhood Mania." The percentage of women completing M.A. and Ph.D. degrees declined as the birth rate climbed. Not only did the attitude of women toward competition in the academic world change, but the attitudes of academic men toward women changed for the worse. During this strange interlude, attention to the history of women faded; even areas of American life in which women had traditionally played important roles went unstudied. When families in America were once again growing and the role of the homemaker was exalted in the media, the historical study of the family languished. The study of political, diplomatic, and economic elites characterized the historiography of these years.

Since the early 1960s the fortunes of the history of women have changed as each of the trends that characterized the preceding decades was reversed. Feminism and feminist issues have gained renewed popularity. In the late 1950s, the birth rate once again began to fall. Each year the number of young women choosing to continue their education increased. Although the proportion of women holding Ph.D.'s in history has not yet reached the level of the 1920s, it has risen dramatically since the nadir of the 1950s. At the same time the attitudes of male colleagues born since the late 1930s represent a distinct improvement over those of the previous generation. Finally, the 1960s witnessed a revival of interest in social history and the processes of social change that has broadened the concept of legitimate subjects of history. The "new" social history, which studies sexual behavior and sex roles, the effects of demographic change, religious and ethnic conflict, and marriage and the family, has suddenly "rediscovered" women everywhere in the American past.

Before the present revival of women's history, most historians writing on women focused narrowly upon the history of the feminist movement and what Schlesinger called women's "contributions to American national progress." Since this approach characterized the writings of the feminist chroniclers, it was only natural that the

Progressive historians, who were sympathetic to the feminist cause and concerned with reform, carried these views over into professional history. But a more comprehensive approach to the history of women is necessary if we are to recapture the wealth and texture of women's lives in the American past.

A general consideration of the current scholarship suggested to us a rather crude taxonomy which has served to organize the essays in this book. We have divided American history into four chronological periods of rather unequal length, but which nonetheless seem to present a sense of surface continuity in relation to the history of American women. Each section is preceded by an introduction that outlines the major unifying themes of the period and relates the essays to these themes. Within each period we have attempted to include material bearing on the three most distinctive aspects of the history of American women: society's definition of the nature of women and their proper roles; the actual conditions of women and the social and economic functions that they performed; and women's response to their special intellectual, socioeconomic, and political problems. Finally, several essays have been included to show the differential effects of changes in these areas on subgroups of women, in order to take into account the effects of region, class, race, religion, and ethnicity. It is our hope that this relatively simple organizational structure will highlight the importance of the essays and facilitate the integration of this excellent recent scholarship into a more comprehensive framework for the study of the American past.

ᖰSuggested Readings

General Histories and Collections of Essays

Banner, Lois. *Women in Modern America*. Englewood Cliffs, N.J.: Prentice-Hall, 1975.

Berkin, Ruth Carol, and Norton, Mary Beth, eds. *Women of America: A History*. Boston: Houghton Mifflin Co., 1979.

Cantor, Milton and Laurie, Bruce, eds. *Sex, Class and the Woman Worker*. Westport: Greenwood Press, 1977.

Cott, Nancy F. and Pleck, Elizabeth H., eds. *A Heritage of Her Own*. New York: Simon & Schuster, 1979.

Degler, Carl. *At Odds: Women and the Family in America from the Revolution to the Present*. New York: Oxford University Press, 1980.

Demos, John, and Boocock, Sarane Spence, eds. *Turning Points: Historical and Sociological Essays on the Family*. Chicago: University of Chicago Press, 1978.

Flexner, Eleanor. *Century of Struggle: The Women's Rights Movement in the United States*. Cambridge: Harvard University Press, 1975.

George, Carol V.R., ed. *"Remember the Ladies": New Perspectives On Women in American History*. Syracuse: Syracuse University Press, 1975.

Goodfriend, Joyce, and Christie, Claudia. *Lives of American Women: A Survey with Documents*. Boston: Little, Brown & Co., 1981.

Gordon, Michael, ed. *The American Family in Social-Historical Perspective*. New York: St. Martin's Press, 1978.

Gornick, Vivian, and Morgan, Barbara K., eds. *Woman in a Sexist Society: Studies in Power and Powerlessness*. New York: Basic Books, 1971.

Hareven, Tamara K., ed. *Family and Kin in Urban Communities, 1700–1930*. New York: New Viewpoint, 1977.

_____, ed. *Transitions: The Family and Life Course in Historical Perspective*. New York: Academic Press, 1978.

_____, and Vinovskis, Maris A., eds. *Family and Population in Nineteenth Century America*. Princeton: Princeton University Press, 1979.

Harley, Sharon, and Tenborg-Penn, Rosalyn, eds. *The Afro-American Woman: Struggles and Images*. Port Washington, N.Y.: Kenniket Press, 1978.

Harris, Barbara J. *Beyond Her Sphere: Women and the Professions in American History*. Westport, Conn.: Greenwood Press, 1978.

Hartman, Mary, and Banner, Lois W., eds. *Clio's Consciousness Raised: New Perspectives on the History of Women*. New York: Harper & Row, 1974.

Hymowitz, Carol, and Weissman, Michaele. *A History of Women in America*. New York: Bantam Books, 1978.

James, Edward T., and James, Janet W., eds. *Notable American Women, 1607–1950: A Biographical Dictionary*. 3 vols. Cambridge: Harvard University Press, 1971.

James, Janet Wilson, ed. *Women and American Religion*. Philadelphia: University of Pennsylvania Press, 1980.

Kessler-Harris, Alice. *Women Have Always Worked: A Historical Overview*. New York: McGraw-Hill, 1981.

Lerner, Gerda. *The Woman in American History*. Reading, Mass.: Addison-Wesley, 1971.

_____. *The Majority Finds Its Past*. New York: Oxford University Press, 1979.

Oakly, Ann. *Women's Work: The Housewife Past and Present*. New York: Vintage Books, 1974.

Rabb, Theodore K., and Rothberg, Robert I., eds. *The Family in History*. New York: Harper & Row, 1973.

Riegel, Robert E. *American Women: A Story of Social Change*. Teaneck, N.J.: Fairleigh-Dickinson Press, 1970.

Rosaldo, Michelle Zimbalist, and Lamphere, Louise, eds. *Women, Culture and Society*. Stamford: Stamford University Press, 1974.

Rosenberg, Charles, ed. *The Family in History*. Philadelphia: University of Pennsylvania Press, 1975.

Rothman, Sheila. *Woman's Proper Place: A History of Changing Ideas and Practices, 1870 to the Present*. New York: Basic Books, 1978.

Ryan, Mary P. *Womanhood in America From Colonial Times to the Present*. New York: New Viewpoints, 1975.

Sinclair, Andrew. *The Better Half*. New York: Harper & Row, 1965.

Smith, Page. *Daughters of the Promised Land*. Boston: Little, Brown & Co., 1970.

Sochen, June. *Herstory: A Woman's View of American History*. New York: Alfred Publishing Co., 1974.

_____. *Movers and Shakers: American Women Thinkers and Activists 1900–1970*. New York: Quadrangle Books, 1973.

Historiography

Carroll, Berenice A., ed. *Liberating Women's History: Theoretical and Critical Essays*. Urbana: University of Illinois Press, 1976.

Freedman, Estelle B. "The New Woman: Changing Views of Women in the 1920s." *Journal of American History* 61 (1974): 372–93.

Gordon, Ann D., Buhle, Mari Jo, and Schrom, Nancy E. "Women in American Society: An Historical Contribution." *Radical America* 5 (1971): 3–66.

Gordon, Linda, Pleck, Elizabeth, Hunt, Persis, Scott, Marcia, and Ziegler, Rochelle. "A Review of Sexism in American Historical Writing." *Women's Studies* 1 (1972): 133–58.

Green, Rayna. "Review Essay: Native American Women." *Signs* 6 (1980): 248–67.

Jensen, Joan M., and Miller, Darlis. "The Gentle Towners Revisited: New Approaches to the History of Women in the American West." *Pacific Historical Review* 49 (1980): 173–213.

Kruppa, Patricia S. "The American Woman and the Male Historian." *Social Science Quarterly* 55 (1974): 605–14.

Lerner, Gerda. "New Approaches to the Study of Women in American History." *Journal of Social History* 3 (1959): 53–62.

_____. "Women's Rights and American Feminism." *The American Scholar* 40 (1971): 235–48.

_____. "Placing Women in History: Definitions and Challenges." *Feminist Studies* 3 (1975): 5–14.

Norton, Mary Beth. "Review Essay: American History." *Signs* 5 (1979): 324–37.

Potter, David. "American Women and the American Character." In *American Character and Culture: Some Twentieth Century Perspectives*, edited by John A. Hague, pp. 65–84. Deland, Florida: Everett Edwards Press, 1964.

Sickerman, Barbara, Monter, E. William, Scott, Joan Wallach, Schlar, Kathryn Kish. *Recent United States Scholarship on the History of Women*. Washington: American Historical Association, 1980.

Sickerman, Barbara. "A Review Essay: American History," *Signs* 1 (1975): 461–85.

Sklar, Kathryn Kish. "American Female Historians in Context, 1770–1930," *Feminist Studies* 3 (1975): 171–84.

Smith-Rosenberg, Carroll. "The New Woman and the New History," *Feminist Studies* 3 (1975): 185–98.

Watkins, Bari. "Women and History." In *Women on Campus: The Unfinished Liberation*, pp. 95–101. New Rochelle, N.Y.: Change Magazine, 1975.

Zangrando, Joanna Schneider. "Women in the Archives: An Historian's View of the Liberation of Clio." *American Archivist* 36 (April 1972): 203–14.

_____. "Women's Studies in the United States: Approaching Reality." *American Studies International* 14 (Autumn 1975): 15–36.

Anthologies of Primary Sources

Baxandall, Rosalyn, Gordon, Linda, and Reverby, Susan, eds. *America's Working Women: A Documentary History, 1600–Present*. New York: Vintage Books, 1976.

Brownlee, W. Elliot, and Brownlee, Mary H., eds. *Women in the American Economy: A Documentary History, 1675–1927*. New Haven: Yale University Press, 1976.

Buhle, Mary Jo, and Buhle, Paul, eds. *The Concise History of Woman Suffrage*. Urbana: University of Illinois Press, 1978.

Cott, Nancy F., ed. *Root of Bitterness: Documents of the Social History of American Women*. New York: E.P. Dutton & Co., 1972.

Cooper, James L., and Cooper, Sheila M., eds. *The Roots of American Feminist Thought*. Boston: Allyn & Bacon, 1973.

Kraditor, Aileen, ed. *Up From the Pedestal: Selected Writings in the History of American Feminism*. Chicago: Quadrangle Books, 1968.

Lerner, Gerda, ed. *Black Women in White America*. New York: Pantheon Books, 1972.

_____. *The Female Experience*. Indianapolis: Bobbs-Merrill, 1977.

Martin, Wendy, ed. *The American Sisterhood*. New York: Harper & Row, 1972.

Morgan, Robin, ed. *Sisterhood is Powerful*. New York: Vintage, 1970.

Parker, Gail, ed. *The Oven Birds: American Women on Womanhood, 1820–1920*. Garden City, N.Y.: Doubleday, 1972.

Rossi, Alice S., ed. *The Feminist Papers: From Adams to de Beauvoir*. New York: Columbia University Press, 1973.

Seller, Maxine, ed. *Immigrant Women*. Philadelphia: Temple University Press, 1981.

Schneir, Miriam, ed. *Feminism: The Essential Historical Writings*. New York: Random House, 1973.

Scott, Anne F., ed. *The American Woman: Who Was She?* Englewood Cliffs, N.J.: Prentice-Hall, 1972.

Scott, Anne F., and Scott, Andrew M. *One Half the People: The Fight for Women Suffrage.* New York: J.B. Lippincott Co., 1975.

Sochen, June, ed. *The New Feminism in Twentieth Century America.* Lexington, Mass: D.C. Heath and Co., 1971.

1 Colonial Women

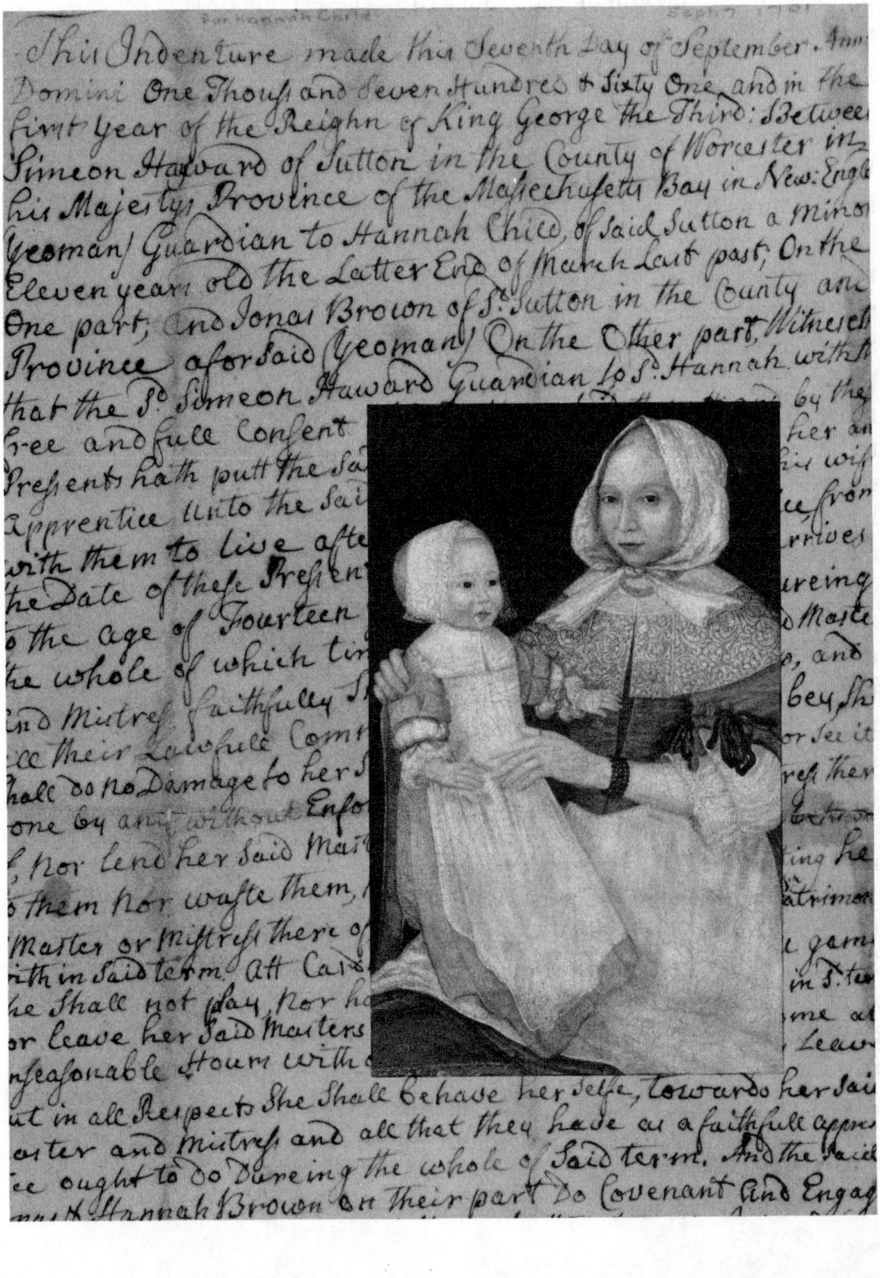

From the settlement of Jamestown until the outbreak of the American Revolution, the colonists struggled to establish a stable society based upon the English model. In each new settlement they recreated familiar social, political and economic institutions in an attempt to reaffirm the ideals and values of English civilization. The new environment and the absence of central authority however, altered institutions and attitudes sometimes immediately, but more often gradually. Colonial society slowly evolved into one quite different from that of the Mother Country; by the mid-eighteenth century, the transplanted Englishman had become a "new man," an American. The effects of this process upon the status of women highlight their anomalous position in American history.

The first mainland colonies were founded as business ventures, and it was not until the decision was made to establish societies in the New World that any significant number of women were transported across the Atlantic. The fact that men outnumbered women throughout the colonial period accounted for the earlier age at which colonial women married and the greater liberties and privileges they enjoyed in relation to European women. Colonial women existed as essential subordinates, however, in a largely patriarchial culture where they were subject to paternal decisions. A father's control of the land gave him the power to determine his daughter's marriage partners and settlements, and to delay property inheritance. Nonetheless, several meliorating circumstances—the scarcity of women, isolation of settlements and a limited labor supply—increased the woman's value to the family and the community. Carl Degler has emphasized that "the wife and mother in the rude settlement on or near the frontier was more than a housekeeper; she was an indispensable part of the apparatus of survival." In an economy dominated by farms and small shops, women worked side by side with men and often ran large plantations or carried on the family business following the death of a husband or father. Of necessity, few jobs were deemed inappropriate for colonial women, and they worked outside the home as blacksmiths and barbers, tanners and tavern keepers. Their contributions, however, were still considered marginal to the market economy.

The lives of most women were generally circumscribed within the family, where wives were expected to be subservient to their husbands. Political rights were almost completely restricted to men as heads of families, and access to the professions was closed to women on the grounds that they should, in the words of John Winthrop, "refrain from such things as proper for men whose minds are stronger." Although colonial Americans considered piety a major feminine grace, only a few denominations allowed women to preach. In general they followed the admonition of St. Paul that "women keep silent in the churches." In "The Case of the American Jezebels," Lyle Koehler discusses Anne Hutchinson, the most famous woman preacher of the colonial era. Koehler focuses on women's frustration with the limitations imposed upon them by traditional roles and by the magistrates' fears of the socially destructive consequences of women's departure from their proper sphere. In this way, he provides an entirely new perspective on the Antinomian controversy of the 1630s in Massachusetts Bay. As Mary Ryan has reminded us, colonial Americans "viewed the whole of society as an intricate series of ranks, a profusion of finely graded positions of authority and subordination, which neither male nor female could circumvent." Violation of gender norms, therefore, seemed to invite moral and civil anarchy threatening the entire social order and undermining the very basis of civilization as they knew it.

The family was an essential element of the community and a sphere in which women shared joint responsibility for a variety of religious, social and economic functions. The roles of husband and wife were less neatly compartmentalized than they would become in the nineteenth century. This cooperation and intimacy between husbands and wives sometimes led colonial women into business and political affairs where they shared their husbands' lives, mending political fences or fomenting revolution.

The Puritan community placed strong emphasis on the social role of the family and on close surveillance of moral life. Yet, the New England colonists were neither so unrealistic about human nature nor so sexually repressive as has often been charged. They were well aware that sexual intercourse was a human necessity and believed that marriage was the proper place for it. Although they were unable to contain all sexual impulses wholly within the bounds of marriage— illicit sexual intercourse was common—the Puritan magistrates encouraged early marriage and took every means to insure peaceful cohabitation. Adultery was severely punished, but divorces and annulments were relatively easy to obtain.

Perhaps the most interesting aspect of the Puritan attitude toward sexual intercourse was the degree to which the magistrates acknowledged and respected sexual needs of women as well as men. John Demos's analysis of the court records of Plymouth in "Husband and Wives" reveals only minor traces of a double standard. Patterns of decision making within the family show that in their day-to-day lives these women stood more nearly equal to their husbands than has generally been supposed. This may explain why foreign observers believed these women occupied a higher status than their European counterparts. Sexual roles were not rigidly defined, and mutuality of obligation and affection often characterized Puritan marriages.

Outside colonial New England, beyond the reaches of the Puritan social order, women retained even more bargaining power regarding their economic status. As Lois Green Carr and Lorena S. Walsh show in "The Planter's Wife," most women who emigrated into seventeenth-century Maryland were indentured servants who married after their term of service. Because they were outnumbered by men, they had a relatively free choice of partners. Once married, women labored to increase their husband's property and status. Recognition of the contribution made by women to the marital partnership led husbands to bequeath more than the customary one-third of their property to wives and, in addition, to name the wives executors of their estates. One such woman was the remarkable Margaret Brent, executrix of the estate of Governor Leonard Calvert. She has been described by Julia Cherry Spruill as one of the "most prominent personages" in Maryland, "whose business and public activities fill many pages of court records."

By the eighteenth century, common social practice, specific legislation, and the development of equity law freed married women from complete domination by their husbands and gave them a certain amount of legal autonomy unknown under the Common Law. In contrast to the English double standard, the New England colonies maintained a single standard of sexual fidelity. In "Divorce and the Changing Status of Women in Eighteenth-Century Massachusetts," Nancy Cott shows that Whiggish trends at the time of the War for Independence resulted in the revival of the Puritan morality that distinguished Republican "virtue" from English "corruption." As a result, divorces, which had been rare, were granted to increasing numbers of women on the grounds of adultery. It should not be forgotten, however, that colonial society was basically masculine in orientation. Attitudes toward women during the period remained traditional, differing little from those of contemporary Europeans. The belief in the inferiority of women was universal. While American women were far better off than their English sisters and in some areas their legal position improved during this period, women, particularly those who were married, suffered numerous legal and social restrictions imposed by the widespread acceptance of the idea of coverture.

During the Revolution, American women aided the patriot cause in a variety of ways. They voiced opposition to the Stamp Act, the hated tea tax and the Coercive Acts; they formed the Daughters of Liberty as a counterpart to the Sons of Liberty. Two famous women, Ester De Berdt Reed and Sara Bache, Benjamin Franklin's daughter, headed an effort to supply troops with badly needed clothing, and many lesser-known women moved into the growing, war-related textile industry. Although the American Revolution produced no great heroine, Molly Pitcher and Margaret Corbin were noted for their courage in battle, and Deborah Sampson Gannett later claimed to have served in the Continental Army disguised as Robert Shurtleff. One Philadelphia woman wrote her husband detailing her support for the Revolution, "I know this—that as free I can die but once; but as a slave I shall not be worthy of life. I have the pleasure to assure you that these are the sentiments of all my sister Americans." Yet the Revolution brought only modest change in women's status or men's attitudes toward them. The brilliant and witty Abigail Adams chided her husband, "I cannot say, that I think you are very generous to the ladies; for whilst you are proclaiming peace and goodwill to men, emancipating all nations, you insist upon retaining an absolute power over all wives."

Joan Hoff Wilson's essay, "The Illusion of Change: Women and the American Revolution," argues that colonial women's gains during these years were due to the sexual imbalance and the labor shortage and thus reflected necessity rather than "any fundamental change in sexist values transplanted from Europe." In tracing economic and demographic changes in the Revolutionary period, Wilson reveals that new technological demands created by the war encouraged a specialization that changed women's economic function. Women's status in the household was reduced and new social institutions, such as schools, increasingly discharged traditional parental responsibilities. The decline of parental authority, the glorification of motherhood, women's circumscribed sphere of influence and growing sexual repression characterized the "family in transition."

The education of women mirrored the society's attitudes. Illiteracy among women was rampant with perhaps as many as two-thirds of the women in sixteenth-century New England unable to sign their names. In the following century, women's literacy improved, but even at the end of the colonial period Kenneth A. Lockridge has shown that "female illiteracy remained quite common and women were always at a distinct disadvantage in obtaining basic education." Even those in school found opportunities limited. In the lower grades, boys and girls attended school together, but beyond that point the colleges, which trained men for the professions, and the grammar schools, which prepared men for the colleges, were closed to women as a matter of course. When coeducation became more popular at the end of the eighteenth century, advocates like Richard Rush emphasized the republic's need for educated mothers rather than the intellectual equality of women. Linda K. Kerber's essay "Daughters of Columbia" traces the post-Revolutionary debate over the proposals of Rush,

Charles Brockden Brown, and Judith Sargent Murray—the author of the "Constantia" letters—for the education of women.

Kerber shows that, even among citizens of the new republic, traditional views of woman's role persisted, and the seemingly radical proposals for their education were limited. Americans of the revolutionary generation were forced to reconcile the role of women with the new political autonomy implicit in Enlightenment thought. "The model republican woman was to be self-reliant," Kerber has written elsewhere, "but her competence did not extend to the making of political decisions. Her political task was accomplished within the confines of her family. The model republican woman was a mother." In this fashion, women were assigned a definite political role in the new republic, but one that integrated traditional female domesticity with the quest for a virtuous citizenry. Women were to take part in the civic culture vicariously through their influence on their sons and husbands.

By the end of the eighteenth century, the lives of American women were undergoing noticeable changes. The ambivalent relationship between motherhood and citizenship was reflected in other areas of life. Improved educational opportunity increasingly narrowed the gap between male and female literacy. The birth rate was declining, and women were gaining control over their own marital and sexual lives. But the close relationship between husband and wife that had characterized the seventeenth century continued to exist only on the frontier and in rural areas where men and women, of necessity, shared the harsh responsibilities of home and family. In the urban areas and among the upper classes, the roles of men and women were becoming more clearly differentiated and the first signs of the so-called Victorian morality appeared. This increasing differentiation of sex roles and the acceptance of English ideals concerning the relations of the sexes was related to the appearance of sharper class distinctions and growing economic specialization, which separated the functions of men and women both physically and psychologically. Page Smith has argued that "in the creation of a middle-class, essentially urban style of life, women who early had shared in the direction of farms and the rigors of pioneer existence, were expected to preside gracefully over drawing rooms." Such changes affected women's self-perceptions and the attitudes of others toward them. Julia Cherry Spruill has noted that "the eighteenth century saw a decline in the vigor and self-reliance of women in wealthier families and a lessening of their influence in public matters."

In the South the idealization of white womanhood was intertwined with the growth of slavery and anxieties concerning miscegenation. The selection by Winthrop Jordan "Fruits of Passion" reveals that racial attitudes and sexual myths were closely related in early America and that the degradation of blacks had deep effects upon white women. In the early eighteenth century the discussion of sex was fairly open, and sexual activity was an accepted part of life. With the development of slavery, sexual relations in the southern colonies became warped, and a distinctive double standard emerged that irreparably scarred southern women of both races.

Little is known about the lives of the many Afro-American women who suffered as slaves in the colonies, but certain things may be inferred from the work of recent historians. Although their status, along with that of Afro-American men, undoubtedly evolved from servant to slave for life, one of the first references to slavery in colonial records concerns a woman; in 1639 a Massachusetts woman refused to allow her master to mate her with a black man on the grounds that such was "beyond her slavery." Early in the eighteenth century the status of slavery was codified and conditions became increasingly severe. Nearly everywhere miscegenation, which had been widespread during the previous century, was outlawed; as the century wore on, manumission grew increasingly difficult. Due to the nature of the tasks to which they were assigned, slave women may have adjusted more easily to their new lives and to the rigors of salvery than did African men. Yet there are numerous instances of resistance to their masters from these women, whose unhappy lives were made harsher by physical and sexual abuse.

The Revolution led to the abolition of slavery in the northern states, but had little positive effect on the status of the vast majority of blacks enslaved below the Mason-Dixon line. Emancipation did bring certain benefits to the free blacks of the North. The black family was strengthened and Afro-American women were able to exercise some leadership in churches and mutual aid societies. There were even modest increases in educational opportunity for free black women. Nonetheless, economic advancement was limited; most black women continued to be employed as domestics. Even freedom itself proved hazardous for black women, who were liable to be kidnapped and resold into slavery.

It is difficult to generalize about the condition of women in colonial America. After the early years, the risk of disease decreased, and both life expectancy and fertility were greater than in England. But the lot of colonial women was neither a uniform nor an easy one. Society in the eighteenth century differed from that in the seventeenth century, and situations of women differed accordingly. The imbalance between the sexes disappeared. Sexual discipline became looser and premarital pregnancy far more common. Class, region, race and status also determined that colonial women led varied lives. While the sexual boundaries were not so clearly drawn as they would become in the nineteenth century, life was difficult for colonial women. Their work was hard; continuous pregnancy and child care jeopardized their health. Death in childbirth was a horror that, in one way or another, touched the life of every woman. The idea that these years represented a "golden age" for women is clearly a myth.

1 ᐟ The Case of the American Jezebels: Anne Hutchinson and Female Agitation during the Years of Antinomian Turmoil, 1636–1640

Lyle Koehler

Between 1636 and 1638 Massachusetts boiled with controversy, and for more than three centuries scholars have attempted to define and redefine the nature, causes, and implications of that controversy. Commentators have described the rebellious Antinomians as "heretics of the worst and most dangerous sort" who were guilty of holding "absurd, licentious, and destructive" opinions,[1] as "a mob scrambling after God, and like all mobs quickly dispersed once their leaders were dealt with,"[2] and as the innocent victims of "inexcusable severity and unnecessary virulence."[3] Other narrators have called the most famous Antinomian, Anne Hutchinson, a "charismatic healer, with the gift of fluent and inspired speech,"[4] another St. Joan of Arc,[5] a rebel with a confused, bewildered mind,[6] and a woman "whose stern and masculine mind . . . triumphed over the tender affections of a wife and mother."[7]

Almost without exception, these critics and defenders of Ms. Hutchinson and the Antinomians have dealt specifically with Antinomianism as a religious movement and too little with it as a social movement.[8] Emery Battis has traced the occupational status of 190

Reprinted by permission.

Mr. Koehler wishes to acknowledge the valuable assistance and encouragement of Karin Rabe, who participated in the analysis of the appeal of Antinomianism to women and sharpened many nuances of expression.

Antinomians and Antinomian sympathizers to examine the secular as well as the religious aspects of the controversy, but his work suffers from one major oversight: only three of his rebels are female.[9] As Richard S. Dunn has rightly observed, "The role of women in colonial life continues to be neglected,"[10] and only one colonial specialist, Michael J. Colacurcio, has been much concerned with women as Antinomians. Colacurcio has argued that sexual tensions were central to the Antinomian controversy, but it is not his primary concern to describe the nature of those tensions. Rather, he focuses on Anne Hutchinson as a "type" of Hawthorne's scarlet lady, Hester Prynne.[11] Dunn's appeal, "We need another view of Ms. Hutchinson,"[12] still entices.

That Anne Hutchinson and many other Puritan women should at stressful times rebel, either by explicit statement or by implicit example, against the role they were expected to fulfill in society is readily understandable, since that role, in both old and New England, was extremely limiting. The model English woman was weak, submissive, charitable, virtuous, and modest. Her mental and physical activity was limited to keeping the home in order, cooking, and bearing and rearing children, although she might occasionally serve the community as a nurse or midwife. She was urged to avoid books and intellectual exercise, for such activity might overtax her weak mind, and to serve her husband willingly, since she was by nature his inferior.[13] In accordance with the Apostle Paul's doctrine, she was to hold her tongue in church and be careful not "to teach, nor to usurp authority over the man, but to be in silence."[14]

In their letters, lectures, and historical accounts many of the Bay Colony men and some of the women showed approval of modest, obedient, and submissive females. Governor John Winthrop's wife Margaret was careful to leave such important domestic matters as place of residence to her husband's discretion, even when she had a preference of her own. She was ashamed because she felt that she had "no thinge with in or with out" worthy of him and signed her letters to him "your faythfull and obedient wife" or "your lovinge and obedient wife." Lucy Downing, Winthrop's sister, signed her chatty letters to her brother, "Your sister to commaund." Elizabeth, the wife of Winthrop's son John, described herself in a letter to her husband as "thy eaver loveing and kinde wife to comande in whatsoeaver thou plesest so long as the Lord shall bee plesed to geve me life and strenge."[15]

Winthrop himself was harshly critical of female intellect. In 1645 he wrote that Ann Hopkins, wife of the governor of Connecticut, had lost her understanding and reason by giving herself solely to reading and writing. The Massachusetts statesman commented that if she "had attended her household affairs, and such things as belong to women, and not gone out of her way and calling to meddle in such things as are proper for men, whose minds are stronger, etc. she had kept her wits, and might have improved them usefully and honorably in the place God had set her." Earlier he had denounced Anne Hutchinson as "a woman of a haughty and fierce carriage, of a nimble wit and active spirit, and a very voluble tongue, more bold then a man, though in understanding and judgement, inferiour to many women."[16]

Winthrop echoed the expectations of the male-dominated society in which he lived, in much the same way as the New England propagandist William Wood and Anne Hutchinson's ministerial accusers did. In 1634 Wood praised the Indian women's "mild carriage and obedience to their husbands," despite his realization that Indian men were guilty of "churlishness and inhumane behavior" toward their wives. Reverend John Cotton arrived in Boston in 1633 and soon requested that women desiring church membership be examined in private since a public confession was "against the apostle's rule and not fit for a women's modesty." At a public lecture less than a year later Cotton explained that the apostle directed women to wear veils in church only when "the custom of the place" considered veils "a sign of the women's subjection." Cambridge minister Thomas Shepard, one of Anne Hutchinson's most severe critics, commended his own wife for her "incomparable meekness of spirit, toward myself especially," while Hugh Peter, a Salem pastor and another of Ms. Hutchinson's accusers, urged his daughter to respect her feminine meekness as "Womans Ornament."[17]

The female role definition that the Massachusetts ministers and magistrates perpetuated severely limited the assertiveness, the accomplishment, the independence, and the intellectual activity of Puritan women. Bay Colony women who might resent such a role definition before 1636 had no ideological rationale around which they could organize the expression of their frustration—whatever their consciousness of the causes of that frustration. With the marked increase of Antinomian sentiment in Boston and Anne Hutchinson's powerful example of resistance, the distressed females were able—as this article will attempt to demonstrate—to channel their frustration into a viable theological form and to rebel openly against the perpetuators of the spiritual and secular status quo. Paradoxically enough, the values that Antinomians embraced minimized the importance of individual action, for they believed that salvation could be demonstrated only by the individual feeling God's grace within.

The process of salvation and the role of the individual in that process was, for the Puritan divines, a matter less well defined. The question of the relative importance of good works (i.e., individual effort) and grace (i.e., God's effort) in preparing man for salvation had concerned English Puritans from their earliest origins, and clergymen of old and New England attempted to walk a broad, although unsure, middle ground between the extremes of Antinomianism and Arminianism. But in 1636 Anne Hutchinson's former mentor and the new teacher of the Boston church, John Cotton, disrupted the fragile theological balance and led the young colony into controversy when he "warned his listeners away from the specious comfort of preparation and re-emphasized the covenant of grace as something in which God acted alone and unassisted."[18] Cotton further explained that a person could become conscious of the dwelling of the Holy Spirit within his soul and directed the Boston congregation "not to be afraid of the word *Revelation*."[19] The church elders, fearing that Cotton's "Revelation" might be dangerously construed to invalidate biblical law requested a clarification of his position.

While the elders debated with Cotton the religious issues arising out of his pronouncements, members of Cotton's congregation responded more practically and enthusiastically to the notion of personal revelation by ardently soliciting converts to an emerging, loosely-knit ideology which the divines called pejoratively Antinomianism, Opinionism, or Familism.[20] According to Thomas Weld, fledgling Antinomians visited new migrants to Boston, "especially, men of note, worth, and activity, fit instruments to advance their designe." Antinomian principles were defended at military trainings, in town meetings, and before the court judges. Winthrop charged the Opinionists with causing great disturbance in the church, the state, and the family, and wailed, "All things are turned upside down among us."[21]

The individual hungry for power could, as long as he perceived his deep inner feeling of God's grace to be authentic, use that feeling to consecrate his personal rebellion against the contemporary authorities. Some Boston merchants used it to attack the accretion of political power in the hands of a rural-dominated General Court based on land instead of capital. Some "ignorant and unlettered" men used it to express contempt for the arrogance of "black-coates that have been at the Ninneversity."[22] Some women, as we will see, used it to castigate the authority of the magistrates as guardians of the state, the ministers as guardians of the church, and their husbands as guardians of the home. As the most outspoken of these women, Anne Hutchinson diffused her opinions among all social classes by means of contacts made in the course of her profession of midwifery and in the biweekly teaching sessions she held at her home. Weld believed that Ms. Hutchinson's lectures were responsible for distributing "the venome of these [Antinomian] opinions into the very veines and vitalls of the People in the Country."[23]

Many women identified with Ms. Hutchinson's rebellious intellectual stance and her aggressive spirit. Edward Johnson wrote that "the weaker Sex" set her up as "a Priest" and "thronged" after her. John Underhill reported he daily heard a "clamor" that "New England men usurp over their wives, and keep them in servile subjection." Winthrop blamed Anne for causing "divisions between husband and wife . . . till the weaker give place to the stronger, otherwise it turnes to open contention," and Weld charged the Antinomians with using the yielding, flexible, and tender women as "an Eve, to catch their husbands also." One anonymous English pamphleteer found in Antinomianism a movement "somewhat like the Trojan horse for rarity" because "it was covered with womens aprons, and bolstered out with the judgement and deep discerning of the godly and reverent."[24]

From late 1636 through early 1637 female resistance in the Boston church reached its highest pitch. At one point, when pastor John Wilson rose to preach, Ms. Hutchinson left the congregation and many women followed her out of the meetinghouse. These women "pretended many excuses for their going out," an action which made it impossible for the authorities to convict them of contempt for Wilson. Other rebels did, however, challenge Wilson's words as he spoke them, causing Weld to comment, "Now the faithfull Ministers of Christ must have dung cast on their faces, and be no better than Legall Preachers, Baals Priests, Popish Factors, Scribes, Pharisees, and Opposers of Christ himselfe."[25]

Included among these church rebels were two particularly active women, Jane (Mrs. Richard) Hawkins and milliner William Dyer's wife Mary, both of whom Winthrop found obnoxious. The governor considered the youthful Ms. Dyer to be "of a very proud spirit," "much addicted to revelations," and "notoriously infected with Mrs. Hutchinson's errors." Ms. Dyer weathered Winthrop's wrath and followed Anne to Rhode Island, but her "addictions" were not without serious consequence. Twenty-two years later she would return to Boston and be hanged as a Quaker.[26] The other of Hutchinson's close female associates, Jane Hawkins, dispensed fertility potions to barren women and occasionally fell into a trance-like state in which she spoke Latin. Winthrop therefore denounced her as "notorious for familiarity with the devill," and the General Court, sharing his apprehension, on March 12, 1638, forbade her to question "matters of religion" or "to meddle" in "surgery, or phisick, drinks, plaisters, or oyles." Ms. Hawkins apparently disobeyed this order, for three years later the Court banished her from the colony under the penalty of a severe whipping or such other punishment as the judges thought fit.[27]

Other women, both rich and poor, involved themselves in the Antinomian struggle. William Coddington's spouse, like her merchant husband, was "taken with the familistical opinions."[28] Mary Dummer, the wife of wealthy landowner and Assistant Richard Dummer, convinced her husband to move from Newbury to Boston so that she might be closer to Ms. Hutchinson.[29] Mary Oliver, a poor Salem calenderer's wife, reportedly exceeded Anne "for ability of speech, and appearance of zeal and devotion" and, according to Winthrop, might "have done hurt, but that she was poor and had little acquaintance [with theology]." Ms. Oliver held the "dangerous" opinions that the church was managed by the "heads of the people, both magistrates and ministers, met together," instead of the people themselves, and that anyone professing faith in Christ ought to be admitted to the church and the sacraments. Between 1638 and 1650 she appeared before the magistrates six times for remarks contemptuous of ministerial and magisterial authority and experienced the stocks, the lash, the placement of a cleft stick on her tongue, and imprisonment. One of the Salem magistrates became so frustrated with Ms. Oliver's refusal to respect his authority that he seized her and put her in the stocks without a trial. She sued him for false arrest and collected a minimal ten shillings in damages. Her victory was short-lived, however, and before she left Massachusetts in 1650 she had managed to secure herself some reputation as a witch.[30]

Mary Oliver and the other female rebels could easily identify with the Antinomian ideology because its theological emphasis on the inability of the individual to achieve salvation echoed the inability of women to achieve recognition on a sociopolitical level. As the woman realized that she could receive wealth, power, and status only through the man, her father or her husband, so the Antinomian realized that he or she could receive grace only through God's beneficence. Thus, women could have found it appealing that in Antinomianism both men and women were relegated vis-à-vis God to the status that women occupied in Puritan society vis-à-vis men, that is, to the status of malleable inferiors in the hands of a higher being. All power, then, emanated from God, raw and pure, respecting no sex, rather than from male authority figures striving to interpret the Divine Word. Fortified by a consciousness of the Holy Spirit's inward dwelling, the Antinomians could rest secure and self-confident in the belief that they were mystic participants in the transcendent power of the Almighty, a power far beyond anything mere magistrates and ministers might muster. Antinomianism could not secure for women such practical earthly powers as sizable estates, professional success, and participation in the church and civil government, but it provided compensation by reducing the significance of these powers for the men. Viewed from this perspective, Antinomianism extended the feminine experience of humility to both sexes, which in turn paradoxically created the possibility of feminine pride, as Anne Hutchinson's dynamic example in her examinations and trials amply demonstrated.

Anne Hutchinson's example caused the divines much frustration. They were chagrined to find that she was not content simply to repeat to the "simple Weomen"[31] the sermons of John Wilson, but that she also chose to interpret and even question the content of those sermons. When she charged that the Bay Colony ministers did not teach a covenant of grace as "clearly" as Cotton and her brother-in-law, John Wheelwright, she was summoned in 1636 to appear before a convocation of the clergy. At this convocation and in succeeding examinations, the ministers found particularly galling her implicit assertion that she had the intellectual ability necessary to judge the truth of their theology. Such an assertion threatened their self-image as the intellectual leaders of the community and the spokesmen for a male-dominated society. The ministers and magistrates therefore sharply criticized Anne for not fulfilling her ordained womanly role. In September 1637 a synod of elders resolved that women might meet "to pray and edify one another," but when one woman "in a prophetical way" resolved questions of doctrine and expounded Scripture, then the meeting was "disorderly." At Anne's examination on November 7 and 8, Winthrop began the interrogation by charging that she criticized the ministers and maintained a "meeting and an assembly in your house that hath been condemned by the general assembly as a thing not tolerable nor comely in the sight of God nor fitting for your sex." Later in the interrogation, Winthrop accused her of disobeying her "parents," the magistrates, in violation of the Fifth Commandment, and paternalistically told her, "We do not mean to discourse with those of your sex." Hugh Peter also indicated that he felt Anne was not fulfilling the properly submissive, nonintellectual feminine role. He ridiculed her choice of a female preacher of the Isle of Ely as a model for her own behavior and told her to consider "that you have stept out of you place, *you have rather bine a Husband than a Wife and a preacher than a Hearer; and a Magistrate than a Subject.*"[32]

When attacked for behavior inappropriate to her sex, Ms. Hutchinson did not hesitate to demonstrate that she was the intellectual equal of her accusers. She tried to trap Winthrop when he charged her with dishonoring her "parents": "But put the case Sir that I do fear the Lord and my parents, may not I entertain them that fear the Lord because my parents will not give me leave?" To provide a biblical justification for her teaching activities, she cited Titus's rule (2:3–4) "that the elder women should instruct the younger." Winthrop ordered her to take that rule "in the sense that elder women must instruct the younger about their business, and to love their husbands." But Anne disagreed with this interpretation, saying, "I do not conceive but that it is meant for some publick times." Winthrop rejoined, "We must . . . restrain you from maintaining this course," and she qualified, "If you have a rule for it from God's word you may." Her resistance infuriated the governor, who exclaimed, "We are your judges, and not you ours." When Winthrop tried to lure her into admitting that she taught men, in violation of Paul's proscription, Anne replied that she throught herself justified in teaching a man who asked her for instruction, and added sarcastically, "Do you think it not lawful for me to teach women and why do you call me to teach the court?"[33]

Anne soon realized that sarcastic remarks would not persuade the court of the legitimacy of her theological claims. Alternatively, therefore, she affected a kind of modesty to cozen the authorities at the same time that she expressed a kind of primitive feminism through double-entendre statements and attacked the legitimacy of Paul's idea of the nonspeaking, nonintellectual female churchmember. When the Court charged her with "prophesying," Anne responded, "The men of *Berea* are commended for examining *Pauls* Doctrine; wee do no more [in our meetings] but read the notes of our teachers Sermons, and then reason of them by searching the Scriptures."[34] Such a statement was on one level an "innocent" plea to the divines that the women were only following biblical prescription. On another level it was an attack on the ministers for presuming to have the final word on biblical interpretation. On yet a third level, since she focused on "Pauls Doctrine" and reminded men that they should take another look at that teaching, her statement was a suggestion that ministerial attitudes toward women ought to be reexamined.

At another point Anne responded to Winthrop's criticism with a similar statement having meaning on three levels. The governor had accused her of traducing the ministers and magistrates and, when summoned to answer this charge, of saying that "the fear of man was a snare and therefore she would not be affeared of them." She replied, "They say I said the fear of man is a snare, why should I be afraid. When I came unto them, they urging many things unto me and I being backward to answer at first, at length this scripture came into my mind

29th Prov. 15. The fear of man bringeth a snare, but who putteth his trust in the Lord shall be safe."[35] Once again, her response was phrased as an "innocent" plea to God to assuage her fears, while at the same time it implied that God was on her side in opposition to the ministers and magistrates. Her statement also told women that if they trusted in God they need not fear men, for such fear trapped them into being "backward" about reacting in situations of confrontation with men.

Anne, although aware of the "backwardness" of women as a group, did not look to intensified group activity as a remedy for woman's down-trodden status. Her feminism consisted essentially of the subjective recognition of her own strength and gifts and the apparent belief that other women could come to the same recognition. A strong, heroic example of female self-assertiveness was necessary to the development of this recognition of one's own personal strength. Anne chose the woman preacher of the Isle of Ely as her particular heroic model; she did, Hugh Peter chided, "exceedingly magnifie" that woman "to be a Womane of 1000 hardly any like to her." Anne could thus dissociate herself from the "divers worthy and godly Weomen" of Massachusetts and confidently deride them as being no better than "soe many Jewes," unconverted by the light of Christ.[36] Other Bay Colony women who wished to reach beyond the conventional, stereotypic behavior of "worthy and godly Weomen" attached themselves to the emphatic example of Anne and to God's ultimate power in order to resist the constraints which they felt as Puritan women.

Fearful that Ms. Hutchinson's example might be imitated by other women, the divines wished to catch her in a major theological error and subject her to public punishment. Their efforts were not immediately successful. Throughout her 1637 examination Anne managed to parry the verbal thrusts of the ministers and magistrates by replying to their many questions with questions of her own, forcing them to justify their positions from the Bible, pointing out their logical inconsistencies, and using innuendo to cast aspersions upon their authoritarianism. With crucial assistance from a sympathetic John Cotton, she left the ministers with no charge to pin upon her. She was winning the debate when, in an apparently incautious moment, she gave the authorities the kind of declaration for which they had been hoping. Raising herself to the position of judge over her accusers, she asserted, "I know that for this you goe about to doe to me, God will ruine you and your posterity, and this whole State." Asked how she knew this, she explained, "By an immediate revelation."[37] With this statement Anne proved her heresy to the ministers and they then took steps to expose her in excommunication proceedings conducted before the Boston church. The divines hoped to expel a heretic from their midst, to reestablish support for the

Puritan way, to prevent unrest in the state and the family, and to shore up their own anxious egos in the process.

The predisposition of the ministers to defame Ms. Hutchinson before the congregation caused them to ignore what she was actually saying in her excommunication trial. Although she did describe a relationship with Christ closer than anything Cotton had envisioned, she did not believe that she had experienced Christ's Second Coming in her own life. Such a claim would have denied the resurrection of the body at the Last Judgment and would have clearly stamped her as a Familist.[38] Ms. Hutchinson's accusers, ignoring Thomas Leverett's reminder that she had expressed belief in the resurrection, argued that if the resurrection did not exist, biblical law would have no validity nor the marriage covenant any legal or utilitarian value. The result would be a kind of world no Puritan could tolerate, a world where the basest desires would be fulfilled and "foule, groce, filthye and abominable" sexual promiscuity would be rampant. Cotton, smarting from a psychological slap Anne had given him earlier in the excommunication proceedings[39] and in danger of losing the respect of the other ministers, admonished her with the words "though I have not herd, nayther do I thinke, you have bine unfaythfull to your Husband in his Marriage Covenant, *yet that will follow upon it.*" By referring to "his" marriage covenant Cotton did not even accord Anne equal participation in the making of that covenant. The Boston teacher concluded his admonition with a criticism of Anne's pride: *"I have often feared the highth of your Spirit and being puft up with your owne parts."*[40]

Both the introduction of the sexual issue into the trial and Cotton's denunciation of Ms. Hutchinson must have had the effect of curbing dissent from the congregation. Few Puritans would want to defend Anne in public when such a defense could be construed as supporting promiscuity. Since Cotton had earlier been sympathetic to the Antinomian cause and had tried to save Anne at her 1637 examination, his vigorous condemnation of her must have confused her following. Cotton even went so far as to exempt the male Antinomians from any real blame for the controversy when he characterized Antinomianism as a women's delusion. He urged that women, like children, ought to be watched, reproved Hutchinson's sons for not controlling her theological ventures, and called those sons "Vipers . . . [who] *Eate through the very Bowells of your Mother,* to her Ruine." Cotton warned the Boston women "to looke to your selves and to take heed that you reaceve nothinge for Truth which hath not the stamp of the Word of God [as interpreted by the ministers] . . . for you see she [Anne] is but a Woman and *many unsound and dayngerous principles are held by her."* Thomas Shepard agreed that intellectual activity did not suit women and warned the congregation that Anne was likely "to seduce and draw away many, Espetially simple Weomen of her owne sex."[41]

The female churchmembers, who would have had good reason to resent the clergy's approach, could not legitimately object to the excommunication proceedings because of Paul's injunction against women speaking in church. Lacking a clearly-defined feminist consciousness and filled with "backward" fear, the women could not refuse to respect that injunction, even though, or perhaps because, Anne had been presented to the congregation as the epitome of despicableness, as a woman of simple intellect, and as a liar, puffed up with pride and verging on sexual promiscuity. This caricature of Anne did not, however, prevent five men, including her brother-in-law Richard Scott and Mary Oliver's husband Thomas, from objecting to her admonition and excommunication. Cotton refused to consider the points these men raised and dismissed their objections as rising out of their own self-interest or their natural affection for Anne.[42]

In Anne's excommunication proceedings the ministers demonstrated that they had found the means necessary to deal effectively with this rebellious woman and a somewhat hostile congregation. At her examination and her excommunication trial Anne attempted to place the ministers on the defensive by questioning them and forcing them to justify their positions while she explained little. She achieved some success in the 1637 trial, but before her fellow churchmembers she found it difficult to undercut the misrepresentation of her beliefs and the attack on her character. Perhaps fearing the banishment which had been so quickly imposed on her associate, John Wheelwright, she recanted, but even in her recantation she would not totally compromise her position. She expressed sorrow for her errors of expression but admitted no errors in judgment and assumed no appearance of humiliation. When Wilson commanded her *as a Leper to withdraw your selfe out of the Congregation,"* Anne rose, walked to the meetinghouse door, accepted Mary Dyer's offered hand, and turned to impugn her accusers' power: "The Lord judgeth not as man judgeth, better to be cast out of the Church then to deny Christ."[43]

During the year and a half following Ms. Hutchinson's excommunication, the Massachusetts ministers and magistrates prosecuted several other female rebels. In April 1638 the Boston church cast out Judith Smith, the maidservant of Anne's brother-in-law, Edward Hutchinson, for her "obstinate persisting" in "sundry Errors." On October 10 of the same year the Assistants ordered Katherine Finch to be whipped for "speaking against the magistrates, against the Churches, and against the

Elders." Less than a year later Ms. Finch again appeared before the Assistants, this time for not carrying herself "dutifully to her husband," and was released upon promise of reformation. In September 1639 the Boston church excommunicated Philip(a?) Hammond "as a slanderer and revyler both of the Church and Common Weale." Ms. Hammond, after her husband's death, had resumed her maiden name, operated a business in Boston, and argued in her shop and at public meetings "that Mrs. Hutchinson neyther deserved the Censure which was putt upon her in the Church, nor in the Common Weale." The Boston church also excommunicated two other women for partially imitating Anne Hutchinson's example: Sarah Keayne was found guilty in 1646 of "irregular prophesying in mixed assemblies," and Joan Hogg nine years later was punished "for her disorderly singing and her idleness, and for saying she is commanded of Christ so to do."[44]

The Salem authorities followed Boston's example in dealing with overly assertive women. In late 1638 the Salem church excommunicated four of Roger Williams's former followers: Jane (Mrs. Joshua) Verin, Mary Oliver, servant Margery Holliman, and widow Margery Reeves. These women had consistently refused to worship with the congregation, and the latter two had denied that the churches of the Bay Colony were true churches.[45] Yet another woman, Dorothy Talby, who was subject to a different kind of frustration, troubled the Essex County magistrates by mimicking Anne Hutchinson's proclamation of "immediate revelation" to justify her personal rebellion. In October 1637 the county court ordered her chained to a post "for frequent laying hands on her husband to the danger of his life, and contemning the authority of the court," and later ordered her whipped for "misdemeanors against her husband." Later, according to Winthrop, she claimed a "revelation from heaven" instructing her to kill her husband and children and then broke the neck of her three-year-old daughter, Difficult. At her execution on December 6, 1638, Ms. Talby continued her defiance by refusing to keep her face covered and expressing a desire to be beheaded, as "it was less painful and less shameful."[46]

Dorothy Talby was one of an increasing number of women to appear before the General Court and the Court of Assistants, an increase which seemed to reflect both a greater rebelliousness in women and a hardening of magisterial attitudes. In the first five years of Puritan settlement only 1.7 percent of the persons convicted of criminal offenses by the Deputies and the Assistants were women. During and after the years of the Antinomian controversy the percentage of female offenders was significantly higher—6.7 percent from 1635 to 1639 and 9.4 percent from 1640 to 1644. If Charles E. Banks's enumeration of 3,505 passengers from ship lists is representative of the more than 20,000 persons who came to Massachusetts between 1630 and 1639, it can be assumed that the number of women did not increase proportionately to the number of men. Banks's ship lists reveal that 829 males and 542 females came to Massachusetts between 1630 and 1634, a number which increased in the next five years to 1,279 males and 855 females. The percentage of females increased only .6 percent, from 39.5 percent between 1630 and 1634 to 40.1 percent between 1635 and 1639.[47] These comparative figures suggest that by 1640 the magistrates could no longer afford to dismiss with verbal chastisement females found guilty of drunkenness, cursing, or pre-marital fornication.[48]

The magistrates not only used the threat of a humiliating court-room appearance and possible punishment to keep female rebels quiet but also levied very stringent penalties on male Antinomian offenders. Anne Hutchinson's son-in-law William Collins was sentenced to pay a £100 fine for charging the Massachusetts churches and ministers with being anti-Christian and calling the king of England the king of Baby-lon. Anne's son Francis, who had accompanied Collins to Boston in 1641, objected to the popular rumor that he would not sit at the same table with his excommunicated mother and, feeling that the Boston church was responsible, called that church "a strumpet." The church excommunicated Francis and the Assistants fined him £40, but neither he nor Collins would pay the stipulated amounts (even when those fines were reduced to £40 and £20) and therefore spent some time in jail.[49]

Besides prosecuting Antinomian sympathizers in church and court, the Massachusetts ministers and magistrates carefully watched new ministers, lest they deliver "some points savoring of familism,"[50] and justified the emergent orthodox position in their sermons and publica-tions. Of these publications, which were directed at audiences both in New and old England, John Cotton's *Singing of Psalmes a Gospel-Ordinance* most significantly asserted the traditional feminine role-response. The Boston teacher, apparently with Ms. Hutchinson in mind, told his readers that "the woman is more subject to error than a man" and continued, "It is not permitted to a woman to speak in the Church by way of propounding questions though under pretence of desire to learn for her own satisfaction; but rather it is required she should ask her husband at home. For under pretence of questioning for learning sake, she might so propound her question as to teach her teachers; or if not so, yet to open a door to some of her own weak and erroneous apprehensions, or at least soon exceed the bounds of womanly mod-esty." Cotton explained that a woman could speak in church only when she wished to confess a sin or to participate in singing hymns.[51]

Other Bay Colony leaders popularized the idea that the intellectual woman was influenced by Satan and was therefore unable to perform the necessary functions of womanhood. Weld described Mary Dyer's abortive birth as "a woman child, a fish, a beast, and a fowle, all woven together in one, and without an head," and wrote of Anne Hutchinson's probable hydatidiform mole as "30. monstrous births . . . none at all of them (as farre as I could ever learne) of humane shape." [52] According to Winthrop's even more garish account of Mary Dyer's child, the still-born baby had a face and ears growing upon the shoulders, a breast and back full of sharp prickles, female sex organs on the rear and buttocks in front, three clawed feet, no forehead, four horns above the eyes, and two great holes upon the back. [53] Wheelwright wrote from his new home in Exeter to attack the governor's farfetched description of these births. That clergyman called Winthrop's monsters "a monstrous conception of his brain, a spurious issue of his intellect," and told that governor that he should know better *then to delude the world with untruths. [For]* I question not his learning, etc. but I admire his certainty or rather impudence: did the man obtestricate [obstetricate] ?"[54]

Despite Wheelwright's effort, Weld's opinion that "as she had vented mishapen opinions, so she must bring forth deformed monsters" impressed the people of the Bay Colony, a people who believed that catastrophic occurrences were evidences of God's displeasure. Some Massachusetts residents viewed the births as the products of both the women's "mishapen opinions" and their supposed promiscuity. Edward Johnson and Roger Clap lamented the "phantasticall madnesse" of those who would hold "silly women laden with their lusts" in higher esteem than "those honoured of Christ, indued with power and authority from him to Preach." A rumor reached England that Henry Vane had crossed the Atlantic in 1637 with Ms. Dyer and Ms. Hutchinson and had "debauched both, and both were delivered of monsters."[55] It was also widely rumored that three of the Antinomian women, Anne Hutchinson, Jane Hawkins, and Mary Oliver, had sold their souls to Satan and become witches. Anne in particular "gave cause of suspicion of witchcraft" after she easily converted to Antinomianism one new male arrival in Rhode Island. [56]

The promotion of the belief that the Antinomian female leaders were witches filled with aberrant lusts and unable to live as proper women was accompanied by an attack on the masculinity of some of the Antinomian men. Although Anne's husband, William, had been a prosperous landowner, a merchant, a deputy to the General Court, and a Boston selectman, Winthrop described him as a "man of very mild temper and weak parts, and wholly guided by his wife." Clap also felt that William Hutchinson and the other Antinomian men were deficient in intellect and judgment. He expressed surprise that any of the men in the movement had "strong parts."[57]

While Massachusetts gossip focused on disordered Antinomian births, lusty Antinomian women, and weak Antinomian men, Winthrop and Cotton tried to convince their English and New England readers that public opinion had been solidly behind Ms. Hutchinson's excommunication. Winthrop contended that "diverse women" objected to this rebel's example and would have borne witness against her "if their modesty had not restrained them." Cotton supported the governor's claim by construing the relative silence at Anne's church trial to mean that the "whole body of the Church (except her own son) consented with one accord, to the publick censure of her, by admonition first, and excommunication after." By asserting this falsehood and ignoring Leverett's admission that many churchmembers wished to stay Anne's excommunication, Cotton made it appear that any person who complained about her censure was contradicting the near-unanimous opinion of the congregation.[58]

The effort to discredit the Antinomians and Antinomian sentiment in the Bay Colony was quite successful. By the late 1640s Antinomianism, in a practical sense, was no longer threatening; the ministers and magistrates had managed to preserve a theological system they found congenial. "*Sanctification* came to be in some Request again; and there were *Notes* and *Marks* given of a good Estate."[59] The position of Massachusetts women within the religious system remained essentially unchanged, while in Rhode Island and nearby Providence Plantations the status of women was somewhat improved. In Providence and Portsmouth the men listened to the wishes of the women and protected the "liberty" of women to teach, preach, and attend services of their choosing. When Joshua Verin, one of the original settlers at Providence, restrained his wife Jane from attending religious services at Roger Williams's home, a town meeting considered the matter. John Greene argued before the townsmen that if men were allowed to restrain their wives, "all the women in the country would cry out." William Arnold rejoined that God had ordered the wife to be subject to her husband and that such a commandment should not be broken merely to please women. According to Winthrop, the townsmen "would have censured Verin, [but] Arnold told them, that it was against their own order, for Verin did that he did out of conscience; and their order was, that no man should be censured for his conscience." Winthrop neglected to record that the town meeting did disfranchise Verin until he declared that he would not restrain his wife's "libertie of conscience," nor did Winthrop mention that Verin had "trodden" his wife "under foot tyrannically and brutishly," endangering her life. After his censure, Verin returned to Salem, and Roger Williams urged Winthrop to prevent this "boisterous and desperate" young man from hauling "his wife with ropes to Salem, where she must needs be troubled and troublesome."[60]

After Anne Hutchinson's arrival and throughout the remainder of the century, women taught and preached in public in Rhode Island. Johnson wrote that in 1638 "there were some of the female sexe who (deeming the Apostle Paul to be too strict in not permitting a room [woman] to preach in the publique Congregation) taught notwithstanding . . . having their call to this office from an ardent desire of being famous." According to Johnson, Anne Hutchinson, "the grand Mistresse of them all, . . . ordinarily prated every Sabbath day, till others, who thirsted after honour in the same way with her selfe, drew away her Auditors."[61] This prating was more purposive than Johnson might have been willing to admit, for Anne soon involved herself in a new controversy, this one springing out of the resentment of many of the poorer inhabitants of the settlement toward Judge (Governor) William Coddington's autocratic rule, his land allotment policy, and his efforts to establish a church resembling closely the Massachusetts example.[62] Allying herself with Samuel Gorton, a religious freethinker and a defender of justice for all men, "rich or poore, ignorant or learned," Anne began to attack the legitimacy of *any* magistracy. Together, she and Gorton managed to foment the rebellion of April 28, 1639, in which the Portsmouth inhabitants formed a new body politic, ejected Coddington from power, and chose William Hutchinson to replace him. William, however, also did not believe in magistracy and soon refused to occupy the office of judge. Coddington, who had fled south with his followers to found Newport, then claimed the judgeship by default, was recognized by the Massachusetts authorities, and proceeded to administer the affairs of Rhode Island.[63] Gorton and at least eleven others responded to Coddington's resumption of power by plotting armed rebellion against him and were ultimately banished from the colony. Anne broke with the Gortonists over that issue, and she and William joined the Newport settlement.[64]

William Hutchinson died at Newport in 1640, and for much of that year Anne was silent. By 1641, however, she had come out of mourning and, according to Winthrop, turned anabaptist. She and "divers" others supported passive resistance to authority, "denied all magistracy among Christians, and maintained that there were no churches since those founded by the apostles and evangelists, nor could any be."[65] Such opinions achieved enough popularity in Rhode Island to contribute to the dissolution of the church at Newport,[66] although not enough to remove Coddington from power. Disgruntled and fearing that Massachusetts would seize the Rhode Island settlements, Anne sought refuge in the colony of New Netherland in 1642, but her stay there was not long. In August 1643 she, William Collins, two of her sons, and three of her daughters were killed by Indians who had quarreled with her Dutch neighbors.[67]

The Massachusetts clergy rejoiced. Not only had God destroyed the "American Jesabel,"[68] but the Lord's vengeance had descended upon her sons and daughters, the poisoned seed. Peter Bulkeley spoke for all the Massachusetts ministers when he concluded, "Let her damned heresies shee fell into . . and the just vengeance of God, by which shee perished, terrifie all her seduced followers from having any more to doe with her leaven."[69] But her "seduced followers" were horrified only at the reaction of the Puritan clergy. Anne's sister, Katherine Scott, commented that the Bay Colony authorities "are drunke with the blod of the saints," and Anne's former Portsmouth neighbor, Randall Holden, blamed those same authorities for forcing Anne first to Rhode Island and ultimately to her death. He reminded them of her partially successful struggle against authority: "you know . . . your great and terrible word magistrate is no more in its original, than masterly or masterless which hath no great lustre in our ordinary acceptation."[70]

Impervious to such protests, the Bay Colony divines considered Anne Hutchinson's death to be the symbolic death of Antinomianism. To these divines she had been the incarnation of the Antinomian evil, and their accounts of the Antinomian stress in Boston accented *her* beliefs, *her* activities, and *her* rebelliousness. The ministers were not as concerned with the important roles played by Coddington, Wheelwright, Vane, and the other male Antinomian leaders because none of these men threatened the power and status structure of society in the concrete way that Anne Hutchinson did. Anne was clearly not, as the ministers might have wished, a submissive quiet dove, content to labor simply in the kitchen and the childbed. She was witty, aggressive, and intellectual. She had no qualms about castigating in public the men who occupied the most authoritative positions. She claimed the right to define rational, theological matters for herself and by her example spurred other women to express a similar demand. Far from bewildered, she thwarted her accusers with her intellectual ability. Perceiving her as a threat to the family, the state, the religion, and the status hierarchy, the Puritan authorities directed their antagonism against Anne's character and her sex. By doing so, they managed to salve the psychological wounds inflicted by this woman who trod so sharply upon their male status and their ministerial and magisterial authority. Their method had a practical aspect as well; it helped restore respect for the ministry and curb potential dissent.

Anne's ability to attract large numbers of women as supporters caused the ministers and magistrates some worry but little surprise, since they believed that women were easily deluded. They chided Anne for choosing a female preacher as a role model and refused to attribute any merit to her at times subtle, at times caustic intellectual ability. They could see only the work of Satan in Anne's aggressiveness and not the more human desire for equal opportunity and treatment which this rebel never hesitated to assert by example in the intellectual skirmishes she had with her accusers throughout her trials. The double oppression of life in a male-dominated society, combined with biological bondage to her own amazing fertility, could not destroy her self-respect. Because of the theologically based society in which she lived, it was easy for her to ally herself with God and to express her self-confidence in religious debates with the leading intellectual authorities. Neither Anne's rebellion nor the rebellion of her female followers was directed self-consciously against their collective female situation or toward its improvement. Specific feminist campaigns for the franchise, divorce reform, female property ownership after marriage, and the like would be developments of a much later era. For Anne Hutchinson and her female associates Antinomianism was simply an ideology through which the resentments they intuitively felt could be focused and actively expressed.

NOTES

1. John A. Albro, ed., *The Works of Thomas Shepard,* I (New York, 1967 [orig. publ. n.p., 1853]), cxvi–cxvii.

2. Darrett B. Rutman, *Winthrop's Boston: Portrait of a Puritan Town, 1630–1649* (Chapel Hill, N. C., 1965), 121.

3. John Stetson Barry, *The History of Massachusetts. The Colonial Period* (Boston, 1855), 261.

4. Andrew Sinclair, *The Emancipation of the American Woman* (New York, 1966), 23.

5. Edith Curtis, *Anne Hutchinson: A Biography* (Cambridge, Mass., 1930), 72–73.

6. Emery Battis, *Saints and Sectaries: Anne Hutchinson and the Antinomian Controversy in the Massachusetts Bay Colony* (Chapel Hill, N. C., 1962), 9, 50–56, 90, admits that Ms. Hutchinson had a "prodigious memory and keen mind," but he believes that she was "wracked with unbearable doubt" as a result of her inability to find a male "mental director." Her husband could not fulfill this need, for he "seems to have lacked the power to provide adequate support and direction for his wife." Ms. Hutchinson's rebellion, according to Battis, grew out of this need for

male guidance and was accentuated by the fact that she was experiencing menopause and felt that "her own inadequacy was at least in part responsible" for the death of two of her children. Of these many reasons for Ms. Hutchinson's restlessness Battis substantiates only his conclusion that she was undergoing menopause. His argument is weakened, however, by anthropological research which ties the psychological distress of menopause to the loss of self-esteem that middle-aged women experience in societies where their status deteriorates at menopause. See Joan Solomon, "Menopause: A Rite of Passage," *Ms.*, I (Dec. 1972), 18. Puritan New England was clearly not such a society, for elderly women could serve as deaconesses and, since they were free from the materialistic proclivities of youth, could furnish venerable examples for younger women. See Benjamin Colman, *The Duty and Honour of Aged Women. A Sermon on the Death of Madam Abigail Foster* (Boston, 1711), 11–30.

7. Peter Oliver, *The Puritan Commonwealth. An Historical Review of the Puritan Government in Massachusetts in its Civil and Ecclesiastical Relations . . .* (Boston, 1856), 181.

8. Anne Hutchinson and the Antinomians have been treated sympathetically in Charles Francis Adams, *Three Episodes of Massachusetts History* (Boston, 1892); Brooks Adams, *The Emancipation of Massachusetts* (Boston, 1887); Winnifred King Rugg, *Unafraid: A Life of Anne Hutchinson* (Boston, 1930); Theda Kenyon, *Scarlet Anne* (New York, 1939); Vernon Louis Parrington, *Main Currents in American Thought: The Colonial Mind* (New York, 1927); Eleanor Flexner, *Century of Struggle: The Woman's Rights Movement in the United States* (Cambridge, Mass., 1959); Elisabeth Anthony Dexter, *Colonial Women of Affairs: A Study of Women in Business and the Professions before 1776* (Boston, 1924); Sinclair, *Emancipation of American Woman*; Rufus M. Jones, *The Quakers in the American Colonies* (New York, 1911); Curtis, *Anne Hutchinson*; Barry, *History of Massachusetts*. Critics of Anne and the Antinomians include Henry Martyn Dexter, *As to Roger Williams, and His "Banishment" from the Massachusetts Plantation; with a Few Further Words Concerning the Baptists, the Quakers, and Religious Liberty* (Boston, 1873); George E. Ellis, "Life of Anne Hutchinson with a Sketch of the Antinomian Controversy in Massachusetts," in Jared Sparks, ed., *The Library of American Biography*, 2d Ser., VI (Boston, 1849); John Gorham Palfrey, *A Compendious History of the First Century of New England . . .* (Boston, 1872); Thomas Jefferson Wertenbaker, *The First Americans, 1607–1690* (New York, 1927); Oliver, *Puritan Commonwealth*; Rutman, *Winthrop's Boston*. More balanced treatments are Edmund S. Morgan, *The Puritan Dilemma: The Story of John Winthrop* (Boston, 1958), and Battis, *Saints and Sectaries*.

9. Battis, *Saints and Sectaries*, 249–307. The three women whom Battis lists as Antinomians are Anne Hutchinson, Jane Hawkins, and Mary Dyer.

10. "The Social History of Early New England," *American Quarterly*, XXIV (1972), 677.

11. "Footsteps of Anne Hutchinson: The Context of *The Scarlet Letter*," *ELH*, XXXIX (1972), 459–494.

12. Dunn, "Social History of Early New England," *Amer. Qtly.*, XXIV (1972), 677.

13. Studies of early 17th-century English attitudes about women appear in Georgiana Hill, *Women in English Life from Mediaeval to Modern Times* (London, 1896); M. Phillips and W. S. Tomkinson, *English Women in Life and Letters*

(London, 1926); Gamaliel Bradford, *Elizabethan Women* (Boston, 1936); Doris Mary Stenton, *The English Woman in History* (London, 1957).

14. I Tim. 2:11–12. St. Paul told the Corinthians: "Let your women keep silence in the churches; for it is not permitted unto them to speak; but they are commanded to be under obedience, as also saith the law. And if they will learn any thing, let them ask their husbands at home; for it is a shame for women to speak in the church" (I Cor. 14:34–35).

15. Margaret Winthrop to John Winthrop, 1624–1630, *The Winthrop Papers* (Boston, 1929–1944), I, 354–355; II, 165, 199; Lucy Downing to John Winthrop, 1636–1640, Massachusetts Historical Society, *Collections*, 5th Ser., I (Boston, 1871), 20, 25, 27; Elizabeth Winthrop to John Winthrop, ca. June 1636, *Winthrop Papers*, III, 267.

16. James Kendall Hosmer, ed., *Winthrop's Journal: "History of New England," 1630–1649*, Original Narratives of Early American History (New York, 1908), II, 225; John Winthrop, *A Short Story of the Rise, reign, and ruine of the Antinomians, Familists and Libertines* in David D. Hall, ed., *The Antinomian Controversy, 1636–1638: A Documentary History* (Middletown, Conn., 1968), 263.

17. William Wood, *New Englands Prospect* . . . (London, 1634), 121–122; Hosmer, ed., *Winthrop's Journal*, I, 107, 120; Michael McGiffert, ed., *God's Plot: The Paradoxes of Puritan Piety, Being the Autobiography and Journal of Thomas Shepard* (Amherst, Mass., 1972), 70; Hugh Peter, *A Dying Fathers Last Legacy to An Only Child: Or, Mr. Hugh Peter's Advice to His Daughter* . . . (Boston, 1717), 22.

18. Morgan, *Puritan Dilemma*, 137. McGiffert's introduction to Shepard's autobiography and journal contains a discussion of the Puritans' problems with assurance. See McGiffert, ed., *God's Plot*, 1–32. Puritan attitudes toward the preparation process are treated comprehensively and perceptively in Norman Pettit, *The Heart Prepared: Grace and Conversion in Puritan Spiritual Life* (New Haven, Conn., 1966).

19. John Cotton, *A Treatise of the Covenant of Grace, as it is despensed to the Elect Seed, effectually unto Salvation* (London, 1671), 177. Cotton's subsequent debate with the other ministers appears in Hall, ed., *Antinomian Controversy*, 24–151.

20. The Familists or Family of Love, a sect which originated in Holland about 1540 and spread to England, gained a largely undeserved reputation for practicing promiscuity. Antinomianism was associated in the Puritan mind with the licentious orgies that accompanied the enthusiasm of John Agricola in 16th-century Germany. Opinionism was a term often used for any theology that the divines disliked. James Hastings, ed., *Encyclopaedia of Religion and Ethics* (New York, 1908–1926), I, 581–582; V, 319; IX, 102.

21. Thomas Weld, "The Preface," to Winthrop, *Short Story*, in Hall, ed., *Antinomian Controversy*, 204, 208–209; Winthrop, *Short Story*, ibid., 253.

22. J. Franklin Jameson, ed., *Johnson's Wonder-Working Providence, 1628–1651*, Original Narratives of Early American History (New York, 1910), 127.

23. Weld, "Preface," to Winthrop, *Short Story*, in Hall, ed., *Antinomian Controversy*, 207.

24. Jameson, ed., *Johnson's Wonder-Working Providence*, 132; John Underhill, *Newes from America; or A New and Experimentall Discoverie of New England* . . .

(London, 1638), reprinted in Mass. Hist. Soc., *Colls.*, 3d Ser., VI (Boston, 1837), 5; Winthrop, *Short Story*, in Hall, ed., *Antinomian Controversy*, 253; Weld, "Preface," to Winthrop, *Short Story, ibid.*, 205–206; *Good News from New England: with An exact Relation of the first planting that Countrey* (1648), reprinted in Mass. Hist. Soc., *Colls.*, 4th Ser., I (1852), 206.

25. John Cotton, *The Way of Congregational Churches Cleared*, in Hall, ed., *Antinomian Controversy*, 423, and Weld, "Preface," to Winthrop, *Short Story, ibid.*, 209.

26. Hosmer, ed., *Winthrop's Journal*, I, 266; Winthrop, *Short Story*, in Hall, ed., *Antinomian Controversy*, 281; Horatio Rogers, "Mary Dyer Did Hang Like a Flag," in Jessamyn West, ed., *The Quaker Reader* (New York, 1962), 168–175.

27. Jameson, ed., *Johnson's Wonder-Working Providence*, 132; Winthrop, *Short Story*, in Hall, ed., *Antinomian Controversy*, 281; Nathaniel B. Shurtleff, ed., *Records of the Governor and Company of the Massachusetts Bay in New England, 1628–1641* (Boston, 1853), I, 224, 329.

28. Hosmer, ed., *Winthrop's Journal*, I, 270.

29. "The Rev. John Eliot's Record of Church Members, Roxbury, Massachusetts," in *A Report of the Boston Commissioners, Containing the Roxbury Land and Church Records* (Boston, 1881), 77.

30. Hosmer, ed., *Winthrop's Journal*, I, 285–286; George Francis Dow, ed., *Records and Files of the Quarterly Courts of Essex County, Massachusetts, 1636–1656*, I (Salem, Mass., 1911), 12, 138, 180, 182–183, 186; John Noble, ed., *Records of the Court of Assistants of the Colony of the Massachusetts Bay, 1630–1644*, II (Boston, 1904), 80, hereafter cited as *Assistants Records;* Sidney Perley, *History of Salem, Massachusetts, 1638–1670*, II (Salem, Mass., 1926), 50; Thomas Hutchinson, *The Witchcraft Delusion of 1692* (Boston, 1870), 6.

31. "A Report of the Trial of Mrs. Anne Hutchinson before the Church in Boston," in Hall, ed., *Antinomian Controversy*, 365.

32. Hosmer, ed., *Winthrop's Journal*, I, 234; "The Examination of Mrs. Anne Hutchinson at the Court at Newtown," in Hall, ed., *Antinomian Controversy*, 312–314, 318; "Trial of Anne Hutchinson before Boston church," *ibid.*, 380, 382–383.

33. "Examination of Mrs. Hutchinson at Newtown," in Hall, ed., *Antinomian Controversy*, 313–316.

34. Winthrop, *Short Story, ibid.*, 268.

35. "Examination of Mrs. Hutchinson at Newtown," *ibid.*, 330.

36. "Trial of Anne Hutchinson before Boston church," *ibid.*, 380. That Ms. Hutchinson chose a woman preacher as a model for her rebellious behavior, instead of the more popular "Spirit-mystic" and "apostle of Ely," William Sedgwick, indicates that Anne had some level of feminist self-awareness and suggests that she was not greatly in need of specifically male guidance. Cotton expressed the view that she was far from satisfied with his guidance. "Mistris *Hutchinson* seldome resorted to mee," he wrote, "and when she did come to me, it was seldome or never (that I can tell of) that she tarried long. I rather think, she was loath to resort much to me, or, to conferre long with me, lest she might seeme to learne somewhat from me." Cotton, *Congregational Churches Cleared, ibid.*, 434. Cotton's testimony may not be completely accurate, as he was writing to wash the Antinomian stain off his own hands.

Little is known about Anne Hutchinson's role-model, the woman of Ely. Thomas Edwards, a contemporary Puritan divine, remarked that "there are also some women preachers in our times, who keep constant lectures, preaching weekly to many men and women. In Lincolnshire, in Holland and those parts [i.e., the parts about Holland in Lincolnshire] there is a woman preacher who preaches (it's certain), and 'tis reported also she baptizeth, but that's not so certain. *In the Isle of Ely (that land of errors and sectaries) is a woman preacher also.*" See his *Gangraena . . .* (London, 1646), Pt. ii, 29, quoted in Battis, *Saints and Sectaries,* 43n.

37. Winthrop, *Short Story,* in Hall, ed., *Antinomian Controversy,* 273, and "Examination of Mrs. Hutchinson at Newtown," *ibid.,* 337.

38. A good discussion of the theological issues surrounding resurrection is provided in Jesper Rosenmeier, "New England's Perfection: The Image of Adam and the Image of Christ in the Antinomian Crisis, 1634 to 1638," *William and Mary Quarterly,* 3d Ser., XXVII (1970), 435–459. Rosenmeier depicts Ms. Hutchinson too explicitly as a Familist without supplying sufficient evidence.

39. Ms. Hutchinson had responded to an argument of Cotton's with the rejoinder, "I desire to hear God speak this and not man." "Trial of Anne Hutchinson before Boston church," in Hall, ed., *Antinomian Controversy,* 358, 362, 355.

40. *Ibid.,* 372. See Battis, *Saints and Sectaries,* 52n.

41. "Trial of Anne Hutchinson before Boston church," in Hall, ed., *Antinomian Controversy,* 369, 370, 365.

42. *Ibid.,* 385–387, 366–368.

43. *Ibid.,* 378, 388, and Winthrop, *Short Story, ibid.,* 307.

44. Richard D. Pierce, ed., *The Records of the First Church in Boston, 1630–1868,* I, in Colonial Society of Massachusetts, *Publications,* XXXIX (Boston, 1961), 22, 25; *Assistants Records,* II, 78, 82; Emil Oberholzer, Jr., *Delinquent Saints: Disciplinary Action in the Early Congregational Churches of Massachusetts* (New York, 1956), 85; "The Diaries of John Hull," American Antiquarian Society, *Archaelogia Americana,* III (Worcester, Mass., 1857), 192n.

45. Joseph B. Felt, *Annals of Salem, Massachusetts,* II (Salem, Mass., 1845), 573, 576, and Charles Henry Pope, *The Pioneers of Massachusetts* (Boston, 1900), 382.

46. Dow, ed., *Essex County Court Records,* I, 6, 9; *Assistants Records,* II, 78; "A Description and History of Salem by the Rev. William Bentley," Mass. Hist. Soc., *Colls.,* 1st Ser., VI (Boston, 1799), 252; Hosmer, ed., *Winthrop's Journal,* I, 282–283; Felt, *Annals of Salem,* II, 420. The attitude of Dorothy Talby's husband may have contributed to the release of her violent inclinations, for on July 1, 1639, he was censured by the Salem church for "much pride and unnaturalness to his wife." Perley, *History of Salem,* II, 52.

47. The author has calculated the percentage of female offenders from the *Assistants Records* and the percentage of male and female arrivals in New England from the ship lists in Charles Edward Banks, *The Planters of the Commonwealth: A Study of the Emigrants and Emigrations in Colonial Times . . .* (Boston, 1930). The increase in female offenders may not seem very significant at first glance. However, if the sex distribution of the Massachusetts population remained stable between 1630 and 1644, which is a big assumption, a z-score comparison of the 1630 to 1634 and the 1635 to 1639 populations yields a result statistically significant at the 5% level. A comparison of the 1630 to 1634 and the 1640 to the 1644 populations yields an even more astounding result which is significant at the 1% level. There is a

1% statistical probability that the increase in female offenders from 1630 to 1644 is due only to chance.

48. Before 1641 the Deputies and Assistants did not prosecute women for fornication or lascivious behavior unless those women were considered "whores" or "sluts." Premarital sexual activity was believed to be sinful, but the male was considered the active, initiatory agent and the female the passive, yielding participant. As a result of this guiding conceptualization, only 2 women but 17 men were convicted of fornication or enticement to fornication between 1630 and 1639. After the assertiveness of many women in the Antinomian unrest had proven to the authorities that women must be held more accountable for their actions, the magistrates began to prosecute both male and female fornicators, including for the first time women who had become pregnant and then married the fathers of their children. Between 1640 and 1644 18 men and 10 women were punished for premarital sexual activities. *Assistants Records*, II, *passim*; Shurtleff, ed., *Mass. Bay Records*, I, II, *passim*.

49. *Assistants Records*, II, 109; Hosmer, ed., *Winthrop's Journal*, II, 38–40; John Cotton to Francis Hutchinson, Mass. Hist. Soc., *Colls.*, 2d Ser., X (1823), 186. In 1633 the Assistants fined Capt. John Stone £100 for assaulting Justice Roger Ludlow and calling him a "just ass." Four years later Robert Anderson was fined £50 for "contempt," but no other reviler of authority was fined more than £20. *Assistants Records*, II, 35, 66.

50. In 1639 the authorities criticized the Rev. Hanserd Knowles for holding "some of Mrs. Hutchinson's opinions" and two years later forced the Rev. Jonathan Burr to renounce certain errors which, wrote Winthrop, "savor[ed] of familism." Hosmer, ed., *Winthrop's Journal*, I, 295; II, 22–23.

51. "Psalm-Singing a Godly Exercise" [*Singing of Psalmes a Gosepl-Ordinance . . .* (London, 1650)], in Edmund Clarence Stedman and Ellen MacKay Hutchinson, eds., *A Library of American Literature From the Earliest Settlement to the Present Time*, I (New York, 1891), 266.

52. Weld, "Preface," to Winthrop, *Short Story*, in Hall, ed., *Antinomian Controversy*, 214. Dr. Paul A. Younge's diagnosis of Ms. Hutchinson's "30. monstrous births" as an hydatidiform mole, a uterine growth which frequently accompanies menopause, is adopted in Battis, *Saints and Sectaries*, 346.

53. Winthrop, *Short Story*, in Hall, ed., *Antinomian Controversy*, 280–281.

54. Charles H. Bell, ed., *John Wheelwright: His Writings, Including His Fast-Day Sermon, 1637, and His Mercurius Americanus, 1645; with a Paper upon the Genuineness of the Indian Deed of 1629, and a Memoir* (Boston, 1876), 195–196.

55. Weld, "Preface," to Winthrop, *Short Story*, in Hall, ed., *Antinomian Controversy*, 214; Jameson, ed., *Johnson's Wonder-Working Providence*, 28; "Roger Clap's Memoirs," in Alexander Young, ed., *Chronicles of the First Planters of the Colony of Massachusetts Bay, from 1623–1636* (Boston, 1846), 360; "From Majr. Scott's mouth," Mass. Hist. Soc., *Proceedings*, 1st Ser., XIII (1873–1875), 132. John Josselyn, a British traveler, wrote that he was surprised to find "a grave and sober person" who told him about Mary Dyer's "monster" on his first visit to Massachusetts in 1639. See his *An Account of Two Voyages to New-England . . .* (London, 1675), 27–28.

56. Hosmer, ed., *Winthrop's Journal*, II, 8.

57. *Ibid.*, I, 299, and "Clap's Memoirs," in Young, ed., *First Planters of Massachusetts*, 360.

58. Winthrop, *Short Story*, in Hall, ed., *Antinomian Controversy*, 307, and Cotton, *Congregational Churches Cleared, ibid.*, 420.

59. George H. Moore, "Giles Firmin and His Various Writings," *Historical Magazine*, 2d Ser., III (1868), 150, quoting Giles Firmin, Πανομογια, *a brief review of Mr. Davis's Vindication: giving no satisfaction* . . . (London, 1693).

60. Hosmer, ed., *Winthrop's Journal*, I, 286–287; John Russell Bartlett, ed., *Records of the Colony of Rhode Island and Providence Plantations, in New England, 1636–1663*, I (Providence, R. I., 1856), 16; Roger Williams to John Winthrop, May 22, 1638, in John R. Bartlett, ed., *The Complete Writings of Roger Williams* (New York, 1963 [orig. publ. Providence, R. I., 1874]), 95–96; Williams to Winthrop, Oct. 1638, *ibid.*, 124.

61. Jameson, ed., *Johnson's Wonder-Working Providence*, 186.

62. Howard M. Chapin, *Documentary History of Rhode Island*, II (Providence, R. I., 1916), 68, 84. Coddington controlled the dispensation of land titles because the original deed to Rhode Island was issued in his name.

63. Edward Winslow, *Hypocrisie Unmasked: A true Relation of the Proceedings of the Governour and Company of the Massachusetts against Samuel Gorton* . . . (London, 1646), 44, 54–55, 67; Hosmer, ed., *Winthrop's Journal*, I, 297, 299; Chapin, *History of Rhode Island*, II, 56–57; William Coddington to John Winthrop, Dec. 9, 1639, *Winthrop Papers*, IV, 160–161; Robert Baylie, *A Dissuasive from the Errours of the Time* . . . (London, 1645), 150.

64. Chapin, *History of Rhode Island*, II, 68, and Winslow, *Hypocrisie Unmasked*, 53, 83.

65. Hosmer, ed., *Winthrop's Journal*, II, 39.

66. Thomas Lechford, *Plain Dealing: or, Newes from New-England* . . . (London, 1642), reprinted in Mass. Hist. Soc., *Colls.*, 3d Ser., III (Boston, 1833), 96.

67. "Letter of Randall Holden, Sept. 15th, 1643," *ibid.*, I (1825), 13, and Samuel Niles, "A Summary Historical Narrative of the Wars in New-England with the French and Indians, in the several Parts of the Country," *ibid.*, VI (1837), 201.

68. Winthrop, *Short Story*, in Hall, ed., *Antinomian Controversy*, 310.

69. Perry Miller, *The New England Mind: The Seventeenth Century* (New York, 1939), 391. Increase Mather saw the hand of God at work again when Anne's son Edward died from Indian wounds in 1675. "It seems to be an observable providence," Mather observed, "that so many of that family die by the hands of the uncircumcised." "Diary of Increase Mather, 1674–87," Mass. Hist. Soc., *Procs.*, 2d Ser., XIII (1900), 400.

70. Katherine Scott to John Winthrop, Jr., 1658, Mass. Hist. Soc., *Colls.*, 5th Ser., I (1871), 96–97, and "Letter of Randall Holden, Sept. 15th, 1643," *ibid.*, 3d Ser., I (1825), 13–15.

2 & Husbands and Wives

John Demos

No aspect of the Puritan household was more vital than the relationship of husband and wife. But the study of this relationship raises at once certain larger questions of sex differentiation: What were the relative positions of men and women in Plymouth Colony? What attributes, and what overall valuation, were thought appropriate to each sex?

We know in a general way that male dominance was an accepted principle all over the Western World in the seventeenth century. The fundamental Puritan sentiment on this matter was expressed by Milton in a famous line in *Paradise Lost:* "he for God only, she for God in him" and there is no reason to suspect that the people of Plymouth would have put it any differently. The world of public affairs was nowhere open to women—in Plymouth only males were eligible to become "freemen." Within the family the husband was always regarded as the "head"—and the Old Colony provided no exceptions to this pattern. Moreover, the culture at large maintained a deep and primitive kind of suspicion of women, solely on account of their sex. Some basic taint of corruption was thought to be inherent in the feminine constitution—a belief rationalized, of course, by the story of Eve's initial treachery in the Garden of Eden. It was no coincidence that in both the Old and the New World witches were mostly women. Only two allegations of witchcraft turn up in the official records of Plymouth,[1] but other bits of evidence point in the same general direction. There are, for example, the quoted words of a mother beginning an emotional plea to her son: "if you would beleive a woman beleive mee. . . ."[2] And why *not* believe a woman?

The views of the Pilgrim pastor John Robinson are also interesting in this connection. He opposed, in the first place, any tendency to regard women as "necessary evils" and greatly regretted the currency of such opinions among "not only heathen poets . . . but also wanton Christians." The Lord had created both man and woman of an equal perfection, and "neither is she, since the creation more degenerated than he from the primitive goodness."[3] Still, in marriage some principles of authority were essential, since "differences will arise and be seen, and so the one must give way, and apply unto the other; this, God and nature layeth upon the woman, rather than upon the man." Hence the proper attitude of a wife towards her husband was "a reverend subjection."[4]

However, in a later discussion of the same matter Robinson developed a more complex line of argument which stressed certain attributes of inferiority assumed to be inherently feminine. Women, he wrote, were under two different kinds of subjection. The first was framed "in innocency" and implied no "grief" or "wrong" whatsoever. It reflected simply the woman's character as "the weaker vessel"—weaker, most obviously, with respect to intelligence or "understanding." For this was a gift "which God hath . . . afforded [the man], and means of obtaining it, above the woman, that he might guide and go before her."[5] Robinson also recognized that some men abused their position of authority and oppressed their wives most unfairly. But *even so*—and this was his central point—resistance was not admissible. Here he affirmed the second kind of subjection laid upon woman, a subjection undeniably "grievous" but justified by her "being first in transgression." In this way—by invoking the specter of Eve corrupting Adam in paradise—Robinson arrived in the end at a position which closely approximated the popular assumption of woman's basic moral weakness.

Yet within this general framework of masculine superiority there were a number of rather contrary indications. They seem especially evident in certain areas of the law. Richard B. Morris has written a most interesting essay on this matter, arguing the improved legal status of colonial women by comparison to what still obtained in the mother country.[6] Many of his conclusions seem to make a good fit with conditions in Plymouth Colony. The baseline here is the common law tradition of England, which at this time accorded to women only the most marginal sort of recognition. The married woman, indeed, was largely subsumed under the legal personality of her husband; she was virtually without rights to own property, make contracts, or sue for damages on her own account. But in the New World this situation was perceptibly altered.

Consider, for example, the evidence bearing on the property rights of Plymouth Colony wives. The law explicitly recognized their part in the accumulation of a family's estate, by the procedures it established for the treatment of widows. It was a basic principle of inheritance in this period—on both sides of the Atlantic—that a widow should have the use or profits of one-third of the land owned by her husband at the time of his death and full title to one-third of his movable property. But at least in Plymouth, and perhaps in other colonies as well, this expressed more than the widow's need for an adequate living allowance. For the laws also prescribed that "if any man do make an irrational and unrighteous Will, whereby he deprives his Wife of her reasonable allowance for her subsistencey," the Court may "relieve her out of the estate, notwithstanding by Will it were otherwise disposed; especially in such case where the Wife brought with her good part of the Estate in Marriage, or hath by her diligence and industry done her part in the getting of the Estate, and was otherwise well deserving."[7] Occasionally the Court saw fit to alter the terms of a will on this account. In 1663, for example, it awarded to widow Naomi Silvester a larger share of her late husband's estate than the "inconsiderable pte" he had left her, since she had been "a frugall and laborious woman in the procuring of the said estate."[8] In short, the widow's customary "thirds" was not a mere dole; it was her *due.*

But there is more still. In seventeenth-century England women were denied the right to make contracts, save in certain very exceptional instances. In Plymouth Colony, by contrast, one finds the Court sustaining certain kinds of contracts involving women on a fairly regular basis. The most common case of this type was the agreement of a widow and a new husband, made *before* marriage, about the future disposition of their respective properties. The contract drawn up by John Phillips of Marshfield and widow Faith Doty of Plymouth in 1667 was fairly standard. It stipulated that "the said Faith Dotey is to enjoy all her house and land, goods and cattles, that shee is now possessed of, to her owne proper use, to dispose of them att her owne free will from time to time, and att any time, as shee shall see cause." Moreover this principle of separate control extended beyond the realm of personal property. Phillips and widow Doty each had young children by their previous marriages, and their agreement was "that the children of both the said pties shall remaine att the free and proper and onely dispose of theire owne naturall parents, as they shall see good to dispose of them."[9] Any woman entering marriage on terms such as these would seem virtually an equal partner, at least from a legal standpoint. Much rarer, but no less significant, were contracts made by women *after* marriage. When Dorothy Clarke wished to be free of her husband Nathaniel in 1686, the Court refused a divorce but allowed a separation. Their estate was then carefully divided up by contract to which the wife was formally a party.[10] Once again, no clear precedents for this procedure can be found in contemporary English law.

The specific terms of some wills also help to confirm the rights of women to a limited kind of ownership even within marriage. No husband ever included his wife's clothing, for example, among the property to be disposed of after his death. And consider, on the other side, a will like that of Mistress Sarah Jenny, drawn up at Plymouth in 1655. Her husband had died just a few months earlier, and she wished simply to "Despose of som smale thinges that is my owne proper goods leaveing my husbands will to take place according to the true Intent and meaning thereof."[11] The "smale thinges" included not only her wardrobe, but also a bed, some books, a mare, some cattle and sheep. Unfortunately, married women did not usually leave wills of their own (unless they had been previously widowed); and it is necessary to infer that in most cases there was some sort of informal arrangement for the transfer of their personal possessions. One final indication of these same patterns comes from wills which made bequests to a husband and wife separately. Thus, for example, Richard Scalis of Scituate conferred most of his personal possessions on the families of two married daughters, carefully specifying which items should go to the daughters themselves and which to their husbands.[12] Thomas Rickard, also of Scituate, had no family of his own and chose therefore to distribute his property among a variety of friends. Once again spouses were treated separately: "I give unto Thomas Pincin my bedd and Rugg one paire of sheets and pilloty . . . I give and bequeath unto Joane the wife of the aforsaid Thomas Pincin my bason and fouer sheets . . . I give and bequeath unto Joane Stanlacke my Chest . . . unto Richard Stanlacke my Chest . . . unto Richard Stanlacke my best briches and Dublit and ould Coate."[13]

The questions of property rights and of the overall distribution of authority within a marriage do not necessarily coincide; and modern sociologists interested in the latter subject usually emphasize the process of decision-making.[14] Of course, their use of live samples gives them a very great advantage; they can ask their informants, through questionnaires or interviews, which spouse decides where to go on vacation, what kind of car to buy, how to discipline the children, when to have company in, and so forth. The historian simply cannot draw out this kind of detail, nor can he contrive any substantial equivalent.

But he is able sometimes to make a beginning in this direction; for example, the records of Plymouth do throw light on two sorts of family decisions of the very greatest importance. One of these involves the transfer of land, and illustrates further the whole trend toward an expansion of the rights of married women to hold property. The point finds tangible expression in a law passed by the General Court in 1646: "It is enacted &c. That the Assistants or any of them shall have full power to take the acknowledgment of a bargaine and sale of houses and lands . . . And that the wyfe hereafter come in & consent and acknowledg the sale also; but that all bargaines and sales of houses and lands made before this day to remayne firm to the buyer notwithstanding the wife did not acknowledge the same."[15] The words "come in" merit special attention: the authorities wished to confront the wife personally (and even, perhaps, privately?) in order to minimize the possibility that her husband might exert undue pressure in securing her agreement to a sale.

The second area of decision-making in which both spouses shared an important *joint* responsibility was the "putting out" of children into foster families. For this there was no statute prescribing a set line of procedure, but the various written documents from specific cases make the point clearly enough. Thus in 1660 "An Agreement appointed to bee Recorded" affirmed that "Richard Berry of Yarmouth with his wifes Concent and other frinds; hath given unto Gorge Crispe of Eastham and his; wife theire son Samuell Berry; to bee att the ordering and Disposing of the said Gorge and his wife as if hee were theire owne Child."[16] The practice of formally declaring the wife's consent is evident in all such instances, when both parents were living. Another piece of legal evidence describes an actual deathbed scene in which the same issue had to be faced. It is the testimony of a mother confirming the adoption of her son, and it is worth quoting in some detail. "These prsents Witnesse that the 20th of march 1657–8 Judith the wife of William Peaks acknowlidged that her former husband Lawrance Lichfeild lying on his Death bedd sent for John Allin and Ann his wife and Desired to give and bequeath unto them his youngest son Josias Lichfeild if they would accept of him and take him as theire Child; then they Desired to know how long they should have him and the said Lawrance said for ever; but the mother of the child was not willing then; but in a short time after willingly Concented to her husbands will in the thinge."[17] That the wife finally agreed is less important here than the way in which her initial reluctance sufficed to block the child's adoption, in spite of the clear wishes of her husband.

Another reflection of this pattern of mutual responsibility appears in certain types of business activity—for instance, the management of inns and taverns ("ordinaries" in the language of the day). All such establishments were licensed by the General Court; hence their history can be followed, to a limited degree, in the official Colony Records. It is interesting to learn that one man's license was revoked because he had recently "buryed his wife, and in that respect not being soe capeable of keeping a publicke house."[18] In other cases the evidence is less explicit but still revealing. For many years James Cole ran the principal ordinary in the town of Plymouth, and from time to time the Court found it necessary to censure and punish certain violations of proper decorum that occurred there. In some of these cases Cole's wife Mary was directly implicated. In March 1669 a substantial fine was imposed "for that the said Mary Cole suffered divers psons after named to stay drinking on the Lords day . . . in the time of publicke worshipp."[19] Indeed the role of women in all aspects of this episode is striking, since two of the four drinking customers, the "divers psons after named," turned out to be female. Perhaps, then, women had considerable freedom to move on roughly the same terms with men even into some of the darker byways of Old Colony life.

The Court occasionally granted liquor licenses directly to women. Husbands were not mentioned, though it is of course possible that all of the women involved were widows. In some cases the terms of these permits suggest retail houses rather than regular inns or taverns. Thus in 1663 "Mistris Lydia Garrett" of Scituate was licensed to "sell liquors, alwaies provided . . . that shee sell none but to house keepers, and not lesse than a gallon att a time;"[20] and the agreement with another Scituate lady, Margaret Muffee, twenty years later, was quite similar.[21] But meanwhile in Middlebury one "Mistress Mary Combe" seems to have operated an ordinary of the standard type.[22] Can we proceed from these specific data on liquor licensing to some more general conclusion about the participation of women in the whole field of economic production and exchange? Unfortunately there is little additional hard evidence on one side or the other. The Court Records do not often mention other types of business activity, with the single exception of milling; and no woman was ever named in connection with this particular enterprise. A few more wills could be cited—for instance, the one made by Elizabeth Poole, a wealthy spinster in Taunton, leaving "my pte in the Iron workes" to a favorite nephew.[23] But this does not add up to very much. The economy of Plymouth was, after all, essentially simple—indeed "underdeveloped"—in most important respects. Farming claimed the energies of all but a tiny portion of the populace; there was relatively little opportunity for anyone, man *or* woman, to develop a more commercial orientation. It is known that in the next century women played quite a significant role in the business life of many parts of New England,[24] and one can view this pattern as simply the full development of possibilities that were latent even among the first generations of settlers. But there is no way to fashion an extended chain of proof.

Much of what has been said so far belongs to the general category of the rights and privileges of the respective partners to a marriage. But what of their duties, their basic responsibilities to one another? Here, surely, is another area of major importance in any assessment of the character of married life. The writings of John Robinson help us to make a start with these questions, and especially to recover the framework of ideals within which most couples of Plymouth Colony must have tried to hammer out a meaningful day-to-day relationship. We have noted already that Robinson prescribed "subjection" as the basic duty of a wife to her husband. No woman deserved praise, "how well endowed soever otherwise, except she frame, and compose herself, what may be, unto her husband, in conformity of manners."[25] From the man, by contrast, two things were particularly required: "love . . . and wisdom." His love for his wife must be "like Christ's to his church: holy for quality, and great for quantity," and it must stand firm even where "her failings and faults be great." His wisdom was essential to the role of family "head"; without it neither spouse was likely to find the way to true piety, and eventually to salvation.

It is a long descent from the spiritual counsel of John Robinson to the details of domestic conflict as noted in the Colony Records. But the Records are really the only available source of information about the workings of actual marriages in this period. They are, to be sure, a negative type of source; that is, they reveal only those cases which seemed sufficiently deviant and sufficiently important to warrant the attention of the authorities. But it is possible by a kind of reverse inference to use them to reconstruct the norms which the community at large particularly wished to protect. This effort serves to isolate three basic obligations in which both husband and wife were thought to share.

There was, first and most simply, the obligation of regular and exclusive cohabitation. No married person was permitted to live apart from his spouse except in very unusual and temporary circumstances (as when a sailor was gone to sea). The Court stood ready as a last resort to force separated couples to come together again, though it was not often necessary to deal with the problem in such an official way. One of the few recorded cases of this type occurred in 1659. The defendant was a certain Goodwife Spring, married to a resident of Watertown in the Bay Colony and formerly the wife and widow of

Thomas Hatch of Scituate. She had, it seems, returned to Scituate some three or four years earlier, and had been living "from her husband" ever since. The Court ordered that "shee either repaire to her husband with all convenient speed, . . . or . . . give a reason why shee doth not." [26] Exactly how this matter turned out cannot be determined, but it seems likely that the ultimate sanction was banishment from the Colony. The government of Massachusetts Bay is known to have imposed this penalty in a number of similar cases. None of the extant records describe such action being taken at Plymouth, but presumably the possibility was always there.

Moreover, the willful desertion of one spouse by the other over a period of several years was one of the few legitimate grounds for divorce. In 1670, for example, the Court granted the divorce plea of James Skiffe "haveing received sufficient testimony that the late wife of James Skiffe hath unlawfully forsaken her lawfull husband . . . and is gone to Roanoke, in or att Verginnia, and there hath taken another man for to be her husband."[27] Of course, bigamy was always sufficient reason in itself for terminating a marriage. Thus in 1680 Elizabeth Stevens obtained a divorce from her husband when it was proved that he had three other wives already, one each in Boston, Barbadoes, and a town in England not specified.[28]

But it was not enough that married persons should simply live together on a regular basis; their relationship must be relatively peaceful and harmonious. Once again the Court reserved the right to interfere in cases where the situation had become especially difficult. Occasionally both husband and wife were judged to be at fault, as when George and Anna Barlow were "severly reproved for theire most ungodly liveing in contension one with the other, and admonished to live otherwise." [29] But much more often one or the other was singled out for the Court's particular attention. One man was punished for "abusing his wife by kiking her of from a stoole into the fier,"[30] and another for "drawing his wife in an uncivell manor on the snow."[31] A more serious case was that of John Dunham, convicted of "abusive carriage towards his wife in continuall tiranising over her, and in pticulare for his late abusive and uncivill carryage in endeavoring to beate her in a deboist manor." [32] The Court ordered a whipping as just punishment for these cruelties, but the sentence was then suspended at the request of Dunham's wife. Sometimes the situation was reversed and the woman was the guilty party. In 1655, for example, Joan Miller of Taunton was charged with "beating and reviling her husband, and egging her children to healp her, bidding them knock him in the head, and wishing his victuals might coak him."[33] A few years later the wife of Samuel Halloway (also of

Taunton) was admonished for "carryage towards her husband . . . soe turbulend and wild, both in words and actions, as hee could not live with her but in danger of his life or limbs."[34]

It would serve no real purpose to cite more of these unhappy episodes—and it might indeed create an erroneous impression that marital conflict was particularly endemic among the people of the Old Colony. But two general observations are in order. First, the Court's chief aim in this type of case was to restore the couple in question to something approaching tranquility. The assumption was that a little force applied from the outside might be useful, whether it came in the form of an "admonition" or in some kind of actual punishment. Only once did the Court have to recognize that the situation might be so bad as to make a final reconciliation impossible. This happened in 1665 when John Williams, Jr., of Scituate, was charged with a long series of "abusive and harsh carriages" toward his wife Elizabeth, "in speciall his sequestration of himselfe from the marriage bed, and his accusation of her to bee a whore, and that especially in reference unto a child lately borne of his said wife by him denied to bee legittimate."[35] The case was frequently before the Court during the next two years, and eventually all hope of a settlement was abandoned. When Williams persisted in his "abuses," and when too he had "himself . . . [declared] his insufficency for converse with weomen,"[36] a formal separation was allowed—though not a full divorce. In fact, it may be that his impotence, not his habitual cruelty, was the decisive factor in finally persuading the Court to go this far. For in another case, some years later, a separation was granted on the former grounds alone.[37]

The second noteworthy aspect of all these situations is the equality they seem to imply between the sexes. In some societies and indeed in many parts of Europe at this time, a wife was quite literally at the mercy of her husband—his prerogatives extended even to the random use of physical violence. But clearly this was not the situation at Plymouth. It is, for example, instructive to break down these charges of "abusive carriage" according to sex: one finds that wives were accused just about as often as husbands. Consider, too, those cases of conflict in which the chief parties were of opposite sex but not married to one another. Once again the women seem to have held their own. Thus we have, on the one side, Samuel Norman punished for "strikeing Lydia, the wife of Henery Taylor,"[38] and John Dunham for "abusive speeches and carriages"[39] toward Sarah, wife of Benjamin Eaton; and, on the other side, the complaint of Abraham Jackson against "Rose, the wife of Thomas Morton, . . . that the said Rose, as hee came from worke, did abuse him by calling of him lying rascall and rogue."[40] In short, this does *not* seem to have been a society characterized by a really pervasive, and operational, norm of male dominance. There is no evidence at all of habitual patterns of deference in the relations between the sexes. John Robinson, and many others, too, may have assumed that woman was "the weaker vessel" and that "subjection" was her natural role. But as so often happens with respect to such matters, actual behavior was another story altogether.

The third of the major obligations incumbent on the married pair was a normal and exclusive sexual union. As previously indicated, impotence in the husband was one of the few circumstances that might warrant a divorce. The reasoning behind this is nowhere made explicit, but most likely it reflected the felt necessity that a marriage produce children. It is worth noting in this connection some of the words used in a divorce hearing of 1686 which centered on the issue of a man's impotence. He was, according to his wife, "always unable to perform the act of generation."[41] The latter phrase implies a particular view of the nature and significance of the sexual act, one which must have been widely held in this culture. Of course, there were other infertile marriages in the same period which held together. But perhaps the cause of the problem had to be obvious—as with impotence—for the people involved to consider divorce. Where the sexual function appeared normal in both spouses, there was always the hope that the Lord might one day grant the blessing of children. Doubtless for some couples this way of thinking meant year after year of deep personal disappointment.

The problem of adultery was more common—and, in a general sense, more troublesome. For adultery loomed as the most serious possible distortion of the whole sexual and reproductive side of marriage. John Robinson called it "that most foul and filthy sin, . . . the disease of marriage," and concluded that divorce was its necessary "medicine."[42] In fact, most of the divorces granted in the Old Colony stemmed from this one cause alone. But adultery was not only a strong *prima facie* reason for divorce; it was also an act that would bring heavy punishment to the guilty parties. The law decreed that "whosoever shall Commit Adultery with a Married Woman or one Betrothed to another Man, both of them shall be severely punished, by whipping two several times . . . and likewise to wear two Capital Letters A.D. cut out in cloth and sewed on their uppermost Garments . . . and if at any time they shall be found without the said Letters so worne . . . to be forthwith taken and publickly whipt, and so from time to time as often as they are found not to wear them."[43]

But quite apart from the severity of the prescribed punishments, this statute is interesting for its definition of adultery by reference to a married (or bethrothed) *woman.* Here, for the first time, we find some indication of difference in the conduct expected of men and women.

The picture can be filled out somewhat by examining the specific cases of adultery prosecuted before the General Court down through the years. To be sure, the man involved in any given instance was judged together with the woman, and when convicted their punishments were the same. But there is another point to consider as well. All of the adulterous couples mentioned in the records can be classified in one of two categories: a married woman and a married man, or a married woman and a single man. There was, on the other hand, no case involving a married man and a single woman. This pattern seems to imply that the chief concern, the essential element of sin, was the woman's infidelity to her husband. A married man would be punished for his part in this aspect of the affair—rather than for any wrong done to his own wife.

However, this does not mean that a man's infidelities were wholly beyond reproach. The records, for example, include one divorce plea in which the wife adduced as her chief complaint "an act of uncleanes" by her husband with another woman.[44] There was no move to prosecute and punish the husband—apparently since the other woman was unmarried. But the divorce was granted, and the wife received a most favorable settlement. We can, then, conclude the following. The adultery of a wife was treated as both a violation of her marriage (hence grounds for divorce) and an offense against the community (hence cause for legal prosecution). But for comparable behavior by husbands only the former consideration applied. In this somewhat limited sense the people of Plymouth Colony do seem to have maintained a "double standard" of sexual morality.

Before concluding this discussion of married life in the Old Colony and moving on to other matters, one important area of omission should at least be noted. Very little as been said here of love, affection, understanding—a whole range of positive feelings and impulses—between husbands and wives. Indeed the need to rely so heavily on Court Records has tended to weight the balance quite conspicuously on the side of conflict and failure. The fact is that the sum total of actions of divorce, prosecutions for adultery, "admonitions" against habitual quarreling, does not seem terribly large. In order to make a proper assessment of their meaning several contingent factors must be recognized; the long span of time they cover, the steady growth of the Colony's population (to something like 10,000 by the end of the century),[45] the extensive jurisdiction of the Court over many areas of domestic life. Given this overall context, it is clear that the vast majority of Plymouth Colony families never once required the attention of the authorities. Elements of disharmony were, at the least, controlled and confined within certain limits.

But again, can the issue be approached in a more directly affirmative way? Just how and how much, did feelings of warmth and love fit into the marriages of the Old Colony? Unfortunately our source materials have almost nothing to say in response to such questions. But this is only to be expected in the case of legal documents, physical remains, and so forth. The wills often refer to "my loveing wife"—but it would be foolish to read anything into such obvious set phrases. The records of Court cases are completely mute on this score. Other studies of "Puritan" ideals about marriage and the family have drawn heavily on literary materials—and this, of course, is the biggest gap in the sources that have come down from Plymouth Colony. Perhaps, though, a certain degree of extrapolation is permissible here; and if so, we must imagine that love was quite central to these marriages. If, as Morgan has shown, this was the case in Massachusetts Bay, surely it was also true for the people of Plymouth.[46]

There are, finally, just a few scraps of concrete evidence on this point. As previously noted, John Robinson wrote lavishly about the importance of love to a marriage—though he associated it chiefly with the role of the husband. And the wills should be drawn in once again, especially those clauses in which a man left specific instructions regarding the care of his widow. Sometimes the curtain of legal terms and style seems to rise for a moment and behind it one glimpses a deep tenderness and concern. There is, for example, the will written by Walter Briggs in 1676. Briggs's instructions in this regard embraced all of the usual matters—rooms, bedding, cooking utensils, "lyberty to make use of ye two gardens." And he ended with a particular request that his executors "allow my said wife a gentle horse or mare to ride to meeting or any other occasion she may have, & that Jemy, ye neger, catch it for her."[47] Surely this kind of thoughtfulness reflected a larger instinct of love—one which, nourished in life, would not cease to be effective even in the fact of death itself.

NOTES

1. The first occurred in 1661, in Marshfield. A girl named Dinah Silvester accused the wife of William Holmes of being a witch, and of going about in the shape of a bear in order to do mischief. The upshot, however, was a suit for defamation

against Dinah. The Court convicted her and obliged her to make a public apology to Goodwife Holmes. *Plymouth Colony Records,* III, 205, 207, 211. The second case (at Scituate, in 1677) resulted in the formal indictment of one Mary Ingham—who, it was said, had bewitched a girl named Mehitable Woodworth. But after suitable deliberations, the jury decided on an acquittal. *Plymouth Colony Records,* V, 223–24.

2. From a series of depositions bearing on the estate of Samuel Ryder, published in *Mayflower Descendant,* XI, 52. The case is discussed in greater detail below, pp. 165–66.

3. *The Works of John Robinson,* ed. Robert Ashton (Boston, 1851), I, 236.

4. *Ibid.,* 239–40.

5. *Ibid.,* 240.

6. Richard B. Morris, *Studies in the History of American Law* (New York, 1930), Chapter III, "Women's Rights in Early American Law."

7. Brigham *The Compact with the Charter and Laws of the Colony of New Plymouth,* 281.

8. *Plymouth Colony Records,* IV, 46.

9. *Ibid.,* 1643–64. For another agreement of this type, see *Mayflower Descendant,* XVII, 49 (the marriage contract of Ephraim Morton and Mistress Mary Harlow). The same procedures can be viewed, retrospectively, in the wills of men who had been married to women previously widowed. Thus when Thomas Boardman of Yarmouth died in 1689 the following notation was placed near the end of his will: "the estate of my wife brought me upon marriage be at her dispose and not to be Invintoried with my estate." *Mayflower Descendant,* X, 102. See also the will of Dolar Davis, *Mayflower Descendant,* XXIV, 73.

10. *Mayflower Descendant,* VI, 191–92.

11. *Mayflower Descendant,* VIII, 171.

12. *Mayflower Descendant,* XIII, 94–96.

13. *Mayflower Descendant,* IX, 155.

14. See, for example, Robert O. Blood, Jr., and Donald M. Wolfe, *Husbands and Wives* (Glencoe, Ill., 1960), esp. ch. 2.

15. Brigham, *The Compact with the Charter and Laws of the Colony of New Plymouth,* 86.

16. *Mayflower Descendant,* XV, 34.

17. *Mayflower Descendant,* XII, 134.

18. *Plymouth Colony Records,* IV, 54.

19. *Plymouth Colony Records,* V, 15.

20. *Plymouth Colony Records,* IV, 44.

21. *Plymouth Colony Records,* VI, 187.

22. *Ibid.,* 141.

23. *Mayflower Descendant,* XIV, 26.

24. Elizabeth Anthony Dexter, *Colonial Women of Affairs* (Boston, 1911).

25. *The Works of John Robinson,* I, 20.

26. *Plymouth Colony Records,* III, 174.

27. *Plymouth Colony Records,* V, 33.

28. *Plymouth Colony Records,* VI, 44–45.

29. *Plymouth Colony Records*, IV, 10.

30. *Plymouth Colony Records*, V, 61.

31. *Plymouth Colony Records*, IV, 47.

32. *Ibid.*, 103–4.

33. *Plymouth Colony Records*, III, 75.

34. *Plymouth Colony Records*, V, 29.

35. *Plymouth Colony Records*, IV, 93.

36. *Ibid.*, 125.

37. *Plymouth Colony Records*, VI, 191.

38. *Plymouth Colony Records*, V, 39.

39. *Ibid.*, 40.

40. *Plymouth Colony Records*, IV, 11.

41. *Plymouth Colony Records*, VI, 191.

42. *The Works of John Robinson*, I, 241.

43. Brigham, *The Compact with the Charter and Laws of the Colony of New Plymouth*, 245–46.

44. *Plymouth Colony Records*, III, 221.

45. There are three separate investigations dealing with this question: Bowen, *Early Rehoboth*, I, 15–24; Joseph B. Felt, "Population of Plymouth Colony," in American Statistical Association *Collections*, I, Pt. ii (Boston, 1845), 143–44; and Bradford, *Of Plymouth Plantation*, xi.

46. See Edmund Morgan, *The Puritan Family* (New York, 1966), esp. 46 ff.

47. *Plymouth Colony Records*, VI, 134–35.

3 ⚭ The Planter's Wife:
The Experience of White Women in Seventeenth-Century Maryland

Lois Green Carr and Lorena S. Walsh

Four facts were basic to all human experience in seventeenth-century Maryland. First, for most of the period the great majority of inhabitants had been born in what we now call Britain. Population increase in Maryland did not result primarily from births in the colony before the late 1680s and did not produce a predominantly native population of adults before the first decade of the eighteenth century. Second, immigrant men could not expect to live beyond age forty-three, and 70 percent would die before age fifty. Women may have had even shorter lives. Third, perhaps 85 percent of the immigrants, and practically all the unmarried immigrant women, arrived as indentured servants and consequently married late. Family groups were never predominant in the immigration to Maryland and were a significant part for only a brief time at mid-century. Fourth, many more men than women immigrated during the whole period.[1] These facts—immigrant predominance, early death, late marriage, and sexual imbalance—created circumstances of social and demographic disruption that deeply affected family and community life.

We need to assess the effects of this disruption on the experience of women in seventeenth-century Maryland. Were women degraded by the hazards of servitude in a society in which everyone had left community and kin behind and in which women were in short supply? Were traditional restraints on social conduct weakened? If so, were women more exploited or more independent and powerful than women who remained in England? Did any differences from English experience which we can observe in the experience of Maryland women survive the

From *William and Mary Quarterly* 34 (October, 1977), pp. 542–571. Reprinted by permission.

transformation from an immigrant to a predominantly native-born society with its own kinship networks and community traditions? The tentative argument put forward here is that the answer to all these questions is Yes. There were degrading aspects of servitude, although these probably did not characterize the lot of most women; there were fewer restraints on social conduct, especially in courtship, than in England; women were less protected but also more powerful than those who remained at home; and at least some of these changes survived the appearance in Maryland of New World creole communities. However, these issues are far from settled, and we shall offer some suggestions as to how they might be further pursued.

Maryland was settled in 1634, but in 1650 there were probably no more than six hundred persons and fewer than two hundred adult women in the province. After that time population growth was steady; in 1704 a census listed 30,437 white persons, of whom 7,163 were adult women.[2] Thus in discussing the experience of white women in seventeenth-century Maryland we are dealing basically with the second half of the century.

Marylanders of that period did not leave letters and diaries to record their New World experience or their relationships to one another. Nevertheless, they left trails in the public records that give us clues. Immigrant lists kept in England and documents of the Maryland courts offer quantifiable evidence about the kinds of people who came and some of the problems they faced in making a new life. Especially valuable are the probate court records. Estate inventories reveal the kinds of activities carried on in the house and on the farm, and wills, which are usually the only personal statements that remain for any man or woman, show something of personal attitudes. This essay relies on the most useful of the immigrant lists and all surviving Maryland court records, but concentrates especially on the surviving records of the lower Western Shore, an early-settled area highly suitable for tobacco. Most of this region comprised four counties: St. Mary's, Calvert, Charles, and Prince George's (formed in 1696 from Calvert and Charles). Inventories from all four counties, wills from St. Mary's and Charles, and court proceedings from Charles and Prince George's provide the major data.[3]

Because immigrants predominated, who they were determined much about the character of Maryland society. The best information so far available comes from lists of indentured servants who left the ports of London, Bristol, and Liverpool. These lists vary in quality, but at the very least they distinguish immigrants by sex and general destination. A place of residence in England is usually given, although it may not represent the emigrant's place of origin; and age and occupation are often noted. These lists reveal several characteristics of immigrants to the Chesapeake and, by inference, to Maryland.[4]

Servants who arrived under indenture included yeomen, husbandmen, farm laborers, artisans, and small tradesmen, as well as many untrained to any special skill. They were young: over half of the men on the London lists of 1683–1684 were aged eighteen to twenty-two. They were seldom under seventeen or over twenty-eight. The women were a little older; the great majority were between eighteen and twenty-five, and half were aged twenty to twenty-two. Most servants contracted for four or five years service, although those under fifteen were to serve at least seven years.[5] These youthful immigrants represented a wide range of English society. All were seeking opportunities they had not found at home.

However, many immigrants—perhaps about half[6]—did not leave England with indentures but paid for their passage by serving according to the custom of the country. Less is known about their social characteristics, but some inferences are possible. From 1661, customary service was set by Maryland laws that required four-year (later five-year) terms for men and women who were twenty-two years or over at arrival and longer terms for those who were younger. A requirement of these laws enables us to determine something about age at arrival of servants who came without indentures. A planter who wished to obtain more than four or five years of service had to take his servant before the county court to have his or her age judged and a written record made. Servants aged over twenty-one were not often registered, there being no incentive for a master to pay court fees for those who would serve the minimum term. Nevertheless, a comparison of the ages of servants under twenty-two recorded in Charles County, 1658–1689, with those under twenty-two on the London list is revealing. Of Charles County male servants (N = 363), 77.1 percent were aged seventeen or under, whereas on the London list (N = 196), 77.6 percent were eighteen or over. Women registered in Charles County court were somewhat older than the men, but among those under twenty-two (N = 107), 5.5 percent were aged twenty-one, whereas on the London list (N = 69), 46.4 percent had reached this age. Evidently, some immigrants who served by custom were younger than those who came indentured, and this age difference probably characterized the two groups as a whole. Servants who were not only very young but had arrived without the protection of a written contract were possibly of lower social origins than were servants who came under indenture. The absence of skills among Charles County servants who served by custom supports this supposition.[7]

Whatever their status, one fact about immigrant women is certain: many fewer came than men. Immigrant lists, headright lists, and itemizations of servants in inventories show severe imbalance. On a London immigrant list of 1634–1635 men outnumbered women six to one. From the 1650s at least until the 1680s most sources show a ratio of three to one. From then on, all sources show some, but not great, improvement. Among immigrants from Liverpool over the years 1697–1707 the ratio was just under two and one half to one.[8]

Why did not more women come? Presumably, fewer wished to leave family and community to venture into a wilderness. But perhaps more important, women were not as desirable as men to merchants and planters who were making fortunes raising and marketing tobacco, a crop that requires large amounts of labor. The gradual improvement in the sex ratio among servants toward the end of the century may have been the result of a change in recruiting the needed labor. In the late 1660s the supply of young men willing to emigrate stopped increasing sufficiently to meet the labor demands of a growing Chesapeake population. Merchants who recruited servants for planters turned to other sources, and among these sources were women. They did not crowd the ships arriving in the Chesapeake, but their numbers did increase.[8]

To ask the question another way, why did women come? Doubtless, most came to get a husband, an objective virtually certain of success in a land where women were so far outnumbered. The promotional literature, furthermore, painted bright pictures of the life that awaited men and women once out of their time; and various studies suggest that for a while, at least, the promoters were not being entirely fanciful. Until the 1660s, and to a less degree the 1680s, the expanding economy of Maryland and Virginia offered opportunities well beyond those available in England to men without capital and to the women who became their wives.[10]

Nevertheless, the hazards were also great, and the greatest was untimely death. Newcomers promptly became ill, probably with malaria, and many died. What proportion survived is unclear; so far no one has devised a way of measuring it. Recurrent malaria made the woman who survived seasoning less able to withstand other diseases, especially dysentery and influenza. She was especially vulnerable when pregnant. Expectation of life for everyone was low in the Chesapeake, but especially so for women.[11] A woman who had immigrated to Maryland took an extra risk, though perhaps a risk not greater than she might have suffered by moving from her village to London instead.[12]

The majority of women who survived seasoning paid their transportation costs by working for a four- or five-year term of service. The kind of work depended on the status of the family they served. A female servant of a small planter—who through about the 1670s might have had a servant[13] —probably worked at the hoe. Such a man could not afford to buy labor that would not help with the cash crop. In wealthy families women probably were household servants, although some are occasionally listed in inventories of well-to-do planters as living on the quarters—that is, on plantations other than the dwelling plantation. Such women saved men the jobs of preparing food and washing linen but doubtless also worked in the fields.[14] In middling households experience must have varied. Where the number of people to feed and wash for was large, female servants would have had little time to tend the crops.

Tracts that promoted immigration to the Chesapeake region asserted that female servants did not labor in the fields, except "nasty" wenches not fit for other tasks. This implies that most immigrant women expected, or at least hoped, to avoid heavy field work, which English women—at least those above the cottager's status—did not do.[15] What proportion of female servants in Maryland found themselves demeaned by this unaccustomed labor is impossible to say, but this must have been the fate of some. A study of the distribution of female servants among wealth groups in Maryland might shed some light on this question. Nevertheless, we still would not know whether those purchased by the poor or sent to work on a quarter were women whose previous experience suited them for field labor.

An additional risk for the woman who came as a servant was the possibility of bearing a bastard. At least 20 percent of the female servants who came to Charles County between 1658 and 1705 were presented to the county court for this cause.[16] A servant woman could not marry unless someone was willing to pay her master for the term she had left to serve.[17] If a man made her pregnant, she could not marry him unless he could buy her time. Once a woman became free, however, marriage was clearly the usual solution. Only a handful of free women were presented in Charles County for bastardy between 1658 and 1705. Since few free women remained either single or widowed for long, not many were subject to the risk. The hazard of bearing a bastard was a hazard of being a servant.[18]

This high rate of illegitimate pregnancies among servants raises lurid questions. Did men import women for sexual exploitation? Does John Barth's Whore of Dorset have a basis outside his fertile imagination?[19] In our opinion, the answers are clearly No. Servants were economic investments on the part of planters who needed labor. A female servant in a household where there were unmarried men must have both provided and faced temptation, for the pressures were great in a society in which men outnumbered women by three to one.

Nevertheless, the servant woman was in the household to work—to help feed and clothe the family and make tobacco. She was not primarily a concubine.

This point could be established more firmly if we knew more about the fathers of the bastards. Often the culprits were fellow servants or men recently freed but too poor to purchase the woman's remaining time. Sometimes the master was clearly at fault. But often the father is not identified. Some masters surely did exploit their female servants sexually. Nevertheless, masters were infrequently accused of fathering their servants' bastards, and those found guilty were punished as severely as were other men. Community mores did not sanction their misconduct.[20]

A female servant paid dearly for the fault of unmarried pregnancy. She was heavily fined, and if no one would pay her fine, she was whipped. Furthermore, she served an extra twelve to twenty-four months to repay her master for the "touble of his house" and labor lost, and the fathers often did not share in this payment of damages. On top of all, she might lose the child after weaning unless by then she had become free, for the courts bound out bastard children at very early ages.[21]

English life probably did not offer a comparable hazard to young unmarried female servants. No figures are available to show rates of illegitimacy among those who were subject to the risk,[22] but the female servant was less restricted in England than in the Chesapeake. She did not owe anyone for passage across the Atlantic; hence it was easier for her to marry, supposing she happened to become pregnant while in service. Perhaps, furthermore, her temptations were fewer. She was not 3,000 miles from home and friends, and she lived in a society in which there was no shortage of women. Bastards were born in England in the seventeenth century, but surely not to as many as one-fifth of the female servants.

Some women escaped all or part of their servitude because prospective husbands purchased the remainder of their time. At least one promotional pamphlet published in the 1660s described such purchases as likely, but how often they actually occurred is difficult to determine.[23] Suggestive is a 20 percent difference between the sex ratios found in a Maryland headright sample, 1658–1681, and among servants listed in lower Western Shore inventories for 1658–1679.[24] Some of the discrepancy must reflect the fact that male servants were younger than female servants and therefore served longer terms; hence they had a greater chance of appearing in an inventory. But part of the discrepancy doubtless follows from the purchase of women for wives. Before 1660, when sex ratios were even more unbalanced and the expanding economy enabled men to establish themselves more quickly, even more women may have married before their terms were finished.[25]

Were women sold for wives against their wills? No record says so, but nothing restricted a man from selling his servant to whomever he wished. Perhaps some women were forced into such marriages or accepted them as the least evil. But the man who could afford to purchase a wife—especially a new arrival—was usually already an established landowner.[26] Probably most servant women saw an opportunity in such a marriage. In addition, the shortage of labor gave women some bargaining power. Many masters must have been ready to refuse to sell a woman who was unwilling to marry a would-be purchaser.

If a woman's time was not purchased by a prospective husband, she was virtually certain to find a husband once she was free. Those famous spinsters, Margaret and Mary Brent, were probably almost unique in seventeenth-century Maryland. In the four counties of the lower Western Shore only two of the women who left a probate inventory before the eighteenth century are known to have died single.[27] Comely or homely, strong or weak, any young woman was too valuable to be overlooked, and most could find a man with prospects.

The woman who immigrated to Maryland, survived seasoning and service, and gained her freedom became a planter's wife. She had considerable liberty in making her choice. There were men aplenty, and no fathers or brothers were hovering to monitor her behavior or disapprove her preference. This is the modern way of looking at her situation, of course. Perhaps she missed the protection of a father, a guardian, or kinfolk, and the participation in her decision of a community to which she felt ties. There is some evidence that the absence of kin and the pressures of the sex ratio created conditions of sexual freedom in courtship that were not customary in England. A register of marriages and births for seventeenth-century Somerset County shows that about one-third of the immigrant women whose marriages are recorded were pregnant at the time of the ceremony—nearly twice the rate in English parishes.[28] There is no indication of community objection to this freedom so long as marriage took place. No presentments for bridal pregnancy were made in any of the Maryland courts.[29]

The planter's wife was likely to be in her mid-twenties at marriage. An estimate of minimum age at marriage for servant women can be made from lists of indentured servants who left London over the years 1683–1684 and from age judgments in Maryland county court records. If we assume that the 112 female indentured servants going to Maryland and Virginia whose ages are given in the London lists served full four-year terms, then only 1.8 percent married before age twenty, but 68 percent after age twenty-four.[30] Similarly, if the 141 women whose ages were judged in Charles County between 1666 and 1705 served out their terms according to the custom of the country, none married before age twenty-two, and half were twenty-five or over.[31] When adjustments are made for the ages at which wives may have been purchased, the figures drop, but even so the majority of women waited until at least age twenty-four to marry.[32] Actual age at marriage in Maryland can be found for few seventeenth-century female immigrants, but observations for Charles and Somerset counties place the mean age at about twenty-five.[33]

Because of the age at which an immigrant woman married, the number of children she would bear her husband was small. She had lost up to ten years of her childbearing life[34] —the possibility of perhaps four or five children, given the usual rhythm of childbearing.[35] At the same time, high mortality would reduce both the number of children she would bear over the rest of her life and the number who would live. One partner to a marriage was likely to die within seven years, and the chances were only one in three that a marriage would last ten years.[36] In these circumstances, most women would not bear more than three or four children—not counting those stillborn—to any one husband, plus a posthumous child were she the survivor. The best estimates suggest that nearly a quarter, perhaps more, of the children born alive died during their first year and that 40 to 55 percent would not live to see age twenty.[37] Consequently, one of her children would probably die in infancy, and another one or two would fail to reach adulthood. Wills left in St. Mary's County during the seventeenth century show the results. In 105 families over the years 1660 to 1680 only twelve parents left more than three children behind them, including those conceived but not yet born. The average number was 2.3, nearly always minors, some of whom might die before reaching adulthood.[38]

For the immigrant woman, then, one of the major facts of life was that although she might bear a child about every two years, nearly half would not reach maturity. The social implications of this fact are far-reaching. Because she married late in her childbearing years and because so many of her children would die young, the number who would reach marriageable age might not replace, or might only barely replace, her and her husband or husbands as child-producing members of the society. Consequently, so long as immigrants were heavily predominant in the adult female population, Maryland could not grow much by natural increase.[39] It remained a land of newcomers.

This fact was fundamental to the character of seventeenth-century Maryland society, although its implications have yet to be fully explored. Settlers came from all parts of England and hence from differing traditions—in types of agriculture, forms of landholding and estate management, kinds of building construction, customary contributions to community needs, and family arrangements, including the role of women. The necessities of life in the Chesapeake required all immigrants to make adaptations. But until the native-born became predominant, a securely established Maryland tradition would not guide or restrict the newcomers.

If the immigrant woman had remained in England, she would probably have married at about the same age or perhaps a little later.[40] But the social consequences of marriage at these ages in most parts of England were probably different. More children may have lived to maturity, and even where mortality was as high newcomers are not likely to have been the main source of population growth.[41] The locally born would still dominate the community, its social organization, and its traditions. However, where there were exceptions, as perhaps in London, late age at marriage, combined with high mortality and heavy immigration, may have had consequences in some ways similar to those we have found in Maryland.

A hazard of marriage for seventeenth-century women everywhere was death in childbirth, but this hazard may have been greater than usual in the Chesapeake. Whereas in most societies women tend to outlive men, in this malaria-ridden area it is probable that men outlived women. Hazards of childbirth provide the likely reason that Chesapeake women died so young. Once a woman in the Chesapeake reached forty-five, she tended to outlive men who reached the same age. Darrett and Anita Rutman have found malaria a probable cause of an exceptionally high death rate among pregnant women, who are, it appears, peculiarly vulnerable to that disease.[42]

This argument, however, suggests that immigrant women may have lived longer than their native-born daughters, although among men the opposite was true. Life tables created for men in Maryland show that those native-born who survived to age twenty could expect a life span three to ten years longer than that of immigrants, depending upon the region where they lived. The reason for the improvement was doubtless immunities to local diseases developed in childhood.[43] A native woman developed these immunities, but, as we shall see, she also married earlier than immigrant women usually could and hence had more children.[44] Thus she was more exposed to the hazards of childbirth and may have died a little sooner. Unfortunately, the life

TABLE 1 Bequests of Husbands to Wives, St. Mary's and Charles Counties, Maryland, 1640 to 1710

	N	Dower or Less	
		N	%
1640s	6	2	34
1650s	24	7	29
1660s	65	18	28
1670s	86	21	24
1680s	64	17	27
1690s	83	23	28
1700s	74	25	34
Totals	402	113	28

Source: Wills, I-XIV, Hall of Records, Annapolis, Md.

tables for immigrant women that would settle this question have so far proved impossible to construct.

However long they lived, immigrant women in Maryland tended to outlive their husbands—in Charles County, for example, by a ratio of two to one. This was possible, despite the fact that women were younger than men at death, because women were also younger than men at marriage. Some women were widowed with no living children, but most were left responsible for two or three. These were often tiny, and nearly always not yet sixteen.[45]

This fact had drastic consequences, given the physical circumstances of life. People lived at a distance from one another, not even in villages, much less towns. The widow had left her kin 3,000 miles across an ocean, and her husband's family was also there. She would have to feed her children and make her own tobacco crop. Though neighbors might help, heavy labor would be required of her if she had no servants, until— what admittedly was usually not difficult—she acquired a new husband.

In this situation dying husbands were understandably anxious about the welfare of their families. Their wills reflected their feelings and tell something of how they regarded their wives. In St. Mary's and Charles counties during the seventeenth century, little more than one-quarter of the men left their widows with no more than the dower the law required—one-third of his land for her life, plus outright ownership of one-third of his personal property. (See Table 1.) If there were no children, a man almost always left his widow his whole estate. Otherwise there were a variety of arrangements. (See Table 2.)

TABLE 2 Bequests of Husbands to Wives with Children, St. Mary's and Charles Counties, Maryland, 1640 to 1710

	N	All Estate		All or Dwelling Plantation for Life		All or Dwelling Plantation for Widowhood		All or Dwelling Plantation for Minority of Child		More than Dower in Other Form		Dower or Less or Unknown	
		N	%	N	%	N	%	N	%	N	%	N	%
1640s	3	1	33	33								2	67
1650s	16	1	6	2	13	1	6	1	6	4	25	7	44
1660s	45	8	18	8	18	2	4	3	7	9	20	15	33
1670s	61	4	7	21	34	2	3	3	5	13	21	18	30
1680s	52	5	10	19	37	2	4	2	4	11	21	13	25
1690s	69	1	1	31	45	7	10	2	3	10	14	18	26
1700s	62			20	32	6	10	2	3	14	23	20	32
Totals	308	20	6	101	33	20	6	13	4	61	20	93	30

Source: Wills, I-XIV.

During the 1660s, when testators begin to appear in quantity, nearly a fifth of the men who had children left all to their wives, trusting them to see that the children received fair portions. Thus in 1663 John Shircliffe willed his whole estate to his wife "towards the maintenance of herself and my children into whose tender care I do Commend them Desireing to see them brought up in the fear of God and the Catholick Religion and Chargeing them to be Dutiful and obedient to her."[46] As the century progressed, husbands tended instead to give the wife all or a major part of the estate for her life, and to designate how it should be distributed after her death. Either way, the husband put great trust in his widow, considering that he knew she was bound to remarry. Only a handful of men left estates to their wives only for their term of widowhood or until the children came of age. When a man did not leave his wife a life estate, he often gave her land outright or more than her dower third of his movable property. Such bequests were at the expense of his children and showed his concern that his widow should have a maintenance which young children could not supply.

A husband usually made his wife his executor and thus responsible for paying his debts and preserving the estate. Only 11 percent deprived their wives of such powers.[47] In many instances, however, men also appointed overseers to assist their wives and to see that their children were not abused or their property embezzled. Danger lay in the fact that a second husband acquired control of all his wife's property, including her life estate in the property of his predecessor. Over half of the husbands who died in the 1650s and 1660s appointed overseers to ensure that their wills were followed. Some trusted to the overseers' "Care and good Conscience for the good of my widow and fatherless children." Others more explicitly made overseers responsible for seeing that "my said child . . . and the other [expected child] (when pleases God to send it) may have their right Proportion of my Said Estate and that the said Children may be bred up Chiefly in the fear of God."[48] A few men—but remarkably few—authorized overseers to remove children from households of stepfathers who abused them or wasted their property.[49] On the whole, the absence of such provisions for the protection of the children points to the husband's overriding concern for the welfare of his widow and to his confidence in her management, regardless of the certainty of her remarriage. Evidently, in the politics of family life women enjoyed great respect.[50]

We have implied that this respect was a product of the experience of immigrants in the Chesapeake. Might it have been instead a reflection of English culture? Little work is yet in print that allows comparison of the provisions for Maryland widows with those made for the widows of English farmers. Possibly, Maryland husbands were making traditional wills which could have been written in the communities they left behind. However, Margaret Spufford's recent study of three Cambridgeshire villages in the late sixteenth century and early seventeenth century suggests a different pattern. In one of these villages, Chippenham, women usually did receive a life interest in the property, but in the other two they did not. If the children were all minors, the widow controlled the property until the oldest son came of age, and then only if she did not remarry. In the majority of cases adult sons were given control of the property with instructions for the support of their mothers. Spufford suggests that the pattern found in Chippenham must have been very exceptional. On the basis of village censuses in six other counties, dating from 1624 to 1724, which show only 3 percent of widowed people heading households that included a married child, she argues that if widows commonly controlled the farm, a higher proportion should have headed such households. However, she also argues that widows with an interest in land would not long remain unmarried.[51] If so, the low percentage may be deceptive. More direct work with wills needs to be done before we can be sure that Maryland husbands and fathers gave their widows greater control of property and family than did their English counterparts.

Maryland men trusted their widows, but this is not to say that many did not express great anxiety about the future of their children. They asked both wives and overseers to see that the children received "some learning." Robert Sly made his wife sole guardian of his children but admonished her "to take due Care that they be brought up in the true fear of God and instructed in such Literature as may tend to their improvement." Widowers, whose children would be left without any parent, were often the most explicit in prescribing their upbringing. Robert Cole, a middling planter, directed that his children "have such Education in Learning as [to] write and read and Cast accompt I mean my three Sonnes my two daughters to learn to read and sew with their needle and all of them to be keept from Idleness but not to be kept as Comon Servants." John Lawson required his executors to see that his two daughters be reared together, receive learning and sewing instruction, and be "brought up to huswifery."[52] Often present was the fear that orphaned children would be treated as servants and trained only to work in the fields.[53] With stepfathers in mind, many fathers provided that their sons should be independent before the usual age of majority, which for girls was sixteen but for men twenty-one. Sometimes fathers willed that their sons should inherit when they were as young as sixteen, though more often eighteen. The sons could then escape an incompatible stepfather, who could no longer exploit their labor or property. If a son was already close to age sixteen, the father might bind him to his mother until he reached majority or his mother died, whichever came first. If she lived, she could watch out for his welfare, and his labor could contribute to her support. If she died, he and his property would be free from a stepfather's control.[54]

What happened to widows and children if a man died without leaving a will? There was great need for some community institution that could protect children left fatherless or parentless in a society where they usually had no other kind. By the 1660s the probate court and county orphans' courts were supplying this need.[55] If a man left a widow, the probate court—in Maryland a central government agency—usually appointed her or her new husband administrator of the estate with power to pay its creditors under court supervision. Probate procedures provided a large measure of protection. These required an inventory of the movable property and careful accounting of all disbursements, whether or not a man had left a will. William Hollis of Baltimore County, for example, had three stepfathers in seven years, and only the care of the judge of probate prevented the third stepfather from paying the debts of the second with goods that had belonged to William's father. As the judge remarked, William had "an uncareful mother."[56]

Once the property of an intestate had been fully accounted and creditors paid, the county courts appointed a guardian who took charge of the property and gave bond to the children with sureties that he or she would not waste it. If the mother were living, she could be the guardian, or if she had remarried, her new husband would act. Through most of the century bond was waived in these circumstances, but from the 1690s security was required of all guardians, even of mothers. Therefore the courts might actually take away an orphan's property from a widow or stepfather if she or he could not find sureties—that is, neighbors who judged the parent responsible and hence were willing to risk their own property as security. Children without any parents were assigned new families, who at all times found surety if there were property to manage. If the orphans inherited land, English common law allowed them to choose guardians for themselves at age fourteen—another escape hatch for children in conflict with stepparents. Orphans who had no property, or whose property was insufficient to provide an income that could maintain them, were expected to work for their guardians in return for their maintenance. Every year the county courts were expected to check on the welfare of orphans of intestate parents and remove them or their property from guardians who abused them or misused their estates. From 1681, Maryland law required that a special jury be impaneled once a year to report neighborhood knowledge of mistreatment of orphans and hear complaints.

This form of community surveillance of widows and orphans proved quite effective. In 1696 the assembly declared that orphans of intestates were often better cared for than orphans of testators. From that time forward, orphans' courts were charged with supervision of all orphans and were soon given powers to remove any guardians who were shown false to their trusts, regardless of the arrangements laid down in a will. The assumption was that the deceased parent's main concern was the welfare of the child, and that the orphans' court, as "father to us poor orphans," should implement the parent's intent. In actual fact, the courts never removed children—as opposed to their property—from a household in which the mother was living, except to apprentice them at the mother's request. These powers were mainly exercised over guardians of orphans both of whose parents were dead. The community as well as the husband believed the mother most capable of nurturing his children.

Remarriage was the usual and often the immediate solution for a woman who had lost her husband.[57] The shortage of women made any woman eligible to marry again, and the difficulties of raising a family while running a plantation must have made remarriage necessary for widows who had no son old enough to make tobacco. One indication of the high incidence of remarriage is the fact that there were only sixty women, almost all of them widows, among the 1,735 people who left probate inventories in four southern Maryland counties over the second half of the century.[58] Most other women must have died while married and therefore legally without property to put through probate.

One result of remarriage was the development of complex family structures. Men found themselves responsible for stepchildren as well as their own offspring, and children acquired half-sisters and half-brothers. Sometimes a woman married a second husband who himself had been previously married, and both brought children of former spouses to the new marriage. They then produced children of their own. The possibilities for conflict over the upbringing of children are evident, and crowded living conditions, found even in the households of the wealthy, must have added to family tensions. Luckily, the children of the family very often had the same mother. In Charles County, at least, widows took new husbands three times more often than widowers took new wives.[59] The role of the mother in managing the relationships of half-brothers and half-sisters or stepfathers and stepchildren must have been critical to family harmony.

Early death in this immigrant population thus had broad effects on Maryland society in the seventeenth century. It produced what we might call a pattern of serial polyandry, which enabled more men to marry and to father families than the sex ratios otherwise would have permitted. It produced thousands of orphaned children who had no kin to maintain them or preserve their property, and thus gave rise to an institution almost unknown in England, the orphans' court, which was charged with their protection. And early death, by creating families in which the mother was the unifying element, may have increased her authority within the household.

When the immigrant woman married her first husband, there was usually no property settlement involved, since she was unlikely to have any dowry. But her remarriage was another matter. At the very least, she owned or had a life interest in a third of her former husband's estate. She needed also to think of her children's interests. If she remarried, she would lose control of the property. Consequently, property settlements occasionally appear in the seventeenth-century court records between widows and their future husbands. Sometimes she and her intended signed an agreement whereby he relinquished his rights to the use of her children's portions. Sometimes he deeded to her property which she could dispose of at her pleasure.[60] Whether any of these agreements or gifts would have survived a test in court is unknown. We have not yet found any challenged. Generally speaking, the formal marriage settlements of English law, which bypassed the legal difficulties of the married woman's inability to make a contract with her husband, were not adopted by immigrants, most of whom probably came from levels of English society that did not use these legal formalities.

The wife's dower rights in her husband's estate were a recognition of her role in contributing to his prosperity, whether by the property she had brought to the marriage or by the labor she performed in his household. A woman newly freed from servitude would not bring property, but the benefits of her labor would be great. A man not yet prosperous enough to own a servant might need his wife's help in the fields as well as in the house, especially if he were paying rent or still paying for land. Moreover, food preparation was so time-consuming that even if she worked only at household duties, she saved him time he needed for making tobacco and corn. The corn, for example, had to be pounded in the mortar or ground in a handmill before it could be used to make bread, for there were very few water mills in seventeenth-century Maryland. The wife probably raised vegetables in a kitchen garden; she also milked the cows and made butter and cheese, which might produce a salable surplus. She washed the clothes, and made them if she had the skill. When there were servants to do field work, the wife undoubtedly spent her time entirely in such household tasks. A contract of 1681 expressed such a division of labor. Nicholas Maniere agreed to live on a plantation with his wife and child and a servant. Nicholas and the servant were to work the land; his wife was to "Dresse the Victualls milk the Cowes wash for the servants and Doe allthings necessary for a woman to doe upon the s[ai]d plantation."[61]

We have suggested that wives did field work; the suggestion is supported by occasional direct references in the court records. Mary Castleton, for example, told the judge of probate that "her husband late Deceased in his Life time had Little to sustaine himselfe and Children but what was produced out of ye ground by ye hard Labour of her the said Mary."[62] Household inventories provide indirect evidence. Before about 1680 those of poor men and even middling planters on Maryland's lower Western Shore—the bottom two-thirds of the married decendents—[63] show few signs of household industry, such as appear in equivalent English estates.[64] Sheep and woolcards, flax and hackles, and spinning wheels all were a rarity, and such things as candle molds were nonexistent. Women in these households must have been busy at other work. In households with bound labor the wife doubtless was fully occupied preparing food and washing clothes for family and hands. But the wife in a household too poor to afford bound labor—the bottom fifth of the married decedent group—might well tend tobacco when she could.[65] Eventually, the profits of her labor might enable the family to buy a servant, making greater profits possible. From such beginnings many families climbed the economic ladder in seventeenth-century Maryland.[66]

The proportion of servantless households must have been larger than is suggested by the inventories of the dead, since young men were less likely to die than old men and had had less time to accumulate property. Well over a fifth of the households of married men on the lower Western Shore may have had no bound labor. Not every wife in such households would necessarily work at the hoe—saved from it by upbringing, ill-health, or the presence of small children who needed her care—but many women performed such work. A lease of 1691, for example, specified that the lessee could farm the amount of land which "he his wife and children can tend."[67]

Stagnation of the tobacco economy, beginning about 1680, produced changes that had some effect on women's economic role.[68] As shown by inventories of the lower Western Shore, home industry increased, especially at the upper ranges of the economic spectrum. In these households women were spinning yarn and knitting it into clothing.[69] The increase in such activity was far less in the households of the bottom fifth, where changes of a different kind may have increased the pressures to grow tobacco. Fewer men at this level could now purchase land, and a portion of their crop went for rent.[70] At this level, more wives than before may have been helping to produce tobacco when they could. And by this time they were often helping as a matter of survival, not as a means of improving the family position.

So far we have considered primarily the experience of immigrant women. What of their daughters? How were their lives affected by the demographic stresses of Chesapeake society?

On of the most important points in which the experience of daughters differed from that of their mothers was the age at which they married. In this woman-short world, the mothers had married as soon as they were eligible, but they had not usually become eligible until they were mature women in their middle twenties. Their daughters were much younger at marriage. A vital register kept in Somerset County shows that some girls married at age twelve and that the mean age at marriage for those born before 1670 was sixteen and a half years.

Were some of these girls actually child brides? It seems unlikely that girls were married before they had become capable of bearing children. Culturally, such a practice would fly in the face of English, indeed Western European, precedent, nobility excepted. Nevertheless, the number of girls who married before age sixteen, the legal age of inheritance for girls, is astonishing. Their English counterparts ordinarily did not marry until their mid- to late twenties or early thirties. In other parts of the Chesapeake, historians have found somewhat higher ages at marriage than appear in Somerset, but everywhere in seventeenth-century Maryland and Virginia most native-born women married before they reached age twenty-one.[71] Were such early marriages a result of the absence of fathers? Evidently not. In Somerset County, the fathers of very young brides—those under sixteen—were usually living.[72]

Evidently, guardians were unlikely to allow such marriages, and this fact suggests that they were not entirely approved. But the shortage of women imposed strong pressures to marry as early as possible.

Not only did native girls marry early, but many of them were pregnant before the ceremony. Bridal pregnancy among native-born women was not as common as among immigrants. Nevertheless, in seventeenth-century Somerset County 20 percent of native brides bore children within eight and one half months of marriage. This was a somewhat higher percentage than has been reported from seventeenth-century English parishes.[73]

These facts suggest considerable freedom for girls in selecting a husband. Almost any girl must have had more than one suitor, and evidently many had freedom to spend time with a suitor in a fashion that allowed her to become pregnant. We might suppose that such pregnancies were not incurred until after the couple had become bethrothed, and that they were consequently an allowable part of courtship, were it not that girls whose fathers were living were usually not the culprits. In Somerset, at least, only 10 percent of the brides with fathers living were pregnant, in contrast to 30 percent of those who were orphans.[74] Since there was only about one year's difference between the mean ages at which orphan and non-orphan girls married, parental supervision rather than age seems to have been the main factor in the differing bridal pregnancy rates.[75]

Native girls married young and bore children young; hence they had more children than immigrant women. This fact ultimately changed the composition of the Maryland population. Native-born females began to have enough children to enable couples to replace themselves. These children, furthermore, were divided about evenly between males and females. By the mid-1680s, in all probability, the population thus began to grow through reproductive increase, and sexual imbalance began to decline. In 1704 the native-born preponderated in the Maryland assembly for the first time and by then were becoming predominant in the adult population as a whole.[76]

This appearance of a native population was bringing alterations in family life, especially for widows and orphaned minors. They were acquiring kin. St. Mary's and Charles counties wills demonstrate the change.[77] (See Table 3.) Before 1680, when nearly all those who died and left families had been immigrants, three-quarters of the men and women who left widows and/or minor children made no mention in their wills of any other kin in Maryland. In the first decade of the eighteenth century, among native-born testators, nearly three-fifths mention other kin, and if we add information from sources other than wills—other probate records, land records, vital registers, and so

	Families N	No Kin % Families	Only Wife % Families	Grown Child % Families	Other Kin % Families
A.					
1640-1669	95	23	43	11	23
1670-1679	76	17	50	7	26
1700-1710	71	6	35[a]	25	34[b]
B.					
1700-1710					
Immigrant	41	10	37	37	17
Native	30		33[c]	10	57[d]

Notes: [a]If information found in other records is included, the percentage is 30.

[b]If information found in other records is included, the percentage is 39.

[c]If information found in other records is included, the percentage is 20.

[d]If information found in other records is included, the percentage is 70.

For a discussion of wills as a reliable source for discovery of kin see n. 78. Only 8
testators were natives of Maryland before 1680s; hence no effort has been made
to distinguish them from immigrants.

Source: Wills, I-XIV.

on—at least 70 percent are found to have had such local connections.
This development of local family ties must have been one of the most
important events of early Maryland history.[78]

Historians have only recently begun to explore the consequences
of the shift from an immigrant to a predominantly native population.[79]
We would like to suggest some changes in the position of women that
may have resulted from this transition. It is already known that as
sexual imbalance disappeared, age at first marriage rose, but it remained
lower than it had been for immigrants over the second half of the
seventeenth century. At the same time, life expectancy improved, at
least for men. The results were longer marriages and more children
who reached maturity.[80] In St. Mary's County after 1700, dying
men far more often than earlier left children of age to maintain their
widows, and widows may have felt less inclination and had less opportunity to remarry.[81]

We may speculate on the social consequences of such changes.
More fathers were still alive when their daughters married, and hence
would have been able to exercise control over the selection of their
sons-in-law. What in the seventeenth century may have been a period

of comparative independence for women, both immigrant and native, may have given way to a return to more traditional European social controls over the creation of new families. If so, we might see the results in a decline in bridal pregnancy and perhaps a decline in bastardy.[82]

We may also find the wife losing ground in the household polity, although her economic importance probably remained unimpaired. Indeed, she must have been far more likely than a seventeenth-century immigrant woman to bring property to her marriage. But several changes may have caused women to play a smaller role than before in household decision-making.[83] Women became proportionately more numerous and may have lost bargaining power.[84] Furthermore, as marriages lasted longer, the proportion of households full of step-children and half-brothers and half-sisters united primarily by the mother must have diminished. Finally, when husbands died, more widows would have had children old enough to maintain them and any minor brothers and sisters. There would be less need for women to play a controlling role, as well as less incentive for their husbands to grant it. The provincial marriage of the eighteenth century may have more closely resembled that of England than did the immigrant marriage of the seventeenth century.

If this change occurred, we should find symptoms to measure. There should be fewer gifts from husbands to wives of property put at the wife's disposal. Husbands should less frequently make bequests to wives that provided them with property beyond their dower. A wife might even be restricted to less than her dower, although the law allowed her to choose her dower instead of a bequest.[85] At the same time, children should be commanded to maintain their mothers.

However, St. Mary's County wills do not show these symptoms. (See Table 4.) True, wives occasionally were willed less than their dower, an arrangement that was rare in the wills examined for the period before 1710. But there was no overall decrease in bequests to wives of property beyond their dower, nor was there a tendency to confine the wife's interest to the term of her widowhood or the minority of the oldest son. Children were not exhorted to help their mothers or give them living space. Widows evidently received at least enough property to maintain themselves, and husbands saw no need to ensure the help of children in managing it. Possibly, then, women did not lose ground, or at least not all ground, within the family polity. The demographic disruption of New World settlement may have given women power which they were able to keep even after sex ratios became balanced and traditional family networks appeared. Immigrant mothers may have bequeathed their daughters a legacy of independence which they in turn handed down, despite pressures toward more traditional behavior.

TABLE 4 Bequests of Husbands to Wives with Children, St. Mary's County, Maryland, 1710 to 1776

	N	All Estate %	All or Dwelling Plantation for Life %	All or Dwelling Plantation for Widowhood %	All or Dwelling Plantation for Minority of Child %	More than Dower in Other Form %	Dower or Less or Unknown %	Maintenance or House Room %
1710-1714	13	0	46	0	0	23	31	0
1715-1719	25	4	24	4	0	28	36	4
1720-1724	31	10	42	0	0	28	23	3
1725-1729	34	3	29	0	0	24	41	3
1730-1734	31	6	16	13	0	29	35	0
1735-1739	27	0	37	4	4	19	37	0
1740-1744	35	0	40	0	3	23	34	0
1745-1749	39	3	31	8	0	31	28	0
1750-1754	43	2	35	7	0	16	40	0
1755-1759	34	3	41	3	0	41	12	0
1760-1764	48	2	46	10	2	13	27	0
1765-1769	45	4	27	11	2	18	33	4
1770-1774	46	4	26	7	0	37	26	0
1775-1776	19	5	32	26	0	5	32	0
Totals	470	3	33	7	1	24	31	1

Source: Wills, XIV-XLI.

It is time to issue a warning. Whether or not Maryland women in a creole society lost ground, the argument hinges on an interpretation of English behavior that also requires testing. Either position supposes that women in seventeenth-century Maryland obtained power in the household which wives of English farmers did not enjoy. Much of the evidence for Maryland is drawn from the disposition of property in wills. If English wills show a similar pattern, similar inferences might be drawn about English women. We have already discussed evidence from English wills that supports the view that women in Maryland were favored; but the position of seventeenth-century English women—especially those not of gentle status—has been little explored.[86] A finding of little difference between bequests to women in England and in Maryland would greatly weaken the argument that demographic stress created peculiar conditions especially favorable to Maryland women.

If the demography of Maryland produced the effects here described, such effects should also be evident elsewhere in the Chesapeake. The four characteristics of the seventeenth-century Maryland population—immigrant predominance, early death, late marriage, and sexual imbalance—are to be found everywhere in the region, at least at first. The timing of the disappearance of these peculiarities may have varied from place to place, depending on date of settlement or rapidity of development, but the effect of their existence upon the experience of women should be clear. Should research in other areas of the Chesapeake fail to find women enjoying the status they achieved on the lower Western Shore of Maryland, then our arguments would have to be revised.[87]

Work is also needed that will enable historians to compare conditions in Maryland with those in other colonies. Richard S. Dunn's study of the British West Indies also shows demographic disruption.[88] When the status of wives is studied, it should prove similar to that of Maryland women. In contrast were demographic conditions in New England, where immigrants came in family groups, major immigration had ceased by the mid-seventeenth century, sex ratios balanced early, and mortality was low.[89] Under these conditions, demographic disruption must have been both less severe and less prolonged. If New England women achieved status similar to that suggested for women in the Chesapeake, that fact will have to be explained. The dynamics might prove to have been different;[90] or a dynamic we have not identified, common to both areas, might turn out to have been the primary engine of change. And, if women in England shared the status—which we doubt—conditions in the New World may have had secondary importance. The Maryland data establish persuasive grounds for a hypothesis, but the evidence is not all in.

NOTES

1. Russell R. Menard, "Economy and Society in Early Colonial Maryland" (Ph.D. diss., University of Iowa, 1975), 153-212, and "Immigrants and Their Increase: The Process of Population Growth in Early Colonial Maryland," in Aubrey C. Land, Lois Green Carr, and Edward C. Papenfuse, eds., *Law, Society, and Politics in Early Maryland* (Baltimore, 1977), 88-110, hereafter cited as Menard, "Immigrants and Their Increase"; Lorena S. Walsh and Russell R. Menard, "Death in the Chesapeake: Two Life Tables for Men in Early Colonial Maryland," *Maryland Historical Magazine,* LXIX (1974), 211-227. In a sample of 806 headrights Menard found only two unmarried women who paid their own passage ("Economy and Society," 187).

2. Menard, "Immigrants and Their Increase," Fig. 1: William Hand Browne *et al.,* eds., *Archives of Maryland* (Baltimore, 1883-   ). XXV, 256, hereafter cited as *Maryland Archives.*

3. Court proceedings for St. Mary's and Calvert counties have not survived.

4. The lists of immigrants are found in John Camden Hotten, ed., *The Original Lists of Persons of Quality; Emigrants; Religious Exiles; Political Rebels; . . . and Others Who Went from Great Britain to the American Plantations, 1600-1700* (London, 1874); William Dodgson Bowman, ed., *Bristol and America: A Record of the First Settlers in the Colonies of North America, 1654-1685* (Baltimore, 1967 [orig. publ. London, 1929]); C. D. P. Nicholson, comp., *Some Early Emigrants to America* (Baltimore, 1965); Michael Ghirelli, ed., *A List of Emigrants to America, 1682-1692* (Baltimore, 1968); and Elizabeth French, ed., *List of Emigrants to America from Liverpool, 1697-1707* (Baltimore, 1962 [orig. publ. Boston, 1913]). Folger Shakespeare Library, MS. V.B. 16 (Washington, D.C.), consists of 66 additional indentures that were originally part of the London records. For studies of these lists see Mildred Campbell, "Social Origins of Some Early Americans," in James Morton Smith, ed., *Seventeenth-Century America: Essays in Colonial History* (Chapel Hill, N.C., 1959), 63-89; David W. Galenson, " 'Middling People' or 'Common Sort'?: The Social Origins of Some Early Americans Reexamined," *William and Mary Quarterly* (forthcoming). See also Menard, "Immigrants and Their Increase," Table 4.1, and "Economy and Society," Table VIII-6; and Lorena S. Walsh, "Servitude and Opportunity in Charles County," in Land, Carr, and Papenfuse, eds., *Law, Society, and Politics in Early Maryland*, 112-114, hereafter cited as Walsh, "Servitude and Opportunity."

5. Campbell, "Social Origins of Some Early Americans," in Smith, ed., *Seventeenth-Century America,* 74-77; Galenson, " 'Middling People' or 'Common Sort'?" *WMQ* (forthcoming). When the ages recorded in the London list (Nicholson, comp., *Some Early Emigrants*) and on the Folger Library indentures for servants bound for Maryland and Virginia are combined, 84.5% of the men (N = 354) are found to have been aged 17 to 30, and 54.9% were 18 through 22. Of the women (N = 119), 81.4% were 18 through 25; 10% were older, 8.3% younger, and half (51.2%) immigrated between ages 20 and 22. Russell Menard has generously lent us his abstracts of the London list.

6. This assumption is defended in Walsh, "Servitude and Opportunity," 129.

7. *Ibid.*, 112-114, describes the legislation and the Charles County data base. There is some reason to believe that by 1700, young servants had contracts more often than earlier. Figures from the London list include the Folger Library indentures.

8. Menard, "Immigrants and Their Increase," Table I.

9. Menard, "Economy and Society," 336–356; Lois Green Carr and Russell R. Menard, "Servants and Freedmen in Early Colonial Maryland," in Thad W. Tate and David A. Ammerman, eds., *Essays on the Chesapeake in the Seventeenth Century* (Chapel Hill, N.C., 1979); E. A. Wrigley, "Family Limitation in Pre-Industrial England," *Economic History Review*, 2d Ser., XIX (1966), 82–109; Michael Drake, "An Elementary Exercise in Parish Register Demography," *ibid.*, XIV (1962), 427–445; J. D. Chambers, *Population, Economy, and Society in Pre-Industrial England* (London, 1972).

10. John Hammond, *Leah and Rachel, or, the Two Fruitfull Sisters Virginia and Mary-land . . .* , and George Alsop, *A Character of the Province of Mary-land . . .* , in Clayton Colman Hall, ed., *Narratives of Early Maryland, 1633–1684*, Original Narratives of Early American History (New York, 1910), 281–308, 340–387; Russell R. Menard, P. M. G. Harris, and Lois Green Carr, "Opportunity and Inequality: The Distribution of Wealth on the Lower Western Shore of Maryland, 1638–1705," *Md. Hist. Mag.*, LXIX (1974), 169–184; Russell R. Menard, "From Servant to Freeholder: Status Mobility and Property Accumulation in Seventeenth-Century Maryland," *WMQ*, 3d Ser., XXX (1973), 37–64; Carr and Menard, "Servants and Freedman," in Tate and Ammerman, eds., *Essays on the Chesapeake*; Walsh, "Servitude and Opportunity," 111–133.

11. Walsh and Menard, "Death in the Chesapeake," *Md. Hist. Mag.*, LXIX (1974), 211–227; Darrett B. and Anita H. Rutman, "Of Agues and Fevers: Malaria in the Early Chesapeake," *WMQ*, 3d Ser., XXXIII (1976), 31–60.

12. E. A. Wrigley, *Population and History* (New York, 1969), 96–100.

13. Menard, "Economy and Society," Table VII-5.

14. Lorena S. Walsh, "Charles County, Maryland, 1658–1705: A Study in Chesapeake Political and Social Structure" (Ph.D. diss., Michigan State University, 1977), chap. 4.

15. Hammond, *Leah and Rachel*, and Alsop, *Character of the Province*, in Hall, ed., *Narratives of Maryland*, 281–308, 340–387; Mildred Campbell, *The English Yeoman Under Elizabeth and the Early Stuarts*, Yale Historical Publications (New Haven, Conn., 1942), 255–261; Alan Everitt, "Farm Labourers," in Joan Thirsk, ed., *The Agrarian History of England and Wales, 1540–1640* (Cambridge, 1967), 432.

16. Lorena S. Walsh and Russell R. Menard are preparing an article on the history of illegitimacy in Charles and Somerset counties, 1658–1776.

17. Abbot Emerson Smith, *Colonists in Bondage: White Servitude and Convict Labor in America, 1607–1776* (Chapel Hill, N.C., 1947), 271–273. Marriage was in effect a breach of contract.

18. Lois Green Carr, "County Government in Maryland, 1689–1709" (Ph.D. diss., Harvard University, 1968), text, 267–269, 363. The courts pursued bastardy offenses regardless of the social status of the culprits in order to ensure that the children would not become public charges. Free single women were not being overlooked.

19. John Barth, *The Sot-Weed Factor* (New York, 1960), 429.

20. This impression is based on Walsh's close reading of Charles County records. Carr's close reading of Prince George's County records, and less detailed examination by both of all other 17th-century Maryland court records.

21. Walsh, "Charles County, Maryland," chap. 4; Carr, "County Government in Maryland," chap. 4, n. 269. Carr summarizes the evidence from Charles, Prince George's, Baltimore, Talbot, and Somerset counties, 1689–1709, for comparing punishment of fathers and mothers of bastards. Leniency toward fathers varied from county to county and time to time. The length of time served for restitution also varied over place and time, increasing as the century progressed. See Charles County Court and Land Records, MS, L #1, ff. 276–277, Hall of Records, Annapolis, Md. Unless otherwise indicated, all manuscripts cited are at the Hall of Records.

22. Peter Laslett and Karla Osterveen have calculated illegitimacy ratios—the percentage of bastard births among all births registered—in 24 English parishes, 1581–1810. The highest ratio over the period 1630–1710 was 2.4. Laslett and Osterveen, "Long Term Trends in Bastardy in England: A Study of the Illegitimacy Figures in the Parish Registers and in the Reports of the Registrar General, 1561–1960," *Population Studies*, XXVII (1973), 267. In Somerset County, Maryland, 1666–1694, the illegitimacy ratio ranged from 6.3 to 11.8. Russell R. Menard, "The Demography of Somerset County, Maryland: A Preliminary Report" (paper presented to the Stony Brook Conference on Social History, State University of New York at Stony Brook, June 1975), Table XVI. The absence of figures for the number of women in these places of childbearing age but with no living husband prevents construction of illegitimacy rates.

23. Alsop, *Character of the Province*, in Hall, ed., *Narratives of Maryland*, 358.

24. Maryland Headright Sample, 1658–1681 (N = 625); 257.1 men per 100 women; Maryland Inventories, 1658–1679 (N = 584); 320.1 men per 100 women. Menard, "Immigrants and Their Increase," Table I.

25. A comparison of a Virginia Headright Sample, 1648–1666 (N = 4,272) with inventories from York and Lower Norfolk counties, 1637–1675 (N = 168) shows less, rather than more, imbalance in inventories as compared to headrights. This indicates fewer purchases of wives than we have suggested for the period after 1660. However, the inventory sample is small.

26. Only 8% of tenant farmers who left inventories in four Maryland counties of the lower Western Shore owned labor, 1658–1705. St. Mary's City Commission Inventory Project, "Social Stratification in Maryland, 1658–1705" (National Science Foundation Grant GS-32272), hereafter cited as "Social Stratification." This is an analysis of 1,735 inventories recorded from 1658 to 1705 in St. Mary's, Calvert, Charles, and Prince George's counties, which together constitute most of the lower Western Shore of Maryland.

27. Sixty women left inventories. The status of five is unknown. The two who died single died in 1698. Menard, "Immigrants and Their Increase," Table I.

28. Menard, "Demography of Somerset County," Table XVII; Daniel Scott Smith and Michael S. Hindus, "Premarital Pregnancy in America, 1640–1971: An Overview," *Journal of Interdisciplinary History*, V (1975), 541. It was also two to three times the rate found in New England in the late 17th century.

29. In Maryland any proceedings against pregnant brides could have been brought only in the civil courts. No vestries were established until 1693, and their jurisdiction was confined to the admonishment of men and women suspected of fornication unproved by the conception of a child. Churchwardens were to inform the county court of bastardies. Carr, "County Government in Maryland," text, 148–149, 221–223.

30 The data are from Nicholson, comp., *Some Early Emigrants.*

31. Charles County Court and Land Records, MSS, C #1 through B #2.

32. Available ages at arrival are as follows:

Age under	12	13	14	15	16	17	18	19	20	21	22	23	24	25	26	27	28	29	30
Indentured (1682–1687)			1	1	6	2	9	9	8	29	19	6	5	6	2	3	1	2	3
Unindentured (1666–1705)	8	5	12	4	7	18	16	13	34	9	11	2	1	1					

Terms of service for women without indentures from 1666 on were 5 years if they were aged 22 at arrival; 6 years if 18–21; 7 years if 15–17; and until 22 if under 15. From 1661 to 1665 these terms were shorter by a year, and women under 15 served until age 21. If we assume that (1) indentured women served 4 years; (2) they constituted half the servant women; (3) women under age 12 were not purchased as wives; (4) 20% of women aged 12 or older were purchased; and (5) purchases were spread evenly over the possible years of service, then from 1666, 73.9% were 23 or older at marriage, and 66.0% were 24 or older; 70.8% were 23 or older from 1661 to 1665, and 55.5% were 24 or older. Mean ages at eligibility for marriage, as calculated by dividing person-years by the number of women, were 24.37 from 1666 on and 23.42 from 1661 to 1665. All assumptions except (3) and (5) are discussed above. The third is made on the basis that native girls married as young as age 12.

33. Walsh, "Charles County, Maryland," chap. 2; Menard, "Demography of Somerset County," Tables XI, XII.

34. The impact of later marriages is best demonstrated with age-specific marital fertility statistics. Susan L. Norton reports that women in colonial Ipswich, Massachusetts, bore an average of 7.5 children if they married between ages 15 and 19; 7.1 if they married between 20 and 24; and 4.5 if they married after 24. Norton, "Population Growth in Colonial America: A Study of Ipswich, Massachusetts," *Pop. Studies*, XXV (1971), 444. Cf. Wrigley, "Family Limitation in Pre-Industrial England," *Econ. Hist. Rev.*, 2d Ser., XIX (1966), 82–109.

35. In Charles County the mean interval between first and second and subsequent births was 30.8, and the median was 27.3 months. Walsh, "Charles County, Maryland," chap. 2. Menard has found that in Somerset County, Maryland, the median birth intervals for immigrant women between child 1 and child 2, child 2 and child 3, child 3 and child 4, and child 4 and child 5 were 26, 26, 30, 27 months, respectively ("Demography of Somerset County," Table XX).

36. Walsh, "Charles County, Maryland," chap. 2.

37. Walsh and Menard, "Death in the Chesapeake," *Md. Hist. Mag.*, LXIX (1974), 222.

38. Menard, using all Maryland wills, found a considerably lower number of children per family in a similar period: 1.83 in wills probated 1660–1665; 2.20 in wills probated 1680–1684 ("Economy and Society," 198). Family reconstitution not surprisingly produces slightly higher figures, since daughters are often under-recorded in wills but are recorded as frequently as sons in birth registers. In 17th-century Charles County the mean size of all reconstituted families was 2.75. For marriages contracted in the years 1658–1669 (N = 118), 1670–1679 (N = 79), and 1680–1689 (N = 95), family size was 3.15, 2.58, and 2.86, respectively. In

Somerset County, family size for immigrant marriages formed between 1665 and 1695 (N = 41) was 3.9. Walsh, "Charles County, Maryland," chap. 2; Menard, "Demography of Somerset County," Table XXI.

39. For fuller exposition of the process see Menard, "Immigrants and Their Increase."

40. P. E. Razell, "Population Change in Eighteenth-Century England. A Reinterpretation," *Econ. Hist. Rev.*, 2d Ser., XVIII (1965), 315, cites mean age at marriage as 23.76 years for 7,242 women in Yorkshire, 1662–1714, and 24.6 years for 280 women of Wiltshire, Berkshire, Hampshire, and Dorset, 1615–1621. Peter Laslett, *The World We Have Lost: England before the Industrial Age*, 2d ed. (London, 1971), 86, shows a mean age of 23.58 for 1,007 women in the Diocese of Canterbury, 1619–1690. Wrigley, "Family Limitation in Pre-Industrial England," *Econ. Hist. Rev.*, 2d Ser., XIX (1966), 87, shows mean ages at marriage for 259 women in Colyton, Devon, ranging from 26.15 to 30.0 years, 1600–1699.

41. For a brief discussion of Chesapeake and English mortality see Walsh and Menard, "Death in the Chesapeake," *Md. Hist. Mag.*, LXIX (1974), 224–225.

42. George W. Barclay, *Techniques of Population Analysis* (New York, 1958), 136n; Darrett B. and Anita H. Rutman, " 'Now-Wives and Sons-in-Law': Parental Death in a Seventeenth-Century Virginia County," in Tate and Ammerman, eds., *Essays on the Chesapeake*; Rutman and Rutman, "Of Agues and Fevers," *WMQ*, 3d Ser., XXXIII (1976), 31–60. Cf. Peter H. Wood, *Black Majority: Negroes in Colonial South Carolina from 1670 through the Stono Rebellion* (New York, 1974), chap. 3.

43. Walsh and Menard, "Death in the Chesapeake," *Md. Hist Mag.*, LXIX (1974), 211–227; Menard, "Demography of Somerset County."

44. In Charles County immigrant women who ended childbearing years or died before 1705 bore a mean of 3.5 children (N = 59); the mean for natives was 5.1 (N = 42). Mean completed family size in Somerset County for marriages contracted between 1665 and 1695 was higher, but the immigrant-native differential remains. Immigrant women (N = 17) bore 6.1 children, while native women (N = 16) bore 9.4. Walsh, "Charles County, Maryland," chap. 2; Menard, "Demography of Somerset County," Table XXI.

45. Among 1735 decedents who left inventories on Maryland's lower Western Shore, 1658–1705, 72% died without children or with children not yet of age. Only 16% could be proved to have a child of age. "Social Stratification."

46. Wills, I, 172.

47. From 1640 to 1710, 17% of the married men named no executor. In such cases, the probate court automatically gave executorship to the wife unless she requested someone else to act.

48. Wills, I, 96, 69.

49. *Ibid.*, 193–194, 167, V, 82. The practice of appointing overseers ceased around the end of the century. From 1690 to 1710, only 13% of testators who made their wives executors appointed overseers.

50. We divided wills according to whether decedents were immigrant, native born, or of unknown origins, and found no differences in patterns of bequests, choice of executors, or tendency to appoint overseers. No change occurred in 17th-century Maryland in these respects as a native-born population began to appear.

51. Margaret Spufford, *Contrasting Communities: English Villagers in the Sixteenth and Seventeenth Centuries* (Cambridge, 1974), 85–90, 111–118, 161–164.

52. Wills, I, 422, 182, 321.

53. For example, *ibid.*, 172, 182.

54. Lorena S. Walsh, " 'Till Death Do Us Part': Marriage and Family in Charles County, Maryland, 1658–1705," in Tate and Ammerman, eds., *Essays on the Chesapeake.*

55. The following discussion of the orphans' court is based on Lois Green Carr, "The Development of the Maryland Orphans' Court, 1654–1715," in Land, Carr, and Papenfuse, eds., *Law, Society, and Politics in Early Maryland*, 41–61.

56. Baltimore County Court Proceedings, D, ff. 385–386.

57. In 17th-century Charles County two-thirds of surviving partners remarried within a year of their spouse's death. Walsh, "Charles County, Maryland," chap. 2.

58. See n. 26.

59. Walsh, " 'Till Death Do Use Part,' " in Tate and Ammerman, eds., *Essays on the Chesapeake.*

60. *Ibid.*

61. *Maryland Archives*, LXX, 87. See also *ibid.*, XLI, 210, 474, 598, for examples of allusions to washing clothes and dairying activities. Water mills were so scarce that in 1669 the Maryland assembly passed an act permitting land to be condemned for the use of anyone willing to build and operate a water mill. *Ibid.*, II, 211–214. In the whole colony only four condemnations were carried out over the next 10 years. *Ibid.*, LI, 25, 57, 86, 381. Probate inventories show that most households had a mortar and pestle or a hand mill.

62. Testamentary Proceedings, X, 184–185. Cf. Charles County Court and Land Records, MS, I #1, ff. 9–10, 259.

63. Among married decedents before 1680 (N = 308), the bottom two-thirds (N = 212) were those worth less than £150. Among all decedents worth less than £150 (N = 451), only 12 (about 3%) had sheep or yarn-making equipment, "Social Stratification."

64. See Everitt, "Farm Labourers," in Thirsk, ed., *Agrarian History of England and Wales*, 422–426, and W. G. Hoskins, *Essays in Leicestershire History* (Liverpool, 1950), 134.

65. Among married decedents, the bottom fifth were approximately those worth less than £30. Before 1680 these were 17% of the married decedents. By the end of the period, from 1700 to 1705, they were 22%. Before 1680, 92% had no bound labor. From 1700 to 1705, 95% had none. Less than 1% of all estates in this wealth group had sheep or yarn-making equipment before 1681. "Social Stratification."

66. On opportunity to raise from the bottom to the middle see Menard, "From Servant to Freeholder," *WMQ*, 3d Ser., XXX (1973), 37–64; Walsh, "Servitude and Opportunity," 111–133, and Menard, Harris, and Carr, "Opportunity and Inequality," *Md. Hist. Mag.*, LXIX (1974), 169–184.

67. Charles County Court and Land Records, MS, R #1, f. 193.

68. For 17th-century economic development see Menard, Harris, and Carr, "Opportunity and Inequality," *Md. Hist. Mag.*, LXIX (1974), 169–184.

69. Among estates worth £150 or more, signs of diversification in this form appeared in 22% before 1681 and in 67% after 1680. Over the years 1700–1705,

the figure was 62%. Only 6% of estates worth less than £40 had such signs of diversification after 1680 or over the period 1700–1705. Knitting rather than weaving is assumed because looms were very rare. These figures are for all estates. "Social Stratification."

70. After the mid-1670s information about landholdings of decedents becomes decreasingly available, making firm estimates of the increase in tenancy difficult. However, for householders in life cycle 2 (married or widowed decedents who died without children of age) the following table is suggestive. Householding decedents in life cycle 2 worth less than £40 (N = 255) were 21% of all decedents in this category (N = 1,218).

	£0–19				£20–39		
	Deced-ents	Land Unkn.	With Land	With Land	Deced-ents	Land Unkn.	With Land	With Land
	N	N	N	%	N	N	N	%
To 1675	10	0	7	70	34	2	29	91
1675 on	98	22	40	53	113	16	64	66

In computing percentages, unknowns have been distributed according to knowns.

A man who died with a child of age was almost always a landowner, but these were a small proportion of all decedents (see n. 45).

Several studies provide indisputable evidence of an increase in tenancy on the lower Western Shore over the period 1660–1706. These compare heads of households with lists of landowners compiled from rent rolls made in 1659 and 1704–1706. Tenancy in St. Mary's and Charles counties in 1660 was about 10%. In St. Mary's, Charles, and Prince George's counties, 1704–1706, 30–35% of householders were tenants. Russell R. Menard, "Population Growth and Land Distribution in St. Mary's County, 1634–1710" (ms report, St. Mary's City Commission, 1971, copy on file at the Hall of Records); Menard, "Economy and Society," 423; Carr, "County Government in Maryland," text, 605.

71. Menard, "Immigrants and Their Increase," Table III; n. 40 above.

72. Menard, "Demography of Somerset County," Table XIII.

73. *Ibid.*, Table XVII; P. E. H. Hair, "Bridal Pregnancy in Rural England in Earlier Centuries," *Pop. Studies*, XX (1966), 237; Chambers, *Population, Economy, and Society in England*, 75; Smith and Hindus, "Premarital Pregnancy in America," *Jour. Interdisciplinary Hist.*, V (1975), 537–570.

74. Menard, "Demography of Somerset County," Table XVIII.

75. Adolescent subfecundity might also partly explain lower bridal pregnancy rates among very young brides.

76. Menard develops this argument in detail in "Immigrants and Their Increase." For the assembly see David W. Jordan, "Political Stability and the Emergence of a Native Elite in Maryland, 1660–1715," in Tate and Ammerman, eds., *Essays on the Chesapeake*. In Charles County, Maryland, by 1705 at least half of all resident landowners were native born. Walsh, "Charles County, Maryland," chaps. 1, 7.

77. The proportion of wills mentioning non-nuclear kin can, of course, prove only a proxy of the actual existence of these kin in Maryland. The reliability of such a measure may vary greatly from area to area and over time, depending on the character of the population and on local inheritance customs. To test the reliability of the will data, we compared them with data from reconstituted families

in 17th-century Charles County. These reconstitution data draw on a much broader variety of sources and include many men who did not leave wills. Because of insufficient information for female lines, we could trace only the male lines. The procedure compared the names of all married men against a file of all known county residents, asking how many kin in the male line might have been present in the county at the time of the married man's death. The proportions for immigrants were in most cases not markedly different from those found in wills. For native men, however, wills were somewhat less reliable indicators of the presence of such kin; when non-nuclear kin mentioned by testate natives were compared with kin found by reconstitution, 29% of the native testators had non-nuclear kin present in the county who were not mentioned in their wills.

78. Not surprisingly, wills of immigrants show no increase in family ties, but these wills mention adult children far more often than earlier. Before 1680, only 11% of immigrant testators in St. Mary's and Charles counties mention adult children in their wills; from 1700 to 1710, 37% left adult children to help the family. Two facts help account for this change. First, survivors of early immigration were dying in old age. Second, proportionately fewer young immigrants with families were dying, not because life expectancy had improved, but because there were proportionately fewer of them than earlier. A long stagnation in the tobacco economy that began about 1680 had diminished opportunities for freed servants to form households and families. Hence, among immigrants the proportion of young fathers at risk to die was smaller than in earlier years.

In the larger population of men who left inventories, 18.2% had adult children before 1681, but in the years 1700–1709, 50% had adult children. "Social Stratification."

79. Examples of some recent studies are Carole Shammas, "English-Born and Creole Elites in Turn-of-the-Century Virginia," in Tate and Ammerman, eds., *Essays on the Chesapeake*; Jordan, "Political Stability and the Emergence of a Native Elite in Maryland," *ibid.*; Lois Green Carr, "The Foundations of Social Order: Local Government in Colonial Maryland," in Bruce C. Daniels, ed., *Town and Country: Essays on the Structure of Local Government in the American Colonies* (Middletown, Conn., 1978); Menard, "Economy and Society," 396–440.

80. Allan Kulikoff has found that in Prince George's County the white adult sex ratio dropped significantly before the age of marriage rose. Women born in the 1720s were the first to marry at a mean age above 20, while those born in the 1740s and marrying in the 1760s, after the sex ratio neared equality, married at a mean age of 22. Marriages lasted longer because the rise in the mean age at which men married—from 23 to 27 between 1700 and 1740—was more than offset by gains in life expectancy. Kulikoff, "Tobacco and Slaves: Population, Economy, and Society in Eighteenth-Century Prince George's County, Maryland" (Ph.D. diss., Brandeis University, 1976), chap. 3; Menard, "Immigrants and Their Increase."

81. Inventories and related biographical data have been analyzed by the St. Mary's City Commission under a grant from the National Endowment for the Humanities, "The Making of a Plantation Society in Maryland" (R 010585-74-267). From 1700 through 1776 the percentage of men known to have had children, and who had no adult child at death, ranged from a low of 32.8% in the years 1736–1738 to a high of 61.3% in the years 1707–1709. The figure was over 50% for 13 out of 23 year-groups of three to four years each. For the high in 1707–1709 see comments in n. 78.

82. On the other hand, these rates may show little change. The restraining effect of increased parental control may have been offset by a trend toward increased sexual activity that appears to have become general throughout Western Europe and the United States by the mid-19th century. Smith and Hindus, "Premarital Pregnancy in America," *Jour. Interdisciplinary Hist.*, V (1975), 537–570; Edward Shorter, "Female Emancipation, Birth Control, and Fertility in European History," *American Historical Review*, LXXVIII (1973), 605–640.

83. Page Smith has suggested that such a decline in the wife's household authority had occurred in the American family by—at the latest—the beginning of the 19th century (*Daughters of the Promised Land: Women in American History* [Boston, 1970], chaps. 3, 4).

84. There is little doubt that extreme scarcity in the early years of Chesapeake history enhanced the worth of women in the eyes of men. However, as Smith has observed, "the functioning of the law of supply and demand could not in itself have guaranteed status for colonial women. Without an ideological basis, their privileges could not have been initially established or subsequently maintained" (*ibid.*, 38–39). In a culture where women were seriously undervalued, a shortage of women would not necessarily improve their status.

85. Acts 1699, chap. 41, *Maryland Archives*, XXII, 542.

86. Essays by Cicely Howell and Barbara Todd, printed or made available to the authors since this article was written, point out that customary as opposed to freehold tenures in England usually gave the widow the use of the land for life, but that remarriage often cost the widow this right. The degree to which this was true requires investigation. Howell, "Peasant Inheritance in the Midlands, 1280–1700," in Jack Goody, Joan Thirsk, and E. P. Thompson, eds., *Family and Inheritance: Rural Society in Western Europe, 1200–1800* (Cambridge, 1976), 112–155; Todd, " 'In Her Free Widowhood'; Succession to Property and Remarriage in Rural England, 1540–1800" (paper delivered to the Third Berkshire Conference of Women Historians, June 1976).

87. James W. Deen, Jr., "Patterns of Testation: Four Tidewater Counties in Colonial Virginia," *American Journal of Legal History*, XVI (1972), 154–176, finds a life interest in property for the wife the predominant pattern before 1720. However, he includes an interest for widowhood in life interest and does not distinguish a dower interest from more than dower.

88. Richard S. Dunn, *Sugar and Slaves: The Rise of the Planter Class in the English West Indies, 1624–1713* (Chapel Hill, N.C., 1972), 326–334. Dunn finds sex ratios surprisingly balanced, but he also finds very high mortality, short marriages, and many orphans.

89. For a short discussion of this comparison see Menard, "Immigrants and Their Increase."

90. James K. Somerville has used Salem, Massachusetts, wills from 1660 to 1770 to examine women's status and importance within the home ("The Salem [Mass.] Woman in the Home, 1660–1770," *Eighteenth-Century Life*, I [1974], 11–14). See also Alexander Keyssar, "Widowhood in Eighteenth-Century Massachusetts: A Problem in the History of the Family," *Perspectives in American History*, VIII (1974), 83–119, which discusses provisions for 22 widows in 18th-century Woburn, Massachusetts. Both men find provisions for houseroom and care of the widow's property enjoined upon children proportionately far more

often than we have found in St. Mary's County, Maryland, where we found only five instances over 136 years. However, part of this difference may be a function of the differences in age at widowhood in the two regions. Neither Somerville nor Keyssar gives the percentage of widows who received a life interest in property, but their discussions imply a much higher proportion than we have found of women whose interest ended at remarriage or the majority of the oldest son.

4 ♀ Divorce and the Changing Status of Women in Eighteenth-Century Massachusetts

Nancy F. Cott

When a neighbor asked John Backus, silversmith of Great Barrington, Massachusetts, in 1784, why he kicked and struck his wife, John replied that "it was Partly owing to his Education for his father often treated his mother in the same manner."[1] John's mother may have tolerated that abuse but his wife did not: she complained of his cruelty, desertion, and adultery, and obtained a divorce.

This epitome of two generations' marital strife, one item in early Massachusetts divorce records, suggests how valuable such records may be to the interpretation of marriage and family life in the past. Divorce proceedings not only elucidate customs and ideals of marriage; they also disclose the marital behavior of the litigants. The history of divorce practice documents sex-role expectations, permits comparison between the obligations and freedoms of husbands and of wives, and provides a test of the double standard of sexual morality. Divorce records from provincial Massachusetts are especially interesting because the years they cover are those least explored in studies of marriage and family in New England. Historians have yet to explain the transition from "Puritan" to "Victorian" standards, but current research has begun to suggest that unrest and change in patterns of sexual and familial behavior were conspicuous during the eighteenth century.[2] Records of divorce in provincial Massachusetts illuminate these little-known aspects of individuals' lives.[3]

From the *William and Mary Quarterly* 33 (October 1976): 586–614. Reprinted by permission.

Ms. Cott is a member of the Department of History and the American Studies Program at Yale University. She wishes to acknowledge her indebtedness to David H. Flaherty and Hiller B. Zobel for helpful research suggestions, and to Douglas L. Jones for comments on an earlier draft. Shorter versions of this paper were read at the Conference on Women in the Era of the American Revolution, George Washington University, July 1975, and at Princeton University, November 1975.

Massachusetts divorce proceedings between 1692 and 1786 can be fairly readily traced because they took place (with a few notable exceptions) before one body, a "court" composed of the governor and his Council.[4] One hundred twenty-two wives and 101 husbands filed 229 petitions in all (six wives petitioned twice).[5] So far as their occupational and residential characteristics are known, the petitioners included the whole range of types in the population. Slightly more than a quarter of them lived in Boston, the others in all varieties of towns, from the smallest to the largest, the most remote to the most advantageously located.[6] Almost 63 percent of the petitioners disclosed the occupation of the man of the family. Thirty-two percent of these cases involved families of artisans or traders; 22 percent, husbandmen or yeomen; and another 22 percent, mariners or fishermen. About 17 percent originated in families in which the husbands had the more prestigious status of gentlemen, merchants, professionals, ship captains, or militia officers; and the remaining 7 percent involved families at the lower end of the occupational scale—laborers, truckmen, and servants. Although one would need to know the petitioners' wealth to ascertain their economic standing or to judge how accurately they typified the Massachusetts population, it is likely that the great majority—perhaps three-fourths—occupied the "middling ranks."[7] Whether or not they were a representative sample, the group included all varieties of the Massachusetts population, urban and rural dwellers, rich and poor.

The petitioners had an easier time gaining divorce in provincial Massachusetts than they would have had in the mother country.[8] In England marital controversies were judged by the ecclesiastical courts, and these courts applied canon law, under which a valid marriage was regarded as indissoluble. True divorce (*divortium a vinculo matrimonii*), allowing the partners to remarry, was never granted unless a marriage was judged null to begin with, on grounds such as consanguinity, bigamy, or sexual incapacity. Such causes as adultery, desertion, or cruelty warranted only separation from bed and board (*divortium a mensa et thoro*), which sustained the legal obligations of marriage, excepting cohabitation, and did not allow either partner to remarry. At the end of the seventeenth century, in order to relieve the stringency of ecclesiastical rule for noblemen whose wives were adulterous, the House of Lords began to dissolve marriages by private act. Only a select group could take advantage of this avenue to divorce. The cost often amounted to several thousand pounds, because a petitioner was expected to have first obtained a decree of divorce *a mensa* and a civil judgment against the adulterers. The Lords passed only about ninety private acts of divorce between 1697 and 1785, all resting on adultery charges and all awarded to husbands.[9] Divorce *a vinculo* from a valid marriage was more frequent in Massachusetts during the second period. Between 1692 and 1786, 110 divorces were granted in the province on grounds other than those considered legitimate by the English ecclesiastical courts—63 to men, 47 to women—and England and Wales had a population of almost seven million in 1765, when the Massachusetts population was under 250,000.[10]

The authority of the governor and Council over divorce originated in provincial statute. No causes for divorce were codified, however, and their divorce policy combined elements of English practice. Puritan divorce theory, seventeenth-century Massachusetts precedents, and innovation. Opposing canon law, Puritan divorce theory held that marriage was a civil contract which could and should be dissolved for such breaches as adultery, long absence, or irremediable cruelty.[11] In the seventeenth century the civil courts of Massachusetts tried to effect this theoretical position, so far as is shown by the results of forty known petitions between 1639 and 1692. The county courts and the General Court, as well as the Court of Assistants (predecessor to the Council) judged petitions for divorce, even after the Code of 1660 gave jurisdiction to the assistants. They annulled marriages on grounds of consanguinity, bigamy, and sexual incapacity, and dissolved them for long absence and for adultery alone or in combination with desertion, neglect, or cruelty. No clear decrees of separate bed and board have been discovered, but our knowledge of seventeenth-century divorce proceedings is probably incomplete.[12]

When the governor and Council assumed more uniform jurisdiction over divorce after 1692, they granted annulments, divorces (literally, dissolutions of marriage bonds) allowing the innocent party to remarry, and decrees of separate bed and board.[13] The years 1754 to 1757 formed a curious exception. During that period, for reasons not apparent in the historical record, the governor and Council declined to dissolve valid marriages and decreed separate bed and board for petitioners who formerly and subsequently would have been granted divorce.[14] In 1755, 1756, and 1757, six petitioners whose spouses were adulterous sought relief from the General Court and obtained legislative divorces instead of divorce decrees. These legislative divorces were the only ones enacted under the provincial charter of 1691.[15] In passing them the General Court assumed the role of Parliament in England; and in two of the six, the governor and Council filled the role of the English ecclesiastical courts by granting prior decrees of separate bed and board. Since they were legislative acts, these divorces were subject to review by the imperial Board of Trade, as was all colonial legislation. Reporting on the first three in 1758, the board called them "extraordinary" and "liable to great objections." The specific points of disapproval highlighted some of the differences between English and Massachusetts divorce policy. All three suits—two of them brought by women—rested on adultery charges. The divorces granted to the two women were called unprecedented, "the first of their kind . . . in the colonies or elsewhere." Moreover, the proofs of adultery were not clear enough; criminal conviction of the adulterers had not preceded the three divorce bills; and only one was supported by a prior decree of separate bed and board. Beyond these objections, which seemed sufficient grounds for disallowance, doubt existed whether any colonial legislature had the right to assume the parliamentary prerogative of granting divorces. The board referred the matter to the attorney-general and the solicitor-general for a decision whether to disallow the acts or declare them null; but no hearing took place, and these divorce bills and the subsequent three in Massachusetts were apparently allowed to stand.[16]

The interlude of legislative divorce in Massachusetts clarified the advantage the province gained through its usual practice of divorce by decree. If Massachusetts had taken the legislative route, the history of divorce there would probably have been quite different. Legislative divorces might well have been disallowed for lack of conformity to English practice, or declared null for invading the authority of Parliament. In fact, between 1769 and 1773 several colonial acts of legislative divorce, passed in Pennsylvania, New Jersey, and New Hampshire, met this fate. The crown's resentment of them resulted in a directive of 1773 to all royal governors to withhold consent from any divorce act passed by a colonial legislature.[17] This order halted divorce in the colonies other than Massachusetts until the Revolution, but in that province both petitions for and grants of divorce continued to multiply. Petitioners no longer resorted to the General Court, for in 1760, after investigating their own precedents for dissolving marriages before 1755, the governor and Council returned to the policy of decreeing divorces *a vinculo*.[18]

TABLE 1   Number of Petitions/Number of Favorable Decrees, by Decade

Peti-tioners	1692-1704	1705-1714	1715-1724	1725-1734	1735-1744	1745-1754	1755-1764	1765-1774	1775-1786	Total
All	7/5	6/5	5/2	9/4	23/15	21/11	26/16	46/24	86/61	229/143
Female	4/3	3/2	4/1	4/1	8/4	12/6	12/7	29/13	53/37	128/74
Male	3/2	3/3	1/1	5/3	15/11	9/5	14/9	18/11	33/24	101/69

Note: Favorable decrees include divorce, annulment, and separate bed and board.

Divorce petitions and decrees showed a general pattern of increase during the eighteenth century in Massachusetts. As Table 1 indicates, more than half of the petitions and decrees between 1692 and 1786 occurred after 1764, and more than a third of them after 1774. This striking concentration took place without any change in the laws regarding divorce. What caused it? The population grew, but not nearly as rapidly as did the number of petitions. The incidence of petitions per decade increased by 77 percent from 1755–1764 to 1765–1774, and by 61 percent from 1765–1774 to 1775–1784, while the white population grew by approximately 5.7 percent from 1760 to 1770, and by approximately 14 percent from 1770 to 1780.[19]

Perhaps the governor and Council became more willing to consider and grant divorces after 1765, thus encouraging larger numbers of petitioners. In these pre-Revolutionary years the Council may have been more assertive in its divorce practice, which opposed England's, just as it became more independent of the royal prerogative in political matters, and more sympathetic to the whig leaders in the legislature.[20] Two decrees of the early 1770s in particular indicated that the Council would proceed on its own initiative in divorce actions whether or not the governor agreed. The Council alone declared Abigail Bradstreet separated from her husband in 1771, and James Richardson divorced from his wife in 1772, although Gov. Thomas Hutchinson did not judge these decrees warranted by the evidence and would not sign them.[21]

The chronological coincidence of the concentration of divorce petitions with the War for Independence suggests a causal link. We might suppose that wartime disruption of families led to an increase of petitions, but there is little direct evidence of this. Very few petitions originated from war-related grievances, such as a married man's adultery with a campfollower or a woman's pregnancy while her husband was absent in military service.[22] Gauged by the evidence of prenuptial pregnancy, premarital sexual relations increased dramatically during the mid- to late eighteenth century—suggesting the possibility of a similar rise in adultery—but that phenomenon antedated the war.[23]

Most likely, divorce petitions increased not because spouses more often had legitimate marital grievances but because they were more often motivated to respond to marital wrongs by seeking divorce. Perhaps, then, the rise in divorce related in a general way to the War for Independence in the sense that a certain personal outlook—one that implied self-assertion and regard for the future, one that we might label more "modern" than "traditional"—may have led a person to seek divorce and also to support American independence.[24] The evidence that aggrieved spouses desired to have their marriages ended officially, rather than taking more traditional measures such as "self-divorce" through desertion, or resigning themselves to the ties of unsatisfactory marriages, suggests a modernization of attitudes.[25] Communication about the granting of divorces may also have had a cumulative effect: the more divorces were allowed, the more likely it became for a discontented spouse to consider the possibility. Especially in small towns, news of divorces being obtained must have encouraged more men and women to petition. The growth in petitions seems to indicate that more individuals were asserting control over the direction of their lives and were refusing to be ruled by unhappy fates—characteristics which are also considered "modern." In the Revolutionary period this kind of self-assertion may have gone along with an enhanced sense of citizenship and legal rights. Not only men claimed the rights of citizens. At least one Boston woman in 1784 and another in 1785 petitioned "as a citizen of this Commonwealth" for a hearing of her case.[26]

More wives than husbands sued for divorce during the period 1692–1786, and the concentration of women's petitions during the Revolutionary years was more marked than that of men's. One can only speculate whether these figures mean that women generally had more marital grievances or that their grievances were growing faster or being more readily voiced. Several variables hindered or encouraged men and women to seek divorce. A man might hesitate because he was shy of the authorities, hated to arouse adverse publicity about his marriage, or could not afford the expense, whatever it was; or because the worth of his wife's domestic service seemed to outweigh her transgressions. Male domination of colonial public life suggests, however, that men were less shy of the authorities than were women, better able to stand adverse publicity about their marriages without risking their entire reputation, significantly more independent economically, and better equipped than women to pay legal expenses. A man could also take the initiative in acquiring a second spouse.

All the feelings that might have kept men from suing for divorce probably affected women even more intensely. Consider the doubts and anguish of Abigail Bailey as she pondered whether to seek divorce from her husband, who had committed incest with their daughter and had also had sexual liaisons with several other women. "Whether it would be consisted [sic] with faithfulness to suffer him to flee, and not be made a monument of civil justice, was my query. The latter looked to me inexpressibly painful. And I persuaded myself, that if he would do what was right, relative to our property, and would go to some distant place, where we should be afflicted with him no more, it might be sufficient; and I might be spared the dreadful scene of prosecuting my husband."[27]

Women apparently expected less success with their petitions than did men. While men always asked for divorce (dissolution of the bonds of marriage), women frequently equivocated; they requested divorce or, if that were not possible, whatever separation the governor and Council were willing to grant.[28] Perhaps other wives who had cause did not even petition because they did not expect to win. According to the most recent study, illiteracy handicapped half or more of the female population in initiating civil actions, compared to 10 or 20 percent of the male population. The female petitioners were distinguished by their literacy: almost three-quarters of them (two-thirds of the non-Boston residents) could sign their names.[29] The high rate of literacy among female petitioners suggests that they may have been a group self-selected by stronger-than-average initiative or education, who did not fully represent the frequency of wives' dissatisfaction in marriage.

Whatever the inhibitions, powerful reasons urged unhappy wives to sue for divorce—reasons that did not so affect husbands. Self-preservation compelled wives whose husbands were physically abusive. A woman whose husband deserted or failed to provide for her gained little advantage from marriage, and the marriage contract hindered her from supporting herself because her property and earnings legally belonged to her husband. Many women pointed this out. In her petition of 1759, for example, Henrietta East Caine of Boston lamented that while her marriage contract lasted, "her Friends will not supply her with Goods to carry on her business as before." Another Boston woman warned that she and her three children would become public charges if she remained subject to her husband, whereas if divorced "she apprehends she shall be able to find Friends that will place her in some business to maintain herself and children." Sarah Backus claimed in 1783 that she "would be content by the most penurious industry to gain a support for herself and Child, but every Idea of comfort is banished from her Breast when she reflects, that by Law her Person is subjected to be controuled by a man possessing no one tender sentiment, but on the contrary under the entire dominion of every criminal and foul pollution."[30]

Sixty-eight percent of the husbands and 58 percent of the wives succeeded in gaining favorable action on their petitions, but 67 percent of the husbands gained freedom to remarry, in contrast to only 45 percent of the wives. Sixteen of the seventeen separations from bed and board granted during the period went to wives. When petitioners failed to obtain favorable action, it was more often because their suits remained unresolved than because they were dismissed. Fewer than 15 percent of the women's and 11 percent of the men's petitions were

TABLE 2 Petition Results

	Male Petitions	Female Petitions	All
Divorce	64	51	115
Annulment	4	7	11
Separate bed and board	1	16	17
Dismissed or not granted	11	19	30
Unresolved	21	35	56
Total	101	128	229

actually dismissed, but more than 27 percent of the women's and 20 percent of the men's never resulted in decrees. (See Table 2.) It is unclear if the lack of resolution of these cases reflected some aim of the court or the petitioner, or whether the records are faulty or missing. No significant pattern of economic or geographic discrimination, or unusual lack of clarity in the cases, appears to account for the fate of these petitions; but the percentages reveal that women's petitions were slightly more likely than men's to suffer this end.[31]

Analysis of the suits by cause clarifies the comparison of men's and women's experiences and of the results of their petitions. All suits involved invalidity or breach of the marriage contract. The causes (and the numbers of petitions) can be categorized as follows:[32]

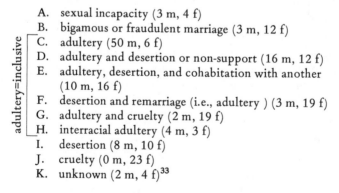

A. sexual incapacity (3 m, 4 f)
B. bigamous or fraudulent marriage (3 m, 12 f)
C. adultery (50 m, 6 f)
D. adultery and desertion or non-support (16 m, 12 f)
E. adultery, desertion, and cohabitation with another (10 m, 16 f)
F. desertion and remarriage (i.e., adultery) (3 m, 19 f)
G. adultery and cruelty (2 m, 19 f)
H. interracial adultery (4 m, 3 f)
I. desertion (8 m, 10 f)
J. cruelty (0 m, 23 f)
K. unknown (2 m, 4 f)[33]

adultery=inclusive

The first two causes, sexual incapacity and invalid marriage, warranted annulment, but the governor and Council were not always consistent in wording when they granted petitions on these grounds. Two of the three men's petitions charging their wives with incapacity for coitus were granted after court-appointed "discreet Matrons" confirmed the charges, one by annulment (1739) and the other by dissolution of marriage bonds (1781). This is unremarkable, except that the one husband waited five years after marrying, and the other, eight, before petitioning for divorce.[34] Men fared better than women in this category of suits. None of the three women's petitions to the governor and Council was granted: one was dismissed and the others were left unresolved, although in one of these cases the husband acknowledged his debility. In a unique instance, however, the General Court in 1780 enacted a legislative annulment of a marriage upon proof of the wife's complaint that her husband was impotent.[35]

Twelve female and three male petitioners pursued divorce for the second cause that warranted annulment—bigamous or fraudulent marriage. Two men, in 1762 and 1770, proved their wives to be biga- mists, and their marriages were declared null. Another argued that his recent marriage was invalid because he had been tricked into it, while drunk, by kinfolk of a young woman who was pregnant with his child. The governor and Council believed him and ruled the marriage null.[36] Women also had considerable success in ending bigamous marriages. Nine of the twelve wives' petitions were granted, six by annulment and three by dissolution, while three others remained unresolved.[37] Women's petitions against bigamous husbands revealed some of the vagaries of marriage in eighteenth-century Massachusetts. In only two instances had the husband's prior marriage taken place long before and in another country.[38] In five, the husband's prior marriage occurred in another New England town between two and eight years earlier (and in one other case, fifteen years earlier).[39] Six of the bigamous husbands had also deserted, either to return to their first wives or to marry third wives.[40] These cases, especially when considered together with cases involving desertion, suggest the ease and perhaps the appeal of running away from one partner and finding another—the traditional "self-divorce." Husbands more frequently made such escapes and new starts than did wives. Twelve wives but only three husbands charged bigamy (category B); sixteen wives but only ten husbands complained of their spouses' desertion

TABLE 3 Proportion of Petitions Receiving Favorable Decrees, 1692-1786

	All Causes	Adultery-Inclusive Only	Adultery-Exclusive Only
Male petitioners	68%	72%	50%
Female petitioners	58%	65%	47%

Note: Favorable decrees include divorce, annulment, separate bed and board.

and adulterous cohabitation with another (E); nineteen wives but only three husbands charged their partners with desertion and remarriage (F); ten wives but eight husbands petitioned on grounds of desertion alone (I). Men moved more easily from place to place, it seems; certainly, according to custom, they, and not women, took the initiative in deciding to marry or remarry.

The bulk of the petitions—84 percent of the husbands', 59 percent of the wives'—included the grievance of adultery. Men had more success than women in adultery-inclusive causes, but both sexes fared better in these causes than in others. (See Table 3.) The comparison between men's and women's experiences in suing on grounds of adultery is especially interesting because it can inform us of the presence of a double standard of sexual morality. Were men's and women's infidelities considered equally cause for divorce? The cultural heritage of Massachusetts contained equivocal answers to this question. Despite the seventh commandment, English tradition enshrined the double standard, forgiving a husband's sexual transgressions but calling a wife's abhorrent. As mentioned earlier, all the parliamentary divorces for adultery in the eighteenth century were awarded to husbands, none to wives. Decorum among the aristocracy required wives to ignore their husbands' extramarital affairs.[41] In Massachusetts, however, Puritan religious values strongly infused the English tradition. Puritan ideology, partially to repudiate aristocratic manners, demanded fidelity of both partners. From the sixteenth century through the eighteenth, Puritan reformers attacked the double standard by advocating chastity before marriage, and fidelity after, for men as well as women.[42]

It is striking that in Massachusetts half of all the men's petitions named adultery as the sole major grievance (C), and that these petitions had a high rate of success: 70 percent resulted in divorce, only 4 percent were dismissed, and the remaining quarter did not result in decrees.[43] To obtain divorce a petitioner had to produce two eyewitnesses to the act of adultery or a confession from the accused spouse, or show record of criminal conviction of the adulterers, or of the failure of the accused to answer the court summons. Alternatively, a male petitioner might show that his wife had become pregnant in his absence. In England prior court conviction of the adulterers was prerequisite to a bill of divorce; but in Massachusetts civil court action only seldom, and randomly, preceded or accompanied divorce suits.[44] Usually the governor and Council themselves determined the justice of the adultery charge. Since a wife's adultery was virtually sure cause for divorce, it was not unknown for a restless husband to "frame" his wife by setting up her seduction or by bribing deponents to testify that they had seen adultery committed. In several cases such plots by the husband were manifest or inferable.[45] The two husbands whose petitions were dismissed brought witnesses who incriminated the accused wives, but the court suspected bribery and believed the wives' contrary testimony.[46]

Clearly, the governor and Council would grant divorce to a man whose spouse committed adultery. Would they grant it to a woman for the same cause? There was no English precedent for such action. Only one suit from seventeenth-century Massachusetts has been found in which a wife sought and received a divorce for the sole cause of adultery—and this decree was subsequently reversed on the husband's appeal.[47] Women in eighteenth-century Massachusetts could be said to have taken a cue from these negative precedents. In contrast to the weight of men's petitions, not a single wife petitioned for the sole grievance of adultery until 1774, and only six did so between 1774 and 1786. Unless we assume that husbands displayed much more virtue than wives, the difference between the numbers of petitions from men and from women in this category (C) suggests a deeply entrenched double standard of marital fidelity. Whether individual women thought that men's adultery warranted divorce remains uncertain; but we can logically conclude that before 1774 women did not expect to obtain divorce for that reason alone and so did not petition.

We can gain an approximation of the governor and Council's response to petitions grounded on husbands' adultery alone, before 1774, by looking at decrees in the other adultery-inclusive categories (D through H). Husbands' suits in these categories, dependent on their substantiation of the adultery charges, had great success. More than four-fifths of their petitions changing adultery and desertion (D), or adultery, desertion, and cohabitation (E), resulted in divorce. Few husbands petitioned on the other adultery-inclusive grounds, and only the ones who proved adultery won their suits. By contrast, the pre-Revolutionary governor and Council gave a woman very little reason to expect divorce for her spouse's infidelity. Seven out of twelve female petitioners before 1774 obtained divorces by proving their partner's desertion, adultery, and remarriage (F), but these decrees took bigamy, as well as adultery, into account.[48] Fourteen women petitioned the governor and Council on other adultery-inclusive grounds prior to 1773. Eight of these received no decrees; one suit with apparent proof of the adultery was dismissed; and three—two of which charged adultery and cruelty—gained decrees of separate bed and board, the same decree which women's petitions charging cruelty alone could obtain.[49] Only two of the fourteen wives won divorces, and their cases were not conclusive on the question of adultery. Sarah Mitchell of Deerfield, who brought suit in 1718 on grounds of her husband's "fornication" with a black woman, obtained a divorce and the return of her marriage portion as well. The uniqueness of the decree suggests that not the adultery, but its interracial nature, was the crucial factor.[50] Hannah Rolfe of Lancaster made the other successful petition, in 1752. Her grievances included desertion, adultery, and cohabitation; her husband Ezra had been jailed for fornicating with a minor and for failing to provide for his bastard child, and he absconded to avoid answering Hannah's petition.[51]

Seventeen hundred and seventy-three was a turning point. In that year, two women who petitioned on the grounds of adultery and cruelty were granted not separate bed and board, but divorce, for the specified cause of adultery. The original notation on Sarah Gould's petition recorded a unanimous decision for separate bed and board, but the formal decree of March 2, 1773, declared her marriage dissolved. Martha Air's petition a few months later resulted in an unequivocal dissolution of marriage bonds on account of Adam Air's adultery.[52] After that, women began to petition for divorce on the sole ground of adultery. The governor and Council (or the Council alone, between 1776 and 1780) granted five out of the six such petitions during the next twelve years. The increasing number of wives who brought other adultery-inclusive charges also obtained divorces, and almost all of these decrees went on to the record as owing specifically to the adultery charge.[53] (See Table 4.)

These decrees were not quite as unprecedented as they may seem at first glance. In the 1750s, during the interval when the governor and Council declined to dissolve marriages, three women obtained bills of divorce from the General Court on adultery-inclusive grounds. The first was Mary Clapham, wife of a gentleman. After obtaining a decree of separate bed and board from the governor and Council because of her husband's desertion and adulterous cohabitation with a woman in Nova Scotia, she petitioned the General Court, "in whom she appre- hend[ed] the Power to be vested," to dissolve her marriage and assign her alimony. The court obliged her first request, citing as William Clapham's "Violation of his Marriage Contract" his "leaving the said Mary, cohabiting and committing adultery with Another Woman."[54] The two other women who appealed successfully to the General Court both charged their husbands with adultery and desertion. Mary Parker, also a gentleman's wife, obtained her divorce because, the bill said, "Phineas Parker has for sundry Years pass'd left the said Mary, and stands convict[ed] of committing Adultery with another woman." The act granted at the plea of Lydia Kellogg, wife of a laborer of Sunderland, declared only that "it appears to this court that the said Ephraim [Kellogg] has been guilty of the crime of adultery."[55]

TABLE 4 Adultery-inclusive Charges Number of Petitions/Number of Favorable Decrees

	1692-1704	1705-1714	1715-1724	1725-1734	1735-1744	1745-1754	1755-1764	1765-1774	1775-1786	Total
C										
Men	2/1	1/1		2/1	6/6	4/2	9/5*	12/8	14/11	50/35*
Women								1/1	5/4	6/5
D										
Men					2/2	1/1	1/1	4/2	8/6	16/12
Women						2/0	2/2*	2/0	6/5	12/7*
E										
Men	1/1						2/2*	1/0	6/6	10/9*
Women					1/1	2/2*		2/0	11/8	16/11
F										
Men		1/1				2/0				3/1
Women	1/1		3/0	2/1	1/1	1/1	1/1	3/2	7/6	19/13
G										
Men							1/0		1/0	2/0
Women						1/1**		6/3**	12/7	19/11**
H										
Men					1/1	1/1	2/2			4/4
Women				1/1				1/0	1/1	3/2

Note:
 *Includes legislative divorce.
 **Includes separate bed and board.

The General Court seems to have been more liberal in granting divorces to women before 1773 than were the governor and Council. In enacting bills of divorce for three wives during the 1750s the court presaged actions which the Council would take during, but not before, the Revolutionary period.[56] The legislative divorces, viewed together with the Council's decrees after 1773, suggest that the more whiggish and the more representative the authority, the more likely it was to treat male and female adultery equally as cause for divorce. The transformation of the Council's attitude toward male adultery would be simpler to explain if it had occurred in 1776, when the composition of the Council changed radically. Though some new members replaced old ones in 1773, specific changes in membership do not clearly account for the new pattern of decrees beginning in that year.[57]

Divorce actions in Massachusetts may have paralleled larger political struggles, but did changes in divorce policy also move against the double standard and advance equality between the sexes? In several ways the record of petitions and decrees implies an improvement in women's status. The great increase in the number of women's petitions after 1764 suggests that women were becoming less resigned to their circumstances and were taking more initiative to end unsatisfactory marriages. Women's petitions were more concentrated in the period after 1764 than were men's.[58] The proportion of petitions including adultery charges rose for both sexes, but more emphatically for wives. (See Table 5.) The higher the proportion of adultery-inclusive petitions, the greater success petitioners were likely to have. In fact, both male and female petitioners fared better between 1765 and 1786, but only on account of decrees made after independence. From 1765 through 1774 an unusually high proportion of suits remained unresolved, reducing petitioners' chances of favorable action. The proportion of unresolved petitions jumped from 23 percent for the years 1692–1764 to 41 percent for 1765–1774, and then dropped to 13 percent for 1775–1786. This noteworthy improvement in efficiency, along with the rise in the proportion of adultery-inclusive petitions, increased petitioners' likelihood of gaining favorable decrees. Because of the added factor of the new treatment of male adultery, wives' rate of success improved dramatically from 49 percent between 1692 and 1774 to 70 percent between 1775 and 1786; husbands' rate of success rose only from 66 percent to 73 percent. Wives' rate of success almost equalled that of husbands' during the decade after independence.

It is tempting to propose from this evidence that the Revolutionary era ushered in a "new deal" that recognized the injustice of the double standard, evened obligations of marital fidelity, and made redress within marriage more accessible to women. To an extent, however small, acceptance of male adultery as grounds for divorce moved in these directions. Motives for the change in the treatment of male adultery probably originated, however, more in men's political intentions than in their desire for sexual justice. Revolutionary rhetoric, in its repudiation of British "vice," "corruption," "extravagance," and "decadence," enshrined ideals of republican virtue—of personal and national simplicity, honesty, frugality, and public spirit. In the view of Revolutionary leaders, republicanism required a moral reformation

TABLE 5 Proportion of All Petitions Containing Adultery Charge

	1692–1764	1765–1774	1775–1786
Male petitioners	78%	94%	91%
Female petitioners	40%	50%	79%

of the American people as well as a political transformation, because a republic's success depended on the virtue of its citizens. As John Adams wrote to his wife Abigail in July 1776, "the new Governments we are assuming . . . will require a Purification from our Vices, and an Augmentation of our Virtues or they will be no Blessings." Samuel Adams stated in 1777, "We shall succeed if we are virtuous. . . . I am infinitely more apprehensive of the Contagion of Vice than the Power of all other Enemies."[59] The dynamism of the words "virtue" and "vice," in Revolutionary usage, derived at least in part from their sexual connotation.[60] Rejection of British "corruption" implied a critique of the traditionally loose sexual standards for men of the British ruling class. The republican ideology of private as well as public virtue also produced an emphasis on marital fidelity, because it focused on the family as the training ground of future citizens. It was wholly consistent that judges in Massachusetts, where patriotic rhetoric evoked Puritan conceptions of righteousness (and thus Puritan standards of fidelity), no longer saw male adultery as venial but called it sufficient grounds for divorce. Such a change in standards for male conduct may well have produced a divorce policy that had the appearance of improving women's marital status.

Petitioners also brought suits on account of important marital breaches other than adultery—namely, desertion (I) and cruelty (J). Desertion suits were the least successful among all the categories. Of ten wives who charged desertion—all but one abandoned for more than three years—only two achieved any favorable result. Five of the petitions were not resolved. Three more were dismissed, suggesting that the governor and Council regarded a husband's willful desertion in itself as insufficient cause to dissolve a marriage.[61] One wife who asked only for her conjugal right to restoration of maintenance, since her husband had deserted long before, obtained her object. The court formalized the couple's agreement for yearly maintenance payments by the husband.[62] In the other successful suit Abigail Bradstreet, whose complaints included cruelty as well as desertion, won a decree of separate bed and board with maintenance payments.[63]

Among the eight men who sued because of their wives' desertion, the earlier petitioners fared better than the later. The court declared John Emery of Newbury separated from his wife in 1710 on his complaint that she slandered him and refused to live with him. Two other men obtained divorces on desertion pleas. John Ferre, a husbandman of Springfield, petitioned in 1718 and was ordered by the governor and Council to post notification that if his wife did not return within six months she would be divorced. Ferre obeyed, his wife did not return, and in 1719 the divorce was granted. Jonathan Fletcher's petition of 1734 stated that his wife had departed sixteen years earlier, after two months of marriage. In this case the governor and Council took the unusual step of declaring both parties single and free to marry, the marriage portion to be returned.[64] After 1734, however, men's desertion pleas all failed. The court gave John Williston's petition in 1737 only a first reading, apparently, and dismissed other petitions in 1739, 1740, 1743, and 1786.[65] These dismissals contradicted the implication of the Ferre and Fletcher cases, and they force the general conclusion that desertion alone, whether by wife or husband, was not considered sufficient cause for divorce. Why not? Certainly desertion violated the marriage contract. In Puritan theory desertion warranted divorce. Under canon law, on the contrary, desertion was not even grounds for separate bed and board unless it was combined with cruelty.[66] Excepting the Ferre and Fletcher cases, the governor and Council acted as though canon law controlled their decisions on desertion.[67] Perhaps the New World offered too great opportunities for desertion for the court to wish to establish desertion as reason for divorce.

Canon law rather than Puritan precept appears to have guided the decisions in cruelty cases as well. Puritan divorce theory allowed divorce for incorrigible enmity between spouses or for dangerous abuse, but canon law prescribed only separate bed and board. Of the twenty-three Massachusetts petitions entered on grounds of cruelty, nine obtained decrees of separate bed and board, three more were settled by separations based on mutual consent, six were dismissed for insufficient evidence, and five were left unresolved. Not a single one gained divorce. However, not all of these petitions asked for divorce. All of the petitioners in this category were women, and almost two-thirds of them requested only separate bed and board with maintenance. It is difficult to tell whether this reflected their pragmatism or their personal preference. Divorce was virtually impossible to obtain for this cause, but separate bed and board was possible. To gain a separation, with alimony, may have seemed a satisfactory solution to the grievance, especially for older women who did not foresee marrying again. Yet even separate bed and board was not easy to obtain, as the six dismissals attested. In all but one of these six cases the wives asked only for separation and maintenance, but the governor and Council would not grant the plea.[68]

Women who petitioned on grounds of cruelty were significantly more urban—and thus perhaps more sophisticated—than petitioners in general. Fourteen of the twenty-two[69] lived in Boston, three in towns immediately outside Boston, two in other large port towns, and only three in smaller, more remote locations. Perhaps urban women had higher standards for kind treatment in marriage than did rural women, or more readily took official steps to combat physical abuse. Urban women also predominated, though not as strongly, among wives petitioning on grounds of adultery and cruelty (G): ten of the nineteen lived in Boston and three in towns nearby.

The governor and Council usually judged requests for maintenance in cases in which they decreed separate bed and board, although a provincial statute of 1695 located jurisdiction over alimony in the Superior Court of Judicature. Alimony ordinarily took the form of regular cash payments, the amount varying with the husband's wealth.[70] Gentlemen's wives, who married with considerable portions, might ask only for the return or use of their own former property to support themselves. Mary Arthur of Boston did so in 1754 when she sought separation from her husband because of his nine years of abuse. After she obtained the separation, a second petition was required before the Council awarded her her household goods and the income from her Boston real estate.[71] The governor and Council assigned to another Bostonian, in lieu of the alimony she requested, the rent and profit of her own real property, removing it from her husband's control. Yet she was not permitted to sell the lands, which were uncultivated and produced no profit, without petitioning again for that privilege. Upon her plea, the General Court enacted a bill allowing her to sell and convey the lands as though she were single, but the Privy Council disallowed it.[72] These alimony arrangements revealed starkly how the marriage bond circumscribed the legal and economic individuality of women.[73]

In three separate bed and board decrees after 1780 the governor and Council failed to mention alimony, although the Massachusetts constitution of 1780 put the matter under their jurisdiction. They granted *divorce* with alimony to two women petitioners, however— the only two such decrees between 1692 and 1786—although no extraordinary characteristics of the cases explain why.[74] It may be that divorced women had earlier sought alimony from the superior courts. Sarah Griffin (Sarah Gould before her divorce) filed a petition for this purpose with the Superior Court of Judicature of Suffolk County on August 31, 1773, but the court appears to have taken no action.[75]

It is doubtful how well the assignment of alimony worked to provide for separated or divorced wives. In those four cases in which the couple mutually agreed to separation and maintenance no complaints followed.[76] But six of the nine decrees of separate bed and board with alimony were succeeded by further petitions from the wives, because their husbands had not made the required payments.[77] Petitioners who won separate bed and board thus had an ambiguous success, not being allowed to remarry, nor released from the economic constraints of the marriage contract, nor guaranteed current support. The husband's provision of alimony, like his support during marriage, was required by law and enforceable by compulsory process, but his performance actually depended on his own conscientiousness and goodwill.

The records of divorce in Massachusetts are most interesting for what they reveal about men's and women's respective power and advantages within marriage. The alimony petitions emphasize something the divorce suits as a whole suggest, that while marriage was a contract—a covenant, in contemporary language—it was a contract between unequals with disparate obligations. Sexual fidelity and good conduct were expected of both partners, but fidelity was not regularly enforced upon husbands by the threat of divorce until the mid-1770s, and a husband's abusive conduct never warranted divorce. The husband's characteristic obligation was provision of support; the wife's, obedient service. In this, marriage resembled an indenture between master and servant; and, indeed, the marriage relation was only one of a number of dependency relations—such as parent-child and master-servant—in traditional society. The husband's obligation— enhanced by his control over his wife's property and labor—was unequivocal. In a case, for example, in which an aggrieved wife returned to her parents' household, her father sued her husband for the cost of maintaining her during that time, and his view of the husband's responsibility was upheld in court.[78] The wife performed her part in her subjection. Like a servant in relation to a master, she contributed continual service and received support. Besides working in the household (many deponents in divorce cases mentioned the industry of wives), she was expected to use frugally what her husband provided. Amos Bliss of Rehoboth felt he had a valid complaint against his wife Phebe because she "behaved herself unfriendly and unsubjectedly toward him; and . . . had linked herself in friendship with her father's Family against him; who . . . had ocationed a great Deal of Trouble, as well as Loss, to his Interest; and he Represented her to be Very Disloyal towards his person: and wastefull and Careless of his provisions and goods"; but Amos was willing to invite Phebe home again if she would act the good and obedient wife and "be in subjection to him."[79] The indenture-like nature of marriage appeared in the practice of a husband's "advertising" his runaway wife, warning others not to harbor or trust her, and refusing responsibility for her debts. A husband would not be bound to provide for his wife if he could not command her services, and he could compel her services by preventing her from obtaining support elsewhere.

Since marriage resembled an indenture contract, divorce should have been more readily available for varieties of nonperformance such as desertion or cruelty. That it was not suggests, first, that the sexual definition of marriage was its essence, and, second, that English divorce policy had more influence on eighteenth-century Massachusetts than might appear at first glance. Although marriage was regarded as a civil contract, and Massachusetts had no ecclesiastical courts, decisions in desertion and cruelty suits were almost entirely consistent with English application of canon law. On the whole, however, Massachusetts divorce practice diverged significantly from that of England. A much wider range of individuals—a laborer, a poor woman, a black servant— were able to obtain divorce with freedom to remarry, while in England only very rich men had that opportunity. In addition, the procedure was simpler than the parliamentary process. No prior ecclesiastical decree or criminal conviction of the adulterers was necessary in adultery cases, although the latter sufficed to warrant divorce. What was more innovative, women were able to obtain divorce with freedom to remarry and after 1773 did so on approximately the same terms as men. When in 1786 Massachusetts enacted a divorce law to codify the practice that had evolved, it allowed divorce for consanguinity, bigamy, impotency, or adultery *in either partner*, and separate bed and board for extreme cruelty.[80]

Throughout the period 1692-1786 husbands found it easier than wives to obtain divorce—not a surprising circumstance, since men also had the legal and economic independence which married women lacked, occupied all political and religious offices, were more literate than women, exercised greater control over geographic moves and choice of spouse, and by the terms at the marriage covenant could command their wives' obedience. It is more remarkable that the number of women's petitions and their rate of success accelerated during the century, so that in the decade after independence more than half again as many women as men pursued divorce, and their rate of success was almost the same. Divorce pleas by both sexes increased during the Revolutionary period, and efficiency in treating them improved, reflecting modernization of both personal values and bureaucratic procedure. The disproportionate growth in women's petitions suggests that they, even more than men, had rising expectations in marriage; and the changing treatment of their petitions implies that wives' objections were being regarded more seriously—that their status within the family had risen in the eyes of authorities.

The equalization of the consequences of adultery by either spouse, which was unmistakably the reason for the increasing success of women petitioners, may have signified a retreat from hierarchical models and an advance toward ideals of complementarity in the prevailing conception of the marriage relationship. In Hingham, Massachusetts, Daniel Scott Smith has found a consonant change in marriage patterns—a move away from parental control in the direction of individual autonomy in marriage choice—beginning markedly in the Revolutionary years. Smith sees the departure from the stable, parent-run system of selecting spouses as evidence of the "erosion and collapse of traditional family patterns in the middle to late eighteenth century."[81] Furthermore, on the basis of her analysis of New England funeral sermons Lonna Malmsheimer affirms that views of women altered significantly during these years. No longer stressing the rigid subordination of wife to husband as they had done earlier, although still insisting on the importance of the wife's domestic service, the sermons began to focus on friendship, complementarity, and emotional bonds between spouses. The seventeenth-century linkage of woman with moral evil, Eve's legacy, gave way to a new image of woman as a being ruled by conscience and religion.[82] Additionally, writers in contemporary Boston magazines seem to have been preoccupied with the reciprocal obligations and advantages of the sexes. They, too, idealized the complementary nature of men's and women's marital roles: an essayist in the Boston *Gentleman's and Lady's Town and Country Magazine,* for example, of September 1784, described "matrimonial felicity" as the uniting of two congenial souls, "the man all truth, the woman all tenderness; he possessed of cheerful solidity, she of rational gaiety; acknowledging his superior judgment she complies with all his reasonable desires, whilst he, charmed with such repeated instances of superior love, endeavors to suit his requests to her inclinations."[83]

By the last quarter of the eighteenth century both parties were evidently restating the terms of the "indenture" of marriage. The divorce court's reprobation of male adultery newly defined one limit to the marital contract. This indicated an improvement in the position of wives, although it did not change their economic status, the essence of their dependency. By making men culpable for adultery, the court may also have heralded a new ideology of sexual roles—one that would encourage families in the young Republic to produce upright citizens. Stricter standards for men's marital fidelity helped enforce ideals of republican character and counteract British social models. The assumption that men could resist the temptation of adultery also implied a nontraditional view of woman[84]—not the devil-as-woman Eve, whose seductiveness absolved men of their sexual transgressions, but the angel-as-woman Pamela, who upheld and typified sexual virtue.

NOTES

1. Deposition of William Whiting, Jr., Suffolk Court Files #129846, Suffolk County Court House, Boston, 106.

2. Robert V. Wells, "Quaker Marriage Patterns in a Colonial Perspective," *William and Mary Quarterly*, 3d Ser., XXIX (1972, 415-442; Daniel Scott Smith, "Parental Power and Marriage Patterns: An Analysis of Historical Trends in Hingham, Massachusetts," *Journal of Marriage and the Family*, XXXV (1973), 419-439; Daniel Scott Smith and Michael Hindus, "Premarital Pregnancy in America, 1640-1966," *Journal of Interdisciplinary History*, VI (1975), 537-570.

3. See Nancy F. Cott, "Eighteenth-Century Family and Social Life Revealed in Massachusetts Divorce Records," *Journal of Social History*, X (1976), where these documents are used to investigate questions about privacy and community, relations among conjugal-family and extended-family members, and romantic love and sex.

4. In June 1692 the General Court declared that "all controversies concerning marriage and divorce shall be heard and determined by the governor and council." *Acts and Resolves, Public and Private, of the Province of Massachusetts Bay . . .* Boston, 1869-1922), I, chap. 25, sec. 4, 61. The state constitution of 1780 confirmed this practice, until "An Act for Regulating Marriage and Divorce" of Mar. 16, 1786, located jurisdiction over divorce suits in the Supreme Judicial Court held for each county. *Acts and Resolves of Massachusetts, 1784-1785* (Boston, ca. [1892]), 564-567.

5. The most informative records are the original petitions and depositions preserved for most of the cases between 1739 and 1786 in volumes 793-796 of the Suffolk Court Files. Similar documents from some earlier cases appear in volume IX of the Massachusetts Archives, at the Archives Dept., State House, Boston. A single bound manuscript volume labeled "Divorces, 1760-1786," hereafter cited as "Divorces," located with the Suffolk Files, summarizes most of the divorce petitions and decrees between those dates. Mass. Archives, CXL, contains a fairly complete record of divorces between 1780 and 1786. Additional cases before 1780 have been recovered from the executive records of the Council, also at the Archives Dept., hereafter cited as Council Recs. Surprisingly, the Council Records do not contain the most inclusive recording of petitions and decrees; their completeness varies considerably through the years. The legislative records of the Council, a separate series in the Archives Dept. called Court Records, have been used in those cases that involved legislation.

6. The overrepresentation of Bostonians—for the city held only 6% of the province's population in 1765—was at least partially owing to the requirement that petitioners appear before the governor and Council at their sessions in Boston. The legislation of 1786 shifted jurisdiction over divorce to the superior courts held in each county because of remote petitioners' difficulty in getting to Boston. I have estimated the geographical distribution of petitioners by using the population figures in the 1764-1765 provincial census, obviously not an exact means since the divorce cases span almost a century, but the only one available. Place of residence was disclosed in almost 90% of the suits. On the basis of 1764-1765 population figures, 24.6% of petitioners resided in towns of less than 1,000 pop.; 22.6% in towns of 1,000 to 1,999; 15.9% in towns of 2,000 to 2,999; 8.2% in towns of 3,000 to 5,000; and 28.7% in Boston. More than two-fifths of the petitioners

lived in the populous counties of Suffolk and Essex; a slightly smaller proportion in the eastern counties of Middlesex, Worcester, Bristol, Plymouth, Barnstable, and Dukes; and the remainder (slightly under a fifth) in the remote and lightly populated counties of Hampshire, Berkshire, Cumberland, Lincoln, and York. See J. H. Benton, *Early Census Making in Massachusetts* (Boston, 1905).

7. There are some interesting differences between the occupational levels of male petitioners and female—the latter judged by their *husbands'* occupations, however. Among the 122 wives, 73 disclosed the occupations of their husbands. Fifteen percent were esquires, gentlemen, or merchants; 4% doctors or officers; 19% husbandmen or yeomen; 16% mariners or fishermen; 37% craftsmen or traders; and 8% laborers, servants, or truckmen. Among the 101 husbands, 67 disclosed their occupations. Only 4.5% were esquires, gentlemen, or merchants; 9% professionals or officers; 25% husbandmen or yeomen; 28% mariners (reflecting the high incidence of adultery on the part of wives whose husbands were at sea for long periods); 27% craftsmen or traders; and 6% the lower occupations.

8. They may have had an even easier time in Connecticut, which had the most liberal divorce policy of all the colonies; both judicial and legislative divorces were granted there. Between 1740 and 1789, 174 superior court divorces were recorded in Hartford County alone. Henry S. Cohn, "Connecticut's Divorce Mechanism: 1636–1969," *American Journal of Legal History*, XIV (1970), 43, n. 39.

9. This discussion of English divorce practice relies on George Elliott Howard, *A History of Matrimonial Institutions, Chiefly in the United States and England* . . . (Chicago, 1904), II, 52–57, 77–85, 92–93, 102–107; Reginald Haw, *The State of Matrimony* (London, 1952), 74–89; Oliver McGregor, *Divorce in England* (London, 1957), 1–12; Joseph W. Madden, *Handbook of the Law of Persons and Domestic Relations* (St. Paul, Minn., 1931), 256–260; and L. Kinvin Wroth and Hiller B. Zobel, eds., *The Legal Papers of John Adams*, I (Cambridge, Mass., 1965), 280–285. The several accounts of divorce in England differ slightly in their estimates of numbers of parliamentary divorces before 1800.

10. The population figure for England and Wales is estimated from a table in J. D. Chambers, *Population, Economy, and Society in Pre-Industrial England* (London, 1972), 108.

11. The document best illustrating Puritan divorce reform theory in England is the *Reformatio Legum Ecclesiasticarum*, authorized by Parliament and drafted by eminent divines in 1552. The *Reformatio* regarded marriage as a civil contract rather than an indissoluble sacred bond, omitted mention of separate bed and board, allowed dissolution of marriage for adultery, desertion, continued absence without news, or unmitigable enmity or cruelty by either spouse—and was never put into effect. Howard, *Matrimonial Institutions*, II, 78–79.

12. *Ibid.*, 331–338; Edmund S. Morgan, *The Puritan Family: Religion and Domestic Relations in Seventeenth-Century New England* (New York, 1966), 35–37; John Demos, *A Little Commonwealth: Family Life in Plymouth Colony* (New York, 1970), 92–97; D. Kelly Weisberg, "Under Greet Temptations Heer: Women and Divorce in Puritan Massachusetts." *Feminist Studies*, 11 (1975), 183–194. Since Howard's list of divorce suits for the period 1692–1786 is incomplete (he lists only 10 suits), it is likely that his list of 40 for the period 1639–1692 is similarly fragmentary.

13. Wroth and Zobel, eds., *Legal Papers of Adams*, I, 282, erroneously states that jurisdiction to grant divorce *a vinculo* was ambiguous after 1692 and that the governor and Council did not grant divorces between 1692 and 1760.

14. They did so despite a law enacted by the General Court in 1755, empowering them to enforce their decrees in divorce suits by ordering imprisonment for disobedience. *Acts and Resolves, Mass. Bay*, III, chap. 15, 782.

15. The acts are in *ibid.*, VI, 165, 169, 170, 173, 174, 177, and can be corroborated in Court Recs., XX, 337–338, 346, 351–352, 373, 379, 460, 461, 468, XXI, 97, 157, 161, 329, 497, 500, 517, 540, XXII, 40. Howard, *Matrimonial Institutions*, II, 340, errs in saying that "after 1692 the legislature does not seem to have interfered in divorce suits either on appeal or in the first instance."

16. Report of the Lords of Trade, June 6, 1758, Mass. Arch., XXII, 9–10. See also *Acts and Resolves, Mass. Bay*, VI, vi–vii, and Joseph Henry Smith, *Appeals to the Privy Council from the American Plantations* (New York, 1950), 582–585. Smith points out that in 1741 the Lords disallowed a Jamaica act of legislative divorce passed in 1739.

17. See William Renwick Riddell, "Legislative Divorce in Colonial Pennsylvania," *Pennsylvania Magazine of History and Biography*, LVII (1933), 175–180; Thomas R. Meehan, " 'Not Made Our of Levity': Evolution of Divorce in Early Pennsylvania," *ibid.*, XCII (1968), 441–464; Leonard Woods Labaree, ed., *Royal Instructions to British Colonial Governors, 1670–1776*, I (New York, 1935), 154–155.

18. A bill "for enabling the Governor and Council to grant Divorces from the Bands of Matrimony," passed by the House of Representatives in Aug. 1757, never became law because the Council neglected or declined to concur. Mass. Arch., IX, 419; *Journals of the House of Representatives of Massachusetts, 1757*, XXXIV (Meriden, Conn., 1961), 105. On July 30, 1759, the Council appointed four of its members to investigate the precedents of divorce actions before 1756. Why the Council had so short a collective memory—when several members had been on the Council in the early 1750s—is puzzling. The committee reported (accurately) on Nov. 10, 1759, that the Council had decreed seven divorces and one separation between 1747 and 1754. See Mass. Arch. IX, 432–434, and Council Recs., XIV, 122, 134. Another influence leading to the Council's resumption of divorce by decree may have been Gov. Thomas Pownall's message of Feb. 2, 1760, which touched on the Council's power as a divorce court. Josiah Quincy, Jr., *Reports of Cases Argued and Adjudged in the Superior Court of Judicature of the Province of Massachusetts Bay between 1761 and 1772* (Boston, 1865), 573–579.

19. The white population of Massachusetts in 1780 was about five-and-a-half times as large as it had been in 1690, but there were twelve times as many petitions and decrees in the years 1775–1786 as in 1692–1704. Population data are from U.S. Bureau of the Census, *Historical Statistics of the United States: Colonial Times to 1957* (Washington, D.C., 1960).

20. See Francis G. Walett, "The Massachusetts Council, 1766–1774: The Transformation of a Conservative Institution," *WMQ*, 3d Ser., VI (1949), 605–627.

21. Abigail Bradstreet v. Joseph Bradstreet, Suffolk Files #129762, "Divorces," 68–70; James Richardson v. Hannah Richardson, Suffolk Files #129769, "Divorces," 70–72.

22. For example, Chloe Welch v. Luke Welch, Suffolk Files #129790, "Divorces," 122–125, and Andrew Gage v. Elizabeth Gage, Suffolk Files #129829, "Divorces," 192–193; see also Ann Lovell v. John Lovell, Jr., Suffolk Files #129778.

23. See Smith and Hindus, "Premarital Pregnancy," *Jour. Interdisciplinary Hist.*, VI (1975), 537–570.

24. See Kenneth A. Lockridge, "Social Change and the Meaning of the American Revolution," *Jour. Soc. Hist.*, VI (1973), 403–439, for several hypothetical models of "preparedness" for the War for Independence.

25. On modernization in New England see *ibid.*, and two articles by Richard D. Brown: "Modernization and the Modern Personality in Early America, 1600–1865: A Sketch of a Synthesis," *Jour. Interdisciplinary Hist.*, II (1972), 201–228, and "The Emergence of Urban Society in Rural Massachusetts, 1760–1820," *Journal of American History*, LXI (1974), 29–51. For a typology of the "modern" personality see Alex Inkeles, "Making Men Modern: On the Causes and Consequences of Individual Change in Six Developing Countries," *American Journal of Sociology*, LXXV (1969), 208–225, and "The Modernization of Man," in Myron Weiner, ed., *Modernization: The Dynamics of Growth* (New York, 1966), 138–150.

26. See Sarah Vernon v. William Vernon, Suffolk Files #129840, petition, 78, and Rebecca Simpson v. Ebenezer Simpson, *ibid.* #129854, petition, 140.

27. *Memoirs of Mrs. Abigail Bailey . . . written by herself . . .* , ed. Ethan Smith (Boston, 1815), 58–59. Mrs. Bailey eventually did petition and obtain a divorce in 1792.

28. For example, Mary Fairservice v. John Fairservice (1767), petition in "Divorces," 40–42; Sarah Gould v. William Gould (1773), Suffolk Files #129772, petition, 56; Sarah Kingsley v. Enoch Kingsley (1771), Suffolk Files #129773, petition, 58; Martha Air v. Adam Air (1773), Suffolk Files #129779, petition, 85.

29. Kenneth A. Lockridge, *Literacy in Colonial New England: An Enquiry into the Social Context of Literacy in the Early Modern West* (New York, 1974), esp. tables on pp. 24 and 41, indicates that Boston women's ability to sign moved from about 40% in 1700 to a peak of 68% in 1758–1762, and then fell to 60% by 1787, while rural women's ability remained below 40% for the whole period, and that Boston men's ability to sign moved from about 75% in 1700 to 80% in 1758–1762, while rural men's ability moved from 65% to 75%. Literacy data (signature or mark) appeared for 96 female divorce petitioners and 56 male petitioners. Sixty-one percent of these female petitioners before 1765 could sign—all of the 9 Boston women, and 8 of the 19 non-Boston women. Seventy-eight percent of the female petitioners between 1765 and 1786 could sign, including 16 of the 20 Boston women and 37 (77%) of the 48 non-Boston women. Among 17 male petitioners before 1765, 94% could sign—that is, all except one black man of Boston, a servant. Of 39 male petitioners between 1765 and 1786, 95% could sign—all of the 8 Boston men and all but two of the 31 non-Boston men. If Lockridge's figures are correct for the general population, both male and female divorce petitioners, as judged by ability to sign, had literacy above the norm. For a control group independent of Lockridge's study, there are the scores of deponents who testified in the divorce cases. They suggest a different norm. The ability to sign of 495 male deponents was 98.4%; it was 100% among the 64 deponents before 1765, and 98.1% among the 431 deponents between 1765 and 1786. The ability to sign of 224 female deponents was 58%; it was 68% among 50 deponents before 1765 and fell to 55.1% among the 174 deponents between 1765 and 1786. Both male and female deponents included large proportions of low-status persons, such as hired laborers and domestic servants, but the male deponents also included many of high status.

30. Henrietta Maria East Caine v. Hugh Caine, Suffolk Files #129736, "Divorces," 2–3; Mary Hunt v. Richard Hunt (1761), "Divorces," 8–9; Sarah Backus v. John Backus, Suffolk Files #129846, 100. See also Sarah Bloget v. John Bloget, Mass. Arch., IX, 211.

31. Ten of the unresolved petitions—seven from women and three from men—show no sign of ever having been read by the Council. If these petitions are removed from the comparison, the difference between the number of men's and the number of women's petitions left unresolved (after at least a first reading) diminishes.

32. In a few cases it is debatable whether the suit should be placed in one category or another: I and J in particular tend to overlap. Any of the adultery causes, C through H, might have included the charge of illegitimate offspring; as a divorce charge, this was included rather as a means of proving adultery than as a separate grievance.

33. The records are so sparse in this category that the charges are not apparent. Rachel Draper won her divorce in 1709, and Joseph Hale's suit was dismissed in 1779; the results of the four others remain as mysterious as the charges. Rachel Draper v. John Draper, Council Recs., V, 124; Mary Parce v. John Parce, *ibid.*, XVIII, 100; Experience Simpson v. husband, *ibid.*, XXIV, 392; Elizabeth Laud v. David Laud, Mass. Arch., CXL, 194; Joseph Hale (or Hail) v. Isabella Hale, Council Recs., XXIII, 64, 76, 414; Thomas Patter v. wife, *ibid.*, XXIII, 64.

34. Jesse Turner v. Grace Turner, Suffolk Files #129727, Council Recs., X, 331, 378; George Sherman v. Phebe Sherman, Suffolk Files #129796, Council Recs., XXIII, 92, XXIV, 206, 301, XXVI, 104, "Divorces," 137-140. Jeremiah Ingraham petitioned for divorce from Mercy Ingraham for this cause in 1733, after 15 years of marriage, but his charge was not substantiated and his petition was dismissed. Council Recs., IX, 464, 533.

35. Sarah Maggin v. William Maggin (dismissed, 1736), Council Recs., X, 47; Elizabeth Bredeen v. Joseph Bredeen (1744), Suffolk Files #129728, Council Recs., XI, 151, 156, 174-175, 184; Judith Walker v. Simeon Walker (1773), Suffolk Files #129777; "An Act for dissolving the Marriage of Philip Turner and Mercy Turner," *Acts and Resolves, Mass. Bay*, VI, 229.

36. William Davidson v. Hannah Davidson (1762), "Divorces," 16-17; Samuel Lefebvre v. Sarah Lefebvre (1770), Suffolk Files #129758, "Divorces," 57-59; Gill Belcher v. Mary Finney alias Belcher (1739), Suffolk Files #129726, Mass. Arch., IX, 228-229, Council Recs., X, 254-315.

37. Annulled: Susanna T. Kennet v. Edward Kennet (1694), Council Recs., II, 290; Reliance Drew v. John Drew (1737), *ibid.*, X, 79, 122; Elizabeth Eldredge v. Ezekiel Eldredge (1751), Suffolk Files #129730, Mass. Arch., IX, 354-356, Council Recs., XII, 219; Rachel Wormley v. John Wormley (1765), Suffolk Files #129744, "Divorces," 33-34; Mary Bates v. Henry Bates (1771), Suffolk Files #129759, "Divorces," 59-62; Mehetabel Nicholson v. Joshua Nicholson (or Nickerson) (1771), Suffolk Files #129761, "Divorces," 62-64. Marriage dissolved: Rebecca Wansford v. Nicholas Wansford (1698), Council Recs., II, 562; Mary Hamilton alias Arthur v. George Arthur (1756), Mass. Arch., IX, 399-402, Council Recs., XIII, 140; Sibble Babcock v. George Babcock (1784), Suffolk Files #129835, "Divorces," 202-203. Not resolved: Abigail Hamen v. John Hamen (1748), Mass. Arch., IX, 321–323, Council Recs., XII, 46; Henrietta Maria East Caine v. Hugh Caine, Suffolk Files #129736, "Divorces," 2-3; Mary Drinkwater v. William Drinkwater (1771), Suffolk Files #129765.

38. Mary Arthur and Henrietta Maria East Caine.

39. Abigail Hamen, Elizabeth Eldredge, Mary Bates, Mehetabel Nicholson, Mary Drinkwater, and Sibble Babcock.

40. Reliance Drew, Abigail Hamen, Mary Arthur, H. M. E. Caine, Rachel Wormley, and Mary Bates. One petitioner, Mary Arthur, had already been granted separate

bed and board because of her husband's cruelty. Perhaps wives would not have complained of the bigamy if their husbands had not compounded the insult with other grievances.

41. See Keith Thomas, "The Double Standard," *Journal of the History of Ideas,* XX (1959), 195–216, and, for an example of such advice, [George Savile], *The Lady's New Year's Gift, or, Advice to a Daughter* (London, 1688).

42. Thomas, "Double Standard," *Jour. Hist. Ideas,* XX (1959), 203–205.

43. At least 17 of the 50 adulteries charged in husbands' petitions occurred while the husband was absent at sea or on a military campaign. In almost all of the cases in which bastard offspring were mentioned, the husband had been absent for a year or more. The wives' partners in adultery were neighbors, hired laborers, boarders, or, in a few cases, casual visitors or traveling campanions.

44. Only six of the male petitioners in category C gave evidence of prior court actions. Three were actions to punish the adulterers: Benjamin Bucklin v. Rebeccah Bucklin (1737), Council Recs., X, 112, 121; Thomas Gelpin v. Abigail Gelpin (1743), Mass. Arch., IX, 263–267, Council Recs., XI, 65–66, 73–74; George Raynord v. Mary Raynord (1752), Suffolk Files #129729, Council Recs., XII, 268. Three were actions for the husband to collect money damages from the wife's lover: Thomas Hammet v. Abigail Hammet (1767), Suffolk Files #129747, "Divorces," 37–40; James Dougherty v. Mary Dougherty (1768), Suffolk Files #129750, "Divorces," 45–48; Joshua Gay v. Sarah Gay (1778), Suffolk Files #129784, "Divorces," 101–103, Council Recs., XXII, 46, 48.

45. For example, Jacob Brown v. Ruth Brown (1758), Mass. Arch., IX, 420–428, Council Recs., XIII, 350, 354; Russell Knight v. Mary Knight (1766), Suffolk Files #129745, "Divorces," 35–37, Mass. Arch., IX, 446–447; Andrew Shank v. Sarah Shank (or Schenk) (1772), Suffolk Files #129766; James Richardson v. Hannah Richardson (1772), Suffolk Files #129769, "Divorces," 70–72; William Sturgis v. Sarah Sturgis (1778), Suffolk Files #129785, "Divorces," 104–106, Council Recs., XXII, 256, 320; Samuel Hemenway v. Hannah Hemenway (1782), Suffolk Files #129804. The legal process attendant on a divorce petition was meant to insure justice to the accused spouse; he or she was allowed to be present when depositions to support the petitioner were taken, and was able to bring his or her own witnesses.

46. Andrew Shank v. Sarah Shank (1772), Suffolk Files #129766; Samuel Hemenway v. Hannah Hemenway (1782), *ibid.* #129804.

47. Howard, *Matrimonial Institutions,* II, 334. But John Demos, *Little Commonwealth*, 97, has found in 17th-century Plymouth Colony records a divorce and favorable settlement granted to one woman who chiefly complained of her husband's "act of uncleanes" with another woman.

48. "An Act against Adultery and Polygamy," passed June 6, 1794, made polygamy (that is, marrying again while one's first spouse was living) a felony punishable by death. *Acts and Resolves, Mass. Bay,* I, 171–172.

49. Not decided: Ann Hall v. William Hall, category D (1753), Mass. Arch., IX, 370–373; Kezia Downing v. Nathaniel Downing, D (1765), Suffolk Files #129742; Lydia Sharp v. Boston (a black), D (1773), *ibid.* #129775; Marcy Robinson v. Leonard Robinson, E. (1770), *ibid.* #129755; Sarah Wheeler v. Valentine Wheeler, E (1772), *ibid.* #129792; Hannah Medberry v. Ebenezer Medberry, G (1767), *ibid.* #129746; Eunice Mountfort v. Benjamin Mountfort, G (1771), *ibid.* #129760; Lucy Foster v. Benjamin Foster, H (1775), Mass. Arch., IX, 393–395. Dismissed: Elizabeth Shaw v. John Shaw, D (1748), *ibid.*, 324, Council Recs., XII, 57. Separate

bed and board: Mary Clapham v. William Clapham, E (1754), Suffolk Files #129733, Council Recs., XII, 349; Eleanor Gray v. Samuel Gray, G (1747), Mass. Arch., IX, 296–311, Council Recs., XII, 12; Mary Fairservice v. John Fairservice, G (1767), Suffolk Files #129749, "Divorces," 40–44.

50. Sarah Mitchell v. Michael Mitchell, Council Recs., VI, 305, 621. The older definition of adultery, incorporating the double standard, hinged on the involvement of a married *woman*. Thus a married man's sexual transgression could still be called fornication, if his partner was single.

51. Hannah Rolfe v. Ezra Rolfe, Mass. Arch., IX, 357–358, Council Recs., XII, 218, 239.

52. Sarah Gould v. William Gould, Suffolk Files #129772, notation on petition, 56; also "Divorces," 78–80. Martha Air v. Adam Air, Suffolk Files #129779, "Divorces," 81–82.

53. Between 1774 and 1786, 5 of the 6 women who charged adultery and desertion, 8 of the 11 who brought suits on account of adultery, desertion and cohabitation, 7 of the 8 who alleged adultery, desertion and remarriage, 7 of the 13 whose grievances was adultery and cruelty, and one whose husband committed interracial adultery all obtained decrees of divorce from the governor and Council. These figures differ slightly from the 1775–1786 column of Table 4 because they include the cases of 1774.

54. Court Recs., Dec. 4, 1754, XX, 337–338; Mass. Arch., IX, 381–382; "An Act to dissolve the Marriage of Mary Clapham with William Clapham and to allow her to marry again," *Acts and Resolves*, Mass. Arch., VI, 165. The Council later awarded Mary her household furniture, worth £100. Council Recs., XII, 386.

55. Mary Parker v. Phineas Parker, Mass. Arch., IX, 374–380, Council Recs., XII, 337, *Acts and Resolves, Mass. Bay*, VI, 169; Lydia Kellogg v. Ephraim Kellogg, Mass. Arch., IX, 403–413, *Acts and Resolves, Mass. Bay*, VI, 173. The Parker and Kellogg divorce acts, and two of the three legislative divorces obtained by male petitioners, were passed without prior decrees of separate bed and board from the governor and Council. Only in the Parker case was prior court conviction of the adulterer mentioned. The men's cases were John Farnum, Jr., v. Elizabeth Farnum, Mass. Arch., IX, 396–398, *Acts and Resolves, Mass. Bay*, VI, 170; Jonah Galusha v. Sarah Galusha, Mass. Arch. IX, 414, *Acts and Resolves, Mass. Bay*, VI, 174, Court Recs., XX, 329; and Daniel McCarthy v. Mary McCarthy, Suffolk Files, #129734, Mass. Arch., IX, 418, Council Recs., XIII, 259, 262, *Acts and Resolves, Mass. Bay*, VI, 177. The three cases reviewed by the Board of Trade in 1758 were Clapham's, Parker's, and Farnum's.

56. Between 1760 and 1773 seven women filed adultery-inclusive petitions and none obtained divorce, although Mary Fairservice, with a plea of adultery and cruelty, obtained separate bed and board. See n. 49.

57. "Divorces" list names of Council members present at each decision.

58. See Table 1. Half of all men's but 63% of all women's petitions occurred after 1764.

59. John Adams to Abigail Adams, July 3, 1776, and Samuel Adams to John Langdon, Aug. 7, 1777, in Gordon S. Wood, *The Creation of the American Republic, 1776–1787* (Chapel Hill, N.C., 1972), 123–124.

60. Ian Watt, "The New Woman: Samuel Richardson's *Pamela*," in Rose Laub Coser, ed., *The Family: Its Structure and Functions* (New York, 1964), 281–282,

points out that "the eighteenth century [in England] witnessed a tremendous narrowing of the ethical scale, a redefinition of virtue in primarily sexual terms. . . . The same tendency can be seen at work on the ethical vocabulary itself: words such as virtue, propriety, decency, modesty, delicacy, purity, came to have the almost exclusively sexual connotation which they have since very largely retained."

61. Howard, *Matrimonial Institutions*, II, 333, lists two late 17th-century cases in which women petitioned on account of their husbands' desertion and failure to provide, and the assistants declared the marriages dissolved, but no comparable 18th-century women's suits had that result. The presumption of the law was that seven years' absence by one spouse allowed the other to remarry. The "Act against Adultery and Polygamy" of 1694 (*Acts and Resolves, Mass. Bay*, I, 171–172) exempted from its punishments any person whose spouse had been overseas for seven years or absent more than seven years, so perhaps the Council assumed that decrees of divorce were unnecessary. Two suits dismissed, however, involved absences of five and six years.

62. That is, this was a separate bed and board arrangement by mutual consent. Ann Vansise v. Cornelius Vansise, "Divorces," 44–45.

63. Abigail Bradstreet v. Joseph Bradstreet, Suffolk Files #129762, "Divorces," 68–70. Her lawyer, John Adams, argued her case according to canon law. See Wroth and Zobel, eds., *Legal Papers of Adams*, I, 280–285.

64. John Emery v. Abigail Emery, Council Recs., V, 180. (Abigail also petitioned unsuccessfully for divorce from John for cruelty, Mass. Arch., IX, 162–163.) John Ferre v. Elizabeth Ferre, Council Recs., VII, 165; Jonathan Fletcher v. wife, *ibid.*, IX, 552, 565.

65. The duration of the wife's absence is not apparent in these cases, except in the last, John Chapin v. Margaret Chapin, Suffolk Files #129856, in which it was three years. One probable reason why John's suit failed was that Margaret was willing to be divorced. Divorce was an adversary process in Massachusetts; separate bed and board, but never divorce, was decreed on the basis of a couple's mutual agreement. Any apparent collusion on the part of the couple to gain divorce invalidated the suit, so that, ironically, one way for a husband or wife to stop a divorce proceeding was to agree to it. See, for example, Sarah Rust v. Francis Rust (Jan. 1784), Suffolk Files #129833, "Divorces," 199–200; and Sarah Rust v. Francis Rust (June 1784), Suffolk Files #129836, "Divorces," 204–205. Cf. n. 80.

66. Wroth and Zobel, eds., *Legal Papers of Adams*, I, 284; Howard, *Matrimonial Institutions*, II, 52–54.

67. Possibly the change from granting of divorces for wives' desertions before 1735 to dismissing such pleas later represented an "anglicization" of divorce policy. The appearance of separate bed and board decrees during the 18th century, when none, according to Howard, was made during the previous century, supports such a theory; but the change in treatment of male adultery in 1773 opposes it. Cf. John Murrin, "Anglicizing an American Colony: The Transformation of Puritan Massachusetts" (Ph.D. diss., Yale University, 1966); Kenneth A. Lockridge, "Land, Population, and the Evolution of New England Society, 1630–1790," *Past and Present*, XXXIX (1968), 62–80; and Kenneth A. Lockridge, *A New England Town, The First Hundred Years: Dedham, Massachusetts, 1636–1736* (New York, 1970), 167–180.

68. The records remaining for five of the six cases are not extensive enough to allow evaluation of the "sufficiency" of the cruelty alleged. One woman whose

petition was dismissed sued a second time, however, bringing additional evidence, and then won separate bed and board. Mary Lobb v. George Lobb, Suffolk Files #129800, "Divorces," 145–148. In the sixth case, the wife gave evidence of enormous cruelty, but the governor and Council accepted her husband's promise henceforth to treat her kindly as reason to dismiss her petition. Apparently their judgment was mistaken, for the wife petitioned again less than a year later, indicating that her plight had not improved. Margaret Knodle v. Frederick Knodle (1764), Suffolk Files #129743, "Divorces," 32.

69. There were 23 suits but only 22 petitioners, since Mary Lobb petitioned twice (n. 68).

70. *Acts and Resolves, Mass. Bay*, I, 209. Some of the alimony awards made by the governor and Council in separate bed and board decrees were as follows: Anne Leonard v. Henry Leonard (a turner, of Boston), in 1743, 5s. per week (Mass. Arch., IX, 268–294, Council Recs., XI, 69, 113–114); Eleanor Gray v. Samuel Gray (a yeoman, of Pelham, Hampshire County), 1747, £6 per year (Mass. Arch., IX, 296–311, Council Recs., XII, 12); Mary Fairservice v. John Fairservice (a trader of Boston), 1767, £12 yearly (Suffolk Files #129749, "Divorces," 40–44); Lucy Purnam v. Scipio Purnam (a truckman, of Newburyport), 1768, 6s. per month (Suffolk Files #129751, "Divorces," 48–51). This last was the most bizarre suit on grounds of cruelty. The couple were black; Lucy accused Scipio not only of treating her cruelly but also of attempting to sell her as a slave. Scipio denied the charges and brought witnesses who impugned Lucy's character. Eventually he agreed to the official separation but objected strongly to paying alimony, claiming "she is at least as well able to support herself as he is himself and Family. "See Suffolk Files #129751, 124.

71. Mary Arthur v. George Arthur, Suffolk Files #129733b, Council Recs., XII, 371, 385.

72. Mary Hunt v. Richard Hunt, "Divorces," 6–11, Council Recs., XIV, 268, 270, 277; "An Act for enabling Mary Hunt to dispose and Convey her lands and interest in Holden," passed Apr. 24, 1762, disallowed by Privy Council Mar. 16, 1763, *Acts and Resolves, Mass. Bay*, VI, 187–188.

Alexander Keyssar, "Widowhood in Eighteenth-Century Massachusetts: A Problem in the History of the Family," *Perspectives in American History*, VIII (1974), esp. 100–103, 114–118, points out that widows commonly faced similar problems: as dower they received the use and profit of one-third of their husbands' real property but not the right to dispose of it. "Dozens" of widows in 18th-century Massachusetts petitioned the General Court to be enabled to dispose of real property because it was not profitable to them. Keyssar's conclusion that "the legal structure aimed at the sustenance, rather than the economic freedom, of widows" (p. 103) could apply to the position of wives separated from their husbands.

73. Under common law all of a woman's personal property and earnings became her husband's upon marriage, and while she retained title to any real estate she owned, her husband gained the right to its use and income. A husband could not liquidate his wife's real property without her consent—this was the root of the quarrel in Bradstreet v. Bradstreet (n. 63)—but neither could she sell it of her own accord.

74. Sarah Wheeler v. Valentine Wheeler, Suffolk Files #129792, "Divorces," 128–131, 144–145, Council Recs., XXV, 181, 400, XXVI, 118; Sarah Sawyer v. Abel Sawyer, Suffolk Files #129827, "Divorces," 188–191. Cf. Sarah Vernon v. William Vernon, Suffolk Files #129849, "Divorces," 216–217, 222–224, for an explicit refusal of alimony after a divorce decree.

75. See Suffolk Files #91716. Her petition is in John Adams's handwriting, according to Worth and Zobel, eds., *Legal Papers of Adams*, I, 285n.

76. Ann McAlpine v. William McAlpine (1763), Suffolk Files #129737—no information on amount of settlement. Ann Vansise v. Cornelius Vansise (1768), "Divorces," 44–45—alimony of £10 yearly. Ann Lovell v. John Lovell (1773), Suffolk Files #129778—wife received her own estate and earnings. Ann Gardner v. David Gardner (1783), *ibid.*, #129813, "Divorces," 168–170—settlement of £40 plus wife's retention of dower rights.

77. See the Bradstreet, Gray, and Purnam cases cited in nn. 63 and 70, and Elizabeth Keith v. Mark Keith, Suffolk Files #129738, "Divorces," 24–27, Mass. Arch., IX, 441–442; Mary Fairservice v. John Fairservice (1770), Suffolk Files #129756, "Divorces," 56–57; Mary Hamilton alias Arthur v. George Arthur (1756), Mass. Arch., IX, 399–492, Council Recs., XIII, 140. Those that did not produce subsequent complaints were Thankfull Winehall's case of 1710, which is very sparsely documented (Council Recs., V, 238); Ann Leonard's settlement of 5s. per week; and Mary Hunt's award of her own property (see nn. 70 and 72).

78. William Sturgis v. Sarah Sturgis, Suffolk Files #129785, "Divorces," 104–106, Council Recs., XXII, 256, 320. See also Burditch v. Sturgis, Suffolk Files #102540.

79. Amos Bliss v. Phebe Bliss, Suffolk Files #129799, depositions of Silvanus Martin and Eleazar Bliss, 49, 43.

80. This law, passed Mar. 16, 1786 (*Acts and Resolves, 1784-1785,* 564–567), also stated that no divorce would be granted if the adultery or cruelty were occasioned by collusion in order to obtain divorce, or if both spouses committed adultery.

81. Smith, "Parental Power and Marriage Patterns," *Jour. Marriage and Family,* XXXV (1973), 426.

82. Lonna Myers Malmsheimer, "New England Funeral Sermons and Changing Attitudes toward Women, 1672-1792" (Ph.D. diss., University of Minnesota, 1973).

83. *Gentleman's and Lady's Town and Country Magazine* (Sept. 1784), 194. See also Herman R. Lantz *et al.*, "Pre-Industrial Patterns in the Colonial Family in America: A Content Analysis of Colonial Magazines," *American Sociological Review*, XXXIII (1968), 413–426.

84. Malmsheimer, "New England Funeral Sermons," finds this kind of shift in ideology in funeral sermons.

5 ᵍThe Illusion of Change:
Women and the American Revolution

Joan Hoff Wilson

Since the 1920s an increasing number of historians have argued that during the colonial period women enjoyed a less sex-stereotyped existence than at any time until recently, despite the absence of any significant number of organized or individual feminists. This argument is largely an exaggeration based on inadequate samplings of the small group of women who worked outside the home, or the few who actually appeared in probate records, paid taxes, wrote wills, or asserted their legal and political rights through petitions and occasional voting.

It is true, however, for most of the period up to 1750 that conditions *out of necessity* increased the functional independence and importance of all women. By this I mean that much of the alleged freedom from sexism of colonial women was due to their initial numerical scarcity and the critical labor shortage in the New World throughout the seventeenth and eighteenth centuries. Such increased reproductive roles (economic as well as biological) reflected the logic of necessity and *not any fundamental change* in the sexist, patriarchal attitudes that had been transplanted from Europe. Based on two types of scarcity (sex and labor), which were not to last, these enhanced functions of colonial women diminished as the commercial and agricultural economy became more specialized and the population grew.

A gradual "embourgeoisement" of colonial culture accompanied this preindustrial trend toward modern capitalism. It limited the number of high status roles for eighteenth-century American women just as it had for

From *The American Revolution: Explorations in the History of American Radicalism*, edited by Alfred F. Young. Copyright © 1976 by Northern Illinois University Press. By permission of the publisher.

seventeenth-century English and European women. Alice Clark, Margaret George, Natalie Zemon Davis, and Jane Abray have all argued convincingly that as socioeconomic capitalist organization takes place, it closes many opportunities normally open to women both inside and outside of the family unit in precapitalist times. The decline in the status of women that accompanied the appearance of bourgeois modernity in England, according to Margaret George, "was not merely a relative decline. Precapitalist woman was not simply relatively eclipsed by the great leap forward of the male achiever; she suffered rather, an absolute setback."[1]

In the New World this process took longer but was no less debilitating. Before 1800 it was both complicated and hindered by the existence of a severe labor shortage and religious as well as secular exhortations against the sins of idleness and vanity. Thus, colonial conditions demanded that all able-bodied men, women, and children work, and so the ornamental, middle-class woman existed more in theory than in practice.

The labor shortage that plagued colonial America placed a premium on women's work inside and outside the home, particularly during the war-related periods of economic dislocation between 1750 and 1815. And there is no doubt that home industry was basic to American development both before and after 1776. It is also true that there was no sharp delineation between the economic needs of the community and the work carried on within the preindustrial family until after the middle of the eighteenth century. Woman's role as a household manager was a basic and integral part of the early political economy of the colonies. Hence she occupied a position of unprecedented importance and equality within the socioeconomic unit of the family.[2]

As important as this function of women in the home was, from earliest colonial times, it nonetheless represented a division of labor based on sex-role stereotyping carried over from England. Men normally engaged in agricultural production; women engaged in domestic gardening and home manufacturing—only slave women worked in the fields. Even in those areas of Massachusetts and Pennsylvania that originally granted females allotments of land, the vestiges of this practice soon disappeared, and subsequently public divisions "simply denied the independent economic existence of women." While equality never extended outside the home in the colonial era, there was little likelihood that women felt useless or alienated because of the importance and demanding nature of their domestic responsibilities.[3]

In the seventeenth and eighteenth centuries spinning and weaving were the primary types of home production for women and children (of both sexes). This economic function was considered so important that legal and moral sanctions were developed to insure it. For example, labor laws were passed, compulsory spinning schools were established "for the education of children of the poor," and women were told that their virtue could be measured in yards of yarn.[4] So from the beginning there was a sex, and to a lesser degree a class and educational, bias built into colonial production of cloth, since no formal apprenticeship was required for learning the trade of spinning and weaving.

It has also been recognized that prerevolutionary boycotts of English goods after 1763 and later during the war increased the importance of female production of textiles both in the home and in the early piecework factory system. By mid-1776 in Philadelphia, for example, 4,000 women and children reportedly were spinning under the "putting out system" for local textile plants.[5]

The importance of those few women who fulfilled other economic roles *in addition to* their household activities is not so readily demonstrable. The documentation about bonafide female entrepreneurs remains highly fragmentary and difficult, if not impossible, to analyze with statistical accuracy.[6] Many, if not most, appear to be the widows of "men who had been less affluent." If we take Philadelphia as representative of greater urban specialization and utilization of female workers due to the shortage of labor,[7] we find a significant number of women in only three entrepreneurial occupations up to 1776: shopkeeping, innkeeping, and crafts-making. The first two were obviously sex-role based in that most of the early retail stores and taverns were located in private homes and simply represented an extension of normal household duties. Although craftswomen also often sold their products directly from their individual dwellings, their work was not always related to traditional domestic tasks. Thus, Philadelphia women engaged in roughly thirty different trades ranging from essential to luxury services. They included female silversmiths, tinworkers, barbers, bakers, fish picklers, brewers, tanners, ropemakers, lumberjacks, gunsmiths, butchers, milliners, harnessmakers, potash manufacturers, upholsterers, printers, morticians, chandlers, coachmakers, embroiderers, dry cleaners and dyers, woodworkers, staymakers, tailors, flour processors, seamstresses, netmakers, braziers, and founders.[8]

It is this impressive array of female artisans in Philadelphia and other colonial towns that has led to the conclusion that work for women was much less sex-stereotyped in the seventeenth and eighteenth centuries than it was to become in the nineteenth. The validity of this claim has yet to be documented by a comparative analysis of female artisans in different areas. On the one hand, women found themselves in these essential and nonfamilial roles because they were substituting for dead or absent husbands; on the other hand, it was not considered "inappropriate" according to prevailing socioeconomic norms for women to engage in this wide variety of occupations, carry on the family business if widowed, or become a skilled artisan while still married. Single and married women operating their own shops and taverns were an even more common fact of colonial life.[9]

From tavern licenses issued in Philadelphia, for example, it is clear that between 1762 and 1776 no less than 17 percent, and even as much as 22 percent, of all tavern operators were women,[10] and these figures do not include those women who may have been operating illegally without licenses.[11] Such fragmentary evidence shows there were at least ninety-four female shopkeepers operating in Philadelphia between 1720 and 1776, and that in 1717 nine out of twenty-eight, or 32 percent, of all shopkeepers taking out "freedoms" were women. None of these businesswomen seem to have been given any special attention or consideration—not even the six who signed the nonimportation agreement of 25 October 1765. At the moment there is no way of knowing how representative these figures on innkeepers or "she-merchants" are for other colonial towns on the eve of the American Revolution.[12]

The increasing commercial and agricultural specialization prior to 1776,[13] affected all Americans, but particularly women, whether they were the vast rural majority who engaged in home production or the few who became entrepreneurs in the cities and towns. Probably the most significant changes were an erratic rise in the standard of living and a substantial increase in the number of landless proletarians in the major urban areas. There is now evidence that the uneven and unequal distribution of wealth as shown for Boston existed as well in Philadelphia, Newport, and New York City. Any amount of economic inequality was particularly devastating for widows, who often had dependents to support. The economic plight of the increasingly large number of widows also led to an expansion of their legal rights before 1776, so that they could convert real property into capital for personal support or investment purposes.[14]

American living standards fluctuated with the unequal prosperity that was especially related to wars. Those engaging in craft production and commerce were particularly hard hit after 1750, first by the deflation and depression following the French and Indian War (1754–1763), and then by the War for Independence. In fact, not only were the decades immediately preceding and following the American Revolution ones of economic dislocation, but the entire period between 1775 and 1815 has been characterized as one of "arrested social and economic development." These trends, combined with increased specialization, particularly with the appearance of a nascent factory system, "initiated a decline in the economic and social position of many sections of the artisan class." Thus with the exception of the innkeeping and tavern business, all of the other primary economic occupations of city women were negatively affected by the periodic fluctuations in the commercial economy between 1763 and 1812.[15]

Women artisans and shopkeepers probably suffered most during times of economic crisis because of their greater difficulty in obtaining credit from merchants. Although research into their plight has been neglected, the documents are there—in the records of merchant houses showing women entrepreneurs paying their debts for goods and craft materials by transferring their own records of indebtedness, and in court records showing an increased number of single women, especially widows sued for their debts, or in public records of the increased number of bankrupt women who ended up on poor relief lists or in debtors' prisons or who were forced to become indentured servants or earn an independent living during hard times.[16]

It was also a difficult time for household spinners and weavers, about whom a few more facts are known. First, this all-important economic function increasingly reflected class distinctions. In 1763 one British governor estimated that only the poor wore homespun clothes, while more affluent Americans bought English imports. Second, it was primarily poor women of the northern and middle colonies who engaged in spinning and weaving for pay (often in the form of credit rather than cash), while black slave women and white female indentured servants performed the same function in the South. Naturally women in all frontier areas had no recourse but to make their own clothing. Beginning with the first boycotts of British goods in the 1760s, women of all classes were urged to make and wear homespun. Several additional "manufactory houses" were established as early as 1764 in major cities specifically for the employment of poor women. Direct appeals to patriotism and virtue were used very success-fully to get wealthier women to engage in arduous home-spinning drives, but probably only for short periods of time.[17]

Thus all classes of women were actively recruited into domestic textile production by male patriots with such pleas as, "In this time of public distress you have each of you an opportunity not only to help to sustain your families, but likewise to call your mite into the treasury of the public good." They were further urged to "cease trifl-ing their time away [and] prudently employ it in learning the use of the spinning wheel."[18] Beyond any doubt the most well-known appeal was the widely reprinted 9 November 1767 statement of advice to the "Daughters of Liberty" which first appeared in the *Massachusetts Gazette*. It read in part:

First then throw aside your high top knots of pride
Wear none but your own country linen.
Of economy boast. Let your pride be the most
To show cloaths of your make and spinning.

Peak periods in prerevolutionary spinning and weaving were reached during every major boycott from 1765 to 1777. But the war and inflation proved disruptive. For example, we know that the United Company of Philadelphia for Promoting American Manufactures, which employed 500 of the city's 4,000 women and children spinning at home, expired between 1777 and 1787, when it was revived. The record of similar organizations elsewhere was equally erratic.[19]

It is common for developing countries with a labor shortage to utilize technological means to meet production demands. After the war, the new republic proved no exception, as the inefficiency and insufficiency of household spinners became apparent. Ultimately the "putting out" system was replaced entirely by the factory that employed the same women and children who had formerly been household spinners. It took the entire first half of the nineteenth century before this process was completed, and when it was, it turned out to be at the expense of the social and economic status of female workers.[20]

At the beginning of this process, however, the early cotton mills in the last quarter of the eighteenth century utilized skilled immigrants of both sexes. In fact, according to one recent study, the years between 1763 and 1812 constituted the "non-verbal period of industrial technology" in American history. During this time English technological "know-how" was transferred to the United States primarily through artificers who either owned, could build, or could operate the latest "labour-saving machines." In July 1788, for example, the Pennsylvania Society located a woman who owned a twisting mill and immediately employed her "on the best Terms." How many of these migrating artisans were women is not yet precisely known.[21]

Direct employment in these early cotton textile mills was the final way, therefore, in which changing economic conditions affected women. Such employment did not represent a new economic function for women—it simply shifted their place of work from the home to the factory. Economic nationalists like Secretary of the Treasury Alexander Hamilton recognized the contributions of women in the production of cloth under the traditional "domestic system." At the same time he recommended, in his well-known *Report on Manufacturers* of 1791, that women and children be utilized in the factory production of cotton goods. All economic nationalists, both Federalist and Republican, openly recognized that the labor of women and children would have to be exploited if the nation were to industrialize.[22]

The position was reinforced in the 1790s by male moralists who preached that poor women who did not take up factory work would be "doomed to idleness and its inseparable attendants, vice and guilt." Through at least the War of 1812, this unholy alliance temporarily prolonged the pragmatic colonial idea that "woman's place was . . . not in the home, . . . but wherever her 'more important' work was."[23] Now, however, this idea became the basis for making a class distinction between women that had not been possible throughout most of the preindustrial colonial period. In other words, the potential economic contribution of women to the new textile industry contrasted sharply with the propagandistic rhetoric of the 1780s and the 1790s, which portrayed them as preservers of republican virtue, exclusively within the home as patriotic wives and educators.

Each role could be (and was) justified in the name of nationalism. But each projected distinctly different future tasks for women, depending upon their socioeconomic status. One led to the dual capitalist exploitation of women as a reserve supply of cheap labor in industry and the home, without any increase in their economic power or personal status; the other led to a less functional and isolated position of women within the modern, middle-class nuclear family, whose domestic duties and responsibilities gradually declined until they consisted primarily of improving male manners and nurturing children. Both were necessary for rapid industrialization in the nineteenth century.

While the industrialization that the War of 1812 stimulated did more to hasten these class distinctions (as well as the low status and alienating features of women's work inside and outside of the home) than did the American Revolution, the latter set the stage for what was to follow both in the attitudes toward women it fostered and the requirements it set for economic growth.

Before, during, and after the Revolution, American women were experiencing important demographic changes that ultimately contributed to their socioeconomic subordination in the modern world. These demographic factors were of such an evolutionary nature, however, that few seem to have been directly affected by the Revolution itself, save for the temporary disruption of the nuclearity of family life, as men left home to participate in political or military activities, and for the lowering of sexual and moral standards that normally accompany wars.

To date most social demographers have concentrated on the seventeenth and early eighteenth centuries rather than the revolutionary period. Nonetheless, much can be inferred from recent studies of family reconstitution about the condition of women on the eve of the American Revolution. While regional differences remain to be studied,[24] significant strides have been taken with vital statistics from about a half dozen small New England communities, which suggest trends for the colonial household in that area. Since such figures could not be obtained from traditional literary sources, earlier assumptions about mortality rates, domestic stability, family size, child raising, education, male-female sex roles, and even remarriage rates are now being questioned.[25]

In general, living conditions in New England (but not in the South) appear to have been more stable and healthy, especially in the seventeenth century, than they were in England and Europe. Thus, there is evidence of increased longevity for adults, decreased deaths from childbirth, and lower mortality rates for infants and adolescents. And contrary to what was commonly thought, the duration of first marriages was quite high— ranging from between twenty and twenty-five years in some New England towns—while remarriage of widows was less likely than once assumed.[26]

Even the much heralded and first significant demographic fact about colonial women, namely their scarcity, has been cast into a new light by social demographers. It is true, for example, that men outnumbered women by three to one in the initial immigration to New England, and by six to one in the early Virginia settlements. Nevertheless, this extreme imbalance in the sex ratio soon succumbed to the high fertility level among colonial women and to lower mortality rates in the New England colonies at the beginning of the eighteenth century. In the middle and southern colonies fertility was also high, but so were mortality rates. Consequently, in these areas immigration continued to play an important role not only in maintaining population growth but also in contributing to a sex imbalance. In colonies like Virginia and Maryland, for example, there were still about three men for every two women in 1700. Even though women colonists in the South showed a greater resistance than men to disease during the "seasoning" process, they remained scarce for the next twenty or thirty years. In contrast, by 1700 the larger New England coastal towns and small eastern settlements actually experienced a surplus of unmarried women, which continued to increase and whose significance has yet to be evaluated by historians.[27]

By 1750, at least northern colonial America could no longer be considered a "paradise on earth for women," where every free, white female could marry and where a stable, parental dominated marriage system or family of orientation (birth) prevailed. It was in the throes of a "demographic crisis." Among other things, this meant that the age gap narrowed between men and women at the time of their first marriages, with men generally marrying slightly earlier and women slightly later. In addition to facing the possibility of not being able to marry, or remarry, in the case of widows, by the time of the Revolution women had been gradually adjusting to changing courtship and marriage patterns, loosened sexual mores, smaller family size, and (among the wealthier, better educated) to more permissive theories from foreign authors about child raising, romantic love, and sex-stereotyped definitions of feminity.[28] All of these demographic alterations were part of the process of family modernization—that is, the evolution from the family of orientation to the family of procreation. This transition was most pronounced in the late eighteenth and early nineteenth centuries, and is therefore coincidentally connected but not substantially affected by the Revolution.

It was the changing position of women within this gradually evolving conjugal household and its declining socioeconomic importance in general that posed the most serious demographic problems for the revolutionary generation of women—not the exact size or structure of the family unit, which continued to vary from region to region and within local communities. In other words, except for the actual years in which the war was fought, colonial women found more and more of their traditional familial duties and responsibilities syphoned off as the economy became more commercially specialized and as other social institutions such as schools became more commonplace. Only women living in the most isolated frontier areas escaped this experience of declining importance and function within the family unit, and their position was far from enviable because of the physical and mental harshness of frontier life.[29]

The difficult task of documenting this trend toward modernization of the conjugal household through family reconstitution analysis is far from complete. But we do know, for example, that there was no dramatic shift from the so-called extended family structure to a nuclear one. Through the seventeenth and early eighteenth centuries New World households appear to have been largely nuclear in structure, with women of completed fertility producing an average of seven to eight children. The number of children borne by New England women declined in the last half of the eighteenth century to five or six. Once mortality rates and other factors are considered, however, the average number of free persons in each household varied from a crowded 9.3 in Boston to 6.7 in some of the interior counties of Massachusetts in 1764 to an average of around 5.8 (or 6.1 if slaves are included) per household by 1790. Despite this slight decrease both in the number of children borne and in household size in the course of the eighteenth century, average American families were still larger than those in England and Europe. No drastic decline in marital fertility rates and household size occurred in the United States until after 1850.[30]

Nonetheless, even this relatively small decline prior to 1800 is interesting both for what it did and did not represent. First, it should be noted that it occurred in urban and rural areas and among all religious groups (including the Quakers). With few exceptions it is doubtful that this can be considered conscious family limitation, yet for reasons not yet clear American parents were beginning to consider large families a liability after 1760. But they did not generally have the modern, small target families in mind. Second, there is some, albeit far from conclusive, evidence from letters and diaries that fewer children and smaller family units produced more intimate, sentimental, and affectionate relationships. This in turn is said to have contributed to the growth of individualism, modern concepts of self and ego development among children, and romantic love ties between husbands and wives. By and large, however, the more permissive, less authoritarian child-centered family of procreation simply had not evolved by 1776, as some scholars have claimed. While there are isolated private examples of a more sentimental view of children and a tendency to glorify motherhood, neither became an established practice until after 1800 in the United States. The same is true of the concept of romantic love that finally led to marriage as a "free act" of the couple involved rather than a parentally controlled affair.[31]

It appears that most eighteenth-century women, even those who had read Locke and Rousseau, were still primarily occupied with how to conquer the wills of their children rather than with the development of individual independence. If anything, the slightly smaller household usually meant that mothers, often weakened or ill from frequent pregnancies, were placed in greater direct contact with their children, since there were fewer relatives or servants present. This led at least upperclass colonial women (and aristocratic foreigners who visited them) in the last half of the century to complain about the recalcitrance of American children and the personal burden they had become. "You can not conceive how my time is taken up," Ester Edwards Burr, the mother of Aaron Burr, confided to her journal in 1756. "Sometimes I never sit down a whole day unless to vittles." Pamela Sedgwick of Massachusetts confided to a spinster friend that she no sooner would "snatch a moment from a crying infant," than two or three of her other "ungoverned children" would begin to make noise the like of which was "as distracting to the brain as a confused din of arms to a timid soldier." She finally wrote her often-absent husband Theodore Sedgwick, in 1790, that she was "tired of living a widow and being at the same time a nurse." Poorer women had neither the time nor the literacy to record their impressions of child raising, but it is doubtful that they were any less strict or less burdened than their better educated counterparts by the late eighteenth century.[32]

A much better indication of the transitional stage of the American family on the eve of the Revolution can be found in the general decline of parental economic control over the marriages of their children. Once again, this generalization applies more to the wealthier than the poorer segment of colonial society. During the seventeenth and up to the middle of the eighteenth century parental control had been exercised largely through delayed property inheritance or the need to support a widowed mother. Such authority was undermined, however, as the legal rights of widows were gradually expanded to make them less economically dependent on their male children, and as primogeniture became less feasible as a means of controlling the marital pattern of eldest sons— it actually made the younger ones, according to Thomas Jefferson, "independent of, and disobedient to their parents."[33]

In the case of women, the increase in those who remained unmarried or who married out of normal sibling sequence was an early indication of the decline in parental authority, and hence a weakening of the family of orientation. Another indication of the gradual separation of girls from their family of birth can be found in the significant drop in the percentage of mother-daughter name-sharing. Before 1700, in Hingham, Massachusetts, 98.5 percent of all families with three or more daughters named one after the mother. By 1780 this had dropped to 53.2 percent, and the practice was to decrease even more by the end of the nineteenth century, although less rapidly for boys than girls because of the potential inheritance value of having the same name as one's father or other close male relative.[34]

Probably the most important, yet often overlooked, of all the indices of changing family patterns was the unprecedented increase in premarital pregnancies among white Americans in the last half of the eighteenth century. A peak in the number of so-called "short-term" babies conceived before marriage was reached between 1761 and 1800, when 16.7 percent of all first babies were born under six months of marriage, 27.2 percent under eight and one-half months, and 33 percent under nine months. The overall figure of 30 percent for premarital pregnancies just before and after the American Revolution was not approximated again until the 1960s. Both high periods reflect more than a simple breakdown in sexual mores encouraged by such external factors as wars, the religious revivalism of the mid-eighteenth century, or the counterculture of the last decade.[35]

Instead, premarital pregnancies are perhaps the strongest demographic indication we have of the family in a period of transition and hence unable to enforce conventional controls over sexual behavior. They represent "a collision between an unchanging and increasingly antiquated family structure and a pattern of individual behavior which is more a part of the past than a harbinger of the future." In other words, a dramatic rise in premarital relations does not mean that all other traditional patterns of the established family in any given time period are also abruptly changed or abandoned. Indeed, premarital pregnancies were no more condoned in the last half of the eighteenth century than they are today, but in both instances they do symbolize a generational conflict and a revolt of the young that presage changing power relationships within conjugal households, which may or may not be liberalizing.[36]

In the case of this first peak period, the process of family change was not completed until the 1820s and 1830s, with the appearance of the established nuclear family of procreation. This new family pattern was not only characterized by the sentimentalization of children and the glorification of motherhood, but also ideally by more consensus, affection, and contractual relations than had existed in the more authoritarian family of orientation. Nonetheless, it was within this newly established, child-oriented household that the socioeconomic functions of women were severely limited and from which sexual restrictions and inhibitions emanated, culminating finally in the excessive sexual repression of the late nineteenth century.[37]

This is not to say that any class of women of the revolutionary generation understood what was happening to the family in the last half of the eighteenth century. In such periods of transition it is common that discrepancies increase between familial attitudes (thought) and behavior (function). It must be remembered that they were accustomed to relying upon external, primarily religious and economic, controls over sexual behavior. As the authority of all orthodox religion began to break down, premarital relations assumed class and gender overtones that had not previously existed. What has been called "a sexually permissive subculture" thus emerged more quickly among poorer groups as colonial society became more economically stratified. Most important, it was encouraged or at least passed on intergenerationally from lower-class mothers to their daughters largely through the practice of bundling. While women like Abigail Adams and Mercy Warren worried over how best to instill virtue in their offspring, at the other end of the social scale young girls were told that bundling was "no sin nor shame, for we your mothers did the same."[38]

At the same time we find male patriots quickly capitalizing on the popularity of the political analogy that symbolized the colonies as children in revolt against the "monstrous" mother country. Yet it is equally evident that they did not want to contribute any further to the generational conflict already in progress or to the generally ambiguous, if not actually contradictory, state of the family of orientation by 1776.[39] Nonetheless, it is difficult to imagine that such antiparental, antifemale rhetoric did not further undermine the existing precarious position of family life during the revolutionary years. It would not be until the first quarter of the nineteenth century, however, that lower-class premarital practices would merge with upper-class theories on permissive child raising and romantic love and courtship to complete the breakdown of the family of orientation and replace it with the family of procreation. Even the best educated women could not realize that they were demographically on their way toward modernization within the family of procreation that offered them the "cult of true womanhood" in place of collective validation and a sense of individual worth. Nor could they be expected to have anticipated other "double standard" limitations associated with this new family pattern, such as increased vicarious fulfillment through their husbands or male children and the psychic burden of the permissive child-centered household that epitomized individualism and modern ego development—for men.[40] Assuming that the rhetoric of the Revolution and the trauma of war had not temporarily obfuscated their view of the future, it is doubtful if the most perspicacious women of this generation could have discerned the degree to which demography, and not the separation from England, would determine the destiny of their daughters and grandchildren.

NOTES

1. Margaret George, *One Woman's "Situation": A Study of Mary Wollstonecraft* (Urbana: University of Illinois Press, 1970), p. 16; idem, "From 'Goodwife' and 'Mistress'," pp. 155–56; Natalie Zemon Davis, "Women on Top: Sexual Inversion and Political Disorder in Early Modern Europe," in *Society and Culture in Early Modern France: Eight Essays* (Stanford, Calif.: Stanford University Press, 1975), p. 126; Jane Abray, "Feminism and the French Revolution," *AHR* 80 (February 1975): 44; Alice Clark, *Working Life of Women in the Seventeenth Century* (New York: Augustus M. Kelley, 1968; reprint of the original 1919 Cass edition), pp. 9–13, 93–149.

2. Edith Abbott, *Women in Industry: A Study in American Economic History* (New York: Source Book Press, 1970; reprint of original 1910 Appleton edition), pp. viii, 11–12; Meta Stern Lilienthal, *From Fireside to Factory* (New York: Rand School of Social Science, 1916), pp. 7–15; Mary P. Ryan, *Womanhood in America: From Colonial Times to the Present* (New York: New Viewpoints, 1975), pp. 21–22, 26, 32, 64.

3. Herbert B. Adams, "Allotments of Land in Salem to Men, Women and Maids," *Essex Institute Historical Collections* 19 (1882): 167–75; Ryan, *Womanhood in America*, p. 35; Edmund S. Morgan, *American Slavery—American Freedom: The Ordeal of Colonial Virginia* (New York: W. W. Norton, 1975), pp. 235, 310.

4. Miriam Schnier, "Women in the Revolutionary Economy," paper delivered April 1975, Organization of American Historians Convention, pp. 2–3; Cotton Mather, *Ornaments for the Daughters of Zion, or the Character and Happiness of a Virtuous Woman* (London: Thomas Parkhurst, 1694), pp. 6–7; Abbott, *Women in Industry*, pp. 20–34; Marcus Wilson Jernegan, *Laboring and Dependent Classes in Colonial America, 1607–1783* (New York: Frederick Ungar Publishing Co., 1931), pp. 84–128; Leonard, *Dear-Bought Heritage*, pp. 156–87; Morgan, *American Slavery—American Freedom*, pp. 321–24. The primary purpose of compulsory education in the colonies was to teach a trade to prevent pauperism and only secondarily to educate for literacy.

5. Frances May Manges, "Women Shopkeepers, Tavernkeepers and Artisans in Colonial Philadelphia" (Ph.D. diss., University of Pennsylvania, 1958), p. 35; Henretta, *Evolution of American Society*, p. 194.

6. Mary Beth Norton, "Eighteenth-Century American Women: The Loyalists as a Test Case," paper delivered at Second Berkshire Conference on the History of Women, 27 October 1974, p. 10. This study of a cross section of female Loyalists indicates only 9.2 percent worked outside the home. Whether these figures are representative of most late eighteenth-century women remains to be documented.

7. For examples of the expansion of female services and functions in port towns, ranging from paid domestic servants, wet nurses, and prostitutes to that of a small group of wealthy women consumers, see Ryan, *Womanhood in America*, pp. 73, 86–87, 91–99; Virginia Bever Platt (Bowling Green State University), "The Working Women of Newport, Rhode Island," paper delivered at 1975 Conference on Women in the Era of the American Revolution. According to Platt's figures, female laborers in Newport (whether free, indentured, or hired-out as slaves, and regardless of race) were paid approximately 30 percent less than the lowest paid unskilled, free, white male workers and 20 percent less than hired-out male slaves.

8. Abbott, *Women in Industry*, pp. 13–20, 149–56; Manges, "Women Shopkeepers, Tavernkeepers and Artisans," pp. xxxi–xxxii, 40–41, 44(n. 101), 69–117(n. 290); Carl Bridenbaugh, *The Colonial Craftsman* (Chicago: University of Chicago Press, Phoenix Books, 1961; reprint of original 1950 New York University Press edition), pp. 105–8; Earle, *Colonial Dames and Good Wives*, pp. 45–87; Carl Holliday, *Women's Life in Colonial Days* (New York: Frederick Ungar Publishing Co., 1922), pp. 291–312; Elisabeth Anthony Dexter, *Colonial Women of Affairs: Women in Business and the Professions in America before 1776*, 2d ed., rev. (Boston: Houghton Mifflin Co., 1931), passim; Ryan, *Womanhood in America*, pp. 34, 92–94.

9. Daniel Scott Smith, "Family Limitation, Sexual Control and Domestic Feminism in Victorian America," *Feminist Studies* 1 (Winter-Spring 1973): 46; Manges, "Women Shopkeepers, Tavernkeepers and Artisans," pp. xii–xxiii, 40–115, 118–119; Page Smith, *Daughters of the Promised Land* (Boston: Little, Brown and Co., 1970), p. 54; Carl N. Degler, *Out of Our Past: Forces that Shaped Modern America* (New York: Harper and Brothers, 1959), pp. 59–60; Mary R. Beard, *Women as Force in History*, pp. 78–80, 106–21. For more details about the socioeconomic activities of colonial women, see Julia Cherry Spruill, *Women's Life and*

Work in the Southern Colonies (New York: W. W. Norton & Co., 1972; reprint of original 1938 University of North Carolina Press edition), pp. 255-313, 340-66; Earle, *Colonial Dames and Good Wives*, pp. 45-87; Holliday, *Woman's Life in Colonial Days*, pp. 291-312; Elisabeth Anthony Dexter, *Career Women of America, 1776-1840* (Clifton, N.J.: Augustus M. Kelley Publishers, 1972; reprint of original 1950 Houghton Mifflin edition), passim; Leonard, *Dear-Bought Heritage*, pp. 118-236; Abbott, *Women in Industry*, pp. 10-47; Helen Campbell, *Women Wage Earners: Their Past, Their Present, and Their Future* (New York: Arno Press, 1972; reprint of original 1893 Roberts Brothers edition), pp. 57-76; Annie Nathan Meyer, *Woman's Work in America* (New York: Henry Holt and Co., 1891), passim; Benson, *Women in Eighteenth-Century America*, pp. 34-78, 100-35.

10. Manges, "Women Shopkeepers, Tavernkeepers and Artisans," p. xxiii. Manges's figures indicate that the low of 17 percent was recorded from July 1763 to July 1764 when 52 women were granted licenses out of a total of 308. The high of 22 percent was recorded from July 1770 to July 1771 when 60 women were granted licenses out of a total of 284. Between 1762 and 1776 the average number of years that each woman held a tavern license was 3.8, according to my analysis of her figures. For Boston taverns, see Carl Bridenbaugh, *Cities in Wilderness: The First Century of Urban Life in America, 1624-1742* (New York: Alfred A. Knopf, 1955) p. 72; idem, *Colonial Craftsmen*, pp. 121-22.

11. Manges, "Women Shopkeepers, Tavernkeepers and Artisans," pp. xxiii, 71, 75, 76, 78-81 (n. 205), 96, 116, 118.

12. Elisabeth Anthony Dexter's widely quoted statement that approximately 10 percent of all colonial shop managers or "she-merchants" in Boston were women is obviously based on an inadequate sampling of newspaper advertisements. On the other hand she provides evidence for the relative decline in women shopkeepers in the post-revolutionary period and their almost exclusive relegation to the sale of dry goods and clothes for their own sex. See Dexter, *Colonial Women of Affairs*, pp. 34-35, 37-38, 162-65; idem, *Career Women of America*, p. 139.

13. See Bernard Bailyn, *The New England Merchants in the Seventeenth Century* (New York: Harper & Row, Harper Torchbook, 1964; reprint of original 1955 Harvard University Press edition), passim; Richard B. Morris, *Government and Labor in Early America* (New York: Columbia University Press, 1946), pp. 1-54; Thomas C. Cochran, *Business in American Life*, pp. 28-57; idem, "The Business Revolution," *The American Historical Review* 79 (December 1974); 1449-66; Samuel Rezneck, "The Rise and Early Development of Industrial Consciousness in the United States, 1760-1830," *Journal of Economic and Business History* 4 (August 1932): 784-86; David J. Jeremy, "British Textile Technology Transmission to the United States: The Philadelphia Region Experience, 1770-1820," *Business History Review* 47 (Spring 1973): 24-29; Henretta, *Evolution of American Society*, pp. 95-112, 714-200; Manges, "Women Shopkeepers, Tavernkeepers and Artisans," pp. 8, 14-15, 17, 20, 25, 33, 37, 38, 42, 118.

14. James Henretta, "Economic Development and Social Structure in Colonial Boston," *William and Mary Quarterly* 22 (January 1965): 80-83, 85; Philip J. Greven, Jr., *Four Generations: Population, Land and Family in Colonial Andover, Massachusetts* (Ithaca: Cornell University Press, 1970), pp. 281-82; Richard L. Bushman, *From Puritan to Yankee: Character and the Social Order in Connecticut, 1690-1765* (Cambridge: Harvard University Press, 1967), pp. 267-88; Burrows and Wallace, "American Revolution," pp. 255-67; Jacob M. Price, "Economic

Function and the Growth of American Port Towns in the Eighteenth Century," *Perspectives in American History* 8 (1974): 130–37; Allan Kulikoff, "The Progress of Inequality in Revolutionary Boston," *William and Mary Quarterly* 28 (July 1971): 376, 378, 380, 383–84, 388–89, 406–9; James T. Lemon and Gary B. Nash, "The Distribution of Wealth in Eighteenth Century America: A Century of Changes in Chester County, Pennsylvania, 1693–1802," *Journal of Social History* 2 (1968–1969): 9–12; Kenneth Lockridge, "Land, Population and the Evolution of New England Society, 1630–1790," *Past and Present*, no. 39 (April 1968), pp. 62–80; Alexander Keyssar, "Widowhood in Eighteenth-Century Massachusetts: A Problem in the History of the Family," *Perspectives in American History* 8 (1974): 100–101, 114–15, 117–18; Platt, "Working Women of Newport," pp. 8, 11.

15. Henretta, *Evolution of American Society*, pp. 42, 72, 159, 188–89; idem, "Economic Development and Social Structure in Colonial Boston," pp. 72–92.

16. Henretta, *Evolution of American Society*, p. 196; Morris, *Government and Labor*, pp. 188–207, 354–63; *AFC*, 4:258; Manges, "Women Shopkeepers, Tavern-keepers and Artisans," pp. 34–35, 69; F. T. Carlton, "Abolition of Imprisonment for Debt in the United States," *Yale Review* 17 (1908): 339–44; Spruill, *Women's Life and Work*, pp. 338–39; Keyssar, "Widowhood in Eighteenth-Century Massachusetts," pp. 112–13; Kulikoff, "The Progress of Inequality in Revolutionary Boston," pp. 383–84, 408–9.

17. Platt, "Working Women of Newport," pp. 9–10; William R. Bagnall, *The Textile Industries of the United States* (New York: Augustus M. Kelley, 1971; reprint of the original 1893 Riverside Press edition), pp. 28–88; Rolla M. Tryon, *Household Manufactures in the U.S., 1640–1860* (Chicago: University of Chicago Press, 1917), pp. 58–59, 100–107, 112–15; Victor S. Clark, *History of Manufactures in the United States*, vol. 1, *1607–1860* (New York: Peter Smith, 1949; reprint of the original 1929 Carnegie Institution edition), pp. 116, 117, 188–91; Jernegan, *Laboring and Dependent Classes*, p. 18; Caroline Gilman, ed., *Letters of Eliza Wilkinson* (New York: Arno Press, 1969; reprint of original 1839 Samuel Colman edition), p. 105; Schneir, "Women in the Revolutionary Economy," p. 8, passim; Leonard, *Dear-Bought Heritage*, pp. 188–99.

18. Quoted from the *Pennsylvania Packet*, 7 August 1775 and 19 December 1774.

19. Jeremy, "British Textile Technology Transmission," pp. 28–29; Abbott, *Women in Industry*, pp. 36–37; Herbert Heaton, "The Industrial Immigrant in the United States, 1783–1812," *Proceedings of the American Philosophical Society* 95 (1951): 522–23; Rezneck, "Industrial Consciousness," pp. 786–90, 795–96; Cometti, "Women in American Revolution," pp. 332–33; Bagnall, *Textile Industries*, pp. 79–88; Leonard, *Dear-Bought Heritage*, pp. 199–203.

20. Cochran, "Business Revolution," pp. 1455, 1465; Abbott, *Women in Industry*, pp. 37–47; Jeremy, "British Textile Technology Transmission," pp. 31, 47; Manges, "Women Shopkeepers, Tavernkeepers and Artisans," pp. 27, 35, 37, 44–70, 119–20; Gerda Lerner, "The Lady and the Mill Girl: Changes in the Status of Women in the Age of Jackson," in *Our American Sisters*, eds. Jean E. Friedman and William G. Shade (Boston: Allyn and Bacon, 1973), pp. 89–90; Leonard, *Dear-Bought Heritage*, pp. 203–7; Elizabeth Faulkner Baker, *Technology and Women's Work* (New York: Columbia University Press, 1964), pp. 12–13; Abbott, *Women in Industry*, pp. 95–97, 109–47.

21. Jeremy, "British Textile Technology Transmission," pp. 24–52, 53–56 (quotations from pp. 29–30); Heaton, "Industrial Immigrant," p. 519; Mildred Campbell,

"English Emigration on the Eve of the American Revolution," *The American Historical Review* 61 (October 1955): 4, 6–7. Campbell's study showed that out of 6,000 emigrants to the New World from December 1773 to April 1776, 12 percent or 720 of these were adult females, of whom 23 percent or 165 "were working women with some skill or occupation" outside of that of housewife. Hopefully, the study in progress by David J. Jeremy will reveal a clearer picture of their contribution to the transmission of textile skills and technology between Britain and America.

22. Abbott, *Women in Industry*, pp. 46, 47, 88; Jeremy, "British Textile Technology Transmission," p. 36; Jacob E. Cooke, ed., *The Reports of Alexander Hamilton* (New York: Harper and Row, 1964), pp. 130–31. For the ways in which economic nationalists rationalized the exploitation of female labor, see Rezneck, "Industrial Consciousness," pp. 790–99.

23. Cochran, "Business Revolution," p. 1465; Baker, *Technology and Women's Work*, pp. 6–7. For earlier Puritan references to the "sin of idleness," see n. 61 below.

24. For demographic studies of the southern colonies see Lorena S. Walsh and Russell R. Menard, "Death in the Chesapeake: Two Life Tables for Men in Early Colonial Maryland," *Maryland Historical Magazine* 69 (Summer 1974): 211–27; Wesley Frank Craven, *White, Red, and Black: The Seventeenth-Century Virginian* (Charlottesville, Va: University of Virginia Press, 1971); Russell R. Menard, "Immigration to the Chesapeake Colonies in the Seventeenth Century: A Review Essay," *Maryland Historical Magazine* 68 (1973): 323–29; Irene W. D. Hecht, "The Virginia Muster of 1624/5 as a Source for Demographic History," *William and Mary Quarterly* 30 (1973): 65–92.

25. I am referring here to recent works on demography and social structure by John Demos, Philip J. Greven, James Henretta, Kenneth A. Lockridge, Robert V. Wells, Daniel Scott Smith, Darrett Rutman, Alexander Keyssar, and Richard Alterman that question some of the earlier prescriptive conclusions reached by Bernard Bailyn, Edmund Morgan, Oscar Handlin, Arthur W. Calhoun, Perry Miller, and Thomas Johnson based on research into literary sources.

26. Henretta, *Evolution of American Society*, pp. 12–13; Greven, *Four Generations*, pp. 21–40, 29, 110–11, 192–94; David E. Stannard, "Death and the Puritan Child," *American Quarterly* 26 (December 1974): 463–66; Keyssar, "Widowhood in Eighteenth-Century Massachusetts," pp. 88–94, 108–9; Walsh and Menard, "Death in the Chesapeake," pp. 222–27; Maris A. Vinovskis, "Mortality Rates and Trends in Massachusetts Before 1860," *Journal of Economic History* 32 (March 1972); 184–89, 190–91, 194–203, 212–13; John Demos, "Notes on Life in Plymouth Colony," *William and Mary Quarterly* 22 (1965): 271–72.

27. Daniel Scott Smith, "The Demographic History of Colonial New England," *Journal of Economic History* 32 (March 1972): 170–73; Herbert Moller, "Sex Composition and Correlated Culture Patterns of Colonial America," *William and Mary Quarterly* 2 (April 1945): 118, 124–25; Henretta, *Evolution of American Society*, p. 172; Greven, *Four Generations*, pp. 121–22; John Demos, "Families in Colonial Bristol, Rhode Island: An Exercise in Historical Demography," in *Quantitative History*, eds. D. K. Rowney and J. Q. Graham, Jr. (Homewood, Ill: Dorsey Press, 1969), pp. 301, 305; Keyssar, "Widowhood in Eighteenth-Century Massachusetts," pp. 95–97. Between 1721 and 1760 as many as 15 percent of all adult women remained unmarried at least until the age of 45 in certain towns in Massachusetts and Rhode Island.

28. Moller, "Sex Composition," p. 140; Demos, "Life in Plymouth," pp. 272–73, 275–76; Henretta, *Evolution of American Society*, p. 132; Bruce E. Steiner, "Demographic Studies," *New England Quarterly* 43 (September 1970), 482–89; Daniel Scott Smith, "Parental Power and Marriage Patterns: An Analysis of Historical Trends in Hingham, Massachusetts," *Journal of Marriage and the Family* 35 (August 1973): 419–28; Ryan, *Womanhood in America*, pp. 106–111; Greven, *Four Generations*, pp. 272–75; Smith and Hindus, "Premarital Pregnancy," pp. 561–64.

29. Smith, "Parental Power and Marriage Patterns," p. 427; Keyssar, "Widowhood in Eighteenth-Century Massachusetts," pp. 117–18; Ryan, *Womanhood in America*, pp. 86–91. Since none of the new demographic studies have dealt with actual frontier conditions I see no reason to deny the validity of the axiom that "the frontier was great for men and dogs, but hell for horses and women." There is a tendency among some historians who have recently rediscovered the functional importance of women within the seventeenth century colonial household to confuse conditions in newly settled coastal areas with those of frontier America, which continued well into the nineteenth century. The former were generally organized efforts characterized by the immediate establishment of stable family life and kinship networks, while the latter were often isolated and unplanned or poorly planned ventures into the wilderness where male dominance reigned supreme and where isolated women, whether they were there as status symbols, slaves, civilizers, or prostitutes, had no institutionalized protection (such as the proximity of their families of orientation) from the physical hardships imposed both by the environment and the men. It appears that this dominance diminished to some degree as the first elements of law and order were introduced and small communities with more balanced sex ratios developed—only to return when these settlements became fully "civilized" and well within the cultural and economic standards set by the older coastal towns. By saying this, I do not want to diminish the socioeconomic importance of the western frontier woman; but at the same time I do not want to romanticize it.

30. Smith, "Parental Power and Marriage Patterns," pp. 421, 427; idem, "Demographic History of Colonial New England," pp. 165 (n. 2), 170–73; Greven, *Four Generations*, 14–16, 30, 111–13, 118–23, 261–68; Wilson H. Grabill, Clyde V. Kiser, and Pascal K. Whelpton, "A Long View," in *The American Family in Social-Historical Perspective*, ed. Michael Gordon (New York: St. Martin's Press, 1973), pp. 375, 379; idem, eds. *The Fertility of American Women* (New York: John Wiley and Sons, 1958), pp. 9–10; Philip J. Greven, Jr., "The Average Size of Families and Households in the Province of Massachusetts in 1764 and in the United States in 1790: An Overview," in *Household and Family in Past Time*, ed. Peter Laslett (London: Cambridge University Press, 1972), pp. 551, 556, 557–58, 559; Demos, "Families in Colonial Bristol," pp. 297, 299, 305.

31. J. William Frost, *The Quaker Family in Colonial America* (New York: St. Martin's Press, 1973), pp. 70, 86–88; Robert V. Wells, "Family Size and Fertility Control in Eighteenth-Century America: A Study of Quaker History," *Population Studies* 25 (1971): 73–82; idem, "Demographic Change and the Life Cycle of American Families," *Journal of Interdisciplinary History* 2 (Spring 1975): 743–49; Smith, "Parental Power and Marriage Patterns," pp. 421, 426; idem, "Demographic History of Colonial New England," pp. 166, 178, 179 (n. 17), 180 (n. 19), 182–83; Grabill, Kiser, and Whelpton, "A Long View," pp. 383–84; Ryan, *Womanhood in America*, pp. 48, 62, 121, 124–35; Lawrence Stone, "The Massacre of

the Innocents," *New York Review of Books*, 14 November 1974, p. 31; Greven, *Four Generations*, pp. 279–84; Bushman, *Puritan to Yankee*, pp. 183–95, 235–66; Burrows and Wallace, "American Revolution," pp. 255–67, 283–89; Gordon S. Wood, "Rhetoric and Reality in the American Revolution," *William and Mary Quarterly* 23 (1966): 25–31; John J. Waters, Jr., *The Otis Family in Provincial and Revolutionary Massachusetts* (Chapel Hill: University of North Carolina Press, 1968), pp. 128–34; David J. Rothman, "A Note on the Study of the Colonial Family," in *Education in American History*, ed. Michael B. Katz (New York: Praeger Publishers, 1973), pp. 22–28; Steiner, "Demographic Studies," pp. 482–89. All statements, even those as qualified as Greven's (p. 282), about the transition taking place in the family unit being complete in 1776, must be viewed with caution especially when Burrows and Wallace suggest (p. 283), "families provide the political system with the personality type it requires."

32. John F. Walzer, "Eighteenth-Century American Childhood," in *The History of Childhood*, ed. Lloyd deMause (New York: The Psychohistory Press, 1974), pp. 352–53, 358, 360–75, 378 (n. 50); Ann Hulton, *Letters of a Loyalist Lady* (Cambridge: Harvard University Press, 1927), pp. ix, 37, 49–50, 63; Spruill, *Women's Life and Work*, pp. 55–63; Stewart Mitchell, ed., *New Letters of Abigail Adams, 1788–1801* (Boston: Houghton Mifflin Co., 1947), pp. xxviii–xxix, 35–36, 109, 129, 130–31, 174; Philip J. Greven, Jr., ed., *Child-Rearing Concepts, 1628–1861* (Ithaca, Ill.: F. E. Peacock Publishers, 1973), pp. 1–6, 46–51, passim. Also see n. 14 for the child-rearing views of Abigail Adams and Mercy Warren.

33. Keyssar, "Widowhood in Eighteenth-Century Massachusetts," pp. 87–91, 100–101, 114, 117, 118; Smith, "Parental Power and Marriage Patterns," pp. 420–24; Greven, *Four Generations*, pp. 72–99, 280–86; Demos, "Notes on Life in Plymouth Colony," pp. 273–75; idem, *Little Commonwealth*, pp. 149–70; (on pages 169–70 Demos appears to contradict some of his own evidence and Greven's by denying "that parents deployed their ownership of property so as to maintain effective control over their grown children" in the seventeenth century); Paul Leicester Ford, ed., *The Words of Thomas Jefferson* (New York: G.P. Putnam's Sons, 1904), 2:269.

34. Joseph E. Illick, "Child-Rearing in Seventeenth-Century England and America," in *History of Childhood*, pp. 324–25; Smith, "Parental Power and Marriage Patterns," pp. 425–26 (n. 9).

35. Smith and Hindus, "Premarital Pregnancy," pp. 537, 561, passim; Daniel Scott Smith, "The Dating of the American Sexual Revolution: Evidence and Interpretation," in *American Family in Social-Historical Perspective*, p. 323; Moller, "Sex Composition," pp. 142–45; Arthur W. Calhoun, *A Social History of the American Family* (New York: Barnes and Noble, 1917), vol. 1; *Colonial Period*, pp. 51–64; Greven, *Four Generations*, pp. 113–16; Demos, "Families in Colonial Bristol, R. I.," p. 306; Henretta, *Evolution of American Society*, pp. 132–33.

36. Smith and Hindus, "Premarital Pregnancy," pp. 537–41, 549, 553 (quotation), 555–60.

37. Ibid., Greven, *Child-Rearing Concepts*, pp. 4–5. See also nn. 48 and 50 above.

38. Smith and Hindus, "Premarital Pregnancy," pp. 547–51. Bundling has been described by these two authors as "an eighteenth century compromise between persistent parental control and pressures of the young to subvert traditional familial authority" (p. 556). See n. 14 for views of Adams and Warren on virtue.

39. Ibid., p. 557; Michael Paul Rogin, *Fathers and Children* (New York: Alfred A.

Knopf, 1975), pp. 30, 34. See n. 50 above and section on education for confirmation of conservative views about the family held by the Founding Fathers.

40. Rogin, *Fathers and Children*, pp. 63–64, 70–71. For representative examples of the general submissiveness and the vicarious aspects of the lives of the middle- and upper-class women in the late eighteenth century which ultimately led to a culmination of the double standard in the cult of idleness and "true womanhood," see Linda Grant De Pauw, "The American Revolution and the Rights of Women: The Feminist Theory of Abigail Adams," paper delivered at the 1975 meeting of the Organization of American Historians; Hulton, *Letters of a Loyalist Lady*, p. 6; Woody, *History of Women's Education*, 1:133–34; Alice Morse Earle, ed., *Diary of Anna Green Winslow: A Boston School Girl of 1771* (Detroit: Singing Tree Press, 1970; reprint of the original 1894 Houghton Mifflin edition), passim; Eliza Southgate Bowne, *A Girl's Life Eighty Years Ago* (New York: Charles Scribner's Sons, 1887), pp. 15–19, 50–51; Ethel Armes, ed., *Nancy Shippen: Her Journal Book: The International Romance of a Young Lady of Fashion of Colonial Philadelphia with Letters to Her and About Her* (Philadelphia: J. B. Lippincott, 1935), pp. 41–42, passim; AFC, 2:407; 3:xxxiii; 4:210, 221, 258; Keith Thomas, "The Double Standard," *Journal of the History of Ideas* 20 (April 1959): 195–216; E. Willett Cunington, *Feminine Attitudes in the Nineteenth Century* (New York: MacMillan and Co., 1936), pp. 201–35; Barbara Welter, "The Cult of True Womanhood: 1820–1860," *American Quarterly* 18 (Summer 1966): 151–74; Ryan, *Womanhood in America*, pp. 137–91.

6 ᎦDaughters of Columbia: Educating Women for the Republic, 1787–1805

Linda K. Kerber

"I expect to see our young women forming a new era in female history," wrote Judith Sargent Murray in 1798.[1] Her optimism was part of a general sense that all possibilities were open in the post-Revolutionary world; as Benjamin Rush put it, the first act of the republican drama had only begun. The experience of war had given words like "independence" and "self-reliance" personal as well as political overtones; among the things that ordinary folk had learned from wartime had been that the world could, as the song had it, turn upside down. The rich could quickly become poor, wives might suddenly have to manage family businesses; women might even, as the famous Deborah Gannett had done, shoulder a gun. Political theory taught that republics rested on the virtue of their citizens; revolutionary experience taught that it was useful to be prepared for a wide range of unusual possibilities.[2]

A desire to explore the possibilities republicanism now opened to women was expressed by a handful of articulate, urban, middle-class men and women. While only a very few writers—Charles Brockden Brown, Judith Sargent Murray, Benjamin Rush—devoted extensive attention to women and what they might become, many essayists explored the subject in the periodical literature. In the fashion of the day, they concealed their identity under pseudonyms like "Cordelia," "Constantia," or, simply, "A Lady." These expressions came largely from Boston, New York, and Philadelphia: cities which were the centers of publishing. The vitality of Philadelphia, as political and social capital, is well known; the presence of so many national legislators in the city, turning up as they did at dances and dinner parties, was no doubt intellectually invigorating, and not least for the women of Philadelphia. In an informal way, women shared many of the political excitements of the city. Philadelphia was the home of the Young Ladies' Academy, founded in 1786, with explicitly fresh ideas about women's education, and an enrollment of more than a hundred within two years; Benjamin Rush would deliver his "Thoughts upon Female Education" there. The first attempt at a magazine expressly addressed to women was made by the Philadelphia *Lady's Magazine and Repository.* Two of the most intense anonymous writers—"Sophia" and "Nitidia"—wrote for Philadelphia newspapers. And after the government moved to Washington, Joseph Dennie's *Port Folio* solicited "the assistance of the ladies," and published essays by Gertrude Meredith, Sarah Hall, and Emily Hopkinson. Boston and New York were not far behind in displaying similar interests: in New York, Noah Webster's *American Magazine* included in its prospectus a specific appeal for female contributors; the *Boston Weekly Magazine* was careful to publish the speeches at the annual "Exhibition" of Susanna Rowson's Young Ladies' Academy.

Most jouranlists' comments on the role and functions of women in the republic merged, almost imperceptibly, into discussions of the sort of education proper for young girls. A pervasive Lockean environmentalism was displayed; what people were was assumed to be dependent on how they were educated. "Train up the child in the way he should grow, and when he is old he will not depart from it"; the biblical injunction was repeatedly quoted, and not quoted idly. When Americans spoke of what was best for the child they were also speaking—implicitly or explicitly—of their hopes for the adult. Charles Brockden Brown, for example, is careful to provide his readers with brief accounts of his heroines' early education. When we seek to learn the recipe for Murray's "new era in female history" we find ourselves reading comments on two related themes: how young women are to be "trained up," and what is to be expected of them when they are old.

If the republic were to fulfill the generous claims it made for the liberty and competence of its citizens, the education of young women would have to be an education for independence rather than for an upwardly mobile marriage. The periodicals are full of attacks on fashion, taking it for an emblem of superficiality and dependence. The Philadelphia *Lady's Magazine* criticized a father who prepared his daughters for the marriage market: "You boast of having given your daughters an education which will enable them 'to shine in the first circles.' . . . They sing indifferently; they play the harpsichord indifferently; they are mistresses of every common game at cards . . . they . . . have just as much knowledge of dress as to deform their persons by an awkward imitation of every new fashion which appears. . . . Placed in a situation of difficulty, they have neither a head to dictate, nor a hand to help in any domestic concern."[3] Teaching young girls to dress well was part of the larger message that their primary lifetime goal must be marriage; in this context, fashion became a feature of sexual politics. "I have sometimes been led," remarked Benjamin Rush, "to ascribe the invention of ridiculous and expensive fashions in female dress entirely to the gentlemen in order to divert the ladies from improving their minds and thereby to secure a more arbitrary and unlimited authority over them."[4] In the marriage market, beauty, flirtatiousness, and charm were at a premium; intelligence, good judgment, and competence (in short, the republican virtues) were at a discount. The republic did not need fashion plates; it needed citizens— women as well as men—of self-discipline and of strong mind. The contradiction between the counsel given to young women and their own self-interest, as well as the best interests of the republic, seemed obvious. The marriage market undercut the republic.[5]

Those who addressed themselves to the problem of the proper education for young women used the word "independence" frequently. Sometimes it was used in a theoretical fashion: How, it was asked, can women's minds be free if they are taught that their sphere is limited to clothing, music, and needlework? Often the context of independence is economic and political: it seemed appropriate that in a republic women should have greater control over their own lives. "The *dependence* for which women are uniformly educated" was deplored; it was pointed out that the unhappily married woman would quickly discover that she had "neither liberty nor property."[6]

The idea that political independence should be echoed by a self-reliance which would make women as well as men economically independent appears in its most developed form in a series of essays Judith Sargent Murray published in the *Massachusetts Magazine* between 1792 and 1794, and collected under the title *The Gleaner* in 1798. Murray insisted that instruction in a manual trade was especially appropriate in a republic, and decried the antiegalitarian habit of assuming that a genteel and impractical education was superior to a vocational one. She was critical of fathers who permitted their sons to grow up without knowing a useful skill; she was even more critical of parents who "pointed their daughters" toward marriage and dependence. This made girls' education contingent on a single event; it offered them a single image of the future. "I would give my daughters every accomplishment which I thought proper," Murray wrote, "and to crown all, I would early accustom them to habits of industry and order. They should be taught with precision the art economical; they should be enabled to procure for themselves the necessaries of life; independence should be placed within their grasp." Repeatedly Murray counseled that women should be made to feel competent at something: "A woman *should reverence herself.*"[7]

Murray scattered through the *Gleaner* essays and brief fictional versions of self-respecting women, in the characters of Margaretta, Mrs. Virgilius, and Penelope Airy. In his full-length novel *Ormond,* published in 1799, Charles Brockden Brown imagined a considerably more developed version of a competent woman. Constantia Dudley is eminently rational. When her father is embezzled of his fortune she, "her cheerfulness unimpaired," sells "every superfluous garb and trinket," her music and her books; she supports the family by needlework. Constantia never flinches; she can take whatever ill fortune brings, whether it is yellow fever or the poverty that forces her to conclude that the only alternative to starvation is cornmeal mush three times a day for three months. Through it all, she resists proposals of marriage, because even in adversity she scorns to become emotionally dependent without love.[8]

Everything Constantia does places her in sharp contrast to Helena Cleves, who also "was endowed with every feminine and fascinating quality." Helena has had a genteel education; she can paint, and sing, and play the clavichord, but it is all fashionable gloss to camouflage a lack of real mental accomplishment and self-discipline. What Brown called "exterior accomplishments" were acceptable so long as life held no surprises, but when Helena meets disaster, she is unprepared to maintain her independence and her self-respect. She falls into economic dependence upon a "kinswoman"; she succumbs to the "specious but delusive" reasoning or Ormond, and becomes his mistress. He takes advantage of her dependence, all the while seeking in Constantia a rational woman worthy of his intelligence; eventually, in despair, Helena kills herself.[9]

The argument that an appropriate education would steel girls to face adversity is related to the conviction that all citizens of a republic should be self-reliant. But the argument can be made independent of explicit republican ideology. It may well represent the common sense of a revolutionary era in which the unexpected was very likely to happen; in which large numbers of people had lived through reversals of fortune, encounters with strangers, physical dislocation. Constantia's friend Martinette de Beauvais has lived in Marseilles, Verona, Vienna, and Philadelphia; she had dressed like a man and fought in the American Revolution; after that she was one of the "hundreds" of women who took up arms for the French.[10] Constantia admires and sympathizes with her friend; nothing in the novel is clearer than that women who are not ready to maintain their independence in a crisis, as Constantia and Martinette do, risk sinking, like Helena, into prostitution and death.

The model republican woman was competent and confident. She could ignore the vagaries of fashion; she was rational, benevolent, independent, self-reliant. Writers who spoke to this point prepared lists of what we would now call role models: heroines of the past offered as assurance that women could indeed be people of accomplishment. There were women of the ancient world, like Cornelia, the mother of the Gracchi; rulers like Elizabeth of England and the Empress Catherine of Russia; a handful of Frenchwomen: Mme. de Genlis, Mme. Maintenon, and Mme. Dacier; and a long list of British intellectuals: Lady Mary Wortley Montagu, Hannah More, Elizabeth Carter, Mrs. Knowles (the Quaker who had bested Dr. Johnson in debate), Mary Wollstonecraft, and the Whig historian Catharine Macaulay.[11] Such women were rumored to exist in America; they were given fictional embodiment by Murray and Brown. Those who believed in these republican models demanded that their presence be recognized and endorsed, and that a new generation of young women be urged to make them patterns for their own behavior. To create more such women became a major educational challenge.

Writers were fond of pointing out that the inadequacies of American women could be ascribed to early upbringing and environmental influences. "Will it be said that the judgment of a male of two years old, is more sage than that of a female of the same age?" asked Judith Sargent Murray. "But ... as their years increased, the sister must be wholly domesticated, while the brother is led by the hand through all the flowery paths of science." The *Universal Asylum* published a long and thoughtful essay by "A Lady" which argued that "in the nursery, strength is equal in the male and female." When a boy went to school, he immediately met both intellectual and physical challenge; his teachers instructed him in science and language, his friends dared him to fight, to run after a hoop, to jump a rope. Girls, on the other hand, were "committed to illiterate teachers, ... cooped up in a room, confined to needlework, deprived of exercise." Thomas Cooper defined the problem clearly: "We first keep their minds and then their persons in subjection," he wrote. "We educate women from infancy to marriage, in such a way as to debilitate both their corporeal and their mental powers. All the accomplishments we teach them are directed not to their future benefit in life but to the amusement of the male sex; and having for a series of years, with much assiduity, and sometimes at much expense, incapacitated them for any serious occupation, we say they are not fit to govern themselves."[12]

Schemes for the education of the "rising generation" proliferated in the early republic, including a number of projects for the education of women. Some, like those discussed in the well-known essays of Benjamin Rush and Noah Webster, were theoretical; others took the form of admitting girls to boys' academies or establishing new schools for girls. There were not as many as Judith Sargent Murray implied when she said: "Female academies are everywhere establishing," but she was not alone in seeing schools like Susanna Rowson's Young Ladies' Academy and the Young Ladies' Academy of Philadelphia as harbingers of a trend. One pamphlet address, written in support of the Philadelphia Academy, expressed the hope that it would become "a great national seminary" and insisted that although "stubborn prejudices still exist . . . we must (if open to conviction) be convinced that *females* are fully capable of sounding the most profound depths, and of attaining to the most sublime excellence in every part of science."[13]

Certainly there was a wide range of opinion on the content and scope of female education in the early republic. Samuel Harrison Smith's essay on the subject, which won the American Philosophical Society's 1797 prize for the best plan for a national system of education, began by proposing "that every male child, without exception, be educated."[14] At the other extreme was Timothy Dwight, the future president of Yale, who opened his academy at Greenfield Hill to girls and taught them the same subjects he taught to boys, at the same time and in the same rooms.[15] But Dwight was the exception. Most proposals for the education of young women agreed that the curriculum should be more advanced than that of the primary schools but somewhat less than that offered by colleges and even conventional boys' academies. Noah Webster thought women should learn speaking and writing, arithmetic, geography, belles-lettres; "A Reformer" in the *Weekly Magazine* advocated a similar program, to which practical instruction in nursing and cooking were added. Judith Sargent Murray thought women should be able to converse elegantly and correctly, pronounce French, read history (as a narrative substitute for novels, rather than for its own interest or value), and learn some simple geography and astronomy.[16] The best-known proposal was Benjamin Rush's; he too prescribed reading, grammar, penmanship, "figures and bookkeeping," geography. He added "the first principles of natural philosophy," vocal music (because it soothed cares and was good for the lungs) but not instrumental music (because, except for the most talented, it seemed a waste of valuable time), and history (again, as an antidote to novel reading).

Rush offered his model curriculum in a speech to the Board of Visitors of the Young Ladies' Academy of Philadelphia, later published and widely reprinted under the title "Thoughts upon Female Education Accommodated to the Present State of Society, Manners and Government in the United States of America." The academy claimed to be the first female academy chartered in the United States; when Rush spoke, on July 28, 1787, he was offering practical advice to a new school. Rush linked the academy to the greater cause of demonstrating the possibilities of women's minds. Those who were skeptical of education for women, Rush declared, were the same who opposed "the general diffusion of knowledge among the citizens of our republics." Rush argued that "female education should be accommodated to the state of society, manners, and government of the country in which it is conducted." An appropriate education for American women would be condensed, because they married earlier than their European counterparts; it would include bookkeeping, because American women could expect to be "the stewards and guardians of their husbands' property," and executrices of their husbands' wills. It would qualify them for "a general intercourse with the world" by an acquaintance with geography and chronology. If education is preparation for life, then the life styles of American women required a newly tailored educational program. [17]

The curriculum of the Young Ladies' Academy (which one of the Board of Visitors called "abundantly sufficient to complete the female mind") included reading, writing, arithmetic, English grammar, composition, rhetoric, and geography. It did not include the natural philosophy Rush hoped for (although Rush did deliver a dozen lectures on "The Application of the Principles of Natural Philosophy, and Chemistry, to Domestic and Culinary Purposes"); it did not include advanced mathematics or the classics. [18]

In 1794 the Young Ladies' Academy published a collection of its graduation addresses; one is struck by the scattered observations of valedictorians and salutatorians that reading, writing, and arithmetic were not enough. Priscilla Mason remarked in her 1793 graduation address that while it was unusual for a woman to address "a promiscuous assembly," there was no impropriety in women's becoming accomplished orators. What had prevented them, she argued, was that "our high and mighty Lords . . . have denied us the means of knowledge, and then reproached us for the want of it. . . . They doom'd the sex to servile or frivolous employments, on purpose to degrade their minds, that they themselves might hold unrivall'd, the power and pre-eminence they had usurped." Academies like hers enabled women to increase their knowledge, but the forums in which they might use it were still unavailable: "The Church, the Bar, and the Senate are shut against us."[19]

So long as the propriety of cultivating women's minds remained a matter for argument, it was hard to press a claim to public competence; Priscilla Mason was an exception. Rush had concluded his advice to the Young Ladies' Academy by challenging his audience to demonstrate "that the cultivation of reason in women is alike friendly to the order of nature and the private as well as the public happiness." But meeting even so mild a challenge was difficult; "bluestocking" was not a term of praise in the early republic. "Tell me," wrote the Philadelphian Gertrude Meredith angrily, ". . . do you imagine, from your knowledge of the young men in this city, that ladies are valued according to their mental acquirements? I can assure you that they are not, and I am very confident that they never will be, while men indulge themselves in expressions of contempt for one because she has a *bare elbow*, for another because she . . . never made a *good pun, nor smart repartee. . . .* [Would they] not titter . . . at her expense, if a woman made a Latin quotation, or spoke with enthusiasm of Classical learning?"[20] When Gertrude Meredith visited Baltimore, she found that her mildly satirical essays for the *Port Folio* had transformed her into a formidable figure: "Mrs. Cole says she should not have been more distressed at visiting Mrs. Macaulay the authoress than myself as she had heard I *was so sensible,* but she was very glad to find I was so free and easy. You must allow," she concluded dryly, "that this compliment was elegantly turned." A similar complaint was made by an essayist whom we know only as "Sophia":

> A woman who is conscious of possessing, more intellectual power than is requisite in superintending the pantry, and in adjusting the ceremonials of a feast, and who believes she, in conforming to the will of the giver, in improving the gift, is by the wits of the other sex denominated a learned lady. She is represented as disgustingly slovenly in her person, indecent in her habits, imperious to her husband, and negligent of her children. And the odious scarecrow is employed, exactly as the farmer employs his unsightly bundle of rags and straw, to terrify the simple birds, from picking up the precious grain, which he wishes to monopolize. After all this, what man in his sober senses can be astonished, to find the majority of women as they really are, frivolous and volatile; incapable of estimating their own dignity, and indifferent to the best interests of society. . . ?[21]

These women were not creating their own paranoid images of discouragement. The same newspapers for which they wrote often printed other articles insisting that intellectual accomplishment is inappropriate in a woman, that the intellectual woman is not only invading a male province, but must herself somehow be masculine. "Women of masculine minds," wrote the Boston minister John Sylvester John Gardiner, "have generally masculine manners, and a robustness of person ill calculated to inspire the tender passion." Noah Webster's *American Magazine,* which in its prospectus had made a special appeal to women writers and readers, published the unsigned comment: "If we picture to ourselves a woman . . . firm in resolve, unshaken in conduct, unmoved by the delicacies of situation, by the fashions of the times, . . . we immediately change the idea of the sex, and . . . we see under the form of a woman the virtues and qualities of a man." Even the *Lady's Magazine,* which had promised to demonstrate that "the FEMALES of Philadelphia are by no means deficient in *those talents,* which have immortalized the names of a *Montagu,* a *Craven,* a *More,* and a *Seward,* in their inimitable writings," published a cautionary tale, whose moral was that although "learning in men was the road to preferment . . . consequences very opposite were the result of the same quality in women." Amelia is a clergyman's only daughter; she is taught Latin and Greek, with the result that she becomes "negligent of her dress," and "pride and pedantry grew up with learning in her breast." Eventually she is avoided by both sexes, and becomes emblematic of the fabled "white-washed jackdaw (who, aiming at a station from which nature had placed him at a distance, found himself deserted by his own species, and driven out of every society)." For conclusion there was an explicit moral: "This story was intended (at a time when the press overflows with the productions of female pens) . . . to admonish them, that . . . because a few have gained applause by studying the dead languages, all womankind should [not] assume their Dictionaries and Lexicons; else . . . (as the Ladies made rapid advances towards manhood) we might in a few years behold a sweepstakes rode by women, or a second battle at Odiham, fought with superior skill, by Mesdames Humphries and Mendoza."[22]

The prediction that accomplishment would unsex women was coupled with the warning that educated women would abandon their proper sphere; the female pedant and the careful housekeeper were never found in the same person. The most usable cautionary emblem for this seems to have been Mary Wollstonecraft, whose life and work linked criticism of women's status with free love and political radicalism. Mary Wollstonecraft's *Vindication of the Rights of Women* was her generation's most coherent statement of what women deserved and what they might become. The influence of any book is difficult to trace, and although we know that her book was reprinted in Philadelphia shortly after its publication in 1792, it would be inaccurate to credit Wollstonecraft with responsibility for raising in America questions relating to the status of women. It seems far more likely that she verbalized effectively what a larger public was already thinking or was willing to hear; "In very many of her sentiments," remarked the Philadelphia Quaker Elizabeth Drinker, "she, as some of our friends say, *speaks my mind.*"[23]

Wollstonecraft's primary target was Rousseau, whose definition of woman's sphere was a limited one: "The empire of women," Rousseau had written, "is the empire of softness, of address, of complacency; her commands are caresses; her menaces are tears." Wollstonecraft perceived that to define women in this way was to condemn them to "a state of perpetual childhood"; she deplored the "false system of education" which made women "only anxious to inspire love, when they ought to cherish a nobler ambition, and by their abilities and virtues exact respect." Women's duties were different from those of men, but they similarly demanded the exercise of virtue and reason; women would be better wives and mothers if they were taught that they need not depend on frivolity and ignorance. Wollstonecraft ventured the suggestion that women might study medicine, politics, and business, but whatever they did, they should not be denied civil and political rights, they should not have to rely on marriage for assurance of economic support, they should not "remain immured in their families groping in the dark."[24]

If, in some quarters, Mary Wollstonecraft's work was greeted as the common sense of the matter, in others it was met with hostility. The *Vindication* was a popular subject of satire, especially when, after the author's death in childbirth in 1797, William Godwin published a *Memoir* revealing that she had lived with other men, and with Godwin himself before her pregnancy and their marriage. Critics were then freed to discount her call for reform as the self-serving demand of a woman of easy virtue, as Benjamin Silliman did throughout his *Letters of Shahcoolen.* Timothy Dwight, who had taken the lead in offering young women education on a par with young men, shuddered at Wollstonecraft and held "the female philosopher" up to ridicule in "Morpheus," a political satire which ran for eight installments in the *New-England Palladium.*[25] Dwight called Wollstonecraft "an unchaste woman," "a sentimental lover," "a strumpet"; as Silliman had done, he linked her radical politics to free love. " 'Away with all monopolies,' " Dwight has her say. " 'I hate these exclusive rights; these privileged orders. I am for having everything free, and open to all; like the air which we breathe. . . .' "

" 'Love, particularly, I suppose, Madam [?]' "

" 'Yes, brute, love, if you please, and everything else.' "[26] Even Charles Brockden Brown's feminist tract *Alcuin* concluded with a long gloss on the same theme: to permit any change in women's status was to imply the acceptance of free love. Alcuin, who has been playing the conservative skeptic, concludes that once it is established that marriage "has no other criterion than custom," it becomes simply "a mode of sexual intercourse." His friend Mrs. Carter protests energetically that free love is not at all what she wanted; " 'because I demand an equality of conditions among beings that equally partake of the same divine reason, would you rashly infer that I was an enemy to the institution of marriage itself?' " Brown lets her have the last word, but he does not make Alcuin change his mind.[27]

Dwight had one final charge to make against Wollstonecraft; he attacked her plea that women emerge from the confines of their families. " 'Who will make our puddings, Madam?' " his protagonist asks. When she responds: " 'Make them yourself,' " he presses harder: " 'Who shall nurse us when we are sick?' " and, finally, " 'Who shall nurse our children?' " The last question reduces the fictional Mary to blushes and silence.[28]

It would not, however, reduce Rush, or Murray, or Brown, to blushes and silence. (Nor, I think, would it have so affected the real Mary Wollstonecraft.) They had neither predicted that women would cease their housewifely duties nor demanded that women should. Priscilla Mason's demand that hitherto male professions be opened to women was highly unusual, and even she apologized for it before she left the podium. There were, it is true, some other hints that women might claim the privileges and duties of male citizens of the republic. In *Alcuin,* Mrs. Carter explains her intense political disappointment through the first two chapters, arguing that Americans had been false to their own revolutionary promises in denying political status to women. "If a stranger questions me concerning the nature of our government, I answer, that in this happy climate all men are free: the people are the source of all authority; from them it flows, and to them, in due season, it returns ... our liberty consists in the choice of our governors: all, as reason requires, have a part in this choice, yet not without a few exceptions ... females ... minors ... the poor ... slaves. ... I am tired of explaining this charming system of equality and independence." St. George Tucker, commenting on Blackstone, acknowledged that women were taxed without representation; like "aliens ... children under the age of discretion, idiots, and lunatics," American women had neither political nor civil rights. "I fear there is little reason for a compliment to our laws for their respect and favour to the female sex," Tucker concluded. As Tucker had done, John Adams acknowledged that women's experience of the republic was different from men's; he hesitantly admitted that the republic claimed the right "to govern women without their consent." For a brief period from 1790 to

1807, New Jersey law granted the franchise to "all free inhabitants," and on occasion women exercised that right; it is conceivable that New Jersey might have stood as a precedent for other states. Instead, New Jersey's legislature rewrote its election law; the argument for political competence was taken no further.[29]

All of these were hesitant suggestions introduced into a hostile intellectual milieu in which female learning was equated with pedantry and masculinity. To resist those assumptions was to undertake a great deal; it was a task for which no one was ready; indeed, it is impossible to say that anyone really wanted to try. Instead, the reformers would have been quick to reply, with Brown's Mrs. Carter, that they had no intention of abandoning marriage; that they had every intention of making puddings and nursing babies; that the education they demanded was primarily to enable women to function more effectively within their traditional sphere, and only secondarily to fulfill demands like Priscilla Mason's that they emerge from it. People were complaining that American women were boring, frivolous, spending excessive amounts of money for impractical fashions; very well, a vigorously educated woman would be less likely to bore her husband, less likely to be a spendthrift, better able to cope with adverse fortune. Judith Sargent Murray versified an equation:

> Where'er the maiden Industry *appears,*
> *A thrifty contour every object wears;*
> *And when fair* order *with the nymph combines,*
> *Adjusts, directs, and every plan designs,*
> *Then* Independence *fills her peerless seat,*
> *And lo! the matchless trio is complete.*

Murray repeatedly made the point that the happiness of the nation depended on the happiness of families; and that the "felicity of families" is dependent on the presence of women who are "properly methodical, and economical in their distributions and expenditures of time." She denied that "the present enlarged plan of female education" was incompatible with traditional notions of women's duties: she predicted that the "daughters of Columbia" would be free of *"invidious and rancorous passions"* and "even the semblance of pedantry"; "when they become wives and mothers, they will fill with honour the parts allotted them."[30]

Rarely, in the literature of the early Republic, do we find any objection to the notion that women belong in the home; what emerges is the argument that the Revolution had enlarged the significance of what women did in their homes. Benjamin Rush's phrasing of this point is instructive; when he defined the goals of republican women, he was careful not to include a claim to political power: "The equal share that every citizen has in the liberty and the possible share he may have in the government of our country make it necessary that our ladies should be qualified to a certain degree by a peculiar and suitable education, *to concur in instructing their sons in the principles of liberty and government.*" The Young Ladies' Academy promised "not wholly to engross the mind" of each pupil, "but to allow her to prepare for the duties in life to which she may be destined." Miss P.W. Jackson, graduating from Mrs. Rowson's Academy, explained what she had learned of the goals of the educated woman: "A woman who is skilled in every useful art, who practices every domestic virtue . . . may, by her precept and example, inspire her brothers, her husband, or her sons, with such a love of virtue, such just ideas of the true value of civil liberty . . . that future heroes and statesmen, who arrive at the summit of military or political fame, shall *exaltingly declare, it is to my mother I owe this elevation.*" By their household management, by their refusal to countenance vice, crime, or cruelty in their suitors and husbands, women had the power to direct the moral development of the male citizens of the republic. The influence women had on children, especially on their sons, gave them ultimate responsibility for the future of the new nation.[31]

This constellation of ideas, and the republican rhetoric which made it convincing, appears at great length in the Columbia College commencement oration of 1795. Its title was "Female Influence"; behind the flowery rhetoric lurks a social and political message:

> Let us then figure to ourselves the accomplished woman, surrounded by a sprightly band, from the babe that imbibes the nutritive fluid, to the generous youth just ripening into manhood, and the lovely virgin. . . . Let us contemplate the mother distributing the mental nourishment to the fond smiling circle, by means proportionate to their different powers of reception, watching the gradual openings of their minds, and studying their various turns of temper. . . . Religion, fairest offspring of the skies, smiles auspicious on her endeavours; the Genius of Liberty hovers triumphant over the glorious scene. . . . Yes, ye fair, the reformation of a world is in your power. . . . Reflect on the result of your efforts. Contemplate the rising glory of confederated America. Consider that your exertions can best secure, increase, and perpetuate it. The solidity and stability of the liberties of your country rest with you; since Liberty is never sure, 'till Virtue reigns triumphant. . . . Already may we see the lovely daughters of Columbia asserting the importance and the honour of their sex. It rests with you to make this retreat [from the corruptions of Europe] doubly peaceful, doubly happy, by banishing from it those crimes and corrup-

tions, which have never yet failed of giving rise to tyranny, or anarchy. While you thus keep our country virtuous, you maintain its independence. . . .[32]

Defined this way, the educated woman ceased to threaten the sanctity of marriage; the bluestocking need not be masculine. In this awkward—and in the 1790s still only vaguely expressed—fashion, the traditional womanly virtues were endowed with political purpose. A pivotal political role was assigned to the least political inhabitants of the Republic. Ironically, the same women who were denied political identity were counted on to maintain the republican quality of the new nation. "Let the ladies of a country be educated properly," Rush said, "and they will not only make and administer its laws, but form its manners and character."[33]

When Americans addressed themselves to the matter of the role of women, they found that those who admired bluestockings and those who feared them could agree on one thing: in a world where moral influences were fast dissipating, women as a group seemed to represent moral stability. Few in the early republic demanded, in a sustained way, substantial revisions in women's political or legal status; few spoke to the nascent class of unskilled women workers. But many took pride in the assertion that properly educated republican women would stay in the home and, from that vantage point, would shape the characters of their sons and husbands in the direction of benevolence, self-restraint, and responsible independence. They refuted charges of free love and masculinization; in doing so they created a justification for woman as household goddess so deeply felt that one must be permitted to suspect that many women of their generation were *refusing* to be household goddesses.[34] They began to make the argument for intelligent household management that Catharine Beecher, a generation later, would enshrine in her *Treatise on Domestic Economy* as woman's highest goal. The Daughters of Columbia became, in effect, the Mothers of the Victorians. Whether Judith Sargent Murray, Charles Brockden Brown, or Benjamin Rush would have approved the ultimate results of their work is hard to say.

NOTES

1. *The Gleaner*, III (Boston, 1798), 189.
2. Montesquieu's comment that republics differed from other political systems

by the reliance they placed on virtue is explored in Howard Mumford Jones, *O Strange New World* (New York, 1964), p. 431.

3. August 1792, pp. 121–123.

4. "Thoughts upon Female Education, Accommodated to the Present State of Society, Manners, and Government in the United States of America" (Philadelphia and Boston, 1787). Reprinted in Frederick Rudolph, ed., *Essays on Education in the Early Republic* (Cambridge, Mass., 1865), p. 39.

5. "The greater proportion of young women are trained up by thoughtless parents, in ease and luxury, with no other dependence for their future support than the precarious chance of establishing themselves by marriage: for this purpose (the men best know why) elaborate attention is paid to external attractions and accomplishments, to the neglect of more useful and solid acquirements. . . . [Marriage is the] *sole* method of procuring for themselves an establishment." *New York Magazine,* August 1797, p. 406. For comment on the marriage market, see letter signed "A Matrimonial Republican" in Philadelphia *Lady's Magazine,* July 1792, pp. 64–67; "Legal Prostitution, Or Modern Marriage," Boston *Independent Chronicle,* October 28, 1793. For criticism of fashion, see *American Magazine,* December 1787, p. 39; July 1788, p. 594; *American Museum,* August 1788, p. 119; *Massachusetts Mercury,* August 16, 1793; January 16, 1795.

6. *New York Magazine,* August 1797, p. 406; Philadelphia *Universal Asylum and Columbian Magazine,* July 1791, p. 11.

7. Murray, *Gleaner,* I, 168, 193.

8. Charles Brockden Brown, *Ormond; Or the Secret Witness,* ed. by Ernest Marchand (New York, 1799; reprinted 1937, 1962), p. 19.

9. *Ibid.,* pp. 98–99.

10. "It was obvious to suppose that a woman thus fearless and sagacious had not been inactive at a period like the present, which called forth talents and courage without distinction of sex, and had been particularly distinguished by female enterprise and heroism." *Ibid.,* p. 170.

11. For examples of such lists, see: Murray, *Gleaner,* III, 200–219; John Blair Linn, *The Powers of Genius: A Poem in Three Parts* (Philadelphia, 1802); Philadelphia *Weekly Magazine,* August 4, 11, 1798; *Port Folio,* February 12, 1803; September 27, 1806; Philadelphia *Minerva,* March 14, 1795. For the admiration expressed by Abigail Adams and Mercy Otis Warren for Catharine Macaulay, see Abigail Adams to Isaac Smith, Jr., April 20, 1771; Abigail Adams to Catharine Sawbridge Macaulay, n.d., 1774; Mercy Otis Warren to Abigail Adams, January 28, 1775; in L. H. Butterfield, ed., *Adams Family Correspondence,* I (Cambridge, Mass., 1963), 76–77, 177–179, 181–183. For the circle of English "bluestockings," in the 1780s, see M. G. Jones, *Hannah More* (Cambridge, 1952), pp. 41–76.

12. *Massachusetts Magazine,* II (March 1790), 133; *Universal Asylum* and *Columbian Magazine,* July 1791, p. 9; Thomas Cooper, "Propositions Respecting the Foundation of Civil Government," in *Political Arithmetic* (Philadelphia [?], 1798), p. 27. See also *Boston Weekly Magazine,* May 21, 1803, pp. 121–122; *American Museum,* January 1787, p. 59; Philadelphia *Lady's Magazine,* June 1792.

13. J. A. Neale, "An Essay on the Genius and Education of the Fair Sex," Philadelphia *Minerva,* April 4, March 21, 1795.

14. *Remarks on Education: Illustrating the Close Connection between Virtue and Wisdom* (Philadelphia, 1798), reprinted in Rudolph, *Essays on Education,* p. 211.

Smith did acknowledge that female instruction was important, but commented that concepts of what it should be were so varied that he feared to make any proposals, and despaired of including women in the scheme he was then devising. "It is sufficient, perhaps, for the present, that the improvement of women is marked by a rapid progress and that a prospect opens equal to their most ambitious desires" (p. 217). The other prizewinner, Samuel Knox, proposed to admit girls to the primary schools in his system, but not to the academies or colleges. Knox's essay, "An Essay on the Best System of Liberal Education," may be found in Rudolph, *Essays on Education,* pp. 271–372.

15. Charles E. Cunningham, *Timothy Dwight: 1752–1817: A Biography* (New York, 1942), pp. 154–163.

16. Noah Webster, "Importance of Female Education," in *American Magazine,* May 1788, pp. 368, 369. This essay was part of his pamphlet *On the Education of Youth in America* (Boston, 1790), conveniently reprinted in Rudolph, *Essays on Education,* pp. 41–78. *Weekly Magazine,* April 7, 1798; Murray, *The Gleaner,* I, 70–71.

17. Benjamin Rush, "Thoughts upon Female Education," in Rudolph, *Essays on Education,* pp. 25–40. See also the comments of the Reverend James Sproat, a member of the Board of Visitors, June 10, 1789, in *The Rise and Progress of the Young Ladies' Academy of Philadelphia; Containing an Account of a Number of Public Examinations and Commencements; the Charter and Bye-Laws; Likewise, a Number of Orations delivered by the Young Ladies, and several by the Trustees of Said Institution* (Philadelphia, 1794), p. 24.

18. Benjamin Say, "Address," December 4, 1789, in *Rise and Progress of the Young Ladies' Academy,* p. 33; Benjamin Rush, *Syllabus of Lectures, Containing the Application of the Principles of Natural Philosophy* . . . (Philadelphia, 1787). Rush, of course, was waging his own crusade against the classics as inappropriate in a republic; he argued elsewhere that to omit Latin and Greek would have the beneficial effect of diminishing "the present immense disparity which subsists between the sexes, in the degrees of their education and knowledge." When his contemporaries omitted the classics from the female curriculum it was usually because they thought women's minds were not up to it. Rush, "Observations upon the Study of the Latin and Greek Languages," in *Essays, Literary, Moral and Philosophical* (Philadelphia, 1798), p. 44.

19. Priscilla Mason, "Oration," May 15, 1793, in *Rise and Progress of the Young Ladies' Academy,* pp. 90–95. See also the valedictory oration by Molly Wallace, June 12, 1792, *ibid.,* pp. 73–79.

20. Letter signed M.G., "American Lounger," *Port Folio,* April 7, 1804.

21. Gertrude Meredith to David Meredith, May 3, 1804, Meredith Papers, Historical Society of Pennsylvania; Philadelphia *Evening Fireside,* April 6, 1805.

22. *New-England Palladium,* September 18, 1801; *American Magazine,* February 1788, p. 134; *Lady's Magazine,* January 1793, pp. 68–72. (The "battle at Odiham" refers to a famous bare-knuckle prize fight, one of the earliest major events in the history of boxing, fought in 1788 by Daniel Mendoza and Richard Humphries in Hampshire, England.) Other attacks on female pedantry, which express the fear that intellectual women will be masculine, are found in the *American Magazine,* March 1788, pp. 244–245 ("To be lovely you must be content to be women . . . and leave the masculine virtues, and the profound researches of study to the province of the other sex"); *New-England Palladium,* September 4, 18, December 4,

1801, March 5, 9, 1802; Benjamin Silliman, *Letters of Shahcoolen, a Hindu Philosophy, Residing in Philadelphia; To His Friend, El Hassan, an Inhabitant of Delhi* (Boston, 1802), pp. 23–24, 62; *American Museum*, December 1788, p. 491; *Boston Weekly Magazine*, March 24, 1804, p. 86 ("Warlike women, learned women, and women who are politicians, equally abandon the circle which nature and institutions have traced round their sex; they convert themselves into men").

23. *Extracts from the Journal of Elizabeth Drinker, from 1759 to 1807, A.D.*, ed. by Henry D. Biddle (Philadelphia, 1889), p. 285. The entry is dated April 22, 1796.

24. Mary Wollstonecraft, *A Vindication of the Rights of Woman, With Strictures on Political and Moral Subjects* (New York, 1891), pp. 23, 149–156.

25. *New-England Palladium*, November 24, 27, December 8, 11, 15, 1801; March 2, 5, 9, 1802. Identification of Dwight as author is made by Robert Edson Lee, "Timothy Dwight and the Boston *Palladium*," *New England Quarterly*, XXXV (1962), 229–239.

26. *New-England Palladium*, March 9, 1802.

27. Charles Brockden Brown and Lee R. Edwards, *Alcuin: A Dialogue* (New York, 1971), pp. 44–88.

28. *New-England Palladium*, March 9, 1802.

29. Brown, *Alcuin*, pp. 32–33; St. George Tucker, *Blackstone's Commentaries: With Notes of Reference, to the Constitution and Laws, of the Federal Government of the United States, and of the Commonwealth of Virginia*, II (Philadelphia, 1803), 145, 445; John Adams to James Sullivan, May 26, 1776, in *The Works of John Adams*, ed. by Charles Francis Adams, IX (1856), 375–379; Edward Raymond Turner, "Women's Suffrage in New Jersey: 1790–1807," *Smith College Studies in History*, I (1916), 165–187. Opposition to woman suffrage apparently surfaced after women voted as a bloc in an unsuccessful attempt to influence the outcome of an Essex County election in 1797.

30. *Gleaner*, I, 161, 12, 29, 191, 190.

31. Rush, "Thoughts upon Female Education," in Rudolph, *Essays on Education*, p. 28 (my italics); "On Female Education," *Port Folio*, May 1809, p. 388; *Boston Weekly Magazine*, October 29, 1803.

32. *New York Magazine*, May 1795, pp. 301–305.

33. Rush, "Thoughts upon Female Education," in Rudolph, *Essays on Education*, p. 36.

34. See, for example, *Boston Weekly Magazine*, December 18, 1802; *Weekly Magazine*, March 3, 1798; *Port Folio*, February 12, 1803, March 3, 1804, April 20, 1805.

7 ୬ Fruits of Passion: The Dynamics of Interracial Sex

Winthrop D. Jordan

When Europeans met Africans in America the result was slavery, revolt, the sociability of daily life, and, inevitably, sexual union. The blending of black and white began almost with the first contact of the two peoples and has far outlasted the institution of chattel slavery.

The tensions which arose may be viewed in several interrelated ways. The Englishmen who came to America brought with them not merely a prevalent social mood but also certain specific sexual standards and certain more or less definite ideas about African sexuality. Many of them came with more or less explicit intentions as to the proper character of the communities they wished to establish in the wilderness. These intentions were not always, or perhaps ever, fully realized; they were deflected—again sometimes more, sometimes less— by conditions in the New World. One of the most important deflectors was the development of a racial slavery which itself became one of the New World's "conditions," though of course the character of this condition was not everywhere the same. The Negro was encountered in very different contexts in the various English colonies. Particularly important in making for differences in the Englishman's reaction to interracial sex was the demographic pattern which developed during the first quarter of the eighteenth century; variations in the numbers of the

Derived from *White Over Black: American Attitudes Toward the Negro, 1550–1812* by Winthrop D. Jordan. Copyright © 1968 The University of North Carolina Press. Published by the Institute of Early American History and Culture, Williamsburg. Reprinted by permission of the publisher.

races and of the sexes in the English colonies may be shown to be almost determinative in shaping certain attitudes.

REGIONAL STYLES IN
RACIAL INTERMIXTURE

Miscegenation was extensive in all the English colonies, a fact made evident to contemporaries by the presence of large numbers of mulattoes. It is impossible to ascertain how much intermixture there actually was, though it seems likely there was more during the eighteenth century than at any time since. Although miscegenation was probably most common among the lower orders, white men of every social rank slept with black women. Almost everyone who wrote anything about America commented upon this fact of life.

No one thought intermixture was a good thing. Rather, English colonials were caught in the push and pull of an irreconcilable conflict between desire and aversion for interracial sexual union. The prerequisite for this conflict is so obvious as to be too easily overlooked: desire and aversion rested on the bedrock fact that white men perceived Negroes as being *both alike and different* from themselves. Without perception of similarity, no desire and no widespread gratification was possible. Without perception of difference, on the other hand, no aversion to miscegenation nor tension concerning it could have arisen. Without perception of difference, of course, the term *miscegenation* had no meaning. Given these simultaneous feelings of desire and aversion, it seems probable that of the two the latter is more demanding of explanation. The sexual drive of human beings has always, in the long run, overridden even the strongest sense of difference between two groups of human beings and, in some individuals, has even overridden the far stronger sense which men have of the difference between themselves and animals. What demands explanation, in short, is why there was *any* aversion among the white colonists to sexual union with blacks.

In most colonies virtually all the offspring of interracial unions were illegitimate, though legally sanctified interracial marriage did occur, especially though not exclusively in New England. Miscegenation in colonial America, as has been true since, typically involved fornication between white men and black women, though the inverse combination was common, far more so than is generally supposed. Probably a majority of interracial marriages in New England involved Negro men and white women of "the meaner sort." In the plantation colonies, although there were occasional instances of white women marrying black men, legitimization of this relationship was unusual.

Public feeling against miscegenation was strong enough to force itself over the hurdles of the legislative process into the statute books of many English continental colonies. As early as the 1660's the Maryland and Virginia assemblies had begun to lash out at miscegenation in language dripping with distaste and indignation. By the turn of the century it was clear in many continental colonies that the English settlers felt genuine revulsion for interracial sexual union, at least in principle. Two northern and all the plantation colonies legally prohibited miscegenation. Though there were exceptions, the weight of community opinion was set against the sexual union of white and black, as the long-standing statutory prohibitions indicated. In significant contrast, none of the British West Indian assemblies prohibited extramarital miscegenation.

In the West Indian colonies especially, and less markedly in South Carolina, the pattern of miscegenation was far more inflexible than in the other English settlements. White women in the islands did not sleep with black men, let alone marry them. Nor did white men actually marry Negroes or mulattoes. Yet white men commonly, almost customarily, took Negro women to bed with little pretense at concealing the fact. Edward Long of Jamaica described the situation: "He who should presume to shew any displeasure against such a thing as simple fornication, would for his pains be accounted a simple blockhead; since not one in twenty can be persuaded, that there is either sin; or shame in cohabiting with his slave." Negro concubinage was an integral part of island life, tightly interwoven into the social fabric.

It is scarcely necessary to resort to speculation about the influence of tropical climate in order to explain this situation, for life in the islands was in large degree shaped by the enormous disproportion of Negroes to white settlers and characterized by brutal nakedness of planter domination over the slaves. In the West Indian islands and to less extent South Carolina, racial slavery consisted of unsheathed dominion by relatively small numbers of white men over enormous numbers of Negroes, and it was in these colonies that Negro men were most stringently barred from sexual relations with white women. Sexually, as well as in every other way, Negroes were utterly subordinated. White men extended their dominion over their Negroes to the bed, where the sex act itself served as ritualistic re-enactment of the daily pattern of social dominance.

Congruent to these regional differences in slavery and interracial relationships were the bedrock demographic facts which so powerfully influenced, perhaps even determined, the kind of society which emerged in each colony. With blacks overwhelmingly outnumbering whites in the various islands (ten to one in Jamaica), and with whites outnumbering Negroes everywhere on the continent except South Carolina, it was inevitable that radically dissimilar social styles should have developed in the two areas. As a French traveler perceptively characterized this dissimilarity in 1777: "In the colonies of the Antilles, most of the colonists are people who have left their homeland with the intention of rebuilding their fortunes. Far from settling in the islands, they look upon them merely as a land of exile, never as a place where they plan to live, prosper, and die. On the other hand, the Anglo-American colonists are permanent, born in the country and attached to it; they have no motherland save the one they live in; and, although London formerly was so considered, they have clearly proved that they held it in less esteem than they did the prosperity, tranquility, and freedom of their own country." The West Indian planters were lost not so much in the Caribbean as in a sea of blacks. They found it impossible to re-create English culture as they had known it. They were corrupted by living in a police state, though not themselves the objects of its discipline. The business of the islands was business, the production of agricultural staples; the islands were not where one really lived, but where one made one's money. By contrast, the American colonists on the continent maintained their hold upon their English background, modifying it less for accommodating slavery than for winning the new land. Unlike the West Indian planters, they felt no need to be constantly running back to England to reassure themselves that they belonged to civilization. Because they were conscious of having attained a large measure of success in transplanting their own society, they vehemently rejected any trespass upon it by a people so alien as the Negroes. The islanders could hardly resent trespass on something which they did not have.

It was precisely this difference which made the Negro seem so much more alien on the continent than on the islands, and miscegenation accordingly less common. For a West Indian to have declared, with Judge Samuel Sewall of Boston, that Negroes "cannot mix with us and become members of society, ... never embody with us and grow up into orderly Families, to the Peopling of the Land" would have been false by reason of the extensive blending of the races in the islands and meaningless because the "peopling" of the islands had already been accomplished—by Africans. Americans on the continent stood poised for a destiny of conquering a vast wilderness, while Englishmen in the little crowded islands looked forward down a precipice of slave rebellion, or at best a slippery slope of peaceful but inevitable defeat. Certainly the bustling communities on the continent had good reason to feel that they had successfully established a beachhead of English civilization in America. They possessed optimism, self-confidence, and a well-defined sense of Englishness, a sense which came automatically to bear when they were confronted with peoples who seemed appreciably dissimilar. When large numbers of very dissimilar people threatened the identity of the continental colonists, their response was rejection of those people in the mind and a tendency to perceive them as being. more dissimilar than ever. For the sense of dissimilarity fed on itself: once the cycle was started, the differences between white Americans and "others," which first sparked anxiety and rejection, loomed progressively larger and generated further anxiety and rejection.

Certainly many Americans on the continent became convinced that the American people were not intended to be Negroes. Benjamin Franklin, who was as fully attuned to American destiny as anyone, nervously expressed the idea that the continent should belong to "White People." "I could wish their Numbers were increased. Why increase the Sons of Africa, by Planting them in America, where we have so fair an Opportunity, by excluding all Blacks and Tawneys, of increasing the lovely White and Red? But perhaps I am partial to the Complexion of my Country," he concluded with his usual self-conscious good sense, "for such Kind of Partiality is natural to Mankind." Franklin was expressing an important feeling, one which a famous Virginian, William Byrd, expressed more directly: "They import so many Negros hither, that I fear this Colony will some time or other be confirmed by the Name of New Guinea."

It was more than a matter of colonial Americans not wanting to give their country over to Africans. Miscegenation probably did not seem so much a matter of long-term discoloration as an immediate failure to live up to immemorial standards. Here again, the intentions which drove English overseas expansion were of crucial importance. The colonists' conviction that they must sustain their civilized condition wherever they went rendered miscegenation a negation of the underlying plan of settlement in America. Simply because most blacks were chattel slaves, racial amalgamation was stamped as irredeemably illicit; it was irretrievably associated with loss of control over the baser passions, with weakening of traditional family ties, and with breakdown of proper social ordering. Judge Sewall's "orderly Families" were rendered a mockery by fathers taking slave wenches to bed.

At the same time it would be a mistake to suppose that the *status* of Negroes in itself aroused white aversion to intermixture; the physical difference was of crucial importance. Without that difference there could never have developed well-formulated conceptions about sexual relations between Africans and Europeans in America. Although perhaps there was some feeling that the laws which prevented racial intermingling helped prevent blacks, as one astute foreign observer put it, "from forming too great opinions of themselves," the underlying reason for their passage was that these mixtures were "disagreeable" to white men.

MASCULINE AND FEMININE MODES IN CAROLINA AND AMERICA

On the face of things it seems paradoxical that the one region on the continent which had become demographically most like a new Guinea should have been the one in which white men seemed least anxious about interracial sexual activity. While permanent unions between persons of the two races normally were quiet or secretive affairs elsewhere on the continent, in South Carolina and particularly in Charleston they were not. It was the only city worthy of the name in the plantation colonies. It was an elegant, gay, extravagant city, where men took advantage of certain of their opportunities in more overt, more relaxed, and probably more enterprising fashion than in the colonies to the north. They possessed an abundance of black women. The result may best be described by a visiting merchant from Jamaica (where the atmosphere surrounding interracial sex was so utterly different from New England), who wrote from Charleston in 1773: "I know of but one Gentleman who professedly keeps a Mulatto Mistress and he is very much pointed at: There are swarms of Negroes about the Town and many Mulattoes, and by the Dress of the Girls, who mostly imitate their Mistresses, I have no doubt of their Conversations with the whites, but they are carried on with more privacy than in our W. India Islands." "As I travell'd further North," the Jamaican visitor continued concerning his trip from Charleston to North Carolina, "there were fewer Negroes about the Houses, and these taken less notice of, and before I finish'd my Journey North, I found an empty House, the late Tenant of which had been oblig'd by the Church Wardens to decamp on Account of his having kept a Black Woman. Dont suppose Fornication is out of Fashion here," he added reassuringly about North Carolina, "more than in other Places, No! the difference only is, that the White Girls monopolize it."

Here was an important regional difference in social "fashion." Charleston was the only English city on the continent where it was at all possible to jest publicly concerning miscegenation. In 1736 the

South-Carolina Gazette published some frank advice to the bachelors and widowers of Charleston: "that if they are in a Strait for Women, to wait for the next Shipping from the Coast of Guinny. Those African Ladies are of a strong, robust Constitution: not easily jaded out, able to serve them by Night as well as Day. When they are Sick, they are not costly, when dead, their funeral Charges are but . . . an old Matt, one Bottle Rum, and a lb. Sugar [.] The cheapness of a Commo-di-ty becomes more taking when it fully Answers the end, or T____l." Next week another writer replied in obvious determination not to be out-done in indelicacy of expression: "In my Opinion, our Country-Women are full as capable for Service either night or day as any African Ladies whatsoever. . . . In all Companies wheresoever I have been, my Country-Women have always the praise for their Activity of Hipps and humoring a Jest to the Life in what Posture soever their Partners may fancy, which makes me still hope that they'll have the Preference before the black Ladies in the Esteem of the Widowers and Batchelors at C____town." Next week the *Gazette* published still another verse.

If these contributions to the *South-Carolina Gazette* were a trifle raw by the standards of a modern family newspaper, they reflected more than eighteenth-century literary frankness about sex. Newspapers elsewhere on the continent did not publish similar discussions of interracial sex, though everywhere (including Boston) they published some none-too-delicate pieces concerning sexual matters. Only in Charleston was it possible to debate publicly, "Is sex with Negroes right?"

This distinctiveness was owing partly to South Carolina's distinctive economic and social history. The preponderance of slaves in the low country tended to give white men a queasy sense that perhaps they were marooned, a feeling that their society was irrevocably committed to Negro slavery and that somehow their mere Englishness had lost its savor in the shuffle for plantation prosperity. The effect of this uneasi-ness was to make men feel like both fleeing and embracing Negro slavery all at once: hence the common annual flights from the planta-tions to Charleston and from South Carolina to northern cities and England, the negation of cherished traditional liberties in the slave codes, the importation of more and more slaves, the continual efforts to encourage white immigration, and not least, the simultaneous em-bracing of Negro women and rejection of the ensuing offspring. Caught as they were in powerful crosscurrents, it is no wonder that white men in Charleston joked nervously about their sexual abandon.

For white women the situation was different, and here again the Charleston area seems to have been characterized by attitudes somewhere midway between those of the West Indies and further north. In the islands, where English settlers were most thoroughly committed to a Negro slave society and where strenuous attempts to attract more white settlers had been unavailing, white women were, quite literally, the repositories of white civilization. White men tended to place them protectively upon a pedestal and then run off to gratify their passions elsewhere. For their part white women, though they might propagate children, inevitably held themselves aloof from the world of lust and passion, a world which reeked of infidelity and Negro slaves. Under no circumstances would they have attempted, any more than they would have been allowed, to clamber down from their pedestal to seek pleasures of their own across the racial line. In fact white women in the West Indies tended to adhere rigidly to the double sexual standard which characterized English sexual mores and to refrain more than in the continental colonies from infidelity with white men. The oppressive presence of slavery itself tended to inhibit the white woman's capacity for emotional, sexual, and intellectual commitment. She served principally an ornamentive function, for everything resembling work was done by Negro slaves. Visitors to the islands were almost universally agreed in describing her life as one of indolence and lassitude, though some were impressed by a formal, superficial gaiety. Her choices were to withdraw from the world or to create an unreal one of her own.

The white women of the Charleston area were less tightly hemmed in. Nevertheless, they rarely if ever established liaisons with Negro men, as happened in the South Carolina back country. Some visitors to the city were struck by their desiccated formality, which seems now to betray the strains imposed by the prevailing pattern of miscegenation. One traveler from Philadelphia described his unfavorable impressions in Charleston by first lamenting that the "superabundance of Negroes" had "destroyed the activity of whites," who "stand with their hands in their pockets, overlooking their negroes." In his letter of 1809 (known only as published much later in the century with some Victorian censorship at the end), he went on to say,

> These, however, are not one tenth of the curses slavery has brought on the Southern States. Nothing has surprised me more than the cold, melancholy reserve of the females, of the best families, in South Carolina and Georgia. Old and young, single and married, all have that dull frigid insipidity, and reserve, which is attributed to solitary old maids. Even in their own houses they scarce utter anything to a stranger but yes or no, and one is perpetually puzzled to know whether it proceeds from awkwardness or dislike. Those who have been at some of their Balls [in Charleston] say that the ladies hardly even speak or smile, but dance with as much gravity, as if they were performing some ceremony of devotion. On the contrary,

the negro wenches are all sprightliness and gayety; and if report be not a defamer—

The dissipation of the white gentleman was as much a tragedy for his white lady as for him. A biracial environment warped her affective life in two directions at once, for she was made to feel that sensual involvement with the opposite sex burned bright and hot with unquenchable passion and at the same time that any such involvement was utterly repulsive.

If women were particularly affected by the situation in South Carolina, white persons of both sexes in *all* the English colonies were affected in a more general way by the tensions involved in miscegenation. Though these tensions operated in white men rather differently than in white women, it seems almost self-evident that the emergent attitudes toward Negroes possessed a unity which transcended differences between the two sexes. Put another way, out of a pattern of interracial sexual relationships which normally placed white men and white women in very different roles, there arose a common core of belief and mythology concerning the Negro which belonged to neither sex but to white American culture as a whole. The emergence of common beliefs out of divergent experiences was of course principally a function of the homogenizing effect of culture upon individual experience, but it is important to bear in mind that the *functional* significance of beliefs about the Negro may have been very different for white women than for white men even when the beliefs themselves were identical. Since the English and colonial American cultures were dominated by males, however, sexually-oriented beliefs about the Negro in America deprived principally from the psychological needs of men and were to a considerable extent shaped by specifically masculine modes of thought and behavior. This is not to say the American attitudes toward the Negro were *male* attitudes but merely that when one talks about *American* attitudes toward anything (the frontier, the city, money, freedom, the Negro) one is using a shorthand for attitudes common to both sexes but predominantly male in genesis and tone.

NEGRO SEXUALITY
AND SLAVE INSURRECTION

As for these ideas or beliefs about the Negro, many seem startlingly modern. Least surprising, perhaps, was the common assumption that black women were especially passionate, an idea which found literary or at least literate expression especially in the *South-Carolina Gazette* and in West Indian books. The Negro woman was the sunkissed embodiment of ardency:

> *Next comes a warmer race, from sable sprung,*
> *To love each thought, . . . to lust each nerve is strung;*
>
> · · ·
>
> *These sooty dames, well vers'd in Venus's school,*
> *Make love an art, and boast they kiss by rule.*

If such amiable assessments found their way into public print, one can imagine what tavern bantering must have been like.

Plainly white men were doing more than reporting pleasant facts. For by calling the Negro woman passionate they were offering the best possible justification for their own passions. Not only did the black woman's warmth constitute a logical explanation for the white man's infidelity, but, much more important, it helped shift responsibility from himself to her. If she was *that* lascivious—well, a man could scarcely be blamed for succumbing against overwhelming odds.

Attitudes toward the Negro male were more complex and potentially far more explosive. The notion that black men were particularly virile, promiscuous, and lusty was of course not new in the eighteenth century, but the English colonists in America showed signs of adding a half-conscious and revealingly specific corollary: they sometimes suggested that black men lusted after white women. There was probably some objective basis for the charge, since sexual intercourse with a white woman must in part have been for black men an act of retribution against the white man. For different reasons there was also good basis for the common feeling that only the most depraved white woman would consent to sleep with a Negro, since white women of the lowest class had the least to lose in flouting the maxims of society and the most reason to hate them. No matter how firmly based in fact, however, the image of the sexually aggressive Negro was rooted even more firmly in deep strata of irrationality. For it is apparent that white men projected their own desires onto Negroes: their own passion for black women was not fully acceptable to society or the self and hence not readily admissible. Sexual desires could be effectively denied and the accompanying anxiety and guilt in some measure eased, however, by imputing them to others. It is not we, but others, who are guilty. It is not we who lust, but they. Not only this, but white men anxious over their own sexual inadequacy were touched by a racking fear and jealousy. Perhaps the Negro better performed his nocturnal offices than the white man. Perhaps, indeed, the white man's woman really wanted the Negro more than she wanted him.

Significantly, these tensions tended to bubble to the surface especially at times of interracial crisis when the colonists' control over their Negroes appeared in jeopardy. During many scares over slave conspiracies, for instance, reports circulated that the Negroes had plotted killing all white persons except the young women, whom they "intended to reserve for themselves." In fact these charges were ill-founded at best, for there is no evidence that any Negroes in revolt ever seized any white women for their "own use," even though rebellious slaves certainly had opportunity to do so during the successful insurrections in the West Indies and also at Stono in South Carolina.

From these indications it seems more than likely that fears of Negro sexual aggression during periods of alarm over insurrection did not represent direct response to actual overt threat, but rather a complex of reactions in the white man. Any group faced with a real threat of serious proportions is inclined to sense, even on a conscious level, a sexual element in the opponents' aggressiveness—as many have identified Communism with free love. Any black insurrection, furthermore, threatened the white man's dominance, including his valuable sexual dominance, and hence the awful prospect of being overthrown was bound to assume a sexual cast. And finally, white men anxious and guilty over their own sexual aggressiveness were quick to impute it to others, especially at a time of interracial crisis. One has only to imagine the emotions flooding through some planter who had been more or less regularly sleeping with some of his slave wenches when he suddenly learned of a conspiracy among their male counterparts; it was virtually inevitable that his thoughts turn in a torrent of guilt to the "safety" of his wife.

DISMEMBERMENT, PHYSIOLOGY, AND SEXUAL PERCEPTIONS

The white man's fears of Negro sexual aggression were equally apparent in the use of castration as a punishment in the colonies. This weapon of desperation was not employed by angry mobs in the manner which became familiar after Emancipation. Castration was dignified by specific legislative sanction as a lawful punishment in Antigua, the Carolinas, Bermuda, Virginia, Pennsylvania, and New Jersey. It was sometimes prescribed for such offenses as striking a white person or running away: employed in this way, castration was a not irrational method of slave control, closely akin to the Jamaica law which authorized severing one foot of a runaway. Yet castration was not simply another of the many brands of hideous cruelty which graced the colonial criminal codes: it was reserved for Negroes and occasionally Indians. In some colonies, laws authorizing castration were worded so as to apply to all blacks whether free or slave. As a legal punishment castration was a peculiarly American experiment, for there was no basis for it in English law. Indeed officials in England were shocked and outraged at the idea, calling castration "inhumane and contrary to all Christian Laws," "a punishment never inflicted by any Law [in any of] H.M. Dominions." Some Americans thought the practice necessary to restrain a lecherous and barbarous people; Englishmen thought the barbarity was on the other side.

Castration of blacks clearly indicated a need in white men to persuade themselves that they were really masters and in all ways masterful, and it illustrated dramatically the ease with which white men slipped over into treating their Negroes like their bulls and stallions whose "spirit" could be subdued by emasculation. In some colonies, moreover, the specifically sexual aspect of castration was so obvious as to underline how much of the white man's insecurity about blacks was fundamentally sexual. The Pennsylvania and New Jersey laws passed early in the eighteenth century (and quickly disallowed by authorities in England) prescribed castration of Negroes as punishment for one offense only, attempted rape of a white woman. Still more strikingly, Virginia's provision for castration of Negroes, which had been on the books for many years and permitted castration for a variety of serious offenses, was repealed in 1769 for humanitarian reasons, but the repealing statute specifically declared that it might still be inflicted for one particular offense—rape or attempted rape of a white woman.

The concept of the Negro's aggressive sexuality was reinforced by what was thought to be an anatomical peculiarity of the Negro male. He was said to possess an especially large penis. The idea was considerably older even than the exegesis on Ham's offense against his father offered by West African travelers. Indeed the idea without question predated the settlement of America and possibly even the Portuguese explorations of the West African coast. Several fifteenth-century map makers decorated parts of Africa with little naked figures which gave the idea graphic expression, and in due course, in the seventeenth century, English accounts of West Africa were carefully noting the "extraordinary greatness" of the Negroes' "members." By the final quarter of the eighteenth century the idea that the Negro's penis was larger than the white man's had become something of a commonplace in European scientific circles. Whether it was a commonplace in popular circles in the English colonies is more difficult to ascertain, since it was scarcely the sort of assertion likely to find its way into print even if a great many people talked about it. Certainly the idea was not unheard of, for as an officer in the First Pennsylvania Regiment commented pointedly in his journal about the Negro boys waiting on Virginia dinner tables: "I am surprized this does not hurt the feelings of this fair Sex to see these young boys of about Fourteen and Fifteen years Old to Attend them. these whole nakedness Expos'd and I can Assure you It would Surprize a person to see these d___d black boys how well they are hung."

Partly because their relationships with blacks were structured by daily contact, Negroes seemed more highly sexed to the colonists than did the American Indians. The magnitude of the differentiation they made between the two aboriginal peoples on this score was so great as to suggest that it reflected not merely the immediate circumstances in which the colonists found themselves but the entirety of English historical experience since the beginning of expansion overseas. Far from finding Indians lusty and lascivious, they discovered them to be notably deficient in ardor and virility. (Eventually and almost inevitably a European commentator announced that the Indian's penis was smaller than the European's.) And the colonists developed no image of the Indian as a potential rapist: their descriptions of Indian attacks did not include the Indians "reserving the young women for themselves." In fact the entire interracial sexual complex did not pertain to the Indian. In the more settled portions of the colonies, Englishmen did not normally take Indian women to bed, but neither did an aura of tension pervade the sexual union of red and white. Of the various laws which penalized illicit miscegenation, none applied to Indians, and only North Carolina's (and Virginia's for a very brief period) prohibited intermarriage. On the contrary, several colonists were willing to allow, even advocate, intermarriage with the Indians—an unheard of proposition concerning Negroes.

MULATTO OFFSPRING IN A
BIRACIAL SOCIETY

Inevitably, miscegenation resulted in children. Somehow they had to be accommodated to a system of racial slavery whose strictest logic their existence violated. How were mulattoes to be treated? Were they to be free or slave, acknowledged or denied, white or black? The ways in which American colonials answered these questions are profoundly revealing. The question arose, of course, in the cultural matrix of purpose, accomplishment, self-conception, and social circumstances of settlement in the New World. Inevitably the fruits of interracial sex grew differently in different contexts of self-identification.

As far as the continental colonies were concerned, it is easy to detect a pattern which has since become so familiar to Americans that they rarely pause to think about it or to question its logic and inevitability. The word *mulatto* is not frequently used in the United States. For social purposes a mulatto is termed a "Negro." Americans lump together both socially and legally all persons with perceptible admixture of African ancestry, thus making social definition without regard to genetic logic; white blood becomes socially advantageous only in overwhelming proportion. This peculiar bifurcation seems to have existed almost from the beginning of English contact with Africans. The word *mulatto,* borrowed from the Spanish, was in English usage from about 1600 and was probably first used in Virginia records in 1666. Thereafter laws dealing with Negro slaves began to add "and mulattoes," presumably to make clear that mixed blood did not confer exemption from slavery. From the first, every English continental colony lumped mulattoes with Negroes in their slave codes and in statutes governing the conduct of free Negroes: the law was clear that mulattoes and Negroes were not to be distinguished for different treatment.

In addition to the statutory homogenization of all persons of African ancestry, mulattoes do not seem to have been accorded higher status than Negroes in actual practice. Whatever the case in other countries or in later centuries, mulattoes seem generally to have been treated no better than unmixed Africans. The diaries, letters, travel accounts, and newspapers of the period do not indicate any pronounced tendency to distinguish mulattoes from Negroes, any feeling that their status was higher and demanded different treatment. These sources give no indication, for instance, that mulattoes were preferred as house servants or concubines. There was a relatively high proportion of mulattoes among manumitted slaves, but probably this was owing to the desire of some masters to liberate their own offspring.

The existence of a rigid barrier between whites and those of African ancestry necessarily required a means by which the barrier could on occasion be passed. Some accommodation had to be made for those persons with so little African blood that they appeared to be white, for one simply could not go around calling apparently white persons Negroes. Once the stain was washed out visibly it was useless as a means of identification. Thus there developed the silent mechanism of "passing." Such a device would have been unnecessary if those of mixed ancestry and appearance had been regarded as midway between white and black. It was the existence of a broad chasm which necessitated the sudden leap which passing represented.

It is possible to find direct evidence of successful passing, but unfortunately there is no way of telling how *many* blacks were effectively transformed into whites. Passing was difficult but not impossible, and it stood as a veiled, unrecognized, and ironic monument to the American ideal of a society open to all comers. But the problem of evidence is insurmountable. The success of the passing mechanism depended upon its operating in silence. Passing was a conspiracy of silence not only for the individual but for a biracial society which had drawn a rigid color line based on visibility. Unless a white man was a white man, the gates were open to endless slander and confusion.

That the existence of such a line in the continental colonies was not predominantly the effect of the English cultural heritage is suggested by even a glance at the English colonies in the Caribbean. The social accommodation of mixed offspring in the islands followed a very different pattern from that on the continent. It was regarded as improper, for example, to work mulattoes in the fields—a fundamental distinction. One observer wrote that mulatto slaves "fetch a lower price than blacks, unless they are tradesmen, because the purchasers cannot employ them in the druggeries to which negroes are put too; the colored [i.e. mulatto] men, are therefore mostly brought up to trades or employed as house slaves, and the women of this description are generally prostitutes." Though the English in the Caribbean thought of their society in terms of white, colored, and black, they employed a complicated battery of names to distinguish persons of various racial mixtures. This terminology was borrowed from the neighboring Spanish, but words are never acquired unless they fulfill a need. While the English settlers on the continent borrowed one Spanish word to describe all mixtures of black and white, the islanders borrowed at least four—*mulatto, sambo, quadroon,* and *mestize*—to describe differing degrees of intermixture.

The connection between the status of mulattoes and the prevailing pattern of miscegenation is obvious. Mulattoes in the West Indies were products of accepted practice, something they assuredly were not in the continental colonies. In the one area, they were the fruits of a desire which society tolerated and almost institutionalized; in the other, they represented an illicit passion which public morality unhesitatingly condemned. On the continent, unlike the West Indies, mulattoes represented a practice about which men could only feel guilty.

The colonist on the American continent, therefore, remained firm in his categorization of mixed-bloods as belonging to the lower caste. It was an unconscious decision dictated perhaps in large part by the weight of Negroes on his community, heavy enough to be a burden, yet not so heavy as to make him abandon all hope of maintaining his own identity, physically and culturally. Interracial propagation was a constant reproach that he was failing to be true to himself. Sexual intimacy strikingly symbolized a union he wished to avoid. If he could not restrain his sexual nature, he could at least reject its fruits and thus solace himself that he had done no harm. Perhaps he sensed as well that continued racial intermixture would eventually undermine the logic of the racial slavery upon which his society was based. For the separation of slaves from free men depended on a clear demarcation of the races, and the presence of mulattoes blurred this essential distinction. Accordingly he made every effort to nullify the effects of racial intermixture. By classifying the mulatto as a Negro he was in effect denying that intermixture had occurred at all.

♀ Suggested Readings for Part I

Akers, Charles. *Abigail Adams*. Boston: Little, Brown & Co., 1979.

Benson, Mary Sumner. *Women in Eighteenth Century America*. New York: Columbia University Press, 1935.

Block, Ruth H. "American Feminine Ideals in Transition: The Rise of the Moral Mother, 1785–1815." *Feminist Studies* 4 (1978): 101–26.

Berlin, Ira. "The Revolution in Black Life." In Alfred F. Young, ed., *The American Revolution*, edited by Alfred F. Young. DeKalb: Northern Illinois University Press, 1976.

Cott, Nancy. "Eighteenth Century Family and Social Life Revealed in Massachusetts Divorce Records." *Journal of Social History* 10 (1976): 20–43.

Cowing, Cedric B. " Sex and Preaching in the Great Awakening." *American Quarterly* 30 (1968): 624–44.

Demos, John. "Underlying Themes in the Witchcraft of Seventeenth Century New England." *American Historical Review* 75 (1970): 1311–1326.

Gladwin, Lee A. "Tobacco and Sex: Some Factors Affecting Non-Marital Sexual Behavior in Colonial Virginia." *Journal of Social History* 12 (1978): 57–75.

Greven, Philip J. *Four Generations: Population, Land and Family in Colonial Andover, Massachusetts*. Ithaca: Cornell University Press, 1970.

Kerber, Linda. *Women of the Republic*. Chapel Hill: University of North Carolina Press, 1980.

_____. "The Republican Mother: Women and the Enlightenment—An American Perspective." *American Quarterly* 28 (1976): 187–205.

Keyssan, Alexander. "Widowhood in Eighteenth-Century Massachusetts: A Problem in the History of the Family." *Perspectives in American History* 8 (1974): 83–119.

Kulikoff, Alan. "The Beginnings of the Afro-American Family in Maryland." In *Law, Society and Politics in Early Maryland*, edited by A.C. Land, L.G. Carr, and E.G. Papenfuse. Baltimore: The Johns Hopkins University Press, 1977.

Lockridge, Kenneth A. *Literacy in Colonial New England*. New York: W.W. Norton & Co., 1974.

Masson, Margaret W. "The Typology of the Female Model for the Regenerate: Puritan Preaching, 1690–1730." *Signs* 2 (1976): 304–315.

Meehan, Thomas R. " 'Not Made Out of Levity': Evolution of Divorce in Early Pennsylvania." *Pennsylvania Magazine of History and Biography* 42 (1968): 441–464.

Mills, Gary B. "Coincoin: An Eighteenth Century 'Liberated' Woman." *Journal of Southern History* 42 (1976): 205–222.

Morgan, Edmund S. *The Puritan Family*. Boston: Boston Public Library, 1944.

_____. "The Puritans and Sex." *New England Quarterly* 15 (1942): 591–607.

Mullin, Gerald W. *Flight and Rebellion: Slave Resistance in Eighteenth Century Virginia*. New York: Oxford University Press, 1972.

Newman, Debra L. "Black Women in the Era of the American Revolution in Pennsylvania." *Journal of Negro History* 66 (1976): 276–89.

Norton, Mary Beth. *Liberty's Daughters: The Revolutionary Experiences of American Women, 1750-1800.* Boston: Little, Brown & Co., 1980.

———. "Eighteenth Century Women in Peace and War: The Case of the Loyalists." *William and Mary Quarterly* 33 (1976): 386-409.

Scholten, Catherine. " 'On the Importance of the Obstetrik Art': Changing Customs of Childbirth in America, 1760-1825." *William and Mary Quarterly* 34 (1977): 426-45.

Smith, Daniel Scott. "Parental Power and Marriage Patterns: An Analysis of Historical Trends in Hingham, Massachusetts." *Journal of Marriage and the Family* 35 (1973): 424-26.

———, and Hindus, Michael S. "Premarital Pregnancy in America, 1640-1971: An Overview and Interpretation." *Journal of Interdisciplinary History* 5 (1975): 535-70.

Spruill, Julia Cherry. *Women's Life and Work in the Southern Colonies.* Chapel Hill: University of North Carolina Press, 1938.

Stone, Lawrence. *The Family, Sex and Marriage in England, 1500-1800.* New York: Harper & Row, 1977.

Thompson, Roger. *Women in Stuart England and America.* London: Routledge and Kegan Paul, 1974.

Ulrich, Laurel Thatcher. "Virtuous Women Found: New England Ministerial Literature, 1668-1735." *American Quarterly* 28 (1976): 20-40.

Wells, Robert V. "Family Size and Fertility Control in Eighteenth Century America." *Population Studies* 25 (1971): 73-82.

———. "Quaker Marriage Patterns in Colonial Perspective." *William and Mary Quarterly* 29 (1972): 415-42.

2 &Victorian Images

Nineteenth-century Americans were haunted by the prospect that unprecedented change in the nation's economy would bring social chaos. In the years following 1820, after several decades of relative stability, the American economy entered a period of sustained and extremely rapid growth that continued to the end of the nineteenth century. Accompanying this growth was a structural change that featured increasing economic diversification and a gradual shift in the nation's labor force from agriculture to manufacturing and other non-agricultural pursuits.

Although the birth rate continued to decline from the high level of the colonial period, the population roughly doubled every generation during the century. As the population grew, its makeup also changed. Massive waves of immigration brought new ethnic groups into the country. Geographic and social mobility—downward as well as upward—touched almost everyone. Local studies indicate that nearly three-quarters of the population—in the North and South, in the emerging cities of the Northeast, and in the restless rural counties of the West—changed their residence each decade. As a consequence, David Donald has written, "social atomization affected every segment of society," and it seemed to many Americans that "all the recognized values of orderly civilization were gradually being eroded."

Rapid industrialization and increased geographic mobility in the nineteenth century had special implications for American women because these changes reinforced the social distinctions that had become manifest in the post-Revolutionary period. In the context of extreme competitiveness and dizzying social change, the Victorian home lost many of its earlier functions and came to serve as a haven of tranquillity and order. As the size of American families decreased, the roles of husband and wife became more clearly differentiated than ever before. In the middle class especially, men participated in the productive economy while women ruled the home and served as the custodians of civility and culture. The intimacy of colonial marriage was rent, and a gulf that at times seemed unbridgeable was created between husbands and wives.

Along with the heightened differentiation of male and female spheres of influence, the life styles of middle-class women became increasingly distinct from those of their lower-class sisters. Gerda Lerner focuses upon the ways in which social and economic change in the early nineteenth century affected the status of women of different classes in "The Lady and the Mill Girl." Medicine, law, business, and science—all areas in which women had played at least modest roles in the colonial period—became increasingly professional. Consequently, they were closed to middle-class women, who were expected to conform to the Victorian model of true womanhood—the gracious lady. At the same time, lower-class women were being forced out of their homes and into the expanding factory system, creating a second social type—the mill girl. "In the urbanized and industrialized Northeast the life experience of middle-class women was different in almost every respect from that of lower-class women."

The Victorian idealization of womanhood continued an earlier trend, the consequences of which are difficult to weigh. The position of the middle-class woman in the nineteenth century was indeed ambiguous, and it typifies the paradoxical role women have played throughout American history. Women became objects of both adoration and domination. Their moral superiority to the brutish and materialistic male was readily acknowledged, but their sphere of influence was confined to the family and the home. Women were accorded the power of intuition in a world that paid homage to reason; they were given a monopoly on piety, purity, and submissiveness in a society that increasingly trivialized these virtues. Although they gained greater control over their sexual lives, causing the birth rate to decline, women paid for this boon with their own desexualization. Denial of women's sexual pleasure and glorification of the womb symbolized female sexuality in the nineteenth century. Mary Ryan has stated bluntly, "Once active sexual desire and the organ of sexual pleasure, the clitoris, had been all but eradicated from female physiology, the nineteenth century gynecologist proceeded to elevate a woman's reproductive system to a position of biological hegemony."

However, the Victorian image was a malleable one; it could be manipulated to justify often conflicting life styles and be made to serve the interests of both reaction and reform. Ronald Hogeland has shown that the Victorian conception of womanhood could accommodate at least four distinct life styles, which he refers to as ornamental, romanticized, evangelical, and radical, each generating different forms of political behavior. The attitudes underlying the "cult of true womanhood" that characterized increasingly industrial, bourgeois New England differed in emphasis, if not content, from the values that idealized ladylike gentility in the plantation South. Men shaped each of these life styles and defined the proper sphere of women's activity in a limited fashion that assured male domination of society, politics, and the economy. Yet the association of women with the moral welfare of society allowed them to find within what the abolitionist, Sarah M. Grimke, ironically called, "the bonds of womanhood," a certain identity and sense of purpose that served many of their own needs.

The culture of Victorian America, which generated the "cult of true womanhood," was dominated by a form of evangelical Protestantism that led to what Ann Douglas termed the "feminization of American culture" in the nineteenth century. Americans had long distinguished between the faculties of the head and the heart, and at this time these faculties became increasingly defined as respectively masculine and feminine. Piety became a uniquely female response; and women, by their sheer numbers in the churches, molded the nature of Victorian religion. Disestablishment had made ministers more dependent upon their congregations for support, and they turned to the growing number of women parishioners as natural allies. Sympathetic to women's frustrations, the clergy encouraged them to take an active role in religious activities. A wide variety of church-related voluntary organizations grew up in the early nineteenth century to support missions, education, and moral reform.

In the selection "Religion and the Bonds of Womanhood," Nancy F. Cott examines the feminization of religion in New England. She illustrates the increasing tendency of ministers to associate a religious temperament with femininity as women "flocked into the churches and church related organizations." Cott shows, however, that, for the women involved, adherence to evangelical Christianity brought opportunity for legitimate self-expression and was a source of identity and purpose as part of a "community of peers." In reality, women found modest ways to benefit from the restricting Victorian image of true womanhood.

For no one did the contradiction between the image and the reality stand out more sharply than for the Southern lady, about whom Anne F. Scott has written so eloquently. In no other section of the country did the "ornamental" style of womanhood become so much a part of the sustaining myths of the society. In contrast to the image of the somewhat frivolous Southern belle sweeping about the plantation in an imported gown, exuding virtue, charm, and accomplishment, most Southern ladies assumed many burdensome tasks related to the domestic administration of the plantation system. In her essay "Women's Perspective on the Patriarchy of the 1850s," Scott supplements her earlier work by showing how the realities of life for the Southern lady conflicted with the "domestic metaphor" that underlay the Southerner's conception of an organic and patriarchal society. Although there is good reason to doubt that these women coldly resisted the pleasures of the flesh, the conflict between the ideal of motherhood and the attendant dangers of pregnancy and childbirth was one of the greatest sources of unhappiness for Southern women. Combined with the gnawing sense of betrayal derived from knowledge of their husband's sexual relations with slave women, the conditions of Southern life helped to create discontent among "the female portion of the population" within what proslavery propagandist Langdon Cheves predicted would be "the most splendid empire upon which the sun has ever shown."

No organized women's movement, however, appeared in the antebellum South. When the Southern states seceded, women gave the rebellion their hearty support, supplying food and clothing for Confederate soldiers, nursing the sick and wounded, and assuming many tasks on the home front that had formerly been performed by men. Although women did benefit from the radical Reconstruction governments, many were more adamant than were Southern men in their opposition to Reconstruction. Eliza Frances Andrews's diary bristles with hostility toward the self-righteous "crack-brained fanatic" Yankees. "They have placed our people in the most humiliating position possible to devise," she wrote in 1865, "where we are obliged either to submit to the insolence of our own servants or appeal to our Northern masters for protection, as if we were slaves ourselves—and that is what they are trying to make us."

Of course, most women in nineteenth-century America could not afford to aspire to the bourgeois definition of true womanhood. Recent studies support the slaveholders' contention that the conditions of the free blacks were miserable and indicate that in the North as well as the South they were plagued by declining economic status and increased family disorganization in the decades preceding the Civil War. But the most obvious contradiction to the Victorian stereotype was presented by the nearly two million black women held in bondage within the fifteen slave states of ante-bellum America. The patriarchal image of the contented slave is no more accurate than that of the contented Southern lady serving her appointed master.

In many ways slavery bore more heavily upon women than upon men. The abolitionists—particularly female abolitionists—emphasized the degradation of women and the destruction of the family inherent in the economic and social relations structured by the "peculiar institution." Most scholars have repeated the abolitionists' depiction of slavery, but they have ignored the ways in which the abolitionist perspective reflected the Victorian image of womanhood. Two themes were prevalent in this indictment: slavery destroyed the family through the sale of children and through the refusal to legalize the marriage bond; and slavery encouraged the sexual exploitation of slave women by masters and their white retainers.

Recent studies suggest that claims of the total brutalization of women under slavery have been exaggerated since resistance took many forms. Family ties among the slaves were far stronger than previous accounts have suggested. These intimate family relationships helped the slaves come to terms with the system. Historians such as Herbert Gutman have convincingly demonstrated the dominance of the two-parent household in the slave quarters. Refuting the white myth of licentious and promiscuous blacks, enslaved yet free of social constraint, he has shown that prenuptial sex coexisted with marital fidelity, as in many premodern societies. Within the slave community sexual behavior followed a well-structured pattern determined by the experience of slavery and cultural predisposition rather than by the dictates of white society. This is best illustrated by the slaves' taboo against marrying blood-cousins, which went unnoticed by whites and which stood in stark contrast to planter practices. Sale of slaves undoubtedly did not break up as many families as the abolitionists believed, although every black woman knew that her "chill'n could be sold away. . . ." Critics have claimed that abolitionists' views of the sexual exploitation of enslaved black women were warped by the extreme sexual repression within their own lives. However, documentary evidence clearly supports the widespread belief that miscegenation was rampant and that it was a central element of the society that scarred the lives of both black and white women.

In contrast to the most recent works on slavery that generalize about the day-to-day life of the slave, Loren Schweninger's "A Slave Family in the Ante Bellum South" focuses upon the life of a single slave, Sally, the matriarch of the Thomas-Rapier family. His sensitive portrayal of her life adds a personal dimension to our understanding of what E. Franklin Frazier called "motherhood in bondage," and it supports recent studies emphasizing the desire of blacks after the Civil War to establish the legitimacy of their marriages and to provide the necessary basis for a stable family life. Although black men often attempted to emulate the Victorian ideal, black women, of necessity, continued to play the important role they had assumed under slavery. Until undermined by economic and political discrimination, such attempts to establish stable family ties were surprisingly successful.

Most working women in nineteenth-century America were not black, and the plight of those whom Lerner has associated with the image of the "mill girl" was an arduous one. The vast majority of adult women married and continued to work within their homes, meeting the multitude of demands placed upon them as farm women or attempting to master the fundamentals of "domestic science" detailed in the plethora of housekeeping manuals directed to middle-class women in the mid-nineteenth century. Ironically, as social and economic change created conditions that generated the cult of domesticity, an increasing number of unmarried women moved out of the home and into the ranks of paid labor. The most common job open to such women—that of domestic servant—represented little more than an extension of their former occupational role. Although the majority of working women continued to be domestics at the end of the century, the factory system employed large numbers of women because of their low labor cost and the relative scarcity of male workers. A handful of errant romantics have extolled the "freedom of the factory," but the women in the factories were generally secondary earners working to supplement a meagre family income.

At its inception, the Waltham or "boarding house" system of labor organization compared more closely to the idyllic view of the factory and did not conflict directly with the Victorian conception of true womanhood. In contrast to the Rhode Island or "family" system which, as its name suggests, was based upon the employment of whole families, the key feature of the Waltham system was the exploitation of young women, mostly with rural origins. For relatively short periods of time, they lived in company-owned boarding houses supervised by matronly housemothers. Generally these young women worked in order to send a brother to school or to provide themselves with an adequate trousseau. As the most famous of their number, Lucy Larcom, said in her autobiography, they were "happy in the knowledge that, at the longest, our employment was only to be temporary."

However, reality never conformed completely to the portrait of the Waltham system sketched in the pages of the *Lowell Offering*, a periodical written by mill girls and actively supported by mill owners, who wished to popularize a favorable image of their factories. In the two decades before the Civil War, that reality was changing and the Waltham system was deteriorating. During these years, wages in the textile industry, which had always been low, began to decline relative to wages paid by other jobs employing mostly women. Mill owners successfully resisted employee demands for improved working conditions and shorter hours. As a result, more children were drawn into the mills, and native-born women were increasingly replaced by the incoming flood of Irish and other immigrants. A few highly skilled women imported from Scotland were sufficiently well paid to save a portion of their earnings and to use their jobs in the mills to improve their lot. But thousands of unskilled immigrant women, who endured long hours and low pay in the textile mills of New England and the sweatshops of New York and Philadelphia, barely survived. By 1865, New York City alone had nearly 75,000 women workers struggling at the edge of poverty. Consequently, prostitution was extremely widespread.

In "Working Class Women in the Gilded Age," Daniel J. Walkowitz examines a specific group of mid-nineteenth-century mill girls, the cotton textile workers of Cohoes in upstate New York. As elsewhere, the Irish and, to a lesser degree, the French Canadians were displacing native-born women workers. Walkowitz traces the effect of work in the mills on the lives of women of different ethnic groups and emphasizes the way in which patterns of marriage and family structure varied along ethnic lines. Although mill girls shared a collective experience in their encounter with the "Dark Satanic Mills," their response to this situation and its effect upon their lives can only be fully understood in terms of the ethnic differences that characterized their society.

Victorian America, however, was still based upon agricultural production. It was not until 1920 that the census revealed more people living in urban than in rural areas. The largest single group of adult women in the nineteenth century were farmwives. This was true in every section of the country, and in the agricultural press the image of the farmwife challenged that of the lady as the ideal woman. Frontier women have been portrayed in a variety of ways: the "gentle tamers" who brought civilization to the wild west; the "sunbonneted helpmates" who worked next to their husbands in the fields; and the "bad women" who were dancehall queens, prostitutes, and outlaws. Most frontier women were simply farmwives, and although most farmwives did not live on the frontier, they performed similar roles from Maine to Missouri. Glenda Riley details the harsh and complicated lives of such women in " 'Not Gainfully Employed': Women on the Iowa Frontier, 1833–1870." Providing meals, caring for the sick, raising children and burying the dead were all in women's hands. One can easily understand why the Granger movement that followed the Civil War appealed to women seeking social contact and a release from the drudgery of farm life.

Throughout the nineteenth century, a minority of women left the confines of their middle-class homes to join the vast array of reform movements that characterized the period. Early in the century, they became involved in the work of a growing number of benevolent societies, and by the 1840s the outlines of what would become "the woman movement" were clear. American feminism was part of the general ferment of humanitarian reform that appeared in the antebellum period. Religious enthusiasm attracted increasing numbers of women to antislavery, temperance, pacifism, prison reform, and other causes of these years.

Although women constituted a majority of the supporters of abolition and temperance, they were generally denied leadership positions within these movements and often found men objecting to their activity on the grounds that it was inappropriate for women to speak publicly. Even among the radical abolitionists the question of women's participation was a divisive issue. Criticism of women who would assume "the place and tone of man as a public reformer" prompted Sarah Grimke to write her *Letters on the Equality of the Sexes* in defense of her reform activities. Other women reformers considered separate action to secure civil and political rights equal to those of men. After being barred from taking their seats at the World Anti-Slavery Convention in 1840 simply because of their sex, Lucretia Mott and Elizabeth Cady Stanton moved increasingly toward a more vigorous assertion of women's rights. In 1848 they called together a convention at Seneca Falls, New York, which issued its own declaration of independence proclaiming that "all men and women are created equal." This launched the struggle "to secure to themselves their sacred right to the elective franchise."

In "Women's Rights before the Civil War," Ellen C. DuBois traces the emergence of the women's rights movement. Like other writers on the subject, she finds the origins of women's activism in evangelical religion and political abolitionism. DuBois, however, emphasizes the problems faced in the infancy of the women's movement and the importance of factional splits within the abolition movement over the issue of women's participation. She also argues that the demand for the vote which came to be the focus of the women's movement was essentially radical and feminist, because in the context of nineteenth-century political theory it implied a challenge to the concept of a separate woman's sphere of influence and "the assumption of male authority over women."

Although the Civil War raised feminists' expectations of success in their battle for the vote, the passage of the Fifteenth Amendment granting the right to vote to black men created a crisis in feminist ranks. Women had contributed in many ways to the Northern war effort. Mary Livermore was one of the leaders of the United States Sanitary Commission that employed thousands of women who distributed food and medical supplies; Dorothea Dix served as the superintendent of women nurses for the Army; and Elizabeth Stanton and Susan B. Anthony formed the National Women's Loyal League to support the Thirteenth Amendment that abolished slavery. Because of the work of these women and others such as "Mother" Bickerdyke and Harriet Tubman, feminists assumed that reformers would rally to the cause of women's suffrage. However, most Radical Republicans, who felt that black male suffrage was vital for the freedmen, thought that tying it to women's suffrage would mean inevitable defeat. Although Northern Democrats mocked women's suffrage and tried to use it along with the shibboleth of miscegenation to defeat the Fifteenth Amendment, most feminists refused to sacrifice women's suffrage to the cause of the black male. They consequently broke with those who insisted that it was "the Negro's hour."

Subsequently, the suffrage movement split into two groups. The National Woman Suffrage Association, led by Stanton and Anthony, concerned itself with a variety of reform causes and was decidedly the more radical of the two groups. The more conservative American Woman Suffrage Association, headed by Lucy Stone and her husband Henry Blackwell, stuck more closely to the single issue of the vote. In subsequent years, both groups agitated for women's suffrage with little success.

While recent historians have disputed the consequences of this split for the development of feminism in America, few would deny that the majority of women reformers in the years following the Civil War were at best "social feminists" who built their reform activities upon the idea of women's moral superiority. Their efforts were limited to such issues as social purity and temperance, which were designed to relieve women and society of the worst consequences of vulgar masculinity. Even when women did secure the vote, as they did in Wyoming in 1869, it was often the product of social forces over which women in general, and the Eastern feminist movement in particular, had little control. The suffrage victory in Wyoming was the product of an effort to reestablish Eastern ideas of order, refinement, and culture in the West.

Thus even the success of women's suffrage in the western states, which were the first to allow women to vote, reaffirmed the pervasiveness of the Victorian image of women as the guardian of culture and civilization. Throughout this period, most Americans, women as well as men, treated feminist demands with apathy or disgust. In his book *Sex and Education*, E.M. Clarke argued that college education would "desex" women. Opponents of equal suffrage insisted that it would undermine the family and endanger the entire social order. Women such as Eliza Francis Andrews agreed that a woman's "business is to refine and elevate society. . . . Her mission is moral rather than intellectual, domestic, rather than political." The feminine intellect was deemed incapable of dealing with civic affairs. Until the twentieth century, the advocates of women's suffrage scored few successes because opposition from their own sex encouraged the hostility of men.

8 ⚥ The Lady and the Mill Girl: Changes in the Status of Women in the Age of Jackson

Gerda Lerner

The period 1800–1840 is one in which decisive changes occurred in the status of American women. It has remained surprisingly unexplored. With the exception of a recent, unpublished dissertation by Keith Melder and the distinctive work of Elisabeth Dexter, there is a dearth of descriptive material and an almost total absence of interpretation.[1] Yet the period offers essential clues to an understanding of later institutional developments, particularly the shape and nature of the women's rights movement. This analysis will consider the economic, political and social status of women and examine the changes in each area. It will also attempt an interpretation of the ideological shifts which occurred in American society concerning the "proper" role for women.

Periodization always offers difficulties. It seemed useful here, for purposes of comparison, to group women's status before 1800 roughly under the "colonial" heading and ignore the transitional and possibly

From *American Studies Journal* X (Spring 1969). Reprinted by permission.

Research for this article was facilitated by a research grant provided by Long Island University, Brooklyn, N.Y., which is gratefully acknowledged.

The generalizations in this article are based on extensive research in primary sources, including letters and manuscripts of the following women: Elizabeth Cady Stanton, Susan B. Anthony, Abby Kelley, Lucretia Mott, Lucy Stone, Sarah and Angelina Grimke, Maria Weston Chapman, Lydia Maria Child and Betsey Cowles. Among the organizational records consulted were those of the Boston Female Anti-Slavery Society, the Philadelphia Female Anti-Slavery Society, Anti-Slavery Conventions of American Women, all the Woman's Rights Conventions prior to 1870 and the records of various female charitable organizations.

atypical shifts which occurred during the American Revolution and the early period of nationhood. Also, regional differences were largely ignored. The South was left out of consideration entirely because its industrial development occurred later.

The status of colonial women has been well studied and described and can briefly be summarized for comparison with the later period. Throughout the colonial period there was a marked shortage of women, which varied with the regions and always was greatest in the frontier areas.[2] This (from the point of view of women) favorable sex ratio enhanced their status and position. The Puritan world view regarded idleness as sin; life in an underdeveloped country made it absolutely necessary that each member of the community perform an economic function. Thus work for women, married or single, was not only approved, it was regarded as a civic duty. Puritan town councils expected single girls, widows and unattached women to be self-supporting and for a long time provided needy spinsters with parcels of land. There was no social sanction against married women working; on the contrary, wives were expected to help their husbands in their trade and won social approval for doing extra work in or out of the home. Needy children, girls as well as boys, were indentured or apprenticed and were expected to work for their keep.

The vast majority of women worked within their homes, where their labor produced most articles needed for the family. The entire colonial production of cloth and clothing and partially that of shoes was in the hands of women. In addition to these occupations, women were found in many different kinds of employment. They were butchers, silversmiths, gunsmiths, upholsterers. They ran mills, plantations, tan yards, shipyards and every kind of shop, tavern and boarding house. They were gate keepers, jail keepers, sextons, journalists, printers, "doctoresses," apothecaries, midwives, nurses and teachers. Women acquired their skills the same way as did the men, through apprenticeship training, frequently within their own families.[3]

Absence of a dowry, ease of marriage and remarriage and a more lenient attitude of the law with regard to woman's property rights were manifestations of the improved position of wives in the colonies. Under British common law, marriage destroyed a woman's contractual capacity; she could not sign a contract even with the consent of her husband. But colonial authorities were more lenient toward the wife's property rights by protecting her dower rights in her husband's property, granting her personal clothing and upholding pre-nuptial contracts between husband and wife. In the absence of the husband, colonial courts granted women "femme sole" rights, which enabled them to conduct their husband's business, sign contracts and sue. The relative social freedom of women and the esteem in which they were held was commented upon by most early foreign travelers in America.[4]

But economic, legal and social status tell only part of the story. Colonial society as a whole was hierarchical, and rank and standing in society depended on the position of the men. Women did not play a determining role in the ranking pattern; they took their position in society through the men of their own family or the men they married. In other words, they participated in the hierarchy only as daughters and wives, not as individuals. Similarly, their occupations were, by and large, merely auxiliary, designed to contribute to family income, enhance their husbands' business or continue it in case of widowhood. The self-supporting spinsters were certainly the exception. The underlying assumption of colonial society was that women ought to occupy an inferior and subordinate position. The settlers had brought this assumption with them from Europe; it was reflected in their legal concepts, their willingness to exclude women from political life, their discriminatory educational practices. What is remarkable is the extent to which this felt inferiority of women was constantly challenged and modified under the impact of environment, frontier conditions and a favorable sex ratio.

By 1840 all of American society had changed. The Revolution had substituted an egalitarian ideology for the hierarchical concepts of colonial life. Privilege based on ability rather than inherited status, upward mobility for all groups of society and unlimited opportunities for individual self-fulfillment had become ideological goals, if not always realities. For men, that is; women were, by tacit consensus, excluded from the new democracy. Indeed their actual situation had in many respects deteriorated. While, as wives, they had benefitted from increasing wealth, urbanization and industrialization, their role as economic producers and as political members of society differed sharply from that of men. Women's work outside of the home no longer met with social approval; on the contrary, with two notable exceptions, it was condemned. Many business and professional occupations formerly open to women were now closed, many others restricted as to training and advancement. The entry of large numbers of women into low status, low pay and low skill industrial work had fixed such work by definition as "woman's work." Women's political status, while legally unchanged, had deteriorated relative to the advances made by men. At the same time the genteel lady of fashion had become a model of American femininity and the definition of "woman's proper sphere" seemed narrower and more confined than ever.

Within the scope of this article only a few of these changes can be more fully explained. The professionalization of medicine and its impact on women may serve as a typical example of what occurred in all the professions.

In colonial America there were no medical schools, no medical journals, few hospitals and few laws pertaining to the practice of the healing arts. Clergymen and governors, barbers, quacks, apprentices and women practiced medicine. Most practitioners acquired their credentials by reading Paracelsus and Galen and serving an apprenticeship with an established practitioner. Among the semi-trained "physics," surgeons, and healers, the occasional "doctoress" was fully accepted and frequently well rewarded. County records of all the colonies contain references to the work of the female physicians. There was even a female Army surgeon, a Mrs. Allyn, who served during King Philip's war. Plantation records mention by name several slave women who were granted special privileges because of their useful service as midwives and "doctoresses."[5]

The period of the professionalization of American medicine dates from 1765, when Dr. William Shippen began his lectures on midwifery in Philadelphia. The founding of medical faculties in several colleges, the standardization of training requirements, and the proliferation of medical societies intensified during the last quarter of the eighteenth century. The American Revolution dramatized the need for trained medical personnel, afforded first hand battlefield experience to a number of surgeons and brought increasing numbers of semi-trained practitioners in contact with the handful of European-trained surgeons working in the military hospitals. This was an experience from which women were excluded. The resulting interest in improved medical training, the gradual appearance of graduates of medical colleges and the efforts of medical societies led to licensing legislation. In 1801 Maryland required all medical practitioners to be licensed; in 1806 New York enacted a similar law, providing for an examination before a commission. By the late 1820's all states except three had set up licensing requirements. Since most of these laws stipulated attendance at a medical college as one of the prerequisites for licensing, women were automatically excluded.[6] By the 1830's the few established female practitioners who might have continued their practice in the old ways had probably died out. Whatever vested interest they had had was too weak to assert itself against the new profession.

This process of preemption of knowledge, institutionalization of the profession and legitimation of its claims by law and public acceptance is standard for the professionalization of the sciences, as George Daniels has pointed out.[7] It inevitably results in the elimination of fringe elements from the profession. It is interesting to note that women had been pushed out of the medical profession in sixteenth-century Europe by a similar process.[8] Once the public had come to accept licensing and college training as guarantees of up-to-date practice, the outsider, no matter how well qualified by years of experience, stood no chance in the competition. Women were the casualties of medical professionalization.

In the field of midwifery the results were similar, but the process was more complicated. Women had held a virtual monopoly in the profession in colonial America. In 1646 a man was prosecuted in Maine for practicing as a midwife.[9] There are many records of well trained midwives with diplomas from European institutions working in the colonies. In most of the colonies midwives were licensed, registered and required to pass an examination before a board. When Dr. Shippen announced his pioneering lectures on midwifery, he did it to "combat the widespread popular prejudice against the man-midwife" and because he considered most midwives ignorant and improperly trained. [10]

Yet he invited "those women who love virtue enough, to own their Ignorance, and apply for instruction" to attend his lectures, offering as an inducement the assurance that female pupils would be taught privately. It is not known if any midwives availed themselves of the opportunity.[11]

Technological advances, as well as scientific, worked against the interests of female midwives. In sixteenth-century Europe the invention and use of the obstetrical forceps had for three generations been the well-kept secret of the Chamberlen family and had greatly enhanced their medical practice. Hugh Chamberlen was forced by circumstances to sell the secret to the Medical College in Amsterdam, which in turn transmitted the precious knowledge to licensed physicians only. By the time the use of the instrument became widespread it had become associated with male physicians and midwives. Similarly in America, introduction of the obstetrical forceps was associated with the practice of male midwives and served to their advantage. By the end of the eighteenth century a number of male physicians advertised their practice of midwifery. Shortly thereafter female midwives also resorted to advertising, probably in an effort to meet the competition. By the early nineteenth century male physicians had virtually monopolized the practice of midwifery on the Eastern seaboard. True to the generally delayed economic development in the Western frontier regions, female midwives continued to work on the frontier until a much later period. It is interesting to note that the concepts of "propriety" shifted with the prevalent practice. In seventeenth-century Maine the attempt of a man to act as a midwife was considered outrageous and illegal; in mid-nineteenth century America the suggestion that women should train as midwives and physicians was considered equally outrageous and improper.[12]

Professionalization, similar to that in medicine with the elimination of women from the upgraded profession, occurred in the field of law. Before 1750, when law suits were commonly brought to the courts by the plaintiffs themselves or by deputies without specialized legal training, women as well as men could and did act as "attorneys-in-fact." When the law became a paid profession and trained lawyers took over litigation, women disappeared from the court scene for over a century.[13]

A similar process of shrinking opportunities for women developed in business and in the retail trades. There were fewer female storekeepers and business women in the 1830's than there had been in colonial days. There was also a noticeable shift in the kind of merchandise handled by them. Where previously women could be found running almost every kind of retail shop, after 1830 they were mostly found in businesses which served women only.[14]

The only fields in which professionalization did not result in the elimination of women from the upgraded profession were nursing and teaching. Both were characterized by a severe shortage of labor. Nursing lies outside the field of this inquiry since it did not become an organized profession until after the Civil War. Before then it was regarded peculiarly as a woman's occupation, although some of the hospitals and the Army during wars employed male nurses. These bore the stigma of low skill, low status and low pay. Generally, nursing was regarded as simply an extension of the unpaid services performed by the housewife—a characteristic attitude that haunts the profession to this day.

Education seems, at first glance, to offer an entirely opposite pattern from that of the other professions. In colonial days women had taught "Dame schools" and grade schools during summer sessions. Gradually, as educational opportunities for girls expanded, they advanced just a step ahead of their students. Professionalization of teaching occurred between 1820–1860, a period marked by a sharp increase in the number of women teachers. The spread of female seminaries, academies and normal schools provided new opportunities for the training and employment of female teachers.

This trend which runs counter to that found in the other professions can be accounted for by the fact that women filled a desperate need created by the challenge of the common schools, the ever-increasing size of the student body and the westward growth of the nation. America was committed to educating its children in public schools, but it was insistent on doing so as cheaply as possible. Women were available in great numbers and they were willing to work cheaply. The result was another ideological adaptation: in the very period when the gospel of the home as woman's only proper sphere was preached most loudly, it was discovered that women were the natural teachers of youth, could do the job better than men and were to be preferred for such employment. This was always provided, of course, that they would work at the proper wage differential—30–50% of the wages paid male teachers was considered appropriate. The result was that in 1888 in the country as a whole 63% of all teachers were women, while the figure for the cities only was 90.04%.[15]

It appeared in the teaching field, as it would in industry, that role expectations were adaptable provided the inferior status group filled a social need. The inconsistent and peculiar patterns of employment of black labor in the present-day market bear out the validity of this generalization.

There was another field in which the labor of women was appreciated and which they were urged to enter—industry. From Alexander Hamilton to Matthew Carey and Tench Coxe, advocates of industrialization sang the praises of the working girl and advanced arguments in favor of her employment. The social benefits of female labor particularly stressed were those bestowed upon her family, who now no longer had to support her. Working girls were "thus happily preserved from idleness and its attendant vices and crimes" and the whole community benefitted from their increased purchasing power.[16]

American industrialization, which occurred in an underdeveloped economy with a shortage of labor, depended on the labor of women and children. Men were occupied with agricultural work and were not available or willing to enter the factories. This accounts for the special features of the early development of the New England textile industry: the relatively high wages, the respectability of the job and relatively high status of the mill girls, the patriarchal character of the model factory towns and the temporary mobility of women workers from farm to factory and back again to farm. All this was characteristic only of a limited area and of a period of about two decades. By the late 1830's the romance had worn off; immigration had supplied a strongly competitive, permanent work force willing to work for subsistence wages; early efforts at trade union organization had been shattered and mechanization had turned semiskilled factory labor into unskilled labor. The process led to the replacement of the New England-born farm girls by immigrants in the mills and was accompanied by a loss of status and respectability for female workers.

The lack of organized social services during periods of depression drove ever greater numbers of women into the labor market. At first, inside the factories distinctions between men's and women's jobs were blurred. Men and women were assigned to machinery on the basis of local need. But as more women entered industry the limited number of occupations open to them tended to increase competition among them, thus lowering pay standards. Generally, women regarded their work as temporary and hesitated to invest in apprenticeship training, because they expected to marry and raise families. Thus they remained untrained, casual labor and were soon, by custom, relegated to the lowest paid, least skilled jobs. Long hours, overwork and poor working conditions would characterize women's work in industry for almost a century.[17]

Another result of industrialization was in increasing differences in life styles between women of different classes. When female occupations, such as carding, spinning and weaving, were transferred from home to factory, the poorer women followed their traditional work and became industrial workers. The women of the middle and upper classes could use their newly gained time for leisure pursuits: they became ladies. And a small but significant group among them chose to prepare themselves for professional careers by advanced education. This group would prove to be the most vocal and troublesome in the near future.

As class distinctions sharpened, social attitudes toward women became polarized. The image of "the lady" was elevated to the accepted ideal of femininity toward which all women would strive. In this formulation of values lower class women were simply ignored. The actual lady was, of course, nothing new on the American scene; she had been present ever since colonial days. What was new in the 1830's was the cult of the lady, her elevation to a status symbol. The advancing prosperity of the early nineteenth century made it possible for middle class women to aspire to the status formerly reserved for upper class women. The "cult of true womanhood" of the 1830's became a vehicle for such aspirations. Mass circulation newspapers and magazines made it possible to teach every woman how to elevate the status of her family by setting "proper" standards of behavior, dress and literary tastes. *Godey's Lady's Book* and innumerable gift books and tracts of the period all preach the same gospel of "true womanhood"—piety, purity, domesticity.[18] Those unable to reach the goal of becoming ladies were to be satisfied with the lesser goal—acceptance of their "proper place" in the home.

It is no accident that the slogan "woman's place is in the home" took on a certain aggressiveness and shrillness precisely at the time when increasing numbers of poorer women *left* their homes to become factory workers. Working women were not a fit subject for the concern of publishers and mass media writers. Idleness, once a disgrace in the eyes of society, had become a status symbol. Thorstein Veblen, one of the earliest and sharpest commentators on the subject, observed that it had become almost the sole social function of the lady "to put in evidence her economic unit's ability to pay." She was "a means of conspicuously unproductive expenditure," devoted to displaying her husband's wealth.[19] Just as the cult of white womanhood in the South served to preserve a labor and social system based on race distinctions, so did the cult of the lady in an egalitarian society serve as a means of preserving class distinctions. Where class distinctions were not so great, as on the frontier, the position of women was closer to what it had been in colonial days; their economic contribution was more highly valued, their opportunities were less restricted and their positive participation in community life was taken for granted.

In the urbanized and industrialized Northeast the life experience of middle class women was different in almost every respect from that of the lower class women. But there was one thing the society lady and the mill girl had in common—they were equally disfranchised and isolated from the vital centers of power. Yet the political status of women had not actually deteriorated. With very few exceptions women had neither voted nor stood for office during the colonial period. Yet the spread of the franchise to ever wider groups of white males during the Jacksonian age, the removal of property restrictions, the increasing numbers of immigrants who acquired access to the franchise, made the gap between these new enfranchised voters and the disfranchised women more obvious. Quite naturally, educated and propertied women felt this deprivation more keenly. Their own career expectations had been encouraged by widening educational opportunites; their consciousness of their own abilities and of their potential for power had been enhanced by their activities in the reform movements of the 1830's; the general spirit of upward mobility and venturesome entrepreneurship that pervaded the Jacksonian era was infectious. But in the late 1840's a sense of acute frustration enveloped these educated and highly spirited women. Their rising expectations had met with frustration, their hopes had been shattered; they were bitterly conscious of a relative lowering of status and a loss of position. This sense of frustration led them to action; it was one of the main factors in the rise of the woman's rights movement.[20]

The women, who in 1848 declared boldly and with considerable exaggeration that "the history of mankind is a history of repeated injuries and usurpations on the part of man toward woman, having in direct object the establishment of an absolute tyranny over her," did not speak for the truly exploited and abused working woman.[21] As a matter of fact, they were largely ignorant of her condition and, with the notable exception of Susan B. Anthony, indifferent to her fate. But they judged from the realities of their own life experience. Like most revolutionaries, they were not the most downtrodden but rather the most status deprived group. Their frustrations and traditional isolation from political power funneled their discontent into fairly utopian declarations and immature organizational means. They would learn better in the long, hard decades of practical struggle. Yet it is their initial emphasis on the legal and political "disabilities" of women which has provided the framework for most of the historical work on women. For almost a hundred years sympathetic historians have told the story of women in America from the feminist viewpoint. Their tendency has been to reason from the position of middle class women to a generalization concerning all American women. This distortion has obscured the actual and continuous contributions of women to American life.[22] To avoid such a distortion, any valid generalization concerning American women after the 1830's should reflect a recognition of class stratification.

For lower class women the changes brought by industrialization were actually advantageous, offering income and advancement opportunities, however limited, and a chance for participation in the ranks of organized labor. They, by and large, tended to join men in their struggle for economic advancement and became increasingly concerned with economic gains and protective labor legislation. Middle and upperclass women, on the other hand, reacted to actual and fancied status deprivation by increasing militancy and the formation of organizations for women's rights, by which they meant especially legal and property rights.

The four decades preceding the Seneca Falls Convention were decisive in the history of American women. They brought an actual deterioration in the economic opportunities open to women, a relative deterioration in their political status and a rising level of expectation and subsequent frustration in a privileged elite group of educated women. The ideology still pervasive in our present-day society regarding woman's "proper" role was formed in those decades. Later, under the impact of feminist attacks this ideology would grow defensive and attempt to bolster its claims by appeals to universality and pretentions to a history dating back to antiquity or, at least, to *The Mayflower.* Women, we are told, have always played a restricted and subordinate role in American life. In fact, however, it was in mid-nineteenth-century America that the ideology of "woman's place is in the home" changed from being an accurate description of existing reality into a myth. It became the "feminine mystique"—a longing for a lost, archaic world of agrarian family self-sufficiency, updated by woman's consumer function and the misunderstood dicta of Freudian psychology.

The decades 1800–1840 also provide the clues to an understanding of the institutional shape of the later women's organizations. These would be led by middle class women whose self-image, life experience and ideology had largely been fashioned and influenced by these early, transitional years. The concerns of middle class women—property rights, the franchise and moral uplift—would dominate the women's rights movement. But side by side with it, and at times cooperating with it, would grow a number of organizations serving the needs of working women.

American women were the largest disfranchised group in the nation's history, and they retained this position longer than any other group. Although they found ways of making their influence felt continuously, not only as individuals but as organized groups, power eluded them. The mill girl and the lady, both born in the age of Jackson, would not gain access to power until they learned to cooperate, each for her own separate interests. It would take almost six decades before they would find common ground. The issue around which they finally would unite and push their movement to victory was the "impractical and utopian" demand raised at Seneca Falls—the means to power in American society—female suffrage.

NOTES

1. Keith E. Melder, "The Beginnings of the Women's Rights Movement in the United States: 1800–1840" (Diss. Yale, 1963). Elisabeth A. Dexter, *Colonial Women of Affairs: Women in Business and Professions in America before 1776* (Boston, 1931); *Career Women of America: 1776–1840* (Francestown, N.H., 1950).

2. Herbert Moller, "Sex Composition and Corresponding Culture Patterns of Colonial America," *William and Mary Quarterly,* Ser. 3, II (April, 1945), 113–153.

3. The summary of the status of colonial women is based on the following sources: Mary Benson, *Women in 18th Century America: A Study of Opinion and Social Usage* (New York, 1935); Arthur Calhoun, *A Social History of the American Family,* 3 vols. (Cleveland, 1918); Dexter, *Colonial Women;* Dexter, *Career Women;* Edmund S. Morgan, *Virginians at Home: Family Life in the 18th Century* (Williamsburg, 1952); Julia C. Spruill, *Women's Life and Work in the Southern Colonies* (Chapel Hill, 1938).

4. E. M. Boatwright, "The political and legal status of women in Georgia: 1783–1860," *Georgia Historical Quarterly,* XXV (April, 1941). Richard B. Morris, *Studies in the History of American Law* (New York, 1930), Chap. 3. A summary of travelers' comments on American women may be found in: Jane Mesick, *The English Traveler in America: 1785–1835* (New York, 1922), 83–99.

5. For facts on colonial medicine the following sources were consulted: Wyndham B. Blanton, *Medicine in Virginia,* 3 vols. (Richmond, 1930); N. S. Davis, M.D.,

History of Medical Education and Institutions in the United States. . . . (Chicago, 1851); Dexter, Career Women; K. C. Hurd-Mead, M.D., A History of Women in Medicine: from the earliest Times to the Beginning of the 19th Century (Haddam, Conn., 1938); Geo. W. Norris, The Early History of Medicine in Philadelphia (Philadephia, 1886); Joseph M. Toner, Contributions to the Annals of Medical Progress in the United States before and during the War of Independence (Washington, D.C., 1874). The citation regarding Mrs. Allyn is from Hurd-Mead, Women in Medicine, 487.

6. Fielding H. Garrison, M.D., An Introduction to the History of Medicine (Philadelphia, 1929). For licensing legislation: Davis, 88–103.

7. George Daniels, "The Professionalization of American Science: the emergent period, 1820–1860," paper delivered at the joint session of the History of Science Society and the Society of the History of Technology, San Francisco, December 28, 1965.

8. Hurd-Mead, Women in Medicine, 391.

9. Ibid., 486.

10. Betsy E. Corner, William Shippen Jr.: Pioneer in American Medical Education (Philadelphia, 1951), 103.

11. Ibid.

12. Benjamin Lee Gordon, Medieval and Renaissance Medicine (New York, 1959), 689–691. Blanton, Medicine, II, 23–24; Hurd-Mead, Women in Medicine, 487–88; Annie Nathan Meyer, Woman's Work in America (New York, 1891). Harriot K. Hunt, M.D., Glances and Glimpses or Fifty Years Social including Twenty Years Professional Life (Boston, 1856), 127–140. Eleanor Flexner, Century of Struggle: The Woman's Rights Movement in the United States (Cambridge, Mass., 1959), 115–119.

13. Sophie H. Drinker, "Women Attorneys of Colonial Times," Maryland Historical Society Bulletin, LVI, No. 4 (Dec., 1961).

14. Dexter, Colonial Women, 34–35, 162–165.

15. Harriet W. Marr, The Old New England Academies (New York, 1959), Chap. 8; Thomas Woody, A History of Women's Education in the United States, 2 vols. (New York, 1929) H, 100–109, 458–460, 492–493.

16. Matthew Carey, Essays on Political Economy . . . (Philadelphia, 1822), 459.

17. The statements on women industrial workers are based on the following sources: Edith Abbot, Women in Industry (New York, 1910), 66–80; Edith Abbot, "Harriet Martineau and the Employment of Women in 1836," Journal of Political Economy, XIV (Dec., 1906), 614–626; Matthew Carey, Miscellaneous Essays (Philadelphia, 1830), 153–203; Helen L. Sumner, History of Women in Industry in the United States, in Report on Condition of Women and Child Wage-Earners in the United States, 19 vols. (Washington, D.C., 1910), IX. Also: Elizabeth F. Baker, Technology and Woman's Work (New York, 1964), Chaps. 1–5.

18. Emily Putnam, The Lady: Studies of certain significant Phases of her History (New York, 1910), 319–320. Barbara Welter, "The Cult of True Womanhood: 1820–1860," American Quarterly, XVIII, No. 2, Part I (Summer, 1966), 151–174.

19. Veblen generalized from his observations of the society of the Gilded Age and fell into the usual error of simply ignoring the lower class women, whom he dismissed as "drudges . . . fairly content with their lot," but his analysis of women's role in "conspicuous consumption" and of the function of women's fashions is

unsurpassed. For references see: Thorstein Veblen, *The Theory of the Leisure Class* (New York, 1962, first printing, 1899), 70–71, 231–232. Thorstein Veblen, "The Economic Theory of Woman's Dress," *Essays in Our Changing Order* (New York, 1934), 65–77.

20. Like most groups fighting status oppression women formulated a compensatory ideology of female superiority. Norton Mezvinsky has postulated that this was clearly expressed only in 1874; in fact this formulation appeared in the earliest speeches of Elizabeth Cady Stanton and in the speeches and resolutions of the Seneca Falls Conventions and other pre-Civil War woman's rights conventions. Rather than a main motivating force, the idea was a tactical formulation, designed to take advantage of the popularly held male belief in woman's "moral" superiority and to convince reformers that they needed the votes of women. Those middle class feminists who believed in woman's "moral" superiority exploited the concept in order to win their major goal—female equality. For references see: Norton Mezvinsky, "An Idea of Female Superiority," *Midcontinent American Studies Journal,* II, No. I (Spring, 1961), 17–26. E. C. Stanton, S. B. Anthony and M. J. Gage, eds., *A History of Woman Suffrage,* 6 vols. (New York, 1881–1922), I, 72, 479, 522, 529 and *passim.* Alan P. Grimes, *The Puritan Ethic and Woman Suffrage* (New York, 1967), Chaps. 2 and 3.

21. Stanton *et al, History of Woman Suffrage,* I, 70.

22. Mary R. Beard, *Woman as Force in History: A Study of Traditions and Realities* (New York, 1946).

9 ✑ Religion and the Bonds of Womanhood

Nancy F. Cott

Woman was "fitted by nature" for Christian benevolence, announced a Presbyterian minister in Newburyport, Massachusetts, in 1837— "religion seems almost to have been entrusted by its author to her particular custody." As he saw it, Christianity had performed a unique service for women by bringing them social advantages as well as spiritual hope, and women had incurred a corresponding obligation.[1] The numbers and activity of women in New England churches suggest that they found benefits indeed in their religious devotion—but did their perception of the benefits and the minister's exactly coincide?

The Puritans who settled Massachusetts Bay worshipped a patriarchal God, but as early as the mid-seventeenth century women outnumbered men in the New England churches. While the church hierarchy remained strictly male the majority of women in their congregations increased, and ministers felt compelled to explain it.[2] "As there were three Marys to one John, standing under the Cross of our Dying Lord," Cotton Mather wrote in 1692, "so still there are far more Godly Women in the World, than there are Godly Men; and our Church Communions give us a Little Demonstration of it." Mather offered two explanations for the persistent pattern. Because of Eve's sins God had decreed that woman's lot would include subjection to man, and pain in childbirth; but he had mercifully converted these curses into blessings. The trials that women had to endure made them "tender," made them seek consolation, and thus turned them toward God and piety. Mather also thought that women had more opportunity and

---

From *The Bonds of Womanhood: "Woman's Sphere in New England, 1780–1835.* (New Haven: Yale University Press, 1977). Reprinted by permission of Yale University Press.

time to devote to "soul-service" than men had because they were ordinarily at home and had little "Worldly Business." Two decades later, when the Reverend Benjamin Colman praised women for showing "more of the Life & Power of Religion" than men, he discerned similar causes: women's "natural Tenderness of Spirit & Your Retiredness from the Cares & Snares of the World; so more especially in Your Multiplied Sorrows the curse pronounc'd upon our first Mother Eve, turn'd into the greatest blessing to Your Souls." Writers later in the eighteenth century dropped the references to Mother Eve and focused instead on the religious inclination "naturally" present in female temperament. In the British work *A Father's Legacy to his Daughters,* which was widely reprinted in New England after 1775, Dr. John Gregory maintained that women were more "susceptible" to religion because of their "superior delicacy," "modesty," "natural softness and sensibility of . . . dispositions," and "natural warmth of . . . imagination." (Men, he assumed, naturally had harder hearts and stronger passions, and were more dissolute and resistant to religious appeal because of the greater freedom they enjoyed.) Gregory also thought that women needed the consolations of religion, since they suffered great difficulties in life yet could "not plunge into business, or dissipate [them] selves in pleasure and riot" (as men might) for diversion. An influential British Evangelical named Thomas Gisborne made a similar appraisal of women's religious inclinations at the turn of the century, giving more weight, however, to women's distress and fear in childbirth as motivations of their piety.[3]

By the early nineteenth century New England ministers took for granted that women were the majority among Christians. They had assimilated the eighteenth-century argument that "women are happily formed for religion" by means of their "natural endowments" of sensibility, delicacy, imagination, and sympathy.[4] It testified how far New England Protestantism had become a matter of "the heart" rather than "the head" between the seventeenth and the nineteenth century—just as it had become a religion chiefly of women rather than men—that such characteristics manifested a "religious" temperament.[5] Recalling Christ's blessing of the meek and merciful, the Reverend Joseph Buckminster asked a Boston women's organization in 1810 if it was "surprising, that the most fond and faithful votaries of such a religion should be found among a sex, destined by their very constitution, to the exercise of the passive, the quiet, the secret, the gentle and humble virtues?" Men, the "self-styled lords of Creation," pursued wealth, politics or pleasure, but "the dependent, solitary female" sought God. Because of their softheartedness women were attuned to Christianity, Buckminster thought, and they appreciated Christianity because it valued domestic life. He summed up dramatically, "I believe that if Christianity should be compelled to flee from the mansions of the great, the academies of the philosophers, the halls of legislators, or the throng of busy men, we should find her last and purest retreat with women at the fireside; her last altar would be the female heart; her last audience would be the children gathered around the knees of a mother; her last sacrifice, the secret prayer, escaping in silence from her lips, and heard perhaps only at the throne of God."[6] Christianity was essentially female, his pronouns revealed.

Buckminster and his colleagues developed a powerful rationale for women's special obligations to Christianity. They reasoned that women's devotion to the religion was only fair recompense for the gospel's service in elevating them to their "proper" rank. Only Christianity, they claimed, made "men willing to treat females as equals, and in some respects, as superiors"; only Christianity "exalt[ed] woman to an equal rank with man in all the felicities of the soul, in all the advantages of religious attainment, in all the prospects and hopes of immortality"; only Christianity redeemed human nature from the base passions and taught reverence for domestic relations.[7] Drawing comparisons from history and from other cultures (readily at hand because of the foreign-mission movement), ministers affirmed that New England women owed their social rank to the progress of Christian civilization. This was an omnipresent theme.[8]

Contrasts between the condition of women in New England and in the countries to which missionaries traveled made it plausible that the Christian gospel had "civilized" men's attitudes to women. To appeal to a female charitable society for funds in 1829, the male trustees of the New Hampshire mission society asserted that "heathen" women were "ignorant—degraded—oppressed—enslaved. They are never treated by the other sex as companions and equals. They are in a great measure outcasts from society. They are made to minister to the *pleasures* of man; they are made to do the *work* of men; but, admitted to the enjoyment of equal rights, and raised to the respectability and happiness of free and honourable social intercourse, they are not." New Hampshire women by contrast were respected and free, and had access to knowledge.[9] Rebeccah Lee, wife of the pastor in Marlborough, Connecticut, urged this point of view on the members of several female societies there. "To the Christian religion we owe the rank we hold in society, and we should feel our obligations," she declared.

> It is that, which prevents our being treated like beasts of burden—which secures us the honourable privilege of human companionship in social

life, and raises us in the domestic relations to the elevated stations of wives and mothers. Only seriously reflect upon the state of our sex, in those regions of the globe unvisited and unblessed with the light of Christianity; we see them degraded to a level with the brutes, and shut out from the society of lordly *man*; as if they were made by their Creator, not as the companions, but as the slaves and drudges of domineering masters. . . . Let each one then ask herself, how much do I owe?[10]

The "feminization" of Protestantism in the early nineteenth century was conspicuous.[11] Women flocked into churches and church-related organizations, repopulating religious institutions. Female converts in the New England Great Awakening between 1798 and 1826 (before the Methodist impact) outnumbered males by three to two.[12] Women's prayer groups, charitable institutions, missionary and education societies, Sabbath School organizations, and moral reform and maternal associations all multiplied phenomenally after 1800, and all of these had religious motives. Women thus exercised as fully as men the American penchant for voluntary association noted by Tocqueville in the 1830s, but women's associations before 1835 were *all* allied with the church, whereas men's also expressed a variety of secular, civic, political, and vocational concerns.[13]

This flowering of women's associational activities was part of the revival movement of the early nineteenth century in which Protestants tried to counteract religious indifference, rationalism, and Catholicism and to create an enduring and moral social order. Ministers were joined by lay persons, often (not always) of wealthy and conservative background, in giving the Awakening its momentum. They interpreted the aftermath of the French Revolution in the 1790s as proof of the dangers of a "godless" society, and feared that the American republic, with its growing urban populations, its Catholic immigrants, its Western inhabitants far from New England culture and clergy, might fall victim to similar "godless" influence. They saw religious education not only as a means to inculcate true faith but as a route to salvation on this earth, since it could teach the restraints demanded for an orderly society. The lay activities of the revival intended education, religious conversion, and the reformation of individual character whether they took the form of distributing bibles and tracts among the urban poor and Western frontier residents, raising money to train ministers or missionaries to evangelize the unchurched, setting up Sabbath schools for children to begin the business of Christian training early, or other myriad forms.[14]

Ministers' religious and denominational aims, conservatives' manipulation of religious benevolence for social control, humanitarians' perceptions of the needs of the poor, and women's orientation toward religious and gender-group expression all contributed to the proliferation of Christian women's societies. Since the prayer meetings called during religious revivals were often sex-segregated, they could serve as prototypes of religious organizations exclusively for women. The British Evangelical movement also supplied explicit models of charitable and humanitarian efforts by women.[15] These several motives and predispositions help to explain the extraordinarily swift rise and geographical dispersion of women's religious benevolent associations. Under the combined forces of local ministers, agents of national benevolent organizations and individual women who took to heart their obligations, female religious and charitable societies were established in all the larger cities of New England shortly after the turn of the century—in Middlebury and Montpelier, Concord and Portsmouth, Portland and Eastport, Providence and Newport, Hartford and New Haven, Boston, Salem, and Newburyport. Small towns in Vermont such as Jericho Center, Danville, Cornwall, Thetford, and Castleton had female religious and missionary societies before 1816. Scores of religious charitable societies were formed among New Hampshire women in rural towns between 1804 and 1814. With the encouragement of agents of the New Hampshire Bible Society, women founded local affiliates in 138 towns between 1820 and 1828. Women belonged to dozens of female charitable societies and "education" societies (which raised funds to educate ministers) in Connecticut towns by 1815; and societies for prayer, for propagation of the gospel, for missionary and charitable purposes were even more numerous in Massachusetts. The Boston Female Society for Missionary Purposes corresponded with 109 similar societies in 1817–18.[16]

Why did women support religion so faithfully? Perhaps Cotton Mather's and Benjamin Colman's reasoning deserves some credence. The specter of death in childbirth repeatedly forced women to think on the state of their souls. And women's domestic occupations may have diverted them from piety less than the "snares" of the world did men; besides, ministers and pious women made every effort to conflate domestic values with religious values. Domestic occupations offered women little likelihood of finding a set of values and symbols to rival the ones proposed by evangelical Christianity. For women at home in New England society, Christian belief had a self-perpetuating force that was not likely to be disrupted by experience that would provide alternative and equally satisfying explanations.[17] Yet women whose occupations took them outside the home, and single women generally, were prominent in the female religious community. Early factory workers participated in revivals, as Catherine Sedgwick, a Unitarian opposed to evangelical fervor, reported to her brother in

1833: "We have had the religious agitators among us lately—They have produced some effect on the factory girls & such light & combustible materials."[18] Perhaps the eighteenth-century reasoning about women's temperament suiting them for Christian faith had a deeper truth. Characteristics expected in women and in Christians—those of the "tender heart"—increasingly coincided during the eighteenth century, because women supported Christianity more consistently than men, and became ministers' major constituency.[19] By the early nineteenth century, the clergy claimed that women supported (or should support) Christianity because it was in the interest of their sex to do so; that reassured the faithful, whether or not it accurately described their motives.

It is less than satisfying, however, to attribute New England women's religiosity to their mortal risks in childbirth or to a socialization process that inculcated domestic piety and "Christian" temperament in them. Skeptics at the time suggested other reasons. Harriet Martineau, a witty and politically astute British visitor who criticized hypocrisies in American women's expected roles, noticed that "in New England, a vast deal of [women's] time is spent in attending preachings, and other religious meetings: and in paying visits, for religious purposes, to the poor and sorrowful." She even found it plausible "that they could not exist without religion," but considered that an unhealthy circumstance. Women were "driven back upon religion as a resource against vacuity," in her view.[20]

(Although Martineau seems to have meant vacuity of *mind* rather than *time*, some evidence suggests that women without pressing demands on their time were indeed the *most* devoted to religion. Single women or childless wives not responsible for the whole of their own support were the most likely to record their religious musings unfailingly. Abigail Brackett Lyman began a journal of that sort in her teens when she made a public profession of faith, and continued, as she reflected several years later, "to inscribe nothing in my journal but devotional exercises from the period abovementioned till some time after my marriage when cares increasing & being obliged to entertain considerable company I found it impossible to continue this laudable practice." Another ardent convert remarked plaintively, while she was still single, "Most of my associates were settled in life but I saw that those who had been zealous and devoted before their marriage had mostly declined in piety when pressed with the domestic cares of a family. I said to myself Why is it so? It cannot be because there is anything in that state subversive of piety for it is of Divine appointment."[21])

Martineau's insight was still more piercing. She said women "pursue[d] religion as an occupation" because they were constrained from exercising their full range of moral, intellectual, and physical powers in other ways. With an extension of her allusion religious activities can be seen as a means used by New England women to define self and find community, two functions that wordly occupations more likely performed for men. Traditionally, of course, religion had enlightened individuals of both sexes about their identity and placed them in a like-minded community; but women's particular needs and the configuration of religious institutions at this time enhanced those social functions. In an era when Protestantism was a "crusade," when ministers presented evangelical Christianity as embattled and yet triumphant, religious affiliation announced one's identity and purpose. "I made religion the principal business of my life," Nancy Thompson summarized the effect of her conversion at nineteen. Abigail Lyman exhorted herself in 1800 (before the Second Great Awakening had progressed widely) "to Live up to the Professions of Religion I had made—to dare to be singular in this day when iniquity abounds."[22]

Religion stretched before the convert a lifetime of purposeful struggle holding out heartening rewards. It provided a way to order one's life and priorities. The evangelical theology of the early nineteenth century made that process of ordering amenable to personal choice. "The salvation of our precious souls is not to be effected independent of our exertions," Lyman wrote in her journal, "—we are free agents and as such should work out our salvation with fear and trembling. . . . We may believe and rely on the faith of Revelation— and form our actions and tempers by its pure and perfect precepts—or we may resist the truth—appose [sic] its influence & harden our hearts in sin—either the one or the other all are constantly doing." Yet an individual made the religious choice in submission to God's will rather than through personal initiative. The morphology of religious conversion echoed women's expected self-resignation and submissiveness while it offered enormously satisfying assurance to converts. Nancy Meriam, a devout young woman of Oxford, Massachusetts, recorded in her religious notes of 1815, "There is sweetness in committing ourselves to God which the world knows nothing of. The idea that I am intirely [sic] in the hands of God fills my mind with a secret pleasure which I cannot describe."[23]

Yet religious identity also allowed women to assert themselves, both in private and in public ways. It enabled them to rely on an authority beyond the world of men and provided a crucial support to those who stepped beyond accepted bounds—reformers, for example. Women dissenters from Ann Hutchinson to Sarah Grimké displayed the subversive potential of religious belief. Religious faith also allowed women a sort of holy selfishness, or self-absorption, the result of the self-examination intrinsic to the Calvinist tradition. In contrast to the self-abnegation required of women in their domestic vocation, religious commitment required attention to one's own thoughts, actions, and prospects. By recording their religious meditations women expressed their literacy and rising self-consciousness in a sanctioned mode. Vigilance for their souls and their conformity to God's requirements compelled them to scrutinize their lives. And the more distinctly Christianity appeared a preserve of *female* values, the more legitimate (and likely) it became for religious women to scrutinize their gender-role. If the popular sales of the published memoirs of female missionaries are any guide, that model of religious commitment, which proposed a submission of self that was simultaneously a pronounced form of self-assertion, had wide appeal. Time and again women who made note of little reading except the Bible read the memoirs of Mrs. Newell, missionary to Burma (1814), and responded perhaps as a young matron of Woodmont, Connecticut, did: "O that I could feel as she did . . . , it appears to me as though I had ought to feel willing to contribute freely to spread the gospel among the heathen."[24]

No other avenue of self-expression besides religion at once offered women social approbation, the encouragement of male leaders (ministers), and, most important, the community of their peers. Conversion and church membership in the era of the Second Great Awakening implied joining a community of Christians. As historians have noted, the individual convert in the revival entered "a community of belief in which he [or she] was encouraged to make a decision that would be a positive organizing principle for his [or her] own life." During these decades the sacramental dimension of the church faded in the light of a new conception, "a voluntary association of explicitly convinced Christians for the purpose of mutual edification in the worship of God and the propagandization of the Christian faith as the group defined it." Because the vigor of religion had sunk during the late eighteenth century, the "awakened" Christian community defined itself to an unusual extent by its adversary and evangelical relation to the outside world, as well as by its intramural purposes. "He that is not with us said the Saviour is against us," Abigail Lyman reiterated.[25]

Being a Christian in this period meant becoming a member of a voluntary community not only in a psychological but in a literal sense, for piety implied group evangelical activity. Associative activity flowed naturally from church membership. The motive to advance personal piety and the cause of Christianity, together with the desire to act cooperatively, and (often) the local minister's support, influenced women to form associations even before they had specific aims. The process of organization of the Female Religious and Cent Society in Jericho Center, Vermont, seems to have been typical. In 1805 a number of women joined together because they wished to "do good" and aid the cause of religion, but they did not know what path to take. They began meeting for prayer. (This was the simplest form religious association took, and probably the most widespread, but also the most difficult to find record of.[26]) With their minister's assistance they formed a society and began to raise money for the missionary movement. The articles of their society proclaimed in 1806 that they would meet fortnightly "for social prayer and praise and religious instruction and edification." They also pledged mutual support and group intimacy, resolving that "all persons attending the meeting shall conduct themselves with seriousness and solemnity dureing [sic] the Exercises nor shall an Illiberal remark be made respecting the performance of any of the members, neither shall they report abroad any of the transactions of the society to the prejudice of any of its members." The society prospered. In 1816, when it joined with a Young Ladies' Society that had been formed in 1812 under another minister's guidance, and founded the Female Cent Society of Jericho, the new group had seventy members.[27]

Women's diaries reveal the efforts, and the high esteem, given to religious associations. As a young matron in Greenfield, Massachusetts, in 1815 Sarah Ripley Stearns joined a group of "youthful females" who hoped to improve themselves in piety. The same year she helped found a female charitable society, with the goal of aiding destitute children to attend school and church. She noted when the "band of associated females" met at her house, and remarked that their "Benevolent Institution" was one of her chief sources of enjoyment. In 1816 she endeavored to found a maternal association, a "Juvenile Institution," and a "heathen school society." She carried on these activities during the years in which she bore three children, despite her laments that household cares left her little time for diary writing, pious reading, or church attendance.[28]

Sarah Connell Ayer of Maine involved herself even more thoroughly. Although her youth had been frivolous, the deaths of four infants during her first five years of marriage turned her increasingly to religion and its community of consolation. (The deaths of children, in these years, may have given women more powerful motivation toward religiosity than ever did fears of their own mortality in childbirth.) By the time Sarah Ayer was twenty-four she saw nothing more pleasant "than to spend an evening in conversation with a few pious friends." In early 1816 she belonged to a female missionary society, prayer meeting, and donation society in Portland, and was devoted to her orthodox Congregationalist minister. After giving birth to two children who survived, she joined the Maternal Association and found its meetings "profitable." In 1822 her husband's appointment as surveyor of the port induced the family to move to Eastport. There Mrs. Ayer found the Congregationalist minister too Unitarian for her taste, and missed her Portland friends greatly. "We loved to meet together, to talk of Heaven as our final home, Christ as our Saviour; we shared each others joys and sorrows, and found the one heightened and the other alleviated by sympathy. Ah! how prone am I to murmur when things go contrary to my own inclinations," she wrote in her diary. Soon, however, she reestablished comparable activities in Eastport. At first she discovered a compatible community among the Baptists, and then worked with a small group of orthodox Congregationalists—seventeen women and three men—to set up a church to her preference. By the late 1820s she participated in a maternal association, a female prayer society, a benevolent society, and Sabbath School class.[29]

The ease with which women moved among evangelical societies, and participated in several at once, suggests that associating under the ideological aegis of evangelical Christianity mattered more to them than the specific goals of any one group. The founding members of the Female Religious Biographical and Reading Society (or "Berean Circle") associated in 1826 because they were "convinced of the importance and utility of the benevolent associations of the present day, and wish[ed] to unite our efforts in the same worthy objects, and also desir[ed] to improve and impress our own minds by obtaining religious instructions."[30] The occurrence of such associations in virtually every Protestant church implied that professing faith had come to include participating in group activity. Whether local ministers, state organizations, or pious individuals launched them, such associations created peer groups which became part of their members' definition of Christian piety.

The chosen Christian community also entered into a woman's self-definition. Rachel Willard Stearns, who set herself off from her Congregational family by converting to Methodism, exemplified that effect in a pronounced way. She appreciated the Methodist small-group meetings, she said, because "if we have been gay or trifling, or anger or revenge have had a place in our hearts, we do not wish to go, if we stay away, then the others will think there is something wrong. . . . I am thankful that I have placed myself under the watch-care and discipline of a church, where when I do wrong they will tell me of it. . . ."[31] Stearns's Methodism brought her to an especially intense religious self-concept; but religion performed an analogous social function for women in traditional denominations.

Within their Christian peer groups women examined their own behavior, weighed the balance between self and sacrifice in their lives, and sought appropriate models. In October 1828 the Berean Circle discussed the question, "Can an individual who is more strongly activated by selfish motives than by a view to the glory of God be a Christian?" They recorded their conclusions: "If their *habitual prevailing* motives are selfish they cannot; for the most important point in conversion is the change from selfishness to benevolence. We are not required to be so disinterested as to leave our own *chief* happiness out of view. This subject led to much interesting conversation." Several years later the group was engaged in similar topics, pursuing such questions as "Is an ungoverned temper, proof of an unsanctified heart?" Women's remarks in diaries suggest unanimously the deep satisfaction derived from occasions for discussion. One recorded that her meeting provided "much pleasure," another that it was "instructive and entertaining," a third that "I returned much refreshed in spirit."[32]

A shift in ministers' views also encouraged women's religious activities. The seventeenth-century clergy had tended to stress Eve's legacy, and hence to focus on woman being the "first in transgression." During the eighteenth century, ministers turned their attention from Eve to other promising models of female character in the Bible, in order to justify the idea that women could bear the standard of the religious community.[33] From the 1790s to the 1820s ministers of several denominations endorsed the view that women were of conscientious and prudent character, especially suited to religion. Drawing often on the text of Proverbs 31, they showed the model Christian woman to be a modest and faithful wife, an industrious and benevolent community member, and an efficient housekeeper who did not neglect the refinements of life. Fervently they described how pious women could influence others in the community and in their own families. From Baptists to Unitarians, clergymen agreed that family religion communicated from parents to children was the natural, divinely approved, most effective means of reproducing true Christian character.[34] By the pastors' own admission, mothers had more impact on children in this regard than fathers did. The reasoning of a Wolfborough, New Hampshire, Sabbath School convention reiterated the pervasive idea that mothers (and by extension, all women) propagated religion best. They resolved in 1834: "Whereas the influence of females on little children ordinarily determines their future character and eternal destiny, and as it has been most effectually exerted in bringing them to Christ, therefore, *Resolved,* that it is the sacred duty of all females to use every effort to promote the cause of Sabbath Schools."[35]

No other public institution spoke to women and cultivated their loyalty so assiduously as the churches did. Quickened by religious anxiety and self-interest, the clergy gave their formulations of women's roles unusual force. They pinned on women's domestic occupation and influence their own best hopes. Their portrayal of women's roles grew in persuasive power because it overlapped with republican commonplaces about the need for virtuous citizens for a successful republic. It gained intensity because it intersected with new interest in early childhood learning. Ministers declared repeatedly that women's pious influence was not only appropriate to them but crucial for society. "We look to you, ladies," said Joseph Buckminster, "to raise the standard of character in our own sex; we look to you, to guard and fortify those barriers, which still exist in society, against the encroachments of impudence and licentiousness. We look to you for the continuance of domestick purity, for the revival of domestick religion, for the increase of our charities, and the support of what remains of religion in our private habits and publick institutions."[36]

Ministers addressed women as a sex and, at the same time, as an interest group in the polity that had special civil and social responsibilities and special powers to defend its interests. "I address you as a class," said a Boston pastor to the mothers of the Mount Vernon Maternal Association, "because your duties and responsibilities are peculiar."[37] Ministers viewed women's sex-role as a social role, in other words. It meant no lessening of women's consciousness of the responsibilities borne to them by gender that the interests and obligations proposed to them were the ministers' own interests, and that the latter looked ahead to a rising generation of sons (the *men* who would lead society). Under ministers' guidance women could conclude that their sex shared not simply a biological but a social purpose. They were entrusted with the morals and faith of the next generation. According to prevailing conceptions of republican virtue, this was a task having political impact.[38]

NOTES

1. Jonathan Stearns, *Female Influence, and the True Christian Mode of Its Exercise: A Discourse delivered in the 1st Presbyterian Church in Newburyport, July 30, 1837* (Newburyport: John G. Tilton, 1837), p. 11. He had to qualify his assertion with "almost," I assume, in order to encourage male church-goers and also to account for the exclusion of women from the ministry.

2. Women's majority did not increase in a linear fashion from the seventeenth to the nineteenth centuries because during the Great Awakening of the 1740s proportionally more men converted than during nonrevival years. On the sex ratio among church members during the seventeenth century see Edmund S. Morgan, "New

England Puritanism: Another Approach," *WMQ* 3d ser., 18 (1961):236–42; Darrett Rutman, "God's Bridge Falling Down—'Another Approach' to New England Puritanism Assayed," *WMQ* 3d ser., 19 (1962):408–21; on the early eighteenth century see Cedric Cowing, "Sex and Preaching in the "Great Awakening," *AQ* 20 (1968):625–34; J. Bumsted, "Religion, Finance and Democracy in Massachusetts: The Town of Norton as a Case Study," *JAH* 57 (1971):817–31; James Walsh, "The Great Awakening in the First Congregational Church of Woodbury, Connecticut, *WMQ* 3d ser., 28 (1971):543–52; Gerald F. Moran, "Conditions of Religious Conversion in the First Society of Norwich, Connecticut, 1718-1744," *JSH* 5 (1972):331–43; Philip J. Greven, Jr., "Youth, Maturity, and Religious Conversion: A Note on the Ages of Converts in Andover, Massachusetts, 1711-1749," *Essex Institute Historical Collections* (April 1972):119–34; on the early nineteenth century see Nancy F. Cott, "Young Women in the Second Great Awakening" *FS* 3 (1975): 15–29; Donald Mathews, "The Second Great Awakening as an Organizing Process," *AQ* 21 (1969), esp. p. 42; Whitney R. Cross, *The Burned-Over District* (New York: Harper Torchbooks, 1965), esp. pp. 84–89; and Barbara Welter, "The Feminization of Religion in Nineteenth-Century America," in Mary Hartman and Lois Banner, eds., *Clio's Consciousness Raised* (New York: Harper Torchbooks, 1973).

3. Cotton Mather, *Ornaments for the Daughters of Zion* (Cambridge, Mass., 1692), pp. 44–45; Benjamin Colman, *The Duty and Honour of Aged Women* (Boston, 1711), pp. ii–iii; Dr. John Gregory, *A Father's Legacy to his Daughters* (London: John Sharpe, 1822), pp. 11–12; Thomas Gisborne, *An Enquiry into the Duties of the Female Sex* (London, reprinted Philadelphia: James Humphreys, 1798), pp. 182–83. I cite these English works because of the evidence that they were read in New England; on this, see Nancy F. Cott, "In the Bonds of Womanhood: Perspectives on Female Experience and Consciousness in New England, 1780-1830" (Ph.D. diss., Brandeis University, 1974), pp. 225–27.

4. Quotation from Daniel Chaplin, *A Discourse Delivered before the Charitable Female Society in Groton [Massachusetts], October 19, 1814* (Andover, Mass., 1814), p. 9.

When I speak of "New England ministers' views" in what follows, my opinions primarily derive from my reading of 65 sermons concerning or addressed to women between 1792 and 1837, of which 54 were written between 1800 and 1820, and 57 were delivered to meetings of female associations in New England towns and cities. The denomination best represented were the trinitarian Congregationalists, who contributed at least a third of the sermons, while Unitarian Congregationalists, Presbyterians, Episcopalians, Baptists, and others together gave the rest. Denominational differences did not perceptibly vary ministers' assessments of women's roles, however. But note that I am not dealing here with the Methodist contribution or the influence of Charles G. Finney's revivalism, which occurred chiefly after 1835 in New England. I have presented the ministers' views in greater detail in "In the Bonds of Womanhood," chap. 3.

5. Jonathan Edwards was, of course, a central figure in this transformation.

6. Joseph Buckminster, "A Sermon Preached before the Members of the Boston Female Asylum, September 1810," hand-copied and bound with other printed sermons to the BFA, pp. 7–9, BPI.

7. Chaplin, *A Discourse*, p. 12; Pitt Clarke, *A Discourse Delivered before the Norton Female Christian Association on . . . June 13, 1818* (Taunton, Mass., 1818), p. 11; Samuel Worcester, *Female Love to Christ* (Salem, Mass., 1809), pp. 12–13.

8. E.g., see Daniel Clark, *The Wise Builder, a Sermon Delivered to the Females of the 1st Parish in Amherst, Mass.* (Boston, 1820), pp. 17-18, 23-24; John Bullard, *A Discourse, delivered at Pepperell, September 19, 1815, before the Charitable Female Society* (Amherst, N.H., 1815), pp. 9-10; Benjamin Wadsworth, *Female Charity an Acceptable Offering* . . .(Andover, Mass., 1817), pp. 27-28; David T. Kimball, *The Obligation and Disposition of Females to Promote Christianity* . . . (Newburyport, 1819), p. 4.

9. *16th Annual Report on the concerns of the Female Cent Institution, New Hampshire* (Concord, N.H., 1829), pp. 3-4 (quotation), 4-6.

10. Mrs. Rebeccah Lee, *An Address, Delivered in Marlborough, Connecticut, September 7, 1831* (Hartford, 1831), p. 4. She also noted, "There is not a town or village in our country, perhaps, where females are not actively engaged in this good cause, and from us much is expected in the present day."

11. The term is Barbara Welter's, in "The Feminization of Religion."

12. See Ebenezer Porter, *Letters on Revivals of Religion* (Andover, Mass.: The Revival Association, 1832), p. 5; and Cott, "Young Women in the Second Great Awakening." Beginning in 1830 Methodist evangelism under Charles G. Finney encouraged women's religious activity, particularly their public praying, more vigorously than other denominations. On the contribution of Methodist practice to Congregational and Presbyterian revival measures in the northeast before Finney, see Richard Carwardine, "The Second Great Awakening in the Urban Centers: An Examination of Methodism and the 'New Measures'," *JAH* 59 (1972):327-41.

Studies of many individual communities will be necessary before the precise impact of the revivals of the sex ratio among church members can be ascertained. Recent historical research on the Second Great Awakening suggests that the proportion of men among the converts was greater during revival years than ordinary years, but only large enough to reduce the female majority somewhat, not to undermine it. See Mary P. Ryan, "A Woman's Awakening: Revivalist Religion in Utica, New York, 1800-1835," paper delivered at the Third Berkshire Conference on the History of Women, Bryn Mawr, Pa., June 10, 1976, and Paul E. Johnson, "A Shopkeeper's Millennium: Society and Revivals in Rochester, N.Y., 1815-1837" (Ph.D. diss., University of California at Los Angeles, 1975).

13. See Alexis de Tocqueville, *Democracy in America,* ed. Phillips Bradley (New York: Vintage Books, 1945), 1:198-205, 2:114-18, 123-28. Cf. Richard D. Brown, "The Emergence of Voluntary Associations in Massachusetts, 1760-1830," *Journal of Voluntary Action Research* 2 (1973), esp. 68-70.

14. See Clifford S. Griffin, "Religious Benevolence as Social Control, 1815-1860," *MVHR* 44 (1957), esp. 440-42; Charles I. Foster, *An Errand of Mercy: The Evangelical United Front, 1790-1837* (Chapel Hill, N.C.: University of North Carolina Press, 1960). A recent critique by Lois Banner, "Religious Benevolence as Social Control: A Critique of an Interpretation," *JAH* 60 (1973):23-41, stresses the organizational dynamics of the Protestant denominations and the sincere educational and humanitarian aims of proponents.

15. Merle Curti, "American Philanthropy and the National Character," *AQ* 10 (1958):425. The first female charitable institution in the United States, the Society for the Relief of Poor Widows and Small Children, was founded in 1796 in New York by a newly arrived Scotswoman, Isabella M. Graham, on the model of a London institution for poor relief.

16. The formation of the national benevolent societies, such as the American Bible Society, the American Sabbath School Association, etc., did not occur until 1815 and after. Documentation of the existence of women's associations occurs in the titles of ministers' sermons, in printed constitutions and reports and manuscript records of the societies themselves, in women's diaries and letters, and in local histories. In addition to titles listed in the Suggested Readings, see documents from the Jericho Center Female Religious Society, Cent Society, and Maternal Association, and constitution and rules of the Maternal Association in Dorchester, Mass., Dec. 25, 1816, CL; documents of the Charitable Female Society in the 2d parish in Bradford, 1815–21, of the West Bradford Female Temperance Society, 1829–34, of the Female Religious, Biographical, Reading Society (Berean Circle), 1826–32, of the Belleville Female Benevolent Society, or Dorcas Society, 1839–40, and of the Hamilton Maternal Association, 1834–35, EI; *Report on the Concerns of the New Hampshire Cent Institution* (Concord, 1814, 1815, 1816); *The Rules, Regulations, Etc. of the Portsmouth Female Asylum* (Portsmouth, 1815); Edward Aiken, *The First Hundred Years of the New Hampshire Bible Society* (Concord, 1912), p. 66; Mrs. L. H. Daggett, ed., *Historical Sketches of Women's Missionary Societies in America and England* (Boston, n.d.), p. 50; *Annual Reports of the Education Society of Connecticut and the Female Education Society of New Haven* (New Haven, 1816–26); *An Account of the Rise, Progress, and Present State of the Boston Female Asylum* (Boston, 1803); *Constitution of the Salem Female Charitable Society, Instituted July 1st, 1801* (printed circular, 1801); *Reminiscences of the Boston Female Asylum* (printed, Boston, 1844); *Account of the Plan and Regulations of the Female Charitable Society of Newburyport* (Newburyport, 1803); *A Brief Account of the Origin and Progress of the Boston Female Society for Missionary Purposes, with extracts from the reports of the society in May 1817 and 1818* (Boston, 1818); *Report of the Boston Female Society for Missionary Purposes* (Boston, 1825); *Constitution of the Female Samaritan Society instituted in Boston, Nov. 19, 1817 and revised 1825* (Boston, 1833); *Constitution of the Female Society of Boston and the Vicinity for Promoting Christianity among the Jews, instituted June 5, 1816* (Boston, n.d.); *Constitution of the Fragment Society, Boston, founded 1817* (Boston, 1825); *Constitution of the Female Philanthropick Society, instituted Dec. 1822* (Boston, 1823); *Boston Fatherless and Widows Society, founded 1817, Annual Report* (Boston, 1836); *Second Annual Report, Third Annual Report, of the Boston Female Moral Reform Society* (Boston, 1837, 1838); *Constitution of the Maternal Association of Newburyport* (printed, 1815); *Constitution of the Maternal Association of the 2d Parish in West-Newbury, adopted Sept. 1834* (printed, n.d.); *Constitution of the Maternal Association* (Dedham, Mass., n.d.); *Constitution of the Maternal Association of the New Congregational Church in Boston, Mass., organized Oct. 6, 1842* (Boston, 1843); *Diary of Sarah Connell Ayer* (Portland, Me., 1910), pp. 213–15, 226, 228, 237, 285–307; diary of Mary Hurlbut, Feb. 10, 1833, CHS. See also Keith Melder, " 'Ladies Bountiful': Organized Women's Benevolence in Early Nineteenth-Century America," *New York History* 48 (1967): 231–54; Mary B. Treudley, "The Benevolent Fair: A Study of Charitable Organizations Among Women in the First Third of the Nineteenth Century," *Social Service Review* 14 (1940):506–22.

17. This line of argument was suggested to me by Gordon Schochet's reasoning about patriarchalism in the seventeenth century in "Patriarchalism, Politics, and Mass Attitudes in Stuart England," *Historical Journal* 12 (1959), esp. 421–25.

18. Catherine Sedgwick to Robert Sedgwick, Sept. 15, 1833, Sedgwick Collection, MHS. See also the diary of Mary Hall, a Lowell operative, NHHS; and Almond H. Davis, ed., *The Female Preacher, or Memoir of Salome Lincoln* (Providence, R.I., 1843).

19. Lonna Malmsheimer suggests that the numerical predominance of women in New England churches forced adjustments in ministers' views of their character during the eighteenth century, in "New England Funeral Sermons and Changing Attitudes toward Women, 1672-1792" (Ph.D. diss., University of Minnesota, 1973).

20. Harriet Martineau, *Society in America* (New York: Saunders and Otley, 1837), 2:255-57, 229, 363. Martineau strenuously objected to women working to raise money to educate young clerics (as they did in "education" societies); see pp. 363, 415-20.

21. Journal of Abigail Brackett Lyman, Jan. 1, 1800, in Helen Roelker Kessler, "The Worlds of Abigail Brackett Lyman" (M.A. thesis, Tufts Univ., 1976), appendix A; "A Short Sketch of the life of Nancy Thomson [sic]," autobiographical fragment in the diary of Nancy Thompson (Hunt), c. 1813, CHS. See also the journal of Mary Treadwell Hooker, 1795-1812, CSI.

22. "Short Sketch," diary of Nancy Thompson, c. 1808; journal of Abigail Brackett Lyman, Jan. 30, 1800; see also diary of Lucinda Read, March 30, 1816, MHS.

23. Journal of Abigail Brackett Lyman, Oct. 3, 1802; Nancy Meriam, "Religious Notes, 1811-15," April 9, 1815, WHS; also see Cott, "Young Women in the Second Great Awakening," on this theme. William McLoughlin summarizes the idea of "compliance with the terms of salvation" thus: "The process of conversion . . . became a shared act, a complementary relationship. Man striving and yearning; God benevolent and eager to save; the sinner stretching out his hands to receive the gift of grace held out by a loving God. This belief in man's free will or his partial power to effect his own salvation had in earlier Calvinist days been condemned as the heresy of Arminianism. For this reason most nineteenth-century ministers preferred to call themselves Evangelicals." *The American Evangelicals 1800-1900* (New York: Harper Torchbooks, 1968), p. 10.

24. Diary of Mrs. S. Smith, March 29, 1825, CSL. See also the diary of Mary Treadwell Hooker; diary of Sarah Ripley Stearns, May 1, 1814, and March 19, 1815, Stearns Collection, S.L.; correspondence between Almira Eaton and Weltha Brown, 1812-22, Hooker Collection, SL.

25. Richard D. Birdsall, "The Second Great Awakening and the New England Social Order," *Church History* 39 (1970):357; Sidney E. Mead, "The Rise of the Evangelical Conception of the Ministry in America, 1607-1850," in H. Richard Niebuhr and Daniel L. Williams, eds., *The Ministry in Historical Perspective* (New York: Harper and Bros., 1956), p. 224; journal of Abigail Brackett Lyman, Oct. 3, 1802. Historians of religion consistently maintain that during the last two decades of the eighteenth century American churches "reached a lower ebb of vitality . . . than at any other time in the country's religious history," in the words of Sydney E. Ahlstrom, *A Religious History of the American People* (New Haven: Yale University Press, 1972), p. 365. Douglas Sweet protests that consensus in "Church Vitality and the American Revolution," *Church History* 45 (1976):341-57. The Second Great Awakening, beginning in the late 1790s, decisively changed the religious climate. Estimates for New England, which generally was the region of highest church affiliation, are unavailable, but Winthrop S. Hudson estimates that church members in the United States as a whole increased from 1

out of 15 in the population in 1800, to 1 out of 8, in 1835, raising the churches' "constituency" from 40 percent to 75 percent of the population; *Religion in America: An Historical Account* (2d ed., New York: Scribners, 1973), pp. 129–30.

26. Mary Orne Tucker mentions her attendance at such a meeting in her diary, April 12, 1802, EI; see also *The Writings of Nancy Maria Hyde of Norwich, Conn.* (Norwich, 1816), pp. 182–83, 189–90, 192–93, 201–02, 203–05.

27. Documents of the Jericho Center, Vermont, Female Religious Society, Cent Society, and Maternal Associations. By 1824 the Cent Society had 120 subscribers.

28. Sarah Ripley Stearns diary, 1814–17, esp. Dec. 24, 1815, March 2, March 31, July 14, Oct. 13, 1816, June 1817.

29. *Diary of Sarah Connell Ayer 1805–1835,* pp. 209, 211, 213, 214, 215, 225, 226, 228, 231–33, 236–37, 239–40, 254, 278, 282–305. There is a gap in the diary between 1811 and 1815, the years in which Ayer bore and buried her first four children.

30. Record book of the Female Religious, Biographical, Reading Society (the Berean Circle), 1826–32, EI. The society was probably located near Newburyport, though its exact location is not clear.

31. Diary of Rachel Willard Stearns, July 19, 1835, Stearns Collection, SI.

32. Record book of the Berean Circle, Oct. 15, 1828, Jan. 17, 1832; Mary Orne Tucker diary, April 12, 1802; *The Writings of Nancy Maria Hyde,* pp. 189–90; diary of Nancy Meriam, May 12, 1819, WHS.

33. See Malmsheimer, "New England Funeral Sermons."

34. See, for example, Amos Chase, *On Female Excellence* (Litchfield, Conn., 1792); John C. Ogden, *The Female Guide* (Concord, N.H., 1793); George Strebeck, *A Sermon on the Character of the Virtuous Woman* (New York, 1800); William Lyman, *A Virtuous Woman the Bond of Domestic Union and the Source of Domestic Happiness* (New London, Conn., 1802); Nathan Strong, *The Character of a Virtuous and Good Woman* (Hartford, 1809); Ethan Smith, *Daughters of Zion Excelling* (Concord, N.H., 1814); Daniel Clark, *The Wise Builder* (Boston, 1820); and Cott, "In the Bonds of Womanhood," pp. 105–15.

35. Quoted by Henry C. Wright in his journal, 6:135, June 18, 1834, HCL.

36. Buckminster, "A Sermon Preached . . . 1810," pp. 24–25.

37. Pastor's address appended to *Constitution of the Maternal Association of the New Congregational Church* (Boston, 1843), p. 5.

38. E.g., Ward Cotton told the women of Boylston, Massachusetts, that bringing domestic missionaries to unchurched Western residents would be "the means not only of the salvation of their souls, but also of the political salvation of our country." *Causes and Effects of Female Regard to Christ* (Worcester, 1816), p. 13.

10 ⚮ Women's Perspective on the Patriarchy in the 1850s

Anne Firor Scott

Southern women were scarcely to be seen in the political crisis of the 1850s. Historical works dealing with that crucial decade seldom mention a woman unless it is in a footnote citing a significant letter from a male correspondent. In women's own diaries and letters the burgeoning conflict between the North and South almost never inspired comment before John Brown's raid and rarely even then.

At the same time, women were a crucial part of one southern response to the mounting outside attack on slavery. The response was an ever more vehement elaboration of what has been called the "domestic metaphor," the image of a beautifully articulated, patriarchal society in which every southerner, black or white, male or female, rich or poor, had an appropriate place and was happy in it. "The negro slaves of the South are the happiest, and, in some sense, the freest people in the world," George Fitzhugh wrote, describing the happy plantation on which none were oppressed by care.[1] "Public opinion," he stoutly maintained, "unites with self-interest, domestic affection, and municipal law to protect the slave. The man who maltreats the weak and dependent, who abuses his authority over wife, children, or slaves is universally detested." Slavery, Fitzhugh thought, was an admirable educational system as well as an ideal society.[2]

What Fitzhugh argued in theory many planters tried to make come true in real life. "My people" or "my black and white family" were phrases that rolled easily from their tongues and pens. "I am friend and

From *Journal of American History* 61 (June 1974). Reprinted by permission.

well wisher both for time and eternity to every one of them . . ." a North Carolinian wrote to his slave overseer upon the death of a slave, expressing sorrow that he could not be present for the funeral.[3] This letter was one in a series of fatherly letters to that particular slave, and the writer, a bachelor, offered similar fatherly guidance to his grown sisters, as he doled out their money to them.

Even as planters tried to make the dream come true, they could not hide their fear and doubt. "It gave me much pleasure to see so much interest manifested," one wrote his wife, reporting that the slaves had inquired about her health and welfare, "and I am convinced that much of it was sincere."[4] Quick panic followed rumors of insurrection, and when the war came many planters took the precaution of moving their slaves as Yankee armies approached. For those who enjoy poetic justice there is plenty to be found in the pained comments of loving patriarchs when their most pampered house servants were the first to depart for Yankee camps.

Women, like slaves, were an intrinsic part of the patriarchal dream. If plantation ladies did not support, sustain, and idealize the patriarch, if they did not believe in and help create the happy plantation, which no rational slave would exchange for the jungle of a free society, who would? If women, consciously or unconsciously, undermined the image designed to convince the doubting world that the abolitionists were all wrong, what then?

Some southern men had doubts about women as well as slaves. This is clear in the nearly paranoid reaction of some of them to the pronouncements and behavior of "strong-minded" women in the North. Southern gentlemen hoped very much that no southern lady would think well of such goings-on, but clearly they were not certain.[5] Their fears had some foundation, for in the privacy of their own rooms southern matrons were reading Margaret Fuller, Madame de Stael, and what one of them described as "decided women's rights novels."[6]

Unlike the slaves, southern women did not threaten open revolt, and when the war came they did not run to the Yankees. Instead they were supportive, as they worked to feed and clothe civilians and the army, nurse the sick, run the plantations, supervise the slaves, and pray for victory. Yet even these activities were partly an indirect protest against the limitations of women's role in the patriarchy. Suddenly women were able to do business in their own right, make decisions, write letters to newspaper editors, and in many other ways assert themselves as individual human beings. Many of them obviously enjoyed this new freedom.[7]

Even before the war women were not always as enthusiastic in their support of the patriarchy as slavery's defenders liked to believe. To the assertion that "The slave is held to *involuntary service*," an Alabama minister responded:

> So is the wife. Her relation to her husband, in the immense majority of cases, is made for her, and not by her. And when she makes it for herself, how often, and how soon . . . would she throw off the yoke if she could! O ye wives, I know how superior you are to your husbands in many respects—not only in personal attraction . . . in grace, in refined thought, in passive fortitude, in enduring love, and in a heart to be filled with the spirit of heaven. . . . I know you may surpass him in his own sphere of boasted prudence and worldly wisdom about dollars and cents. Nevertheless, he has authority, from God, to rule over you. You are under service to him. You are bound to obey him in all things. . . . you cannot leave your parlor, nor your bed-chamber, nor your couch, if your husband commands you to stay there![8]

The minister was speaking to a northern audience and intended, no doubt, to convince northern women that they should not waste energy deploring the servitude of the slave since their own was just as bad, but surely this Alabama man shaped his understanding of married life in his home territory.

The minister's perception is supported in a little volume entitled *Tales and Sketches for the Fireside,* written by an Alabama woman for the purpose of glorifying southern life and answering the abolitionists. Woman's influence, she wrote,

> is especially felt in the home circle; she is the weaker, physically, and yet in many other respects the stronger. There is no question of what she can bear, but what she is obliged to bear in her positions as wife and mother, she has her troubles which man, the stronger, can never know. Many annoying things to woman pass unnoticed by those whose thoughts and feelings naturally lead them beyond their homes.

The writer added that since men were so restless, God in his wisdom designed women to be "the most patient and untiring in the performance . . . of duties." Weariness almost leaps from her pages. Not only is she bitter about the burdens of woman's lot, she also feels keenly the one-sidedness of those burdens and the failure of men even to notice.[9]

Personal documents provide even more detailed evidence of female discontent in the South of the 1850s. Unhappiness centered on women's lack of control over many aspects of their own sexual lives and the sexual lives of their husbands, over the institution of slavery which they could not change, and over the inferior status which kept them so powerless.[10]

The most widespread source of discontent, since it affected the majority of married women, was the actuality of the much glorified institution of motherhood. Most women were not able to control their own fertility. The typical planter's wife was married young, to a husband older than herself, and proceeded to bear children for two decades. While conscious family limitation was sometimes practiced in the nineteenth century, effective contraception was not available, and custom, myth, religion, and men operated to prevent limitation. With the existing state of medical knowledge it was realistic to fear childbirth and to expect to lose some children in infancy.[11]

The diary of a Georgia woman shows a typical pattern of childbearing and some reactions to it. Married in 1852 at the age of eighteen to a man of twenty-one, she bore her first child a year later. In the summer of 1855, noting certain telltale symptoms, she wrote "I am again destined to be a mother . . . the knowledge causes no exhilirating feelings . . . [while] suffering almost constantly . . . I cannot view the idea with a great deal of pleasure."[12] The baby was born but died in a few weeks, a circumstance which she prayed would help her live more dutifully in the future. A few months later she was happily planning a trip to the North because "I have no infant and I cannot tell whether next summer I will be so free from care . . . ,"[13] but in four days her dreams of travel vanished abruptly when morning nausea led her to wonder whether she was "in a peculiar situation, a calamity which I would especially dread this summer."[14] Her fears were justified, and she had a miscarriage in August. There was no rest for the weary. By January 1857 she was pregnant again, and on her twenty-fourth birthday in April 1858 she was pregnant for the fifth time in six years, though she had only two living children. Diary volumes for the next two years are missing, but in December 1862 she recorded yet another pregnancy, saying "I am too sick and irritable to regard this circumstance as a blessing *yet awhile.*"[15] A year later with the house being painted and all in confusion she jotted the illuminating comment: "I don't wonder that men have studys which . . . I imagine to be only an excuse for making themselves comfortable and being out of the bustle and confusion of . . . housekeeping . . . and children."[16] She also expressed bitter opposition to the practice of sending pregnant slaves to work in the fields. By February 1865, after four years of war, she was writing "unfortunately I have the prospect of adding again to the little members of my household. . . . I am sincerely sorry for it."[17] When the child was born prematurely in June the mother thanked God that it did not live. By 1869, this woman had managed to relegate her husband to a separate bedroom, and, for good measure, she kept the most recent infant in her bed, as effective a means of contraception as she could devise.[18] Later she reflected that she had never "been so opposed to having children as many women I know."[19]

The difference between the male and female angle of vision is illustrated in the life of a South Carolina woman, a niece of James L. Petigru, married to a cousin ten years her senior. She gave birth to six children in the first nine years of her marriage, and her uncle—normally a wise and perceptive human being—wrote to the young woman's mother: "Well done for little Carey! Has she not done her duty . . . two sons and four daughters and only nine years a wife? Why the Queen of England hardly beats her. . . ."[20] If the uncle had had access to the correspondence between "little Carey" and her planter husband he might not have been so quick to congratulate her. It seems likely from the evidence of these letters that her three-month sojourns with her mother in the summers were partly motivated by a desire to prolong the time between babies, but no sooner did her lonesome husband come to visit than she was pregnant again.[21]

This woman had a faithful family doctor who moved into her household when time for her confinement drew near, but even his comforting presence did not prevent her fears of death each time. Mrs. Thomas, writer of the first diary, relied on a slave midwife, her mother, and a town doctor. Both these women loved their children and cared for them, though with ample assistance before the war. Yet each privately insisted that she would have preferred a much longer time between babies. As the Alabama minister quoted earlier suggested, however, a woman could not leave her bedchamber or her couch without her husband's permission.[22]

Women's private feelings about constant childbearing provide one example of unhappiness which was masked by the cheerful plantation image. The behavior of the patriarchs themselves in other realms of sexual life was another source of discontent. The patriarchal ideal which called for pure, gentle, pious women also expected a great deal of men: that they should be strong, chaste, dignified, decisive, and wise. Women who lived in close intimacy with these men were aware of the gap between the cavalier of the image and the husband of the reality, and they were also aware that those who had the greatest power were also—by women's standards—the most sinful. A diarist summarized an afternoon of sewing and conversation in Richmond County, Georgia:

> We were speaking of the virtue of men. I admitted to their general depravity, but considered that there were some noble exceptions, among those I class my own husband. . . .[23]

The entry revealed a certain uneasiness even about the noble exception, since the writer added that if her faith in her husband should be destroyed by experience her happiness on earth would end, and added

"between husband and wife this is (or should be) a forbidden topic."
She was twenty-two.

This notation parallels one in a more familiar dairy. Observing the
goings-on of the low-country aristocracy, Mary Boykin Chesnut wrote:
"Thank God for my country women, but alas for the men! They are
probably no worse than men everywhere, but the lower their mistresses
the more degraded they must be. . . ."[24] Chesnut's comment revealed
the dual nature of male depravity: sexual aberration in general and
crossing the racial barrier in particular. Concern on this topic was an
insistent theme in the writings of southern women and continued to be
so long after emancipation. It may be significant that they did not
blame black women, who might have provided convenient scapegoats.
The blame was squarely placed on men. "You have no confidence in
men," wrote one husband; "to use your own phrase 'we are all hum-
bugs,' " adding that he himself was a great sinner though he did not
specify his sin.[25]

Miscegenation was the fatal flaw in the patriarchal doctrine. While
southern men could defend slavery as "domestic and patriarchal,"
arguing that slaves had "all the family associations, and family pride,
and sympathies of the master," and that the relationship between
master and slave secured obedience "as a sort of filial respect," southern women looked askance at the fact that so many slaves quite literally
owed their masters filial respect.[26] "There is the great point for the
abolitionists . . . ," one wrote.[27] While some southern reviewers blasted
"the fiend in petticoats" who wrote Uncle Tom's Cabin, southern
women passed copies of the book from hand to hand.

Impressive evidence of the pervasiveness of interracial sex and its
effects on the minds and spirits of white women, gathered thirty years
ago, has recently found its way into print. James Hugo Johnston
examined 35,000 manuscript petitions to the Virginia legislature.
Among these documents were many divorce petitions in which white
women named slave women as the cause of their distress. In some
petitions wives told the whole story of their marriages, throwing much
light on what could happen to the family in a slave society. One
testified that her husband had repeated connection with many slaves,
another protested several black mistresses who had been placed in her
home and had treated her insolently. Yet another recounted a complicated story in which her brother had tried to force her husband to send
away his black mistress, without success. In several cases the husband's
attention to his mulatto children, sometimes in preference to his
legitimate children, was offered in evidence. The stories run on and on
until one is surfeited with pain and tragedy from the white woman's
point of view, pain which could doubtless be matched from the black

woman's point of view if it had been recorded. Many petitioners candidly described their husbands' long attachment to black mistresses, and their reluctance to give them up. Johnston also adduced evidence of the tortured efforts white men made to provide for their mulatto children, efforts corroborated by Helen Catterall's compilation of legal cases dealing with slavery.[28]

If so much evidence found its way into the official records of the state of Virginia, how much is there yet unexamined in the records of other slave states, and how much more was never recorded because women suffered in silence rather than go against religion, custom, and social approval to sue for divorce by a special act of the legislature? Johnston, from his close acquaintance with the documents, surmised that there must have been many women who calmly or sullenly submitted to becoming "chief slave of the master's harem," a phrase attributed to Dolley Madison.[29]

Even apart from miscegenation, the general sexual freedom society accorded to men was deeply resented by women. A thread of bitterness runs through letters describing marital problems, the usual assumption being that male heartlessness could be expected. The double standard was just one more example of how unfairly the world was organized:

> As far as a womans being forever 'Anathema . . .' in society for the same offence which in a man, very slightly lowers, and in the estimation of some of his own sex rather elevates him. In this I say there appears to be a very very great injustice. I am the greatest possible advocate for womans purity, in word, thought or deed, yet I think if a few of the harangues directed to women were directed in a point where it is more needed the standard of morality might be elevated.[30]

Ten years later the same woman had not changed her mind: "it occurs to me that if virtue be the test to distinguish man from beast the claim of many Southern white men might be questionable. . . ."[31]

In addition to the widely prevailing skepticism with which women viewed the pretensions of their lords and masters (a label often used with a measure of irony), there was widespread discontent with the institution of slavery. "I never met with a lady of southern origin who did not speak of Slavery as a sin and a curse—the burden which oppressed their lives," Harriet Martineau observed in her autobiography.[32]

In Virginia, after the Nat Turner rebellion, twenty-four women joined in a petition to the legislature, noting that though "it be unexampled, in our beloved State, that females should interfere in its political concerns," they were so unhappy about slavery that they were willing to break the tradition. They urged the legislature to find a way to abolish slavery.[33] An overseer of wide experience told Chesnut in 1861 that in all his life he had met only one or two women who were not abolitionists.[34] William Gilmore Simms, reviewing *Uncle Tom's Cabin* in the *Southern Quarterly Review,* made clear his understanding of the opposition to slavery among southern women.[35]

Of course Martineau and the overseer exaggerated to make a point, and the Virginia petitioners were unusual. Women of slaveholding families responded ambiguously to the life imposed on them. Some accepted it without question. Others, complaining of the burden of slavery, nevertheless expected and sometimes got a degree of personal service which would have been inconceivable to women in the free states.[36] It was also true that few were philanthropic enough to give up a large investment for a principle. It is further clear that most southern women accepted, with a few nagging questions, the racial assumptions of their time and place.

Even with these conditions many women of the planter class had strong doubts about either the morality or the expediency of slavery, as the following statements indicate. "Always I felt the moral guilt of it, felt how impossible it must be for an owner of slaves to win his way into Heaven."[37] "But I do not hesitate to say . . . that slavery was a curse to the South—that the time had come in the providence of God to give every human being a chance for liberty and I would as soon hark back to a charnel house for health inspiration as to go to the doctrines of secession, founded on the institution of slavery, to find rules and regulations. . . ."[38] "When the thunderbolt of John Brown's raid broke over Virginia I was inwardly terrified, because I thought it was God's vengeance for the torture of such as Uncle Tom."[39] "I will confess that what troubles me more than anything else is that I am not certain that *Slavery is right.*"[40] "When will it please our God to enfranchise both the holders and the slaves from bondage? It is a stigma, a disgrace to our country. . . ."[41] "In 1864 I read Bishop Hopkins' book on slavery. He took the ground that we had a right to hold the sons of Ham in bondage. . . . Fancy a besotted, grinding, hardfisted slave driver taking up a moral tone as one of God's accredited agents!!"[42]

One doubter suggested that she would happily pay wages to her house servants if her husband would agree, and another thought slaves ought to be permitted to choose their own masters. Still another devoted all her time to teaching slaves to read and write, even though to do so was illegal, and to providing a Sunday school for slave children. [43]

Moral doubts were further complicated by strong personal attachments between white and black women. A South Carolina woman went into mourning in 1857 when her favorite slave died, and her sister wrote that "She loved Rose better than any other human being." [44]

Another member of the same family insisted that her brother and brother-in-law keep promises made to slaves whom she had sold within the family. A Virginia woman, seeking permission to free her slave woman and keep her in the state, contrary to the law, testified to her "strong and lasting attachment to her slave Amanda."[45] Such phrases were not uncommon among southern women.

For every woman who held slavery to be immoral, or who simply loved individual slaves, there were dozens who hated it for practical reasons. "Free at last," cried one white woman when she heard of the Emancipation Proclamation. "If slavery were restored and every Negro on the American continent offered to me," wrote another, "I should spurn them. I should prefer poverty rather than assume again the cares and perplexities of ownership. . . ."[46] Such quotations could be multiplied. They are typified by a diary entry in the fall of 1866 expressing relief "that I had no Negro clothes to cut out this fall O what a burden, like that of Sinbad the Sailor, was the thought of 'Negro clothes to be cut out.' "[47]

Motherhood, happy families, omnipotent men, satisfied slaves—all were essential parts of the image of the organic patriarchy. In none of these areas did the image accurately depict the whole reality.

For women as for the slaves, open revolt was made difficult by many constraints. Though women had complaints, they shared many of the assumptions of men, and, at least intermittently, enjoyed the role and status of the landholding aristocracy. Discontent does not automatically lead to a clear idea of alternatives, and few, if any, southern women in the 1850s had visions of a multiracial society based on freedom, much less equality. Nor did they conceive of fundamental change in the patterns of marriage and family which bound them so tight. Some, to be sure, found widowhood a liberating experience.[48]

The ideology of woman's liberation, which was being worked out in the North by Sarah Grimké, Margaret Fuller, Elizabeth Cady Stanton, and others, had only begun to take shape in the minds of southern women, but signs of change can be found. A letter written from Yazoo, Mississippi, in 1849 to the *Southern Ladies Companion* complained about an article which seemed to imply that only men were part of mankind:

> Woman is not, or ought not to be, either *an article* to be turned to good account by the persons who compose "this life" [men] nor a plaything for their amusement. She ought to be regarded as forming a part of mankind herself. She ought to be regarded as having as much interest or proprietorship in "this life" as anyone else. And the highest compliment to be paid her is that she is useful to herself—that in conjunction with the rest of mankind, in works of virtue, religion and morality, the sum of human

happiness is augmented, the kingdom of the Savior enlarged and the glory of God displayed.[49]

By the 1850s some echoes of the woman's rights debate which had erupted in the North in 1848 began to reach southern ears. A violent attack on the Woman's Rights Convention held in Worcester, Massachusetts, in 1851 appeared in the *Southern Quarterly Review,* written by a distinguished southern woman, Louisa Cheves McCord.[50] A closer look at McCord's own history is instructive with respect to built-in constraints. Daughter of Langdon Cheves, she was outstandingly able both as a writer and as an administrator. Yet she used her ability to defend the whole southern domestic metaphor, including slavery. One has only to imagine her born in Boston instead of Charleston to find in Louisa McCord all the makings of a Margaret Fuller or an Elizabeth Cady Stanton.

What was the significance of this widespread discontent? Public decisions are rooted in private feelings, and the psychological climate in any society is one of the most important things a social or political historian needs to understand. The South by 1860 was in a high state of internal tension, as feelings of guilt and fear of the future mounted. The part played by slaves themselves, as well as by women, in exacerbating these tensions is just now beginning to be examined. Speaking of the American Revolution, Charles Francis Adams once remarked that it "drew its nourishment from the sentiment that pervaded the dwellings of the entire population," and added, "How much this home sentiment did then, and does ever, depend upon the character of the female portion of the people, will be too readily understood by all to require explanation."[51] What Adams called "the home sentiment" was in the South of 1860 an unstable and hence explosive mixture of fear, guilt, anxiety, and discontent with things as they were. How much this stemmed from the unhappiness of "the female portion of the population" is not yet well understood, but it is worth a good deal of study.

NOTES

1. George Fitzhugh, *Cannibals All! or Slaves Without Masters* (Cambridge, Mass., 1960), p. 18.

2. William Pettigrew to Mose, July 12, 1856, Pettigrew Family Papers (Southern Historical Collection, University of North Carolina).

4. Charles Pettigrew to Caroline Pettigrew, Oct. 18, 1857, *ibid.*

5. Anne Firor Scott, *The Southern Lady: From Pedestal to Politics 1830–1930* (Chicago, 1970), 20–21.

6. *Corinne,* Madame de Stael's famous feminist novel, appeared often in lists of books read by southern women. Even Mary Wollstonecraft was not entirely unknown in the South. See William R. Taylor, *Cavalier and Yankee: The Old South and the American National Character* (New York, 1961), 162–67, for discussion of a pervasive malaise among ante bellum southern women.

7. See H. E. Sterkx, *Partners in Rebellion: Alabama Women in the Civil War* (Rutherford, N.J., 1970), for the most recent collection of evidence concerning the extraordinary vigor and range of southern women's activities during the war. It is important to note that this essay does not treat all classes of women. There were eight million southerners in 1860, of whom the largest part were ordinary farmer folk, slaves, and free blacks. This majority was ruled, politically, economically, and socially, by a small top layer, the large and medium-sized plantation owners who had money, or at least credit, slaves, and power. From their ranks came the proslavery philosophers, the mythmakers, the leaders of opinion. From their ranks came the most visible southerners, the minority which the rest saw and heard. It was members of this minority who consciously or unconsciously clung to the idea of the beautiful organic society so well described in George Fitzhugh, *Sociology for the South: or the Failure of Free Society* (Richmond, 1954). It was women of this minority who were called upon to play the appropriate role, to live up to the image of the southern lady. Other women, farmer's wives and daughters and illiterate black women, were part of society and in some inarticulate way doubtless helped to shape it, but historians have just begun to forge tools which may permit an examination of their role. For insights into southern society, see Steven A. Channing, *Crisis of Fear: Secession in South Carolina* (New York, 1970).

8. Fred A. Ross, *Slavery Ordained of God* (Philadelphia, 1859), 54–56.

9. R. M. Ruffin, *Tales and Sketches for the Fireside* (Marion, Ala., 1858).

10. For other sources of women's unhappiness, especially the desire for education, see Scott, *Southern Lady.* This essay concentrates on areas of complaint directly related to the patriarchal myth. Of course the education some women hoped for, had it been available, would have indirectly undermined the patriarchy.

11. See *Annual Report to the Legislature of South Carolina Relating to the Registration of Births, Deaths and Marriages for the Year Ending December 13, 1856* (Columbia, S. C., 1857). Though the report acknowledges grave deficiencies in its fact gathering, this early venture into vital statistics supports generalizations suggested here. For comparative purposes the report includes some statistics from Kentucky which are also supportive. Of the deaths recorded in South Carolina in 1856, nearly one half were children under the age of five and nearly one fourth were children under one year. Of marriages in the same year, 5.7 percent were of men under twenty, while 40.4 percent of the women were under that age. Nearly one half of the men and three fourths of the women who married in 1856 were under twenty-five. One fourth of the men but only 9.4 percent of the women married between the ages of twenty-five and thirty. A cohort analysis of selected groups of southern women patterned on Robert V. Wells' study of Quakers might be useful, if data could be found. See Robert V. Wells, "Demographic Change and the Life Cycle of American Families," *Journal of Interdisciplinary History,* II (Autumn 1971), 273–82. Analysis of the biographical sketches of 150 low-country

planters prepared by Chalmers Gaston Davidson provides further evidence of the age gap between husbands and wives. Davidson's study is based on 440 South Carolinians who had 100 or more slaves on a single estate. (Although fifty of the planters were women—a somewhat startling fact—his information is always about the men these women married.) The majority of the men were one to ten years older than their wives in first marriage. For second marriages the age difference increased, as it did for third and fourth marriages. In cases where the woman was older than her husband (twenty-three in all), the age gap was usually up to five years, though three women were more than ten years older than their husbands. Chalmers Gaston Davidson, *The Last Foray: The South Carolina Planters of 1860: A Sociological Study* (Columbia, S. C., 1971), 170–267.

12. E. G. C. Thomas Diary, June 26, 1855 (Department of Manuscripts, Duke University).

13. *Ibid.*, May 26, 1856.

14. *Ibid.*, June 1, 1856.

15. *Ibid.*, Dec. 1862.

16. *Ibid.*, Dec. 31, 1863.

17. *Ibid.*, Feb. 12, 1865.

18. *Ibid.*, Jan. 29, 1869.

19. *Ibid.*, Nov. 29, 1870.

20. James Petigru Carson, *Life, Letters and Speeches of James Louis Petigru: The Union Man of South Carolina* (Washington, 1920), 441.

21. Letters of Charles and Caroline Pettigrew, 1856–1861, Pettigrew Family Papers.

22. The degree to which maternity shaped women's lives emerges from any random examination of family histories. For example, Charles and Mary Pratt Edmonston of North Carolina had their first child in 1812, their last in 1833. During those twenty-one years Mrs. Edmonston bore eleven children, four of whom died in infancy. Mrs. Andrew McCollum of Louisiana bore ten children between 1840 and 1855, including one set of twins. Three died in infancy. During 180 months of married life, she spent ninety in pregnancy and seventy in nursing babies, since she did not use wet nurses. Thus in all her married life there was one month when she was neither pregnant nor nursing a baby. Margaret Ann Morris Grimball, wife of South Carolinian John B. Grimball, married at twenty and had a child every two years for eighteen years. At seventeen Varina Howell of Mississippi married Jefferson Davis who was thirty-five and a widower. Children were born in 1852, 1855, 1857, 1861, and 1864. Georgian David Crenshaw Barrow married Sarah Pope who bore him nine children in seventeen years, then died. John Crittenden's wife bore seven children in thirteen years. Robert Allston of South Carolina married Adele Petigru, ten years his junior. She bore ten children in seventeen years of whom five lived to maturity. Examples could be multiplied indefinitely, but far more useful would be a careful demographic study of selected southern counties, tidewater and upcountry, to give a firm underpinning to this kind of impressionistic evidence.

23. Thomas Diary, April 12, 1856.

24. Mary Boykin Chesnut, *Diary from Dixie*, Ben Ames Williams, ed. (Boston, 1949), 21–22.

25. Charles Pettigrew to Caroline Pettigrew, July 10, 1856, Pettigrew Family Papers.

26. Quoted in Severn Duvall, *"Uncle Tom's Cabin:* The Sinister Side of the Patriarchy," *New England Quarterly,* XXXVI (March 1963), 7–8. This perceptive article deserves serious attention from social historians.

27. Thomas Diary, Jan. 2, 1858.

28. James Hugo Johnston, *Race Relations in Virginia & Miscegenation in the South 1776–1860* (Amherst, 1970); Helen Tunnicliff Catterall, *Judicial Cases concerning American Slavery and the Negro* (2 vols., Washington, 1926). See also Guion Griffis Johnson, *Ante-Bellum North Carolina: A Social History* (Chapel Hill, 1937), 221, for evidence that cohabitation with a Negro was the second most important cause for divorce in North Carolina.

29. Johnston, *Race Relations in Virginia,* 237.

30. Thomas Diary, Feb. 9, 1858.

31. *Ibid.,* May 7, 1869.

32. Harriet Martineau, *Harriet Martineau's Autobiography: With Memorials by Maria Weston Chapman* (3 vols., London, 1877), II, 21.

33. Augusta County Legislative Petitions, 1825–1833 (Virginia State Library, Richmond).

34. Chesnut, *Diary from Dixie,* 169.

35. William Gilmore Simms, review of *Uncle Tom's Cabin, Southern Quarterly Review,* VIII (July 1853), 216, 233.

36. Their expectations may be illustrated by the E. G. C. Thomas family in its poverty-stricken postwar phase still requiring, so they thought, a person to cook, a person to clean, a person to wash and iron, one to do the chores, and a carriage driver. See Thomas Diary, 1868–1869, as Mrs. Thomas details her search for reliable domestic help among the freed people. One complication was that it was considered unethical to hire fine servants who had once belonged to friends.

37. John Q. Anderson, ed., *Brokenburn: The Journal of Kate Stone 1861–1868* (Baton Rouge, 1955), 8.

38. Rebecca L. Felton, "The Subjection of Women," pamphlet 19, Rebecca L. Felton Papers (Manuscript Division, University of Georgia).

39. Mrs. Burton [Constance Cary] Harrison, *Recollections Grave and Gay* (New York, 1912), 42.

40. Thomas Diary, Sept. 23, 1854.

41. Martha E. Foster Crawford Diary, Feb. 7, 1853, Feb. 3, 1854 (Department of Manuscripts, Duke University).

42. Hope Summerell Chamberlain, *Old Days in Chapel Hill, being the Life and Letters of Cornelia Phillips Spencer* (Chapel Hill, 1926), 93.

43. John Q. Anderson, "Sarah Anne Ellis Dorsey," Edward T. James and others, eds., *Notable American Women 1607–1950: A Biographical Dictionary* (3 vols., Cambridge, Mass., 1971), I, 505–06. There were southern men who opposed slavery, too, but theirs was usually an economic, not a moral critique.

44. Jane P. North to Caroline Pettigrew, Nov. 16, 1857, Pettigrew Family Papers.

45. J. H. Easterby, ed., *The South Carolina Rice Plantation as Revealed in the Papers of Robert F. W. Allston* (Chicago, 1945), 149.

46. Caroline Merrick, *Old Times in Dixie* (New York, 1901), 19. Mary A. H. Gay of Georgia, quoted in Matthew Page Andrews, *Women of the South in Wartime* (Baltimore, 1920), 334.

47. Thomas Diary, Sept. 20, 1866.

48. A study of planter's widows would be interesting. Many of them conducted plantations with considerable success, and as they necessarily came in contact with the outside world in business they began to develop more forceful personalities and interest in politics as well. For example, Jane Petigru North, sister of the famous James L. Petigru, was widowed early and ran one plantation owned by her brother and then another owned by her son-in-law, Charles L. Pettigrew. She did not hesitate to take full responsibility, and like her brother she was an outspoken supporter of the Union down to the moment of secession.

49. *Southern Ladies Companion,* II (1848), 45.

50. [Louisa Cheves McCord] L. S. M., *Southern Quarterly Review,* V (April 1852), 322–41. See also Margaret Farrand Thorp, "Louisa Susannah Cheves McCord," James and others, eds., *Notable American Women,* II, 451–52.

51. Charles Francis Adams, *Letters of Mrs. Adams with an Introductory Memoir by her grandson* (Boston, 1848), xix.

11 ❧ A Slave Family in the Ante Bellum South

Loren Schweninger

Twentieth century scholars of Afro-American history have offered two basically different interpretations concerning the effect of slavery on the black family. In his famous 1932 study *The Negro Family in the United States,* Negro sociologist E. Franklin Frazier asserted that slavery destroyed the black family. Fundamental economic forces and material interests, he said, shattered even the toughest bonds of black familial sentiments and parental love.[1] Supporting Frazier in the 1959 comparative analysis, *Slavery: A Problem in American Intellectual and Institutional Life,* white historian Stanley M. Elkins listed four reasons for the destruction of the black slave family: sexual exploitation, separation, miscegenation, and restrictive legal codes. "The law could permit no aspect of the slave's conjugal state to have an independent legal existence."[2] In an examination of the urban South, historian Richard C. Wade likewise concluded that "For a slave, no matter where he resided, a house was never a home. Families could scarcely exist in bondage. The law recognized no marriage."[3] And Daniel P. Moynihan, in his 1965 report, re-iterated that slavery had an extremely negative effect on the black family.[4]

Recently, three writers have put forth a far more optimistic view of the black family in bondage. Herbert Gutman, Robert Abzug and John Blassingame contend that strong family loyalties developed among slaves. Admitting the obvious institutional barriers, they argue that

From the *Journal of Negro History* 60 (January 1975). Reprinted by permission of The Association for the Study of Afro-American Life and History, Inc.

bondsmen used the family as a shelter against the brutalities of the Southern slave system. "Although it was weak, although it was frequently broken," Professor Blassingame writes in The Slave Community, a psychological study of Blacks in bondage, "the family provided an important buffer, a refuge from the rigors of slavery."[5] Thus, though asking the same basic question of the way in which the institution of slavery affected the black family, scholars have advanced two fundamentally different interpretations.

An investigation of one slave family will not end the controversy. In a limited sense it can only tell us about a family, and one that was in many respects very fortunate.[6] The members of the Thomas-Rapier slave family received an education; achieved a degree of economic independence; and eventually became free or at least "quasi-free." Moreover, they belonged to extremely permissive and beneficent masters. They lived in an urban environment (as did only 10% of the South's slave population), and hired out, though it was against the law. But, like many other Blacks in the ante bellum South, they too suffered the pains of separation (living in Alabama, Tennessee, and Canada); sexual exploitation (the slave mother bore three sons by three different white men); and the legal denial of the slave family. Yet, in spite of these institutional barriers or perhaps because of them, the members of the Thomas-Rapier family maintained their integrity. Indeed, as seen in a rare collection of slave letters, notes, and autobiographical reminiscences, they preserved a cohesive family unit for three generations. In a larger sense, then, an investigation of one slave family can perhaps shed some light on the family experiences of many slaves in the ante bellum South.

Born in Albemarle County, Virginia, about 1790, the black slave, Sally, grew up on the 1500-acre tobacco plantation of Charles S. Thomas, a friend and neighbor of Thomas Jefferson.[7] At a young age she was sent to the fields. Working from sun-up to sundown, season to season, and year to year, she (along with forty-one other slaves on the "big gang"), prepared beds, planted seeds, transplanted shoots, "wormed and topped" young plants, hung, and then stripped, sorted and bundled the final product. When she was about eighteen, Sally suffered (or accepted) the sexual advances of a white man (probably John Thomas, the owner's eldest son); and in September 1808, she gave birth to a mulatto boy, John. Some years later she gave birth to a second mulatto child, Henry.[8] As Virginia law required that progeny take the status of the mother, both children were born in bondage, but as part of the Thomas Trust Estate, they were protected against sale or separation.[9] Consequently, when one of the heirs of the estate (again probably John) joined the westward movement of slaveholders across the Appalachians into the Cumberland river valley about 1818, Sally, John and Henry were transported to the fast growing town of Nashville, Tennessee.[10]

The city offered many opportunities. With the master's permission, Sally hired out as a cleaning lady, a practice common among urban slaves, and secured an agreement to retain a portion of her earnings. She then rented a two-story frame house on the corner of Deaderick and Cherry Streets in the central business district. Converting the front room into a laundry, and manufacturing her own soap (blending fats, oils, alkali and salt in a small vat in the front room), she established a business of cleaning clothes. She soon built up a thriving trade.[11] At the same time Sally arranged for her eldest son, John, to hire out as a waiter and poll boy to river barge Captain Richard Rapier,[12] who was plying the Cumberland–Tennessee–Mississippi river trade, between Nashville, Florence (Alabama), and New Orleans;[13] and arranged for Henry to hire out as an errand boy to various "white gentlemen" around Nashville. Part of their earnings, along with her own, she saved in a tea cannister, which she hid in the loft, hoping someday to be able to purchase "free papers" for the children. "However, that might cost as much as $2000!" Undeterred, she conscientiously set aside part of her earnings every month, and by early 1826, she had saved over $300.[14]

Though thirty-six years old, Sally was still an attractive woman. In October 1827, in the house on Deaderick Street she gave birth to a third mulatto son, James.[15] The father was the famous ante bellum Judge John Catron, but according to the state law, which, like the law in Virginia, assigned progeny the status of the mother, James was born in bondage. "Now my own father presided over the supreme court of Tennessee [and served as a justice on the United States Supreme Court]," James later recalled, "[but] he had no time to give me a thought. He gave me 25 cents once, [and] if I [were] correctly informed, that is all he ever did for me."[16] With three children, John nineteen, Henry about sixteen, and James, Sally despaired that she might not be able to save enough to free her family.

But her despair soon turned to joy. She received word in 1829 that her eldest son had been emancipated. "I bequeath one thousand dollars to my executors for the purpose of purchasing the freedom of the mulatto boy, John, who now waits on me, and belongs to the Estate of Thomas," Richard Rapier stipulated in his will, and the Alabama General Assembly, the only legal emancipator of slaves in the state, passed a law freeing "a certain male slave by the name of John H. Rapier."[17] Then, she saw an opportunity to free Henry. With the final settlement of the Thomas Estate in 1834, "Sally and the two mulatto

The Genealogy of a Slave Family

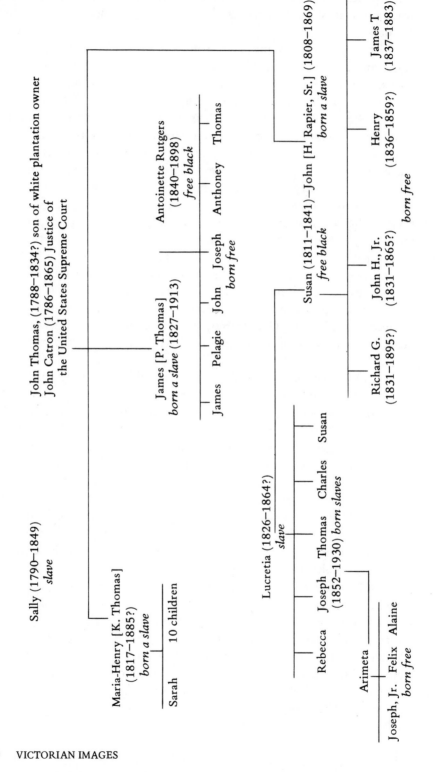

boys," reverted to one John Martin, an affable young man who wanted to sell a part of his inheritance for a quick profit. Fearing that her children would be sold "down river to Mississippi," Sally urged Henry to escape. Heeding his mother's advice, Henry fled through upper Tennessee and Kentucky but was captured near Louisville and confined to a guard house. He managed to work off his leg-chains one night, however, steal down to the Ohio River, untie a boat, and drift into the current. "The night was cold," Henry wrote afterwards. "I headed the yawl downstream, sculled over the falls and made for the Indiana shore. There I found a man who freed my hands."[18] Taking the surname Thomas, he travelled to Buffalo, New York, where he opened a barber shop.[19]

Shortly after Henry's escape, Sally went to Ephraim H. Foster, a prominent Tennessee lawyer, and asked for assistance in putting James out of Martin's reach. "Will you talk with him [Martin] and see what he will take for the boy," she asked. "Very well, Aunt Sally," Foster replied, "I will see him and let you know what can be done." A few days later Foster told her that Martin wanted $400. "I have saved only $350," Sally explained, but quickly added: "Now if you, Col. Foster, will pay the fifty and make it four hundred, have the bill of sale made to yourself, you can hold James in trust until I return [the] money. I want you to be his protector." Foster agreed and the bargain was sealed. A short time later, she paid off the debt and received a bill of sale, "free papers," for six-year-old James.[19] Even then, however, he was not free. The law required emancipated Blacks to secure a manumission deed from the county court, and "thereupon immediately leave Tennessee."[20] Thus, despite having "free papers," James was still legally a slave.

But neither the law nor slavery seemed to curtail his activities. As a young boy, he performed a variety of chores for his mother: keeping salt in the hopper for making soap, cutting wood for the fire place, cleaning up around the house, and delivering clothes to customers. He also enrolled in the Nashville school for Blacks. Thomas recalled sitting on splintery benches, in a drafty one-room school house and listening to ill-prepared lessons on such basic subjects as "the fundamentals of reading." In addition, he remembered that the school remained open only a few months each year, the pupils, or "scholars," had to pay a very high $4 tuition fee, and that free Blacks Rufus Conrad, Daniel Watkins and Samuel Lowery taught at the school from time to time. "But often," he said, "there was no school because there was no teacher." In 1836, for instance, a black teacher, described as "a fine scholar," was taken out by whites and whipped nearly to death. "Tennesseans generally opposed educating blacks," he recalled, "they might want the same as whites." But young James had an intense desire to learn and quickly mastered the basics of mathematics, reading and writing.[21]

Having secured a rudimentary education, James hired out as an apprentice barber. Working with bondsman Frank Parrish, who had earlier established a barber shop on Public Square, he quickly learned the trade.[22] "James [is] still with Frank Parrish and has the character of a good barber, So a Gentleman told me," his brother, John Rapier, observed in 1843. "He is well thought of by the Gentlemen. James has manners to please almost anyone who does not let their prejudice go far on account of color."[23] Two years later James was still with Parrish, earned $12 a month, and at the same time had begun violin lessons with one Gordan McGowan. "James will make a man of musick I think. He seems to be very fond of it."[24] Having served a five-year apprenticeship, in 1846, he opened his own barber shop. The nineteen-year-old slave established his shop in the house where he had grown up (and where his mother still operated her cleaning business), at 10 Deaderick Street. The location was ideal. Within a few steps of several banking houses, newspapers, and law firms, as well as the county court house, Market Square, and the Capitol, "the place on Deaderick," he explained, "was convenient to bankers, merchants, lawyers, politicians, and professional men." He counted among his customers six famous Tennesseans: William Carroll, one time governor; E. S. (Squire) Hall, an important businessman; General William Harding, owner of Bellemeade Estate; Ephraim Foster, a Whig political leader; and William G. (Parson) Brownlow, the Civil War governor.[25] Francis Fogg, the well-known Davidson County lawyer, visited the Thomas shop daily. "He returns to us in the evening," Mrs. Fogg noted approvingly, "with face smooth and curls nicely arranged."[26]

While attending to his duties as a barber, James listened attentively to conversations that took place among his customers. "They had time to talk in the barber shop. Nobody seemed in a great hurry. Everything was discussed—social, commercial, political and financial." He remembered conversations about the abolitionists, the advancement of cotton on the Liverpool market, the magetism and sporting proclivities of Andrew Jackson, plantation acreage along the Mississippi, and fugitive slaves. Once, he recalled being sharply questioned about runaway Blacks. "You have a brother living in Buffalo, New York, I believe," General Harding asked pointedly. "Yes," was the reply. "Well he treated me in a gruff manner. I went to ask him if he knew anything about a boy who ran off from me. I told him I only wanted to see him. I had come to Buffalo for that purpose. I received a very cold and indifferent reply." James could do little but apologize for his brother's "rudeness." Though he usually remained silent when the conversation turned to such controversial issues; at times he ventured an opinion on the slavery question. Once, for example, while shaving a young Virginia lawyer, he defended the Wilmot Proviso, a proposal to prohibit slavery in the newly acquired Mexican territories. "The set back I got caused me to be careful in the future. Among other things he told me I had no right to listen to a gentleman's conversation."[27] Despite such "set backs," James built up a flourishing business. Charging 25 cents for a haircut, 15 cents for a shave, and $1 for occasionally extracting teeth, he operated one of the most prosperous "tonsorial establishments" in Nashville. In the city's first business directory (published in 1853), he advertised in large boldface print: "JAS. THOMAS, BARBER SHOP, 10 Deaderick St."[28]

Meanwhile, Sally's other two children, freedman John H. Rapier and fugitive Henry Thomas, were also prospering as barbers. Rapier opened a shop in Florence, Alabama, soon saved over $500, purchased a white frame house on Court Street in the downtown district, and like James, converted the house into a place of business as well as a residence. In 1831, he married Susan, a free Black from Baltimore, Maryland, and in the next decade the couple had four children: Richard, John Jr., Henry and James.[29] After his wife's death in childbirth at the age of twenty-nine, he purchased a sixteen-year-old slave, Lucretia, and between 1848 and 1861, they had five slave children, the youngest named Susan.[30] During the ante bellum period Rapier acquired real estate holdings in Alabama, the Minnesota Territory, and Canada, purchased valuable railroad stock, and saved $2000 in cash. By 1860, he was one of the wealthiest free Blacks in Alabama, with about $10,000.[31]

Henry Thomas also opened a barber shop. Locating in the basement of Buffalo's elegant hotel Niagara, he too built up a lucrative trade. About 1835, he married a black woman, Maria, and they had eleven children, ten boys and a girl, Sarah.[32] In 1852, to avoid apprehension by slave catchers (who were encouraged by the 1850 Fugitive Slave Law), he moved to the black community of Buxton, Canada West. With resources he had saved as a barber, he purchased one hundred acres of wilderness land, built a log house, cleared the trees, and put in a crop of corn, wheat and barley.[33] "The settlement improves slowly, but prospects are good for its success," he noted in 1856. "The lumber mill is making improvements for the neighborhood. Soon the railroad will pass through. The school is flourishing. I have six acres in wheat and 2 in barley."[34] Thus, using one of the few profitable occupations open to ante bellum Blacks, James, John and Henry were all able to achieve a degree of financial independence.

The members of the slave family were also successful at maintaining close family ties. Though separated by hundreds, even thousands of miles, though forbidden to travel in certain regions, and though denied postal privileges, they kept in close touch. As a slave and also when he was a free Black, John Rapier Sr. frequently visited Nashville. And between 1838 and 1846, he arranged for all four of his children to attend school in the Tennessee capital and to stay with their slave uncle and slave grandmother. "John and James are so [well] pleased with their grandmother [and school], he noted in 1843, "that they do not want to come home, so James writes."[35] A couple of years later he added: "My two sons that are with mother are well when I last hear[d] from them. I entend to go up to Nashville in the course of ten or twelve days and See them all." On that occasion Rapier confessed that he had not been to Tennessee in nearly a year. "I am extremely anxious to See the family again," he said, promising to deliver a letter from his brother, which had been smuggled into the South from the North. After a visit to the Tennessee capital, he wrote to "Brother Henry": "Mother looks as young as she did 8 years ago and works as hard and hardly takes time to talk to you." Forwarding other family news, he said that "Brother James" was doing extremely well as a barber; and of his sons, he proudly observed that Richard wrote in an excellent hand; Henry wanted to continue his education; James read extremely well "for a little boy of his age [6] and training;" and "John has wrote me two letter and writes very plain for a boy of eight, . . . and has as much taste for reading as any child I know off and is very good in arithmetic."[36] Rapier not only journeyed to Tennessee often, but about once a year, he travelled to New York or Canada.[37] After one such sojourn, he expressed concern for Brother Henry's future in the North. "I told him to buy [more] land in that country and to pay the taxes. [But] I am fearful that Brother Henry will come to want in [Canada] as I am of the opinion that [it] is poor farming country."[38] For their parts, Henry and James also expressed a deep concern for the welfare of the slave family. Henry usually concluded his letters with the simple, but significant, line: "All the family is well and wishes to be remembered to you."[39] And James Thomas wrote: "A letter from your hands [John Rapier Jr.] offers me a great deal of pleasure to say nothing of the family news it imparts."[40] It seems that separation, an inherent part of the institution of slavery, had little effect on the spiritual unity of the slave family.

There was also a solidarity among the members of the Rapier family. Deeply concerned about the welfare of his children, John Rapier offered them advice on everything from economic matters to questions of morality: "Settle your debts," "Save your money," "Stay away from liquor," he admonished "The Four Boys." "Stick closer to work and Say nothing and do nothing but what is right and you will do well my sons."[41] In 1845 he wrote Richard, who was attending school in Buffalo and living with Henry Thomas: "Study your books so I can hold you up as an example to your lettle Brothers. You are blessed if you will look at your situation. You have kind relations who are anctious to see you grow up an ornament to society."[42] Perhaps the best expression of the spiritual unity of the Rapier family was written by James Thomas Rapier, James P. Thomas's namesake and one of Sally's twenty-six grandchildren. Also living with fugitive Henry Thomas, and attending school in Buxton, he wrote:

> In our boyhood . . . all four of us boys were together. We all breathed as one. [Now] we are scattered abroad on the face of the Earth. Do you ever expect to see us all together again? I do not. Just look where we are . . . John in [Minnesota]. Myself in the north. Henry and Dick in California. Father in Alabama. Did you ever think how small our family is?[43]

Among the Rapiers, as well as the Thomases, there was an almost religious devotion to the institution of the family.

The ability of the slave family to remain so close seems all the more remarkable in the face of the legal restrictions placed on Blacks. Statutes forbade a free Black from either visiting with slaves, or travelling from one state to another, both on penalty of being sold into slavery. Laws prohibited slaves from owning personal property, renting real estate, earning money, or securing an education. "No person shall hire to any slave," one Tennessee code pronounced, "the time of said slave."[44] Lawmakers prescribed a ten year prison sentence to anyone helping a slave to escape, forging a pass for a slave, harboring a runaway or inciting a Black to defy a white; and laid down the death penalty for Blacks convicted of assaulting or molesting a white woman, maliciously setting fire to a barn, preparing any poison, or conspiring to revolt. "A ring leader or Chief Instigator of any plot to rebel or murder any white," one law stated, "may be lawfully killed [on sight], if it is not practicable, otherwise, to arrest and secure him."[45] Nashville ordinances required free Blacks to pay a capitation (head) tax of $1 or $2, register at the court house, and "carry free papers on their person at all times." Blacks without such papers were to be treated as slaves. Moreover, Negroes were not permitted to walk the streets after dark, enter tippling houses, make weird noises, or gather within the city limits for any purpose, except public worship, and Blacks attending church were to be supervised by whites.[46]

But the slave family disregarded the elaborate code governing Blacks. Sally hired out, earned money, rented a house, and operated a business. "Mother lived so long at the corner of Deaderick and Cherry Streets," James Thomas remarked later, "that the people of Nashville thought she [was free] and owned the property." She moved about the city with little hindrance, boarded her grandchildren as they attended school, and secretly advised Henry to escape to the North.[47] In a similar manner James Thomas hired out, earned money and established a business. He eventually accumulated a large amount of personal property—furniture, mirrors, clothes, and about $1000 in cash, and while still a slave, became the manager of one of the largest barbering establishments in Nashville. He travelled to various parts of the city without a pass, entertained free Blacks in his home, and attended black church meetings. At one such gathering he recalled the black congregation, mostly slaves, singing until 12 o'clock at night. "The owners," he wrote, "seemed to care very little how much religion their servants got. They seemed to encourage it."[48] In much the same way John Rapier and Henry Thomas acquired personal property, hired out, earned as much as $50 a month, and, despite the laws against the movement of Blacks, travelled throughout the South, North, and Canada. Rapier even assisted a slave, Sam Ragland, to escape on one occasion.[49] In short, the slave family was not in the least constrained by the restrictive black codes.

Sally's dream that all of her children secure their freedom finally came true in 1851, when her youngest son, James, asked Ephraim Foster to present a manumission petition to the Davidson County court. The slave and his master appeared at the courthouse in Nashville on March 6. "James has always maintained an exemplary character," Foster told the nine-judge panel hearing the case. "He has been industrious, honest, moral, humble, polite and had conducted himself as to gain the confidence and respect of whites. He is a man of great worth in his place." The testimony of such an eminent Tennessean swayed the magistrates and, after a short deliberation, they ordered "the slave James, otherwise called James [P.] Thomas, emancipated and forever set free." Thomas now addressed the court himself. He requested immunity from the 1831 law requiring manumitted Blacks to leave Tennessee. "I have deported myself in a manner requiring the confidence of whites. I have always earned a good living. I would be greatly damaged having to Start anew in some Strange Country." The judges, after receiving the required $500 good behavior bond, granted the immunity. James P. Thomas thus became the first black man in the county, perhaps the state, under the stringent emigration law of 1831, to gain legally both freedom and residency.[50]

A short time before James gained his freedom, however, Sally died of cholera.[51] A woman of great drive and dedication, she had devoted her life to freeing her children. She had hired out, started a business, and gladly put up her life savings to purchase "free papers" for James. She had also assisted Henry in his quest for freedom. Due in part to her unwavering efforts, the slaves John H. Rapier, Sr., Henry K. Thomas, and James P. Thomas, all gained free status before the Civil War. In addition, the Thomases and Rapiers all found great strength in the slave family. Members of these families were quite successful: John entered politics during Reconstruction; Henry farmed hundreds of acres in Canada; and James acquired property in St. Louis valued at $250,000;[52] while Sarah Thomas became a school teacher, James T. Rapier a Congressman, and John Rapier, Jr. a surgeon, stemmed from the security they found in the slave family.[53] It seems that for the black slave Sally, sexual exploitation, miscegenation, separation, and legal restrictions—the very forces designed, in part, to destroy the black family—gave impetus, *not* to disintegration and disunity, but to an extraordinary feeling of family loyalty, unity, and love. For Sally, her children, and her grandchildren, the slave family was indeed "a refuge from the rigors of slavery."

NOTES

1. E. Franklin Frazier, *The Negro Family in the United States* (Chicago: University of Chicago Press, 1939), pp. 40, 41; "The Negro Slave Family," *Journal of Negro History XV* (April, 1930), pp. 198–259.

2. Stanley M. Elkins, *Slavery: A Problem in American Institutional and Intellectual Life* (Chicago: University of Chicago Press, 1959), pp. 53, 54.

3. Richard C. Wade, *Slavery in the Cities: The South, 1820–1860* (New York: Oxford University Press, 1964), pp. 117–121.

4. Lee Rainwater and William L. Yancey, *The Moynihan Report and the Politics of Controversy* (Cambridge, Massachusetts: The Massachusetts Institute of Technology Press, 1967), pp. 61, 62, 414, 415.

5. Herbert Gutman is working on a book length study of the black family. See: Tamara K. Hareven, editor, *Anonymous Americans: Explorations in Nineteenth-Century Social History* (Englewood Cliffs, N.J.: Prentice-Hall, Inc., 1971), p. 209; Robert H. Abzug, "The Black Family During Reconstruction," in Nathan I. Huggins, Martin Kilson and Daniel M. Fox, *Key Issues in the Afro-American Experience* (New York: Harcourt Brace Jovanovich, Inc., 1971), pp. 26–41; John

W. Blassingame, *The Slave Community: Plantation Life in the Ante-Bellum South* (New York: Oxford University Press, 1971), chapter III.

6. It is not the purpose of this paper to enter the contemporary sociological debate on the origins of the "black matriarchy." As it happened, the central figure in this slave family was a woman. All three of her slave children, however, became dominant fathers, maintaining their marriages for twenty-six, forty-two, and thirty years respectively. In addition, it is not the purpose of this essay to differentiate between the family attitudes of the mother, who remained in bondage, and her children, who eventually gained their freedom. Their family attitudes were for the most part the same.

7. "The Autobiographical Reminiscences of James P. Thomas," Moorland-Spingarn Collection, Howard University, Washington, D.C., [1911], p. 1; hereafter "Thomas Autobiography." In the original manuscript many of the pages are out of place and un-numbered. Thus the page numbers cited are only approximate; Albemarle County Probate Records, Deed Books, Book XXXII (January 2, 1835), p. 89; *ibid.,* Book VI (July 14, 1814), p. 26; *ibid.,* Book IX (November 17, 1825), p. 260; The Genealogy of a Slave Family.

8. "Thomas Autobiography," pp. 2–7; U.S. Census Office, Sixth Census of the United States, "Population Schedules for Lauderdale County, Alabama," Vol. IV, 1840, p. 104.

9. Winthrop Jordan, *White Over Black: American Attitudes Toward the Negro, 1550–1812* (Chapel Hill: University of North Carolina Press, 1968), p. 76; Albemarle County Probate Records, Deed Books, Book XXXII (January 2, 1835), pp. 89, 90.

10. "Thomas Autobiography," pp. 3–6.

11. *Ibid.; The Nashville Business Directory* (Nashville: Printed by John P. Campbell, 1855), *passim;* "Miscellaneous Notes of James P. Thomas," Moorland-Spingarn Collection, Howard University, Washington, D.C., n.p.

12. Richard Rapier, described as "a large fleshy man weighing over 200 pounds," settled in Nashville about 1799. Soon he was transporting large quantities of tobacco to New Orleans and returning with sugar, teas and coffee. In 1806 he formed a "copartnership" with Lemuel T. Turner and James Jackson.

13. Davidson County Probate Records, Minutes, Vol. C. (July 1801), p. 405; *The Tennessee Gazette and Metro District Advertiser Repository,* March 29, 1898; *The Clarion,* September 27, 1808; *The Imperial Review and Cumberland Repository,* May 5, 1808; *The Democratic Clarion and Tennessee Gazette,* May 19, 1812, May 31, 1814.

14. "Thomas Autobiography," chapter 1; "Miscellaneous Notes of James P. Thomas," Moorland-Spingarn Collection, Howard University, Washington, D.C., n.p. (See page 33)

15. "Thomas Autobiography," p. 7.

16. *Ibid.,* chapter 1; *Acts Passed at the First and Second Session of the Nineteenth General Assembly of the State of Tennessee* (Nashville: Allen Hall and A. S. Heiskel, Printers to the State, 1832), pp. 167–170.

17. Lauderdale County Probate Records, Wills, Vol. VI (June 3, 1824), p. 117; *Acts of the Eleventh Annual Session of the General Assembly of the State of Alabama* (Tuscaloosa: McGuire, Henry and Walker, 1830), p. 36; Richard Rapier, Auburn, California, to James P. Thomas, December 14, 1877, Rapier Papers,

Moorland-Spingarn Collection, Howard University, Washington, D.C., hereafter Rapier Papers.

18. "Thomas Autobiography," chapter 1; "Miscellaneous Notes of James P. Thomas," Moorland-Spingarn Collection, Howard University, Washington, D.C., n.p.; John H. Rapier, Sr., Florence, Alabama, to Henry K. Thomas, Buffalo, New York, February 28, 1843, Rapier Papers; A. M. Simmons, Cincinnati, Ohio, to Henry K. Thomas, Buffalo, New York, May 26, 1836, *ibid.; Buffalo City Directory* (Buffalo: Horatio N. Walker, Publisher, 1844), p. 213.

19. "Thomas Autobiography," pp. 1–6.

20. *Acts Passed at the First and Second Session of the Nineteenth General Assembly of the State of Tennessee* (Nashville: Allen Hall and A. S. Heiskel, Printers to the State, 1832), p. 167; Robert William Fogel and Stanley L. Engerman in their statistical study *Time on the Cross: The Economics of American Negro Slavery* (Boston, 1974) also conclude that the slave family was a viable institution, but they, like most historians concerned with the peculiar institution, emphasize the role and attitudes of whites. They suggest that the Negro family survived for three basic reasons: the desire of planters to promote family stability (to increase the output of contented slaves); the extreme reluctance of owners to break up family units; and the Victorian attitudes among the planting class, which made miscegenation extremely rare, resulting in a miniscule percent of mulattoes in the ante bellum South (7.7 in 1850 and 10.4 in 1860). Besides the impressionistic evidence used by the two cliometricians to support their contentions, the dubious relationship between the extent of sexual exploitation and the percent of mulattoes in the South in a given year (which is itself upon question), and the mis-interpretation of the quantified evidence concerning the break up of families on the New Orleans auction block between 1804–1862 (the authors suggest 84 percent of the sales involved unmarried individuals, but failed to reveal that the slave's familial status was generally not recorded), the greatest weakness of the study is the obvious inadequacy of quantification methods in evaluating the slave family. Statistical evidence does not reveal the feelings of interdependence, unity, and cohesiveness that black family members in bondage felt for one another. Robert William Fogel and Stanley L. Engerman, *Time on the Cross: The Economics of American Negro Slavery* (Boston, 1974), pp. 126–144.

21. "Thomas Autobiography," chapters 1, 2; "Miscellaneous Notes of James P. Thomas," Moorland-Spingarn Collection, Howard University, Washington, D.C.; James P. Thomas, Nashville, Tennessee, to John H. Rapier, Jr., St. Paul, Minnesota Territory, October 3, 1856.

22. The Nashville *Republican,* April 21, 1836; The Nashville *Daily Republican Banner,* April 9, 1841; Davidson County Probate Records, Minutes, Book E (October 4, 1853), pp. 563–564. Many times, as in this instance, probate court cases included biographical material about Blacks to illustrate their "good character." Davidson County Probate Records, Wills and Inventories, Vol. 16 (November 28, 1854), pp. 429–430.

23. John H. Rapier, Sr., Florence, Alabama, to Henry K. Thomas, Buffalo, New York, February 28, 1843, Rapier Papers.

24. John H. Rapier, Sr., Florence, Alabama, to Richard Rapier, Buffalo, New York, April 8, 1845, Rapier Papers.

25. "Thomas Autobiography," chapters 1, 2, 3; *The Nashville General Business Directory* (Nashville: The Daily American Book and Job Printing Office, 1853),

1–20; For the early business and financial activities of E. S. Hall in Nashville, see: John Claybrooke Papers, Manuscript Division, State Library and Archives, Nashville, Tennessee; For the activities of the other whites mentioned, see: Philip Hamer, *Tennessee: A History,* Vol. I (New York: American Historical Society, 1935), pp. 282, 370, 381, 475; "Leadership in Nashville: Biographical Sketches of 116 of the Most Prominent Citizens in Nashville," Catherine Pilcher Avery Papers, Manuscript Division, State Library and Archives, Nashville, Tennessee; "Old Days in Nashville, Tennessee: Reminiscences by Jane Thomas," (no relation to James Thomas), reprints from the Nashville *Daily American,* 1895–1896 in Jane Thomas Papers, Manuscript Division, State Library and Archives, Nashville, Tennessee; *The Official Political Manual of the State of Tennessee* (Nashville, Tennessee: Marshall and Bruce, 1890), p. 180.

26. Ellen S. Fogg, Nashville, Tennessee, to E. H. Foster, Louisville, Kentucky, February 15, 1849, Ephraim Foster Papers, Manuscript Division, State Library and Archives, Nashville, Tennessee.

27. "Thomas Autobiography," chapter 2.

28. *Nashville Business Directory* (Nashville: Daily American Book and Job Printing Office, 1853), p. 68.

29. Richard Rapier, Auburn, California, to James P. Thomas, December 14, 1877, Rapier Papers; In this letter Richard, John Rapier's eldest son, refers to his date and place of birth. In the "Diary and Notes of John H. Rapier, Jr.," March 10, 1857, Rapier Papers; John, Rapier's third son, likewise refers to his birth date; U.S. Census Office, Sixth Census of the United States, "Population Schedules for Lauderdale County, Alabama," Vol. IV, (1840), p. 104; James T. Rapier, Florence, Alabama to John H. Rapier, Jr., St. Paul, Minnesota Territory, September 27, 1858, Rapier Papers; "Thomas Autobiography," p. 73; *Alabama State Sentinel,* November 25, 1867; The inscription on Susan Rapier's tombstone reads: "Sacred to the memory of Susan Rapier. Born in Baltimore, Md. 25 of December 1811 departed this life at Florence Alabama 10 of March 1841—also her two infant children Jackson and Alexander—Depart my friends and dry up your tears for I must lie hear [sic] till Christ appears."

30. U.S. Census Bureau, Sixth Census of the United States, Population Schedules for Lauderdale County, Alabama," Vol. IV, (1840), p. 104; United States Census Bureau, Seventh Census of the United States, Populations Schedules for Lauderdale County, Alabama," Vol. I, (1850), p. 293; United States Census Bureau, Eighth Census of the United States, Vol. VI (1860), p. 39.

31. John H. Rapier, Sr., Florence, Alabama, to Richard Rapier, Buffalo, New York, April 8, 1845, Rapier Papers; John H. Rapier, Sr., Florence, Alabama, to John H. Rapier, Jr., St. Paul, Minnesota Territory, September 16, 1857, Rapier Papers; Lauderdale County Probate Records, Wills and Inventories, Vol. B (September 13, 1869), pp. 78–80, Land Deeds, Book II (May 3, 1844), p. 78; Book XVI (August 7, 1858), p. 324; The Florence *Gazette,* March 5, 1862; Loren Schweninger, "John H. Rapier, Sr.: A Slave and Freedman in the Antebellum South," *Civil War History*/Vol. 20, (March 1974), p. 31.

32. A. M. Simmons, Cincinnati, Ohio, to Henry K. Thomas, Buffalo, New York, May 26, 1836, Rapier Papers; *Buffalo City Directory* (Buffalo: Horatio N. Walker, Publisher, 1844), p. 213; John H. Rapier, Sr., Florence, Alabama, to Henry K. Thomas, Buffalo, New York, February 28, 1843, Rapier Papers; "Thomas Autobiography," chapter 1; *Buffalo City Directory* (Buffalo: Jewett, Thomas and Company, Commercial Advertiser Office, 1847–48), p. 158.

33. Henry K. Thomas, Buxton, Canada West, to John H. Rapier, Sr., Florence, Alabama, October 27, 1856, Rapier Papers; James T. Rapier, Buxton, Canada West, to John H. Rapier, Jr., St. Paul, Minnesota Territory, June 26, 1857, Rapier Papers; "Thomas Autobiography," chapter 1.

34. Henry K. Thomas, Buxton, Canada West, to John H. Rapier, Sr., Florence, Alabama, October 27, 1856, Rapier Papers.

35. John H. Rapier, Sr., Florence, Alabama, to Henry K. Thomas, Buffalo, New York, February 28, 1843, Rapier Papers.

36. John H. Rapier, Sr., Florence, Alabama, to Richard Rapier, Buffalo, New York, April 8, 1845, Rapier Papers.

37. "The Autobiography of William King," (1890), p. 255, King Papers, Public Archives of Canada, Ottawa, Ontario; King, who founded Buxton, reminisced about Rapier's frequent visits to Toronto and Buxton during the 1850's; John H. Rapier, Sr., Florence, Alabama, to John H. Rapier, Jr., Minnesota Territory, September 16, 1857, Rapier Papers.

38. John H. Rapier, Sr., Florence, Alabama, to John H. Rapier, Jr., Minnesota Territory, September 15, 1856, Rapier Papers.

39. Henry K. Thomas, Buxton, Canada West, to John H. Rapier, Sr., October 27, 1856, Rapier Papers; March 13, 1857; Henry's only daughter Sarah wrote to John Rapier, Jr.: "Through Papa and James I would like to give you some news . . . Mama and Papa are well as is the rest of the family and they sent their compliments. We shall all feel very much pleased if you make a visit to this place." Sarah Thomas, Buxton, Canada West, to John H. Rapier, Jr., Minnesota Territory, March 10, 1857, Rapier Papers.

40. James P. Thomas, St. Louis, Missouri, to John H. Rapier, Jr., Minnesota Territory, June 17, 1858, Rapier Papers.

41. John H. Rapier, Sr., Florence, Alabama to John H. Rapier, Jr., Minnesota Territory, September 15, 1856, Rapier Papers; John H. Rapier, Sr., Florence, Alabama to John H. Rapier, Jr., Benton County, Minnesota Territory, December 13, 1856, Rapier Papers.

42. John H. Rapier, Sr., Florence, Alabama, to Richard Rapier, Buffalo, New York, April 8, 1845, Rapier Papers.

43. James Rapier, Buxton, Canada West to John H. Rapier, Jr., Little Falls, Minnesota Territory, January 27, 1857, Rapier Papers.

44. *Acts Passed at the First Session of the Fourteenth General Assembly of the State of Tennessee* (Knoxville: Heiskell and Brown, Public Printers to the State, 1821), p. 34; *Acts Passed at the Second Session of the Fourteenth General Assembly of the State of Tennessee* (Knoxville: Heiskell and Brown, Printers to the State, 1822), p. 22; *Acts Passed at the First Session of the Fifteenth General Assembly of the State of Tennessee* (Murfreesborough: J. Norvell and G. A. and A. C. Sablett, 1823), p. 76; *Acts Passed at the Extra Session of the Sixteenth General Assembly of the State of Tennessee* (Knoxville: Heiskell and Brown, 1927), 31–33; *Acts Passed at the First and Second Session of the Nineteenth General Assembly of the State of Tennessee* (Nashville: Allen A. Hall and A. S. Heiskell, Printers to the State, 1932), pp. 165–170.

45. *Private Acts Passed at the Called Session of the Nineteenth General Assembly of the State of Tennessee* (Nashville: Allen A. Hall and F. S. Heiskell, Printers, 1832), pp. 5, 6; *Public Acts Passed at the First Session of the Twentieth General Assembly of the State of Tennessee* (Nashville: Allen A. Hall and F. S. Heiskell,

Printers to the State, 1833), pp. 2, 3, 75, 76, 14, 87, 94, 99, 100, 215, 216; *Public Acts Passed at the First Session of the Twenty-first General Assembly of the State of Tennessee* (Nashville: S. Nye and Co., Printers, 1836), pp. 92, 145, 146, 167; *Acts Passed at the First Session of the Twenty-third General Assembly of the State of Tennessee* (Nashville: J. Geo. Harris, Printer to the State, 1840), pp. 82, 83; *Acts Passed by the First Session of the Twenty-fourth General Assembly of the State of Tennessee* (Murfreesborough: Cameron and Company, Printers to the State, 1842), pp. 229, 230; *Acts of the State of Tennessee Passed at the First Session of the Twenty-sixth General Assembly* (Knoxville: James C. Moses, 1846), p. 278; *Acts of the State of Tennessee Passed at the First Session of the Twenty-eighth General Assembly* (Nashville: McKennie and Watterson, Printers to the State, 1850), p. 30; *Acts of the State of Tennessee Passed at the First Session of the Twenty-eighth General Assembly* (Nashville: McKennie and Watterson, Printers to the State, 1850), p. 304; *Acts Passed at the First Session of the Twenty-ninth General Assembly* (Nashville: McKennie Printers, 1852); pp. 120, 521; *Acts of the State of Tennessee Passed at the First Session of the Thirtieth General Assembly* (Nashville: McKennie and Brown, Book and Job Printers, 1854), pp. 121, 122, 157; *Acts of the State of Tennessee Passed at the First Session of the Thirty-first General Assembly* (Nashville: Printed by G. C. Torbett and Company, 1856), pp. 71, 77; William Imes, "The Legal Status of Free Negroes and Slaves in Tennessee," *Journal of Negro History,* IV (July 1919), pp. 260, 261.

46. *Revised Laws of the City of Nashville* (Nashville: Union and American Steam Press, 1854), pp. 147, 154–58; *Revised Laws of the City of Nashville* (Nashville: Harvey M. Watterson Printers, 1850), pp. 124–26; *Acts Passed at the First Session of the Twenty-fifth General Assembly of the State of Tennessee* (Nashville: L. Gifford and E. G. Eastman, Printers, 1844), p. 18.

47. "Thomas Autobiography," chapter 1.

48. *Ibid.;* "Miscellaneous Notes of James P. Thomas," Moorland-Spingarn Collection, Howard University, Washington, D.C., n.d.; James P. Thomas, Louisville, Kentucky, to John H. Rapier, Jr., St. Paul, Minnesota Territory, March 1, 1856, Rapier Papers; James P. Thomas, Nashville, Tennessee, to John H. Rapier, Jr., Minnesota Territory, October 3, 1856, Rapier Papers.

49. Loren Schweninger, "John H. Rapier, Sr.: A Slave and Freedman in the Antebellum South," Vol. 20, *Civil War History* (March 1974), *passim.*

50. "Thomas Autobiography," pp. 1–8; Davidson County Probate Records, Minute Book E (March 6, 1851), pp. 134, 135.

51. "Thomas Autobiography," p. 1; James Thomas said that his mother died in a cholera epidemic in 1850, but it was probably in the spring of 1849, when hundreds of Nashvillians died from the dreaded disease.

52. The Florence *Journal,* September 18, 1869; Assessors Records, City of St. Louis, Plate 1874–1876, number B65, Blk 300, 301, 691; Assessors Records, City of St. Louis, Tax Books for 1871, Book 17 (1871), pp. 20–21; Probate Records of the City of St. Louis, Warranty Deeds, Book 452 (August 13, 1872), pp. 470, 471; "Autobiography of William King," pp. 355–360.

53. James T. Rapier, Montgomery, Alabama, to William King, Buxton, Ontario, July 7, 1872, King Papers; Loren Schweninger, "James Rapier and Reconstruction," (PH.D. dissertation, Chicago, 1972), *passim.*

12 ♀ Working-Class Women in the Gilded Age: Factory, Community, and Family Life Among Cohoes, New York, Cotton Workers

Daniel J. Walkowitz

In much of the recent work characterized as the "New Urban History," sociologists and historians have focused on the relationship between social mobility and behavior within the nineteenth-century working class.[1] To a large extent this scholarship has tried to grapple with the question often posed by the New Left: "Whatever happened to the revolution?" Two alternative arguments have generally been put forth concerning working-class oppression and united or individual efforts towards social amelioration. In the first case, the oppressed working class organized and struggled—even violently—to gain some affluence and security through the labor movement. In the second case, workers individually achieved some mobility, and consequently little or no united effort was made to win a social revolution.[2] Something, however, of both these views may be correct: workers lived and worked under oppressive conditions, but workers achieved some significant

This is an expanded version of a paper read at the annual meeting of the American Historical Association in Boston, December 30, 1970. Data for the paper were compiled from the United States manuscript census schedules for the city of Cohoes, Albany County, New York: Census Office, 8th Census of Population, 1860; Census Office, 8th Census of Manufactures 1860; Census Office, 10th Census of Population, 1880; and, 10th Census of Manufactures, 1880. Especially helpful also was Arthur Masten, *History of Cohoes, New York, From its Earliest Settlement to the Present Time* (Albany, 1877).

measure of social mobility. Furthermore, considerable violence did occur in labor struggles, but no social revolution occurred.

These seeming paradoxes hinge on the contrast between working-class mobility as it was perceived by the members of the working class themselves and the attempt to make some "objective" assessment of the parameters of that mobility. This essay intends to examine the ways in which the cultural experience of the predominantly immigrant working class might have distorted their view of their social conditions and impaired their ability to focus on the origins of their oppression. Consequently, working-class violence, rather than being directed at the manufacturer, was directed at the ranks of the unemployed ready to claim their jobs. In this way, the working class did not engage in aggressive violence to win a social revolution so much as it fought defensive struggles to protect its modest gains.

Working-class behavior is not merely a response to objective social conditions but is fundamentally shaped by the *perception* of those conditions. Historians have correctly emphasized the poverty and fragility of working-class economic and social existence during the Gilded Age. For instance, a New York State Assembly Committee investigating laboring conditions declared that the testimony of 17 randomly selected employees of the Harmony cotton mills in Cohoes, New York, "very clearly establishes . . . [that] very few families are enabled to save money, while a majority of them barely manage to make both ends meet at the close of the year."[3] But these harsh social realities must be viewed in the context of the expectations—the social dream—and the alternatives open to the working-class community. While violence marked the struggle to control the conditions of industrial life, the equation between poverty and violent social behavior is not precise. The history of the Cohoes cotton worker community is a case in point.

Cohoes, New York, is a small city located eight miles north of Albany on the west bank of the Hudson River at the confluence of that river and the Mohawk River. The cotton mills of Cohoes provided job opportunities in light industry for female laborers, opportunities that helped to create an unusual social community: the mills attracted a high percentage of working women and almost one quarter of the cotton worker families was headed by a woman. Confronted by the values of Puritan America, subjected to the social paternalism of the Harmony Corporation and sensitive to the demands of their own ethnic traditions, these women were immersed in a patriarchal culture. What kind of security and status, then, could Cohoes offer these women and their families? And, equally important, how did security and status function? The history of Cohoes' cotton workers demonstrates that the factory and the community helped both to sustain the mill operatives and to secure some social mobility for them. However, the small degree of status and security they attained did not liberate them from economic and social worries; rather, these modest gains restricted their field of vision and alienated them from their own social reality. It is within this context that we must view labor violence that erupted in Cohoes during the early 1880s.

During the 1870s, in the midst of a national economic storm that produced many financial failures, bitter strikes and violence, the Harmony Mills had offered relative industrial calm—with the not inconsiderable financial security and stability that this represented, especially for the immigrant working-class family. The depression compelled the Harmony Mills to close only one month during that entire decade; and while wages fell, the workers never struck. However, the tone and temper of Cohoes industrial life changed suddenly in 1880. In that year, and in 1882, extended strikes were fought. The strikes and lockouts began usually over further wage reductions, but at their core was a conflict over union recognition and power. These struggles culminated in violent mob scenes where angry women cotton workers and their children confronted imported Swedish "scab" workers and their police bodyguards.

Why was the Cohoes labor movement dormant during the 1870s, and why did disorder and violence erupt after 1880? If as E.P. Thompson suggests,[4] class is a relationship between people, a shared consciousness, what then were the dominant needs and values that influenced working-class behavior? What institutions were most valuable to them? And what effect did the industrial experience have on the position and attitudes of women in nineteenth-century Cohoes? Did it permit them some measure of independence; did it give them some role in community life; did they suffer a loss of status by having to leave the home to work? Central to our concern is the relationship between the factory, the community and the cotton worker and her family.

Since the Industrial Revolution, woman as worker has been seen as a contradiction in terms, as some sort of sin against nature. This attitude underlay the widely held belief that for women to work would, as Richard Ely wrote in 1893, mean "the scattering of the members of the family and the breakdown of the home. . . ."[5] Carroll D. Wright, writing in the Tenth United States Census in 1880 identified the factory as the culprit: "The factory system necessitates the employment of women and children to an injurious extent, and consequently its tendency is to destroy family life and ties and domestic habits, and ultimately the home."[6] Wright's implications were clear: since the factory system removed mother from the home, it destroyed the family; therefore, remove women from the factory and the family would be saved.

Although they have disagreed on the causes, many historians have accepted the view that the working-class family was disorganized. Oscar Handlin has suggested, for example, that the urban industrial slum, "the disorganizing pressure of the environment," and not the factory, weakened the family.[7] In this way, the city, the factory and the immigrant experience, each have received the blame for the disorganization of the working-class family.

The history of the Cohoes, New York, cotton worker community, suggests the need to reconsider the impact of the factory and the city on the lives of the cotton worker and her family. Quite early in its history Cohoes had one distinct feature: by 1860 it had become a company town. Although both wool and cotton mills gave the city its title as the Spindle City, the Harmony Mills Company dominated the city, and by 1864 monopolized the town's cotton industry. But the Harmony Company controlled much more than Cohoes' cotton industry. In association with the wool manufacturers, company officials constituted an interlocking directorate that held virtually every major political and financial post in the city throughout this period.[8] And lastly, the company maintained considerable economic influence over the working-class community. The company built and rented the more than 800 brick tenement houses and five boarding houses that spread over Harmony Hill, the city's first ward where the cotton workers all lived. In addition, Harmony Mill paternalism oversaw the workers' lives from the child's attendance at the Sabbath School to the family's weekly food purchased from the Company Store. Consequently, strike issues included not only wages and hours, but also such complaints as the credit system under which the cotton workers bought their food and the rent deducted from the family's pay.

The cotton mills, led by the Harmony Company, more than kept pace with the growth of the overwhelmingly working-class inhabitants of Cohoes, whose population numbered only 1,850 residents in 1840, 8,800 in 1860 and 19,416 in 1880. Consequently, while approximately one out of every four Cohosiers worked as a cotton hand in 1860, the ratio had risen to almost one in three in 1880. Most important, 60 percent of these cotton workers were women, and in 1860 more than half were immigrant Irish, while in 1880 four out of every five cotton workers were either first or second generation Irish or French-Canadian immigrants.

The experience of Cohoes suggests, however, that the factory and the working-class community play a more ambiguous part in the life of workers and their families than is traditionally thought. The cotton workers organized in response to this corporative omnipresence, and their activities touched all aspects of social life in the Harmony Hill community. The working class organized around the factory. Led by the skilled male spinners and female weavers, cotton workers organized unions which struck and won a wage advance in the Harmony Mills in 1858. During and immediately after the Civil War, the union activity waned, but the cotton workers did participate in the Short Hour Movement, the Workingman's Party and in the Workingman's Cooperative Store. Since working-class culture on Cohoes' Harmony Hill was also ethnic culture, mass strike rallies were addressed in both French and English to help unite the Irish and French Canadians around their common problems and needs. For certain issues involved social conditions which these people experienced together. So, to their laboring, political and ethnic activities must be added their role within the Harmony Hill community. For almost all cotton workers and their families lived on the Hill. There these workers had constructed a full and complex network of fraternal, religious and political clubs and institutions that offered them entertainment, security and some cultural nourishment. Usually several members of each family and occasionally whole families worked in the mills. These workers were not concerned only with narrow economic questions, but saw union activity as vital to the security of their family and community, security some had traveled as much as 3,000 miles to achieve. Thus, we have to view the working-class woman in the full context of her community. But before we can begin to understand behavior within the working-class community, we need to identify the workers and their families and see what changes took place in the Harmony Hill community between 1860 and 1880.

For Lucy Larcom[9] and her fellow workers in the 1830s, the cotton mill might have seemed like a boarding school for young ladies; but in Cohoes in 1857 the image of the factory and the factory girl had drastically changed. In reply to a series of letters from "A Factory Girl" in the local newspaper, a town teacher explains why she held these girls in contempt: "I *do* claim to be superior to the vulgar herd with which our factories are stocked, and I *do* consider them unfit to associate with me, or to move in the same society to which I belong. Such, too, is the sentiment of all 'Upper Tendom.' "[10] For the "elite" of Cohoes society who may well have spent their own girlhood in the mills, factory life had lost status. But it remains to be seen whether it had lost status for the large masses of Cohosiers who now worked in the mills.

The manuscript United States Census of Population for Cohoes in 1860 does not distinguish between cotton and wool workers,[11] but the average textile worker in the town was not a native American by birth.[12] Factory life had become predominantly an immigrant experience. More than one half the employees in 1860 were either Irish immigrants or their children, only one quarter were native Americans, while English and French-Canadian hands each constituted less than one tenth of the workers. The typical cotton worker had more than a single social and cultural identity: this worker was both Irish and female. Moreover, the Harmony Mills cotton hand was most likely an unskilled and unmarried woman between the ages of 15 and 25. Four out of every five Irish women between the ages of 15 and 19 worked in the mills in 1860 (Table 3).

Although fewer women and young men were employed among the other ethnic groups, they followed a common pattern: children entered the mills in their early teens and left increasingly in their twenties. Women then married and men found employment outside the mills. Only English males remained in the mills. Usually married and of middle-age they worked as skilled spinners, weavers, dressers and carders. The husbands of other cotton mill workers found other jobs. Americans established themselves in trades or business outside the factory, while the Irish and French-Canadians became unskilled day laborers on the Erie and Champlain canal network or on the factory maintenance staff.[13]

Thus, even before the Civil War, immigrant Irish families had found work for their children in the Harmony Mills. While the Irish clearly dominated the mills, they were joined by a sizable number of native American workers. Other ethnic groups also moved readily into the mills in numbers equal to their relative share of the city's population. Finally, the factory did not draw mothers away from their families. When they married and began raising families women did not work. Their children worked. The additional income especially from unmarried daughters could be put to good advantage. As Stephan Thernstrom discovered among the Newburyport Irish, income provided by the children enabled the family to gain some small measure of the security Ireland had not afforded—property. Similarly in the Cohoes working-class community of 1860, it was mainly a few families headed by Irish cotton workers who accumulated property: 11 percent of these Irishmen owned property in 1860, compared to only 5.9 percent of the Englishmen, 1.8 percent of the Americans and none of the French Canadians.

Cohoes differed from the early New England textile town. Not only did young immigrant Irishwomen dominate the Cohoes cotton mills in 1860, but also by this time weaving remained the only skilled trade in which women still readily found employment: slightly more than half

TABLE 1 Factory (Textile) Workers (FW) and Ethnicity, 1860, and Cotton Workers (CW) and Ethnicity, 1880

1860*	Male	Female	Total	Percent of Population	FW† (%)
All Textile					
Workers	778	1103	1881	28.3	100.0
(Ten and Over)	41.4%	58.6%			
Native American	197	293	490	22.8	26.0
	40.2%	59.8%			
Irish	377	617	994	31.6	52.8
	37.9%	62.1%			
English	101	74	175	30.0	9.3
	57.7%	42.3%			
Fr. Canadian	50	74	124	26.2	6.5
	40.3%	59.7%			
*1880**					
All Cotton					
Workers	1280	1964	3244	21.3	100.0
(Ten and Over)	39.5%	60.5%			
Native American	136	148	284	9.1	8.8
	47.9%	52.1%			
Irish	514	958	1472	26.8	45.4
	34.9%	66.1%			
English	151	111	262	19.2	8.1
	57.6%	42.4%			
Fr. Canadian	435	674	1109	24.6	34.2
	39.2%	60.8%			

*Manuscript Census of Population data.

†Percentages of ethnic groups do not total 100% because small numbers of Scottish and German workers are omitted.

the Cohoes weavers in 1860 were women. The number of skilled workers distinguished by the census leaves much to be desired. But while the English filled skilled positions in the mills considerably in excess of their relatively small numbers in the town, Irishmen and women held skilled as well as unskilled positions (Table 2). This evidence shows the Irishmen did more than dig ditches and lay railroad track and Irishwomen worked in other than domestic services.[14] While the relative concentration of female English weavers was six times that of the Irish, in Civil War Cohoes, Irishwomen held as many skilled posts as weavers as did workers of American and English extraction. Native Americans still held about one quarter of the jobs, but by 1860 Cohoes' cotton mills had become largely Irish "institutions."

Between 1860 and 1880, Cohoes' Harmony Mills expanded greatly. New hands were needed to operate her spinning mules and looms. But

TABLE 2 Percentage and Relative Concentration* of Skilled and Un-skilled Cotton Workers in Ethnic Groups, 1860 and 1880

1860	Unskilled		Skilled		Spinners (Males)	Dressers Carders (Males)
	Males	Females	Males	Females		
USA	25.3%	26.5%	2.4%	32.6%	16.6%	46.1%
	80	84	8	103	52	145
IRE	48.4%	55.9%	36.6%	32.6%	25.0%	7.6%
	107	114	81	67	55	17
ENG.	12.9%	6.7%	46.3%	32.6%	50.0%	30.7%
	130	86	468	418	505	310
FR. CAN	6.4%	6.7%	0.0%	0.0%	0.0%	7.6%
	86	97	0	0	0	103
N:	778	1103	41	46	12	13
1880						
USA	10.6%	7.5%	11.1%	2.0%	0.0%	9.0%
	53	37	58	10	0	44
IRE	40.2%	48.8%	44.4%	72.9%	60.0%	54.5%
	117	139	127	200	175	159
ENG	11.8%	5.7%	11.1%	14.5%	33.3%	22.7%
	122	70	117	177	342	233
FR. CAN	34.0%	34.3%	0.0%	4.1%	0.0%	4.5%
	121	114	0	14	0	16
N:	1280	1964	9	48	30	22

*Proportion among gainful workers in all occupations = 100.

how had the characteristics of the average cotton worker and her family changed during these decades? And again, in what ways did these changes reflect the absence of union activity and relative quiescence of the Cohoes' cotton worker then?

During the two decades in question, the most dramatic change in the mill labor force involved the native American and French-Canadian ethnic groups. Whereas one out of every four unskilled textile workers in Cohoes in 1860 had been of native American extraction, and less than one in ten had been of French Canadian origin, by 1880 the percentages were virtually reversed (Table 1). The Harmony Mills population had doubled, but the number of native American workers was almost one half its 1860 figure. The 124 French-Canadian textile workers counted in 1860, for instance, had increased by 1880 ninefold to 1,109 in the cotton mills alone; the number of native Americans dropped 42 percent during this period from 490 to 284. Almost half the workers were still Irish, but better than one in three unskilled cotton hands were of French-Canadian ancestry. Native American and English workers now comprised less than one in ten of each group. Even under the pressure represented by the influx of large numbers of

TABLE 3 Percentage of Cohoes Men and Women of an Age and Ethnic Group Employed as Cohoes Factory (Textile) Workers, 1860

Ethnicity	Age 10–14	15–19	20–29	30–39	40+
American	5.4%	57.2%	34.8%	13.3%	6.9%
Irish	14.7%	81.9%	47.7%	13.7%	6.2%
Females					
English	11.5%	50.8%	31.8%	21.8%	9.2%
French Canadian	11.1%	77.0%	26.0%	12.1%	0.0%
American	6.4%	50.3%	24.9%	13.7%	7.4%
Irish	16.4%	67.6%	29.4%	18.1%	8.8%
Males					
English	3.6%	40.5%	52.1%	44.3%	23.6%
French Canadian	7.8%	58.0%	27.1%	25.0%	10.7%

"cheap" employable French-Canadian immigrant laborers, the Irish found additional employment in the mills. Similarly, the French Canadians found Harmony Hill to be a hospitable textile center. It is true that almost all teenage members of the family had to work for subsistence wages and everyone in the community depended heavily on company paternalism. The Harmony Mills, however, offered these people steady employment, solid brick-construction housing and a steady though meagre income. The French Canadian had found a home and, with friends, had established a community.

Although each ethnic group had distinct work patterns that reflected its separate cultural background, there were similarities among them. Two out of every three cotton workers in 1880 were female. The Irish and French Canadians maintained this ratio, while in contrast, the number of American-born men and women was almost even, and the number of English male workers continued as in 1860 to exceed the number of females in the mills. Native Americans had left the mills: 22.8 percent of the native population age ten and over labored in the textile mills in 1860, but by 1880 the percentage had dropped to 9.1 percent. Otherwise, among each of the three large immigrant ethnic groups—the Irish, French Canadians and English—the percentage of cotton workers remained about one out of every four or five "adults." Finally, as in 1860, the English continued to show a work pattern different from the other groups: the average English cotton hand was more likely to be a married male who was older than was his Irish, French-Canadian or native-American counterpart.

Thus, the typical unskilled cotton hand in 1880 was probably an Irish or French-Canadian woman. Not only was she a young unmarried woman, but the reverse was equally true: if one was a young Irish or

French-Canadian girl growing up in Cohoes, the chance that she once worked, still worked or would shortly work in the Harmony Mills was most probable. It was also likely that she started work in the mills at an earlier age in 1880 than she would have in 1860, especially if she was of French-Canadian extraction (Table 4).

The percentage of workers under twenty remained at about 50 percent in both census years, but the percentage of children under 14 employed tripled between 1860 and 1880 from 7.4 percent of the entire work force in 1860 to 24.1 percent in 1880. And while the increase was more marked among boys than girls, both vastly increased; and children from all ethnic groups worked. The average age of the workers remained fairly constant, at approximately 20. However, the average age of the women *did* vary with ethnicity: for instance, two out of every three female French-Canadian cotton workers were *under* 20, while the same percentage of English were *over* 20. These differences suggest different attitudes toward the child's role in the family and the birth rate among the different ethnic groups. A higher number of English women did not work. The key here is that fewer English children worked. Married Englishwomen did not flock to the mills; rather, they appear to have remained at home and to have kept their daughters home or in school. This decision might have been motivated by a variety of concerns. The desire of the English to educate or protect their daughters, cultural animosities and the fear of loss of status through association with the mass of mostly Irish and French-Canadian cotton workers may serve as explanations. For the Irish and newly arrived French-Canadian family, there was much more to be gained than lost by working in the mills. Children increasingly could and had to work the exhausting 72 hour week under frequently dangerous conditions at absurdly low salaries; but their income enabled mother to stay home with the youngest children. For a young Irish woman or man the mills also offered the prospect of some occupational mobility.

TABLE 4 Percentage of Female Factory (Textile) Workers, 1860, and Cotton Workers, 1880, in Selected Ethnic Groups Who Are under Twenty Years Old

	Age	U.S.A.	Ire.	Eng.	Fr. Can.
1860	0–14	2.7%	7.1%	10.5%	6.4%
	15–19	36.5	48.5	38.2	63.5
	Under 20	39.2	55.6	48.7	69.9
1880	0–14	16.7	15.6	13.5	27.3
	15–19	27.5	32.5	24.3	38.7
	Under 20	44.2	48.1	37.8	66.0

Achievement therefore related to the fortunes of the family. Many Irish appeared to have become skilled weavers and spinners as early as 1860. And by 1880 the Irish filled a majority of the skilled cotton mill positions. Irishwomen comprised 72.9 percent of the female weavers, and their sons and husbands fared equally well. Skilled Irishmen constituted 60 percent of the spinners and 54.5 percent of the dressers, carders and loom harness makers in 1880.

Consequently, while young girls of English and native-American origin may no longer have found factory work desirable, Irish and French-Canadian families wanted and easily obtained employment for their teenage daughters and sons and unmarried young women. So how may we evaluate the economic gains and social mobility experienced by the average cotton worker and her family between 1860 and 1880? High costs and low incomes made steady employment essential, and the Harmony Mills provided it.[15] The hours were long, the work among the whirling machines dangerous, but the Irish family procured work for as many children, relatives and neighbors as might turn up, and gained skilled positions. A few even translated money earned into some small property holdings. In this way, the history of Cohoes' working-class Irish and French Canadians suggests the need to reconsider Thernstrom's conclusion that the nineteenth-century working class did not exhibit the economic and social mobility celebrated in the American success myth.[16]

Thernstrom measured mobility in industrial and economic terms: occupational mobility and change in real estate and personal estate holdings. But these useful indices are too narrow. To grasp more fully the significance and character of social mobility in America, historians need to consider the goals and aspirations of the worker and her family on the one hand, and the form and function of status and power on the other. We can then assess the impact of technology, economic pressures and attitudes toward women. Might it not, for example, be the full realization of a social dream for the cotton worker family, freshly arrived in the new country with memories of famine still vivid, to find ample and steady employment in the mills, to maintain the security of the tenement home and to develop community fellowship? Cohoes' Irish found full employment in the Harmony Mills, and during the 20 years they increasingly dominated the skilled crafts. Life was not easy. But unlike many other factories during the depression, the Harmony Mills continued to provide regular monthly pay checks throughout the 1870s. The Company also maintained some unusually fine living conditions: well constructed apartments, paved streets, even some garbage collection and manicured lawns with room for a small garden. Compared to what one saw and heard of English manufacturing districts, and relative to the sorry conditions that impelled them to leave either Ireland or Quebec, it is easy to understand their desire to defend this small but for them not insignificant measure of security. Moreover, a woman had only to look at her Irish neighbors on the other side of town who worked at more menial service jobs—housekeepers and washerwomen—to recognize her preferred status. As the local newspaper noted, Cohoes' textile mills' employment of women made it "next to impossibility [sic] to get competent, reliable girls, who are willing to do housework at any price." The women had "the feeling that as operatives in the mills they take a higher place in the social scale than is accorded them when they do housework. The fact is, they don't like the idea of being servants, or being treated as such, and unless compelled by lack of the employment of their choice they avoid it with scorn."[17] So by 1880, as far as she was concerned, the cotton worker had achieved some measure of both status and security.

But what impact did the factory have on the cotton worker family? Did the company town tear the family apart? While there were considerable economic strains on the Cohoes cotton worker families, it is significant that working-class marriage patterns strikingly resembled the nonfactory family Richard Sennett described in the middle-class community of Union Park in Chicago during this same period. Except for the important presence of child labor among the working class, there appear to be surprisingly few structural differences between these working-class and middle-class families.

Whatever differences did exist between the marriage patterns of Union Park middle-class families and Cohoes cotton worker families seem to have arisen as much from the various ethnic cultural experiences as from disparities in economic position. For example, the percentage of married workers in the Harmony Mills follows the same pattern found in middle-class Union Park.[18] The average cotton worker couple married only when the husband had reached his early thirties, most likely when he felt somewhat more financially secure (Table 5). For the vast majority of the couples, no wide age difference separated the wife and husband (Table 6). In more than 80 percent of the marriages, the wife was less than ten years younger than the husband. And only Englishwomen married younger men with any frequency. Among 15.6 percent of all couples the wife was older than her husband, but among English couples the percentage was 25.3 percent. Women usually left the mills when they were married to assume the role of wife, mother and homemaker. But what of the relative size of the working-class and middle-class family? Once the family formed, conventional wisdom has it that the working class multiplied while the middle class exercised some reproductive restraint. Quoting Sennett on Union

TABLE 5 Percentage Married Within an Age Group, 1880, Among Cohoes Cotton Workers and Chicago's Union Park

Age	Workers	Middle Class Union Park Chicago*	Age
15–19	0.8%	3.5%	15–19
20–29	16.2%	20.4%	20–24
		43.0%	25–29
30–39	61.8%	60.3%	30–34
		60.3%	35–39
40–49	74.2%	70.7%	40–44
		72.0%	45–49
50–59	89.3%		

Percentage Married Within an Age Group by Sex and Ethnicity, 1880, Among Cohoes Cotton Workers

	Age	Ire.	Fr. Can.	Ethnicity Eng.	USA	Total
Females	20–29	8.0%	11.5%	13.0%	25.0%	10.3%
	30–39	44.2%	31.4%	83.3%	17.6%	41.0%
Males	20–29	24.0%	32.3%	39.3%	52.5%	29.1%
	30–39	80.7%	78.5%	91.6%	76.9%	90.6%

*Sennett, *Families Against the City*, 105.

Park, "A host of sexual taboos and the prohibition of child labor in this middle-class community made abstinence not only possible but a compelling necessity."[19] Cohoes, however, suggests again that the most important variable in terms of family size was ethnicity. The ratio of children under ten to the adult population in each ethnic group in 1860 (the "survival rate") demonstrates that family planning crossed class lines: the English and Irish couples averaged 30 percent and the French Canadians almost 50 percent more children than the couples of native-American extraction.[20] Finally, intermarriage figures between persons of different ethnic background demonstrate further the impact of ethnic culture. Almost 40 percent of the working-class English and native Americans who married wed outside of their own ethnic group. In contrast, French Canadians and Irish almost never married outside their ethnic community.[21] The reasons for this low rate of intermarriage would seem to be twofold: the Catholic injunction against marriage outside the religion, and the exclusiveness of both *Canadien* and Irish nationalist culture. In sum, working-class marriage patterns shared

TABLE 6   Age Differences Between Husbands and Wifes of Cotton Worker Families, 1880

	Marriages (N)	Wife Older (%)	Husbands 0–9 yr. older (%)	Wife less than 5 yr. older Husbands; 0–9 yr. older (%)
Ir.	303	15.8	69.7	81.6
Fr. Can.	105	11.6	80.0	87.7
U.S.A.	50	12.0	72.0	80.0
Eng.	75	25.3	65.4	82.7
Other	18	16.7	66.6	77.7
Total	601	15.6	71.9	83.0

many of the same concerns for tradition, security and stability as the middle-class marriage. Each ethnic group, however, expressed these concerns in different forms of behavior.

Working-class households on Harmony Hill in 1880 again resembled those in Union Park. As in that middle-class community, working-class Cohosiers predominantly lived in nuclear families. By contemporary standards, however, cotton worker families experienced considerable disorganization. In a culture that celebrated a traditional two-parent family and the guiding role of the father, one-parent families, especially when headed by a woman, were considered incomplete and hence "disorganized." But it is crucial to examine the origins and dimensions of this "disorganization." Three quarters of the Irish and English male- or female-headed households were nuclear families (Table 7). These households, composed of first and second generation immigrants, were nuclear after the 3,000-mile migration. Households headed by native Americans or French Canadians had a percentage of families augmented by both relatives and boarders almost twice that of the other two groups. But it was the high percentage of one-parent families that distinguished the cotton worker family from other working-class and Chicago middle-class families.

One out of every four Cohoes cotton worker families on Harmony Hill was a "broken" family—a family headed by one parent. One-parent Irish families had raised the percentage considerably: 28.8 percent of the Irish families were "broken," compared to only about 14 percent of the families of other ethnic groups. Furthermore, almost all of these "broken" families were female-headed. Thus, almost one-quarter of the Harmony Hill families were headed by a "widow"—a woman whose husband had either left her or died. Family structure among the iron workers of Troy, New York, across the river, suggests that this extra-

TABLE 7 Cotton Worker Household and Family Structure in Cohoes, 1880—
Ward One, Harmony Hill

Households	Ire.	Can.	USA	Eng.	Other	Total
Nuclear	323	125	35	63	18	564
	72.7%	67.9%	60.3%	77.8%	81.8%	71.5%
Extended	42	20	6	8	2	78
	9.5%	10.9%	10.3%	9.9%	9.1%	9.9%
Augmented	65	38	15	10	2	130
	14.6%	20.7%	25.9%	12.3%	9.1%	16.5%
Mixed Adult Group* (MAG) & Single	14	1	2	0	0	17
	3.2%	0.5%	3.5%	0.0%	0.0%	2.2%
	444	184	58	81	22	789
*Families***						
Whole	302	157	47	71	17	594
	68.0%	85.3%	81.0%	87.7%	77.3%	75.3%
"Broken"	128	26	9	10	5	178
	28.8%	14.1%	15.5%	12.3%	22.7%	22.6%
Percentage of "broken" families headed by a female	89.8%	88.5%	88.9%	80.0%	80.0%	88.8%
Average No. Cotton Wkers/ Family†	2.75	3.63	1.67	2.04	–	2.79

*The two boarding houses are not included.

**MAG & Singles not included.

†Based on first 250 families enumerated in Ward One.

ordinary rate of family "disorganization" reflected conditions peculiar to the textile industry more than it did the general character of working-class life. Sennett found 10.9 percent of the Union Park families to be without one parent. Troy's iron workers, both skilled and unskilled, lived in "broken" homes to about the same extent.[22]

Differences did occur, however, *between* ethnic groups. In Troy and Cohoes the rate of one-parent Irish families outdistanced the other groups. Combining skilled and unskilled Troy iron workers, approximately 15 percent of the Irish, 6 percent of the English, and 10 percent of the native Americans lived in "broken" homes. Thus working-class and middle-class household and family structure strongly resembled one another: both were nuclear families with two parents. Differences were ethnic and industrial—in our case, especially among the Irish and the cotton industry. Why were so many of the cotton worker families one-parent in structure? Widowed women may have taken their families to Cohoes where their children could find employment in the Harmony Mills' light industry. Almost all the widows were over 40 years old with teenage children, and the cotton mills made it possible for mother to stay home with the youngest children while the older children earned the family's income.

Thus Cohoes' cotton worker families were more "disorganized" than Troy's iron worker families. But the high incidence of nuclear families suggests a problem with the term "disorganization." The term exposes the historical prejudice against the one-parent family and ignores the tensions that may have wracked many two-parent families. In addition, the cotton mill may have provided employment and a financial refuge for the widowed family. Thus Sennett's categories may be inadequate to understand the pressures on the nineteenth-century working-class family. In fact almost nine of every ten non-Irish cotton worker families were two-parent headed. Sennett is correct, however, when he insightfully suggests the importance of the stable family in a changing and complex industrial city. According to Sennett, "The family was enshrined out of a sense of its peril in the city."[23] For Sennett, fear that the stability and security of the family would not be maintained became a "guiding force" in the history of the nineteenth-century American city. The middle class clung to the family as the one stable institution in the midst of a rapidly changing world. Although the pressures on the family were immense, the family did not constitute the workers' single supportive institution. On the contrary, the factory and community also structured their social life. Thus, the working class, and the Irish in particular, made an effort to get their daughters and sons unskilled and skilled jobs in the mills and membership in the network of city fraternal and religious associations.

Why, however, was the Irish family so distinctly scarred? In her pioneering study of working-class Irish in mid-nineteenth-century London, Lynn Lees showed the continued dominance of the nuclear family in the Irish household, noted the similarity between the Irish and the English working-class family and concluded that the Irish had not suffered any unusual breakdown.[24] Lees, however, failed to adequately distinguish between families headed by two parents and those in which only one parent was present. In this regard, we were not told whether or not the Irish in London differed from the English. The evidence in both Troy and Cohoes suggests that the Irish family structure—though not household structure—differed from that of the other major ethnic groups present in these two cities. Statistics compiled by the United States Immigration Commission in 1910 corroborate this evidence: the Commission *Reports* listed 12.4 percent of the immigrant cotton workers born in Ireland as widowed, compared to percentages of 5.9 percent of the French Canadians and 7.1 percent for the English.[25] Significantly, these *Reports* suggested that this difference largely disappeared within one generation. For the second generation immigrant family—the first born in the United States—the percentage of Irish widows more nearly approximates the percentages for the other groups: the percentages for the American-born Irish, English and Canadian respectively are 5.9 percent, 4.8 and 3.8 percent. So, though some of the distinctions between the family structure of the Irish and other ethnic groups appear at face value to have diminished with a generation of acclimation, acculturation and without a 3,000-mile migration, the situation of the immigrant Irish family remains somewhat unique. The fragile Irish family reflected the problems that worried the immigrant in industrial America, i.e., considerable prejudice, high mortality and the intense pressures of industrial capitalism. But the higher number of one-parent Irish families may also have reflected distinct ethnic values. We may offer some preliminary suggestions for this. Peasant, semifeudal Irish cultural traditions celebrated Irish community life and kinship and then were patriarchal. Beyond this, though, the Irish families' willingness to allow young girls out of the home and into the factory during adolescence suggests that the Irish husband subscribed to a set of traditional family values distinctly different from those held by men of Protestant English and American origins. Lastly, the Irish peasants' culture had unregimented preindustrial work rhythms. Adjustment required by factory life, with its highly disciplined work patterns, made the Irish industrial experience disruptive and alienating.[26] Although more work needs to be done in this area, we see the importance of ethnic culture in shaping working-class experience.

What then can we say about the cotton workers and their families, their community and their adjustment to factory life during the Gilded Age? The history of Patrick Dillon and his family illustrates the life of one representative cotton worker family in Cohoes.[27] Patrick Dillon probably left Ireland with his wife Ellen and their six children during the potato famine. They arrived in New York around 1850, and by 1860 had added three more children to their family. At the outbreak of the Civil War the now 11-member family lived in a four- or five-room company tenement at 4 Willow Street in the heart of the Harmony Hill Community. The family had managed to save approximately 300 dollars, but it had not been easy; four members of the family worked full time. Every morning the 45-year-old head of the household left home before six for work as a day laborer. The two eldest sons, Michael and William, age 20 and 18 respectively, answered the call of the Harmony Mills' bell, and walked down the street to the mill for a six-o'clock start, too. And Patrick, the 16-year-old son, joined his father as a day laborer. The father and son possibly worked on one of the canal or railroad labor gangs involved in area construction. They may well, however, have also worked for the Harmony Company—building new tenements or enlarging the newly acquired Ogden Mills. Mother, meanwhile, had her hands full at home. Matthew, age 14, and the 12-year-old twin girls did not yet work and only six-year-old James attended school. In addition, not only was Mrs. Dillon pregnant, but the baby, Bridget, who had only just celebrated her first birthday, and Margaret, age three, must have required considerable attention.

Meanwhile the men came home for lunch on their 40-minute noon break and then returned to the mills. At half past six the bell rang to close the mills for another day. For these 12 hours of work an adult common laborer received $0.75, while a skilled mule spinner received as much as $1.50. Women and especially children who labored in the mills received considerably less: an unskilled "back boy," for example, received $0.30 for his 12-hour day. When the monthly pay day arrived, the tenement house rent of between $5 and $7 was simply deducted from the salary.[28]

What happened to the Dillons during the next two decades? Did the family unit survive intact, did the family remain financially solvent and did they remain to establish themselves within the Cohoes' community? Patrick Dillon, Sr., had died late in the 1860s, but his widow continued to maintain the home on Willow Street. Family economics required that Mrs. Dillon open her small home to another family—John Kanal, his wife and two children—and to a boarder. Of her children, Patrick, Jr., died suddenly in 1870 at the age of 26 (shortly after his marriage) and James died September 15, 1874, at the age of 19—both from causes that are undisclosed. Michael and Matthew reappear periodically in the city directory as operatives in the Harmony Mills. Finally, while the older girls had most likely married, William, the second eldest son 20 years earlier, by 1880 had become head of the family, still located in their Willow Street tenement. The family once again sustained itself without boarders. William Dillon's first wife had died but he had remarried. His second wife, Elizabeth, was 15 years his junior, and was only nine years older than his son Patrick, now 15.[29] William now ran a "saloon" but his three youngest sisters, now 19, 20 and 22 years old, together with Patrick worked in the Harmony Mills, much as the family had for the past 20 years. Over the years the Dillon family had secured a place within the community for its remaining numbers but there had been many deaths in the family and most at relatively young ages.

Work in the mills had hardly changed. Wages for the now ten and a half to 11-hour day had dropped back from the high level maintained between 1867 and 1875 to their 1864 level: for a day's work a common laborer now received $1.12½, a skilled spinner $1.75, and a back boy $0.42. The Harmony Company continued throughout this period to play a central part in the life of the Dillon family: the Willow Street tenement remained a focus for the family, and the mills continuously employed the teenagers and adult Dillons and so helped to sustain the family. In fact, five of the seven members of the family in 1880 worked—four of them in the cotton mills. And, five years later the Dillons evidently felt secure enough to permit young Patrick, now 20 years old, to leave the mills and return to school. While living at home, Patrick Dillon—the grandson of his namesake who arrived in American almost 40 years earlier—had become a "student," with the considerable occupational and social mobility American society afforded the educated man. Though for many of his relatives, mobility had been only from the mills to the grave, young Patrick had achieved an avenue both he and the dominant American culture could celebrate.

Like other families in Cohoes, the lives of the Dillon family extended beyond the factory and was fuller and richer than this industrial portrait suggests. On Cohoes' Harmony Hill, the Irish and French-Canadian cotton workers like the Dillons had established by 1880 a diverse and full community replete with ethnic, religious, social and political club life. There were separate Irish and French Catholic churches; the Irish organized the Fenians and the Land League, and the French formed the St. Jean Baptiste Society; a French newspaper, *La Patrie Nouvelle*, was begun in the city in 1876; each ethnic group formed benevolent societies; and while Cohoes Irishmen usually voted Democratic, it was not uncommon for French Republican groups to form before the fall elections.

Carl Wittke has emphasized the competition between the Irish and the French Canadians. This competition supposedly stemmed from the French-Canadian support of the Republican Party and their reluctance to organize.[30] There were, however, certain fundamental similarities in their experience as well. Whether the workers were Irish like the Dillons, or French Canadian, both were Catholic, both came to America in search of economic advancement. Both worked side by side in the mills and were neighbors on the Hill. And together both struggled against the manufacturers to preserve their jobs and to control their work conditions. Work for the women and children in the Mills was indeed taxing. But through the depression, families like the Dillons gained some security and status. There were openings in skilled positions and some families had even become property holders. The factory did not provide "pin money," especially in the case of the large number of widowed families. The factory offered women jobs and made it possible to hold the female-headed family together and to maintain a nuclear family. In this way, rather than destroying the family, for the cotton workers, the Harmony Mill helped to sustain it.

In addition, urban Harmony Hill did not necessarily alienate the family. While living conditions left something to be desired, the close relationships and organization of the community also helped sustain the cotton worker family. When the workers went out on strike, the whole city was affected. Community pressure helped to maintain the strike: some businessmen offered discounts and contributions to striking workers; one woman, for instance, complained to the local press that the family above her had been persecuting her family for working, and that the day before she had been hit on the head by a bottle thrown by one of them; various tenants who wanted to work complained of "bulldozing"—intimidation from striking neighbors. But community pressures weakened the strikers, too; many striking weavers would return to Cohoes to work because they and their girls were homesick. As Miss O'Brien wrote from Forestdale, R.I., "This [Forestdale] is a very pretty place, but not like home [Cohoes]."[31]

So, why did violence erupt in Cohoes in the early 1880s? This seemingly optimistic portrait was deceptive. The family, community life and occupational mobility in the factory were enclaves against a threatening and insecure urban industrial life. Cohoes cotton workers lived in poverty. That they could endure three wage reductions during the 1873–1877 depression demonstrates how their depressed lives had lowered their expectations. At least the Harmony Company had not closed. In this way, they felt they had gained some success and had established a home. But they continued to live on the edge of fear—low pay, technological changes in the industry and an always ample supply of surplus labor threatened to destroy the small part of the social dream they had been able to realize. In addition, the increasing competition of industrial capitalism demanded increased production, lower costs and greater efficiency. To secure and maintain their profits the Harmony Mill manufacturers felt it necessary to reduce wages and control all aspects of mill life. Unions stood in their way. When the cotton workers' wages were reduced for the fourth time in seven years, they saw their minimal success, status and security threatened. Central to the struggle was control. At issue were not simply salaries, but the survival of the entire community. When, after six months of strikes, the manufacturers brought in disciplined, Protestant, Swedish immigrant families to replace the strikers, the women and children cotton workers responded directly and vigorously. They gathered at the mill entrances to "greet" the Swedes with stones. Police were brought in to protect the "scabs," and violence ensued. Although the strike was crushed, the working-class community then united and two months later elected the strike leader to the State Assembly.

In conclusion, the behavior of the Cohoes cotton worker community suggests the need to understand the place of ethnic traditions in the context of working-class achievements and perception. Furthermore, we need to reassess the impact of the community and factory on the working-class family. Many working-class cotton mill families *were* broken. Child labor was necessary. Industrial capitalism divested the worker of control over work conditions and threatened the family's quest for social and economic security. Both the factory and the urban experience intensified the problems of adjustment for preindustrial peoples, subjecting them to new and alienating work and to the strange heterogeneity of the city. But it must be remembered that by 1880 both the factory and the community had come to sustain the cotton worker family, and especially the female-headed household, in important ways. Together the mills and community provided another avenue to social fulfillment and achievement for the Irish and French Canadians of Harmony Hill. Thus, ironically, the argument that urged women to be taken out of the factory did much to rob many families of their one vital source of income. For in the textile mills at least, the women who worked not only needed the money desperately, but were usually unmarried adolescents, not mothers. Lastly, the Cohoes cotton worker community illustrates the *embourgeoisement* of the working class; the working class had begun to acquire certain middle-class attitudes about the values of status, security, property and the privatized nuclear family. Thus the final irony of cotton worker mobility: on the road to success, the pressures of industrial capitalism had reduced the cotton worker and her family to perceptual cripples, alienated from and by their own conditions. Cohoes' working class did engage in violence, but the violence was defensive—an attempt to protect their modest social position. There is perhaps no greater testimony to how difficult these people's lives had been, how fragile their economic existence remained and how fearfully they faced the future, than the energetic manner in which the women of Cohoes' Harmony Hill cotton worker community defended and celebrated the modicum of status and security they had achieved. Enmeshed in this difficult, fragile and fearful existence, the working-class dream had become a nightmare.

NOTES

1. See Richard Sennett and Stephan Thernstrom, eds., *Nineteenth-Century Cities: Essays in the New Urban History* (New Haven: 1969).

2. There are, of course, variations on each theme. The first view is widespread in the literature of the labor movement. (One popular refinement of this view emphasizes the considerable oppression of the working class and argues that this suffocated its radicalization.) The second view is expressed by Stephan Thernstrom in the conclusion to his article in a New Left anthology. Stephan Thernstrom, "Urbanization, Migration, and Social Mobility in Late Nineteenth-Century America" in *Towards a New Past: Dissenting Essays in American History*, Barton J. Bernstein, ed. (New York: 1968), 158–75.

3. New York State Bureau of Statistics of Labor, *2nd Annual Report, 1884* Legislative Assembly Document 26 (1882), "Establishing the Fact of the Existence of Child Labor in the State," (Albany: 1885), 112.

4. Edward P. Thompson, *The Making of the English Working Class* (New York: 1963), 9–10.

5. Richard Ely, "Introduction," in Helen S. Campbell, *Women Wage-Earners* (Boston: 1893), n.p.

6. Carroll D. Wright, quoted in Campbell, 90.

7. Oscar Handlin, *The Uprooted* (New York: 1951), 167.

8. The biography of William E. Thorn, the agent and treasurer of the Harmony Company from 1867 to 1910, well exemplifies the social, financial and political institutions that Cohoes textile manufacturers controlled. Thorn was both the son-in-law of Commodore Cornelius Vanderbilt and the nephew of Thomas Garner, the owner of the Harmony Mills. After coming to Cohoes in 1867, Thorn served on the Board of Directors of the Cohoes Company (the water power company), was secretary and treasurer of the Cohoes Gas Light Company (both controlled by the Garner interests), was director and first president of the Manufacturers' Bank of Cohoes and was instrumental in organizing the Cohoes Mechanics' Savings Bank. Finally Thorn was elected mayor of Cohoes in 1878 and 1880 and served as a Republican Presidential elector in 1892. See James H. Manning, *New York State Men* (Albany: 1920).

9. Lucy Larcom, *A New England Girlhood* (New edition, New York: 1961). See Edith Abbott, *Women in Industry: A Study in American Economic History* (New York, 1918), 114–16. Abbott writes of the Lowell, Massachusetts, mills that "all operatives were required to live in the company boarding houses . . . organized to resemble . . . big boarding schools." And, "Lowell had a high reputation for good order, morality, piety, and all that was dear to the old-fashioned New Englander's heart."

10. "A Factory Girl" to the editor, *Cohoes Cataract,* April 18, 1857.

11. One encounters various problems working with census data. In Cohoes all mill hands are simply enumerated in the 1860 Census of Population as "Works in Factory." The Census of Manufactures, however, suggests that the cotton and wool worker situation did not vary much. The statistics from the Census of Population for textile workers closely approximates the Census of Manufactures data for the Harmony and other cotton mills in the city. Therefore, one must interpolate from the former to the latter. In 1880 cotton workers and sections of town are distinguished.

12. Unless otherwise indicated the father's place of birth is used to define ethnicity. Thus a native American is someone whose father was born in the United States.

13. The percentage of Irish and French-Canadian men in their thirties and forties who worked as laborers doubled and tripled respectively the percentage of those in their twenties. The actual number also rose markedly. For example, 49 Irishmen or 17.2 percent of those Irishmen in their twenties were laborers, but among those in their forties the number rose to 95 or 54.3 percent.

14. See Oscar Handlin, *Boston's Immigrants, 1790–1865: A Study in Acculturation* (Cambridge, Mass.: 1941), 61–75; Thomas N. Brown, *Irish-American Nationalism: 1870–1890* (Phila.: 1966), 18–19; William V. Shannon, *The American Irish* (New York: 1963), 28, 95; Carl Wittke, *The Irish in America* (Baton Rouge, La.: 1956).

15. In 1880, between four and five people worked in the average Irish and French Canadian household respectively; in contrast, only two or three people worked in the average English and American cotton worker household.

16. Stephan Thernstrom, *Poverty and Progress: Social Mobility in a Nineteenth Century City* (Cambridge, Mass.: 1964), 146.

17. *Cohoes Daily News,* May 11, 1881.

18. See Richard Sennett, *Families Against the City: Middle-Class Homes of Industrial Chicago, 1872–1890* (Cambridge, Mass.: 1970), 105.

19. Sennett, *Families Against the City,* 118.

20. Comparative birth rates for Cohoes in 1860 can be approximated by comparing the ratio between the adult population of each ethnic group and the number of children in that group below a given age. (I have chosen age ten, but the figure can be adjusted easily.) Multiplied by one thousand, the birth rate (actually a "survival rate") per thousand population in 1860 reads:

Native Americans	209
English	263
Irish	277
French Canadians	308

21. Only six of 298 French Canadians in Cohoes Harmony Hill (2.0 percent) married someone from another ethnic group. Forty-two of 596 Irish men or women (7.0 percent) intermarried.

22. Thirteen and eight-tenths percent and 12.2 percent of Troy's skilled and unskilled iron workers respectively lived in one-parent households. See Daniel J. Walkowitz, "Statistics and the Writing of Working-class Culture: The iron workers of Troy, New York, 1860–1880," forthcoming, 1972, in a book edited by Herbert G. Gutman.

23. Sennett, *Families Against the City,* 116–19.

24. Lynn Lees, "Patterns of Lower-class Life: Irish Slum Communities in Nineteenth-Century London," in *Nineteenth-Century Cities,* 359–85.

25. U.S. Immigration Commission, *Reports of the Immigration Commission to Congress,* 1910, 10, part 3, *Immigrants in Industries,* 154–55.

26. Thompson, 436–44.

27. This biographical sketch is based upon the original federal manuscript census schedules. Most important also was the *Troy Directory, also Cohoes...,* 1867–1885; Masten, *History of Cohoes;* and, Census Office, 10th Census, 1880, *Reports,* 20, "Statistics of Wages...," 361–63.

28. Caroline F. Ware, *The Early New England Cotton Manufacture,* 244, presents a picture of the wage structure in New England cotton towns that is sensitive to the dependence of the employee on meagre wages, the ways in which salary was tied to their total social condition through rent and store pay and the reduced wages of women and children.

29. This 15-year age difference between William Dillon and his second wife reflected the usual pattern. When widowers remarried there is almost always a larger age gap with the second wife than with the first. This suggests something of the poor odds against a widow's remarrying. For an extended discussion of this problem, see William J. Goode, *World Revolution and Family Pattern* (New York: 1963), 318–19.

30. Carl Wittke, *We Who Built America* (New York: 1940), 315–28.

31. *Cohoes Daily News,* August 15, 1882.

13 &"Not Gainfully Employed": Women on the Iowa Frontier, 1833–1870

Glenda Riley

To study pioneer women through census data alone can be a frustrating and often deceptive effort. Certainly this is true for Iowa between 1833, when the area was opened for settlement by the Black Hawk Purchase Treaty, and 1870, when the United States Bureau of the Census declared the Iowa frontier "closed." Admittedly, the rich census data available for Iowa reveal a great deal about the population in general. The typical migrant, according to Allan Bogue's reading of the data, was "a married man between the ages of twenty-five and forty-five who had started his family before he moved to the . . . Iowa frontier."[1] The Iowa territorial census of 1838 allows scholars to expand on Bogue's analysis in significant ways. It shows that most of the new arrivals lived in households which averaged 5 to 6 members and with a ratio of 4 men to 3 women. This census also indicates that most people were attached to some type of family and that few people lived alone.[2] The next territorial census in 1840 demonstrates that the preponderance of pioneers were engaged in agricultural pursuits. There were, for example, 10,728 people listed as engaged in agriculture as opposed to 1,594 in manufacturing and trade, while only 348 were grouped in the "learned professions."[3] Summary statistics given in the state census of 1880 confirm that the agrarian-oriented migration persisted throughout Iowa's frontier period with the gross number of farms in Iowa rising from 14,805 in 1850, to 61,163 in 1860, and 116,292 in 1870.[4]

This statistical picture is revealing, and perhaps even predictable, but it leaves many questions unanswered, especially regarding women.

From *Pacific Historical Review* 49 (May 1980). Reprinted with permission.

The census did count white men and women separately (blacks and those born in other countries were frequently lumped together with no differentiation by gender), so it is clear that the white males outnumbered the white females throughout the frontier period.[5]

	1838	1850	1856	1860	1865	1870
Male population	24,355	101,052	278,584	354,493	383,272	625,917
Female population	18,757	91,162	239,291	320,420	346,086	568,103

Anecdotal evidence supports the contention that women were constantly in demand as wives in this family-farm economy, but other jobs they might have held are lost in generalized census categories such as clerks, teachers, editors, hotelkeepers, boardinghouse keepers, and even loafers. Only occasionally did the gender of the census category—such as seamstress, dressmaker, tailoress, or milliner—make it obvious that women were employed outside the home.[6] Even then, however, the marital status of women employed outside the home was unknown. The census did not count single people at all. Only the married and widowed were identified, but even they were not counted by gender.

Clearly, to study Iowa pioneer women through census data requires asking some very modern questions of statistics whose limitations mirror the perspectives and philosophies of another era. This problem is demonstrated, in particular, by the various census reports which summarily group Iowa women under the heading "Not Gainfully Employed." This categorization raises some surprising and, in a sense, shocking questions regarding frontierswomen. Was their labor worth so little that they were not considered workers? Was their contribution to the westward movement so inconsequential that it could be easily dismissed?

These questions cannot be answered in the affirmative since abundant frontier lore pictures pioneer women as hard workers. They were economic producers who manufactured all manner of domestic goods, gave birth to and trained future laborers, helped with "men's" work, and generated small amounts of cash income. Why, then, did census takers label them "not gainfully employed"? The answer is simple. The census did not reflect the actual work of frontier women; rather, it reflected a moneyed society which tended to equate useful work with paid work. During the very early years of American settlement, factors such as barter, trade, subsistence farming, and emergent capitalist structures made it necessary to judge people's labor by standards other than the cash income it earned. But as America became more settled and moved with headlong speed towards its own version of the Industrial Revolution, money and the ability to earn it took on new meaning.

By the 1830s, when the settlement of Iowa was beginning, the eastern United States was already immersed in a system which separated the "paid" worker from the unpaid. Mill girls were employed, farm wives were not. Nursemaids were employed, mothers were not. Businessmen were employed, but the wives who ran their homes and served as their status symbols were not. The idea that the mark of a gainfully employed person was the ability to earn money rapidly became characteristic of American society. Translated into twentieth-century terms, it compels full-time wives and mothers to apologetically proclaim, "I'm *just* a housewife."

Since the idea that domestic work is not gainful work was so pervasive in nineteenth-century America, it is not surprising that census officials sometimes cavalierly extended it to women on the Iowa frontier. In the nineteenth-century East, factories were rapidly taking over women's customary functions of producing foodstuffs, soap, lighting facilities, clothing, and other domestic goods. In the nineteenth-century West, women still produced these goods in their own homes. Frontier women manufactured many items and purchased little, especially in the early years of settlement, because neither the goods nor the cash to obtain them were readily available. By the 1870s, as railroads and cities spilled over the Iowa prairie, this situation had altered radically. But it was too late for the pioneer woman. She went down in history as one who was not gainfully employed.

Revision of this view is long overdue. The frontier woman was not just a domestic drudge whose life was automatically unhappy. Women's diaries, memoirs, and correspondence indicate that she was a full economic producer in her own right within the home. As such, her life could include the same kind of satisfactions that her male counterpart derived from his labor. In fact, the skills she needed in her life's work were of such great consequence that she spent a good portion of her girlhood in apprenticeship to her mother or to another woman to learn them thoroughly.

By the time a frontier woman was of marriageable age, her greatest assets centered around her abilities as a domestic manufacturer. She was rated by her local reputation as a worker in the same way that men were graded as "providers." According to one study on frontier marriage,

> ...The choosing of a mate on the frontier was a matter of economic necessity far and above individual whim. Good health and perseverance were premium assets while the charm and ability to entertain that one values so highly in a society of mechanization and leisure time was only of tangential significance. ... [T]he woman who could not sew nor cook had no place on the frontier.[7]

Mates, then, were chosen primarily as economic partners. It was considered a bonus if they were also compatible. For the typical frontier couple, their wedding day marked not only the beginning of a shared life but the beginning of a shared business venture as well.

If a pioneer woman opted to remain unmarried or was pushed into living alone by circumstances, such as divorce or the death of a mate, her skills were still crucial. Census figures tentatively indicate that most single women on the Iowa frontier were absorbed by other households: parents, children, relatives, or neighbors. In their adoptive family, women had to pull their own economic weight by continuing to render their share of household services. As in other parts of the country, these unattached females were often assigned the task of spinning flax, wool, and other fibers into thread. This phenomenon left its mark upon the American language in the word spinster (spin-ster) meaning an unmarried woman.

Regardless of their marital status, women were absolutely necessary to the frontier economy. Since domestic labor was so diverse in orientation, it is difficult to know where to begin a discussion of its nature. The picture given by one Iowa man regarding his mother's labors gives some idea of their vast scope.

> Mother bore and cared for the babies, saw that the floor was white and clean, that the beds were made and cared for, the garden tended, the turkeys dressed, the deer flesh cured and the fat prepared for candles or culinary use, that the wild fruits were garnered and preserved or dried, that the spinning and knitting was done and the clothing made. She did her part in all these tasks, made nearly all the clothing and did the thousand things for us a mother only finds to do.[8]

His description clearly indicates that his mother was the chief laborer within the home. It was her responsibility to process the raw materials generated in the fields outside of the home. The woman and her home, or in other words, the worker and her workplace, were the key link in turning unusable raw materials into consumable finished goods. She was therefore to her family what the factory was to an industrialized society.

Of all the products that she manufactured, food required the most continuous attention. In an age when people worked long, physically taxing hours and consumed thousands of calories per day to sustain themselves, food preparation was at the hub of domestic activity. Unlike the women of later eras, a pioneer woman had to rely on her own talents and resources for every step from processing through storing to actual preparation.

The first step, processing, began with the gathering of raw foodstuffs. Many of these, such as corn and wheat, were produced by the men of the family. However, the women were often responsible for obtaining vegetables, fruits, herbs, eggs, and milk. Although the men usually did the heavier jobs, such as harrowing and planting the vegetable patch, women did the weeding, picking, and "digging taters." Women also gathered wild and domestic fruits, beginning with currants and cherries in June and ending with strawberries later in the summer. Furthermore, planting herb gardens, gathering wild herbs, collecting eggs, and sometimes even milking the cows fell to the lot of the women. Their labor, combined with the produce of the fields, of farm stock, and of hunting, provided a myriad of raw materials which could be processed into many varieties of usable, and often appetizing, foodstuffs.

Naturally, corn was a staple of the Iowa pioneer's diet. It was eaten fresh, but was also stored for use during the long winter months when fresh foods were unavailable. Drying sweet corn took place during the hottest days of late August when the ears were husked, scalded, and then stripped of the kernels which were spread on pans, covered by a mosquito net, and placed on the roof in the sun. If rain threatened, the pans were rushed back into the house and placed in the oven for drying. This dried corn would later reappear in many forms—cornbread, mush, corncakes, and corn pone.[9] Corn was also commonly processed into hominy, a favorite food served with milk and some sort of sweetener. The following description of hominy-making was passed on by May Ramsay:

> They had a hopper made out of wood up on a stand where they put the wood ashes and made lye. Grandmother would take corn and boil it in lye water until the shell would come off. (That was in a big kettle outdoors). Then take the corn to the well and wash it until she had all the lye off. I remember how I watched her and wondered about it. It sure made good hominy when it was washed enough.[10]

Eggs and milk constituted two other standards of the pioneer menu. Milk, of course, was frequently churned into butter. Matilda Peitzke Paul remembered that it was a tedious and time-consuming process.

> ... the milk was put in pans to cool and left long enough for the cream to come to the top which was about 24 hours, then the cream was

skimmed off with this kind of skimmer and kept in a cool place if there was one, until there was enough cream to make several pounds of butter in a dash churn. . . . I remember how I used to dread to have mother call me and tell me to help with the churning. It seemed as if the butter never would come [since] sometimes it did take for hours to churn.[11]

Another woman lived near a creek with a shelving rock under the bank where she kept her milk and butter cold even on the hottest summer days. She was an expert butter maker and in 1857, when she sent her "roll of butter, daintily marked and as smooth as marble" to the local fair she easily captured first place.[12]

By the end of the fall, the family's cellar had been transformed into a storehouse which would gradually surrender its precious treasure throughout the long winter. Amelia Murdock Wing always retained fond memories of her family's well-stocked cellar:

A barrel of kraut was made in the fall; chunks of pork were salted down; fruit was canned and kept in long, heavy wooden boxes, many kinds of vegetables could be kept there throughout the winter. . . . In our cellar there was a floor of rock, always cleanly scrubbed. There was a long table for use in handling the milk and butter, and a wooden dash-churn stood beside it. There was a large cupboard whose tin doors had holes for ventilation, and this was where the milk, cream and butter was kept. No one had ice in those days, but our cellar was cool.[13]

Processing of foodstuffs was primarily a summertime chore, but converting food supplies into edible meals was a continual task to be faced day after day, year after year, often with only the most rudimentary kitchen equipment as an aid. During the early years of settlement, the most common cooking utensil on the Iowa frontier was a black iron kettle suspended on an iron crane which swung in and out of the open fireplace. This was complemented by a Dutch oven which consisted of a rather flatbottomed pot with an iron lid. This oven was set directly in the hot coals and often covered over with coals. Another common implement was a long-handled frying pan, used for both meat and flapjacks which were fried over the open fire. Large meat strips, such as turkey, venison, or pork, might be cooked by suspending it over the fire on a tightly twisted piece of string. As the string unwound it acted as a kind of spit which turned the meat slowly and allowed it to brown evenly. Bread was also baked by the open fire by spreading the dough over a "johnnycake" board, propping the board up to face the fire, and then turning it until the heat of the fire produced a nicely browned loaf. Sarah Nossaman's directions for this bread gives a good idea of the talent and experience required.

Take a board eighteen inches long and eight inches wide, round the corners off and make the edges thinner than the middle, spread it with well-made corn dough, set it on edge before a hot fire in a fireplace, and it will bake nice and brown, then turn and bake the other side the same way, then you have corn bread that no one will refuse.[14]

Despite the limitations, many pioneer women gained reputations as competent cooks, an achievement which was particularly difficult when the few receipt (recipe) books that did exist gave directions in terms of a pinch and a handful. Kitturah Belknap was especially pleased after a fleece-sorting party because her women friends were impressed with her chicken dinner and old-fashioned pound cake. "Now my name is out as a good cook," she rejoiced, "so am alright for good cooking makes good friends."[15] Another Iowa woman discovered that she could earn money to purchase her first store-bought clothes by hiring out as a cook. Working with one other woman over an open fireplace in Bonaparte around 1840, she prepared all the meals for forty-five men building a mill. For this feat she was paid the grand sum of seventy-five cents per week which, according to her, "was the best wages that had ever been paid in the country at that time."[16]

Regardless of the rude conditions, the diversity of pioneer menus seemed almost unlimited. On one occasion, Belknap treated her guests to stewed chicken, fried cakes, sausage, and mashed potatoes. Another time she prepared a Christmas dinner for twelve people that would tax the dexterity of a modern cook equipped with all the latest appliances. Her bill of fare, as she called it, was rather extensive:

Firstly; for bread, nice light rolls; cake, doughnuts; for pie, pumpkin; preserves, crab apples and wild plums; sauce, dried apples; meat first round: roast spare ribs with sausage and mashed potatoes and plain gravy; second round: chicken stewed with the best of gravy; chicken stuffed and roasted in the Dutch oven by the fire.[17]

When confronted by a shortage of some kind, which was frequently the case, many pioneer cooks made up the difference with their own creativity. Harriet Bonebright-Closz recalled that her family lacked a rolling pin which was essential to biscuit making. Instead, they used a wooden stick, peeled fresh daily. "When it could not be found," she said, "the biscuit dough was rolled with a fresh ear of corn—or mayhap, the cob."[18] Belknap often found herself without the kind of fruit that she needed for preserves so she devised a clever imitation. She squeezed the juice from watermelon, boiled it down to syrup, added some muskmelons and crabapples, cooked them with a little sugar, and produced a substance which at least tasted like preserves. According to her, "You have nice preserves to last all winter (and they are fine when you have nothing better and sugar 12-1/2 c. a lb. and go 40 miles after it)."[19]

Belknap's comment regarding sugar points up the problem that most frontier cooks faced in obtaining sugar, salt, and other spices. Often herbs from their own gardens sufficed for seasonings, but salt had to be purchased, as did sugar, and both were usually very expensive by pioneer standards. In 1856 Sarah Kenyon complained to her mother that sugar was $1.00 for eight to nine pounds and molasses was 85¢ per gallon.[20] Another source listed sugar as wholesaling for 9-8/10 cents per pound in 1856, 9 cents per pound in 1861, and jumping to 23-1/2 cents per pound by 1864 due to the inflationary effects of the Civil War.[21] It is little wonder that frontierswomen did what they could to find substitutes. Sweeteners, of course, were more easily replaced than salt. Women kept their eye out for a bee tree which they might rob of its highly prized honey. They tapped maple trees for sap which was boiled down into maple molasses[22] or converted into maple sugar at a "sugaring-off" in the fall.[23] And they stripped cane to produce molasses, a commodity considered so important that children were often kept home from school to help with the "stripping."

As settlements thickened and frontier towns increased in size and number, the problems of the pioneer cook were somewhat alleviated. Her sparse utensils were augmented by tinware, pewter ware, and various types of pots and pans. Her open fireplace with its pot and crane was replaced by a stove, often with "newfangled gadgets" such as warming ovens. And her stock of foodstuffs was enhanced by the goods offered in the rapidly spreading stores and emporiums.

Those people who could afford the new cooking utensils, stoves, and other food items found them very convenient. The articles of food offered by the new grocers included staples such as flour and salt, but shopkeepers also catered to the appetites of migrants hungry for delicacies that they had enjoyed in their former homes. In 1855 the *Iowa Sentinel* of Fairfield advertised a shipment of raisins and figs as well as fresh Baltimore peaches and strawberries.[24] Oysters were particularly esteemed by Iowans, many of whom were former New Englanders. In 1857 the *Iowa Sentinel* announced the opening of the "Young America Oyster and Lunch Saloon," which claimed that "its patrons, at all hours, will be served with Oysters in every style, also with Welch Rabbits, Hot Cakes and Coffee, Venison, Steaks, Game, etc."[25] Inland merchants also reacted to the demand for oysters, and in 1861 the *Waterloo Courier* heralded a shipment of "Celebrated Baltimore Fresh Oysters."[26]

Of course, the less settled regions of the Iowa frontier did not enjoy such luxuries until the coming of the railroads, primarily after the Civil War. In 1856 Sarah Kenyon's sister Mary mentioned making a meal of "punkin flap jacks" and a few slices of venison, then grumbled that "we don't have anything but 'taters' and punkin here."[27] Even as late as 1869, a newly arrived family of migrants in Clay County subsisted for an entire winter on little more than "sod house soup" made of chunks cut off a "half-of-beef" and mixed with the meager vegetable supply they had brought along.[28]

But as complex and demanding as food processing and preparation were, they only accounted for one segment of the frontierswoman's workday. She was also responsible for domestic commodities manufactured from food byproducts, such as soap and lighting facilities. Both required constant attention on her part in order to stockpile the food wastes which in turn would become her raw materials.

Soap-making involved three separate processes: collecting grease, fat, and tallow from meat; saving wood ashes for lye; and boiling the two together in the correct proportion to create a substance known as soft soap. Collection of grease was a year-long procedure. Drip pans were carefully positioned under spitted meat to catch the drippings and all leftover grease from frying was put aside. Any nonedible scraps of fat from cuts of meat were also diligently hoarded. By spring, there was usually a sizable accumulation of waste grease and fat. This was enlarged upon by the addition of scraps of fat saved from the spring butchering of hogs and beeves.

Wood ashes were also collected throughout the year, but these had to be transformed into lye before they were ready to be combined with the grease. Janette Stevenson Murray described this procedure in detail:

> One neighbor leached lye from wood ashes kept in a barrel. This was perforated in the bottom and set on an inclined board. A circle was chiseled out on the board outside the bottom of the barrel with a groove at the lower edge to let the seeping water run into a wooden pail. This yellow water was the lye. The barrel was kept full of ashes and every once in a while more water was poured over them.[29]

Soap-making was done out-of-doors in the spring with the children joining in. The lye and grease were carefully measured into a large iron kettle, a fire was stoked under the kettle, and the concoction was boiled until the women judged it to be of the proper consistency. Matilda Peitzke Paul stated that "This had to be watched most of the time to be kept from boiling over. In the mean time the water was being poured into the leach several times a day until the lye was too weak to hold up an egg, for then it was too weak to make soap."[30]

Once the mixture foamed up and had been carefully stirred together, it was poured into crocks or wooden boxes lined with cloth. When it hardened, usually in a day or two, it was cut into "bars" and stored away in kegs, wrapped in hay, or just piled lattice-fashion on cellar shelves for use during the coming year. Some women refined the method even further by using pure tallow, rendered from beef fat and molded in pans, to make a whiter soap for clothes, dishes, and hands while they used cracklings and scraps to make a darker laundry soap.[31]

Attitudes toward soap-making seemed to vary widely. Amelia Murdock Wing remembered it as a "process we enjoyed."[32] Paul, however, rather sourly commented that "it took plenty of work to make it."[33] At any rate, soap-making apparently continued to be a home function for a good many years, for there is little evidence, either in manuscript form or in the advertisements of the time, that it was marketed very widely during the pioneer years.

Providing light for pioneer homes called for another skill on the part of domestic women artisans during the early period when kerosene was unavailable. Many families simply relied on the fireplace to light their homes. As soon as possible this scanty light was supplemented by the easiest type of lighting fixture known on the frontier—the saucer lamp. This was merely a saucer, usually of wood, filled with some kind of grease with a piece of twisted rag inserted in it as a wick. The grease might be excess cooking fat, lard tallow, goose grease, or melted lard. Margaret Archer Murray said that their first lights were "grease lamps we had a shallow dish first took a soft rad [rag] twisted it then dipped one end in melted lard layed that end up on side of dish pored the melted lard over that then it was ready to light."[34] Similarly, Sarah Kenyon wrote that "Our light consists of a saucer filled with coons oil with a rag in it."[35]

By modern standards, it is amazing that pioneers managed to complete all their tasks adequately or efficiently with such defective lighting. Since evening and long winter afternoons were crucial work periods for pioneers, it meant that they often mended harness, made nails, carved furniture, processed food, and sewed the family's clothing by the flickering light of fireplaces and saucer lamps. Bonebright-Closz mentioned in passing that her mother "did much of the family sewing beside the feeble ray of this type of light,"[36] while Margaret Murray went into a little more detail:

> Mother did all her sewing and knitting by that [saucer light] and the light from the fireplace and she sure had a lot of it to do . . . . Mother made all our cloths by hand knit all our stockings and mittens by lamp light.[37]

As soon as they could afford it, most frontierswomen began to produce candles to light their homes. These were of two basic types, the tallow dip and the molded candle, both of which involved some capital investment in supplies. In the case of tallow dips, the tallow itself could be rendered at home from meat fats, but the wicking had to be purchased. Labor was supplied by women who went through the following procedure once every year.

> She filled the wash boiler with tallow; then, she put wicks over some little round sticks and dipped them in the hot tallow and hung them in a row above the boiler. By the time the last stick was hung up, the first sticks were cool enough to dip again. Thus the work proceeded until the candles were of the right size.[38]

Molded candles required not only the purchase of wicking, but an initial investment in an iron candle mold. Paul recalled that her family had a mold that held one dozen candles. "The wick," she explained, "had to be bought at a store and run through the center of each one after that the tallow was melted and poured into the mold and left till perfectly cold and hard."[39] Janette Murray gave a similar account of the process:

> Pieces of candlewick, cut in proper length, were laid over the sticks across the top of the mold, shaken down, pulled through the small holes at the bottom and tied tightly. The molds were then filled with melted tallow and set outdoors to cool. After heating a moment in the morning, the cream-colored candles could be lifted out.[40]

Most frontierswomen were justifiably proud of their skills and their results. Certainly, no frontier homestead could have survived without them. Furthermore, no frontier family would have been clothed if frontier women had not fit the manufacture of garments into their already crowded schedules. During the first years of frontier settlement, the manufacture of apparel was both difficult and time-consuming. Since commercially produced yardgoods were not generally marketed as yet, early frontierswomen had to begin literally with plants, such as flax, and with animals, such as sheep, to obtain the fibers that would eventually become thread, then cloth, and finally clothing.

Flax and wool, both ubiquitous on the Iowa frontier, required hours of monotonous work before they could be spun into thread. Raw flax was "combed" by throwing the fibers over a hackle and pulling them through its teeth. This hackle was usually made of a wooden base with close-set iron prongs projecting upwards from it.

A hackle resembled a medieval instrument of torture, or perhaps a bed of nails, and was just as dangerous if a woman was not alert and agile while using it. Wool was not hackled but was carded with a crude curry-comb type of instrument. Although not as dangerous as a flax hackle, the carding comb also called for patience and endurance on the part of the woman operating it. Once the fibers were combed into smooth strands they were spun into thread on a treadle-powered spinning wheel. The spinning wheel occupied a place of honor in many cabins and consumed untold hours of the pioneer woman's time. It was, however, only the second step in an extensive process. Next the thread had to be woven into cloth: flax into linen cloth; wool into woolen cloth; and flax and wool into linsey-woolsey cloth. This cloth was then colored with dyes that women produced themselves from plants such as indigo, red oak bark, and sumac berries. Finally, the cloth was ready to be laboriously hand-stitched into a finished garment.

Naturally, women got help with these jobs whenever they possibly could, both by inviting in friends to help and by sending the fibers out to a carding machine or the thread to a weaving mill. In 1853, for instance, the *Wapello Intelligencer* advertised a commercial wool carding service in the town of Wapello.[41] But Margaret Murray's description indicates that while her mother did get some help, she alone was responsible for many tiresome tasks.

> After the shearing was done she washed the fleeces then hand picked the wool to get out the burs and the like often had wool picking invite a few women for the day. After that the wool was sent to the carding machine and made into rolls then mother had to spin it into yarn then have that woven into cloth some for jeans for mens cloths and flannel for us children and apart of the yarn for kniting then she did all the coloring.[42]

Belknap's recollections were very much the same. "All this winter I have been spinning flax and tow [coarse, broken fibers of flax] to make some summer clothes," she wrote. "Now the wool must be taken from the sheep's back, washed and picked and sent to the carding machine and made into rolls, then spun, colored and wove ready for next winter." Another year she gave a fuller account:

> I'm the first one to get at the wool (25 fleeces). Will sort it over, take off the poor short wool and put it by to card by hand for comforts. Then sort out the finest for flannels, and the courser for jeans for the men's wear. I find the wool very nice and white but I do hate to sit down alone to pick wool so I will invite about a dozen old ladies in an in a day they will do it all up.[43]

When her wool came home from the carding machine, she was pleased with the nice rolls that were all ready to spin. She first planned to spin her stocking yarn, estimating that she could spin two skeins a day and double and twist it during the evening while her husband read the history of the United States.[44]

Later, Belknap spun thread for the simple dresses which satisfied most women in those years. In 1840, she was elated to get a new calico dress for Sunday and one new homemade dress for everyday. She recalled: "It was cotton warp colored blue and copper and filled with pale blue tow filling so it was striped one way and was almost as nice as gingham." The following year she added a new blue and red flannel dress to her wardrobe. "I am going to try and make me one dress every year," she commented, "then I can have one for nice and with a clean check apron I would be alright."[45]

Besides their own dresses, women also sewed dresses for the young girls of the family and jeans and cotton shirts for the men and boys. All buttonholes had to be painstakingly worked in by hand to accommodate the hooks, eyes, and buttons that were used for fastening. In addition, warm stockings, mittens, mufflers, and wristlets for all were knitted from wool. Hats were plaited from straw or wild grass gathered in the fields. And sunbonnets were made to extend out over the face approximately four inches using pasteboard slats, a design which Bonebright-Closz described as such "an obstruction to sight and an impediment to hearing" that most young women let them hang loosely down their backs rather than using them as a protection from the prairie sun as intended.[46]

As merchants and dry goods stores began to appear, women looked to them to supply them with yardgoods and other sewing materials. In 1862, Sarah Kenyon said she could buy thin cotton cloth for 20 cents, calico for 20 cents, sheeting for 30 cents, thread for 10 cents a spool, but "needles its almost impossible to get." Although she did not give quantities with her prices, her list does signify that these goods were being sold in her area of Plum Creek, Kossuth County, in the north central portion of Iowa by the time of the Civil War.[47]

A survey of some frontier newspapers shows that these goods were widely sold much sooner in areas located along well-traveled routes of settlement and trade. As early as 1836, the *DuBuque Visitor* advertised ready-made clothing and "Calicoes, Ginghams, Muslins, Cambricks, Laces, Ribbands."[48] That fall they featured ads for dry goods, including "Sattinettes, Cassimeres and brodd Cloths."[49] In 1837, the *Iowa News*, also in Dubuque, announced "Ready Made Clothing from New York."[50] And by 1844, Dubuque's *Iowa Territorial Gazette and*

Advertiser carried ads for "Hats, Hats," a "Fashionable Milliner and Dress Maker," "Hats and Bonnets," and "Rich Fancy Goods."[51]

Burlington, also located on the Mississippi River, became another supply center. The *Burlington Daily Hawk-Eye and Telegraph* of the 1850s was filled with commercial notices appealing "to the Ladies." One offered "30 pieces fine linen thread edging," assorted black silk lace edging, lisle and silk gloves, black silk mitts, and kid gloves.[52] A few years later the People's Store advertised calicoes, ginghams, silk goods, linens, fancy goods, boots and shoes, with the claim that "The stock is not, and cannot be surpassed in the West."[53] The new Philadelphia Dry Goods and Milliners insisted that "the best, handsomest and cheapest goods, and the greatest bargains" were to be found in their establishment.[54]

Nearby inland towns did their best to compete for the expanding market. In 1854, Mt. Pleasant's *Weekly Observer* called for "Ladies! Ladies!! Ladies!!!" to notice new stocks of "Lawn Satin, Silk and Crepe Bonnets of the latest styles," and "Ribbons, Flowers, caps, and every variety in the millinery lines." They also offered "Fowler's system of cutting dresses taught in 3 lessons for $3, with model patterns cut to fit the figure for 25 cts."[55] Gradually, such goods were marketed in the more interior portions of Iowa, but it was not a smooth east to west movement. Business development gravitated first around the Mississippi River and secondly around the Missouri River. This was due in part to the early steamboats that plied both rivers, bringing settlers and trade goods. Though the Missouri River was more difficult for steamboats to navigate, towns along its banks, particularly Kanesville (Council Bluffs), benefitted because of the many migrants passing through in their journey to the Far West.

These business developments do not fit well with the popular stereotype of frontierspeople in their rough homespun and animal skin clothing. Moreover, they do not support the image of grinding poverty throughout the prairieland of frontier days. At least in pioneer Iowa, those kinds of conditions were brief and transitory for most frontierspeople. Relative prosperity allowed many Iowans not only to purchase dry goods, ready-made clothes, and accessories, but also to acquire the sewing machine. By the 1850s, the spinning wheel no longer held the place of honor in most Iowa pioneer homes nor was all sewing any longer done by hand. The treadle sewing machine was making its presence felt on many parts of the Iowa frontier. With its many variations in design and price, its ability to lighten work, and its increasing accessibility, it was to the frontier woman what the McCormick reaper was to the frontier farmer. In 1855, a *Davenport Gazette* advertisement for a Wheeler, Wilson and Company's Superior Sewing Machine slightly overstated the effects of the revolution in the domestic manufacture of clothing: "by the use of these machines very much of that which has been a drudgery become but a pleasant task."[56]

That people were purchasing and using sewing machines was substantiated by frequent mention of them in women's diaries and memoirs. Although the machines were foot-powered and rudimentary by today's standards, many women discovered that they relieved them of hundreds of wearying hours of hand-stitching. The new machines also made more complicated fashions possible and allowed the young women of the family to take over a good share of the family sewing at an earlier age than had been possible when they had to be carefully taught various types of stitches. A case in point was Alice Money, a young girl who did all the sewing for her family in the 1860s, including muslin undergarments with yards of ruffles and tucks, calico dresses lined and trimmed with more ruffles, tucks, and bias binding, and shirts and suits for the boys and men. She must have treadled hundreds of miles on her family's early model of a Wheeler and Wilson machine which was said to have "made a noise like a threshing machine and ran almost as hard."[57]

In addition to the production of clothing, women were also saddled with its complex and tiring care. In an era which predated commercial laundries, dry cleaners, or even washing machines, all apparel had to be handled with the utmost care. Brocades and silks were wrapped in sheets and hung away in spare closets. Most women had at least one "good" dress. This was made of black silk and saw her through weddings, funerals, and other special occasions. She would remake it in the latest fashion every four or five years so that it would last most of her lifetime. According to Janette Murray, these and other fancy dresses were made at home or by a local seamstress. "The silk," she explained, "was heavy and rich and the dresses were made with so much lining, crinoline, and boning that they almost stood alone."[58]

Everyday clothing, along with bedding and other linens, had to be washed by hand. On washing day, large wooden washtubs were first laboriously filled with water hauled in from the well and heated by the fireplace or stove. A washboard and some soft soap completed the list of necessary equipment. Women then proceeded to rub the clothing back and forth over a convoluted scrub board. When this step was concluded, the garment was hand wrung and hung outside to dry. In inclement weather the wash was hung and draped about the kitchen to drip on the heads of those working below.

Almost everything, including sheeting, required ironing. This was done with heavy, solid iron flatirons. Several of these were heated in the fireplace or stove while an ironing table was placed near by.

As one iron cooled during use, it was carried to the source of heat and exchanged for a hot iron. All ruffles, tucks, fluting, and other frills were ironed in some small flatirons made with various types of ridging especially for this purpose. Many garments had to be starched, and it took a particularly skillful woman to know just when to remove the iron so that the telltale marks of scorched starch would not be left behind.

As Paul mentioned at several points in her memoirs, all of the frontierswomen's duties, from feeding a family through clothing them, "made plenty of work."[59] But on another level, the outcome of her labors also plainly indicated her degree of skill as an artisan in a society which judged a person by immediate results rather than by wealth, family name, or social class. Her ability and industry in the manufacture of suitable domestic wares could determine the "comfort level" of her family's existence in frontier Iowa. Furthermore, her family depended on her as a kind of paraprofessional in a society which quite often lacked pharmacists, doctors, and morticians. Frontierswomen, in addition to all their other capabilities, became accomplished herbalists. After women picked the herbs in the woods or from their own gardens, they dried them and then brewed them into medicinal teas, tonics, bitters, or prepared them as poultices.

As apothecaries, women were guided not only by the family knowledge that had been passed on to them, but by the recipes for medicine, which often outnumbered the recipes for food in the early receipt books, or by a "doctor book" if the family was fortunate enough to own one. Many herbs, which are now ignored by most medical practitioners in the age of antibiotics, were pressed into service as medicine. Crowder listed a few of the most popular used by her mother in treating her own family as well as the many neighbors who depended on her competence in time of illness.

> Many wild plants were used as medicines, most of them steeped and drunk as tea. Among these were "Culver's root" taken, "for the liver." The dandelion, both as extract and as wine, was used for the same purpose. Tonics were made from the butterfly weed, sweet flag root, sassafras bark, and boneset . . . . For colds, pennyroyal, prairie balm, and horse mint were popular remedies. Mullen was used externally for pleurisy. . . . Smartweed was used externally for boils. Cubeb berries were smoked for catarrh.[60]

Bonebright-Closz added some others to Crowder's list: "skunk-oil and goose-grease, sulphur and sorghum, rhubarb and butternut pills, boneset and burdock bitters, sassafras and smartwood tea, slippery-elm salve and plaintain poultices."[61]

These home remedies were augmented, when possible, by prepared medicines such as quinine, morphine, and particularly whisky. When Paul was struck by a poisonous rattlesnake, the affected foot was kept in fresh mud for six hours and she was dosed with whisky. "This one poison," she dryly remarked, "offset another."[62] Bonebright-Closz was especially graphic in her description of the medicinal use of whisky.

> Whisky was the base for all bitters and the vehicle for internal and external application. It was, in fact, an all around remedial rejuvenator. . . . It was taken as an eye-opener before breakfast and a victual settler after meals, an exhilarator between them, and as a nightcap at bedtime. . . . [W]hiskey served in sociability as it did in sickness.[63]

By the 1860s there were also hundreds of patent medicines on the market in Iowa, all offering instant relief for any ailment. Although commercially prepared medications were available, whether they were truly efficacious is an unanswerable question. If, as Bonebright-Closz believed, whisky was actually the base for many of them, they probably did bring a measure of relief to the sufferer, if not a measure of cure. Doctors, on the other hand, were too few or too far away to be prevailed upon for medical care in most cases. So if common preventive medicine, such as the spring doses of sulphur and molasses or the little bag of asafetida (gum resin with a garlic-like odor) tied around a person's neck, did not successfully ward off illness, then it was often up to the women of the family to become both doctor and nurse.

When Sarah Kenyon's husband fell victim to a serious cold, she insisted that "John would have roared if I had not quelled him with morphene." She treated his symptoms by putting "the physic and hoar hound tea to him nice and kept him on water porridge the next day."[64] Mary Ann Ferrin had a much more difficult time curing her husband of what she called "that terrible Foe, chills and fever." After two weeks of treatment, he was finally attacked by a "sinking chill" which alarmed her because she had no "doctor's medicine" in the house. She prepared hot teas for him to drink, rubbed his limbs vigorously, and "applied hot flannels wrung out of strong mint tea to his stomach and bowels." She continued to give him ginger tea, and in a few days his chills were broken and, to her great relief, he gradually regained his strength.[65]

Ellen Strang's diary gives a particularly good account of her own determined yet unsuccessful treatment of her younger sister for an "Ague chill." Ellen first put mustard poultices on her sister's feet, wrists, and neck and gave her Jamaica Ginger tea once every hour. The next day she tried mustard poultices, and by the end of the week called a doctor who brought her some "medicine." Ellen continued the Jamaica Ginger tea and various poultices through the next week with only occasional success. By the third week the patient felt better, then had a sudden relapse. Ellen responded by rubbing the child's limbs with whisky, giving her more Jamaica Ginger tea, using mustard water to soak her hands and feet, binding sulphur on the joints of her hands and feet, and feeding her meals of corn meal gruel and flour porridge. She finally gave her quinine measured out on the point of a pen knife every two hours and some "powders" brought by the doctor, but after these long weeks of suffering, the little girl died.[66]

Strang's diary temporarily stopped here so there is no record of her feelings regarding the death of her sister nor any description of the funeral. From other sources, it is clear that "laying out the dead" was also assigned to the women, who again used herbs to prepare the body. The explanation behind such tasks being assigned to the women is partly practical and partially ideological. Women were in the house most of the hours of the day so they were present to provide constant service. On the ideological level, women were seen as "natural" care-takers of the sick and dead due to the "greater sensibilities" imputed to them by nineteenth-century cultural norms. Because they were female, they were thought to have an inherent widsom and softness that men lacked. This also at least partially explains why men were normally excluded from childbirth, a mysterious business which was usually handled by the mother-to-be, a female midwife, and perhaps a few female friends or relatives.

Procreation was encouraged on the frontier both to aid popula-tion growth and to provide future laborers for the family farm or other business. Therefore, besides all her other duties, a frontiers-woman was also expected to produce and rear future laborers. Once she completed the pregnancy and the birth, a woman was charged with the primary, if not sole, responsibility of supervising her child, assuming that the child survived infancy. It might be added that since women were in the home more than men it was again only "natural" that they should be charged with the task of child care. Actually this was probably more of an eastern perception than a western reality, for in Iowa at least, many women did leave the home to do farm work, carrying their children with them in ingenious ways. Paul hauled up water from the well with her baby tied to her in her apron "to keep her from being trampled on by the thirsty cattle." When she helped her husband with the field work, she took her baby with her and "put her in a large box where she could play" while Paul worked. Even when at home she combined child care with work: "I done all my washing by hand rubbing every garment, and often stood on one foot while rubbing, and rocking the baby's cradle with the other foot, to keep her from waking up."[67]

If the children were indeed to become laborers on the family farm, the assignment of early child care to the mother meant in practice that she become the trainer, organizer, and overseer of the family labor force. Therefore, besides her own functions as a worker/producer, she was also thrust into a supervisory position. As manager of the home, she quickly initiated the young children into the tasks of food processing, soap making, candle making, spinning and weaving, knitting, and the like. In their early years, both boys and girls were expected to share in these tasks; there are even cases of Iowa boys taking part in stocking knitting and quilt piecing. As the children advanced in age, a division of labor of sorts began to appear with the boys assuming more of the outdoor chores and the girls more of the indoor work. It was common for boys to be sent for fuel and water, to help with the planting, to help with the stock, and to work in the fields, while the girls continued with the production of food, soap, candles, and with the care of the younger children.

Yet these role divisions were not absolute; the nature of the tasks and the available labor supply quite often determined who would undertake what job. Herding of stock was often assigned to boys and girls alike. Children as young as six and seven were sent out to follow the sound of the bell strapped around the lead cow's neck and to persuade the herd to stop grazing and return home for milking.[68] In addition to this chore, Matilda Paul remembered that as a child she carried in wood for the cook stove, hauled water, and fed the calves in the morning and evening, as well as assisting with the more traditional female-oriented household duties. Along with the other younger children, she also worked in the fields, dropping corn and potatoes into the rows at planting time while older children followed along behind with hoes and covered the holes. Other jobs followed:

> When the corn first came up we had to stay out in the field and chase the black-birds to keep them from digging and eating the corn as fast as it came up. It was our work in spring to pull weeds for the hogs for feed. About the middle of June we used to pick wild strawberries. . . . We often had to watch our cattle to keep them out of other peoples as well as out of our own fields. . . . Before I was old enough to bind grain I helped carry bundles in piles, ready to be shocked up. . . . I often had to get water from a spring and carry it out to the field for drinking for the workers, before I was old enough to do other field work. Later on I helped bind the grain. . . . We children had to go over the whole field and gather up the roots in piles and when they got dry we used them for fuel. . . . After harvest and haying was done we had to dig the potatoes and husk the corn ready for winter.[69]

The complexities of the frontierswoman's task as superintendent are apparent, but she was also frequently called upon to aid with tasks normally considered "men's work." Because Iowa land was cheap and plentiful, "hiring out" one's labor was usually less attractive than taking up land for oneself. As a result of the scarcity of hired hands, many women were called upon to "fill in" until another source of labor became available. Women drove teams of plow animals, dropped seed, harvested crops, and did many of the other heavy field work that nineteenth-century cultural values said women should not and could not do. Caroline Phelps, for example, helped her trader husband "to pack the skins, as we had no man to help."[70] Paul drove the horses on a reaper during one harvest and the next year she drove a harvester.[71] Sarah Kenyon, along with her children, did a variety of field jobs, including reaping wheat. One year when her husband hired a field hand, she told her mother that things were looking up. "John has hired a man to work for him this Summer," she wrote, and "hope I shall not have to dig quite as much out of doors." But when the hired man quit just before the fall corn harvest she took it philosophically:

> Our hired man left just as corn plucking commenced so I shouldered my hoe and have worked out ever since and I guess my services are just as acceptable as his or will be in time to come to the country.... I wore a dress with my sunbonnet wrung out in water every few minutes and my dress also wet [and] this was all the clothing . . . I wore.[72]

The argument could be made that women doing men's work was a "gainful" employment in that it helped produce a cash crop and/or preserved cash which would have been paid out to a hired laborer. Yet since no actual cash passed into *her* hands and because she was laboring within the family unit, she was still not considered to be gainfully employed. This logic was also applied to her production of surplus domestic goods, such as butter and eggs, which were sold outside the home for cash. Historian Gilbert Fite maintains that butter was a primary cash product on the farmer's frontier, its income often keeping farms financially afloat during the rocky years.[73] Since women produced butter and other cash products, they were bringing in money for the operation of the homestead.

Murray remembered that "mother sold Butter Eggs & Beeswax & anything we could spare off the farm, [and] in the summer and fall we gathered Black Berries wild grapes & anything we raised on the farm that would bring money or exchange for groceries." When her uncle and aunt worked together to build a brick drying kiln, her aunt realized that she could also use the kiln to dry fruit; during the first winter she earned a dollar selling dried peaches.[74] In another case, Belknap discovered that she could add a few coins to the savings box intended for their new home by making a few extra pieces of linen for sale while doing her own spinning and weaving.[75] Crowder recalled her mother being rather successful at producing and selling butter. She took $230 of inheritance money, invested it in milch cows, and from that time on made butter for the market. She packed it away in one hundred pound tubs and stored it in the cellar until fall, when it was hauled to Algona, the nearest market, thirty miles and three days away. The money raised was used for winter clothing and supplies. Hogs were also purchased to consume the surplus milk, and hog-raising became the family's principal industry. Crowder states that many frontier women not only produced income by selling their produce, but were aware of their economic importance to the family in doing so.

> Frequently enough, while the men were learning to farm, the women and children actually supported the families. They raised chicken and eggs for the table, raised the vegetables and fruit, and made butter to sell in exchange for things not produced at home. The women were not unaware of this fact and were quite capable of scoring a point on occasion when masculine attitudes became too bumptious.[76]

Another resource that many women used to generate cash income were their own homes. By taking boarders into their already crowded quarters, they created more work for themselves but brought in some much-needed money. Paul, for instance, took care of her husband, two baby girls, and a hired man, yet she opted to board the local teacher for two dollars a week which, she said, "helped out a little."[77] When a branch of the Rock Island Railroad cut through the Newton farm, the family took in some of the laborers as boarders who, with the family's own five children, created a rather large household to care for.[78] And Emery Bartlett later told his children that "for two or three years, with my utmost exertion and strictist economy, I could scarcely tell whether I was gaining or losing and had it not been for the little money my dear wife saved by taking a few boarders, I must certainly have gone under."[79]

In summarizing these economic functions of frontierswomen, it seems almost incredible to realize that their economic significance in the settlement of the frontier has been largely unrecognized for so many years. Food processing and cooking; soap and candlemaking; spinning, weaving, and sewing; washing and ironing; acting as apothecaries, nurses, doctors, and morticians; producing children, caring for them, and training them as laborers; helping with men's work; and generating cash income was no mean list of accomplishments. Since factories and trained professionals have taken over most of these functions in our own world, it is doubly difficult for us to realize just how much skill and labor were involved. Whether nineteenth-century society or the U.S. Bureau of the Census accepted it or not, these frontierswomen were indeed "gainfully employed."

NOTES

The author wishes to thank the Newberry Library for research support.

1. Allan G. Bogue, *From Prairie to Corn Belt: Farming on the Illinois and Iowa Prairies in the Nineteenth Century* (Chicago, 1968), 22–24.

2. Iowa Census of 1838 (Microfiche, University of Northern Iowa Library), 190–191.

3. Iowa Census of 1840, p. 3.

4. Iowa Census of 1880, p. 57.

5. *Ibid.*, 168–170.

6. Iowa Census of 1856, pp. 12, 19, 25, 31, 35. Another possible source of women's occupations outside the home for the later part of the frontier period is city directories. The 1870 Mt. Pleasant city directory, for example, lists some women's names (with the titles of Miss or Mrs.) along with the occupation of milliner, seamstress, dressmaker, tailoress, dry goods dealer, teacher, assistant principal, and professor of English literature. There were, however, many women's names listed with the title Mrs., but no occupational category or source of support is given for these women. E. H. Annewalt, comp., *Mount Pleasant City Directory: Containing a Catalogue of Inhabitants* (Burlington, Iowa, 1870), 27–58.

7. Edeen Martin, "Frontier Marriage and the Status Quo," *Westport Historical Quarterly*, X (1975), 100.

8. George C. Duffield, "An Iowa Settler's Homestead," *Annuals of Iowa*, VI (1903), 210.

9. Janette Stevenson Murray, "Women of North Tama," *Iowa Journal of History and Politics*, XLI (1943), 296.

10. Edith H. Hurlbutt, "Pioneer Experiences in Keokuk County, 1858–1874," *Iowa Journal of History*, LII (1954), 335.

11. Matilda Peitzke Paul, memoirs, Iowa State Historical Society, Iowa City, Iowa.

12. Bessie L. Lyon, "Grandmother's Story," *Palimpsest*, V (1924), 7.

13. Amelia Murdock Wing, "Early Days in Clayton County," *Annals of Iowa*, XXVII (1946), 280.

14. Sarah Welch Nossaman, "Pioneering at Bonaparte and Near Pella," *ibid.*, XIII (1922), 450.

15. Kitturah Penton Belknap, reminiscences, Iowa State Historical Society, Iowa City, Iowa.

16. Nossaman, "Pioneering at Bonaparte and Near Pella," 446.

17. Belknap, reminiscences.

18. Harriet Bonebright-Closz, *Reminiscences of Newcastle, Iowa, 1848* (Des Moines, 1921), 172.

19. Belknap, reminiscences.

20. Sarah Kenyon to her mother, Aug. 29, 1856, Kenyon Family Papers, Iowa State Historical Society, Iowa City, Iowa.

21. U.S. Bureau of the Census, *Historical Statistics of the United States* (Washington, D.C., 1975), 209.

22. Lida L. Greene, ed., "Diary of a Young Girl," *Annals of Iowa*, XXXVI (1962), 454.

23. Wing, "Early Days in Clayton County," 280.

24. *Iowa Sentinel*, Jan. 11, 1855.

25. *Ibid.*, Feb. 26, 1857.

26. *Waterloo Courier*, April 9, 1861.

27. Mary Ellis to her mother, Nov. 7, 1856, Kenyon Family Papers.

28. Abbie Mott Benedict, "My Early Days in Iowa," *Annals of Iowa*, XVII (1930), 341.

29. Murray, "Women of North Tama," 299.

30. Paul, memoirs.

31. Murray, "Women of North Tama," 298.

32. Wing, "Early Days in Clayton County," 280.

33. Paul, memoirs.

34. Margaret E. Archer Murray, "Memoir of the William Archer Family," *Annals of Iowa*, XXXIX (1968), 360.

35. Sarah Kenyon to her mother, Dec. 1, 1856, Kenyon Family Papers.

36. Bonebright-Closz, *Reminiscences of Newcastle*, 39.

37. Murray, "Memoir of the William Archer Family," 361.

38. Wing, "Early Days in Clayton County," 279.

39. Paul, memoirs.

40. Murray, "Women of North Tama," 299.

41. *Wapello Intelligencer*, May 31, 1853.

42. Murray, "Memoir of the William Archer Family," 361.

43. Belknap, reminiscences.

44. *Ibid.*

45. *Ibid.*

46. Bonebright-Closz, *Reminiscences of Newcastle*, 121.

47. Sarah Kenyon to her mother, Oct. 9, 1862, Kenyon Family Papers.

48. *Dubuque Visitor*, July 6, 1836.

49. *Ibid.*, Sept. 14, 1836.

50. *Iowa News*, July 1, 1837.

51. *Iowa Territorial Gazette and Advertiser*, June 1, 1844.

52. *Burlington Daily Hawk-Eye and Telegraph*, July 23, 1855.

53. *Ibid.*, April 5, 1859.

54. *Ibid.* .

55. *Weekly Observer*, April 20, 1854.

56. *Davenport Gazette*, June 14, 1855.

57. Floy Lawrence Emhoff, "A Pioneer School Teacher in Central Iowa—Alice Money Lawrence," *Iowa Journal of History and Politics*, XXXIII (1935), 378–379.

58. Murray, "Women of North Tama," 307.

59. Paul, memoirs.

60. E. May Lacey Crowder, "Pioneer Life in Palo Alto County," *Iowa Journal of History and Politics*, XLV (1948), 183.

61. Bonebright-Closz, *Reminiscences of Newcastle*, 227.

62. Paul, memoirs.

63. Bonebright-Closz, *Reminiscences of Newcastle*, 229.

64. Sarah Kenyon to her mother, March 18, 1860, Kenyon Family Papers.

65. Mary Ann Ferrin Davidson, "An Autobiography and a Reminiscence," *Annals of Iowa*, XXXVII (1964), 249–251.

66. Greene, "Diary of a Young Girl," 448–455.

67. Paul, memoirs.

68. Crowder, "Pioneer Life in Palo Alto County," 160.

69. Paul, memoirs.

70. Caroline Phelps, diary, Iowa State Historical Society, Iowa City, Iowa.

71. Paul, memoirs.

72. Sarah Kenyon to her mother, Oct. 11, 1861, Kenyon Family Papers.

73. Gilbert C. Fite, *The Farmers' Frontier, 1865–1900* (New York, 1966), 47.

74. Murray, "Memoir of the William Archer Family," 362, 370.

75. Belknap, reminiscences.

76. Crowder, "Pioneer Life in Palo Alto County," 178, 181.

77. Paul, memoirs.

78. Edith H. Hurlbutt, "Pioneer Experiences in Keokuk County, 1858–1874," *Iowa Journal of History*, LII (1954), 331.

79. Emery S. Bartlett, "The Bartlett Family of Poweshiek County," Iowa Historical Museum and Archives, Des Moines, Iowa.

14 ✑ Women's Rights before the Civil War

Ellen Carol DuBois

For many years before 1848, American women had manifested consider-able discontent with their lot. They wrote and read domestic novels in which a thin veneer of sentiment overlaid a great deal of anger about women's dependence on undependable men. They attended female academies and formed ladies' benevolent societies, in which they pursued the widest range of interests and activities they could imagine without calling into question the whole notion of "woman's sphere." In such settings, they probed the experiences that united and restrained them—what one historian has called "the bonds of womanhood."[1] Yet women's discontent remained unexamined, implicit, and above all, disorganized. Although increasing numbers of women were questioning what it meant to be a woman and were ready to challenge their tradi-tional position, they did not yet know each other.

The women's rights movement crystallized these sentiments into a feminist politics. Although preceded by individual theorists like Margaret Fuller, and by particular demands on behalf of women for property rights, education, and admission to the professions, the women's rights movment began a new phase in the history of feminism. It introduced the possibility of social change into a situation in which many women had already become dissatisfied. It posed women, not merely as beneficiaries of change in the relation of the sexes, but as agents of change as well. As Elizabeth Cady Stanton said at the meeting that inaugurated the movement, "Woman herself must do the work."[2]

The pioneers of women's rights pointed the way toward women's discontent organized to have an impact on women's history.

The women's rights movement developed in the dozen years before the Civil War. It had two sources. On the one hand, it emerged from women's growing awareness of their common conditions and grievances. Simultaneously, it was an aspect of antebellum reform politics, particularly of the antislavery movement. The women who built and led the women's rights movement combined these two historical experiences. They shared in and understood the lives of white, native-born American women of the working and middle classes: the limited domestic sphere prescribed for them, their increasing isolation from the major economic and political developments of their society, and above all their mounting discontent with their situation. Women's rights leaders raised this discontent to a self-conscious level and channeled it into activities intended to transform women's position. They were able to do this because of their experience in the antislavery movement, to which they were led, in part, by that very dissatisfaction with exclusively domestic life. Female abolitionists followed the course of the antislavery movement from evangelicism to politics, moving from a framework of individual sin and conversion to an understanding of institutionalized oppression and social reform. This development is what enabled them and other women's rights pioneers to imagine changing the traditional subservient status of women. Borrowing from antislavery ideology, they articulated a vision of equality and independence for women, and borrowing from antislavery method, they spread their radical ideas widely to challenge other people to imagine a new set of sexual relations. Their most radical demand was enfranchisement. More than any other element in the women's rights program of legal reform, woman suffrage embodied the movement's feminism, the challenge it posed to women's dependence upon and subservience to men.

The first episode of the women's rights movement was the 1848 Seneca Falls Convention, organized by Elizabeth Cady Stanton, Lucretia Mott, and several other women. As befitted an enterprise handicapped by the very injustices it was designed to protest, the proceedings were a mixture of womanly modesty and feminist militancy. When faced with the task of composing a manifesto for the convention, the organizers, in Stanton's words, felt "as helpless and hopeless as if they had been suddenly asked to construct a steam engine." Nor was any woman willing to chair the meeting, and the office fell to Lucretia Mott's husband. Yet the list of grievances which the organizers presented was comprehensive. In retrospect, we can see that their Declaration of Sentiments and Resolutions anticipated every demand of nineteenth-century feminism. To express their ideas about women's rights and wrongs, they chose to rewrite the Preamble of the Declaration of Independence around "the repeated injuries and usurpations on the part of man towards woman." On the one hand, this decision reflected their need to borrow political legitimacy from the American Revolution. On the other, it permitted them to state in the clearest possible fashion that they identified the tyranny of men as the cause of women's grievances.[3]

The Seneca Falls Convention was consciously intended to initiate a broader movement for the emancipation of women. For the women who organized the convention, and others like them, the first and greatest task was acquiring the skills and knowledge necessary to lead such an enterprise. In Elizabeth Cady Stanton's words, they had to transform themselves into a "race of women worthy to assert the humanity of women."[4] Their development as feminists, as women able to bring politics to bear on the condition of their sex, had as its starting point the experience they shared with other women. While many accounts of this first generation of feminist activists stress what distinguished them from other women—their bravery and open rebellion—it is equally important to recognize what they had in common with nonfeminists: lack of public skills; lives marked by excessive domesticity; husbands and fathers hostile to their efforts; the material pressures of housekeeping and child-rearing; and the deep psychological insecurity bred by all these factors. A movement is a process by which rebellion generates more rebellion. The women's rights pioneers did not begin their political activities already "emancipated," freed from the limitations that other women suffered. Many of the personal and political resources they drew on to challenge the oppression of women were developed in the course of mounting the challenge itself.

"THE INFANCY OF OUR MOVEMENT"

Even the most committed and militant of the first-generation women's rights activists hesitated on the brink of the public activity necessary to build a feminist movement. Although a successful writer, Frances Dana Gage was as homebound as other women, when she was asked to preside over a women's rights convention in Akron in 1851. She was reluctant, but accepted the responsibility. "I have never in my life attended a regular business meeting," she told her audience, whose vistas were even more circumscribed than hers.[5] When Clarina Nichols delivered the first women's rights address before the Vermont legislature in 1850, her voice broke and her supporters feared that she would fail.

Spurred on by "the conviction that only an eminently successful presentation of her subject could spike the enemy's batteries," she finished her speech, "though her voice was tremulous."[6] Daring to speak out at the first women's rights convention she had ever attended, in 1852, Matilda Joslyn Gage was inaudible to her audience and "trembling in every limb." The mother of four young children at the time, Gage did not plunge seriously into political work until after the war, when her children had grown and domestic responsibilities were less insistent.[7] Abigail Bush spoke for an entire generation of feminists committed to acquiring political skills in service to their sex. When the audience at a convention in Rochester in 1848 called down the women speakers with cries of "louder, louder!" Bush responded: "Friends, we present ourselves here before you, as an oppressed class, with trembling frames and faltering tongues, and we do not expect to be able to speak as to be heard by all at first, but we trust we shall have the sympathy of the audience, and that you will bear with our weakness now in the infancy of our movement. Our trust in the omnipotency of right is our only faith that we shall succeed."[8]

Compared to many other women, Antoinette Brown was relatively self-confident as she prepared herself for public life and women's rights leadership. For three years, she resisted Oberlin College's attempts to drive her from its theological course. Nonetheless, the objection of a respected mentor to her women's rights ideas "put me into such an agony . . . I did wish God had not made me a woman."[9] The opposition of men, particularly the fathers and husbands on whom they were dependent, reinforced women's lack of public experience to restrain their feminist activism. Excluded from the World's Anti-Slavery Convention in London in 1840, Mary Grew returned to Pennsylvania to circulate petitions for a married women's property act. Her abolitionist father, who had encouraged her to do similar work in behalf of the slave, vigorously opposed her.[10] Elizabeth Cady Stanton, who was singularly unafflicted with psychological insecurity, faced her greatest obstacles in her husband and her father. Henry Stanton stubbornly opposed his wife's desire to join in the 1855–1856 canvass of New York, and her father, whom she adored, temporarily disinherited her when she began public lecturing. Her convictions only deepened. "To think," she wrote, "that all in me of which my father would have felt a proper pride had I been a man, is deeply mortifying to him because I am a woman . . . has stung me to a fierce decision—to speak as soon as I can do myself credit. But the pressure on me just now is too great. Henry sides with my friends, who oppose me in all that is dearest to my heart. They are not willing that I should write even on the woman question. But I will both write and speak."[11]

During the late 1850's the focus of Stanton's "domestic bondage" shifted from the opposition of husband and father to the demands of her seven children. "I seldom have one hour undisturbed in which to sit down and write," she complained, while nursing her daughter. "Men who can, when they wish to write a document, shut themselves up for days with their thoughts and their books, know little of what difficulties a woman must surmount to get off a tolerable production."[12] By sharing both political and domestic work with Anthony, she was able to continue leading the women's rights movement for most of this period. But Stanton's last pregnancy was enough to undermine even her exceptional self-confidence and physical strength. "You need expect nothing from me for some time," she wrote to Anthony after the birth of 12½-pound Robert. "I can scarcely walk across the room . . . and have to keep my mind in the most quiet state in order to sleep. . . . He seems to take up every particle of my vitality, soul and body."[13] Four months later, she was still "in no situation to think or write," but succumbed to Anthony's blandishments to prepare a memorial for the New York State legislature. "We have issued bulls under all circumstances," she conceded. "I think you and I can do more even if you must make the pudding and carry the baby."[14]

Unlike Stanton, Lucy Stone and Antoinette Brown assumed domestic responsibilities after they had become prominent women's rights advocates. Stone married Henry Blackwell in 1855, and Brown married his brother Samuel a year later. Brown had seven children; Stone had one, which kept her out of political work for over a decade. "I wish I felt the old impulse and power to lecture . . . , but I am afraid and dare not trust Lucy Stone," Stone wrote to Brown, when her daughter was a year and a half old. "I went to hear E. P. Whipple lecture on Joan d'Arc. It was very inspiring and for the hour I felt as though all things were possible to me. But when I came home and looked in Alice's sleeping face and thought of the possible evil that might befall her if my guardian eye was turned away, I shrank like a snail into its shell and saw that for these years I can be only a mother."[15] Brown experienced this same dilemma. Unable even to keep up a political correspondence because of the press of household obligations, she wrote to Anthony, "This, Susan, is 'woman's sphere.' "[16] Anthony was unsympathetic to her comrade's preference for what she called "the ineffable joys of Maternity," and resentful of the political responsibilities that devolved on her. She wrote to Brown in frustration over Stone's preparations for an important debate: "A woman who is and must of necessity continue for the present at least the representative woman has no right to disqualify herself for such a representative occasion. I do feel that it is so foolish for her to put herself in the position of *maid of all work* and *baby tender*. What man would dream of going before the public on such an occasion as this one night-tired and worn from such a multitude of engrossing cares."[17] Indeed, even though Brown and Stone had foresworn marriage while young girls, Anthony was the only first-generation national women's rights leader who remained single. "Where are you Susan and what are you doing?" Stanton wrote when she hadn't heard from Anthony for some time. "Are you dead or married?"[18]

In the face of such obstacles, the major resource on which women's rights activists drew to support themselves and advance their cause was one another. Like many nineteenth-century women, they formed intense and lasting friendships with other women. Frequently these were the most passionate and emotionally supportive relationships that they had. While feminists' mutual relationships were similar to other female friendships in emotional texture, they were different in their focus on the public and political concerns that made their lives as women unique. The most enduring and productive of these friendships was undoubtedly that of Elizabeth Cady Stanton and Susan B. Anthony, which began in 1851. The initial basis of their inter-dependency was that Anthony gave Stanton psychological and material support in domestic matters, while Stanton provided Anthony with a political education. In an episode repeated often in their first decade together, Anthony called on Stanton when she found herself unable to write a speech for a New York teachers' convention: "For the love of me and for the saving of the reputation of womanhood, I beg you, with one baby on your knee, . . . and four boys whistling, buzzing, hallooing 'Ma, Ma,' set yourself about the work. . . . I must not and will not allow these schoolmasters to say, 'See, these women can't or won't do anything when we do give them a chance.'"[19]

Antoinette Brown and Lucy Stone were also bound by an intense friendship, formed when they were both students at Oberlin. They turned to each other to fortify their common feminism against the assaults of friends and teachers, and, as Brown remembered it, "used to sit with our arms around each other . . . and talk of our friends and our homes and of ten thousand subjects of mutual interest until both our hearts felt warmer and lighter."[20] Their relationship continued to sustain them after they left Oberlin and became abolitionists and women's rights agitators. When Stone was subject to particularly intense harassment for wearing bloomers, Brown offered her support. "Tonight I could nestle closer to your heart than on the night when I went through the dark and the rain and Tappan Hall and school rules—all to feel your arm around me," she wrote, "and to know that in all this wide world I was not alone."[21]

An important aspect of these relationships was overtly political. Given the strength of men's commitment to maintaining their political monopoly, the few women who were fortunate enough to have acquired a political education had to share their skills and knowledge with others. Stanton's contribution to Anthony's political development has already been noted. When Brown and Stone first met, they organized six other women students into "an informal debating and speaking society" to provide the oratorical experience they were denied in Oberlin's "ladies" course. They were so afraid of official intervention that they met in a black woman's home "on the outskirts of town," and occasionally in the woods, with a guard posted "against possible intruders." When Brown returned home to Michigan for a year, she organized another group to discuss women's sphere and women's rights. "We are exceedingly careful in this matter and all move on together step by step," she wrote to Stone. "Some will undoubtedly shrink back when they come to find where they stand and believe they must have been mistaken . . . and a few I hope and believe will go out into the world pioneers in the great reform which is about to revolutionize society."[22]

There were limits, however, to the support women's rights pioneers could offer one another. One such constraint was physical distance. As reformers they traveled to a degree unheard of among pre-Civil War women and, when unmarried, could scarcely be said to have a home. They were usually alone. In addition, the attacks on them for stepping outside women's sphere were constant, severe, and beyond the power of friends to halt or counteract. Brown described for Stone the response she elicited from the townspeople of Oberlin: "Sometimes they warn me not to be a Fanny Wright man, sometimes believe I am joking, sometimes stare at me with amazement and sometimes seem to start back with a kind of horror. Men and women are about equal and seem to have their mouths opened and their tongues loosed to about the same extent." Surrounded on all sides by hostility, women's rights agitators had to work most of the time without the companionship and sisterhood they so prized. "You know we used to wish sometimes that we could live on and have no need of the sympathy of anyone," Brown reminded Stone, after she had left Oberlin, "I have learned to feel so." "What hard work it is to stand alone!" she wrote a few years later. "I am forever wanting to lean over onto somebody but nobody will support me."[23]

In the face of such pressures, some women could not maintain their resolve to challenge women's sphere. One such woman was Letitia Holmes, who was Antoinette Brown's classmate at Oberlin and, like her, committed to becoming a religious teacher. Holmes married a minister, moved with him to Portsmouth, New Hampshire, and found herself in a role she had not anticipated, isolated from any source of support. "You know I have been looked upon as a pastor's wife with the incumbent duties to perform . . . ," she wrote to Brown. "I have been (I was going to say tired to death) receiving calls." An educated woman, she had ambitions beyond her sphere, which were not well received in Portsmouth. "There are but few here who think of women as anything more than slave or a plaything, and they think I am different from most women," she wrote. "I tell them I think not." Despite a sympathetic husband, she could not find an outlet for her talents or knowledge. Her long letter describing her situation to Brown, who was already achieving some prominence as a public lecturer, was a mixture of jealousy and a plea for help. Holmes regretted that she did not have another woman "who seems to be one of us you might say . . . another self of my own sex." She asked Brown for "a list of what books would be advantageous for me to read and study with a view to assist me in preparing for public duties." She also asked for Brown's lectures on women's rights, and offered a glimpse into the pressures operating against her Oberlin education and her strong-minded aspirations: "The thing is just this. I do not see it all as clearly as I should to explain to others and when they bring forward the scriptures I fear for myself." In the end, Holmes continued to believe that she would "go forth," which she never did, and could not understand why she was so "long in beginning."[24]

ABOLITIONIST POLITICS

The abolitionist movement provided the particular framework within which the politics of women's rights developed. From the 1837 clerical attack on the Grimké sisters, through the 1840 meeting of Lucretia Mott and Elizabeth Cady Stanton at the World's Anti-Slavery Convention, to the Civil War and Reconstruction, the development of American feminism was inseparable from the unfolding of the antislavery drama. In tracing the sources of the women's rights movement, Stanton and Anthony cited abolitionism "above all other causes." Mistaking political rhetoric for historical process, historians commonly identify the connection between the two movements as women's discovery of their own oppression through its analogy with slavery.[25] Certainly women's rights leaders made liberal use of the slave metaphor to describe women's oppression. Yet women's discontent with their position was as much cause as effect of their involvement with the anti-slavery movement. What American women learned from abolitionism was less that they were oppressed than what to do with that perception, how to turn it into a political movement. Abolitionism provided them with a way to escape clerical authority, an egalitarian ideology, and a theory of social change, all of which permitted the leaders to transform the insights into the oppression of women which they shared with many of their contemporaries into the beginnings of the women's rights movement.

Women's involvement in abolitionism developed out of traditions of pietistic female benevolence that were an accepted aspect of women's sphere in the early nineteenth century. The feminist militance of Sarah and Angelina Grimké and the women who succeeded them was rooted in this common soil. The abolitionist movement was one of the many religious reforms that grew out of evangelical Protestantism. For the movement's first half-decade, the role women had in it was consistent with that in other benevolent religious efforts such as urban missionary activities and moral reform. Women organized separate antislavery auxiliaries, in which they worked to support men's organizations and gave particular attention to the female victims and domestic casualties of slavery. The Grimkés entered abolitionism on these terms.[26] Unlike other pious activisms, however, abolition had an unavoidably political thrust and a tendency to outgrow its evangelical origins. As the movement became secularized, so did the activities of benevolent women in it. "Those who urged women to become missionaries and form tract societies . . . have changed the household utensil to a living, energetic being," wrote domestic author and abolitionist Lydia Maria Child, "and they have no spell to turn it into a broom again."[27]

The emergence of the Garrisonian wing of the abolitionist movement embodied and accelerated these secularizing processes. In 1837 William Lloyd Garrison was converted by utopian John Humphrey Noyes to the doctrine of perfectionism, which identified the sanctified individual conscience as the supreme moral standard, and corrupt institutions, not people, as the source of sin. In particular, Garrisonians turned on their churchly origins and attacked the Protestant clergy for its perversion of true Christianity and its support of slavery.[28] Garrisonians' ability to distinguish religious institutions from their own deeply-felt religious impulses was an impressive achievement for evangelicals in an evangelical age. The reformulation of antislavery strategy around these beliefs drew Hicksite Quakers, liberal Unitarians, ultraist come-outers, and a disproportionate number of women activists.

The clergy was the major force that controlled women's moral energies and kept pietistic activism from becoming political activism. Garrisonian anticlericalism was therefore critical to the emergence of abolitionist feminism and its subsequent development into the women's rights movement. This was clear in the 1837 confrontation between the Grimké sisters and the Congregational clergy of Massachusetts. In this episode, Garrisonian perfectionism and the limits of women's sphere were inseparable matters. Like women in moral reform and other pious activisms, the Grimkés had been led by their religious vocation to step outside their traditional role. At that point, like other benevolent women, they were confronted by clerical authority and ordered to return to more womanly pursuits. Yet the fact that they were Garrisonians enabled them to hold fast to their religious convictions, reject clerical criticism, and instead indict the churches for being institutional bulwarks of slavery and women's oppression.[29]

Against the power of clerical authority, which had long restrained women's impulses for a larger life, Garrisonian abolition armed women with faith in their own convictions. Although restrained by the fact that her husband was a political abolitionist, Elizabeth Cady Stanton's allegiances were with the Garrisonians. Throughout her young adulthood, she had wrestled unsuccessfully with religious orthodoxy from which Garrisonian anticlericalism liberated her.

> In the darkness and gloom of a false theology, I was slowly sawing off the chains of my spiritual bondage, when, for the first time, I met Garrison in London. A few bold strokes from the hammer of his truth, I was free! Only those who have lived all their lives under the dark clouds of vague, undefined fears can appreciate the joy of a doubting soul suddenly born into the kingdom of reason and free thought. Is the bondage of the priest-ridden less galling than that of the slave, because we do not see the chains, the indelible scars, the festering wounds, the deep degradation of all the powers of the God-like mind?[30]

Almost until the Civil War, conflict with clerical authority remained a central issue for the women's rights movement. The 1854 national convention resolved: "We feel it a duty to declare in regard to the sacred cause which has brought us together, that the most determined opposition it encounters is from the clergy generally, whose teachings of the Bible are intensely inimical to the equality of women with man." Representatives of the clergy pursued their fleeting authority onto the women's rights platform. However, Garrisonian women had learned the techniques of Biblical exegesis in numerous debates over the scriptural basis of slavery. They met clergymen on their own ground, skillfully refuting them quote for quote. "The pulpit has been prostituted, the Bible has been ill-used . . . ," Lucretia Mott contended at the 1854 convention. "The temperance people have had to feel its supposed denunciations. Then the anti-slavery, and now this reform has met, and still continues to meet, passage after passage of the Bible, never intended to be so used."[31] When ministers with national reputations started to offer their support to the women's rights movement in the 1850's, the issue of clerical authority began to recede in importance. It was not a major aspect of postwar feminism, because of changes in both the movement and the clergy.

Women in the Garrisonian abolitionist movement not only absorbed its anticlericalism, but also drew on its principle of the absolute moral equality of all human beings. Because the Garrisonian abolitionists' target was Northern racial prejudice and their goal the development of white empathy for the suffering slave, they focused their arguments on convincing white people of their basic identity with black people. The weakness of this emphasis on the ultimate moral identity of the races was its inability to account for their historical differences. Garrisonians did not develop an explanation for the origins and persistence of racism, and as a result many abolitionists continued to believe that there were biological causes for the inferior position of black people. Instead, Garrisonian abolitionism stressed the common humanity of blacks and whites. Garrisonians formulated this approach as a moral abstraction, but its basis was the concrete demands of the agitational task they faced as abolitionists.[32]

Abolitionist feminists appropriated this belief and applied it to women. The philosophical tenet that women were essentially human and only incidentally female liberated them from the necessity of justifying their own actions in terms of what was appropriate to women's sphere. In other words, Garrisonianism provided an ideology of equality for women to use in fighting their way out of a society built around sexual difference and inequality. The degree to which abolitionist feminists ignored the demands of women's sphere is particularly remarkable because they did so at the same time that the ideology of sexual spheres was being elaborated by benevolent women, in other ways very much like them. To the Congregational clergy's demand that she return "to the appropriate duties and influence of women," Sarah Grimké responded: "The Lord Jesus defines the duties of his followers in his Sermon on the Mount . . . without any reference to sex or condition . . . never even referring to the distinction now so strenuously insisted upon between masculine and feminine virtues. . . . Men and women are CREATED EQUAL! They are both moral and accountable beings and whatever is right for man to do is right for woman."[33] Her belief in sex equality took added strength from Hicksite Quaker doctrine and practices. The Grimkés were followed by other Garrisonian feminists who also refused to justify their efforts in terms of women's sphere. "Too much has already been said and written about woman's sphere," Lucy Stone said in 1854. "Leave women, then, to find their sphere." The 1851 women's rights convention resolved that: "We deny the right of any portion of the species to decide for another portion . . . what is and what is not their 'proper sphere'; that the proper sphere for all human beings is the largest and highest to which they are able to attain."[34]

Just as the Garrisonian emphasis on the moral equality of the races could not account for their historical inequality, the conviction that men and women were morally identical had serious analytical limitations. The women's rights belief in the moral irrelevance of sexual spheres ignored the reality of women's domestic confinement, which made them different from and dependent on men, and gave credence to the doctrine of spheres. Indeed, Garrisonian feminists ignored the question of women's sphere while simultaneously believing in its existence. A women's rights convention in Ohio in 1852 simultaneously resolved: "Since every human being has an individual sphere, and that is the largest he or she can fill, no one has the right to determine the proper sphere of another," and "In demanding for women equality of rights with their fathers, husbands, brothers, and sons, we neither deny that distinctive character, nor wish them to avoid any duty, or to lay aside that feminine delicacy which legitimately belongs to them as mothers, wives, sisters, and daughters."[35] Like other women, women's rights activists believed in the particular suitability of their sex for domestic activities and did not protect a reorganization of the division of labor within the home. They believed that domestic activities were as "naturally" female as childbearing, and as little subject to deliberate social manipulation.[36] The abstract quality of their belief in the moral identity of the sexes did not help them to confront this contradiction in their feminism. Indeed, while permitting the prewar women's rights movement to establish sexual equality as its goal, Garrisonian premises simultaneously held it back from the critical task of examining the sources of sexual inequality.

Along with a philosophical basis, Garrisonian abolitionism provided the women's rights movement with a theory and practice of social change, a strategy that gave direction to its efforts for female emancipation. The core of Garrisonian strategy was the belief that a revolution in people's ideas must precede and underlie institutional and legal reform, in order to effect true social change. "Great political changes may be forced by the pressure of external circumstances, without a corresponding change in the moral sentiment of a nation," Lydia Maria Child wrote in 1842, "but in all such cases, the change is worse than useless; the evil reappears, and usually in a more exaggerated form."[37] Some historians, notably Stanley Elkins and Gilbert Barnes, have mistaken this radical and democratic approach to reform as an anarchistic disregard for the institutional structures of social reality.[38] Garrisonians were not indifferent to institutions, but it is true that they did not specify how changes in popular ideology could be translated into institutional reform. They left this up to the politicians. Instead, they saw themselves as agitators concentrating their energies on provoking public sentiment. While Garrisonian agitation did not develop political mechanisms for ending slavery, it was well suited to the early years of the antislavery movement when the primary problem was overcoming public apathy.

Faced with an equally stubborn and widespread indifference to the oppression of women, women's rights leaders drew on this abolitionist precedent and formulated their task as the agitation of public sentiment. "Disappointment is the lot of woman," Lucy Stone wrote in 1855. "It shall be the business of my life to deepen this disappointment in every woman's heart until she bows down to it no longer."[39] Ernestine Rose described the work as "breaking up the ground and sowing the seed."[40] To Lucy Stone and Susan B. Anthony, both of whom were paid agents of the American Anti-Slavery Society, the role of itinerant feminist agitator came quite naturally. However, it was Elizabeth Cady Stanton who developed the strategy of women's rights agitation most fully, and this was one of the bases of her leadership. Throughout her long political career, she consistently believed that anything that focused public attention on women's oppression was desirable. She wrote in her diary in 1888, "If I were to draw up a set of rules for the guidance of reformers . . . I should put at the head of the list: 'Do all you can, *no matter what*, to get people to think on your reform, and then, if the reform is good, it will come about in due season.' "[41] She did not care whether her efforts generated sympathy or antipathy, as long as they undermined public apathy. Nor did she believe that translating agitation into reform was her function. "I am a leader in thought, rather than numbers," she wrote late in her life, when her methods had become alien to young feminists.[42]

Garrisonian agitation was built around the demand for unconditional, immediate abolition. The intention was both to achieve a concrete reform and to launch an ideological attack on the slaveholding mentality. With this program Garrisonians were able to work simultaneously for the legal abolition of slavery and a revolution in the racial consciousness of whites to give abolition meaning. As Aileen Kraditor has interpreted it, immediate abolition was both the means and the end for Garrisonian antislavery.[43] The demand for woman suffrage functioned in a similar fashion in the women's rights movement. It aimed at both a concrete reform in women's legal status and the education of public opinion to the principle of the equal humanity of the sexes.

The goal was necessarily twofold because, like unconditional abolition, woman suffrage was a radical idea, acknowledged inside and outside the movement as the capstone of women's emancipation.

THE DEMAND FOR WOMAN SUFFRAGE

From the beginning, gaining the franchise was part of the program of the women's rights movement. It was one of a series of reforms that looked toward the elimination of women's dependent and inferior position before the law. The women's rights movement demanded for married women control over their own wages, the right to contract for their own property, joint guardianship over their children, and improved inheritance rights when widowed. For all women, the movement demanded the elective franchise and the rights of citizenship. Compared to legal reforms in women's status articulated before 1848, for instance equal right to inherit real property, the women's rights program was very broadly based, and intentionally so.[44] In particular, the right to control one's earnings and the right to vote were demands that affected large numbers of women—farm women, wives of urban artisans and laborers, millgirls and needlewomen.

While part of this general reform in women's legal status, the demand for woman suffrage was always treated differently from other women's rights. In the first place, it initially met with greater opposition within the movement than other demands did. At the Seneca Falls Convention, Elizabeth Cady Stanton submitted a resolution on "the duty of the women of this country to secure to themselves the sacred right to the elective franchise." Lucretia Mott thought the resolution a mistake, and tried to dissuade her from presenting it. Mott's position may have been based on her Garrisonian objections to involvement in the world of electoral politics, but surely others recoiled from the woman suffrage demand because it seemed too radical. Although the convention passed all other motions unanimously, it was seriously divided over the suffrage. Frederick Douglass, who, himself disfranchised, appreciated the importance of membership in the political community, was Stanton's staunchest supporter at Seneca Falls. The woman suffrage resolution barely passed.[45]

Soon, however, woman suffrage was distinguished from other reforms by being elevated to a preeminent position in the women's rights movement. After the Seneca Falls Convention, there is no further evidence of reluctance within the movement to demand the vote. On the contrary, it quickly became the cornerstone of the women's rights program. A resolution passed at the 1856 national convention may be taken as representative: "Resolved, that the main power of the woman's rights movement lies in this: that while always demanding for woman better education, better employment, and better laws, it has kept steadily in view the one cardinal demand for the right of suffrage: in a democracy, the symbol and guarantee of all other rights."[46]

In keeping with the truth of this resolution, the demand for woman suffrage also generated much more opposition outside the movement. Public opinion and politicians were more sympathetic to feminists' economic demands than to their political ones. In the mid-1850's, state legislatures began to respond favorably to women's lobbying and petition efforts for reforms in property law. By 1860, fourteen states had passed some form of women's property rights legislation. Encouraged by these victories, the movement escalated its demands and shifted its emphasis from property rights to the suffrage. This was clearest in the case of New York. Initially, to gain maximum support for the less controversial demand, activists there circulated separate petitions for property rights and for the vote. As the movement gained strength, however, they included both economic and political demands on a single petition, and, in 1857, presented a unified program to the legislature.[47] Three years later, the New York legislature passed the most comprehensive piece of women's rights legislation in the United States, the Married Women's Property Act. This law granted New York women all the economic rights they demanded, but still refused women the right to vote.[48]

To both opponents and advocates of women's rights, therefore, the demand for woman suffrage was significantly more controversial than other demands for equality with men. Why was this the case? Like the overwhelming majority of their contemporaries, nineteenth-century feminists believed that the vote was the ultimate repository of social and economic power in a democratic society. They wanted that power for women and relied on well-developed natural rights arguments and the rhetorical traditions of the American Revolution and the Declaration of Independence to make their demand. "In demanding the political rights of woman," the 1853 national convention resolved, "we simply assert the fundamental principle of democracy—that taxation and representation should go together, and that, if the principle is denied, all our institutions must fall with it."[49]

The widespread belief in the importance of the ballot which feminists drew on to make their case for woman suffrage is a somewhat elusive aspect of the American political tradition because the extension of the franchise to the masses of white men had been such a gradual process. No organized political movement was required as Chartism had been in Britain. As a result, what the vote meant and promised to antebellum American men was not formalized into an explicit ideological statement, and is that much harder for us to assess in retrospect. However, American white working men seem to have attached considerable importance to their franchise. Even though they did not have to organize to win the vote, they did form working men's parties in every northern state to protect it and give it power. Believing that the vote "put into our hands the power of perfecting our government and securing our happiness," they organized against obstacles to its use, such as indirect elections and caucus nominations.[50] In addition, working men saw the democratic franchise, divested of property qualifications, as a victory against privilege. As a British Chartist put it in 1834, "With us Universal suffrage will begin in our lodges, extend to the general union, embrace the management of trade, and finally swallow up political power."[51] To the degree that organized working men believed that universal white manhood suffrage established the necessary preconditions for social democracy, they looked to their own shortcomings for their failure to achieve such a society. "Our fathers have purchased for us political rights and an equality of privileges," a July Fourth orator chastised the trade unions of Boston in 1834, "which we have not yet had the intelligence to appreciate, nor the courage to protect, nor the wisdom to employ."[52]

Yet these general ideas about the power and importance of the ballot are not sufficient to explain the special significance of the suffrage issue for women. The ideas of democratic political theory were not systematically applied to women until feminist leaders, anxious to challenge the subservient position of women, appropriated those ideas and demanded the vote. Like black men, women were excluded from the actual expansion of the suffrage in the late eighteenth and early nineteenth centuries, but the exclusion of women from political life went even further. Women were so far outside the boundaries of the antebellum political community that the fact of their disfranchisement, unlike that of black men, was barely noticed. The French and American Revolutions greatly intensified awareness of the educational, economic, and social inequality of the sexes, but few Revolutionary leaders considered the inclusion of women in the franchise, and even fewer—perhaps only Condorcet—called for it.[53] Further back in the democratic political tradition, the radical Levellers of seventeenth-century England made the same distinction between women's civil and moral rights, which they advocated, and women's political rights, which they never considered.[54] In large part, the awareness that women were being excluded from the political community and the need to justify this disfranchisement came after women began to demand political equality. Prior to the women's rights movement, those who noticed and commented on the disfranchisement of women were not advocates of woman suffrage, but antidemocrats, who used this exception to disprove the natural right of people to self-government.[55]

On what basis were women excluded from any consideration in the distribution of political power, even when that power was organized on democratic principles? At least part of the answer seems to lie in the concept of "independence," which was the major criterion for enfranchisement in classical democratic political theory, and which acted to exclude women from the political community. Even the radical Tom Paine thought that servants should not have the vote because they were economically and socially dependent on their masters, and "freedom is destroyed by dependence."[56] A contemporary political theorist, C.B. Macpherson, has defined the core of this concept of "independence" as self-ownership, the individual's right to possess his own person: "The essential humanity of the individual consisted in his freedom from the will of other persons, freedom to enjoy his own person and to develop his own capacities. One's person was property not metaphorically, but essentially; the property one had in it was the right to exclude others from its use and enjoyment."[57] Women's traditional relationships to men within their families constituted the essence of dependence. When John Adams considered the question, "Whence arises the right of men to govern the women without their consent?" he found the answer in men's power to feed, clothe, and employ women and therefore to make political decisions on their behalf.[58] Not only were eighteenth- and early nineteenth-century women prohibited from owning real property or controlling wealth; they could not be said even to hold property in themselves. Law and custom granted the husband ownership, not only of his wife's labor power and the wages she earned by it, but of her physical person as well, in the sexual rights of the marriage relation. No people, with the exception of chattel slaves, had less proprietary rights over themselves in eighteenth- and early nineteenth-century America than married women.[59] Until the emergence of feminism, the dependent status that women held was considered natural, and if not right, then inescapable.

Thus, the demand that women be included in the electorate was not simply a stage in the expansion and democratization of the franchise. It was a particularly feminist demand, because it exposed and challenged the assumption of male authority over women. To women fighting to extend their sphere beyond its traditional domestic limitations, political rights involved a radical change in women's status, their emergence into public life. The right to vote raised the prospect of female autonomy in a way that other claims to equal rights could not. Petitions to state legislatures for equal rights to property and children were memorials for the redress of grievances, which could be tolerated within the traditional chivalrous framework that accorded women the "right" to protection. In 1859 the *New York Times* supported the passage of the New York Married Women's Property Act by distinguishing the "legal protection and fair play to which women are justly entitled" from "the claims to a share of political power which the extreme advocates of Women's Rights are fond of advancing."[60] By contrast, the suffrage demand challenged the idea that women's interests were identical or even compatible with men's. As such, it embodied a vision of female self-determination that placed it at the center of the feminist movement. "While we would not undervalue other methods," the 1851 national women's rights convention resolved, "the Right of Suffrage for Women is, in our opinion, the cornerstone of this enterprise, since we do not seek to protect woman, but rather to place her in a position to protect herself."[61]

The feminist implications of the suffrage demand are further evident in the reverberations it sent through the ideology of sexual spheres, the nineteenth-century formulation of the sexual division of labor. Most obviously, woman suffrage constituted a serious challenge to the masculine monopoly of the public sphere. Although the growing numbers of women in schools, trades, professions, and wage-labor were weakening the sexual barriers around life outside the family, most adult women remained at home, defined politically, economically, and socially by their family position. In this context, the prospect of enfranchisement was uniquely able to touch all women, offering them a public role and a relation to the community unmediated by husband or children. While the suffrage demand did not address the domestic side of the nineteenth-century sexual order directly, the connections between public and private spheres carried its implications into the family as well. In particular, the public honor of citizenship promised to elevate women's status in the home and raised the specter of sexual equality there. Women's rights leaders were relatively modest about the implications of the franchise for women's position in the family, anticipating reform of family law and improvement in the quality of domestic relations. Their opponents, however, predicted that woman suffrage would have a revolutionary impact on the family. "It is well known that the object of these unsexed women is to overthrow the most sacred of our institutions . . . ," a New York legislator responded to women's rights petitions. "Are we to put the stamp of truth upon the libel here set forth, that men and women, in the matrimonial relation, are to be equal?"[62] In the introduction to the *History of Woman Suffrage*, Elizabeth Cady Stanton penetrated to the core of this antisuffrage response. "Political rights, involving in their last results equality everywhere," she wrote, "roused all the antagonism of a dominant power, against the self-assertion of a class hitherto subservient."[63]

OBSTACLES TO GROWTH

The process by which women's rights ideas were spread was a highly informal one. As the first activists reached the small towns of New York, Massachusetts, Ohio, and Indiana, their example drew local women out of their isolation. A speech by Lucy Stone impelled two Rockland, Maine, women to become printers.[64] Olympia Brown was brought into the movement when, still a student at Antioch College, she heard author and abolitionist Frances Gage. "It was the first time I had heard a woman preach," she recalled, "and the sense of victory lifted me up."[65] Frances Ellen Burr, who went on to lead suffrage forces in Connecticut, attended a women's rights convention in Cleveland when she was twenty-two. She was surprised at how attracted she was to the militance of the speakers and noted in her diary, "Never saw anything of the kind before." "Lucy Stone . . . is independent in manner and advocates woman's rights in the strongest terms," she wrote; "scorns the idea of *asking* rights of man, but says she must boldly assert her own rights, and *take* them in her own strength."[66] Reports of the Seneca Falls Convention stirred Emily Collins to gather fifteen neighbors into an equal rights society, and draw up a petition to the legislature. "I was born and lived almost forty years in South Bristol, Ontario County—one of the most secluded spots in Western New York," she explained,

> but from the earliest dawn of reason I pined for that freedom of thought and action that was then denied to all womankind. I revolted in spirit against the customs of society and the laws of the State that crushed my aspirations and debarred me from the pursuit of almost every object worthy of an intelligent, rational mind. But not until that meeting at Seneca Falls in 1848, of the pioneers in the cause, gave this feeling of unrest form and voice, did I take action.[67]

Of all the pre-Civil War activists, Susan B. Anthony was the most deliberate about introducing new women to women's rights. Between 1854 and 1860 she made several canvasses of New York. In the innumerable small towns she visited, she tried to locate the people most sympathetic to women's rights. She particularly cultivated the women, encouraging the boldest of them by asking them to preside over the meetings she organized or by staying in their homes overnight.

Occasionally, she discovered a genuinely strong-minded woman, waiting for the women's rights movement to take her up. In Aurora, she found three women wearing bloomers, one of whom she asked to conduct the meeting. "It does my heart good to see them," she wrote in her diary.[68]

Nonetheless, the movement grew slowly. As Stone rationalized after a particularly disappointing lecture tour, "I sell a great many of the tracts, so seed is being scattered that will grow *sometime*."[69] In the wake of their lectures and conventions, Stone, Anthony, and others left a trail of strong-minded women behind them. Sarah Burger attended a women's rights convention in 1853, when she was sixteen. What she heard there convinced her that the University of Michigan should be opened to women and "that women themselves should move in the matter." She located twelve other girls to join with her and in 1858 petitioned the university for admission. She continued her campaign for several years, and, although she had to attend a normal school, the University of Michigan finally admitted women in 1869.[70] Two Ellsworth, Maine, women organized a lecture series on women's rights. Despite threats to the livelihood of one of them, they persisted and the lectures were held.[71] Other local activists, more than we may ever know, launched their own protests, but often the women's rights movement was too small and weak to sustain them. In 1859, Mary Harrington of Claremont, New Hampshire, refused to pay her taxes because she was disfranchised. The tax collector seized her furniture and the local newspaper editor attacked her in print. She was too isolated to do anything more, and her rebellion went underground for the time being. "Such unjust treatment seemed so cruel that I sometimes felt I could willingly lay down my life," she wrote later, "if it would deliver my sex from such degrading oppression. I have, every year since, submissively paid my taxes, humbly hoping and praying that I may live to see the day that women will not be compelled to pay taxes without representation."[72]

Prewar women's rights agitation had an impact on a large number of women who were not ready to speak or act publicly but were convinced that the position of their sex demanded reform. A friend of her sister's invited Antoinette Brown to visit her "to introduce you to my friends here and let them see that you have not got horns. . . . I think I see more and more clearly that the Lord has a work for females to do that they have not understood," she continued, "and I am glad that there are some that are willing to learn and to do what He requires of them."[73] Anthony reported to Stanton that she had been to dinner with Mrs. Finney, the wife of the president of Oberlin. After her husband denounced women's rights, "Mrs. Finney took me to another seat and with much earnestness inquired all about what we were doing and the growth of our movement. . . . Said she you have the sympathy of a large proportion of the educated women with you. In my circle I hear the movement much talked of and earnest hopes for its spread expressed—but these women dare not speak out their sympathy."[74] Women's rights agitators barely knew how many women they were affecting, much less how to encourage their halting sympathies.

Ironically, the Garrisonian politics and abolitionist alliance that had enabled the women's rights movement to develop in the first place were beginning to restrain its continued growth. Like the abolitionists before them, women's rights activists saw themselves as agitators, stirring up discontent. However, they had no way to consolidate the feminist sentiment that their agitation was beginning to create. Once the level of their discontent was raised, there was nothing for most women to do with it. Women's rights activities were organized around a small group who were politically skilled, willing to shoulder the opprobrium of "strongmindedness," and able to commit a great deal of their energies to the movement. Women who were just beginning to develop political skills and sensibilities could not normally find an active role to play. The limitations to growth inherent in the agitational focus of prewar women's rights were embodied in the movement's organizational underdevelopment. There were no national or state organizations. Annual conventions were planned by an informal and constantly changing coordinating committee. Speaking tours and legislative campaigns were highly individualistic matters, which put a premium on personal initiative and bravery. The movement's close political relationship with abolitionism further restrained its organizational growth, in that its ability to rely on the organizational resources of the American Anti-Slavery Society meant that it did not develop its own. Women's rights articles were published in antislavery newspapers, and its tracts were printed with antislavery funds. The surrogate political coherence that abolitionism provided women's rights permitted the movement's leaders to indulge their propensities for individualism without risking the entire women's rights enterprise. The 1852 national convention rejected a proposal for a national women's rights society on the grounds that formal organizations "fetter and distort the expanding mind."[75]

Above all, the prewar women's rights movement depended on abolitionism for its constituency. It is impossible to estimate how many women were touched by women's rights, and how many of these were abolitionists. Still, the movement's strongest, most reliable, and most visible support came from abolitionist ranks, particularly from the women. This dependence on an organized constituency borrowed from abolitionism was particularly marked on the national level. The call for the first national women's rights convention was timed to coincide with the annual meeting of the American Anti-Slavery Society.[76] Abolitionist women provided women's rights with an audience well suited to its first, highly controversial years. Their antislavery activity had already put them outside the pale of respectable womanhood, where they were less likely to be frightened by public hostility. However, the availability of an audience among antislavery women kept feminist leaders from a systematic effort to reach the many women who were not reformers. At the worst, it gave them a kind of disdain for the nonpolitical preoccupations of most women. The fearlessness of female abolitionists sheltered the women's rights movement from a confrontation with the very real fears of male opposition and public disapproval that lay between it and the mobilization of large numbers of women.

Although primarily a source of strength, the relation of women's rights to abolitionism was thus a potential liability as well. The partnership was unequal, with women's rights dependent on abolitionism for essential resources and support. The basic precepts, strategic methods, and organizational forms of Garrisonian abolitionism had sustained the women's rights movement through its first dozen years. On this basis, feminist leaders were able to transform insights into the oppression of women that they shared with many other women into a social movement strong enough to have a future. This achievement raised other political problems—the extent of the movement's reforming ambitions, the nature of its constituency, the organizational form it would take, and above all, its relation to abolitionism. The resolution of these matters was interrupted by the outbreak of the Civil War. Women's rights activists subordinated all other interests to the fate of slavery, and suspended feminist activity for the length of the war. When they returned, four years later, to consider the future of women's rights, the political context within which they did so had been completely altered.

NOTES*

1. Nancy F. Cott, *The Bonds of Womanhood: "Woman's Sphere" in New England, 1780-1835* (New Haven, 1977). On the early nineteenth century, see also Kathryn Kish Sklar, *Catharine Beecher: A Study in American Domesticity* (New Haven,

*Here HWS refers to *History of Woman Suffrage*, ed. by Elizabeth Cady Stanton, Susan B. Anthony, Matilda Joslyn Gage, et al. (Rochester: Susan B. Anthony: New York: National American Woman Suffrage Association, 1881-1922), 6 vols.

1973); Carroll Smith Rosenberg, "Beauty, the Beast and the Militant Woman: A Case Study in Sex Roles and Social Stress in Jacksonian America," *American Quarterly*, 23 (1971), 562–584; and Keith Melder, "The Beginnings of the Woman's Rights Movement in the United States, 1800–1840" (doctoral diss., Yale University, 1964).

2. As quoted in Flexner, *Century of Struggle*, p. 77.

3. On the Seneca Falls convention, see *HWS*, I, 68–73.

4. Stanton to Gerrit Smith, January 3, 1856, *Stanton Letters*, p. 64.

5. *HWS*, I, 111.

6. *HWS*, I, 174.

7. Elizabeth B. Warbasse, "Matilda Joslyn Gage," *NAW*, II, 4.

8. *HWS*, I, 76.

9. Antoinette Brown Blackwell, "Autobiography," unpublished manuscript, 1909, SL, p. 117.

10. Ira V. Brown, "Mary Grew," *NAW*, II, 91.

11. Stanton to Anthony, September 10, 1855, *Stanton Letters*, pp. 59–60. Also see Stanton to Elizabeth Smith Miller, September 20, 1855, *ibid.*, pp. 60–62.

12. Stanton to Anthony, December 1, 1853, *ibid.*, p. 55.

13. Stanton to Anthony, April 2, 1859, Autograph Collection, Vassar College Library.

14. Stanton to Anthony, July 15, 1859, *ibid.*

15. Stone to Antoinette Brown Blackwell, February 20, 1859, Blackwell Family Papers, SL.

16. Antoinette Brown Blackwell to Anthony, October 25, 1859, as quoted in Blackwell, "Autobiography," p. 228.

17. Anthony to Martha Coffin Wright, June 6, 1856, Garrison Family Papers, Sophia Smith Collection (Women's History Archive), Smith College Library; Anthony to Antoinette Brown Blackwell, April 22, 1858, as quoted in Blackwell, "Autobiography," p. 223.

18. Stanton to Anthony, January, 1856, Autograph Collection, Vassar College Library.

19. Anthony to Stanton, June 5, 1856, *Stanton Letters*, pp. 64–65. See Carroll Smith Rosenberg, "The Female World of Love and Ritual: Relations between Women in Nineteenth-Century America," *Signs: Journal of Women in Culture and Society*, 1 (1975), 1–29.

20. Brown to Stone, sometime in 1848, as quoted in A. B. Blackwell, "Autobiography," p. 128.

21. Brown to Stone, February 18, 1854, as quoted in *ibid.*, p. 172.

22. *Ibid.*, pp. 54 and 119.

23. *Ibid.*, pp. 127 (1848), 129 (1848), and 137 (August 4, 1852).

24. Holmes to Brown, March 9, 1851, SL.

25. *HWS*, I, 52. Women's antislavery activities are surveyed in Alma Lutz, *Crusade for Freedom: Women of the Antislavery Movement* (Boston, 1968). Andrew Sinclair locates the origins of women's discontent in the abolitionist movement in *The Emancipation of the American Woman* (New York, 1966),

p. 37. Also see Flexner, *Century of Struggle*, p. 40. The most notable exception to this approach is Melder, "Beginnings of the Woman's Rights Movement."

26. On the evangelical origins of abolitionism, see Bertram Wyatt-Brown, *Lewis Tappan and the Evangelical War against Slavery* (Cleveland, 1969), and Ronald G. Walters, *The Antislavery Appeal: American Abolitionism after 1830* (Baltimore, 1976). On women's early antislavery benevolence, see Keith Melder, "Ladies Bountiful: Organized Women's Benevolence in Early Nineteenth Century America," *New York History*, 48 (1967), 231–254. On the Grimké sisters, see Gerda Lerner, *The Grimké Sisters from South Carolina: Rebels against Slavery* (Boston, 1967).

27. Child, July 23, 1841, *The Liberator*, as reprinted in Aileen S. Kraditor, *Means and Ends in American Abolitionism: Garrison and His Critics on Strategy and Tactics, 1834–1850* (New York, 1967), p. 47. Kraditor is excellent on the emergence of the women's rights issue within abolitionist circles in the late 1830's.

28. Wyatt-Brown, *Lewis Tappan*, and Lewis Perry, *Radical Abolitionism: Anarchy and the Government of God in Antislavery Thought* (Ithaca: Cornell University Press, 1973).

29. Lerner, *Grimké Sisters*, chap. 12. The 1837 Pastoral Letter of the Massachusetts Congregational clergy and the Grimkés' responses are excerpted in *Up from the Pedestal: Selected Writings in the History of American Feminism*, ed. Aileen S. Kraditor (Chicago, 1968), pp. 50–66. For the restraining influence that clerical authority had on women's protofeminism, see Sklar, *Catharine Beecher*, chap. 3.

30. Stanton, "Speech to the 1860 Anniversary of the American Anti-Slavery Society," Elizabeth Cady Stanton Papers, LC.

31. *HWS*, I, 383 and 380.

32. Kraditor, *Means and Ends, passim*, esp. p. 59.

33. Sarah Grimké, *Letters on the Equality of the Sexes and the Condition of Woman: Addressed to Mary S. Parker* (Boston, 1837), p. 16.

34. *HWS*, I, 165 and 826.

35. *HWS*, I, 817.

36. For an account of how these domestic beliefs affected the life of one abolitionist-feminist, see Ellen DuBois, "Struggling into Existence: The Feminism of Sarah and Angelina Grimké," *Women: A Journal of Liberation*, 1 (1970), 4–11.

37. Child, "Dissolution of the Union," *Liberator*, May 20, 1842, as quoted in Kraditor, *Means and Ends*, p. 23. Kraditor provides an excellent analysis of the Garrisonians' agitational approach to social change.

38. Elkins, *Slavery* (Chicago, 1959), and Barnes, *The Antislavery Impulse, 1830–1844* (New York, 1964).

39. *HWS*, I, 165.

40. *HWS*, I, 693.

41. Diary entry, August 20, 1888, *Stanton Letters*, p. 252.

42. Stanton to Olympia Brown, May 8, 1888, Olympia Brown Willis Papers, SL.

43. Kraditor, *Means and Ends, passim*.

44. For an excellent account of the pre-Seneca Falls efforts to improve women's legal position see Margaret M. Rabkin, "The Silent Feminist Revolution: Women and the Law in New York State from Blackstone to the Beginnings of American Women's Rights Movement" (doctoral diss., State University of New York at Buffalo, 1975).

45. On the Seneca Falls Convention see *HWS*, I, 63–75, and Elizabeth Cady Stanton, *Eighty Years and More: Reminiscences, 1815–1897* (New York, 1899), pp. 143–154. In 1849, Lucretia Mott publicly supported woman suffrage, while very clearly maintaining her distance from electoral politics: "Far be it from me to encourage women to vote or take an active part in politics in the present state of our government. Her right to the elective franchise, however, is the same, and should be yielded to her, whether she exercise that right or not" (*HWS*, I, p. 372).

46. *HWS*, I, 634.

47. *HWS*, I, 588–589 and 676–677. The fourteen states were: Massachusetts, Vermont, New Hampshire, Rhode Island, Ohio, Illinois, Indiana, Wisconsin, Connecticut, Texas, Maine, Iowa, Kansas, and Alabama.

48. *HWS*, I, 686–687.

49. *HWS*, I, 834. As one kind of evidence that woman suffrage was considered more radical than other women's rights demands, note that, in Ohio in 1850, a petition for "equal rights" for women received four times as many signatures as a petition for equal suffrage (*HWS*, I, 122). Similarly, at the 1853 National Women's Rights Convention, Clarina I. H. Nichols explained that "the propriety of woman voting" had been the last obstacle to her conversion to women's rights (*ibid.*, p. 355).

50. Frederick Robinson, "An Oration Delivered before the Trade Unions of Boston," (1834) in *Labor Politics: Collected Pamphlets*, ed. Leon Stein and Philip Taft, (New York, 1971), I, 28–29. Also see Walter Hugins, *Jacksonian Democracy and the Working Class: A Study of the New York Workingmen's Movement, 1829–1837* (Palo Alto, Calif., 1960). The one instance during the nineteenth century in which white men had to organize politically to get the vote was in Rhode Island. See Marvin Gettleman, *The Dorr Rebellion* (New York, 1973).

51. Ray Boston, *British Chartists in America, 1838–1900* (Manchester, 1971), p. 2.

52. Robinson, "Oration," p. 6.

53. Marguerite Fisher, "Eighteenth Century Theorists of Women's Liberation," in *"Remember the Ladies": New Perspectives on Women in American History*, ed. Carol V. R. George (Syracuse, N.Y., 1975), pp. 39–47.

54. C. B. Macpherson, *The Political Theory of Possessive Individualism: Hobbes to Locke* (London, 1962), p. 296.

55. See, for instance, Francis Bowman, "Recent Contest in Rhode Island (1834)," in Stein and Taft, *Labor Politics*, I, 421.

56. Eric Foner. *Tom Paine and Revolutionary America* (New York, 1976), pp. 142–144.

57. Macpherson, *Political Theory*, p. 153.

58. Cited in Scott and Scott, *One Half the People*, p. 4.

59. Rabkin, "The Silent Feminist Revolution," *passim*.

60. "Property of Married Women," *New York Times*, April 8, 1859, p. 4.

61. *HWS*, I, p. 825.

62. *HWS*, I, 613.

63. *HWS*, I, 16.

64. Alice Stone Blackwell, *Lucy Stone: Pioneer of Women's Rights* (Boston, 1930), pp. 101–102.

65. Lawrence L. Graves, "Olympia Brown," *NAW*, I, 257, and Olympia Brown Willis, *Acquaintances Old and New among Reformers* (Milwaukee, 1911), p. 10.

66. *HWS*, III, 335.

67. Collins, "Reminiscences," *HWS*, I, 88.

68. Diary entry, January, 1855. Susan B. Anthony Papers, SL.

69. Stone to Susan B. Anthony, November 8, 1855, Blackwell Family Collection, LC.

70. *HWS*, III, 527.

71. *HWS*, III, 365.

72. *HWS*, III, 373–374.

73. Unknown correspondent to Antoinette Brown, November 5, 1852, SL.

74. Anthony to Stanton, May 26, 1856, Elizabeth Cady Stanton Papers, Vassar College Library.

75. *HWS*, I, 540–542. The speaker was Angelina Grimké Weld.

76. *HWS*, I, 216.

໑ Suggested Readings for Part II

Abzug, Robert. "The Black Family During Reconstruction,"In *Key Issues in the Afro-American Experience*, edited by Nathan I. Huggins, Martin Kilson, and Daniel M. Fox. New York: Harcourt Brace Jovanovich, 1971.

Andrews, William D., and Andrews, Deborah C. "Technology and the Housewife in Nineteenth-Century America." *Women's Studies* 2 (1974): 309–28.

Banner, Lois. *Elizabeth Cady Stanton*. Boston: Little, Brown & Co., 1979.

Barker-Benfield, G.J. *The Horrors of the Half-Known Life: Male Attitudes Toward Women and Sexuality in Nineteenth-Century America*. New York: Harper & Row Inc., 1976.

_____. "The Spermatic Economy: A Nineteenth Century View of Sexuality." *Feminist Studies* 1 (1972): 45–74.

Basch, Norma. "Invisible Woman: The Legal Fiction of Marital Unity in Nineteenth Century America." *Feminist Studies* 8 (1979): 346–366.

Berg, Barbara. *The Remembered Gate: Origins of American Feminism—The Woman and the City*. New York: Oxford University Press, 1978.

Berthoff, Rowland. "The Social Order of the Anthracite Region, 1825–1902." *Pennsylvania Magazine of History and Biography* 89 (1965): 261–91.

Blassingame, John. *The Slave Community: Plantation Life in the Ante-bellum South*. New York: Oxford University Press, 1972.

Bridges, William E. "Family Patterns and Social Values in America, 1825–1875." *American Quarterly* 17 (1965): 3–11.

Conrad, Susan P. *Perish the Thought: Intellectual Women in Romantic America, 1830–1860*. New York: Oxford University Press, 1976.

Cott, Nancy F. "Passionlessness: An Interpretation of Victorian Sexual Ideology, 1790–1850." *Signs* 4 (1978): 219–36.

Douglas, Ann. *The Feminization of American Culture*. New York: Alfred A. Knopf, 1977.

Dublin, Thomas. *Women at Work: The Transformation Work and Community in Lowell Massachusetts, 1826–1860*. New York: Columbia University Press, 1979.

_____. "Women Workers and the Study of Mobility." *Journal of Interdisciplinary History* 10 (1979): 647–665.

Epstein, Barbara. *The Politics of Domesticity: Women, Evangelism, and Temperance in Nineteenth-Century America*. New York: Wesleyan University Press, 1981.

Faragher, John Mack. *Women and Men on the Overland Trail*. New Haven: Yale University Press, 1979.

_____, and Stansell, Christine. "Women and their Families on the Overland Trail to California and Oregon, 1842–1867." *Feminist Studies* 2 (1975): 150–66.

Fogel, Robert W. and Engerman, Stanley. *Time on the Cross: The Economics of American Negro Slavery*. Boston: Little, Brown & Co., 1974.

Frazier, E. Franklin. *The Negro Family in the United States*. Chicago: University of Chicago Press, 1939.

Garvan, Anthony N.B. "Effects of Technology on Domestic Life, 1830–1880." In *Technology in Western Civilization*, Vol. I, edited by Melvin Kranzberg and Carroll W. Pursell, Jr., pp. 546–559. New York: Oxford University Press, 1967.

Genovese, Eugene. *Roll Jordan Roll: The World the Slaves Made.* New York: Pantheon Books, 1974.

Ginger, Ray. "Labor in a Massachusetts Cotton Mill, 1853–1860." *Business History Review* 28 (1954): 67–81.

Gitelman, Howard M. "The Waltham System and the Coming of the Irish." *Labor History* 8 (1967): 227–53.

Groneman, Carol. "Working-Class Immigrant Women in Mid-Nineteenth Century New York: The Irish Woman's Experience." *Journal of Urban History* 4 (1978): 255–74.

Gutman, Herbert G. *The Black Family in Slavery and Freedom.* New York: Pantheon Books, 1976.

———. "Persistent Myths About the Afro-American Family." *Journal of Interdisciplinary History* 6 (1975): 81–210.

Hagler, D. Harland. "The Ideal Woman in the Antebellum South: Lady or Farmwife?" *Journal of Southern History* 46 (1980): 405–18.

Haller, John S., and Haller, Robin M. *The Physician and Female Sexuality in Nineteenth Century America.* Urbana: University of Illinois Press, 1974.

Hersh, Blanche Glassman. *The Slavery of Sex.* Urbana: University of Illinois Press, 1978.

Hogeland, Ronald W. "The Female Appendage: Feminine Life-Styles in America, 1820–1860." *Civil War History* 17 (1971): 101–114.

Jeffrey, Julie Roy. *Frontier Women.* New York: Hill & Wang, 1979.

Johnson, James Hugo. *Race Relations in Virginia and Miscegenation in the South, 1776–1860.* Amherst: University of Massachusetts Press, 1970.

Kaser, David. "Nashville's Women of Pleasure in 1860." *Tennessee Historical Quarterly* 23 (1964): 379–82.

Katsman, David. *Seven Days a Week: Women and Domestic Service in Industrializing America.* New York: Oxford University Press, 1978.

Kleinberg, Susan. "Technology and Women's Work: The Lives of Working Class Women in Pittsburgh, 1870–1900." *Labor History* 17 (1976): 58–72.

Kraditor, Aileen S. *Means and Ends in American Abolitionism: Garrison and His Critics on Strategy and Tactics, 1834–1850.* New York: Pantheon Books, 1969.

Larson, T.A. "Woman Suffrage in Western America," *Utah Historical Quarterly* 38 (1970): 7–19.

———. "Emancipating the West's Dolls, Vassals and Hopeless Drudges! The Origins of Woman Suffrage in the West." In *Essays in Western History in Honor of T.A. Larson,* edited by Roger Daniels. Laramie: University of Wyoming, 1971.

Lasch, Christopher. "Emancipated Women." *New York Review of Books.* (July 13, 1967): 28–32.

Lerner, Gerda. *The Grimke Sisters from South Carolina: Rebels Against Slavery.* Boston: Houghton Mifflin, 1967.

Lebsock, Susan D. "Radical Reconstruction and the Property Rights of Southern Women." *Journal of Southern History* 63 (1977): 195–216.

Lumpkin, Katharine DuPre. *The Emancipation of Angelina Grimke.* Chapel Hill: University of North Carolina Press, 1974.

Massy, Mary Elizabeth. *Bonnet Brigades.* New York: Alfred A. Knopf, 1966.

McGraw, Judith A. " 'A Good Place to Work': Industrial Women and Occupational Choice." *Journal of Interdisciplinary History* 10 (1979): 227–48.

McPherson, James. "Abolitionists, Woman Suffrage and the Negro, 1865–1869." *Mid-America* 47 (1965): 40–47.

Melder, Keith E. *Beginnings of Sisterhood: The American Woman's Rights Movement, 1800–1850.* New York: Schocken Books, 1977.

_____. "Ladies Bountiful: Organized Women's Benevolence in Early 19th-Century America." *New York History* 48 (1967): 231–55.

Mills, Gary B. "Miscegenation and the Free Negro in Antebellum 'Anglo' Alabama: A Reexamination of Race Relations." *Journal of American History* 68 (1981): 16–34.

Mohr, James C. *Abortion in America: The Origins and Evolution of National Policy.* New York: Oxford University Press, 1978.

Mott, Frank L. "Portrait of an American Mill Town: Demographic Response in Mid-Nineteenth Century Warren, Rhode Island." *Population Studies* 26 (1972): 147–57.

Morantz, Regina. "Making Women Modern: Middle Class Women and Health Reform in 19th Century America." *Journal of Social History* 10 (1976–77): 490–507.

Muncy, Raymond Lee. *Sex and Marriage in Utopian Communities: Nineteenth Century America.* Bloomington: University of Indiana Press, 1974.

O'Neill, William L. *The Woman Movement: Feminism in the United States and England.* Chicago: Quadrangle Books, 1971.

Owens, Leslie Howard. *This Species of Property: Slave Life and Culture in the Old South.* New York: Oxford University Press, 1976.

Pivar, David J. *Purity Crusade: Sexual Morality and Social Control, 1868–1900.* Westport, Conn.: Greenwood Press, 1973.

Pleck, Elizabeth. "The Two-Parent Household: Black Family Structure in Late Nineteenth-Century Boston." *Journal of Social History* 6 (1972): 1–31.

_____. "A Mother's Wages: Income Earning Among Married Italian and Black Women, 1896–1911." In *The American Family in Social-Historical Perspective,* edited by Michael Gordon, pp. 490–510. New York: St. Martin's Press, 1978.

Rawick, George P. *From Sundown to Sunup.* Westport, Conn.: Greenwood Press, 1972.

Riley, Glenda. "Images of the Frontierswomen: Iowa as a Case Study." *Western Historical Quarterly* 8 (1977): 198–202.

Ripley, C. Peter. "The Black Family in Transition: Louisiana, 1860–65." *Journal of Southern History* 41 (1975): 869–80.

Rosenberg, Charles E. "Sexuality, Class and Role in 19th-Century America." *American Quarterly* 25 (1973): 131–53.

Ryan, Mary. *Cradle of the Middle Class Family: Oneida County, New York, 1780–1865.* Cambridge: Cambridge University Press, 1980.

_____. "A Woman's Awakening: Evangelical Religion and the Families of Utica, N.Y., 1800–1840." *American Quarterly* 30 (1978): 602–23.

_____. "The Power of Women's Networks: A Case Study of Female Moral Reform in Antebellum America." *Feminist Studies* 5 (1979): 66–85.

Scott, Anne F. *The Southern Lady: From Pedestal to Politics, 1830–1930.* Chicago: University of Chicago Press, 1970.

Sklar, Kathryn Kish. *Catherine Beecher: A Study in Domesticity.* New Haven: Yale University Press, 1973.

Smith, Daniel Scott. "Family Limitation, Sexual Control, and Domestic Feminism in Victorian America." *Feminist Studies* 1 (1973): 40–57.

Smith-Rosenberg, Carroll. "Beauty, the Beast and the Militant Woman: A Case Study of Sex Roles and Social Stress in Jacksonian America." *American Quarterly* 23 (1971): 562–84.

————. "The Female World of Love and Ritual: Relations Between Women in Nineteenth Century America." *Signs* 1 (1975): 1–29.

————, and Rosenberg, Charles E. "The Female Animal: Medical and Biological Views of Women in Nineteenth-Century America." *Journal of American History* 60 (1973): 332–56.

Sterkx, H.E. *Partners in Rebellion: Alabama Women in the Civil War.* Teaneck, N.J.: Fairleigh Dickinson University Press, 1970.

Taylor, William R. and Lasch, Christopher. "Two 'Kindred Spirits': Sorority and Family in New England, 1839–1846." *New England Quarterly* 36 (1963): 23–41.

Walters, Ronald G. "The Family and Ante-bellum Reform: An Interpretation." *Societas*

————. "The Erotic South: Civilization and Sexuality in American Abolitionism." *American Quarterly* 25 (1973): 177–201.

Ware, Caroline. *Early New England Cotton Manufacture.* Boston: Houghton Mifflin, 1931.

Welter, Barbara. *Dimity Convictions: The American Woman in the Nineteenth Century.* Athens: Ohio University Press, 1976.

Wiley, Bell Irwin. *Confederate Women.* Westport, Conn.: Greenwood Press, 1975.

Wood, Ann Douglas. "The War Within a War: Women Nurses in the Union Army." *Civil War History* 18 (1972): 197–212.

Yans-McLaughlin, Virginia. *Family and Community: Italian Immigrants in Buffalo, 1880–1930.* Ithaca: Cornell University Press, 1977.

————. "Patterns of Work and Family Organization: Buffalo's Italians." *Journal of Interdisciplinary History* 2 (1971): 299–314.

3 ❧ The Progressive Impulse

Throughout the latter part of the nineteenth century and into the twentieth, urbanization and industrialization proceeded at an ever-increasing pace. Women followed the general migration pattern from country to city, from farm to factory. At all economic levels, women were breaking out of the confines of the home and entering the public arena. For new immigrants and for lower-class women in general, this process brought the dubious emancipation of jobs outside the home in domestic service, sweatshops, and shirtwaist factories. For their wealthier sisters, increased leisure time and education created opportunities to enter the professions and to invest their energies in the cause of social justice. Women became a major element in the Progressive reform coalition, creating a growing tangle of organizations that confronted a wide range of social issues from pornography and prostitution to world peace.

The latter part of the nineteenth century witnessed major changes in thought and behavior that ushered in an era of reform. Among the new generation of reformers were the reform Darwinists, who scathingly criticized nearly all elements of Victorian thought and emphasized "coming to grips with life, experience, process, growth, context and function." Their emphasis on the economic context of social order promised immense benefits to women. Although these thinkers failed to seriously confront many aspects of the nineteenth-century definition of a woman, they challenged the sanctity of social and economic institutions that confined women to a limited sphere of influence. In "Loving Courtship or the Marriage Market?" Sondra R. Herman compares the traditional nineteenth-century view of marriage with the anxious orthodoxy of the social purity movement and the critical analyses of five leading reform Darwinists, including Charlotte Perkins Gilman, the era's most interesting feminist. At the heart of Gilman's brilliant polemic, *Women and Economics*, which emphasized the economic basis of women's subordination to men, was a radical assault on the inequalities and inefficiencies of contemporary marriage. She agreed with radical men like Edward Bellamy and Lester Frank Ward that only a fundamental change in the economic specialization of the sexes could reorient the relationship between husband and wife to make true social progress possible.

At the same time that radical critics were challenging the sanctity of traditional marriage, major shifts were occurring in sexual and marital practices. Urban conditions, including the shrinking dimensions of the household, the growing autonomy of middle-class women due to expanded educational opportunities, and increased employment of women outside the home, produced new patterns of behavior. A startling rise in the rates of illegitimacy and premarital intercourse, which had been falling throughout the nineteenth century, indicated increased sexual activity. Although marriage and childbirth continued to characterize the average woman's life, in the final two decades of the nineteenth century larger numbers of women chose not to marry than at any other time in American history. Those who did were, on the average, older when they decided to marry, and a greater percentage of married women chose not to have children. More startling to contemporaries, however, was the rapid increase in the number of women who sought release from unhappy marriages through divorce. As the percentage of women marrying returned to "normal" after the turn of the century, the United States had the anomalous distinction of both marriage and divorce rates that ranked among the highest in the world.

Expanded opportunities for education drew middle-class women out of the home and into some professions. Under the leadership of Emma Willard and Catherine Beecher, secondary education was increasingly available to women during the years before the Civil War. In 1837 Mary Lyon founded Mount Holyoke Female Seminary, which set an example for the rapid expansion of women's colleges after the war: in 1865, Vassar was established; Smith and Wellesley in 1875; and Bryn Mawr in 1885. Coeducation on the college level emerged first in the Midwest when Oberlin College in Ohio opened its doors to women in the 1830s. After the Civil War, a growing number of state universities followed Oberlin's example.

By the end of the century, over 5,000 women were graduating yearly from the nation's colleges, and the majority moved into the labor force. The number of women doctors increased as medical education (in sexually segregated classes) became available to more women. Through the dogged efforts of women such as Myra Bradwell and Belva Lockwood, who ran for president in 1884 and 1888, resistance to women in the legal profession was gradually eroded. However, most women were excluded from these professions and confined to teaching, nursing, and library work, occupations characterized by low status and low pay.

This unique group, whom Vida D. Scudder termed "the first-generation of college women," became the nucleus of a burgeoning reform movement. Horrified by multiplying slums, contaminated food and water, and unhealthy conditions under which the poor, and particularly poor women, labored, they devoted themselves to serving others in missions overseas and in settlement houses within the urban ghettos. The activities of Lillian Wald and Jane Addams are well known, but the women's organizations that appeared in increasing numbers after 1890 were more typical of the Progressive era. These organizations, which often shared members and sometimes worked together, ranged from the numerous women's clubs that focused on civic improvement—loosely united after 1901 under the aegis of the General Federation of Women's Clubs (GFWC)—to older political groups like the Women's Christian Temperance Union (WCTU).

Beginning with the WCTU, middle-class women gradually moved into a succession of community activities. For thousands of farmwives the populist movement provided an opportunity to become involved in reforms that could alter their traditional role. The expanding progressive impulse even touched the women of the "New South." In "Women and the Southern Farmers Alliance," Julie Roy Jeffrey details the various ways in which North Carolina women participated in the activities of the Alliance. The farmwives she discusses hardly fit the model of the pious, virtuous and submissive, Southern lady who was "the delight and charm of every circle" in which she moved. They were practical, hard-working women well aware of the sexual barriers erected against them. The Populists offered a "spirited attempt to work out a new place for [women] both in theory and practice," but even these male reformers were wary of women's direct participation in politics.

As women who wished to reform the social order increasingly felt their disfranchisement a great handicap, women's suffrage became the focus of the women's movement. In 1890 the warring factions in the suffrage movement made peace and banded together in the National American Woman Suffrage Association under the presidency of Elizabeth Cady Stanton. From 1890 to 1910, the new organization continued to follow the strategy of securing women's suffrage on a state-by-state basis. Although these women had remarkable success in opening school board and municipal elections to women, only a handful of states provided for equal suffrage.

In the next century a new generation of suffrage leaders, represented by Dr. Anna Howard Shaw and Carrie Chapman Catt, led the NAWSA to its final victory. Under the direction of Catt, NAWSA swelled to nearly two million members and concentrated on the enactment and ratification of the Nineteenth Amendment. However, it was not until after 1910 that major strides were made. In quick succession, five far-western states joined with Kansas and Illinois in giving women the vote. Then in 1912, the Progressive party included a women's suffrage plank in its platform. Suffragists waged major campaigns in the populous states of the Midwest and East during 1915, and, although these attempts failed, the results indicated that the possibility of future success was excellent.

At about the same time, the campaign for an amendment to the Constitution was revived through the vigorous action of Alice Paul, a young Quaker woman who had been deeply influenced by her work with the militant English feminists. On returning to the United States, she organized the Congressional Union, which was at first affiliated with the NAWSA but eventually became the basis for the independent Woman's Party. Until 1917 the two groups maintained an uneasy alliance.

It does not diminish the achievement of Catt to argue that the final success of women's suffrage depended not only upon a few heroic national leaders, but also upon the vigorous activity of the rank and file who struggled within the complex web of state politics. In "Leadership and Tactics in the American Suffrage Movement," Sharon Hartman Strom focuses on the campaign for the vote in Massachusetts and the relationship between feminism and progressivism. Strom explains how the suffrage movement, which seemed to have been stymied by a defeat in the Massachusetts referendum of 1895, was revitalized after the turn of the century and grew in power until it swept the ratification of the Nineteenth Amendment before it. She emphasizes the importance of the rank and file to other Progressive reforms and the incorporation by suffragists of some of the radical tactics employed by their English sisters. Strom's study is detailed and complex; it shows once again that differences in ethnicity, religion, and class hindered the unity of the women's movement. She highlights to a greater extent than any previous scholar the intricate political maneuvering between suffragists and Progressives, which led to the final success of the suffrage amendment.

Ironically the Nineteenth Amendment was finally recommended by President Woodrow Wilson as a wartime measure—in response to American women's wholehearted support of World War I. Women had traditionally made up a sizable element of the American peace movement, and, at first, organizations such as NAWSA joined with the radical Woman's Peace Party to oppose American entrance into the war. But once war was declared, the majority of women supported the administration. Anna Howard Shaw, former president of NAWSA, served as head of the National Women's Committee of the Council of National Defense during the war. Although their efforts had little effect on the government, NAWSA worked through state and local branches, rolling bandages for the Red Cross and providing food and clothing for the soldiers. Many other women took over men's jobs in factories and in civil service and worked in Europe with the U.S. Army Corps of Nurses, the Red Cross, and the Salvation Army. Such activities drew wide praise and contributed to women's attainment of suffrage.

By 1920 women reformers had reason to be proud of their accomplishments and to be optimistic about the future. The two major reforms for which women organized and worked during the nineteenth century had been achieved with the enactment of the constitutional amendments providing for prohibition and women's suffrage. Organized women had played an important role in securing protective legislation for child labor, pure food and drugs, and conservation. They also influenced Progressive measures in two other areas traditionally of interest to women—reform of divorce laws and the curbing of prostitution. This impressive body of legislative success in the interest of women has led one scholar to term the Progressive era "the greatest age in the history of American women." However, the achievement of these reforms was not without cost to the women's movement.

Although the conditions of children and working women were ameliorated through the activities of women such as Mary "Mother" Jones, Florence Kelley, the executive secretary of the National Consumers' League, and Elizabeth Gurley Flynn and Rose Schneiderman, who struggled in the interest of the working classes, women workers remained generally unorganized and outside the mainstream of the feminist movement. During the nineteenth century, women's protests against low wages and horrid working conditions seldom provided the basis for long-term organization. Attempts to organize working women made by the Daughters of St. Crispin and later by the Knights of Labor failed; the American Federation of Labor vacillated and was generally unsympathetic to the problem. Feminism and labor radicalism never joined, which prevented working-class women from contributing further to Progressive reform.

Although the percentage of women in industry gradually declined, the number of working women increased with each census. By 1900 working women represented 20 percent of the total female population over sixteen years of age. For the most part, they worked as domestic servants or farm workers, and many still labored in the textile mills. Increasing numbers, however, worked in new white-color jobs as telephone and telegraph operators and secretaries. The lot of most working women was a hard one that improved little until the enactment of Progressive reforms setting minimum wages and controlling hours and conditions of labor. In 1910 the Bureau of Labor reported that most working women were "paid very low wages—wages in many cases inadequate to supply a reasonable standard of living for women dependent upon their own earnings for support."

Only a few women in select areas, such as the garment industry, moved into the labor movement. After 1903 the Women's Trade Union League, organized by Mary Kenny O'Sullivan, attempted with limited success to bring women into the trade union movement. The idea behind the WTUL was to join working-class women and their middle-class female allies in a single organization to improve the wages and working conditions of laboring women. Nancy Schrom Dye illustrates some of the problems within the New York WTUL in her essay, "Creating a Feminist Alliance." Class and ethnic differences among these women undermined a sense of sorority. The League also failed to develop "an analysis which came to terms with both facets of women workers' situation," that is, one that synthesized class and gender in a meaningful explanation.

In the face of adversity, the WTUL did score a few modest successes. They gave crucial support to the New York shirtwaistmakers' strikes of 1909–1910, and were primarily responsible for the establishment of the Women in Industry Division of the Department of Labor during World War I, which eventually became the Woman's Bureau under the direction of Mary Anderson in 1920. The career of the WTUL illustrates both the immense problems involved in organizing women due to the opposition of male workers and the limitations of the women's movement of the Progressive era. As so often in the American past, differences between women had a greater impact on their behavior than the common problems that they faced because of their sex.

As success became a possibility, the increasing concern for tactics undermined the idealism of the movement. In order to gain the unity necessary for effective political pressure, the major women's organizations had to disavow their more militant elements, such as Alice Paul's Women's Party, and ignore the needs and desires of black women. Blacks were involved in the Progressive movement: Ida B. Wells-Barnett led the crusade against lynching, and Mary Church Terrill organized the National Association of Colored Women. A few white women did take a special interest in racial equality. Mary White Ovington, for example, was one of the founders of the National Association for the Advancement of Colored People. But for the most part, the interests of black women were sacrificed to attain Southern support. The CFWC and the WCTU were built upon sectional reconciliation and were strong in the South, but even NAWSA, whose roots stretched back into the abolitionist movement, tolerated racist arguments and gave in to the racist demands of its Southern members. During World War I attempts were made to enlist the support of black women. In "Black Women and the Great War," William J. Breen analyzes the efforts of Alice Dunbar Nelson and the Committee on Women's Defense Work, which resulted in an unusual cooperation between southern white and black women that extended beyond the Committee's original goals into other areas of reform.

Aside from class and ethnic divisions within the movement, feminism was plagued by ideological inconsistencies. In the 1890s the basis of the suffrage argument shifted from natural rights to expediency. Suffragists increasingly related other reform measures to their demand for the vote. They insisted that a purification of the political process would follow the entrance of women into the polling place. Alice Stone Blackwell, the activist daughter of Lucy Stone, believed that "in the main, suffrage and prohibition have the same friends and the same enemies" and urged clergymen to support suffrage because it would augment the power of the churches in "the warfare against the liquor traffic, and the white slave traffic, child labor, impure food, and many other existing evils."

In "Women Reformers and American Culture, 1870–1930," Jill Conway emphasizes the failure of reformers to question basic aspects of traditional sexual stereotypes and their emphasis on the distinctive moral qualities of women. Women like Jane Addams and Lillian Wald "worked within the tradition which saw women as civilizing and moralizing forces within the society." They conceived of women as temperamentally suited to the task of social housekeeping. Because women alone possessed the virtues extolled in Victorian sexual stereotypes, Addams and Wald urged women to move out of the home into efforts for social justice and the reform of politics. Even Charlotte Gilman, who questioned almost every aspect of the subordination of women, believed that motherhood was the biological destiny of women and that women were by nature more peaceful, even-tempered, and less competitive than men. The success of the major progressive reforms was based upon "not the image of women as equals . . . but the image of women as victims."

15 Loving Courtship or the Marriage Market? The Ideal and Its Critics, 1871–1911

Sondra R. Herman

During the last three decades of the 19th century and the first of the 20th, American feminists generally avoided discussion of marital and sexual issues. Fearful of disgracing the movement with scandal, particularly after the Victoria Woodhull affair, and sharing the sexually repressive standards of the age, feminists increasingly turned their attention to the suffrage and the supposed benefits it would bring all of society.

Yet in these same decades of repression a debate *did* arise over marital questions. If the implications of sexuality could not be considered freely, neither could the subject of marriage be avoided. More women were going to work; more were seeking a college education, particularly after the 1890s. More couples were moving to the city. Defenders of traditional marriage promulgated the old ideals of female domesticity, submissiveness and sexual purity in the face of what they thought were some dangerous trends. Critics of American marriage found that male domination, female uselessness and economic depen-

From the *American Quarterly* 25 (May 1973). Copyright © 1973 by the Trustees of the University of Pennsylvania. Reprinted by permission.

A revised version of this paper was presented at the meeting of the Organization of American Historians, April 1972.

The author would like to thank all of the following individuals for helpful comments on an earlier version of this paper, although none should be associated with the positions I have taken in it: Carl N. Degler, Samuel Haber, Anne Sherrill, Carroll Smith-Rosenberg, Warren I. Susman.

dency had distorted marital happiness. Both groups concentrated their attention on the processes of courtship, for here they perceived the sex roles they were either defending or challenging took on most obvious forms.

The debate centered on a peculiar question: Was American courtship a process of practical love-seeking or was it a marriage market? Since we have no evidence that American marriages were in fact marriages of convenience in the 1880s and 1890s any more than earlier, the critics' charge of materialism seemed in large measure a weapon in the battle for female independence. The defense of courtship as love-seeking similarly was part of an effort to keep women at home in an age known for the restlessness of its females.

Both defenders and critics realized that their evaluation of marriage was connected to their evaluations of the whole social order. In general the defenders of traditional marriage implied that America offered opportunity enough for men and contentment for wives if they would only be supportive. The critics of American marriage, at least the five treated here—Edward Bellamy, Lester Frank Ward, Charlotte Perkins Gilman, Thorstein Veblen and Theodore Dreiser—attacked traditional marriage as part of the general injustice of American society. Thus while the debate could not before 1910 take direct sexual terms, it took a social form—defense of or attack upon the social status quo.

The defenders of the status quo were most often Protestant, especially evangelical clergy, conservative women, and doctors who wrote books offering the most traditional marital advice. The critics were intellectuals who refused to acknowledge religious authority and who openly challenged the ideal of fixed sex roles contained in such works. Only toward the end of the era, after 1910 or so, did an actual rebellion against repressive notions of sexuality begin. The debate in the eighties and nineties, while occasionally hinting at discontent with sexual standards, focused on proper sex roles and on woman's economic dependency.

Writers of the marriage manuals frequently asserted that indissoluble matrimony was the foundation of the whole social order. It was a "duty binding upon all well-equipped people who cannot show some larger obligation that is inconsistent with this."[1] It was, first, essential to complete the humanity of each man and woman. The two sexes, more different from one another than alike, needed to enter a human trinity—man, woman, child, so that each could become more truly a self. Celibacy not only meant incompletion, it threatened a sinful life, especially for men. Marriage was essential, secondly, to fulfill the social obligation of parenthood.[2] Sex was an expression of love but essential for reproduction only.

Like the Puritan clergy generations earlier, the marital advisers of the late 19th century assumed that it was completely within the partners' capabilities to make or unmake their marriage. Marital happiness became a duty to be performed not only for the husband and wife's own benefit, but for the sake of the children and society.

Critics of American marriage, on the other hand, believed that marital happiness was deeply influenced by social conditions outside of marriage. They implied by the term "marriage market" that materialistic motives were necessarily present in most marriage choices. Young ladies presented themselves as merchandise for eager young men to marry. The girls, being dependent, had to do so in order to survive. Secondly, the term "market" suggested a terrible impersonality in the exchange of love for support. The harshness of the business world was invading the home itself. Home was no longer a refuge from the cold world, but rather its extension. To correct these conditions, the critics argued, a new social ethic was needed—more independence for women, more freedom to marry outside of one's class, more freedom to reject marriage altogether.

The audience for these strictures was an urban middle class who may have found marital choice freer and more difficult than ever before.[3] The sheer population of neighborhoods, the increasing opportunities for men and women to meet at work, made it virtually impossible for parents to know all the eligibles from whom a son or daughter would make a choice. Some resource had to replace the valuable gossip of the small town. The marriage advice books flowed into the gap. Some of these works, particularly those of doctors promising postnuptial sexual advice, as well as advice as to marital choice, were quite popular. *The Physical Life of Woman* by Dr. George Napheys sold 150,000 copies in its original 1869 edition and was reprinted in 1888. Others appeared to be collections of sermons circulating little further than the clergyman's parish, but clerical works sometimes ran to later editions as well.[4]

The marital advice books attempted to erect barriers against changing values. They cautioned against neglect of the church and against extravagant, worldly women. They upheld static definitions of role, relating these to the protection of the American home from declining moral standards. The major responsibility for creating a moral society, by building the foundations at home, lay with the wife. Unlike the critics, the nuptial guides viewed woman as relatively influential because they valued her role as moral guardian. Home was to provide a haven of tenderness in the cold world, and woman, by nature more emotional than man, was the source of that warmth. Her husband's success and therefore the economic well-being of the family, her children's character, and therefore the moral future of the republic, depended critically upon her patient strength. She, more than anyone else, upheld the ideals of sexual purity and family devotion.[5]

Given such conditions the ministers and doctors wrote fairly uniform descriptions of the good wife, and they castigated behavior that did not conform with their ideals. Men were advised to seek both character and performance in a wife. The prospective bride had to show she could become a thrifty, meticulous housekeeper. But prevalent female extravagance in dress made this requirement difficult to meet. The writers feared that idle wives who ministered only to their husbands' sensual needs were on the increase. Their families were not large enough to occupy them.[6] A wife, secondly, had to identify her future with her husband's completely, listen sympathetically to his plans and comfort him when they failed. And sympathy was needed by the husband. "I counsel the wife to remember in what a severe and terrific battle of life her husband is engaged," preached the Reverend DeWitt Talmage in 1886.[7] The independent college graduate, more in evidence in the next decade, evidently had to learn this submissive, traditional role. Above all, the wife had to be trustworthy, which meant both that she could be her husband's confidante, and that she was sexually pure. No hint of sexual interest should ever touch her manner or conversation. Her reputation, more than her husband's, became the reputation of the entire family. For the most part, the marriage advisers believed that this requirement would be easier to meet than the others. Most asserted or implied that woman's sexual drive was much weaker than man's, although some doctors emphasized that it was not absent altogether.[8] The fulfillment of these feminine ideals—tenderness, chastity, homemaking skills—came with maternity. The requirements of motherhood pervaded the advice literature which was often anti-birth-control literature as well.

Similarly, the prospective husband was regarded in his role as paterfamilias. If a woman's duty was to comfort and serve, a man's was to love and protect. Assuming that man's "animal nature" was much stronger than woman's (yet necessary for the propagation of the race), the doctors and clergy issued stern warnings about the average masculine morality. Women might exercise a softening influence, but they could never reform fundamental wrongs. The girls should avoid men much older than themselves, licentious men, drunkards, gamblers, cold-hearted tyrants, those whose work took them away from home frequently and "despisers of the Christian religion."[9] Of all the post-nuptial failings, man's overabsorption in his business and in the attractions of hotel life were believed most common. Marriage advisers warned wives to stay neat and attractive.[10]

The wife's choice of a husband (but interestingly, not the husband's choice of a wife) was deemed fatal. Presumably the clergy's opposition to divorce would equalize the seriousness of choosing. It did not. Some writers acknowledged that a man could always escape to his club, but a woman had no escape. Was this an implied acknowledgment of the double standard? It is hard to say, for other advisers cautioned men against "lascivious actions which are a drain upon the whole system" and asked them to come to the marriage bed as virginal as their brides.[11]

One factor that increased the dangers of poor choice by the woman, her economic dependence, a major concern of critics, was rarely mentioned by the guides. They may have taken the husband's provider role for granted. Yet this avoidance of any discussion of money appeared to be related to the estimate of woman's weaker sex drive. When a man sought a girl he was following a powerful instinct. The girl, on the other hand, could judge a suitor more rationally.[12] Thus the clergymen avoided any statement implying ecclesiastical approval of women coldly evaluating prospective husbands in terms of earning power.

Having presented marriage as a sacred institution, and home as a refuge from the world's commercialism, the advisers could hardly allow commercial standards of judgment about marriage. To have acknowledged materialistic motives on a general scale would have been to admit precisely what the critics implied—the obligation to Christianize the social order, an order that had so corrupted matrimony. The marital advisers acted on the contrary assumption: the traditional marital relationship was pure. It did not need woman's economic independence to cure its materialism. On the contrary, when marriage was delayed in order to acquire the money for a respectable "establishment," it was the sinner's corruption not society's. Woman's worship of fashion, man's "absurd social ambition," were individual evils, not symptoms of social disorder.[13]

After cautioning their readers about financial extravagance, the preachers presumed to tell lovers how to judge love. Their intentions were clear—to discourage matches of sudden passion and deceptive romance. Sudden falling in love they believed a myth fostered by too much novel reading. A marriage based upon passion was as dangerous as an overcalculating one. Instead, men and women should grow in love, that is, make reasonable and practical choices based upon secure knowledge of one another's characters. Above all, it was important to distinguish passion from love. The first was easily satiated and carnal, but love was at least partially spiritual and entirely unselfish, reasonable and tender. It could pass certain tests which lovers should make before they married. It had the constancy required for indissoluble marriage and responsible parenthood.[14] By emphasizing love's reasonableness, the nuptial counselors gave hardly any hint of the mysterious process by which men and women discovered their mutuality, nor of the possibilities of tragic choices. If one was sensible, the endings were happy. Love, true tender love, was essential to marriage. It was the greatest guarantee of marital and social stability.

Frequently, objections to romantic love merged with objections to marriage across class lines. Harmonious differences in temperament were considered healthy, but not marked differences in status. Cultural incompatibility would destroy such a marriage which might have been motivated by social climbing on the part of the poorer partner. As they feared such class mixtures (and certainly racial and religious mixtures were beyond the pale), so the advisers feared the drowning of an educated, Protestant, older American population in a sea of ignorant, immigrant poor. The urging of practical, compatible marriages sometimes took place in this context.[15]

In spite of the pleas for class compatibility, the Cinderella ideal remained as popular as ever in short stories and plays. Writers usually sought a formula to prove that Cinderella was not a fortune-hunter. In one of the longest-run productions on the New York stage and on the road, Steel McKaye's *Hazel Kirke* (1880), the lovely, submissive miller's daughter fell in love with a titled Englishman, quite unaware of his position. When the inevitable obstacles arose in the form of previously promised marriages of convenience, the hero sacrificed fortune and position to keep Hazel—thereby equalizing their social positions. In most short stories, however, in the women's mass circulation magazines of the first decade of the 20th century, the fortune, hidden during courtship, was revealed and kept at the end as a reward for true love.[16] Although the fiction upheld the Cinderella ideal and the marriage manuals cautioned against it, together they constituted a success literature. Both declared that chastity and virtuous courtship would win rewards—both spiritual and practical.

It is difficult to know just how seriously readers took the advice to marry within their class. Some middle-class families, perhaps chiefly those in the upper middle class, found that neighborhood acquaintance alone was not enough to maintain the lines. When Ethel Sturgis, daughter of the President of the Chicago, Northwestern Bank, became engaged to Francis Dummer, Vice President of the same bank in 1888, she wrote, "I almost tremble to think if love and duty had not coincided, what a struggle our two lives would have been." Ethel's father and Francis' sister had, however, pointed out the virtues of Ethel and Francis to each other.[17] In contrast, when a niece of the famous Doctors Blackwell, Elizabeth and Emily, pursued a young farmer in

Martha's Vineyard, the family placed every possible obstacle in the way of this "common" marriage. In spite of their niece's behavior the aunts assumed a lower moral standard went with the lower class.[18]

In this assumption, the Blackwells reflected an undercurrent of anxiety that ran through some of the purity campaigns of the 1890s and 1900s. The purity crusaders were a diverse group of women, doctors, prohibitionists, later progressives who launched a series of campaigns against prostitution and lax age-of-consent laws. They certainly wanted a single standard of sexual morality—but not only for both sexes, but for all classes as well. They resented society's "heartless discriminations in favor of the rich and the influential."[19] As Benjamin Flower, editor of the *Arena,* a vehicle for the movement, observed: "The immorality and degradation of rapid life among the mushroom aristocracy is matched by the grosser manifestations of immorality in the social cellar . . . [and] the great middle class absorbs the contagion from above and below."[20]

The purity advocates warned against social climbing in marriage, believing that ambitious marriages increased extramarital temptations. Avaricious parents led innocent sons and daughters into such marriages while corrupt churchmen ignored the social consequences.[21] As Nathan G. Hale has pointed out, the purity campaigns for sex education, their muckraking against white slavery, the whole drive for a break in the wall of silence they claimed protected vice, had very different results than they envisioned. The campaigns undermined the old repressive standards.[22] In spite of this contrast in effects, the campaigners upheld the same values as those of the churchmen whose protection of virtue they considered so inadequate. Their ideals remained: chastity, female domesticity, rational love and class compatibility.

The purity campaigners' emphasis upon the social injustices which they thought imperiled the home was one indication among many that Americans were, by the 1880s, more receptive to more radical analyses of their society. No stronger weapon existed in the radical armory than the charge that even the home, the supposed haven of warmth and love, was corrupted by materialism. All of the five critics—Bellamy, Ward, Gilman, Veblen and Dreiser—had reason to challenge the alliance of church, home and business. Edward Bellamy and Lester Frank Ward, for example, had early experienced crises of belief which left them with the idea that the church's repressive sexual standards and the guilt they induced were themselves a source of evil.[23] Economic insecurity had scarred the childhoods of Charlotte Perkins Gilman and Theodore Dreiser. Mrs. Gilman's father had deserted a family of four, offering only occasional financial, and no psychological support. Charlotte, seeing her mother's submissive suffering, could never play the traditional female role. Theodore Dreiser's family disintegrated altogether under the combined disasters of his father's obsessive moralism and frequent unemployment. Thorstein Veblen appeared to have learned his skepticism early by contrasting the life of the hard-working Norwegian American farmers with that of the Yankee middle class. By the time he attended Carleton College, he was a full-fledged rebel.[24] In various ways, then, these critics' early experiences led them to reject the conservative success ethos that shaped traditional marital standards.

Edward Bellamy, whose utopian novel, *Looking Backward* (1888) appealed both to intellectuals and to the general public as a solution to the ills of monopolistic capitalism, did not revolt against his own closely knit family, but first against the remnants of Calvinist dogma which crushed the individual conscience. The destructive sense of guilt, the haunting Nemesis of an evil fate, he considered more psychologically damaging than any evil deed. By the 1870s his vaguely transcendental Religion of Solidarity replaced the old religion and provided the philosophical ground of his utopia, being at once impersonal and social.[25]

While he was in his twenties, in the midst of this religious crisis, Bellamy *had* entertained profound doubts about marriage. Avoiding it himself, he argued that marriage became the grave of the creative man who had to prostitute his talents in order to support dependents. In an unpublished novel, *Eliot Carson,* he toyed with the monastic solution for artists. This could hardly answer for all of society. Bellamy himself finally found it unsatisfactory and married late in his thirties.[26] Yet the question remained: How could men have love and a home without the imprisoning economic dependency of women?

Only when Bellamy turned from his fiction of individual psychological transformation to his utopia of revolutionary social transformation did he find the answer. In *Looking Backward,* the hero Julian awoke in the year 2000 to find a society in which both men and women worked for the state until their forties, and all received state support throughout their lifetimes. Men had the delights of domesticity without its restrictive burdens; women, having simpler homes (and with much of the traditional domestic labor performed publicly), had the interest of working in the world. The price, unfortunately, was considerable regimentation, but Bellamy did not think this an obstacle.[27] Society was rid of inhumane poverty and inequality.

The economic equality of the year 2000 utterly destroyed the marriage market. Men and women married for love alone; there could be no other reasons. Class distinctions in marriage were gone as were the classes themselves. Bellamy believed that such a free marriage system had tremendous genetic implications: "For the first time in human history, the principle of sexual selection with the tendency to preserve and transmit the better types of the race . . . has unhindered operation. The necessity of poverty, the need of having a home, no longer tempt women to accept as fathers of their children men whom they can neither love nor respect. . . . The gifts of the person, mind, and disposition . . . are sure of transmission to posterity."[28]

Thus did Bellamy affirm one of the strongest values of the radical critics of American marriage—the goal of an improved future generation. This goal, which was also implicit in the marital guidebooks' concern for proper parenthood, took a different form in the critics' analysis. They thought about the development of future generations more in post-Darwinian terms. Bellamy had even for a time entertained the idea of stirpiculture.[29] The guides believed that a marriage system which preserved class divisions, and in which the educated produced more children than the poor and uneducated, promised the best future. The critics believed that a class society, and a society of economically dependent women, harmed the future generation. They valued instead what Veblen called the parental bent—concern not just for one's own children, but for all children and for their future.

Bellamy relied upon "nationalism" to destroy the marriage market and he claimed it would end such accompanying evils as female triviality, hypocrisy (induced by 19th century courtship) and the double standard. This last reflected sexual economics more than sexual morality. It protected the purity of dependent married women at a horrible cost in prostitution. Since true ethical behavior could originate only with free choice, and since neither prostitutes nor chaste women were free, true sexual morality could begin only when women were economically independent of men. Such free women could frankly confess their love to men. No longer compelled to please the average man, in order to catch a husband, each woman could develop her own interests and talents. Women would no longer pass on their "mental and moral slavery" to their offspring.[30]

In thus simplifying the problem in economic terms, Bellamy was deferring to the popular, sexually repressive opinion of his day. His brother Charles had offered in a utopian novel, *An Experiment in Marriage* (1889), solutions Edward eschewed—virtually complete communal living, easy divorce and frequent remarriage. Only this system preserved the freshness of love.[31] With his brother's ideals of frank courtship and female equality Edward agreed. But divorce he could not endorse publicly, and he certainly had reservations about the sensuality favored in *An Experiment in Marriage*. Under "nationalism" he suggested the sexual drive would be not more intense but more diffuse, "like light that passes through a prism . . . refracted into many shades and hues."[32] In place of the free divorce system he created in the story "To Whom This May Come" a society of mind readers who recognized their true loves at once (vitiating the need for sensual experimentation). And these mind readers' unions were, of course, more spiritual than passionate, affirming the Bellamy ideal of love—moderate rapture. Since men would not have to support women in the socialist state, intense passion would not be needed to induce marriage. As family relationships declined in intensity, everyone would be "a thousandfold more than now occupied with nature and the next steps of the race."[33]

Like Bellamy, Lester Frank Ward and Charlotte Perkins Gilman attacked the exaggerated sexual differentiation of lives in late 19th century America. While Ward deplored sexual repression, Mrs. Gilman, who had paid the high price of nervous depression, divorce and separation from her daughter to attain autonomy, felt that American marriages *over-emphasized* sensuality. She was never able to accept the freer standards of the war years. In the early seventies Ward launched attacks upon the church, whose doctrines of female submission and indissoluble marriage he held directly responsible for prostitution.[34] Yet he left off his attack as he turned his attention to evolutionary theory and only took up the defense of freer sexual expression in 1903. In the 1890s then both Ward and Gilman criticized American marriage in the only "acceptable" way it could be criticized—by challenging traditional notions of the female role.

Both asserted that female inferiority was not inherent, but developed in the processes of the marriage market. Both extended the discussion to include a naturalistic consideration of the mate-selection process. Ward outlined a woman-centered theory of evolution indicating how the female of the species had abandoned an initially superior status. In all subhuman species, he noted, it was the female, not the male, who transmitted the characteristics of the race. She selected the males with whom to mate. Eventually, however, the females began to select not only the strongest, but the most intelligent mates. At that point, just as primitive man evolved, a crucial transformation took place. The men perceived that it was easier to seize females for mating than to contest for their favors with stronger males, allowing the female to choose the victor. This seizure and rape process, male-dominated mate selection, was the germ of marriage. And men continued to dominate the marriage market until modern times.[35]

Charlotte Perkins Gilman added that this male domination of the market bred a race of frail, backward women. Men chose such women for wives, so the smarter, stronger ones did not reproduce their own kind. But there was an even more crucial reason for female inferiority. Once man had conquered woman and enslaved her, she could no longer hunt for her own food, or provide for her own young as female animals did. Man stood between woman and the challenging environment of the economic world. Women, thus, developed largely through their relationships with men. They developed those traits needed to catch a husband: conformity, flirtatiousness, sexual exaggeration and passivity.[36] Marriageable women, as much as prostitutes, were utterly dependent upon men and in essence sold themselves. "When we confront this fact boldly . . . in the open market of vice, we are sick with horror. When we see the same economic relation made permanent, established by law . . . sanctified by religion, covered with flowers and accumulated sentiment, we think it innocent, lovely, and right. The transient trade we think evil, the bargain for life we think good."[37]

Both Ward and Gilman saw signs, however, that the age of the marriage market was passing. As societies became more complex and more highly civilized, the most fastidious individuals, Ward believed, had difficulty choosing a mate, and tended to decline marriage altogether. This, and the burden of economically unproductive women, made the goal of one indissoluble marriage for each impossible of realization.[38]

Ward asserted that by the end of the 19th century male-dominated selection was fortunately declining. If men continued to select women for their frail, ephemeral beauty, the race would eventually be extinct. But modern men were selecting women for their mental and moral strengths as well as for beauty. By this process they happily increased female influence. More and more *mutual* selection took place. Ward identified this mutual selection with romantic love. Unlike most nuptial guides, he cherished and celebrated romance as not only beautiful for individuals, but beneficial for society. It was the highest form of man's noblest natural instinct—sexual love. When men and women fell in love, they advanced both the race and the civilization. By choosing mates of contrasting temperament and build, they acted out of a natural wisdom to produce well-balanced offspring. Thus the only sound eugenics was obedience to the law of love.[39] Ward, arguing in evolutionary terms, was using a powerful weapon against "practical" marriage advice.

Moreover, romantic love aided civilization just because it rarely ran smooth. For each couple it meant working, struggling, long denial. Out of this yearning struggle came man's deepest inspirations to create in the arts and sciences. And the struggle, unstable in itself, ended in fulfillment, with the onset of calm conjugal love. Society's standards, therefore, should not be sexually repressive. Love was a "higher law" that should prevail over social conventions. Free divorce should be allowed so that marriages contracted out of unromantic motives, loveless, practical marriages could be ended for the sake of romance and the next generation.[40] This combination of romantic idealism and evolutionary science constituted Ward's plea for greater sexual freedom.

Mrs. Gilman was distinctly less enthusiastic about sexual freedom, although she too wanted love unshackled from economic marriage. Her own experiences, her early allegiance to Bellamy's socialism, led her to emphasize the collective life of modern society which she wished women to enter. In her famous *Women and Economics* (1898) she demonstrated that the individualism of the marital relation contradicted and distorted economic relations which tended to collectivity as industries modernized. Man's selfishness for "the sake of the family" was no more reasonable in a cooperative world than woman's isolation at home or overspecialization as to sex. The traditional roles had to and would decay for the world's benefit. Already a complex economy was drawing women out of the home, ending their alienation from creative labor. Primitive household labor was becoming obsolete. Woman's very restlessness in the domestic role indicated a new social consciousness.[41]

Woman's economic independence would not threaten marriage itself, but would end the male-dominated marriage market. Marriage would no longer be a "sexuo-economic" relationship. Women would choose husbands, sublimating immediate sexual attractiveness to the demands of "right parentage." At the same time, female influence would counteract the aggressive tendencies of the man-made world with the values of "peaceful, helpful interservice." A new social environment, reinforcing industrial efficiency, would prevail, making the egalitarian changes in the marriage relationship permanent.[42]

Although he was less hopeful than Mrs. Gilman, Thorstein Veblen made a very similar identification between the peaceful primitive matriarchy of the past and a possible future industrial republic. Like Ward and Gilman he looked backward in order to criticize the present and reconstruct the future. His anthropological economics was so implicitly subversive that readers could only regard their own mores as vestiges of barbarism. In all the Veblenian lexicon the most barbaric institution of all was the patriarchal marriage.

The patriarchy originated when primitive tribes acquired an excess of goods and encountered hostile tribes. Seizing the conquered tribes' goods and women, they eventually made war a way of life. In the transformation into a barbaric society, private ownership, slavery and patriarchal marriage originated. Because only wives and slaves worked, labor was judged irksome. The patriarch displayed his wives as possessions, and he owned the products of their labor. Riches and status came together. "The ownership and control of women is gratifying evidence of prowess and high standing."[43]

When Veblen extended this argument into a work both popular and scholarly, *The Theory of the Leisure Class* (1899), he forged a weapon of considerable power against traditional sex roles. For in stating that the middle-class wife functioned only to display luxury and idleness as proof of her husband's social standing, he touched an area as sensitive with the conservative preachers as with the radical critics. America's traditional values could not encompass idleness or uselessness and Veblen knew this. Moreover, he answered a hopeful strain of the 1890s by stating that in spite of the interference of barbaric capitalism, the processes of modern technology would destroy the patriarchal marriage and allow a reemergence of "the most ancient habits of thought of the race."[44]

Veblen's economics implied goals very similar to those of Bellamy's utopia, Gilman's feminist analysis and Ward's naturalistic sociology. All viewed marriage as an institution distorted by late 19th century capitalistic culture. In its distorted form, in its competitive materialism, it was an impediment to a cooperative future. While the writers of marriage manuals viewed marriage as a sacred absolute, the critics thought it had the tinges of a modern slavery. Nevertheless, they too suggested an ideal marriage at the end of evolutionary change—a relationship personal yet more responsive to community needs, romantic because freed from the man's one-sided economic dominance and responsibilities. In place of the guides' values—home, purity, social order—they cherished woman's economic independence, creative and cooperative labor, romantic love and the parental bent. They grounded these values in a naturalistic Weltanschauung rather than in a traditionally Protestant one.

Only when the repressive sexual ethic met a direct challenge, however, would the revolt against the older morality be launched. Of course, changing behavior itself was such a challenge. But ideologically the challenge, out of a naturalistic framework, was issued by a "new man" with no loyalty to the older, small-town America, to its code or its optimism. Theodore Dreiser confronted the sexual code by depicting directly its everyday violations. His first two novels, *Sister Carrie* (1900) and *Jennie Gerhardt* (1911) grew out of his sister's experiences with the civilized morality. In those works, as in his others, Dreiser painted Americans as they actually stood—unprotected in the lonely urban world. His newspaper experience had told him a great deal about the city's real values in contrast to the small-town pieties.[45] But Dreiser's first lessons began at home.

After witnessing repeated contradictions between the standard 19th century moral conventions and his sisters' escape from poverty through illicit affairs, between his father's gloomy prudery and the life of pleasure his brother, songwriter Paul Dresser, led, Theodore compounded his own naturalistic religion to replace his father's Catholicism. He came to believe that sexual love, infused with the love of natural beauty, was *the* experience initiating men and women into nature's truth. Change was the law of life, and any static institutions or ideals of respectability had to be cast aside if they stood in the way of sheer survival.[46]

In *Sister Carrie* the heroine adapted to the urban world, first by a simple, hardly considered abandonment of virginity, then by a determined struggle and finally by developing into an actress. In choosing to become Drouet's mistress, rather than remain a cold, poorly paid, worn factory-hand, Carrie was taking the first step toward survival and success, rather than toward the traditional downfall and ruin. Her second lover, Hurstwood, destroyed himself not by stealing money or committing adultery, but in a futile effort to retain his middle-class respectability.[47] Carrie knew how to fight; Hurstwood gave up. That was all. Their sexual behavior brought neither punishment nor reward. That was what was most devastating about Dreiser's portraits—his refusal to pass any condemning judgments. Carrie trading her body outside of marriage appeared not a whit more materialistic than Hurstwood's wife trading within marriage, and offering her daughter Jessica in the marriage market.

In *Jennie Gerhardt* (1911) Dreiser drew the contrast between "the grasping legality of established matrimony" and the free flow of love most clearly. Jennie was that most ancient of literary heroines, the woman in love. Full of passionate tenderness, she seemed at one with nature itself. Lester Kane, her lover, heir to a manufacturing fortune, shared a passionate communion with Jennie. But he knew he need never marry her. She was a lower-class girl and marriage was a very practical arrangement. He had hoped to escape it altogether. When business interests and his family dictated otherwise, Kane left Jennie to marry an attractive, rich widow with whom he shared social and intellectual interests. Thus Dreiser portrayed man in the natural world of feeling, a world of great depth, and yet bound to the world of convention, if unable to pay the price of defiance. The conventional world upheld that static institution—marriage—and reversed the natural value of passionate love. That was reason enough for Dreiser's contempt for convention. Jennie, alone, having lost social acceptance, her love and her child, triumphed by sheer affirmation of natural love.[48]

By the time Dreiser wrote this defiance of the marriage market, the age of new sexual standards was beginning. *Jennie Gerhardt* was a critical and popular success. Although his subsequent struggle with *The Genius* (1915) indicated that Comstockery did not die all at once, the tide had turned. Perhaps for this very reason the revolt of the 1880s and 1890s seemed excessive to the new age. Dreiser's attack upon marriage, and especially upon the class divisions marriage upheld, was not repeated, although studies confirmed that Americans continued to marry those of similar wealth and status.[49] To the postwar generation there would be something anachronistic about Gilman's feminism, although American women had not achieved anything approaching her ideal of economic independence.

Above all, the critics' implicit association between marital discontent and the inequalities of late 19th century society seemed too radical for the war and postwar generations. Did social institutions require a thoroughgoing transformation for men and women to enjoy a healthier, franker relationship? In the age of Freud the younger generation doubted it. The double standard was withering, but women were receptive to a new ideology of domesticity. Yet the radicals of the 1880s and 1890s *did* connect social transformation with true freedom for romantic love. The sexually repressive standards of Gilman and Bellamy were distinctly Victorian. But in their attacks upon the home, upon women's economic dependency and upon exaggerated sexual differentiation of roles, the critics appear to speak more to our own generation than they did to the generations that directly succeeded them.

NOTES

1. Delos S. Wilcox, *Ethical Marriage: A Discussion of the Relation of Sex from the Standpoint of Social Duty* (Ann Arbor: Wood-Allen, 1900), p. 10; see also John L. Brandt, *Marriage and the Home* (Chicago: Laird & Lee, 1892), pp. 21–22, 57.

2. Caroline Corbin, *A Woman's Philosophy of Love* (Boston: Lee, Shepard, 1893), p. 13; Minot Judson Savage, *Man, Woman, and Child* (Boston: George Ellis, 1884), pp. 64, 136–37; George McLean, *The Curtain Lifted: Hidden Secrets Revealed* (Chicago: Lewis, 1887), pp. 165–67; James Reed, *Man and Woman: Equal but Unlike* (Boston: Nichols & Noyes, 1870), *passim;* Samuel R. Wells, *Wedlock* (New York: S. R. Wells, 1871), pp. 24–25; William H. Holcombe, *The Sexes Here and Hereafter* (Philadelphia: Lippincott, 1869), p. 166; and George H. Napheys, M.D., *The Physical Life of Woman* (Philadelphia: David McKay, 1888), pp. 57–58.

3. The author is indebted to Prof. Samuel Haber of the University of California, Berkeley for this observation and for pointing out that the very existence of many choices may have popularized the phrase "marriage market."

4. Napheys, *Physical Life,* preface, p. vii. Other doctor works include Henry Hanchett, *Sexual Health* (New York: Charles Harlburt, 1887); Henry Guernsey, *Plain Talks on Avoided Subjects* (Philadelphia: F. A. Davis, 1882); and H. S.

Pomeroy, *The Ethics of Marriage* (New York: Funk & Wagnalls, 1888), commended as an anti-birth-control work in Brevard Sinclair, *The Crowning Sin of the Age* (Boston: H. L. Hastings, 1892), p. 15, and in *Journal of the American Medical Association,* 2 (1888), 309–11. Clerical works or limited edition collections of sermons used as brides' books include: S. D. & Mary Kilgore Gordon, *Quiet Talks on Home Ideals* (New York: Fleming Revell, 1909); Robert F. Horton, *On the Art of Living Together* (New York: Dodd Mead, 1896); and F. B. Meyer, *Lovers Always* (New York: Fleming Revell, 1899). Examples of second editions in marital guide-books are: Wells, *Wedlock* (c. 1869, 1871 ed.); Mrs. E. B. Duffy, *The Relations of the Sexes* (New York: M. L. Holbrook, c. 1876, 1889 ed.); and James R. Miller, D.D., *The Wedded Life* (Presbyterian Board of Publication of Philadelphia, c. 1886, 1894 ed.).

5. Brandt, *Marriage and Home,* pp. 51, 210; Wells, *Wedlock,* p. 173; and Savage, *Man, Woman, and Child,* pp. 33, 37. The same assumptions cropped up in personal correspondence concerning courtships and betrothal. For example, when Austin Baldwin of Savannah became engaged to Louise Maynard of Massachusetts, Baldwin's brother wrote: "It is . . . not the man that makes his wife, but the wife that more often makes the man and I hope my new sister will prove a good advisor and helpmate. . . . If Lou is as good as she is handsome . . . you may date your success in life from the time you were married." T. J. Baldwin to A. Baldwin, May 15, 1872, Baldwin Family Papers, Schlesinger Archives, Radcliffe College. Similarly, Emily Blackwell wrote her sister Elizabeth: "I felt a great deal depended upon the woman he married. If she had been a girl whose ambition was for society . . . it would have spoiled him. Frances will be ambitious for him to choose a worthwhile career, and will support him in any serious work. I believe she will be an excellent influence in his life." Nov. 6, 1904, Blackwell Family Papers, Schlesinger Archives, Radcliffe College.

6. Cortland Myers, *The Lost Wedding Ring* (New York: Funk & Wagnalls, 1902), pp. 100–2; Elizabeth Blackwell, *Counsel to Parents on the Moral Education of their Children* (New York: Brentano, 1883), p. 75; Charles Frederick Goss, *Husband, Wife and Home* (Philadelphia: Vir Publishing, 1905), pp. 33–34; Brandt, *Marriage,* pp. 70–71, 81–85, 85–88; and Miller, *Wedded Life,* pp. 65–67.

7. *The Marriage Ring: A Series of Discourses in Brooklyn Tabernacle* (New York: Funk & Wagnalls, 1886), p. 62. See also Savage, *Man, Woman, and Child,* p. 38; and Miller, *Wedded Life,* pp. 20–21.

8. Napheys, *Physical Life,* pp. 96, 102; Hanchett, *Sexual Health,* p. 37; Brandt, *Marriage,* pp. 80–81.

9. Talmage, *Marriage Ring,* pp. 24–25, 28–29; M. Salmonsen, *From the Marriage License Window* (Chicago: John Anderson, 1887), pp. 100, 103; Savage, *Man, Woman, and Child,* pp. 13–21; and Miller, *Wedded Life,* pp. 31–39, 42–49, 52–54 detail the masculine ideal.

10. Goss, *Husband, Wife, Homes,* pp. 50, 66–68; and Talmage, *Marriage Ring,* pp. 62–64, 66.

11. Guernsey, *Plain Talks,* p. 36; Brandt, *Marriage,* p. 111; Talmage, *Marriage Ring,* pp. 24–25; Myers, *Wedding Ring,* p. 84.

12. Frank N. Hagar, *The American Family: A Sociological Problem* (New York: University Publishing Soc., 1905), pp. 44–45.

13. McLean, *Curtain Lifted,* pp. 161–62; Kate Gannett Wells, "Why More Men Do

Not Marry," *North American Review,* 165 (July 1897), 124; George Shinn, *Friendly Talks About Marriage* (Boston: Jos. Knight, c. 1897), pp. 56–57.

14. Anthony W. Thorald, *On Marriage* (New York: Dodd Mead, 1896), p. 16; Pomeroy, *Ethics of Marriage,* p. 51; Sarah Grand, "Marriage Questions in Fiction: The Standpoint of a Typical Modern Woman," *Living Age,* 217 (Apr. 1898), 73; Corbin, *Woman's Philosophy,* pp. 38–41; Mary Wood-Allen, M.D., *What a Young Woman Ought to Know* (Philadelphia: Vir Publishing, 1893), pp. 200–4; Brandt, *Marriage,* pp. 41–42; and Wells, *Wedlock,* pp. 51–52.

15. Wilcox, *Ethical Marriage,* pp. 25–28; Thorold, *Marriage,* p. 25; Myers, *Wedding Ring,* p. 7; McLean, *Curtain Lifted,* pp. 161–62; Shinn, *Friendly Talks About Marriage,* pp. 31–32; Hagar, *American Family,* pp. 73–74; Sinclair, *Crowning Sin,* pp. 13, 17–18; and Wells, *Wedlock,* pp. 45, 47, 49.

16. Arthur Hobson Quinn, ed., *Representative American Plays* (New York: Appleton-Century, 1930) pp. 435–36, 439–40, 451, 453, 457, 465, 470; and Donald Makosky, "The Portrayal of Women in Wide Circulation Magazine Short Stories, 1905–1955," Diss. University of Pennsylvania 1966, pp. 139–40.

17. Ethel Sturgis to Francis Dummer, June 11, 1888. See also Dummer to Sturgis, Mar. 6, 1888; Mrs. Sturgis to F. Dummer, June 12, 1888; Katherine Dummer to Ethel Sturgis, June 12, 1888; and Katherine Dummer to Francis Dummer, June 12, 1888, Sturgis-Dummer Family Papers, Schlesinger Archives, Radcliffe College.

18. Emily Blackwell to Elizabeth Blackwell, Aug. 13, 1881, Oct. 2, 1881. For a contrasting view within the family see Alice Stone Blackwell to Kitty Barry Blackwell, July 23, 1882, Aug. 27, 1882, Blackwell Family Papers, Schlesinger Archives, Radcliffe College. The marriage took place nevertheless.

19. J. Bellanger, "Sexual Purity and the Double Standard," *Arena,* 11 (Feb. 1895), 373.

20. "Social Conditions as Feeders of Immorality," *Arena,* 11 (Feb. 1895), 410–11. For the way in which the purity movement shifted from an ecclesiastical to a scientific rationale for its positions, see David J. Pivar, "The New Abolitionism: The Quest for Social Purity, 1876–1900," Diss. University of Pennsylvania 1965.

21. Helen Gardiner, *Is This Your Son My Lord?* (Boston: Arena Publishing, 1890), *passim.*

22. *Freud and the Americans: The Beginnings of Psychoanalysis in the United States, 1876–1917* (New York: Oxford Univ. Press, 1971), pp. 252–54.

23. Joseph Schiffman, "Editor's Introduction," *Edward Bellamy: Selected Writings on Religion and Society* (New York: Liberal Arts Press, 1955), pp. xii–iii; Bellamy, *Dr. Heidenhoff's Process* (New York: c. 1880, Ams. Press, 1969), pp. 119–20, 138–39; Ward, "Revealed Religion and Human Progress," from *Iconoclast,* i (Nov. 1, 1870); *Glimpses of the Cosmos* (New York: Putnam, 1918), 1: 91–95; and "The Social Evil," *Iconoclast,* 2 (Aug. 1871), *Glimpses,* 1: 238–41.

24. Carl N. Degler, "Introduction to the Torchbook Edition," Gilman, *Woman and Economics* (New York: Harper & Row, 1966), pp. ix–x; Robert H. Elias, *Theodore Dreiser, Apostle of Nature* (Ithaca: Cornell Univ. Press, 1970), pp. 6, 11–13; and Henry Steele Commager, *The American Mind: An Interpretation of American Thought and Character Since the 1880's* (New Haven: Yale Univ. Press, 1959), pp. 238–39.

25. "The Religion of Solidarity" (1874) in Schiffman, *Bellamy, Religion and*

Society, pp. 15–17; Arthur E. Morgan, *Edward Bellamy* (New York: Columbia Univ. Press, 1955), p. 138.

26. Sylvia E. Bowman, *The Year 2000: A Critical Biography of Edward Bellamy* (New York: Bookman Associates, 1959), pp. 69–70, 279; and Morgan, *Edward Bellamy,* p. 55.

27. *New Nation,* 1 (Mar. 14, 1891), 110; (Apr. 4, 1891), 159.

28. *Looking Backward 2000–1887* (New York: Random House, n.d.), p. 218.

29. "Stirpiculture," *Springfield Daily Union* (Oct. 2, 1875), p. 4. The term, used by John Humphrey Noyes of the Oneida Community and briefly practiced there, meant arranged marriages to bring out the genetic strengths of the partners—the breeding of children. At the same time Bellamy was supporting "common-sense" in marriage which he occasionally identified with "like marrying like" in terms somewhat similar to those of the guides. He thought that marked class differences were accompanied by cultural differences, but he did not raise the objections of fortune hunting, etc. See "Literary Notices," *Springfield Daily Union* (Jan. 30, 1875), p. 6; and (Feb. 6, 1875), p. 6. *Looking Backward* then meant a considerable change in outlook.

30. *Equality,* 10th ed. (New York: Appleton, 1909), pp. 135–38, 140–41.

31. *An Experiment in Marriage: A Romance* (Albany: Albany Book, 1889), pp. 17, 24–25, 96–102, 116–17.

32. *New Nation,* 1 (1891), 298.

33. *The Blindman's World and Other Stories* (New York: Garrett, 1968), pp. 405–6, 408–9; papers B 2-7-10,11 quoted in Arthur E. Morgan, *The Philosophy of Edward Bellamy* (New York: Kings Crown, 1945), pp. 76–77. Bellamy's distrust of passion came early and remained with him; see Morgan, *Bellamy* (biography), p. 81.

34. "Revealed Religion and Human Progress" and "The Social Evil."

35. "Our Better Halves," *Forum,* 6 (Nov. 1888), 266–75: Speech Before the Six O'Clock Club, May 24, 1888, *Glimpses,* 4: 129: and *Dynamic Sociology* (New York: Appleton, 1883), 1: 617, 648.

36. *Our Androcentric Culture or the Man-Made World,* as serialized in *Forerunner,* 1 (Nov. 1909), 23–25; *Women and Economics,* pp. 61–63, 86–88.

37. *Women and Economics,* pp. 63–64.

38. *Dynamic Sociology,* 1: 624–26.

39. *Pure Sociology* (New York: Macmillan, 1903), pp. 381, 384, 398–99. In spite of Ward's appreciation for the importance of the sexual drive, Harriet Stanton Blatch thought he underestimated female sexuality, and even the "pretty clear physiological aim" of those mothers whom the world thought mercenary in pushing their daughters into the marriage market. Blatch to Ward, June 31, 1903, Sept. 2, 1903, Ward Collection, Brown University.

40. *Pure Sociology,* p. 398 n.; pp. 401–3.

41. *Woman and Economics,* pp. 105–7, 143, 154–57, 160; see also "All the World to Her," *Independent,* 55 (July 9, 1903), 1614 for the effects of woman receiving the world through her husband, and her overconcentration upon him.

42. "Man Made World," *Forerunner,* 1 (Dec. 1910), 22–24; (Dec. 1909), 14.

43. "The Barbarian Status of Women," *American Journal of Sociology,* 4 (Jan.

1899), 510; see also pp. 503–4 and "The Beginnings of Ownership" (Nov. 1898), pp. 364–65.

44. "Barbarian Status," p. 514. For Veblen's discussion of feminine beauty and dress in this regard see *The Theory of the Leisure Class* (New York: Modern Library, 1934), pp. 146–48, 179–82.

45. Dreiser, *Dawn* (New York: Liveright, 1931), pp. 173, 264; *A Book About Myself* (London: Constable, 1939), pp. 65–67, 70, 480, 488–89; Malcolm Cowley, "Sister Carrie Her Fall and Rise," *The Stature of Theodore Dreiser*, eds. Alfred Kazin and Charles Shapiro (Bloomington: Indiana Univ. Press, 1965), p. 174.

46. Maxwell Geismar, *Rebels and Ancestors: The American Novel, 1890–1915* (Boston: Houghton Mifflin, 1953), p. 291; John McAleer, *Theodore Dreiser: An Introduction and an Interpretation* (New York: Holt, Rinehart & Winston, 1968), pp. 34–35.

47. *Sister Carrie* (New York: New American Library, 1961), pp. 56, 61–62, 75–76, 84–88, 258, 267, 270–72, 315, 330–31, 421–22, 462.

48. *Jennie Gerhardt: A Novel* (New York: Harper, 1911), pp. 18, 128, 130, 215, 238, 313, 317, 322.

49. August Hollingshead, "Cultural Factors in Selection of Marriage Mates," in Marvin Sussman, ed., *Sourcebook in Marriage and the Family* (Cambridge: Riverside Press, 1955), pp. 43–50; and Richard Centers, "Occupational Endogamy in Marital Selection," ibid., pp. 56–61.

16 ᕲ Women in the Southern Farmers' Alliance: A Reconsideration of the Role and Status of Women in the Late Nineteenth-Century South

Julie Roy Jeffrey

In the spring of 1891, Mrs. Brown, secretary of the Menola Sub-Alliance in North Carolina, welcomed an audience of delegates to the quarterly meeting of the Hertford County Farmers' Alliance. After introductory remarks to both the women and men in the audience, Brown addressed her female listeners directly.

> Words would fail me to express to you, my Alliance sisters, my apprecia-tion of woman's opportunity of being co-workers with the brethren in the movement which is stirring this great nation. Oh, what womanly women we ought to be, for we find on every hand, fields of usefulness opening before us. Our brothers . . . are giving us grand opportunities to show them, as Frances E. Willard says, that "Drudgery, fashion and gossip are no longer the bounds of woman's Sphere."

So enthusiastically was Brown's speech received, that the County Alliance unanimously requested its publication in the official paper of the Farmers' Alliance, the *Progressive Farmer*.[1] In a similar fashion, the Failing Creek Alliance asked the *Progressive Farmer* later that year to reprint a speech Katie Moore had delivered to them. Moore had also spoken before an audience of women and men, and she too had had some special words for the women. " 'Tis not enough that we should be what our mothers were," she told them. "We should be more, since our advantages are superior. . . . This is the only order that allows us equal privileges to the men; we certainly should appre-ciate the privilege and prove to the world that we are worthy to be considered on an equal footing with them"[2]

From *Feminist Studies* 2 (Fall 1975). Reprinted by permission of the publisher, Feminist Studies, Inc., Women's Studies Program, University of Maryland, College Park, Maryland 20742. Roy Jeffrey first appeared in *Feminist Studies*, 2, no. 2/3 (Fall 1975): 72-91.

That the two audiences had approved of these speeches to the point of urging their wider circulation was not surprising. For the slogan of the Southern Farmers' Alliance itself was, "Equal rights to all, special privileges to none." As one Alliance publication explained, "The Alliance has come to redeem women from her enslaved condition, and place her in her proper sphere. She is admitted into the organization as the equal of her brother . . . the prejudice against woman's progress is being removed."[3]

Such statements about the condition of Alliance women were important, for they came from an organization which had millions of members and which was a significant force on the regional and national level in the 1880s and 1890s. In part, the Alliance was a rural protest against the inferior social, economic, and political position its members felt farmers occupied in the emerging urban-industrial society. But, like civil service reformers and other protest groups in the Gilded Age, the Farmers' Alliance argued that the finely balanced two-party system responded only to the demands of special interest groups and political machines rather than to the needs of the people. Alliance members first tried to change this situation by pressing at the state level for control of monopolies and other unfriendly interests and for favorable legislation. Better public schools for rural children, state agricultural colleges, colleges for women, laws controlling the railroads, better prices for farm products were some of the goals the Alliance sought to enable rural classes to survive within a new world. As this strategy proved frustrating, about half of the Alliance membership moved into the Populist party which ran its first presidential candidate in 1892. Although the Populist party ultimately failed, it offered the most serious challenge to the two-party system in the late nineteenth century and contributed to the reshaping of the American political system.[4]

These exhortations and demands emphasizing female equality and opportunity were important, then, because the Alliance was important, but they have an unfamiliar ring in the context of what has generally been known about sex roles and relationships in the post-Civil War South. The accepted interpretation of late nineteenth-century southern society has argued that the model of the southern lady, submissive and virtuous, "the most fascinating being in creation . . . the delight and charm of every circle she moves in," still marked the parameters of appropriate behavior for middle-class women, though the model had been predictably weakened by the traumatic experience of civil war. As for lower-class women, this interpretation suggests, they were "not much affected by role expectations," although "farmers' wives and daughters and illiterate black women . . . in some inarticulate way doubtless helped to shape [society]" and its standards.[5]

Yet an investigation of the Farmers' Alliance in North Carolina, where the Alliance had great success, indicates this explanation does not hold true for that state. If the North Carolina experience is at all typical of other southern Alliance states, and there is little reason to think it is not, the reality of southern attitudes toward women was more complex than recent analyses have allowed.[6] The Civil War had been the initial catalyst for women entering new areas of activities; after the war, poverty and loss of fathers, brothers, husbands, and other male relatives forced many women to run farms, boarding houses, to become seamstresses, postmistresses, and teachers.[7] As the traditional view of woman's sphere crumbled under the impact of the post-war conditions, at least one alternative to the older view emerged in the South—one exemplified by the case of North Carolina. Responsive to social changes stemming from war and defeat, the Alliance in the 1880s and 1890s urged women to adopt a new self-image, one that included education, economic self-sufficiency, one that made a mockery of all false ideas of gentility. The activities and behavior that the Alliance sanctioned were not only considered appropriate for middle-class women but for women on all social levels.[8] Although evidence on the social class composition of the Alliance is limited, recent work suggests that approximately 55 percent of the North Carolina membership owned their land, about 31 percent were tenants, and 14 percent rural professionals. Since many wives and daughters joined the Alliance, it seems reasonable to assume that female membership, like male membership, crossed class lines.[9] Certainly, the new female role was applicable to all of them. Finally, although it was not actually created by Alliance women, the new cultural model was consciously elaborated by some of them, thus offering one way of understanding how middle-class farming women, later deemed "inarticulate" because they left so few written records, perceived and shaped their social role.

Furthermore, a case study of the North Carolina Farmers' Alliance shows that the Alliance also offered numerous rural women the rare privilege of discussing important economic and political issues with men and of functioning as their organizational equals. Few southern institutions offered women similar opportunities. The political party barred them altogether. The Methodist and Baptist churches, which with the Presbyterian claimed a majority of church members, still supported the traditional view that women ought to remain at home although they had allowed women a new area of activity in establishing female missionary societies. This expansion of their sphere was considered to be "no compromise . . . [to] female modesty and refinement," although, in reality, women could and did acquire political experience and skills in them.[10] After 1883, North Carolina women also gained valuable organizational knowledge through their involvement in the Women's Christian Temperance Union. But the W.C.T.U., the church missionary societies and women's clubs of the 1880s were all-female organizations and thus did not offer women the chance to establish a pragmatic working relationship with men as the Alliance would do.[11]

One other rural organization in the South, the Grange, which reached its height of popularity in North Carolina between 1873 and 1875, admitted both sexes before the Alliance did so. Unlike the Alliance, however, the Grange made clear distinctions between most of the offices and ranks women and men could hold. Nevertheless, the Grange clearly provided women with some practical organizational experience with men and, presumably, offered some kind of rough equality. Still, partly because of its Northern origins, the impact of the Grange was limited in the South. In North Carolina, the Grange's total membership never surpassed the 15,000 mark, and by the 1880s, numbers had dwindled.[12] Moreover, since the Grange was primarily an educational body, it failed to provide the same kind of experience for southern women as the Alliance would in the 1880s and 1890s. Ostensibly apolitical, the Alliance was actually devoted to a discussion of the "science of economical government" and was deeply involved in political questions.[13] Within the North Carolina Alliance, the spheres of women and men drew closer as both sexes voted, held office, and discussed together the stirring issues of the day as they had rarely done before.

Within the framework of the Alliance, then, southern women had the opportunity to discuss pressing economic, political, and social questions, to try out ways of behaving in mixed groups and to gain confidence in newly acquired skills. One might expect that a group of women, and perhaps men, eventually emerged whose Alliance experiences would lead them ultimately to demand or sympathize with the greater expansion of woman's role that the organization officially supported. Yet this never happened. At the same time that the Alliance offered new roles and organizational possibilities for women, the meaning of equality for women was constricted by the organization's major goal of reviving southern agriculture. Political rights within the Alliance were not seen as the first step toward political rights outside of the Alliance. The career of the North Carolina Alliance and its inclusion of women in its membership thus offers another kind of study of the slow progress of the women's rights movement in North Carolina and perhaps gives additional clues for its uncertain course in the South as a whole.[14]

The evidence for this study comes from many sources. Most useful is the State Alliance paper, the *Progressive Farmer*,[15] whose policy it was to publish the views of the Alliance membership. Few of these rural correspondents provided the leading articles for the paper, but rather they contributed letters to the correspondence page. Since these long forgotten farm women and men left virtually no other personal records, their letters, some literary, most artless, provide a crucial insight into the grassroots level of the Alliance and an important view of their responses to the opportunities the Alliance held out to them.

Initial interest in a farmers' organization in North Carolina resulted from the depressed state of southern agriculture in the 1880s. By 1886, Colonel Leonidas Polk, editor of the new agricultural weekly, the *Progressive Farmer*, was vigorously urging the paper's readers to organize local farmers' clubs as the basis for a future state wide organization. From the beginning he visualized at least some women in the clubs, for he advised they could be "elected as honorary members." Yet farmers' clubs were not to have a long life in North Carolina. By May 1887 Alliance organizers from Texas, where the agricultural order had originated, had begun to establish local Alliances in North Carolina, while a Carolinian, J. B. Barry, also began recruiting. Polk, aware of the growth potential of the Alliance, joined one of Barry's Alliances in July 1887, and was soon meeting with Texas Alliance leaders to discuss a merger between the Alliance and his farmers' clubs. After the merger was made the North Carolina Alliance grew by leaps and bounds. In the summer of 1888 the membership stood at 42,000. By 1891 the Alliance claimed 100,000 members in over 2,000 local chapters.[16]

Requirements for membership in the Alliance, formalized in the state constitution adopted in October 1887, were far more positive to female members than Polk's farmers' clubs had been. Membership was open to rural white women and men over sixteen years of age who had a "good moral character," believed in "the existence of a Supreme Being," and showed "industrious habits." While men were to pay fifty cents as an initiation fee in addition to quarterly dues of twenty-five cents, women had no required fee or dues, no doubt a recognition of their marginal economic status and their desirablility as members.[17] Membership of both sexes was essential to Alliance goals as state Alliance president, Captain Sydenham B. Alexander, indicated. The purpose of the Alliance, Alexander wrote in 1887 was "to encourage education among the agricultural and laboring classes, and *elevate to higher manhood and womanhood* those who bear the burdens of productive industry."[18]

Alliance leaders did not leave the issue of female participation in the organization to chance but stressed it forcefully. Harry Tracy, a National Lecturer of the order, urged *"the ladies to come out and hear him,"* and warned Alliance members: "The ladies eligible must join the order before we can succeed." Despite emphatic support from the top, however, letters from local Alliances to the *Progressive Farmer*, now the official organ of the North Carolina Alliance, indicate some male resistance to the idea of female members. As the Secretary of the Davidson College Alliance explained: "I think that the ladies are best suited to home affairs." Verbal opposition to female members led one woman to comment, "They don't want us to join, and think it no place for us." Other, more subtle techniques of discouraging female membership seem to have existed. Holding meetings in places where women would be uncomfortable or feel out of place kept the number of female members down. As the correspondent from Lenoir Alliance noted, his Alliance had fifty men and one woman because meetings were held in the court house. As one frequent contributor to the *Progressive Farmer* who favored female members pointed out: "Each Sub-Alliance needs a hall. . . . We cannot urge the ladies to attend until we can seat them comfortably."[19]

Numerous questions addressed to Polk, now secretary of the state Alliance as well as editor of the *Progressive Farmer* indicated that even if not opposed to female membership, men were often hesitant and confused about the membership of women. A variety of questions focused on what women were eligible for membership and, if elected, what their rights should be. Were women, in fact, to have the same "rights and privileges of the male members"?[20] Over and over again Polk replied that women were to have equal rights and privileges; they were to vote on new members, participate in all Alliance business and to know "all the secret words and signs" of the order.[21]

If some men were unenthusiastic about female members, so too were some of the women. As one Allianceman explained: "Our female friends seem to repose great confidence in our ability to conduct the affairs of the Alliance without their direct union and assistance. Indeed, our wives, mothers and sisters have as much as they can do to attend their own business." Other letters from men more enthusiastic about female members agreed that women refused to join because they were "too modest, or think it out of their line."[22] There was even some outright female opposition to Alliance membership as one "bright and energetic young lady," the first woman to join the Alliance in Vance County, discovered when her friends ridiculed "the idea of young ladies joining."[23] The traditional view of woman's sphere, then, constituted a barrier to active female participation in the Alliance, and it was one which female members consciously tried to undermine. When Alliancewomen wrote to the *Progressive Farmer* they frequently urged the other women to overcome feelings of timidity. "Dear Sisters, go to work; don't stay home and die, then say I have something else to do; that will never do," wrote Addie Pigford. "Sisters, what are you doing?" asked Mrs. Carver. "There is work for us to do, and we shall not be found wanting. We can help in many ways, and we must do it."[24]

Opposition and hesitation on the subject of female members obviously existed as the reports of local and county Alliances and male and female correspondents to the *Progressive Farmer* show. But evidence suggests that the message that women were to be encouraged as vigorous participants of the Alliance eventually came through clearly to most local groups. By 1889, for example, the State Line Alliance reported it was planning to discuss the desirability of female members. Rather ruefully, the writer commented: "That indicates *how far we are behind*, but we do not intend to remain there."[25] Questions about membership requirements and privileges, membership breakdowns sent into the *Progressive Farmer*, and local minute books, indicate that women were presenting themselves for membership. Not only did the wives and daughters of male members join but so too did unattached women. As the Alliance grew so did the number of women in the organization. In some cases, women comprised one-third to one-half of local groups.[26] "We can work just as well as the brethren," pointed out one Alliance woman. "If we want to derive good from the Alliance, we must work in love and harmony with our fellow-man"[27]

As thousands of women responded to the Alliance's invitation to join "the great army of reform," there were hints that women felt increasingly at ease in their new organizational role. Although it is difficult to recover the perceptions of these rural women, their letters to the *Progressive Farmer* from 1887 through 1891 can serve as an imperfect measure for their thoughts and feelings about their participation in the Alliance.[28]

One of the most striking aspects of the women's correspondence is the initial hesitation about writing to a newspaper at all. Only one woman communicated to the editor in 1887. Gradually, however, women began to send letters, many of them conscious of departing from past patterns of behavior. "Being a farmer's wife, I am not in the habit of writing for the public prints," wrote the first female correspondent of 1888, a certain Mrs. Hogan who was concerned about stray dogs. Replied the second, "Mr. Editor:—I have never written anything for the public to read, but I feel just now, after reading Mrs. Hogan's trouble . . . that I want to tell her I truly sympathize with her."[29] Other correspondents in 1888 and 1889 often began their letters with the polite request for a "small space" for a few words from a farm woman or with the phrase, "I am but a female." "I suppose your many subscribers will not expect much from a female correspondent," wrote one corresponding secretary, "and if so, they will not be disappointed when they read this article, but if I can be of any service to the Alliance by putting in my little mite, I am willing to do what I can."[30] By 1890 such protestations and expressions of humility had disappeared. A series of letters from Evangeline Usher exemplifies the growing confidence on the part of women that their letters and reports on Alliance activities were appropriate and acceptable. In an early letter, Usher urged other women to write to the paper, with the typical hope that Polk would "give us a little space somewhere." Describing herself as fearful that her letter would go into the wastebasket, she further explained that her feelings of delicacy would prevent her from contributing her Alliance's news regularly. "I already imagine I see Brother 'R' smiling ludicrously at the idea." Within a few months, however, Usher wrote again, confessing "a kind of literary pride in seeing my name in print." By 1889, she could begin her letter, "I feel like I must intrude again, and as I am quite independent of all disfavor, I do not care whether you like the intrusion or not."[31] Though Usher was unusually outspoken, her growing boldness correlates with the straightforward and secure tone women gradually adopted in writing to the paper and suggests their greater feelings of confidence within the organization.[32]

Local reports, letters, and records also give information on another crucial consideration concerning women's involvement in the Alliance. If women only sat on the back benches during Alliance meetings, listening silently while men discussed the great economic and political issues of the day, their membership would have been insignificant. If, on the other hand, women actually helped to run the organization and helped contribute to its success, even if they were not equal in every respect to men, then the Alliance was an important departure from the typical southern organization.

Although there is no indication that women were ever elected to the office of president of local Alliances, they were occasionally, at least, voted into important positions. The Jamestown Alliance Minute Book, for example, records that a year after the subject of female members was first discussed, a woman was elected as assistant secretary; she declined, but two months later was elected as treasurer.[33] Other women held the office of secretary, with the responsibility not only for making "a fair record of all things necessary to be written," but also for "receiving all moneys due" and for communicating with

Secretary Polk.[34] Still others became lecturers or assistant lecturers, both crucial positions since they were to give addresses, lead discussions, and furnish "the material of thought for the future consideration of the members."[35] Women as well as men read papers "on subjects of importance for the benefit of the order." In one Alliance, records show that women conducted the business on an Alliance meeting day.[36] At the county level where meetings were held quarterly, women were included in the membership count on which representation was based, were delegates, and at least one was elected vice-president. Others gave key addresses to large audiences.[37] Women could also be found at the annual meetings of the state Alliance. As the *Progressive Farmer* warmly replied to two women who had written to ask if they could go to the meeting, "You are not only *allowed*, but you will be most cordially welcomed to a seat."[38] Though such evidence is fragmentary, it does imply that many women took an active part in running Alliance affairs.

Women's participation in the Alliance is seen in a variety of other areas too. Several letters to the *Progressive Farmer* noted that women subscribed to the State Business Agency Fund, an important Alliance effort aimed at eliminating middlemen in purchasing fertilizers, groceries, and agricultural goods. Alliance leaders urged local groups to donate at least fifty cents a member to the fund. A few reports show women carrying their financial share. Women also sent in news to the paper, wrote articles, and worked to increase the subscription list, a job which Polk and other leaders saw as vital to Alliance success since they argued that earlier efforts to arouse farmers had foundered on ignorance and lack of proper information.[39]

If not all women were active members of the Alliance, enough were to be reported and praised in the *Progressive Farmer*. Clearly, many women welcomed the chance to work in the organization. Moreover, as their letters indicate, they shared men's interest in the compelling subjects of the day: agricultural cooperation, the role of combines and trusts in creating the farming crisis, the need to diversify southern agriculture, all standard themes for discussion and instruction in Alliance meetings and reading material.[40] But as much as women were involved with such topics, as much as they enjoyed the social conviviality of the Alliance, many must have agreed with the woman who reminded her Alliance, "This is the only order that allows us equal privileges to the man; we certainly should appreciate the privilege."[41]

North Carolina Alliance's support of "equal rights" for women within the organization and of the new role described for them outside it may seem startling, yet it corresponded to the reality of life for southern women in the late 1880s and early 1890s. It would have been surprising if the changes in southern society following the Civil War had failed to result in some ideological reconsideration of women's status. Yet the Alliance's stance was not merely a response to social change in the South. The National Alliance upheld the concept of equal rights. State leaders recognized that the farmer and his wife worked as an agricultural unit. It made sense to involve both in the Alliance for as one farmer pointed out, "We know we can scarcely dispense with the labor of our wives and children on the farm."[42] Furthermore, leaders reasoned that the Alliance could not count on continued enthusiasm and good attendance unless women as well as men came to meetings. "Meetings must be interesting" to spur membership and attendance, one pamphlet pointed out, "and the first step in this direction is to get more women and young people into the Order." At least one member agreed. The presence of women, he wrote, "cheers us on." Clearly, if the Alliance and its work were to prosper, both sexes would have to be involved.[43]

The social composition of the leadership suggests another important reason for the Alliance support for women. Although men like Colonel Polk and Sydenham Alexander, president of the state Alliance, had been or were farmers genuinely concerned with agricultural problems, they were also members of the rural upper-class. Polk had had a long career as planter, army officer, legislator, commissioner of agriculture, and editor. Alexander had headed the state Grange in the 1870s. Other leaders were teachers, doctors, and clergymen.[44] As members of North Carolina's elite, these men partially accepted the traditional view of woman as the beacon of social morality. "If our organization means anything," one prominent supporter of female members wrote, "it means a moral reformation, morality must be our guide. The ladies are and always have been the great moral element in society; therefore *it is impossible to succeed without calling to our aid the greatest moral element in the country.*"[45]

This was how Alliance leaders conceived of the role and importance of women within their organization. But women themselves had their own ideas about their role, as an examination of their letters to the *Progressive Farmer* reveal. The writers stressed their pride in farm life, the need to throw off female passivity, the vital importance of women to the Alliance effort. "While it has been remarked that women are necessary evil," wrote Fannie Pentecost, "let us by our untiring energy, and zeal show them that it is a mistake. . . . We should devise plans and means by which we can assist those who have to bear the burdens of life." In the Alliance, another woman pointed out, women had the unique opportunity of helping men "in the thickest of the fight" by encouragement, prayers, self-denial, and endurance. Some correspondents clearly saw their role as one of moral support, but others visualized a more active role, using words like helpmate or companion to describe how they saw themselves.[46] One woman shaped the female role curiously: "Let us all put our shoulders to this great wheel, the Alliance. We, as sisters of this Alliance may feel we are silent factors in this work; we know we constantly need something to lean upon. . . . Let us so entwine ourselves around our brothers that *should we be taken away* they will feel they are *tottering*." Here, encouragement and support had become the vital activity for women. So, too, one woman from Fair Grove commented that women must be "ready to hold the hands of the strong, should they become weak."[47]

That women perceived themselves occasionally as the major support for men corresponds with the way in which Alliance leaders visualized them. But there was a sharp edge to the role of moral guide as some correspondence revealed. Again, Evangeline Usher provides an insight into this kind of thinking. In a letter of September 1890, Usher wrote that someone had recently sent her a compliment, "saying they were just as strong as Alliance boy as I was an Alliance girl." Evangeline's rather surprising comment was "Brother . . . I only hope you are, for I am one that believes in working and not talking." Other letters and articles convey a similar scepticism of men. "Why," asked assistant lecturer Lizzie Marshburn, "is it that the farmer and laboring class generally, have got no self-will or resolution of their own? . . . as a general rule they have been ever ready to link their destinies with any political aspirant who can get up and deliver a flowerly address of misrepresentation." Allie Marsh told her audience at a Randolph County meeting, "We come to these meetings with an unwritten agreement to take things as they are." Women, she said, were "perfectly content" that men exercise political rights "as long as you are vigilant in making [the ballot box] as efficient as possible." Yet the remainder of her speech suggested that she had found the men "wanting." A letter from still another woman acidly observed, "Some men can't see beyond their nose."[48]

Although most women and men probably agreed upon the function of women's participation within the Alliance, it appears that some Alliance women saw the matter differently and that they suspected that the commonly accepted view of women as the quiet impetus behind male reformers was inadequate. Their letters convey misgivings about the ability of men to persist in their support of reform and implicitly suggest that these women perceived themselves as steadier leaders than the men. As one Alliance woman explained: "My sisters, this is something we should know, that our names are on this list [of reformers] and [we should] regret we could not be allowed this opportunity years ago, for no doubt our country would be in a much better condition to-day had we taken this step." Added another, apparently filled with misgivings about men: "I would earnestly *beg the brethren* when they put their hands to the plow *not to look back . . . if they do,* they will not reap the harvest we all desire. *We must work* and *wait,* and not grow discouraged."[49] Yet, despite these indications that women suspected that they rather than men were possibly the most steadfast and reliable leaders of reform, they were hardly ready to challenge openly the Alliance's basic assumptions because of the positive support the Alliance was already providing for southern women in many areas of life.

Indeed, women's rights within the organization was only part of the Alliance's reformulation of women's status. A woman's role in the Alliance was understood to parallel the more significant role the Alliance suggested women could enjoy in society at large. The *Progressive Farmer's* policy of reporting on the achievements of women who were doctors, surgeons, journalists, lawyers, government workers, even pastors, indicated the wide range of possibilities beyond the conventional one of marriage and motherhood.[50] These career options, of course, depended on educating women, a goal that the Alliance and its official newspaper consistently supported as part of the general attempt to improve all educational facilities for "farmers and laborers."[51]

"The ability of girls," the *Progressive Farmer* stated flatly, "has been found equal to that of boys." As the resolutions of the 1890 State Alliance meeting show, the Alliance went on record that year not only in favor of public schools for boys and girls but also in support of "ample [state] appropriations [for] the training and higher education of females." The paper explained, "The lopsided system of education in North Carolina . . . provides for the education of men and neglects that of women. Gentlemanly instinct, to say nothing of justice and mercy, requires that women should be given as good a chance for education as men possess. . . . Give the noble girls of the State—those who are not able to go to our expensive colleges a chance to get an education," the paper urged. Responding to pressure from the Alliance and other interested groups, the legislature of 1891 appropriated $10,000 a year to establish a normal and industrial training school for girls.[52]

The reason for the Alliance's concern with women's education becomes obvious in the *Progressive Farmer's* discussions of private girls' schools. Traditionally, these schools had stressed teaching female accomplishments to the would-be southern lady of means. But now, the *Progressive Farmer* enthusiastically reported, Salem Female Academy had expanded its offering by establishing a business course featuring music, telegraphy, phonography (shorthand), typing and bookkeeping. Such a course, the *Progressive Farmer* pointed out, was most desirable with its "studies of a practical character, fitting the learners for active avocations when required to depend upon their own efforts in the battle of life." Other schools, the paper urged, ought to follow Salem Academy's example. The fundamental point, the paper emphasized, was that *all* young women of *all* social classes should be prepared for jobs. It was true, of course, that education would help poor girls by enabling them "to make an honest living," but all women ought to learn to be self-sufficient and self-supporting.[53]

Women themselves stressed the importance of economic self-sufficiency. They did not want to "be entirely dependent upon the bounties of others" if they lost their protectors. And, as an additional point in favor of education, one Alliance woman brought up the important question of marriage. Self-sufficiency would allow women to marry because they wanted to, not because they needed financial support. Thus education of a certain kind would help women avoid the "fatal blunder," incompatibility in marriage.[54]

Alliance support for practical education for women was based on a rejection of the concept of gentility which had been such a fundamental component of the idea of the southern lady.[55] The search for a "pale and delicate" complexion, the interest in elaborate clothing and accomplishments were all denounced in the pages of the *Progressive Farmer*. These traditional female concerns were misguided since they undermined the importance of hard work and, thus, the opportunities for female independence. The idea that labor was degrading, the *Progressive Farmer* reminded its readers, was just another unfortunate remnant of slavery, and, in fact, contributed in an important way to poverty itself. True Alliance men and women wanted young people "to see that it is no disgrace, but a high honor, to know how to work and to be able to do it." The feminine ideal was the woman who was independent and practical, educated either to support herself or to marry wisely.[56]

Better education for both sexes was an issue with which many Alliance members sympathized, hoping their children's future would be more promising than their own. Yet the Alliance could not concern itself exclusively with the new options for young women who still had their lives ahead of them. With so many adult female members, the Alliance also considered how to reshape life styles for those women who would never leave the farm for school or a job. "Is the life of the Farmer's wife under present systems, calculated to give her virtue and intelligence full play?" asked the Southern Alliance paper, the *National Economist*. "Is she not a slave and a drudge in many cases?" The

Progressive Farmer gave the answer: there were "thousands and tens of thousands" of farmers' wives "worked to their graves."[57] Improving this dreary situation necessitated a multipronged approach. First, the paper's scientific articles on housekeeping and cooking could show the farmwife how to lighten her work load. Then, too, her husband was to be prodded into helping her out. As one correspondent to the *Progressive Farmer* explained, men needed tough words. "Our Lecturer, in trying to discuss the social feature [of the Alliance], handles husbands quite roughly, but it is received in the proper spirit. If country life is ever made more attractive, there must be more congeniality in spirit and aggressiveness between the one that follows the plow handles and the one of all beings earthly that acts as a helpmeet to man." What were "the conveniences for the good and faithful wife?" asked Colonel Polk. How far did she have to walk to the woodpile or the spring? Had the bloom on her cheeks faded prematurely? These were the subjects, he urged, that ought to be discussed in Alliance circles so that "new life, new energy, new action . . . and new views of life and living" might emerge for both sexes.[58]

The Alliance's concern with helping hard working farmwomen fused with the order's major objective, the overall improvement of agricultural life. To this end, the Alliance sought to discover "a remedy for every evil known to exist and afflict farmers and other producers."[59] The remedy of improved farming methods was especially important as the number of articles in the *Progressive Farmer* attest. The paper argued that the one-crop system was the obvious and basic cause of the state's agricultural depression. Over and over again, the paper and Alliance meetings focused on the need to farm properly and to stay out of debt. Consider the two kinds of farmers, the *Progressive Farmer* urged. One raised cotton on his land, bought milk, bread, hay and fertilizers on credit. The other chose the Alliance route and would prosper. And "his wife, dear devoted woman, instead of wearing out her life in cooking for a lot of negroes to work cotton, has time to look after the adornment and the beautifying of her home, to attend to her milk and butter, eggs, garden, bees, chickens and other poultry, and with all this they have a little time to spare socially with their neighbors and to go to church."[60]

The *Progressive Farmer* might describe the tasks of the wise farmer's wife enthusiastically, but the list of her activities highlights a crucial problem in the Alliance's approach to women. Although the Alliance supported expanding women's rights and privileges, its overall objective was to put farmers on an economic, social, and political parity with other occupations. To do so, or to try to do so, had definite implications for women's lives and shaped the Alliance's conception of equality. If the home was to be made attractive enough to discourage children from abandoning farm life, if it was to be "a place of rest, of comfort, of social refinement and domestic pleasure," then women would have to make it so.[61] If the farm was to stay out of debt, if the farmer was to remain free of the supply merchant by raising as many of his necessities as he could, his wife must help. Woman's "judgement and skill in management may be essential to the success of her husband," one article reminded Alliance readers. "And this responsibility . . . continues to the close of her life."[62]

The Alliance proposed a position for women that embodied an equality of sorts, the economic equality of a diligent coworker. In its recognition of the importance and difficulty of woman's work, the role model differed from that of the southern lady. Nor did the model merely update the characters of the yeoman farmer's family. The Alliance's concern with diversifying southern agriculture, with eliminating the disastrous dependency on the one-crop system, was not an attempt to recreate the small farm and agricultural myth of an idealized past but to create a new kind of farm and a new cast of characters. Agricultural reform, in fact, was seen as part of a modernizing process, and it was favored not only by the Alliance but also by leaders of the New South movement. Spokesmen for each group agreed that the South had to end its colonial status both through substantial industrial growth and through agricultural diversification.[63]

But what were the implications of such a view for women? "The housewife, who, by her industry, transforms the milk from her dairy into butter . . . is as truly a manufacturer as the most purse-proud mill-owner of Britain," explained the *National Economist*. Labeled manufacturers or helpmates, women were to carry a heavy burden in creating the new order.[64] The truth was that even though the Alliance talked of a variety of opportunities available for women, most women in North Carolina would continue to live on the farm, and Alliance leaders thought this right in terms of the world they wished to create. Farm women were important for they would share in the task of restoring agriculture to its rightful position in the economy. Even the Alliance's interest in women's education was partially tied to this goal. If women were to become efficient, modern coworkers in the task of agricultural reconstruction, they needed an education. As Polk explained: "The great and imperative need of our people and our time, is the practical education of the masses. . . . It will be a glorious day for the South when her young ladies, educated in all the higher and refined arts of life, shall boast and without blushing of equal proficiency in the management of the household and the flower-garden."[65]

Moreover, women needed to be educated so that, in turn, they could teach Alliance children, first at home and then at school. Rural children, many Alliance members were convinced, needed a special kind of education, one that embraced "the moral, physical and industrial, as well as the mental training of our children." By providing such an education, women could offer an "invaluable service." For "this system will strengthen the attachment of these classes [to agricultural life] instead of alienating [them] from it . . . it will better qualify them for success and happiness in life . . . increase the opportunity and inclination to adorn the home and practice the social virtues."[66]

Other pragmatic considerations led to the support of women's education. Education could provide poor girls with the opportunity "to make an honest living." Most, but not all, women would marry. To prepare for the possibility of spinsterhood, every careful mother must see not only that daughters were trained in their domestic and spiritual responsibilities, but would also "have them taught a trade or profession and thus equip them fully to 'face the world' if this need shall come to them."[67] No one, not even a woman, ought to be an economic drain on the others. Teaching provided one means of support. So too would factory work, which the Alliance leaders, like spokesmen of the New South movement, hoped would be a growing field of employment. North Carolina's piedmont region, the *Progressive Farmer* enthusiastically suggested, should be covered with factories. "Then we could have money because our boys and girls and women who are now consumers would find constant, honorable and remunerative employment and would thus become self-supporting." Women not only had the option but, indeed, the duty of being self-supporting and of adding "to the general wealth of the place." The more educated and useful women became, "the better for them and for our State."[68]

The part that the Alliance encouraged women to play in southern life was more expansive than the traditional role of the southern lady at the same time that it had definite limitations. Women need no longer cultivate the appearance of genteel passivity; they required education as the preparation for a useful life. But the Alliance defined utility in terms of the organization's over-all objectives, the profitability of agriculture, the prosperity of the state. Thus, it was vital that women learn to be skilled managers or teachers. Whether spinsters or widows, women must never be parasites on their families or on their state. Beneath the rhetoric, the lifestyle the Alliance supported for women was one of constant hard work and low wages, if women were to be paid for their labor at all. These limitations, harsh though they seem, were realistic both in terms of the Alliance's major goals and in terms of available options in the South. As one northern observer testified, "There is yet no rapid development of opportunity for profitable labor for young white women in the South."[69]

There may be yet another reason for the contradictory meaning of equality that the Alliance proposed for women. Despite the support the Alliance gave to an expanded life style for women, Alliance leaders were affected by the circumstances of time, place, and class. Like other well-born Southerners, they had not rejected the traditional view of women as the source of morality and goodness. Because of their moral qualities, women had to participate in the Alliance, but it is doubtful whether North Carolina Alliance leaders would have supported enlarging women's sphere in any way that might threaten their own social or political position.[70]

As the *Progressive Farmer* firmly acknowledged, it had no sympathy with "that spirit which could encourage class feeling or class prejudice. . . . It is . . . *subversive of the social order*."[71] Leaders wanted changes, but not at the expense of social stability. Thus women might share in a kind of social and economic equality with men but they would hardly be offered political rights.

There are few indications that this strategy was unacceptable to the majority of Alliance women. Most letters from women indicate that the new parameters for female behavior were thankfully welcomed. Only occasionally can one discern an undercurrent of unrest, when women remarked on men's failure to be vigorous Alliance fighters or when they pointed out how much better a place the world would be had women, long ago, taken a more active part in shaping it.[72] Then, too, a few women dared to write on political matters, giving their own opinions and urging men to take notice.[73] At least one woman realized how far she had stepped out of her place. After mocking Alliance men who were "willing to wave Alliance principles and swallow the whole Democratic party," she observed, "I could say a good deal more on this line, but will stop, for fear some fool will ask: 'Are you a woman?'"[74]

The *Progressive Farmer* not surprisingly steered away from the explosive issue of women's participation in politics.[75] In two unusual references to the question of women's political rights, however, it is clear that the issue had come up in local meetings. At one county rally, the lecturer told the women, "He did not invite them to suffrage, though it was gaining rapidly in public favor and if they had the ballot they would drive out the liquor traffic of this country and other evils." In Almance County, the Alliance lecturer warned his female listeners, "Do not spend your time in longing for opportunities that will never come, but be contented in the sphere the Lord hath placed you in. If the Lord had intended you for a preacher or lawyer He would have given you a pair of pantaloons."[76]

But the desire to maintain the *status quo* did not automatically succeed. Though Alliance leaders delineated definite boundaries to the theoretical and actual position women might occupy in the world, the fact that suffrage was mentioned at all may indicate a turbid undercurrent of half conscious challenge to the leadership. The way the two Alliance speakers spoke of the suffrage issue suggests that some Alliance circles had discussed it. A few letters to the *Progressive Farmer* and other fragmentary evidence point to the same conclusion. On a visit to North Carolina in 1893, for example, a Mrs. Virginia Durant who had established a suffrage organization in South Carolina, reported she found "suffrage sentiment" of an unfocused kind in the state. Perhaps she sensed incipient interest among those women exposed to the Alliance.[77]

Yet there is not enough evidence to resolve the issue. If there were some support for the further expansion of women's activities through the Alliance, however, it never had the time to grow strong and vocal. For although the Alliance lingered on into the twentieth century, by the mid-1890s it had ceased to be an institution of importance. The failure of Alliance cooperative economic ventures, continued hard times, and a split within the organization over the support of the Populist party all contributed to a decline in membership. A changing political ·climate brought new issues, new questions to the fore; many of them would have conservative implications.[78] By the end of the decade, the shape of southern life would be set. After the Populist challenge, franchise for both poor whites and blacks would be limited and the question of political participation closed. Voting was a privilege, not a right. "Equal rights for all, special privileges for none" was a slogan best forgotten.[79]

Though the Alliance did not survive long enough to dislodge the traditional ideas of woman's sphere, its spirited attempt to work out a new place for her both in theory and practice shows greater complexity in late nineteenth-century attitudes and behavior with respect to sex roles than previously recognized, and suggests that there may have been other attempts to create new roles for women in the South. The Alliance alternative, it is true, fell short of offering women equality in all spheres of life. Primary Alliance goals and the nature of the leadership limited the meaning of equal rights for women. Yet to expect the Alliance to propose full equality for women would be to ignore the influence of both time and place and to expect consistency of thought and action when such consistency rarely exists.

NOTES

1. *Progressive Farmer*, June 23, April 21, 1891.

2. *Progressive Farmer*, December 22, 1891.

3. Nelson A. Dunning, ed., *The Farmer's Alliance History and Agricultural Digest* (Washington: The Alliance Publishing Co., 1891), pp. 309-310. See also *National Economist*, June 6, 1891.

4. For general information on the Alliance see John D. Hicks, *The Populist Revolt: A History of the Farmers' Alliance and the People's Party* (Minneapolis: University of Minnesota Press, 1931), pp. 105, 146; Theodore Saloutos, *Farmer Movements in the South: 1865-1933* (Berkeley: University of California Press, 1960), pp. 85, 123, 282-83; Hugh Talmage Lefler and Albert Ray Newsome, *The History of A Southern State: North Carolina* (Chapel Hill: University of North Carolina Press, 1963), p. 513; John M. Dobson, *Politics in the Gilded Age: A New Perspective on Reform* (New York: Praeger, 1972), pp. 172-75, 183-86.

5. Quoted in Anne Firor Scott, *The Southern Lady: From Pedestal to Politics, 1830-1930* (Chicago: University of Chicago Press, 1970), pp. 4-5, x-xi, and Anne Firor Scott, "Women's Perspective on the Patriarchy in the 1850s," *Journal of American History* 61 (June 1974): 54, note 4.

6. Other areas in the South were more radical in their views about women than North Carolina. See *National Economist*, May 4, May 25, September 1, 1889; March 1, June 14, July 12, July 26, October 25, 1890; June 6, July 25, November 12, 1892. See also Annie L. Diggs, "The Women in the Alliance Movement," *The Arena* 6 (June 1892): 163; Dunning, *Farmer's Alliance*, pp. 308-309; A. D. Mayo, "Southern Women in the Recent Educational Movement in the South," *Bureau of Education Circular of Information*, no. 1 (Washington, D.C.: G.P.O., 1892), pp. 54, 124; Josephine K. Henry, "The New Woman of the New South," *The Arena* 11 (February 1895): 353-62; Saloutos, *Farmer Movements*, chapters 5-7.

7. Scott, *Southern Lady*, chapters 4 and 5.

8. Robert Carroll McMath, Jr., "The Farmer's Alliance in the South: The Career of an Agrarian Institution" (Ph.D. dissertation, University of North Carolina at Chapel Hill, 1972), pp. 88-89; Robert Carroll McMath, Jr., "Agrarian Protest at the Forks of the Creek: Three Subordinate Farmers' Alliances in North Carolina," *The North Carolina Historical Review* 51 (January 1974): 47; Philip Roy Muller, "New South Populism: North Carolina, 1884-1900," (Ph.D. dissertation, University of North Carolina at Chapel Hill, 1971), pp. 33-37, 148-54.

9. McMath, "Farmers' Alliance," pp. 88-89.

10. Quoted in Hunter Dickinson Farish, *The Circuit Rider Dismounts: A Social History of Southern Methodism, 1865-1900* (Richmond: Dietz Press, 1938), pp. 327, 325-26; Scott, *Southern Lady*, pp. 137-41; Anne Firor Scott, "Women, Religion and Social Change in the South, 1830-1930, in *Religion and the Solid South*, ed., Samuel S. Hill, Jr. (Nashville: Abingdon Press, 1972), pp. 93-115; Marjorie Stratford Mendenhall, "Southern Women of a 'Lost Generation,' " *South Atlantic Quarterly* 33 (October 1937): 339-41; Emory Stevens Bucke, ed., *The History of American Methodism* (Nashville: Abingdon Press, 1964), vol. 2, pp. 291-92.

11. Daniel J. Whitener, *Prohibition in North Carolina, 1715–1935* (Chapel Hill: University of North Carolina Press, 1945), pp. 104–105; Scott, *Southern Lady*, pp. 139–52. Men were admitted as honorary members to the W. C. T. U. Another organization that included both women and men was the International Order of The King's Daughters and Sons, established in 1886. As in the W. C. T. U., men played little part in the organizational activities of the charitable group. Easdale Shaw, *The History of the North Carolina Branch of the International Order of The King's Daughters and Sons* (Raleigh: Capital Printing Co., 1929), pp. 3–4.

12. Solon Justus Buck, *The Granger Movement: A Study of Agricultural Organization and Its Political, Economic and Social Manifestations: 1870–1880* (Cambridge: Harvard University Press, 1913), pp. 41–43, 381; Saloutos, *Farmer Movements*, pp. 30–33, 42; Stuart Noblin, *The Grange in North Carolina 1929–1954: A Story of Agricultural Progress* (Greensboro: The North Carolina State Grange, 1954), pp. 2, 3.

13. Saloutos, *Farmer Movements*, pp. 32, 42; Roy V. Scott, *The Reluctant Farmer: The Rise of Agricultural Extension to 1914* (Urbana: University of Illinois Press, 1970), pp. 42–46; *National Economist*, March 14, 1889, June 7, 1890; *Progressive Farmer*, December 1, 1887, January 28, 1890. In 1889, the North Carolina State Alliance decided all political demands were to be sent to local Alliances for their approval. See "Official Circular No. 6," May 27, 1892, John R. Osborne Papers, Duke University, where Alliance secretaries are ordered to present the State Alliance resolution in favor of a secret ballot to their Sub-Alliances "for discussion and ratification."

14. In other parts of the country, the Alliance did radicalize some women and men. O. Gene Clanton, *Kansas Populists: Ideas and Men* (Lawrence: University of Kansas Press, 1969), *passim*. But for the story of the slow-moving suffrage campaign in North Carolina, see A. Elizabeth Taylor, "The Woman Suffrage Movement in North Carolina," *The North Carolina Historical Review* 38 (January and April 1961): 45–62, 173–89; Virginius Dabney, *Liberalism in the South* (Chapel Hill: University of North Carolina Press, 1932), chapter 19.

15. Although major Alliance manuscript collections and records were utilized for this study, the most useful source for it was the official newspaper of the North Carolina Alliance, the *Progressive Farmer*. The weekly paper served as one of the major means of communication between the state Alliance and local and county groups, publishing reports, orders, and instructions for Alliance members and, in turn, including letters and reports from the membership. Its paid circulation, the largest of any North Carolina newspaper of the time, had reached 18,240 by 1891. Actually, the paper reached more readers than this figure indicates since it was passed on and often read aloud at Alliance meetings. See McMath, "The Farmers' Alliance," pp. 200–204; Stuart Noblin, *Leonidas LaFayette Polk: Agrarian Crusader* (Chapel Hill: University of North Carolina Press, 1949), p. 210. Letters and articles for 1886, the year before the Alliance officially adopted the paper are also used since they do not differ in content or tone from what was published later. The *Progressive Farmer* is the best source for this study of Alliance thought and practice not only because of its central role in disseminating and reflecting Alliance views, but because local Alliance records are skimpy, leaders were often concerned with the "major" issues, and few of the women and men left any lasting remains at all aside from their letters to the paper. The *National Economist*, official journal of the Southern Alliance between 1889 and 1893,

also proved helpful as a supplement and contrast to the *Progressive Farmer*, as did other Alliance books and pamphlets.

16. *Progressive Farmer*, March 31, 1886; McMath, "Farmers' Alliance," pp. 82–83; John D. Hicks, "The Farmers' Alliance in North Carolina," *The North Carolina Historical Review* 2 (April 1925): 169. It is difficult precisely to estimate membership in the Southern Alliance or its North Carolina branch. The organization claimed a total membership of 362,970 in July 1888, just a year after recruiting began. Of these, 42,496 or 12 percent were women. By 1890, the Alliance reported it had 3,000,000 members, a figure that some believe was inflated (Saloutos, *Farmer Movements*, p. 77). In North Carolina, the Farmers' Alliance *Daybook*, North Carolina State Archives, Raleigh, notes that the number of local Alliances had reached 2,000 in February 1890. See also *Minutes* of the Farmers' State Alliance, 1887–1893, August 14, 1888, North Carolina State Archives, Raleigh; McMath, "Farmers' Alliance," p. 139.

17. *Minutes*, Farmers' State Alliance, October 4, 1887, August 16, 1888.

18. Reprinted in *Progressive Farmer*, December 8, 1887; my italics.

19. *Progressive Farmer*, July 9, 1889, February 25, 1890, June 23, 1891. *The Sub Alliance and What It Can Accomplish: Report of the Program Committee of the North Carolina Farmers State Alliance* (no date, North Carolina State Archives, Raleigh) emphatically makes the point that female membership is a necessity. See also *Progressive Farmer*, June 11, 1889; July 10, May 22, 1888; July 30, 1889; February 25, 1890; April 8, 1890; June 25, 1889.

20. *Progressive Farmer*, December 18, June 12, December 4, June 12, July 24, 1888, May 14, 1889.

21. Ibid.; also *Progressive Farmer*, March 13, 1888, March 5, 1889.

22. *Progressive Farmer*, May 22, 1888; October 7, 1890. See also July 30, August 6, 1889, September 23, October 7, 1890.

23. *Progressive Farmer*, February 18, 1890, April 17, 1888.

24. *Progressive Farmer*, December 16, March 25, 1890. See also July 24, 1888, June 11, August 6, October 1, 1889; February 11, September 23, 1890; September 22, December 22, 1890; *National Economist*, June 6, 1891. Of course, men were also encouraged to be more vigorous in their support of the Alliance.

25. *Progressive Farmer*, June 11, November 19, 1889.

26. For membership ratios, see the Bethany Alliance Minute Book, John R. Osborne Papers, Duke University, Jamestown Alliance Minute Book, Duke University, and the Mt. Sylvan Alliance Minute Book, North Carolina State Archives, Raleigh. See also the Account Book of Wake City Alliance, Roll Book of L. L. Polk, Sub Alliance No. 2254, Wake County, Polk Papers, in the Southern Historical Collection, University of North Carolina Library, Chapel Hill, and the *Progressive Farmer, passim*. The Wake County Alliance Account Book, which gives membership figures for about 45 local Alliances in that County, indicates that 36 percent of the County's membership in September 1890 were women. A year later this percentage of women had risen to 38 percent.

27. *Progressive Farmer*, February 11, 1890; August 7, May 15, December 11, 1888; August 13, 1889.

28. *Progressive Farmer*, March 10, 1891. There is, of course, the possibility that any woman writing to the newspaper was atypical.

29. *Progressive Farmer*, January 19, 1887; February 16, March 13, 1888.

30. *Progressive Farmer*, April 16, April 30, 1889; October 1, 1889.

31. *Progressive Farmer*, July 24, December 11, 1888; September 23, 1889; see also her letter of March 19, 1889, and February 25, 1890. Interestingly enough, Polk saved a letter from Usher that can be found in his papers. Evangeline Usher to L. L. Polk, December 25, 1889, Polk Papers, in the Southern Historical Collection, University of North Carolina Library, Chapel Hill.

32. A letter from a Kansas woman, Mrs. S. V. P. Johnson to L. L. Polk, April 1, 1892, Polk Papers, in the Southern Historical Collection, University of North Carolina Library, Chapel Hill discusses in detail the difficulties of throwing off female hesitancy, the opportunities she felt the Alliance offered her, and her lack of confidence.

33. Jamestown Alliance Minute Book. She subsequently left this office. "Organizers Report," November 13, 1889, Polk Papers, in the Southern Historical Collection, University of North Carolina Library, Chapel Hill, notes Mrs. J. M. E. Midget as treasurer. Unfortunately, inadequate records make it impossible to discover how many women held office. There are enough casual references to women in office, however, to suggest that female office holders were not unusual.

34. *National Farmers' Alliance and Industrial Union Ritual* (Washington, D.C.: National Economist Publishing Co., 1891). *Progressive Farmer*, May 28, October 1, 1889; September 23, October 7, 1890.

35. *Ritual; Progressive Farmer*, August 6, September 24, 1889. President Alexander stressed the crucial importance of the lecturer's position in characterizing it as "more important than any of the others" (*Minutes*, Farmers' State Alliance, August 13, 1889).

36. *Progressive Farmer*, September 11, 1888; March 31, December 22, 1891.

37. *Progressive Farmer*, June 23, 1891; July 17, October 23, 1888; April 21, 1891. There was clearly some confusion about counting women for representation. W. M. Koonts, secretary of the Davidson County Alliance, wrote to the Bethany Alliance secretary, "You are only entitled to delegates for the *male* members clear on the books." But the previous year Polk, in answer to a question on this very point, had announced that both sexes were to be counted (S. M. Koonts, to John R. Osborne, December 27, 1889, John R. Osborne papers, Duke University, *Progressive Farmer*, July 17, 1888.

38. *Progressive Farmer*, July 9, 1889.

39. "Circular No. 3, North Carolina Farmers' Alliance Business Agency Fund," November 22, 1890, Richard Street Papers, North Carolina State Archives, Raleigh; *Progressive Farmer*, August 13, 1889, July 24, 1888, September 8, 1887; S.B. Alexander to L. L. Polk, November 14, 1885, Polk Papers, Southern Historical Collection, University of North Carolina Library, Chapel Hill; *Progressive Farmer*, May 28, October 1, 1889; Circular, "Important to Sub-Alliances: Please Read at Next Meeting," L. Polk Denmark Collection, North Carolina State Archives, Raleigh.

40. Women reported on crop information and expressed interest in a wide variety of subjects. See *Progressive Farmer*, August 14, November 6, 1888; February 26, April 30, July 9, 1889 for examples.

41. *Progressive Farmer*, December 22, 1891.

42. *Progressive Farmer*, September 11, 1888.

43. *Progressive Farmer*, June 25, 1889. For a similar view, but from Texas, see *National Economist*, September 1, 1889. *The Sub-Alliance and What It Can Accomplish*, pp. 3, 4; *National Economist*, June 7, 1890; *Progressive Farmer*, June 11, 1889.

44. See Noblin, *Polk, passim*; Noblin, *The Grange*, p. 3; McMath, "Farmers' Alliance," pp. 84–88; Muller, "New South Populism," pp. 33–37, 148–54.

45. *Progressive Farmer*, July 9, 1889; March 31, 1891; June 25, 1889; November 12, 1888. The Pleasant Garden Alliance Minute Book, William D. Hardin Papers, Duke University, shows the importance members attributed to moral and orderly conduct at meetings. *Progressive Farmer*, March 24, 1891.

46. *Progressive Farmer*, June 11, 1889; June 23, 1891; for similar views from other southern women, see *National Economist*, July 12, July 26, 1889; October 25, 1890; July 25, 1891.

47. *Progressive Farmer*, July 24, 1888, my italics; *Progressive Farmer*, June 4, 1889.

48. *Progressive Farmer*, September 23, 1890; September 24, 1889; January 22, 1889; February 25, 1890.

49. *Progressive Farmer*, September 22, 1891; December 10, 1889, my italics.

50. These items are generally given without any editorial comments, as were the other items of general interest. For examples, see *Progressive Farmer*, May 18, July 21, October 29, November 17, 1886; February 2, May 8, June 12, July 3, November 6, 1888; August 20, 1889.

51 *Progressive Farmer*, November 10, 1887.

52. *Progressive Farmer*, February 10, 1891; *Minutes*, Farmers' State Alliance, August 14, 1890; *Progressive Farmer*, January 20, 1891 and August 19, 1890; February 18, 1889; Virginia Terrell Lathrop, *Educate a Woman: Fifty Years of Life at the Woman's College of the University of North Carolina* (Chapel Hill: University of North Carolina Press, 1942), pp. xi–xiii.

53. *Progressive Farmer*, June 19, 1888, June 23, 1887, January 12, 1888; February 19, 1889. The objectives of the Normal and Industrial School for girls were "(1) to give young women such education as shall fit them to teach; (2) to give instruction in drawing, telegraphy, typewriting, stenography, and such other arts as may be suitable to their sex and conducive to their usefulness." (quoted in Lathrop, *Educate a Woman*, p. xii).

54. *Progressive Farmer*, June 25, 1889; December 16, 1890.

55. Scott, *Southern Lady*, pp. 4–8.

56. *Progressive Farmer*, March 10, June 30, 1886; April 21, 1887; February 26, June 11, 1889; July 7, February 10, 1886; February 2, 1887; November 20, 1888; September 4, 1888; March 24, 1886.

57. *National Economist*, May 4, 1889. See also W. Scott Morgan, *History of the Wheel and Alliance and the Impending Revolution* (Fort Scott: J. H. Rice & Sons, 1889), pp. 197–99; *Progressive Farmer*, June 2, 1886; September 4, 1888.

58. *Progressive Farmer*, January 19, 1887; June 30, 1886; June 5, 1888; February 28, 1888; December 8, 1886. For another southern view, see *National Economist*, June 14, 1890.

59. Dunning, *The Farmers' Alliance*, p. 257; Saloutos, *Farmer Movements*, p. 85.

60. *Progressive Farmer*, March 26, 1889.

61. *Progressive Farmer*, March 10, April 21, 1886. See *National Economist*, May 25, 1889, in which one of the Alabama Alliance's goals is to "adorn and beautify our homes, and render farm life more attractive."

62. *Progressive Farmer*, January 19, 1887; June 2, 1886; May 28, 1889; May 5, 1887. See also *The Sub-Alliance and What It Can Accomplish*, p. 6.

63. Richard H. Abbott, "The Agricultural Press Views the Yeoman: 1819-1859," *Agricultural History* 42 (January 1968): 35-48, suggests that historians have over-estimated the importance of the myth of the yeoman farmer. See also, Muller, "New South Populism," p. 23; Paul M. Gaston, *The New South Creed: A Study in Southern Mythmaking* (New York: Alfred A. Knopf, 1970), pp. 64-68, 107-108.

64. *National Economist*, April 5, 1889.

65. *Progressive Farmer*, January 12, 1888; May 12, July 7, October 13, 1886; September 15, 1887; November 20, 1888.

66. *Progressive Farmer*, November 10, 1887; *Minutes*, Farmers' State Alliance, August 11, 1892; *Progressive Farmer*, February 19, 1889.

67. *Progressive Farmer*, July 2, and April 21, 1887.

68. *Progressive Farmer*, March 2, 1887; December 8, 1886; July 28, 1887; December 3, 1889.

69. Mayo, "Southern Women," p. 170.

70. As Muller, "New South Populism," notes, p. 149, only men qualified as members of the elite.

71. *Progressive Farmer*, February 2, 1888. See Muller, "New South Populism," pp. 56-57, 177-85, for discussions of the social conservatism of Alliance leaders, pp. 104-105.

72. *Progressive Farmer*, September 22, 1891.

73. *Progressive Farmer*, June 3, September 16, December 23, 1890; July 7, December 15, 1891.

74. *Progressive Farmer*, November 4, 1890.

75. For suffrage discussions, see *National Economist*, March 1, July 12, October 18, October 25, 1890; March 5, November 12, December 24, 1892; January 21, February 18, March 11, 1893.

76. *Progressive Farmer*, September 15, 1891; December 3, 1889. There were occasionally other references to suffrage; see January 22, 1889, for example.

77. Quoted in Taylor, "Woman Suffrage," p. 46.

78. Saloutos, *Farmer Movements*, pp. 122-26; McMath, "Agrarian Protest," pp. 56-63.

79. Gerald Henderson Gaither, "Blacks and the Populist Revolt: Ballots and Bigotry in the New South (Ph.D. dissertation, University of Tennessee, 1972), pp. 151, 201-209; Gaston, *The New South*, pp. 38-39; J. Morgan Kousser, "The Shaping of Southern Politics: Suffrage Restriction and the Establishment of the One Party South, 1880-1910," (Ph.D. dissertation, Yale University, 1971), pp. 139-43; Guion Griffis Johnson, "The Ideology of White Supremacy, 1876-1910," in Fletcher Melvin Green, ed., *Essays in Southern History* (Chapel Hill: University of North Carolina Press, 1949), p. 133.

17 & Leadership and Tactics in the American Woman Suffrage Movement: A New Perspective from Massachusetts

Sharon Hartman Strom

In the fall of 1915 Massachusetts voters defeated an amendment to the state constitution granting women the suffrage by a margin of 132,000 votes. Suffrage workers predicted that defeat because they knew Massachusetts had long been the center of popular and well-organized resistance to votes for women. Yet in 1919, when the Congress of the United States passed the Nineteenth Amendment and sent it to the states for ratification, Massachusetts was the eighth state to ratify, a month after the amendment left Washington. Massachusetts may have been the eastern locus of anti-suffrage sentiment, but it was also the home of a dynamic and politically sophisticated state suffrage movement. Determined women suffragists had gained enough experience by 1919 to crown ten years of innovative and aggressive political agitation with victory.

The history of the woman suffrage movement has traditionally focused on a group of titanic figures: the pioneers, Elizabeth Cady Stanton, Susan B. Anthony, and Lucy Stone; the inspirational leader of the middle years, Anna Howard Shaw; and the great organizer of the final drive for the federal amendment between 1914 and 1920, Carrie Chapman Catt. Accounts by contemporary chroniclers and autobiographies of leaders of the movement are in large part responsible for this focus on a few personalities,[1] and most recent historians have largely

From the *Journal of American History* 62 (September 1975). Reprinted by permission.

taken these uncritical assessments on faith. While historians of other social movements have begun to move away from reliance on such egocentric sources and conclusions, historians of the suffrage movement give the impression that the success of the cause resulted from the drive and determination of these gifted women, especially in the last campaigns for a federal amendment.[2]

Even the most recent histories convey the feeling that the mass of the American movement was curiously isolated from any contact with its foreign counterparts. Although women in both England and America were fighting for the suffrage at the same time and shared a common ideological heritage, surprisingly few women in the American movement seem to be responsible for the adoption of English militant suffragist tactics.[3] Again, a few unusual individuals account for whatever English influence was felt in America: Harriot Stanton Blatch, daughter of the invincible Stanton, and Alice Paul, militant leader of the Woman's party, both of whom spent time working in the English movement and tried to adapt English tactics to the American scene.[4]

The history of the woman suffrage movement in Massachusetts between 1901 and 1919, however, indicates that these assumptions may be incorrect. Although studies of other states' suffrage movements will be required to substantiate these new hypotheses completely, the evidence from Massachusetts shows that extensive changes both within the rank and file of the movement and in the wider arena of social reform, not the aggressive leadership of a few personalities, were responsible for a highly mobilized and efficient organization in the years before World War I. Massachusetts sources also indicate that large numbers of ordinary American women suffragists enthusiastically supported their militant English sisters and consciously adapted militant suffragist tactics to the work in America several years before Paul arrived in Washington.

Massachusetts women have long been downgraded in analyses of the national movement. As the nineteenth-century headquarters of the American Woman Suffrage Association, the more conservative of the national organizations, Boston is usually characterized as the capital of stuffy feminism.[5] New York, the home of the founders of the more radical National Woman Suffrage Association, is usually credited with having produced most of the innovative tactics and aggressive leaders. Stanton and Susan B. Anthony were far more catholic in their reform interests and consistently feminist than Stone and Henry Blackwell. By 1890, however, when the two groups merged to become the National American Woman Suffrage Association (NAWSA), most women in the suffrage movement neither knew nor cared about the original quarrel between the two organizations. In fact, there is every reason to believe that, while the New York movement produced the precinct organization method and such personalities as Blatch and Catt, the woman's movement in Massachusetts was an equally rich source of tactics and workers for the final battle.

The fight in Massachusetts for an amendment to the state constitution granting women the vote in the late-nineteenth century was largely an exercise in futility. The road to final adoption was difficult; passage required a two thirds vote in both houses of two sucessive legislatures, as well as approval by referendum. Before 1880, the suffragists followed a well-established routine. Every year they presented petitions to the state legislature, and then eloquent proponents of woman suffrage testified at the subsequent public hearing in the State House, hoping both to convince legislators and obtain publicity. They also sought endorsement of the suffrage by reformers, editors, politicians, and educators, and, whenever they were invited, spoke in churches and lecture halls. They also organized suffrage societies. But after fifteen years of such work, there was still no evidence that the state legislature would enact a suffrage amendment—the yearly hearings had become a barely noticed ritual.[6]

In 1879 suffragists thought they had made a breakthrough. With the temporary support of the Republicans, who controlled the state, they secured the right for women to vote for and serve on their local school committees. Republicans supported school suffrage partly in recognition of the stake women had in the education of their children, but mostly in the hope that middle-class females would help to combat the growing voting power of Catholic immigrant and working-class men in local communities. The School Suffrage Law was possible because bills regarding local elections required only a simple majority in the state legislature. The state constitution, in effect, specified male voters for state offices.

Members of the Massachusetts Woman Suffrage Association (MWSA) immediately moved to take advantage of their 1879 victory and this constitutional exception. They began to work for an additional form of partial suffrage, the municipal vote, and played down their demands for an amendment to the state constitution, which would give women the same voting rights as men.[7] This change of emphasis from their traditional argument to a more "expedient" one led suffragists to imply that voting women in the cities could clean up urban politics, combat boss rule, and restore the municipal order upset by industrialization and immigration.[8] However, the new strategy of the state suffrage organization proved to be a disaster. MWSA found itself not only again allied with the Woman's Christian Temperance Union but also with the virulently anti-Catholic Loyal Women of America.[9] Even this approach failed to reclaim Republican support. The municipal bill passed in the Massachusetts lower house in 1894 but was defeated in the state senate. Abandoned by the Republicans, suffragists also found their campaign had elicited the strongest statewide anti-suffrage movement in the country, whose leaders now maneuvered to get rid of the municipal voting issue once and for all by proposing a mock referendum in the election of 1895. Women eligible to vote for their school committees were asked to participate. Ignoring the fact that women who voted in the referendum overwhelmingly voted "yes," the antis gloated over the poor turnout; only 4 percent of the eligible female voters went to the polls. For years Massachusetts suffragists had to combat the anti-suffrage position that women should not be given the vote because they did not want it anyway.

With Stone's death in 1893 seeming to foreshadow a general dampening of enthusiasm, the suffrage movement in Massachusetts entered a period of steady decline.[10] Ninety local leagues had been organized in 1889; only twenty-six remained in 1895.[11] Yet by 1908, though there had been no apparent significant change in leadership, the Massachusetts Woman Suffrage Association was among the largest in the country.[12]

Many factors account for the resurgence of the suffrage movement in Massachusetts. The lessons learned in the municipal suffrage referendum of 1895 about the specific nature of Massachusetts politics, general social changes which occurred during the Progressive era, and changes among women, especially those in the upper class, were the most important. One of the effects of urbanization and industrialization in America in the late-nineteenth century was a frantic growth in organizations which for many people took the place of the extended family, the church, and the rural village.[13] The concomitant move of middle- and upper-class women into a limited participation in public life and the professions, especially teaching and social work, gave them new skills and self-confidence. In reform circles, these new talents allowed women to move away from their reliance on male reformers, who had always been somewhat dubious allies, and to create their own organizations.[14]

In Massachusetts these trends were well on their way by the time of the municipal suffrage debacle in 1895. That referendum convinced women suffrage workers that they should concentrate entirely on reaching women, who, they decided, must never again be accused of indifference to their own rights and needs. They also learned that their arguments should be as universal as possible, or combined with specific ones for every special interest group in the state, since arraying themselves against so many power blocs had led to defeat. But the crucial point is that, once having made these decisions, Massachusetts suffragists could act on them because of the proliferation of organizations for women at the turn of the century.

There were three important organizations in Massachusetts that worked in concert with dozens of others to promote the suffrage after 1900: MWSA; the College Equal Suffrage League (CESL); and the Boston Equal Suffrage Association for Good Government (BESAGG). This group of organizations provided the impetus for the resurgence of the woman's vote question. The smallest and most specialized of them, BESAGG, was probably the most important. Founded in 1901, BESAGG was initially a civic organization with committees on the schools, sanitation, temperance, vice reform, peace, and the suffrage. By 1904, however, suffrage work dominated its activities.[15] Three of the founders of BESAGG—Pauline Agassiz Shaw, Mary Hutcheson Page, and Maud Wood Park—are typical of the kind of women who reinvigorated the Massachusetts movement and then worked in the national campaign during its final years.[16] They were well-educated, confident, independent, and determined to become first-class citizens. In 1900 they needed a small organization in which to discuss new ideas, unencumbered by the stodgy membership of MWSA and its older, more conservative leaders—Julia Ward Howe and Mary A. Livermore—who were still using all the old tactics.

The first president of BESAGG, Pauline Agassiz Shaw, was the daughter of world-renowned Harvard professor Louis Agassiz and wife of Quincy A. Shaw, owner of the fabulous Calumet and Hecla mines. The most powerful supporter of suffrage in Massachusetts, Pauline Agassiz Shaw moved in the state's most élite circles of education and wealth. She preferred to work behind the scenes and left decision-making and public speaking to friends like Mary Hutcheson Page and Maud Wood Park. Her money kept BESAGG financially sound, and more than once saved the *Woman's Journal* from ceasing publication. It was rumored upon her death in 1917 that she had donated millions to Boston schools and reform groups.[17]

Perhaps it is because she was so adept at manipulating people and at backstage politics that Mary Hutcheson Page's contributions have been overlooked. Born in 1860 to a family of bankers, she was orphaned at the age of sixteen, left "comfortably off" and almost entirely on her own. Unhappy with her traditional finishing school education, she sought tutoring in mathematics and then enrolled in Massachusetts Institute of Technology as a special student. In 1890 she married George Hyde Page, son of James Page, the headmaster of Dwight School. Despite her four young children, but with the hearty endorsement of her husband, she worked in the suffrage movement all through the 1890s. At first she helped to organize a special "Committee of Work" in Massachusetts to raise money for Catt's Colorado campaign. But she soon turned her hand to work closer to home. BESAGG was born in her Committee of Work in 1901, and it was she who convinced Pauline Agassiz Shaw to become its first president. Her fund-raising abilities and powers of persuasion were legendary within the movement. She raised thousands of dollars through her social contacts and had a special genius for finding the right person to do the right job. Convinced, for instance, that Alice Stone Blackwell was an ineffective chairman of the Executive Board of MWSA, she quietly convinced Alice Stone Blackwell in 1901 to step down and be replaced by her personal choice, Maud Wood Park.[18]

In 1895, the year of the municipal suffrage referendum in Massachusetts, Maud Wood had enrolled in Radcliffe, where the faculty was solidly opposed to suffrage for women, and where there were almost no suffragists among her fellow students. In her senior year she was invited to speak at the annual MWSA dinner because she was one of the few college women interested in suffrage. After her marriage in 1898 to Charles Park, an architect in sympathy with the suffrage cause, she became a devoted worker. In 1900, searching for inspiration, she visited NAWSA's convention in Washington. She came away appalled. The meeting was held in the basement of a church and attended by an audience of about 100 middle-aged and elderly women. The first speaker presented a state report from Missouri in rhyme. Convinced something must be done to attract younger, especially educated, women, Maud Wood Park and a college friend, Inez Haynes, decided that spring to form a new organization, a College Equal Suffrage League. Based at first in Boston, CESL was ingeniously designed to interest two groups of women in suffrage. College alumnae were to form chapters in CESL and then were charged with organizing women currently attending their alma maters. In 1901, Maud Wood Park strengthened her suffrage ties by becoming chairwoman of the Executive Board of MWSA, and by founding BESAGG with Mary Hutcheson Page.[19]

CESL mushroomed in Massachusetts among the numerous new college women graduates, and in 1904 Maud Wood Park was invited by Blatch and Caroline Lexow to set up college leagues in New York State. In 1906 NAWSA asked her to organize leagues throughout the country. Pauline Agassiz Shaw missed her so much that she volunteered to pay her salary for five years if she would return to New England and work full time. Maud Wood Park promised to return eventually, but in the meantime continued to travel; and in 1908 along with M. Carey Thomas, president of Bryn Mawr, formed a national CESL, complete with an executive council. The older and more prestigious Thomas was made president of the league and perhaps partly out of resentment Maud Wood Park, now widowed, took temporary leave of suffrage work in 1909 to embark on a tour to study women throughout the world, predictably financed by Pauline Agassiz Shaw. Although Maud Wood Park was out of the country during the summers of 1909 and 1910, when new tactics were introduced, she had been instrumental in laying the organizational groundwork and returned to Massachusetts for full-time work in 1911.[20]

While women like Mary Hutcheson Page and Maud Wood Park formed new organizations, they also sought to strengthen old ones. By 1901 they held powerful positions in MWSA and had begun vigorous new recruitment activities. They contacted women in all the religious denominations and teachers' societies, sent speakers to chapters of the Massachusetts Federation of Women's Clubs, and set up booths at agricultural and county fairs.[21] MWSA and CESL also quickly moved to take advantage of the arrival in Boston in 1903 of the Women's Trade Union League (WTUL), hoping to strengthen ties with the American Federation of Labor and convert more working women to suffrage. Unions and suffrage groups exchanged speakers and held joint meetings.[22] By 1909 Mary Hutcheson Page reported that 235 unions had endorsed woman suffrage.[23]

For the first time since the Civil War the wealthy and college-educated women who made up the suffrage movement found themselves allied with large and potentially powerful segments of the population. Organized labor, consumers, ethnic groups, and progressive reformers were all, like the suffragists, on the outside looking in at the entrenched Republican establishment and the interests it represented. In Massachusetts this establishment had conspired to defeat all of the truly "modern" measures such as factory regulations, child labor laws, temperance, and the suffrage.[24] Most WTUL women were suffragists, and most suffrage workers were genuinely concerned about the plight of working women.[25] Each group needed the others' support to obtain the legislation they wanted; organized labor could reasonably expect that once women had the vote they would help elect progressive candidates pledged to support regulatory factory legislation. To convince the unions of their potential support, suffragist speakers emphasized what the ballot would do for working women. The alliance between organized labor and suffrage organizations was a long-lived and amicable one. The zeal with which Massachusetts women pursued the friendship indicates they were aware of the important role labor would play in the fight for suffrage.[26]

By 1907 the success of the Massachusetts women in rebuilding the suffrage movement had brought them to the point where they were restless. The movement seemed to have reached a hiatus, in which the convinced reinforced their own convictions. The method of reaching women through the endorsements of prominent citizens, labor leaders, and civic-minded organizations seemed to have reached maximum efficiency. Maud Wood Park, on tour for CESL in 1907, expressed these dissatisfactions to Mary Hutcheson Page from San Francisco:

> You know how we are hampered because we are thought to be merely suffragists, how we can seem to go just so far and no farther. For example, when I want to speak to an audience of college girls it's almost impossible to get them together unless someone of great influence works up the meeting. We rarely get a chance to be heard by uninterested persons. . . .[27]

Maud Wood Park was struggling here to articulate two questions asked more and more frequently by members of the Massachusetts suffrage movement. The first was how the suffragists could gain attention strictly on their own. The second was how they could expand their realm of agitation so as to draw in the uninformed citizen. For ultimately, woman suffrage would have to run the gauntlet of popular opinion before the Massachusetts state constitution could be amended.

The answers to these questions were not always self-evident. For the most part these upper- and middle-class women did not expect suffrage to lead to any fundamental change in woman's special function as wife, mother, and civilizer. To think of themselves as political agitators meant calling into question the whole notion of special spheres of female activity, which was especially prevalent in their age.[28] Once given an inkling of how to overcome these obstacles, however, Massachusetts women did so with remarkably little hesitation.

The hint came not from American leadership or from a more dynamic state suffrage movement but from England. British suffragists had been using more aggressive tactics than their American counterparts for some time, largely as a result of women's involvement with the anti-corn law agitation. Even the more conservative constitutionalist suffrage societies in England considered public speaking and barnstorming campaigns legitimate realms of activity for respectable women.[29] Precisely for this reason, however, these activities failed to stir up much interest or notice. The militant groups, of which Emmeline G. Pankhurst's Women's Social and Political Union (WSPU) was the most famous, sought public attention when they introduced more dramatic tactics: interruptions of political meetings; partisan campaigns in by-elections; and enormous processions through the streets of London, culminating in demonstrations at Westminster. The militants, who were quickly labeled "Suffragettes," got what they bargained for and more;

they were in the headlines for years. Police usually turned the processions into ugly riots, and many women were injured and arrested; a few were killed.[30]

Women in America did not evidently become aware of tactics used for some time by English suffragists until the English militants made them famous on both sides of the Atlantic. Not surprisingly, Mary Hutcheson Page was one of the first Massachusetts women to develop contacts with the militants. In 1908 she initiated a correspondence with Emmeline Pethick-Lawrence, subscribed to the militant paper, *Votes for Women,* and began work on an article concerning the English militant suffragists, which appeared in *Colliers* in 1909.[31] Her attitudes toward the English movement were largely the same as those that were to be expressed by most Massachusetts women over the next few years. She explained that English women had been using constitutional methods for years and had never been taken seriously by any government in power. The women were simply forced to take more aggressive steps, none of them illegal, to make their point. For this they had been beaten, arrested, and imprisoned. She was obviously impressed with the respectable origins of the militants, so much like her own, and found them convincing proof of the sincerity and legitimacy of their motives. She portrayed Pankhurst as a fearless heroine, devoted to the suffrage and the cause of working women. "The suffragettes," she explained, "prefer to go to prison rather than politically recant their dearest convictions; namely, the right to demand the vote in a way that they consider necessary and legal."[32] The cause also received sympathetic treatment in the *Woman's Journal.*[33]

The difficulty for the Massachusetts suffragists lay in deciding what lessons could legitimately be drawn from the English experience. Most important, they had to consider the ways in which the methods used to gain the suffrage in Massachusetts were bound to be different from those employed in England. Pressuring the majority government into supporting the suffrage was only one step in most American states, since constitutional amendments would ultimately have to be approved by the voters.[34] The suffrage movement in America had to gain the spotlight without alienating the voting public. The Massachusetts suffrage organizations, while openly sympathetic with the plight of the English militant suffragists, were more interested in finding out about less defiant tactics that could, nonetheless, bring American women publicity. Some discussion of English tactics, including the open-air meeting, took place at a MWSA meeting in October 1908.[35]

The open-air meeting was perfectly suited to the requirements of the Massachusetts suffragists. It was a dramatic new tactic, for unlike their English sisters American women had typically spoken at only carefully prearranged indoor meetings.[36] It was well-suited to the need the women felt to reach a wider range of people on their own. Moreover, it could be defended as a relatively conservative tactic, since even the constitutional societies in England had long used it. Two English suffrage workers visited Boston during the winter of 1908–1909 and became much-sought-after speakers on the subject of their open-air speaking tours.[37] The result was that in the spring and summer of 1909 a virtual revolution in suffragist tactics took place in Massachusetts. Most of them were consciously adopted from the English movement. One suffragist succinctly summarized the new strategy when she told her colleagues that opposition to suffrage was not the major difficulty in winning the vote:

> We are handicapped by indifference and its resulting ignorance . . . we have got to prove our case, not to a small body of lawmakers, but to a large body of the people, those who elect the lawmakers, and to prove it to them we must make them listen. . . . If they are uninterested it is because you have not made the subject interesting. Make it so. Make it picturesque. This is what the English women have accomplished. Then when you have made it picturesque there is one other step; make it easy . . . you must go to him [the voter].[38]

The first steps taken were naturally a bit tentative and timid, for these suffrage workers were about to do something quite novel for women of their rank and class: they were going to speak, not to prearranged audiences with guaranteed manners, but to whatever assortment of listeners might appear, including the possibly rude or hostile. On May 7 in a meeting of MWSA Mary Hutcheson Page proposed that a storefront in downtown Boston be rented for propaganda work. MWSA, in cooperation with BESAGG, opened a suffrage shop in Tremont Street in late May. Speeches were given there every day at noon.[39] On May 29 the *Woman's Journal* reported that even the New England Woman Suffrage Association was discussing English tactics and concluded that although "it would not be useful in America to smash windows or interrupt public speakers . . . most of the other methods of propaganda work invented in England could be well employed here."[40]

By June more vigorous plans were under way. Again, MWSA and BESAGG cooperated by forming a special joint Votes for Women Committee, headed by Mary Hutcheson Page, which would operate outside both organizations, probably to avoid identifying the more radical tactics with either organization.[41] She promptly sought the best person for the job of directing the first open-air meetings. Her choice, Susan Walker Fitzgerald, the daughter of Admiral John G. Walker, and wife of a wealthy, Harvard-trained lawyer, had majored in political science and history at Bryn Mawr and after her graduation in 1893 had done social work on the West Side of New York. A colleague of Ernest Poole, Robert Hunter, and Lillian Wald, she had served as a truant officer and settlement worker before coming to Boston in 1907.[42]

The women chose the quiet village green of Bedford for their first open-air talk.[43] On June 5 it rained, but on June 12 they held "that first painful meeting" with an audience of about 100. Although they tried to prearrange times and places at first, they soon learned "the only thing to do was to reach a town, take possession of the busiest spot and begin to talk."[44] Under the guidance of Fitzgerald, a small corps of women speakers toured the smaller towns, villages, and vacation spots of Massachusetts during the summers of 1909 and 1910 in automobiles, trolley cars, and trains, outfitted with banners, leaflets, petitions, and "Votes for Women" buttons.[45] One of the travellers delightfully described the routine:

> Picture our party unloading from a street-car in the central square of some little country town. . . . Then we make for the nearest drug store, deposit all our luggage in one corner, and to compensate for its storage all of us are in duty bound to buy sodas. . . . While we drink, the drug clerk is crossexamined as to where the best audience can be collected, time of trolleys, hotel for the night, factories and mills in town, number of employees, men or women, union or non-union, what they manufacture, and a few dozen other similar things. Meanwhile, if the town is large enough for us to require a permit to speak, Mrs. Fitzgerald has interviewed the police. Then our leaflets are unpacked, our flag erected, we borrow a Moxie box from the obliging drug clerk and proceed to the busiest corner of the town square. Our chief mounts the box, the banner over her shoulder, and starts talking to the air, three assorted dogs, six kids, and the two loafers in front of the grocery store just over the way. The rest of us give handbills to all the passers-by and the nearby stores. Within ten minutes our audience has increased from twenty-five to five hundred, according to the time and place. We speak in turn for an hour or more, answer questions, sell buttons, and circulate the petition. Then we leave, generally in undignified haste, to catch our car for the next meeting.[46]

The success of the new tactics was indisputable. The suffragists made converts in their open-air meetings but, more important, gained wide coverage in the newspapers. All summer, reporters and photographers followed them around, delighted with the drama of giving some of Boston's élite families prominent news coverage.[47] As the women steadily became more experienced and accomplished, they tried to invade at least two towns a day and worked six days a week.

Although several dozen women became veteran crowd-handlers, two in particular caught the attention of the press. Florence Luscomb, a 1909 graduate from Massachusetts Institute of Technology in architecture, slim and delicately beautiful, was an aggressive and always self-confident speaker. Her mother, Hannah Knox Luscomb, had long been a suffrage worker and had used her private income to help finance the movement.[48] Margaret Foley may have been the only speaker in the first tours with a working-class background. She grew up in Irish Roxbury, worked in a hat factory, joined the hat-trimmers union, and was eventually put on the local board of WTUL. She was certainly the most colorful of the speakers, for as the Boston *Transcript* rhapsodized, "she stands five feet eight and weighs in at one hundred and forty, but she can easily manage seven feet, turn her brown hair to flame, descend like a mountain of brick and extend her mellifluous accent to megaphonics."[49] Some of the women visited factories and spoke at noon to the workers. Florence Luscomb thought those meetings were especially challenging but claimed the mill audiences were "ready to be entertained," and "often sympathetic in advance."[50] Suffrage workers also distributed thousands of leaflets and gave dozens of speeches at county fairs, sent Margaret Foley up in a balloon, put a float in the Waltham Fourth of July parade, and persuaded the manager of a circus to drape his elephant with a Votes for Women sign.[51]

At home, in the Boston headquarters, the response of most suffrage workers was wholly supportive. The patriarch of the New England movement, Henry Blackwell, heartily endorsed the open-air meetings in the *Woman's Journal,* often combining his kudos with admiration for the English militant suffragists.[52] He died in September 1909, but his daughter, Alice Stone Blackwell, the chief editor of the *Woman's Journal,* was even more enthusiastic about new tactics than her father, and tenaciously defended the Pankhursts through some of their most difficult moments in 1909 and 1910.[53] Noting that English women sold suffrage newspapers on the street, she suggested the same might be done in Boston; and in November 1909, Florence Luscomb and Mabel Ewell entered the ranks of the Boston "newsies," most of whom were working-class boys.[54] This tactic also received much attention in the press and got suffragists, probably for the first time, out onto the streets of Boston.[55]

When Pankhurst visited the city in October, she received a tumultuous greeting from Boston women; and the entire issue of October 16 of the *Woman's Journal* was devoted to the English woman suffrage cause. The first suffrage parade in Boston carried Pankhurst from South Station to Boylston Street suffrage headquarters. More than 2000 people heard the English leader at Tremont Theatre, where she was introduced by Fitzgerald. She stayed in the home of Mary Hutcheson Page. Her visit to the city was capped by a luncheon at the Vendome, where Alice Stone Blackwell compared her to Stone, Henry Blackwell, and the other great reformers.[56]

In December, Foley and Gertrude Cliff invaded the floor of the Boston Stock Exchange and Chamber of Commerce and distributed leaflets advertising the visit of Ethel Snowden, then second in command of WSPU.[57] The total hegemony of the younger generation of more militant Massachusetts women was fittingly symbolized by the appearance of Julia Ward Howe, the most ancient and respectable of all New England feminists, on the same platform with Snowden, who, according to the Boston *Herald*, said that classes or sexes with no redress had eventually to resort to violence.[58]

By 1910, enthusiasm for English tactics was so widespread among Massachusetts suffragists that perhaps the greatest danger to the vitality of their movement lay in losing a feel for what might be appropriate in America and in underestimating their abilities. A more practical atmosphere settled over the Massachusetts movement after the summer of 1911, when two of the most popular open-air speakers in the recent campaigns, Foley and Florence Luscomb, went to the convention of the International Woman Suffrage Alliance in Stockholm. In fact, the main purpose of their trip abroad was to study the English suffrage movement. They spent over a month in London, interviewing leaders of all the suffrage societies, attending meetings, marching in parades, attending demonstrations, visiting Parliament, and selling newspapers.

Florence Luscomb, who kept a detailed diary of what she saw and heard, was obviously in sympathy with the militants and carefully recorded all their tactics and lines of argument that might be useful in America. She was particularly taken with the militant campaigns in by-elections to defeat candidates publically opposed to suffrage. However, she found the English suffrage movement to be more complicated than she had believed. Accustomed to a close alliance between trade union women and suffragists, she was disturbed to learn that many English labor leaders distrusted the Pankhursts and other aristocratic militant suffrage leaders because they were willing to work for a limited franchise for women and ignore the question of universal suffrage for adults. The most militant suffragists were not, evidently, the most radical.[59] In general she came away feeling grateful for American institutions and democratic principles, which, she felt, would make suffrage easier to obtain in America than in England. She was also convinced that American women suffragists were at least as competent as their English counterparts, and she wrote her mother:

> Understand, I am not for a moment disparaging the splendid enthusiasm of the WSPU. . . . But with the exception of Mrs. Pankhurst I did not find

many of their speakers or workers superior . . . their methods, ingenuity, etc., seem no better than our own, when we really set about it. . . . I am coming home more encouraged and pleased with our work than ever.[60]

Foley's new inspiration and self-confidence were also immediately apparent. In the fall of 1911 she set out on a personal campaign to initiate in Massachusetts the English technique of quizzing politicians on their suffrage views at public rallies. She and a group of fellow "hecklers," as they were dubbed in the newspapers, set off by automobile to pursue the Republican campaign through the Berkshires. They were followed by newspaper reporters who gleefully reported the politicos' unsuccessful attempts to escape. She also invaded Tammany Hall, where Congressman James M. Curley and other Democrats recognized her right to speak and gave at least tacit support to woman suffrage.[61] The heckling campaign, although not an official activity of MWSA or BESAGG, was clearly a precursor of future developments.

In 1911 and 1912 the national suffrage movement was at a crossroads over the issue of participation in political campaigns. For years the policy of NAWSA had been one of absolute neutrality. At the national convention in 1912 a major controversy would explode over the party affiliations of several members. After an emotional debate the convention voted to allow its officers to work for the political parties of their choice.[62] For years Henry Blackwell had advocated fierce opposition to anti-suffrage candidates, a form of political partisanship which ultimately would be adopted in the last stages of the federal amendment drive.[63] The successful use of the tactic in England helped to revive interest in it in Massachusetts and in 1909 Alice Stone Blackwell editorialized on its merits in the *Woman's Journal*.[64] Such exhortations could seriously be considered by 1911 because women suffragists in the state were now clearly a significant political force. Morever, the policy was well suited to politics in Massachusetts, where the suffrage issue cut across party lines. Although the entrenched Republicans were the most obvious enemies of the cause, the suffragists skillfully refused to ally with the Progressive, Democratic or Socialist parties except on specific issues, in order to avoid being identified with any potential losers. They concentrated instead on identifying specific enemies, supporting friends, and educating the public on the suffrage issue.

By the summer of 1911 they were ready to overcome the largest center of indifference to suffrage in their state, the city of Boston. The method for reaching city voters and potential women supporters was consciously borrowed from the suffrage workers in New York City who had suggested using the precinct organization method to mobilize city residents for the suffrage cause.[65] In Boston each voter was identified from the registration lists. A suffrage worker visited each voter's residence in the hope of enlisting the women of the house in a new Woman Suffrage party, for which no dues were required. Suffrage literature was also distributed for the voting men. Rallies were held on street corners or party headquarters in every ward of the city, with speeches by women in whichever languages predominated.[66] The door-to-door canvassing was probably the final baptism of fire for the elegant Bostonian suffragists. As the state chairman of ward organization reported after a trial effort in 1910:

> It took some sense of duty, some devotion to our cause, to push us up the dim . . . staircase, to knock at any one of the several non-committal doors on the first shabby landing. Probably the woman who answered knew no English, and stared uncomprehendingly. No matter—you did as well as you could, the children, who have learned English, helped; the Yiddish and Italian flyers helped; and best of all the women, as soon as they knew what it was all about, proved so kindly, so approachable, so open-minded and responsive . . . that whatever the future may hold . . . the pilgrimage through Ward 8 proved of the deepest interest and meaning.[67]

In 1912 suffragists in Massachusetts demonstrated their new political power. They defeated Roger Woolcott, an old enemy, who as chairman of the state senate's Constitutional Amendments Committee, had blocked suffrage bills. In the same year the Progressive party endorsed suffrage, and the Progressive members of the state legislature, supported by pro-suffrage lobbyists, defeated conservative attempts to force another referendum. In coalition with Progressive elements suffragists defeated Levi Greenwood, president of the state senate, in 1913, although his district had been a Republican stronghold for years. By 1914 woman suffrage was supported by the Socialists, the Progressives, the Democrats, the State Federation of Labor, and the new Democratic governor of Massachusetts, David Walsh. In 1914 and 1915 the amendment easily passed both houses of the legislature and was on its way to the voters.[68]

Suffragists in Massachusetts expected to lose the referendum battle and did, but when the federal amendment was passed by Congress in 1919, they quickly remobilized for the ratification drive. Calling on the coalition that had put the state amendment through in 1914 and 1915, they defeated a move by their opponents which would have submitted the amendment to referendum. They collected 135,000 petition signatures in two weeks, and spent an "eleventh hour" session with the chairman of the Federal Relations Committee arguing the legal aspects of ratification. The committee produced a favorable report on the floor of the house, and on June 25 ratification carried by a vote of 185 ayes to 47 noes. There were only five votes against the measure in the senate.[69]

The woman suffrage workers of Massachusetts had, by 1919, transformed a dormant, unimaginative state society of suffragists into a network of aggressive organizations, which mobilized thousands of women, many of them young, in suffrage work and a unique political movement. Their energy and success were stimulated by their own self-confidence, talents, rising aspirations, the example of their English sisters, and the assistance given them by organized labor and other progressive elements in Massachusetts. Their history should remind scholars that while national leaders are important, the rank and file of any movement can be more significant.

NOTES

1. The most widely used original accounts of the suffrage movement are Carrie Chapman Catt and Nettie Rogers Shuler, *Woman Suffrage and Politics: The Inner Story of the Suffrage Movement* (Seattle, 1926); Ida Husted Harper, *The Life and Work of Susan B. Anthony* (3 vols., Indianapolis, 1893–1908); Anna Howard Shaw, *The Story of a Pioneer* (New York, 1915); Elizabeth Cady Stanton, *Eighty Years and More 1815–1897: Reminiscences* (New York, 1898); Elizabeth Cady Stanton, Susan B. Anthony, Matilda Joslyn Gage, and Ida Husted Harper, eds., *The History of Woman Suffrage* (6 vols., Rochester, 1899–1922).

2. Eleanor Flexner, *Century of Struggle: The Woman's Rights Movement in the United States* (New York, 1970), 236; Aileen S. Kraditor, *The Ideas of the Woman Suffrage Movement, 1890–1920* (New York, 1965), 9; William L. O'Neill, *The Woman Movement: Feminism in the United States and England* (London, 1969), 73–78. Alan P. Grimes nearly goes to the other extreme by suggesting that the success of the suffrage movement was due, especially in the West, not so much to the work of suffragists as to generally conservative and irrational social forces which viewed woman suffrage as a means of gaining social control. Alan P. Grimes, *The Puritan Ethic and Woman Suffrage* (New York, 1967).

3. For an analysis of the origins of English and American feminism, see James L. Cooper and Sheila M. Cooper, *The Roots of American Feminist Thought* (Boston, 1973), and O'Neill, *Woman Movement*.

4. Flexner, *Century of Struggle,* 249–53, 263; William L. O'Neill, *Everyone Was Brave: A History of Feminism in America* (Chicago, 1971), 126–27.

5. For example, see Flexner, *Century of Struggle,* 216. The bias in the original sources toward New York may possibly be attributed to several factors: New York women wrote almost all of the published autobiographies; the state of Massachusetts was so notorious among suffragists for its anti-suffrage movement that the hundreds of suffrage activists were often forgotten; New York won a popular

referendum for woman suffrage in 1917 while Massachusetts lost one in 1915, leading to the possible but not necessarily logical conclusion that Massachusetts had a weaker suffrage organization; the official history of the movement was edited by New York women, except Ida Husted Harper, who was a devoted biographer and companion of Susan B. Anthony and enthusiastic champion of Carrie Chapman Catt. Whether in a moment of pique or forgetfulness, Harper managed to avoid including Massachusetts in the index of Volume V of the *History of Woman Suffrage;* sixteen states, including New York, had entries.

6. For a history of the Massachusetts suffrage movement in the nineteenth century, see Lois Bannister Merk's, "Massachusetts and the Woman Suffrage Movement" (doctoral dissertation, Northeastern University, 1961). See also Arthur Mann, *Yankee Reformers in the Urban Age* (Cambridge, Mass., 1954), 205–16.

7. Merk, "Massachusetts and the Woman Suffrage Movement," 58–64.

8. For a discussion of the differences between the "justice" and "expediency" arguments, see Kraditor, *Ideas of the Woman Suffrage Movement,* 43–74.

9. Lois Bannister Merk, "Boston's Historic Public School Crisis," *New England Quarterly,* 31 (June 1958), 172–99.

10. Maud Wood Park, "Massachusetts Woman Suffrage Association: Introductory Notes," June 1943, Woman's Rights Collection (Schlesinger Library, Radcliffe College).

11. *Ibid.;* Merk, "Massachusetts and the Woman Suffrage Movement," 330.

12. NAWSA reported in 1908 that Massachusetts was second only to New York in membership: New York had 27,476; Massachusetts had 19,197; and Illinois had 10,080. *Proceedings of the Annual Convention of the National American Woman Suffrage Association* (Warren, Ohio, 1908), 21–22.

13. See Robert H. Wiebe, *The Search for Order, 1877–1920* (New York, 1967), 111–32, 165.

14. O'Neill, *Everyone Was Brave,* 77–106; Mann, *Yankee Reformers in the Urban Age,* 201–04.

15. *First Report of the Boston Equal Suffrage Association for Good Government, 1901–1903* (Boston, 1903); Maud Wood Park, "Boston Equal Suffrage Association for Good Government. (1901–1907) Introductory Note," Woman's Rights Collection.

16. Mary Hutcheson Page retired from the suffrage movement in 1918 and Pauline Agassiz Shaw died in 1917. Maud Wood Park, as chairwoman of the Congressional Committee of NAWSA from 1917 to 1920, was responsible for directing the work of getting the federal amendment through Congress. For her experiences in Washington, see Maud Wood Park, *Front Door Lobby,* Edna Lamprey Stantial, ed. (Boston, 1960).

17. Edward T. James, Janet Wilson James, and Paul S. Boyer, eds., *Notable American Women, 1607–1950: A Biographical Dictionary* (3 vols., Cambridge, Mass., 1971), III, 278–80; Harper, ed., *History of Woman Suffrage,* V, 337; Boston *Transcript,* Feb. 10, 1917.

18. Katherine Page Hersey, "Mary Hutcheson Page," May 1943, Maud Wood Park, "Mary Hutcheson Page," April 1943, Anthony to Mary H. Page, March 15, 1899, Page Scrapbook, Woman's Rights Collection. See also, National American Woman Suffrage Association, *Victory How Women Won It: A Centennial Symposium, 1840–1940* (New York, 1940), 76. Carrie Chapman Catt knew of Mary Hutcheson

Page's abilities: "*Now,* you are the great persuader . . . I've heard how you go in and camp before your object of entreaty and just smile until she does just what you want." Carrie C. Catt to Mary H. Page, Aug. 12, 1905, Page Scrapbook, Woman's Rights Collection.

19. Lois Bannister Merk, "The Early Career of Maud Wood Park," *Radcliffe Quarterly,* 32 (May 1948), 10–17; Maud Wood Park, "Supplementary Notes," Jan. 1943, and "College Equal Suffrage League Introductory Notes," Dec. 1942, Woman's Rights Collection; "Constitution of the College Equal Suffrage League," May 24, 1905, *ibid.*

20. Park, "College Equal Suffrage League Introductory Notes," Dec. 1942; Park, "College Equal Suffrage League Supplementary Notes," Jan., 1943, Woman's Rights Collection; Pauline A. Shaw to Maud W. Park, April 10, 1907 (copy), *ibid.*

21. Merk, "Massachusetts and Woman Suffrage," 340–56.

22. College Equal Suffrage League, *Minutes,* 1 (Dec. 5, 1906), 64–65, Woman's Rights Collection; Massachusetts Woman Suffrage Association, *Records,* 2 (June 1, 1906 and Oct. 28, 1908), 221, 302, *ibid.*

23. Massachusetts Woman Suffrage Association, *Records,* 2 (Oct. 22, 1909), 348, *ibid.*

24. Whether there was a progressive movement in Massachusetts is debatable. Richard M. Abrams believes the state, with a few exceptions, woman suffrage among them, had enacted most progressive reforms by 1900. He says that Republican leaders, who controlled the government, were "conservative," and when a successful challenge came to their rule, it came from Irish-Americans, not progressives. Since Abrams confines his discussion of woman suffrage to one footnote and excludes women as a political force entirely, his book cannot be considered a comprehensive political study of the period or of the progressive movement in Massachusetts. Richard M. Abrams, *Conservatism in a Progressive Era: Massachusetts Politics 1900–1912* (Cambridge, Mass., 1964). That ethnic leaders in Massachusetts might also be labeled progressives is explored by John D. Buenker, "The Mahatma and Progressive Reform: Martin Lomasney as Lawmaker, 1911–1917," *New England Quarterly,* 44 (Sept. 1971), 397–419.

25. The Women's Trade Union League was organized in Boston, in 1903 at a regular convention of AFL. Although Chicagoans soon dominated the national organization, there was a very strong league in Boston that supported striking women, agitated for labor legislation, organized women workers, and supported feminist causes. Gladys Boone, *The Women's Trade Union Leagues in Great Britain and the United States of America* (New York, 1968).

26. For example, see two accounts of speeches given by Florence Luscomb. Bangor (Maine) *Daily News,* April 22, 1909; Richmond (Virginia) *News Leader,* Oct. 4, 1910. The Woman's Rights Collection has a large number of newspaper clippings and suffrage fliers which attest that women suffragists consistently tried to appeal to labor. See also, Merk, "Massachusetts and Woman Suffrage," 269–74.

27. Maud W. Park to Mary H. Page, Nov. 25, 1907 (copy), Woman's Rights Collection.

28. Aileen S. Kraditor, *Up from the Pedestal: Selected Writings in the History of American Feminism* (Chicago, 1968), 7–13.

29. Constance Rover, *Women's Suffrage and Party Politics in Britain 1866–1914* (London and Toronto, 1967), 61.

30. *Ibid.*, 72–101. See also E. Sylvia Pankhurst, *The Suffragette: The History of the Women's Militant Suffrage Movement 1905–1910* (London, 1911); E. Sylvia Pankhurst, *The Life of Emmeline Pankhurst: The Suffragette Struggle for Women's Citizenship* (New York, 1969).

31. Emmeline Pethick-Lawrence to Mary H. Page, Sept. 16, Nov. 12, 1908, Page Scrapbook, Woman's Rights Collection.

32. Mary Hutcheson Page, "Mr. Asquith's Prisoners," *Colliers,* 43 (May 15, 1909), 17. See also, Mary Hutcheson Page, "Letter to the Editor," Boston *Herald,* March 23, 1909.

33. For example, see "The Struggle in England," *Woman's Journal,* 39 (Oct. 31, 1908), 174; "Events in England," *ibid.,* 39 (Nov. 7, 1908), 178; "An American in England," *ibid.,* 40 (Aug. 14, 1909), 130.

34. Harper succinctly made this point in 1907: "In the United States there are forty-five Parliaments to be reckoned with, and that is only the beginning; for, when a majority of their members have been enlisted, they can only submit the question to the electors. It encounters then such a conglomerate mass of voters as exists nowhere else on the face of the earth, and it is doubtful if under such similar conditions women could get the franchise in any country on the globe." Ida Husted Harper, "Woman Suffrage Throughout the World," *North American Review,* 186 (Sept. 1907), 70.

35. Massachusetts Woman Suffrage Association, *Records,* 2 (Oct. 28, 1908), 303–04, Woman's Rights Collection.

36. There were probably many exceptions to this general rule. The chairwoman of the Meetings Committee of MWSA reported in 1908 that as many as 1000 people a day had been spoken to by suffragists at local fairs that summer and fall. *Ibid.,* 304. The first open-air meetings in Boston took place by accident outside the state house because everyone present could not fit into the building. Boston *Herald,* Feb. 24, 1909.

37. *Woman's Journal,* 40 (Jan. 2, 1909), 3; *ibid.,* 40 (Feb. 20, 1909), 29; *ibid.,* 40 (March 6, 1909) 35.

38. Florence H. Luscomb, "Our Open-Air Campaign," circa 1909, p. 1, Woman's Rights Collection.

39. Massachusetts Woman Suffrage Association, *Records,* 2 (May 7, 1909), 327, *ibid.; Woman's Journal,* 40 (May 29, 1909), 86.

40. *Woman's Journal,* 40 (May 29, 1909), 85.

41. Massachusetts Woman Suffrage Association, *Records,* 2 (June 4, 1909), 335, Woman's Rights Collection; *Fifth Report of the Boston Equal Suffrage Association for Good Government, 1908–1910* (Boston, 1910), 9.

42. "Mrs. Susan W. Fitzgerald," *Woman's Journal,* 41 (Feb. 5, 1910), 21. Susan Walker Fitzgerald served as recording secretary for NAWSA from 1912 to 1915. Another original participant in the Massachusetts open-air meetings, Katherine Dexter McCormick, was treasurer of NAWSA in 1913 and 1914, and first vice-president from 1915 to 1920.

43. The question of which group or individual gave the first open-air meeting in the United States remains in doubt. Scholars have generally accepted the contention of Harriot Stanton Blatch that she pioneered the technique in America, but she admits that her first attempt, a trolley car campaign along the Erie Canal in May 1908, was a dismal failure. See Harriot Stanton Blatch and Alma Lutz, *Challenging*

Years: the Memoirs of Harriot Stanton Blatch (New York, 1940), 107. Winifred Cooley, who reported on the use of such tactics in New York City, claimed a group called the Suffragettes, led by Lydia K. Commander, gave the first open-air meetings in New York City during the winter of 1907–1908. Winifred Cooley, "Suffragists and 'Suffragettes' a Record of Actual Achievement," *World To-Day,* 15 (Oct. 1908), 1066–71. Two English suffrage workers instigated a parade followed by an open-air meeting in Boone, Iowa, in 1908. Louise R. Noun, *Strong-Minded Women: The Emergence of the Woman Suffrage Movement in Iowa* (Ames, 1969), 246. Harriot Stanton Blatch's trolley tour was routinely reported in the *Woman's Journal,* 39 (June 13, 1908), 95, with no editorial comment. The crucial point here is that Massachusetts women were convinced that they had adopted the technique from England, not from New York. Certainly the Massachusetts women were the first moderate organization with a statewide membership to use the tactic systematically and consistently. See Florence H. Luscomb, "Brief Biographical Sketch," 1945, pp. 1–3, Woman's Rights Collection; interview with Florence Luscomb, Nov. 6, 1972, Oral History Project of Rhode Island (University of Rhode Island).

44. *Fifth Report of the Boston Equal Suffrage Association for Good Government,* 9.

45. For a description of the tours, see *ibid.*; Luscomb, "Our Open-Air Campaign"; *Woman's Journal,* 40 (Aug. 28, 1909), 138–39; *Proceedings of the Annual Convention of the National American Woman Suffrage Association* (New York, 1910), 118–19.

46. Luscomb, "Our Open-Air Campaign," 4–5.

47. "Annual Report of the Massachusetts Woman Suffrage Association," *Minutes,* 2 (Oct. 22, 1909), 343, Woman's Rights Collection.

48. Interview with Florence Luscomb, July 18, 19, 1972, Oral History Project of Rhode Island; Luscomb, "Brief Biographical Sketch," 1–2.

49. Clipping, circa 1911, Woman's Rights Collection.

50. Luscomb, "Our Open-Air Campaign," 5.

51. Interview with Florence Luscomb, Nov. 6, 1972, Oral History Project of Rhode Island; Luscomb, "Brief Biographical Sketch," 2–4.

52. For example, see "Open-Air Meetings," *Woman's Journal,* 40 (Aug. 14, 1909), 130; "Contrasting Methods," *ibid.,* 40 (Sept. 11, 1909), 146. Meanwhile the open-air technique had captured the interest of women all over the country. At the 1910 NAWSA convention in Washington, D.C., two Massachusetts women were asked to participate in a symposium presided over by Blatch on open-air meetings and help give a "practical demonstration." Mary Hutcheson Page was asked to lead a meeting on "Practical Methods of Work." When the state of California voted in favor of suffrage for women in 1911, workers there enthusiastically reaffirmed that open-air meetings and publicity in the papers were a crucial factor in their success. By 1911 Anna Howard Shaw endorsed open-air campaigns in her presidential address to the convention and in 1912 the tactic was officially introduced on the national level at a huge rally in Independence Square in Philadelphia. See Harper, ed., *History of Woman Suffrage,* V, 286, 317, 333; *Proceedings of the Annual Convention of the National American Woman Suffrage Association* (New York, 1911), 100–07.

53. "Mrs. Pankhurst's Methods," *Woman's Journal,* 40 (Oct. 23, 1909), 170; "Militant Moods," *ibid.,* 40 (Oct. 30, 1909), 174.

54. "Sell the Woman's Journal," *ibid.*, 40 (Sept. 25, 1909), 154.

55. "Selling the Woman's Journal," *ibid.*, 40 (Nov. 13, 1909), 183; "Selling the Woman's Journal," *ibid.*, 40 (Nov. 20, 1909), 186.

56. "Mrs. Pankhurst in Boston," *ibid.*, 40 (Oct. 30, 1909), 174.

57. "The climax of the excitement came when Miss Gertrude Cliff . . . was gently but firmly escorted from the center of the wheat pit." Boston *American*, Dec. 13, 1909.

58. Boston *Herald*, Dec. 15, 1909.

59. This diary is in the possession of Florence Luscomb.

60. Florence H. Luscomb to Hannah K. Luscomb, June 4, 1911, *ibid.*; Boston *Globe*, April 6, 1911.

61. Boston *Globe*, Sept. 9, 1911; Boston *Herald*, Sept. 16, 1911; Boston *Globe*, Sept. 26, Oct. 10, 1911. The Woman's Rights Collection has a large number of clippings about Margaret Foley's "heckling" in the fall of 1911. See also Harper, ed., *History of Woman Suffrage*, VI, 296.

62. *Ibid.*, V, 342.

63. "Militant Woman Suffrage," *Woman's Journal*, 40 (Feb. 20, 1909), 30; Merk, "Massachusetts and Woman Suffrage," 100. After a federal amendment granting woman suffrage was defeated in the United States Senate in 1918 by two votes, NAWSA decided to work for the defeat of one incumbent senator from each party up for election that year. Senators John Weeks of Massachusetts and Willard Saulsbury of Delaware were defeated. See Flexner, *Century of Struggle*, 310–11.

64. "Non-Partisan Influence," *Woman's Journal*, 40 (Sept. 25, 1909), 154.

65. Ronald Schaffer, "The New York City Woman Suffrage Party, 1909–1919," *New York History*, 43 (July 1962), 268–87.

66. *Sixth Report of the Boston Equal Suffrage Association for Good Government, 1910–1912* (Boston, 1912), 14–16.

67. *Quarterly Report of the Massachusetts Woman Suffrage Association*, June 1910 (Boston, 1910), 14. Ward 8 was the political domain of city boss Martin Lomasney. Although he remained opposed to woman suffrage, he gave the suffragists some assistance in their campaign in his district, perhaps one of the best indications of the political power of the suffrage movement in Massachusetts by 1910. For Lomasney's views on suffrage, see Buenker, "The Mahatma and Progressive Reform," 409–10, 412.

68. For a discussion by Alice Stone Blackwell of this sequence of events, see Harper, ed., *History of Woman Suffrage*, VI, 296–99. See also Luscomb, "Brief Biographical Sketch," 5.

69. Harper, ed., *History of Woman Suffrage*, VI, 301–02; interview with Florence Luscomb, Aug. 27, 1973, Oral History Project of Rhode Island.

18 ❧Creating a Feminist Alliance: Sisterhood and Class Conflict in the New York Women's Trade Union League, 1903–1914

Nancy Schrom Dye

A "small band of enthusiasts who believed that the nonindustrial person could be of service to her industrial sister in helping her find her way through the chaos of industry"[1] formed the Women's Trade Union League of New York late in 1903. The organization's members—a unique coalition of women workers and wealthy women disenchanted with conventional philanthropic and social reform activities—dedicated themselves to improving female laborers' working conditions and their status in the labor movement.

The women who formed the core of the New York Women's Trade Union League's membership were both trade unionists and feminists. As unionists, they worked to integrate women into the mainstream of the American labor movement. As feminists, they tried to make the early twentieth-century women's movement relevant to working women's concerns. To these ends, the WTUL attempted to serve as a link between women workers and the labor movement and as a focal point for unorganized women interested in unionism. The League agitated among unorganized women workers in an effort to educate women to the importance of unionization. In addition, the organization made concerted efforts to change male trade unionists' negative attitudes

From *Feminist Studies* 2 2/3 (1975). Reprinted by permission of the publisher, Feminist Studies, Inc., c/o Women's Studies Program, University of Maryland, College Park, MD 20742.

This paper was originally presented at the Conference on Class and Ethnicity in Women's History, SUNY–Binghamton, September 1974.

toward women. The WTUL offered assistance to municipal labor organizations and often aided local unions during strikes. League members also worked as organizers and helped establish several dozen unions of unskilled and semiskilled women workers in New York City. Most notably, the New York League played an important role in building the shirtwaist makers' union (International Ladies' Garment Workers' Union Local 25) and the white goods workers' union (International Ladies' Garment Workers' Union Local 62). In a later period of its history, particularly during the 1910s and 1920s, the New York League abandoned its singleminded emphasis on union organizing in order to concentrate most of its efforts on the campaigns for woman suffrage and women's protective labor legislation.[2]

Women came to the League from a variety of backgrounds. Many members were young working women who learned of the WTUL through their unions or through League publicity campaigns. Other members were wealthy women. Often college-educated, allies, as upper-class members were called, usually came to the League with experience in charity organizations, social reform societies, or social settlements. The New York City Consumers' League, the working girls' clubs, and the Workingwomen's Society were among the groups dedicated to improving the women's position in the labor force. Such organizations as the Municipal League and the Young Women's Christian Association occasionally conducted investigations of women's working and living conditions. Residents of the city's settlement houses frequently took an interest in working women and in the rapidly growing trade union movement.

The WTUL, however, differed from these organizations in two important respects. First, the League stressed the importance of actual union organizing efforts rather than such customary reform activities as social investigations. Many women joined the League precisely because they were discouraged by the slow approach of social reform organizations or by the elitism of traditional charity work. As Gertrude Barnum, a leading upper-class member in the League's early years, explained,

> I myself have graduated from the Settlement into the trade union. As I became more familiar with the conditions around me, I began to feel that while the Settlement was undoubtedly doing a great deal to make the lives of working people less grim and hard, the work was not fundamental. It introduced into their lives books and flowers and music, and it gave them a place to meet and see their friends or leave their babies when they went out to work, but it did not raise their wages or shorten their hours. It began to dawn on me, therefore, that it would be more practical to turn our energies toward raising wages and shortening hours.[3]

Second, the Women's Trade Union League stressed the importance of cross-class cooperation between upper-class and working-class women, and it was the only early twentieth-century women's organization that attempted to build such an egalitarian, cross-class alliance into its organizational structure. New York League membership was open to any individual who professed her allegiance to the American Federation of Labor and who indicated her willingness to work to unionize New York's women workers. League members stressed that allies as well as workers could be dedicated trade unionists and effective labor organizers.

Examining the day-to-day relationships WTUL members established among themselves and studying the alignments on policy issues makes it possible to observe the dynamics of cross-class cooperation and conflict. Two questions are of particular importance: How successful was the League in establishing an egalitarian, cross-class alliance? What were the sources of conflict within the organization that undermined the alliance?

The success of the New York Women's Trade Union League depended upon maintaining harmony and a sense of purpose within its coalition of workers and allies. The individuals who founded the League did not expect the coalition's stability to be a problem. The first WTUL members—most of whom were settlement residents and social reformers—apparently anticipated few difficulties in relating to one another: women could, they believed, surmount social and ethnic differences and unite on the basis of their common femininity. In this respect, the Women's Trade Union League was typical of the early twentieth-century women's movement. A conviction that women could relate to one another across class lines in the spirit of sisterhood and an emphasis on the special qualities that women shared linked many League members to the larger feminist movement. One of the major ideological strains in American feminism at the turn of the century was that women were different, emotionally and culturally, from men. Unlike mid-nineteenth-century feminists who had inveighed against the notion of a separate sphere for women and who had argued that both sexes shared a common humanity, early twentieth-century feminists, suffragists, and social reformers stressed the importance of sex differences. As WTUL member Rheta Childe Dorr expressed this philosophy,

> Women now form a new social group, separate, and to a degree homogeneous. Already they have evolved a group opinion and a group ideal. . . . Society will soon be compelled to make a serious survey of the opinions and the ideals of women. As far as these have found collective expressions, it is evident that they differ very radically from the accepted opinions and ideals of men. . . . It is inevitable that this should be so.[4]

League members, like other feminists in the early twentieth century, were often vague when they tried to define women's sisterhood. They usually used the term to convey the idea that social class was less important than gender for understanding a woman's status. The primary social dichotomy was a sex distinction rooted in differences between women and men, not classes. Women, some League members argued, shared distinct emotional qualities: they were more gentle and moral than men, more sensitive and responsive to human needs. League members also argued that women, regardless of class, could empathize with one another because they belonged to an oppressed social group.[5] This belief in sisterhood provided the ideological impetus for the League's formation and helps explain why many women joined the organization.

In certain basic respects, members found that their ideal of sisterhood could be realized. As an organization in which both upper-class and working-class women played important roles, and in which working-class and upper-class women could gain knowledge and confidence from one another, the WTUL remained viable for several decades. And it is possible to document many examples of close personal and working relationships within the League that transcended class lines.

In many other respects, however, WTUL members discovered that it was considerably easier to make verbal assertions of sisterhood than it was to put the ideal into practice. In contrast to the League's public affirmation of sorority, the organization's internal affairs were rarely harmonious. Beyond a basic commitment to unionizing women workers and to the American Federation of Labor, there was little upon which women in the League could agree. Far from behaving in sisterly fashion in their day-to-day affairs, members were often at odds with one another over League objectives and policies: Who should be allowed to join the organization? How much money and energy should the League commit to labor organization, to educational activities, to suffrage agitation? Should the League support protective legislation for women? Personal animosity and rancor accompanied debates over WTUL priorities. Leading members frequently submitted resignations or threatened to resign. They wrote angry letters denouncing one another or defending themselves against others' attacks. In short, WTUL women were a contentious lot. "If we have failed in what might be our greatest usefulness to the workers," Leonora O'Reilly, a leading working-class member, concluded wearily in 1914, "it is just in proportion as we have exhausted the energy of our friends and ourselves . . . in periodical tiffs and skermishes [sic]."[6]

What accounted for the high level of animosity within the New York WTUL? It is tempting to single out class conflict as a blanket explanation for the League's factionalism, policy disputes, and difficult personal relationships. Without doubt, class conflict was a reality within the League and a factor which undercut members' attempts to create an egalitarian alliance. Allies and workers came to the organization with different conceptions of social class, different attitudes toward work, and, of course, radically different social, educational, and cultural backgrounds. The ideal of sisterhood notwithstanding, difficulties and misunderstandings between women from different social backgrounds were inevitable. Yet class conflict in and of itself is not an adequate explanation for the controversies that regularly shook the organization. Indeed, social relationships among League members sometimes tended to mitigate serious class conflict. More important, there were no simple class alignments on League issues. Clearly, factors in addition to class conflict were involved.

The women who made up the organization were never able to reconcile their dedication to women as an oppressed minority within the work force and their commitment to the labor movement as a whole. Belief in sisterhood, League members discovered, was not always compatible with a belief in the importance of class solidarity. In other words, League members were unable to develop a satisfactory solution to the problem of women's dual exploitation: were women workers oppressed because they were workers or because they were female? In effect, many controversies which characterized the organization were in large part a reflection of the League's struggle to synthesize feminism and unionism—a struggle that had personal as well as ideological ramifications for many WTUL members.[7]

Although differences in members' social backgrounds did not fully account for the conflicts within the League, they were an important contributing factor. In the organization's first years, from late 1903 through 1906, allies much more readily than working women joined the WTUL. During these years, when the League rarely had more than fifty members, upper-class women dominated the organization numerically. Although the League's first president was a working woman—Margaret Daly, a United Garment Workers organizer—she remained in the League for only a short time. She was succeeded by Margaret Dreier, an ally. With the exception of Daly, all of the WTUL's officers and a small majority of the executive board members were allies. References can be found to young working women who joined the League between 1903 and 1907, but their role in the organization was shadowy—few remained in the League for more than a year or took a vocal role in the organization's activities.[8]

To stem the tide of young college graduates and settlement residents who flocked to the League in its first years, Gertrude Barnum, an ally herself, suggested that the WTUL impose a quota system to limit the number of upper-class members and that prospective allies be required to endorse the principle of the closed shop as a measure of their commitment to the labor movement. The League did not implement either of these policies. The organization's major provision to guard against upper-class domination was contained in its constitution, which stipulated that working women were to hold the majority of executive board positions. In addition, positions of leadership on organizing committees were sometimes reserved for working women. Such safeguards, however, could not change the fact that in the first years allies dominated the organization numerically. Although no one questioned the desirability of large numbers of working-class members, the first members had difficulty recruiting them.

By 1907, the League had established itself and had begun to come to the attention of young working women through its organizing efforts and its support of labor activities. More workers joined the organization. Three of the League's five officers in 1907 were working women, as was a clear majority of the executive board. After the 1909 general shirtwaist strike, in which the WTUL played a central role, workers joined the League in greater numbers than at any time previously. The year after the strike, eight of the ten executive board members were working women. For the rest of the period under consideration, the League's total membership was several hundred individuals, and working women and allies were numerically balanced.[9]

Numerical equality, however, could not solve the more serious problem of upper-class cultural domination—a problem that was always with the WTUL. Most upper-class members were seemingly unconscious of the genteel atmosphere that permeated the League, despite its unpretentious headquarters in dingy Lower East Side flats. Allies apparently saw nothing incongruous about juxtaposing "interpretive dance recitals" with shop meetings or inviting women to stop by for an afternoon of "drinking tea and discussing unionism." For working women, however, the League had an aristocratic air about it. For example, Rose Schneiderman, a young Jewish capmaker who had grown up on the Lower East Side, recalled her amazement when she attended her first League meeting and watched the participants dance the Virginia Reel. She, like many workers, had to overcome initial reluctance to join an organization with so many wealthy, college-educated women. On a personal level, the League's gentility undermined workers' self-confidence and made them feel awkward; on an ideological level, the organization's aristocratic character was foreign and often suspect. "Contact with the Lady does harm in the long run," Leonora O'Reilly declared at one point. "It gives the wrong standard."[10]

Ideally, allies were to extirpate from themselves any trace of the "Lady with something to give to her sisters."[11] They were to make way for working-class members to take the initiative in labor affairs. In short, they were to learn about trade unionism, labor organizing, and working conditions from the women who had first hand experience in such matters. Despite the emphasis on egalitarian relationships between working-class and upper-class members, however, allies often took the lead in day-to-day affairs. In part, this might be explained by the fact that upper-class members had the advantages of good education and financial independence. Then, too, allies were, on the average, ten years older than working-class members, and their age may have given them additional confidence and authority in the League.[12]

The patronizing attitudes of certain allies toward working-class members were evident in the WTUL's educational work. Upper-class members occasionally assumed the self-appointed task of discovering and developing natural leaders among New York City working women. As Mary Beard confided to another League member, "It has been my dream to develop young women to be a help in the awakening of their class. . . ."[13] One young WTUL organizer recorded in her monthly work report that her scheduled activities included writing lessons. ". . . Miss Scott felt that I ought to practice my writing as I would have to do a great deal of it in the future. I put in several days at nothing else but writing. I had two lessons with Mrs. Charles Beard."[14] Instead of working-class members teaching allies to relate to women workers and to be effective organizers, the opposite was sometimes the case.

Such attitudes did not go ignored or uncriticized. Leonora O'Reilly, a working woman with long experience as a garment trades organizer and labor speaker and one of the original members of the League, was particularly vocal in expressing her dislike of college women who came to the labor movement with lofty ideals of feminism and solidarity but who knew nothing about the realities of labor organizing or of working for a living. She was determined that working-class members should not be intimidated by upper-class women's academic and financial advantages. More specifically, she carried on a running campaign against Laura Elliot, an older ally who joined the League in 1910. Elliot offered League members courses in singing, elocution, and art history; she organized a League chorus and took groups of young women workers to museums and concerts. Most members apparently regarded Elliot as an eccentric but harmless individual and paid her little mind. O'Reilly, however, found her ideas pernicious enough to attack. She harangued Elliot about her condescending attempts to save working women by filling them with useless and pretentious notions of culture.

Elliot was hurt and confused by O'Reilly's anger, but insisted that she had a contribution to make to the League.

> You cannot push me out and you cannot make me afraid of any working girl sisters or render me self-conscious before them, I refuse to be afraid to take them to the Metropolitan Museum and teach them and help them. . . . I feel no fear in putting my side of the proposition up to any working girl. I'm not afraid to tell her that I have something to bring her and I'm never afraid that she will misunderstand or resent what I say. She needs my present help just as the whole race needs her uprising. . . .[15]

Workers sometimes asserted that allies, despite good intentions, did not know how to appeal to working women: their experiences and backgrounds were simply too different from those of their constituents to bridge the gap. Pauline Newman, a young Jewish immigrant who joined the League during the 1909 shirtwaist strike, summarized her impressions of upper-class limitations in both the League and the suffrage campaign in her remark: "the 'cultured' ladies may be very sincere . . . I don't doubt their sincereity [sic] but because their views are narrow and their knowledge of social conditions limited, they cannot do as well as some of us can."[16]

Workers' frustration with the well-intentioned but sometimes inept efforts of their affluent colleagues was understandable. Allies, as the executive board admitted at one point, could be "trying."[17] Upper-class members were sometimes responsible for decisions which exasperated working women. On at least one occasion, for example, League officers scheduled a conference on Yom Kippur, despite Jewish members' protestations. In the League's book of English lessons, *New World Lessons for Old World People,* references to Jewish working girls going to church slipped by uncorrected. Only one League ally is known to have studied Yiddish. Some allies held stereotypic conceptions of immigrant women. Jewish women were often described as "dark-eyed," "studious," and "revolutionary" in League literature. Italians were usually "docile," "fun-loving," "submissive," and "superstitious."[18]

Overt class and ethnic conflict in the WTUL reached its peak during a 1914 presidential contest between Rose Schneiderman and Melinda Scott. At the time of the election, Rose Schneiderman was the WTUL's East Side or Jewish organizer. Scott, a skilled hat trimmer and president of an independent union in her trade, served as the League's organizer of American-born women in the neckwear and dressmaking industries. Although both candidates were workers, they represented widely divergent approaches to the problems of organizing women. Schneiderman had always emphasized the importance of reaching immigrant women. Scott was pessimistic about organizing immigrants and advocated a policy of concentrating on American-born workers. Thus, the election involved League attitudes and policies toward immigrants. Nevertheless, support for the two candidates divided along class lines: allies backed Scott while working women voted for Schneiderman.[19] When Scott won by four votes, Pauline Newman related the details to Schneiderman.

> Your vote, with the exception of three or four was a real trade Union vote. On the other hand, the vote for Linda was purely a vote of the social workers. People who have not been near the League for four or five years, came to vote . . . but they could not get the girls from the Union to vote against you. . . . So you see, that nothing was left undone by them to line up a vote for Linda on the ground that you were a socialist, a Jewes [sic] and one interested in suffrage.[20]

Part of the difficulty underlying clashes between allies and workers lay in the fact that the two groups had different conceptions of class. The importance of class differences was usually far more obvious to working women than it was to allies. Upper-class members were not as acutely aware of class antagonism within the League and often downplayed the importance of social background. Many were confused by the emphasis workers placed on class differences. As Laura Elliot wrote to Leonora O'Reilly, "Before I was unconscious about this class and that class and this stupid difference and that stupid difference. Girls were just girls to me, and now you people are putting all sorts of ideas in my head and making me timid and self-conscious."[21]

Many allies believed that with great effort an individual could transcend her social background. Social class was flexible, not immutable. When allies talked of transcending their backgrounds, they were referring to young women from wealthy families who became self-sufficient and who could relate to workers without self-consciousness. Helen Marot, an ally who came from a comfortably affluent Philadelphia family regarded herself as a worker because she worked as the League's secretary and supported herself on her earnings. In similar fashion, Violet Pike, a young woman who joined the League shortly after her graduation from Vassar in 1907, was included among the working women on the executive board because she performed some clerical duties and joined the Bookkeepers, Stenographers, and Accountants' union.[22] Maud Younger, a wealthy ally, was listed on the League's masthead as a representative of the Waitresses' Union because she conducted an investigation of waitresses' working conditions and attended meetings of the union. In a sense, these women were workers, and they were proud of being self-supporting and resisted being categorized in their fathers' class.

Allies and workers came to the League with different conceptions of work as well. Upper-class members frequently had romanticized views of poverty and often regarded self-sufficiency as a kind of luxury. Work meant liberation from the confines of proper femininity. This attitude contributed to allies' naivete concerning the role of work in the lives of female wage-earners. Because they idealized work and equated it with economic and emotional self-sufficiency, many allies never seemed to come to terms with the fact that most women were not independent laborers but part of a family economic unit in which work did not usually connote independent economic status.[23] "Thank God working girls have a chance to be themselves because they earn their own wage and nobody owns them," one typical League article began. "I am pretty sure you are somebody, because you are self-supporting."[24]

That the New York League was characterized by personal, cultural and political strife there can be no doubt. But Pauline Newman's 1914 depiction of an organization sharply divided between "social workers" and "trade unionists" was overdrawn and simplistic. Although it is easy to document class conflict, it is also possible to document experiences that mitigated serious, sustained conflict between upper-class and working-class women. There were cohesive factors as well as divisive tendencies that operated within the League and enabled the organization to function.

League members' personal relationships with one another constituted one factor that undercut the class conflict inherent in the organization. Sisterhood sometimes became a tangible reality in friendships. Mary Dreier, the WTUL's president from 1907 through 1914, and Leonora O'Reilly, for example, maintained a warm personal relationship for many years that survived numerous political and cultural differences between the two women. "You say you wonder whether I would always trust you," Dreier wrote O'Reilly after some disagreement over League policy.

> There doesn't even seem to be such a word as trust necessary between thee and me. . . . I might not always understand, as you might not always understand my activities—but as to doubting your integrity of soul, or the assurance on which trust is built seems as impossible to me as walking on a sunbeam into the heart of the sun for any of us humans—a strange and beautiful mixture of personal and impersonal is my relationship to you and I love you.[25]

Such relationships were not uncommon among League women. Some, like that of Dreier and O'Reilly, cut across class lines. Other close friendships were established between women of the same social background.

It is not surprising that such relationships were common among League members. For many WTUL women, the organization was a full-time commitment, a way of life. Then, too, that League members should form their closest emotional ties with other women is not surprising in light of the social conventions that governed personal relationships in the pre-Freudian culture of the early twentieth century. Emotional attachments between individuals of the same sex were not viewed with the same suspicion that would characterize a later period. Intense relationships involving open expressions of tenderness and affection were accepted as natural.[26]

Then, too, the longer a working woman spent in the League, the more she had in common with an upper-class ally. Both groups of women were atypical in early twentieth-century American society: the majority were single at ages when most women were married, they prided themselves on being independent and self-supporting, and they lived in a gynaecentric environment in which other women were their closest companions, their working colleagues, and their sources of emotional support. Only an extremely mechanistic definition of social class could fail to take into account that these women shared many important life experiences.

Finally, class conflict is not an adequate explanation for the disagreements within the organization for the simple reason that a member's social background did not dictate her stand on League policies. On every important issue, alignments were unclear. Suffrage, traditionally regarded as a middle-class issue, was an important priority for many working-class members. Rose Schneiderman and Pauline Newman were the first members to devote themselves full-time to the suffrage campaign. Ally Helen Marot, on the other hand, resisted the League's growing emphasis on the importance of the vote. Protective labor legislation, an issue that was enormously important in the League's history during the 1910s and 1920s, was a more controversial issue than woman suffrage, but on that issue as well, there were no clear class alignments. Allies and workers could be found on both sides of the question. In short, one cannot argue that only upper-class League members supported such reform issues as protective legislation while only workers supported labor policies such as direct organizing. There is no evidence to support the view that working women saw the League as a labor union and allies viewed it as a social reform organization. Rather, it is clear that factors in addition to class conflict played a role in creating the controversies in which League members found themselves embroiled.[27]

League members, regardless of class background, viewed the WTUL both as a women's organization and as a labor organization. Therein lay the second and perhaps more pervasive source of discord. Members had difficulty reconciling their commitment to organized labor with their commitment to the women's movement. They could not agree on a solution to the problem of women workers' dual exploitation or find a way to reconcile their belief in sisterhood with their belief in the importance of working-class solidarity. If a woman dedicated herself to working for protective legislation or for suffrage, or if she advocated separate unions for women workers, she opened herself to the charge of dividing the working class. If, on the other hand, she stayed away from women's issues entirely, she was guilty of ignoring women's special problems in the work force. This dilemma was real, and neither the League nor the individuals in it fully resolved the question.

Some members felt strongly that dedication to the labor movement should override the League's feminist leanings. In their analysis, the problems of women workers were bound up inextricably with the problems of working men. Class, not gender, was the main concern. True, they said, women suffered discrimination in the labor movement, but such opposition was not insurmountable.

Other members found their primary orientation in the women's movement. Or, as happened more frequently, women first attempted to cooperate with organized labor but ultimately despaired of changing male unionists' attitudes. They dismissed the labor movement and turned to suffrage and protective legislation as ways to ameliorate women workers' conditions.

Helen Marot, the League's secretary and an organizer, epitomized the first, or "woman as worker" position. Although she was never an industrial worker, she never wavered from her conviction that the WTUL should be committed to organized labor as a whole and not to women as a separate group. Female workers, she emphasized, should be regarded as inseparable from male workers: to think otherwise was to impede class solidarity and to denigrate women's capabilities. Throughout her career in the League and in her book, *American Labor Unions,* Marot vigorously opposed any policy that smacked of caste-consciousness. She emphasized that women were difficult to organize because they were unskilled, not because they were female. She was vehement in her opposition to the minimum wage for women, despite the fact that the measure eventually won the approval of many working-class League members. "If women need state protection on the ground that they do not organize as men do," she told the New York State Factory Investigating Commission, "then also do the mass of unskilled, unorganized men who do not appreciate or take advantage of organization. . . . The reasons for trade unionists to oppose State interference in wage rates apply to women workers as they do to men."[28]

Harriot Stanton Blatch, a well-known suffragist, represented the other strain of the WTUL. Unlike Marot, her interest in women workers derived from her involvement in the women's movement, not from a concern with industrial problems. Unions for women were only one aspect of a multifaceted campaign for women's rights, not an end in themselves. For Blatch, any class-related issue was secondary to the vote. In part, expedient 'considerations motivated her participation in the League: she realized that working women's support was vital for the ultimate success of the suffrage movement, and the League offered an avenue by which to reach them. On another level, however, Blatch was convinced that political equality was a prerequisite for any other improvement in women's status. Thus, only when women could vote would they command the respect of the labor movement. And only with suffrage would women develop the confidence to fight for industrial equality. "I have . . . [been] working with the Women's Trade Union League and attending meetings of the women's locals on the E. Side," Blatch wrote Gompers in 1905. "Those young women need stirring up, need independence, and some fight instilled into them. . . . I am understanding of all that the vote would mean to them—[it] would help in the trade union work as nothing else could."[29]

Marot and Blatch were sure of their objectives and their ideological orientation. The problem of women's dual status was not so clearcut for the majority of League members, however. For working-class members, the problems posed by the WTUL's dual commitment to its constituents as women and as workers were particularly vexing. For them, the matter was not only a theoretical and political issue, but frequently a personal dilemma as well. On the one hand, workers identified with their class background. They came to the League with experience in organizing activities and committed to trade unionism. On the other hand, they, like allies, were also feminists. Although workers were less likely than allies to come to the WTUL with an interest in the women's movement and probably became acquainted with the ideas of organized feminism and with the goals of the women's movement through their relationships with allies, most became dedicated feminists. More important, by comparing their experiences in the League with their role in trade unions they often came to a realization that the WTUL offered more opportunities for women to fill autonomous, responsible positions than male-dominated unions did.

Leonora O'Reilly's career in the League provides a good example of working-women's difficulties. Her commitment to the League was always ambivalent. She was faced with what she regarded as a conflict between her class background and her work in a women's organization. This was aggravated by her conviction that any serious attempt to organize working women had to be a feminist as well as a labor effort. An outspoken feminist herself, she recognized the need for an organization such as the League to devote special attention to women. She knew from her own experience as a United Garment Workers' organizer that women could count on little assistance from male unions. For all that, O'Reilly never came to terms with her ambivalence. She vacillated between urging the League to refrain from interfering in union affairs and stressing that the League should implement its policies in an autonomous fashion.[30] Sometimes she exalted the ability of women to fend for themselves in the work force, independent of men. ". . . I want to say to my sisters," she once declared to a WTUL convention, "for mercy's sake, let's be glad if the men don't help us!"[31] From her days in the Working-women's Society in the 1890s, O'Reilly had stressed the importance of sisterhood. She was a dedicated suffragist. On a number of occasions she spoke of "women's real togetherness." "Personally," she wrote, "I suffer torture dividing the woman's movement into the Industrial Group and all the other groups. Women real women anywhere and everywhere are what we must nourish and cherish."[32] Yet at other times, O'Reilly denounced the League as an elitist organization that had no real concern for working-class people. "The League ought to die," she reportedly said at one point, "the sooner the better."[33] Her two resignations from the WTUL in 1905 and in 1914 indicated her continual difficulty in resolving the conflict. In both instances she emphasized that working women would have to organize themselves.[34]

Rose Schneiderman and Pauline Newman exhibited similar confusion and ambivalence about their role as working women in the League. On the one hand, they identified with the East Side immigrant working-class community in which they had grown up. On the other, they regarded themselves as feminists devoted to women's issues. Like O'Reilly, they frequently experienced enough conflict to consider resigning from the League.[35]

Both women were torn between working in the WTUL and devoting themselves to the East Side Jewish labor movement. Yet to work as an organizer for a Jewish union or for the International Ladies' Garment Workers' Union, as both women discovered, was often an isolated and lonely experience. If the WTUL was not sufficiently interested in the progress of the working class and did not sufficiently appreciate efforts and ability to reach immigrant women, the Jewish labor organizations ignored the special problems of women altogether and discriminated against the small number of women organizers. Newman, after several years of unhappy and unrewarding work as an ILGWU organizer concluded that League work was more desirable than she had thought originally: ". . . remember Rose that no matter how much you are with the Jewish people, you are still more with the people of the League and that is a relieff. [*sic*]"[36] It seems clear, therefore, that working women could compare the League favorably with trade unions. The WTUL offered women organizers considerably more autonomy and responsibility than unions did. What was more, the League provided the company of women who shared interests and experiences.

Still, both Schneiderman and Newman continually had difficulty reconciling the women's movement and the labor movement. On occasion, both women denounced the superficial efforts of upper-class philanthropists and reformers to improve industrial conditions. Yet they were the first WTUL members to work as full-time suffrage agitators. Later in the League's history, both were vocal supporters of women's protective legislation, especially of minimum wage statutes and maternity insurance, despite the fact that the labor movement frowned upon the principle of protective legislation in general and upon the minimum wage in particular. During Rose Schneiderman's presidency in the 1920s, the WTUL devoted itself almost exclusively to legislative activity.

The difficulties these women faced were not uncommon. Most League members experienced some conflict between feminism and unionism. The organization's policies also reflected this: during the first decade of its history, from 1903 to 1914, the WTUL downplayed women's special problems in the work force and concentrated on integrating women into the labor movement as workers, while during a later period its members worked hard to implement demands that were relevant only to women workers: suffrage and protective legislation. For League members, explanations for the oppression of working women were always couched in "either/or" terms: either a working woman was exploited as a worker or she suffered as a woman. What the League needed was an analysis which came to terms with both facets of women workers' situation. That analysis was never realized, and the League remained split. Caught between two alternatives, League members frequently were unable to define their purpose or their role.

In short, the Women's Trade Union League had only limited success in achieving its goal of an egalitarian cross-class alliance. Although the League went further than any other women's organization in establishing sustained relations with working women and in grappling with the problems a feminist alliance posed, its internal affairs were rarely harmonious. In part, the organization's difficulties can be attributed to conflict between allies and workers. Both groups' problems in resolving the WTUL's dual commitment to the labor movement and the women's movement also contributed to the difficulties in establishing a cross-class alliance.

NOTES

1. Mary Dreier, "Expansion Through Agitation and Education," *Life and Labor* 11 (June 1921): 163.

2. The New York Women's Trade Union League was an autonomous organization, but it was closely related to a larger body, the National Women's Trade Union League of America. The same individuals founded both organizations in late 1903.

3. *Weekly Bulletin of the Clothing Trades,* March 24, 1905, p. 2.

4. Rheta Childe Dorr, *What Eight Million Women Want* (Boston: Small, Maynard, 1910), p. 5. For a good discussion of the changes in American feminist ideology from the mid-nineteenth century to the early twentieth century, see Aileen Kraditor, *The Ideas of the Woman Suffrage Movement* (New York: Columbia University Press, 1965), Chapter 3.

5. See, for example, Gertrude Barnum, "The Modern Society Woman," *Ladies' Garment Worker* 2 (June 1911): 8. "All women before the laws of the country . . . are of equal rank or lack of rank, being classed without exception with children, idiots, and criminals. With a common sense of injustice, feminine descendents of Patrick Henry, Tom Paine, and Thomas Jefferson ignore social differences and march shoulder to shoulder in campaigns to secure their 'inalienable rights'—to secure the fullest possible social equality with man."

6. Leonora O'Reilly to the executive board, Women's Trade Union League of New York, January 14, 1914, Women's Trade Union League of New York Papers, New York State Labor Library, New York, New York (hereafter cited as WTUL of NY papers).

7. Some historians who have dealt briefly with the Women's Trade Union League have interpreted the discord within the organization and the shift from labor organizing to legislative activity as the result of class conflict between allies, or social reformers, and working women. William Chafe argues, for example, "Reformers viewed the WTUL's primary function as educational, and believed that the interests of the workers could best be served by investigating industrial conditions, securing legislative action, and building public support for the principle of trade unionism. Female unionists, on the other hand, insisted that organizing women and strengthening existing unions represented the League's principal purpose. One group perceived the WTUL as primarily an instrument of social uplift, the other as an agency for labor organization" (Chafe, *The American Woman, Her Changing Social, Economic, and Political Roles, 1920–1970* (New York: Oxford University Press, 1972), p. 71.

8. The New York League was never a large organization. Although it counted several hundred women among its dues-paying members in the years after 1907, few of these individuals played active roles in the League's day-to-day work. In the years from 1903 to 1914, about twenty women formed a core group of members. These women made League policies, served as League officers, organizers, and speakers, and set League priorities. Although the composition of this core group changed from year to year, most of these members devoted most of their time to the organization for at least several years. Using the lists of executive board members, officers, and committee members that are extant, it is possible to reach some conclusions about the changing class composition of the core membership

group. This discussion on membership is based on a more complete treatment in my doctoral dissertation, "The Women's Trade Union League of New York, 1903–1920," (University of Wisconsin, Madison, Wisconsin, 1974).

9. Women's Trade Union League of New York, *Annual Reports,* 1909–1910 to 1913–1914. For a more detailed discussion of membership, see Dye, "The Women's Trade Union League of New York, 1903–1920."

10. Letter to Leonora O'Reilly, 1908. O'Reilly's statement is in the form of a note written to herself on the back of the letter. Leonora O'Reilly Papers, Schlesinger Library, Cambridge, Massachusetts (hereafter cited as Leonora O'Reilly Papers).

11. William English Walling to Leonora O'Reilly, December 1903 (O'Reilly's handwritten note on the back of the letter), Leonora O'Reilly Papers.

12. This statement is based on the compilation of biographical information on the WTUL's core membership group. For more complete information, see Dye, "The Women's Trade Union League of New York."

13. Mary Beard to Leonora O'Reilly, July 21, 1912, Leonora O'Reilly Papers.

14. Report of the Organizer, October, 1915, Women's Trade Union League of New York, WTUL of NY Papers.

15. Laura Elliot to Leonora O'Reilly, March 1911, Leonora O'Reilly Papers.

16. Pauline Newman to Rose Schneiderman, July 16, 1912, Rose Schneiderman Papers, Tamiment Institute, New York University, New York, N.Y. (hereafter cited as Rose Schneiderman Papers).

17. Minutes, Executive Board, Women's Trade Union League of New York, January 25, 1906, WTUL of NY Papers.

18. See, for example, Violet Pike, *New World Lessons for Old World People* (New York: Women's Trade Union League of New York, 1912); Gertrude Barnum, "A Story with a Moral," *Weekly Bulletin of the Clothing Trades,* November 20, 1908, p. 6; Gertrude Barnum, "At the Shirtwaist Factory, A Story," *Ladies' Garment Worker,* 1 (June 1910): 4.

19. Pauline Newman recorded her impressions of the election in three letters to Rose Schneiderman. Pauline Newman to Rose Schneiderman, 1914, Rose Schneiderman Papers.

20. Ibid.

21. Laura Elliot to Leonora O'Reilly, March 1911, Leonora O'Reilly Papers.

22. Women's Trade Union League of New York, *Annual Reports,* 1910–1911, 1911–1912. In both years, Pike is listed as a union representative for the Book-keepers, Steographers, and Accountants' Union.

23. U. S. Congress, Senate, *Report on Condition of Woman and Child Wage-Earners in the United States,* "Wage-Earning Women in Stores and Factories," S. Doc. 645, 61st Cong., 2d sess., 1910, 5: 18, 25, 144. Senate investigators pointed out that New York City had the smallest proportion of self-supporting women of all the major cities investigated.

24. Gertrude Barnum, "Women Workers," *Weekly Bulletin of The Clothing Trades,* July 13, 1906, p. 8.

25. Mary Dreier to Leonora O'Reilly, June 19, 1908, Leonora O'Reilly Papers.

26. Other historical studies have touched upon this phenomenon. See, for example, Christopher Lasch and William Taylor, "Two Kindred Spirits," *New England Quarterly* 36 (Winter 1963): 23–41.

27. This interpretation differs from brief accounts of the WTUL in other works. See, for example, Kraditor, *Ideas of the Woman Suffrage Movement,* Chapter 6, and Chafe, *American Woman,* Chapter 3.

28. New York, Factory Investigating Commission, *Fourth Report of the New York State Factory Investigating Commission, 1915* 1: 774; Helen Marot, *American Labor Unions, By a Member* (New York: Henry Holt, 1915), Chapter 5.

29. Harriot Stanton Blatch to Samuel Gompers, December 30, 1905, American Federation of Labor Papers, Wisconsin State Historical Society, Madison, Wisconsin; Harriot Stanton Blatch, *Challenging Years* (New York: Putnam, 1940).

30. See, for example, Leonora O'Reilly to executive board, Women's Trade Union League of New York, January 14, 1914, WTUL of NY Papers.

31. National Women's Trade Union League, *Proceedings of the Second Biennial Convention, 1909,* p. 26.

32. Leonora O'Reilly to Mary Hay, December 29, 1917, Leonora O'Reilly Papers.

33. Leonora O'Reilly's statement was quoted in a letter from Pauline Newman to Rose Schneiderman, 1914, Rose Schneiderman Papers. Newman wrote, "Mrs. Robins wanted Nora [Leonora O'Reilly] to tell her what she thought of the candidats [sic] but Nora said that, 'this you will never know, but I can tell you what I think of the League, it ought to die, and the sooner the better.'"

34. Minutes, Special Meeting, Executive Board, Women's Trade Union League of New York, November 19, 1915, WTUL of NY Papers.

35. See, for example, Pauline Newman to Rose Schneiderman, February 22, 1912, Rose Schneiderman Papers.

36. Pauline Newman to Rose Schneiderman, April 17, 1911, Rose Schneiderman Papers.

19 Black Women and the Great War: Mobilization and Reform in the South

William J. Breen

Historians have devoted relatively little attention to the study of grass-roots America during World War I. Little is known about how national policies were implemented at the local level and how the American population in general, and American women in particular, were brought into the war effort.[1] Practically nothing has been written concerning the attitude of black women, particularly southern black women, toward the war or about the attempt of the national administration to incorporate them into the general war effort.[2] This paper explores some aspects of the little-known effort made by the Committee on Women's Defense Work of the Council of National Defense (also known as the Woman's Committee) to achieve this aim. Southern black women saw the possibilities for social reform that the wartime situation offered.[3] This reformist thrust is reflected both in the quiet struggle over the appropriate form of wartime organization for black women and in the actual programs adopted. The Woman's Committee maintained a constant, if discreet, pressure on the southern states to integrate black women into the civilian war effort on terms that made many white southerners balk. The war ended too soon for the reform impetus to come to fruition, but the direction of the change was clear.

Little or no thought had been given by the administration to the potential role of women in the event of America's becoming involved in the European war. Once war was declared, the national women's organizations deluged Washington with patriotic offers of assistance. Not quite knowing what to do with these offers, the administration decided to establish a Woman's Committee under the general aegis of

From *The Journal of Southern History* 44 (August 1978), Copyright © 1978 by the Southern Historical Association. Reprinted by permission of the Managing Editor.

the Council of National Defense, a planning body created in 1916 primarily concerned with the problems of industrial mobilization. The major national women's associations were represented on the Woman's Committee, and it was believed that this body would somehow serve as a point of contact between the national government and the general war effort on the one hand and the women of the nation on the other.[4] Once organized, the Woman's Committee divided the work to be done into departments of subcommittees and began to build a nationwide network of state committees.[5]

Although the Council of National Defense, acting in cooperation with the various state governors, had already established men's committees called Councils of Defense in each state, the Woman's Committee insisted on separate state women's organizations in the belief that there was, in fact, some unique role for the women of the country to play in the wartime crisis. As the war progressed both the men's and the women's state committees gradually expanded through the creation of county, township, and eventually community organizations.[6] The ultimate aim was to involve the entire population in the domestic war effort. The anomaly of this objective and the almost totally white membership of these various state committees became increasingly obvious. This was especially so in the southern states, and as time went on groping efforts began to be made to incorporate the black community, both men and women, into the organizational structure.

The pressure to incorporate the black population into the war effort in an organized and systematic way came from several directions. In the Woman's Committee there had been an increasing sense of this need, and many of the state and local organizations had begun to take some faltering steps in that direction by the winter of 1917–1918.[7] In addition, the men's Section on Cooperation with States (later the State Councils Section of the Council of National Defense) began to put pressure on the various state Councils of Defense, particularly in the South, to organize the black population in a systematic manner.[8] In February 1918 the State Councils Section circularized the southern state Councils of Defense with a suggested plan for the establishment of a statewide Negro council as an auxiliary to each state council.[9] Washington followed up this circular with various other communications on the same topic throughout 1918, and this pressure began to bear fruit as more and more of the state councils in the South decided to organize the black male population.[10] By mid-1918 other federal agencies with machinery in the southern states had begun to incorporate the blacks. The Food Administration, the Department of Labor, and the speakers among the Four-Minute Men of the Committee of Public Information all took steps in this direction.[11]

As this pressure to incorporate the black population began to mount, the War Department helped to crystallize the attitude of the Woman's Committee and to force some positive action. In July 1918 Emmet Jay Scott, special assistant to the secretary of war, approached the Woman's Committee because of concern about reports of unrest among the black population stemming mainly from discrimination practiced by whites in war work.[12] He also approached the Woman's Division of the Committee on Public Information over the same matter.[13] Recommending the appointment of a black field representative to work among the black women in the various states, Scott argued that it "would do much to build up the morale" of the black women of the country.[14] He also pressed for the establishment of a separate black woman's council at the national level as a subcommittee of the Woman's Committee in Washington, or, at least, the establishment of councils composed of black women as subcommittees of, and directly responsible to, each state Woman's Committee. Such organizations, he thought, would give the black women of the country some national, or statewide, recognition and encourage active participation in the war effort. In response, the Woman's Committee decided to appoint Alice Dunbar Nelson as a field representative to undertake a trip through the southern states to report on the situation and help stimulate organization among the black women.[15]

Born and educated in New Orleans, Alice Ruth Moore taught literature and published her first book of poems and short stories in 1895. Two years later she moved to New York, began teaching in the Brooklyn schools, and became involved in the National Association of Colored Women, serving as recording secretary between 1897 and 1899. In 1898 she married Paul Laurence Dunbar, a young black poet and literary figure. After her husband died of tuberculosis in 1906, Mrs. Dunbar moved to Wilmington, Delaware, and began to teach at the Howard High School, where she remained for eighteen years, eventually becoming head of the English Department. In 1916 she married Robert John Nelson, editor and publisher of the weekly Wilmington *Advocate* and an activist in the fight for Negro civil rights. During American involvement in the World War Mrs. Nelson was given a year's leave of absence to work as a field representative among the black women for the Woman's Committee.[16]

On her trip through the South Mrs. Nelson was on the alert for signs of disaffection and kept the Washington office informed of what she learned. Predictably, it was a fairly depressing picture. In New Orleans she found the grievance was quite specific "because government employment bureaus here recognize in every colored girl who applies for work only a potential scrub woman, no matter how educated and refined the girl may be."[17] In Alabama and Mississippi the local Red Cross had refused the black women permission to do canteen work at the railroad stations "because they would not permit the colored women to wear the canteen uniform."[18] Understandably, this had caused "some feeling among the colored women."[19] Mrs. Nelson noted that Vicksburg, in particular, "has not been exactly a hot-bed of patriotism among the colored people." The attitude of the black community in the city had been further embittered by a tar-and-feather episode that had occurred a few weeks before Mrs. Nelson's arrival: one of the victims was a black woman whose husband was fighting in France. "Since that time the colored brass band will not lead the colored draftees to the station, seeing no cause for making music."[20] The black women had other causes for complaint in Mississippi. When the Hoover pledge cards for food conservation were distributed, "the white people would not let the colored ministers give them to their congregations. Said colored people needn't sign them, it wasn't necessary. Too much like social equality."[21]

Mrs. Nelson believed that among the Negro community in Mississippi "even the most ignorant, are doing a lot of bitter thinking. . . . It isn't German propaganda either, it's American propaganda, that is working harm among the people."[22] Nevertheless, even though discontented over the deliberate exclusion from official participation in the more important aspects of the war effort, southern black women remained anxious to demonstrate their patriotism when given the opportunity. In Tennessee, for example, Mrs. Nelson found the black women "eager, interested, but not sure of their ground."[23] Even in Mississippi she reported that, overall, "the colored women are alive and anxious to work. . . . "[24]

Mrs. Nelson's reception in the southern states indicated the different perceptions held by the various white state chairmen of the urgency of the problem. Most of the chairmen were polite and quite willing to discuss the problem with her, though many thought the proposed organization to be unnecessary. The chairman of the South Carolina Woman's Committee, for example, saw "no necessity for her [Nelson's] visiting South Carolina at this time to organize," though she was perfectly willing to talk over the matter with Mrs. Nelson.[25] The latter spent "quite an interesting hour discussing problems and threshing out difficulties."[26] In North Carolina, Mrs. J. Eugene (Laura Holmes) Reilley approved the idea of a field representative to work among the black women and was quite willing to discuss the matter with Mrs. Nelson.[27] In Louisiana the state chairman took Mrs. Nelson's visit very personally: "But she is hurt, thinking that I've come to find fault with her work or to spy upon her. . . . will you try to disabuse her mind of the idea that the Committee at Washington thinks she isn't giving the colored women a square deal?"[28] Georgia was the only state where Mrs. Nelson was rebuffed by the state chairman.[29]

If her reception had been cool or lukewarm elsewhere, Mrs. Nelson was overwhelmed by the enthusiasm of her welcome in Florida and Mississippi. Here the white state chairmen were fully aware of the problem and were anxious to do everything in their power to incorporate the black women into the patriotic war effort. In Florida the state chairman arranged for publicity about Paul Laurence Dunbar and his literary work in order to interest the general public in Mrs. Nelson's arrival and invited "a number of prominent white people to come to this meeting to assure the negroes of our interest in their development, and our cooperation in their work."[30] In addition, a speaking itinerary was arranged for Mrs. Nelson throughout the state. Her reception in Mississippi was similarly enthusiastic. There the state chairman, Mrs. Edward McGehee, reported that if she had known the exact date of Mrs. Nelson's arrival, she would have organized a statewide meeting for her, "but as it was I got busy with the long distance phone and telegraph, and made engagements for her in three of the principal cities in the state."[31] Mrs. McGehee was impressed with Mrs. Nelson: "I found her very capable, very intelligent and with good judgement to carry on the work as planned."[32] Mrs. Nelson was equally impressed with the state chairman: "She is delightfully alive, eager and interested. Would keep me in Mississippi indefinitely and feels quite put out that I can spend only a week."[33]

The most contentious issue was not whether to organize the black women in the southern states but what form this proposed organization should take. Only Missouri, a border state, actually thought there was no need at all to organize the black women.[34] Most southern states favored some form of minimal organization of the black population that would ensure a degree of cooperation and coordination with the least likelihood of upsetting existing social relations. Formal, statewide organizations that entailed official recognition of southern black women seemed to imply an unnecessary threat to the existing pattern of race relations in the region.

The central office of the Woman's Committee always acted with extreme caution in discussing the role of Mrs. Nelson and the nature of her trip through the South. The Woman's Committee relied on voluntary cooperation, and there was no possibility of coercing the various state committees into taking a position they did not wish to adopt. Miss Hannah Jane Patterson, the resident director of the Woman's Committee, in writing to the Georgia state chairman made clear that Mrs. Nelson "understands that she is to follow whatever plans you may have, and is to undertake only whatever propaganda and organization work you consider wise at this time."[35] In correspondence with Mrs. Reilley of North Carolina Miss Patterson stressed that "It is, of course, understood that whatever Mrs. Nelson does will be under the direction of the State Chairman."[36] After Mrs. Nelson had left North Carolina Miss Patterson reassured the state chairman that the Washington office was not trying to force a new policy on the state: "The Woman's Committee has adopted no policy with regard to organizing the negroes, but has left the matter to each state to determine. . . . The work which we had in mind is an experiment. We wish to carry it out in accordance with the policies of the State Divisions. . . . "[37]

Organization of the black population was a touchy issue in the southern states and, even though Mrs. Nelson was concerned only with black women, it was important that this undertaking have, if not the support, then at least the acquiescence of the men's state organizations. Writing to Mrs. Samuel Martin (Mildred McPheeters) Inman, state chairman in Georgia, Miss Patterson queried: "I presume that you have already consulted with the State Council of Defense, so that any work undertaken among colored women will be in harmony with the work of the State Council in its work among colored men."[38] Other states were likewise reminded to inform the men's state councils of the proposal to work among the black women.[39] In no way was Mrs. Nelson's visit allowed to appear to threaten the status quo in the southern states.

Despite such deference to the views of the southern chairmen, the national Executive Committee did have a fairly clear idea of the type of organizational structure it believed most desirable. "It is the thought of the [Executive] Committee that the plan . . . of having a section of colored women organized under . . . and responsible to the State Division, would be the best form of organization. This is the plan which has worked out so well in Maryland and Florida."[40] The resident director of the Woman's Committee made these views perfectly clear to Mrs. Nelson in correspondence, adding that these black councils "carry on the same work as the white women and are constantly in consultation with the leaders of the Woman's Committee in their respective districts, whether they be state, county or local."[41] Mrs. Nelson herself considered this type of state organization for the Negro women to be "the only way they would ever become self-reliant."[42]

The views of the Washington office coincided with the aspirations of many of the black women Mrs. Nelson interviewed in her travels through the South. It became increasingly obvious to her that what these black women needed, and wanted, was a semi-independent, statewide organization of their own which would parallel the organization of the white women. For example, in North Carolina Mrs. Nelson commented that Miss Mamie McCullough, chairman of the black war workers at Charlotte, "agreed with me that a separate state organization among the colored people, that is, a colored state chairman, with county chairmen, and local chairmen, would accomplish the best good for the colored people of the state, since it would throw them on their own responsibility and at the same time enable them to reach down into all classes." In a concluding comment on the North Carolina situation Mrs. Nelson wrote: "Miss McCullough and one or two other women whom I saw last evening, tell me that the colored people are simply aching to be put in touch in an official way with the situation."[43]

The southern states exhibited remarkable diversity both in the degree and the type of organization among the black women. Florida stood at one end of the spectrum. It was the only state where Mrs. Nelson considered her visit to have been superfluous: "Florida is so well organized I told them they hardly need me at all." By the time of her visit in August 1918 the black women had a complete organization, which included a black state chairman, black chairmen in each county, and a complete set of committees in each county.[44] Miss Eartha M. White, who had worked with the state labor commissioner, had been appointed state chairman of the black woman's department of the state Woman's Committee. The white state chairman, Mrs. Frank E. Jennings, could not praise her work highly enough.[45] Maryland, which Mrs. Nelson did not visit on her trip, was the only other southern state that had a comparable statewide organization for black women.[46] These two states set an example, but not one enthusiastically emulated in the South as a whole.

Mississippi approximated the Florida model in intention, if not in actual performance. There the energetic white state chairman, Mrs. Edward McGehee of Como, was completely in sympathy with the need for the thorough organization of the black women and had even given up her summer vacation for the first time in her life to stay in Como and push the work.[47] Shortly before Mrs. Nelson's arrival, Mrs. McGehee had appointed a black state chairman to organize the women throughout the state. The woman appointed, Miss Sally Green, was a native of Mississippi, had been a student at Hampton Institute, had taught school for some years, and was currently a county agent for the blacks in Panola County.[48] Mrs. McGehee was so keen to get the black women organized that she paid the salary and expenses of Miss Green out of her own pocket.[49] Mrs. McGehee told the Washington office that she wanted the black women in the state organized "along the same lines that we are," and she circularized her county chairmen asking them to select "the best negro woman you know in your county to work under your supervision, and to assist Sally Green."[50] Miss Green was to work under the joint supervision of Mrs. McGehee and the local county chairman, but the object was to establish a thorough statewide organization of black women. Miss Green began a tour of Mississippi on September 1, 1918.[51] By early October, Mrs. McGehee was reporting "great results."[52]

But Mrs. Nelson found that Florida and Mississippi were the exception rather than the rule. Most southern states tended to approximate the South Carolina model, known as the Sumter County Plan. This did not really go much beyond appointing a local black to cooperate, when needed, with the local county council, and in no sense did it call for a separate black organization. The chairman of the South Carolina Woman's Committee did not see any need to go beyond this form of cooperation.[53] However, Mrs. Nelson's visit to South Carolina spurred on the effort to organize the black women and also altered the views of the white state chairman. She agreed to a plan involving the appointment of a black woman state chairman, with black chairmen in each county, who would establish black units to work with their white counterparts. Although this would take some time to organize, Mrs. Nelson could report that "They hope to get these plans under way for the colored women by the winter."[54]

Most other southern states could boast only a few sporadic examples of black organization concentrated in the major urban areas. In Louisiana, for example, only New Orleans had any organization among the black women. Mrs. Nelson found that the feeling between the races was ideal but, as she remarked, "There isn't any organization, just a lovely cooperation, and general foggy feeling of good-will and sisterly love. . . . " When she inquired about the lack of organization in the state, especially in cities like Baton Rouge, Shreveport, and Alexandria with large black populations, she was told, "Everyone seems to think that the difficulties of accommodation [and] hard travel precluded any 'delicate lady's' going into the hinterland."[55] This was in sharp contrast to the adjoining state of Mississippi, where the indefatigable Mrs. McGehee, the white state chairman, had no fear of distance. There, Mrs. Nelson reported, "The colored women are alive and anxious to work—Mrs. McGehee has seen to that. Little details of 100 or 200 miles have no terrors for her."[56] However, if Louisiana was poorly organized as a state, Mrs. Nelson found the organization in the city of New Orleans to be a model for the rest of the country.

The state Woman's Committee had appointed a special city chairman for New Orleans, Mrs. William Porteour. She appointed a white and a black chairman in each of the seventeen wards in the city and relied on them to develop appropriate local organizations.[57]

On discovering that some of the black chairmen she had initially appointed did not reside in the wards they represented, she insisted on a reorganization to ensure that each ward chairman actually lived in her ward. Mrs. Nelson, who had been invited to the reorganization conference, commented that "I feel more encouraged than at any time since I left Washington. . . . It is, without doubt, one of the finest bits of organization I've ever seen anywhere, and it works."[58] Mrs. Porteour had the additional advantage of excellent cooperation with city officials and departments, including use of the City Council Chamber for one of her organizational meetings—"the first time in the history of the city that a colored or mixed audience ever met in that sacred hall."[59]

The situation in Alabama and Tennessee was uneven but encouraging. The black women in Birmingham, and surrounding Jefferson County, seemed to be quite well organized. Mrs. Nelson described the Jefferson County Woman's Committee as "more thriving, active and alert than any that I have come across anywhere thus far—I mean so far as its work among the colored women is concerned."[60] The situation in other parts of the state was disappointing. In Selma, for example, "It seems there has been no organization there of the colored women—some have been working at the sale of stamps and making sporadic efforts but undirected."[61] In Mobile she found no official organization, but she did discover an independent black women's "War Service Club," which appeared to operate in the same manner as the Woman's Committee, and with all the various departments under the direction of a county chairman. Although she talked with the chairman and other members of the club, Mrs. Nelson reported that she "was unable to elicit any definite information as to their activities. I fear their work is to be done, not accomplished."[62] In Tennessee there were black women's organizations only in Knoxville, Nashville, and Memphis. But the white state chairman was anxious to extend the organization to cover the state. Mrs. Nelson reported that the chairman "is extremely anxious to get the work under way and would keep me in Tennessee indefinitely. I promised to come back."[63]

A slightly different procedure, similar to that followed in Maryland, had been used in Kentucky. There the men's State Council of Defense had organized the black men into a state committee, and, once organized, this committee added two black women to its number. The state Woman's Committee thought this "a very happy solution of the problem, as it is one that can be much better handled by the State than Nationally."[64]

In early 1918 the executive committee of the North Carolina Woman's Committee had discussed the question of a separate state organization for the black women. All agreed, however, that the best results would be obtained by incorporating the blacks into the existing county organizations on the Sumter County Plan, and they adopted a motion to "strenuously advise against setting up separate organization of negroes for Council of Defense work in any Southern State."[65] However, the state chairman, Mrs. Reilley, was anxious to mobilize the black community: "I decidedly approve of a woman coming to work and talk to our colored population and each community can decide just how they prefer to work."[66] Moreover, she was willing to bring the matter of organization of the black community before her committee again in the light of her discussion with Mrs. Nelson.[67]

Mrs. Nelson found Georgia to be the most disappointing of the southern states. Although the state Woman's Committee had appointed a subcommittee on black affairs early in 1918, this had not led to the development of a statewide black women's organization. Mrs. Nelson found the attitude of the white state chairman uncooperative and aloof; Georgia was the only state where she did not meet and talk with the white chairman of the state Woman's Committee.[68] However, while in Atlanta, she did manage to get in touch with Mrs. Alice Dugged Cary, president of the State Federation of Colored Women of Georgia and the chairman of the black subcommittee of the state woman's committee. Mrs. Cary conveyed the impression that the state was relatively well organized as far as the black women were concerned, although more by cities than by counties.[69] Not satisfied with this report—"it was too roseate and indefinite"—Mrs. Nelson stopped at Augusta overnight on her way to South Carolina and talked with Miss Lucy C. Laney, the principal of the Haines Institute and "the best and strongest colored woman in Georgia." Miss Laney's impressions were more critical. She knew of occasional, sporadic bits of war work among the black women in the state but, to her knowledge, no serious organized effort was being made. She was not even aware of the appointment of a black state chairman. Miss Laney introduced Mrs. Nelson to a Mrs. Harrington, the white county chairman of Richmond County, who said the work among the black women in that county was "at a standstill." In summing up the situation in the state Mrs. Nelson commented: "Such is the situation in Georgia—stultified by self-satisfaction in Atlanta."[70]

Mrs. Nelson found that those women actively involved in the effort to organize the black community mirrored their white counterparts. In New Orleans, for example, Mrs. Nelson noted that the black women who were active and anxious to organize a black woman's committee were "for the most part, teachers and college women, with a keen sense of responsibility."[71] In New Orleans the registration of women suggested by the Woman's Committee was put in the hands of a Mrs. Williams, "a colored school principal."[72] In North Carolina Miss McCullough, the black woman Mrs. Reilley relied upon, was a schoolteacher on leave of absence.[73] In Mississippi Mrs. McGehee selected Miss Sally Green, another schoolteacher, who had additional experience as a county agent.[74] In Florida the black state chairman was Miss Eartha M. White, a woman "of unusual ability," who had worked with the state labor commissioner. She was also known as "a leading negro club woman."[75] Naturally enough educated women with organizational experience formed the core around which the bulk of the black women were organized.

The patriotic programs and achievements of the black women during the war paralleled those of the white women. The work tended to fall into two categories. The initial activities followed the traditional, well-defined patterns of women's roles in war. Guided by the programs of the Woman's Committee, a second level of activity sought to go beyond this passive, traditional role and use the wartime crisis to improve social conditions in the nation. The first programs concentrated on the soldier going into battle and on a general display of patriotism on the home front. In the industrial town of Bessemer, Alabama, for example, the black women had an active Council of Defense unit which "made comfort kits for soldiers—with Bibles in each kit. . . . They found wives of soldiers who had gone to camp and helped them, particularly in making layettes for expectant mothers."[76] In Cobb County, on the northern outskirts of Atlanta, Georgia, the black women reported in a similar vein: "The organization was started with 27 women and has seen to it that every colored soldier from Cobb County has a bible to carry with him to the battle front. We fitted up a rest room for our soldiers from Camp Gordon. We showed our patriotism in the grand parade in Atlanta, April 27th., being there with our flags and banners to represent Cobb County."[77] As Mrs. Nelson remarked in discussing the war work among the black women in Birmingham, Alabama, "Most units have concentrated on comfort kits for soldiers and care of soldiers families."[78] Another area of concern for the soldiers was the staffing of canteens at the railroad stations. These canteens were generally run by the Red Cross, and sometimes there was friction between that organization and the black women who wanted to assist. In Alabama and Mississippi, for example, the Red Cross refused to give the black women permission to do canteen work at the railroad stations.[79]

In addition to its concern for the men in uniform, the Woman's Committee pressed its members throughout the states to do everything in their power to conserve and enlarge the existing food supply. This was in response to an obvious wartime need. However, the program went further and constituted an important aspect of the drive for social reform by the women. It offered the long-term hope of a better and more nutritious diet for the population as a whole. From the beginning, the Woman's Committee emphasized the need to produce more food and to conserve existing supplies, especially seasonal produce, with the new canning techniques. The unit of black women in Bessemer, Alabama, for example, canned over one thousand quarts of perishable foodstuffs.[80] In Cobb County, Georgia, the idea of increasing food production and conservation was eagerly accepted: "The motion picture on gardening for the school children was seen by 300 most of whom immediately went to work with war gardens. Prizes have been offered for the best gardens, chickens, pigs and vegetables. We have a knitting class. We are organizing canning clubs. We have now 60 members and an organization of boys, also one of girls."[81] Black women appreciated the importance of this work and actively sought help to implement it. In North Carolina, for example, Mrs. Reilley, the white state chairman of the woman's committee, commented: "We have had big county rallies and talks on well balanced meals and demonstrations by the girls of the county in the way to can—the most approved methods. We are taking the work to the colored people and the other day when I was in Anson County organizing, the colored people heard of it and requested that I speak in the Methodist Episcopal Church, so I did—my first experience but I never had a more attentive audience."[82]

In Florida the food-conservation work was pushed by Miss White, the Negro state chairman and organizer for the state Woman's Committee. In Duval County, with the assistance of the county commissioners, she established a Liberty Kitchen "in the basement of the Negro High School, to teach food substitutes and economy of fuel and a registration bureau was conducted for washerwomen and cooks."[83] In Tampa, the black Baptist preacher and his wife, both college graduates, turned their own kitchen into a demonstration unit for similar work.[84] In September 1918 the chairman of the Florida Woman's Committee reported that "Leon County is doing good Home Demonstration work among the negroes, due to the fine Home Economics Department of the State College for Women, working with the Agricultural Extension Department of the Government."[85] Much of this work built on foundations laid by the home economics extension service of the various state agricultural colleges, which in the previous seven years had helped organize thousands of canning and home demonstration clubs throughout the country. The Department of Agriculture paid the salary of county home demonstration agents in counties that complied with the provisions of the Smith-Hughes Act of 1917.[86]

In addition to such conventional patriotic work, a good deal of the program advanced by the Woman's Committee and taken up by the black women centered on improving the general social conditions of the black community. The war was seen as an opportunity to push social-welfare programs that had been talked about before the war but had received little positive encouragement. Probably the most important area of reform was in the field of public health. A great effort was made by the Woman's Committee, in conjunction with the Children's Bureau of the Department of Labor, to draw attention to the very high infant mortality rate in the United States and to publicize the need for better health services in the community. This was a continuation of a program launched in 1916 under the auspices of the General Federation of Women's Clubs and the Children's Bureau which sought to publicize the need for baby clinics, public nurses, accurate birth registration, purer milk supplies, and the like. The program centered on the baby weighing and measuring program, which the Woman's Committee vigorously supported throughout the country. Mrs. Nelson noted that the program seemed to have worked well in Jackson, Mississippi. She spoke to the black public-health nurse in that city, "who has been doing some excellent work here. The colored babies in Jackson are being weighed and a milk and ice fund is under way."[87]

Not all areas could report such good results. In South Carolina, where very little organization of the black women had been effected, there had been no activity in this area. However, as a direct result of Mrs. Nelson's visit there was agreement that this matter would be taken up as soon as practicable and would begin in Columbia, the state capital.[88] In New Orleans the program ran into some opposition, and Mrs. Nelson reported that there had been some "quiet agitation" among the Negro mothers themselves. Their concern centered around the fact that nothing was done after the babies were weighed and measured, and the mothers therefore regarded it as a waste of time and effort. "If they [babies] are sub-normal and home conditions are poor no effort is made to supply them with Pasteurized milk."[89] In Birmingham Mrs. Nelson found three separate black units working in different sections of the city. Although more was being done there than in New Orleans, some of the complaints were the same: "Babies weighed, but have not been followed up. There is a great deal of misunderstanding about this—some units seeming to think the weighing is an end in itself."[90]

Allied to the baby weighing and measuring program was the related drive to improve recreational facilities for children. In Atlanta Mrs. Nelson found that the Georgia State Federation of Colored Women, working in conjunction with the state woman's committee, had arranged for the establishment in the city of two playgrounds for black children.[91] In Jacksonville, Florida, Mrs. Nelson reported that "the colored women are interested in a playground for colored children, and the men have interested themselves and raised $600 for apparatus and equipment."[92] In the speeches she made to groups of black women throughout the South Mrs. Nelson did not hesitate to stress these aspects of the war program of the Woman's Committee. In Birmingham, before a big evening meeting in the largest black church in the city, she stressed the importance of the nurses' drive, the need for adequate playgrounds for the children, and the need to take measures to safeguard women in industry.[93]

Just as the war opened up job opportunities for white women, so it did on a lesser scale for black women. The central Woman's Committee and the various state committees began to push for nurses' training for black women. The Washington office sent out a list of hospitals where black women could receive training in nursing and the state chairmen usually publicized this information. In Mississippi Mrs. McGehee used the opportunity to encourage the organization of black women in the state, asserting, "I want to enroll them as nurses, as they are so anxious for that training right now. I did not do this in our own enrollment, because I knew I was going to organize them, and they would like so much better to see something that their organization had done at once to give them an opportunity to serve. I thank you for the list of hospitals where they can get training."[94] In New Orleans Mrs. Nelson heard that "colored nurses are 'under way' for city work."[95] In mid-1918 the retiring chairman of the Florida Woman's Committee reported that "They have done specially good service in cities as practical nurses, releasing graduate nurses for overseas service."[96]

There were other areas in which the war opened up new opportunities for black women. In Jacksonville, Florida, for example, the Negro state organizer "supplied a dozen office buildings with negro girls for elevator service to release men. Elevator girls are also being supplied for the hotels and stores, under her direction."[97] Florida went one step further. Under the energetic direction of Miss White, a Mutual Protection League for Working Girls was established for the benefit of those "who had take up the unfamiliar work of elevator girls, bell girls in hotels, and chauffeurs. From this it was not far to a Union of Girls in Domestic Service . . . ."[98]

Mrs. Nelson's southern trip as field representative of the Woman's Committee was a valuable exercise. Although, with a few notable exceptions, she found relatively little formal organization of black women, she did find that, contrary to some rumors, they were patriotic and anxious to be incorporated in a formal way into the domestic war effort. Her reception among the white southern chairmen of the state Woman's Committees was, on the whole, polite and receptive, and in some cases she was able to influence their views on the matter of black organization. Most of the state committees were aware of the need to take concrete steps to incorporate the black community into the war effort, and some were genuinely impressed with the possibilities of the project. Traveling between Alabama and Florida in August 1918, Mrs. Nelson caught that mood in her comment—"Trains slow, distances tremendous, state chairmen importunate."[99] As she journeyed from state to state it was obvious how much the success of the Woman's Committee organization in the states depended on the personal attitudes and organizational abilities of the state chairmen. It varied from state to state and made generalization difficult. In organizing the black women, the problems of the chairmen were compounded by the attitudes of the state governors and the men's state Councils of Defense, who tended to be conservative on that particular issue.[100]

By mid-1918 the war had begun to create pressures for profound social change in domestic America. Chief among these pressures was the need for a more rational approach to the utilization of all resources, including human resources. The potential for social reform inherent in the situation was grasped by southern black women. Their quiet struggle over organization was an important aspect of this battle for social reform. It formed part of the effort to erode the southern caste system and to gain more responsibility and self-respect. Similarly, in the drives for greater food production and conservation, for improved employment opportunities, and particularly in the different aspects of the child-welfare program, southern black women like their white counterparts had an opportunity both to demonstrate their patriotism and to advance social reforms that would have long-term significance for the entire community. The war ended too soon to allow any substantial or permanent social change to take place in the South, but the direction of the change was clear. The white state chairman of Mississippi recognized the opportunity the war offered the black population of her state. In commenting on the need to get the black women organized and involved in the war effort, she wrote: "I am vitally interested in this, and can see its far reaching effect—not alone now—but after the war, when we will need trained hands and brains, for the great work awaiting."[101]

NOTES

1. The most encyclopedic coverage of domestic America during World War I remains Frederic L. Paxson, *America at War, 1917-1918* (Boston, 1939), which is Volume II of his *American Democracy and the World War* (3 vols., Boston and

Berkeley, 1936–1948). Some of the state studies do attempt to come to grips with the question of how national policies were implemented at the state and local levels. Examples of the better studies include Franklin F. Holbrook and Livia Appel, *Minnesota in the War with Germany* (2 vols., St. Paul, Minn., 1928–1932); Benjamin F. Shambaugh, ed., *Chronicles of the World War* (7 vols., Iowa City, Iowa, 1920–1923); Marguerite E. Jenison, comp., *The War-Time Organization of Illinois* (Springfield, Ill., 1923), Volume V of Theodore C. Pease, ed., *Illinois in the World War* (6 vols., Springfield, Ill., 1921–1923). A brief account of the role of women in the war is contained in William L. O'Neill, *Everyone Was Brave: The Rise and Fall of Feminism in America* (Chicago, 1969), 169–224. The best contemporary accounts of the role of women in the war are Ida C. Clarke, *American Women and the World War* (New York, 1918), and Emily N. Blair, *The Woman's Committee, United States Council of National Defense: An Interpretative Report, April 21, 1917, to February 27, 1919* (Washington, 1920).

2. The best contemporary account of the role of black women in World War I is Alice Dunbar-Nelson, "Negro Women in War Work" in Emmett J. Scott, ed., *Scott's Official History of the American Negro in the World War* ([Chicago], 1919), 374–97. A more personal account of wartime work in a government department and organizational work on behalf of southern black women and girls for the War Camp Community Service in the immediate aftermath of the Armistice is Mary C. Terrell, *A Colored Woman in a White World* (Washington, D.C., 1940), Chaps. 25, 32. For a discussion of the administration's attempt to mobilize the black male population see Jane L. Scheiber and Harry N. Scheiber, "The Wilson Administration and the Wartime Mobilization of Black Americans, 1917–18," *Labor History,* X (Summer 1969), 433–58.

3. On the question of domestic reform see Allen F. Davis, "Welfare, Reform and World War I," *American Quarterly,* XIX (Fall 1967), 516–33; and Otis L. Graham, Jr., *The Great Campaigns: Reform and War in America, 1900–1928* (Englewood Cliffs, N.J., 1971), 97–114.

4. For general accounts of the establishment of the Woman's Committee see O'Neill, *Everyone Was Brave,* 169–224; and Blair, *The Woman's Committee,* Chap. 1. The National Association of Colored Women was represented on the general committee of the Woman's Committee.

5. By July 1918 the Woman's Committee had the following departments of work: Registration for Service; Food Production and Home Economics; Food Administration; Women in Industry; Child Welfare; Maintenance of Existing Social Service Agencies; Health and Recreation; Educational Propaganda; Liberty Loan; Home and Allied Relief. See Blair, *The Woman's Committee,* 20–21.

6. It was not until the very end of the war, in mid-September 1918, that these dual organizations in the states finally merged and formed the Field Division of the Council of National Defense.

7. Woman's Committee, Minutes, Meeting of January 29, 1918, p. 278, 13A-C5, Box 570. Records of the Committee on Women's Defense Work, Records of the Council of National Defense, Record Group 62 (National Archives, Suitland Federal Record Center, Md.); hereinafter cited as WC Minutes with date and page number. Except for one citation in note 65, all manuscript materials are from the Records of the Council of National Defense, RG 62.

8. See "Increasing the Patriotic Efforts of the Negroes in the Southern States," January 7, 1918 (unsigned memorandum: Dorothy Pope?), Reports of State

Councils of Defense, Records of the Field Division, 15-C1, Box 908, folder marked "State Councils Section: Negro Organization"; cited hereinafter as Repts. SCD with category and box number.

9. See "General Letter No. 44, February 23, 1918," *ibid*. This circular, issued by the State Councils Section of the Council of National Defense, stressed the valuable assistance that the Negro community, if organized, could give to the war effort in the states and suggested the establishment of Negro county Councils of Defense which would work under the direction of the white county councils. See also Dorothy Pope memorandum, "Response to General Letter No. 44 Calling for Organization of the Negroes," March 15, 1918, *ibid*.

10. See "Organization of Negroes as Conducted by the Southern State Councils" (n.d.: circa July–August 1918. 24 pp. typed memorandum, unsigned), *ibid*.

11. Ernest T. Attwell of Tuskegee Institute was appointed by the Food Administration as a field worker among the Negroes in the South. He later went to Washington and directed the Negro Section of the Food Administration. See John H. Franklin, *From Slavery to Freedom: A History of Negro Americans* (New York, 1969), 471. Dr. George Edmund Haynes of Fisk University was appointed to the specially created post of Director of Negro Economics in the Department of Labor in May 1918. See Scheiber and Scheiber, "The Wilson Administration," 448–49. The Scheibers emphasize (pp. 449–50) that all these efforts by the government agencies were exhortative and patriotic only. There was no emphasis on reform. By contrast, the Woman's Committee made one of the most serious efforts and one that did have more overtly reformist overtones. Alice Dunbar-Nelson believed that "The Council of National Defense made the best organized attempt at mobilizing the colored women of all the war organizations." See Dunbar-Nelson, "Negro Women in War Work," 383.

12. WC Minutes, July 8, 1918, p. 505. For comments on Negro unrest and anxiety see Franklin, *From Slavery to Freedom*, 474–75; and Dunbar-Nelson "Negro Women in War Work," 394.

13. WC Minutes, July 8, 1918, p. 505.

14. The quotation is from Miss Patterson's report of Scott's conversation. See Hannah Jane Patterson to Walter S. Gifford, July 8, 1918, Central Correspondence File, 1918, Records of the Committee on Women's Defense Work, 13A-A2, Box 496, File 79 (cited hereinafter as Corr. CWDW with category, box, and file numbers); WC Minutes, July 8, 1918, pp. 505–506.

15. WC Minutes, July 8, 1918, p. 505.

16. For biographical details see Nick A. Ford, "Alice Dunbar Nelson," in Edward T. James, *et al.*, eds. *Notable American Women 1607–1950: A Biographical Dictionary* (3 vols., Cambridge, Mass., 1971), II, 614–15.

17. Nelson to Patterson, August 14, 1918, Corr. CWDW, 13A-A2, Box 512, File 131.

18. Nelson to Patterson, August 23, 1918, *ibid*.

19. Nelson to Patterson, August 26, 1918, *ibid*. Mrs. Nelson referred to this grievance concerning the Red Cross, specifically in Montgomery, Alabama, and Vicksburg, Mississippi.

20. Nelson to Patterson, August 23, 1918, *ibid*.

21. Nelson to Patterson, August 21, 1918, *ibid*.

22. *Ibid*.

23. Nelson to Patterson, September 10, 1918, *ibid.*

24. Nelson to Patterson, August 19, 1918, *ibid.*

25. Mrs. J. Otey Reid to Patterson, August 20, 1918, Corr. CWDW, 13A-A2, Box 522, File 162.

26. Nelson to Patterson, September 5, 1918, Corr. CWDW, 13A-A2, Box 512, File 131.

27. Mrs. Eugene Reilley to Mrs. Joseph R. Lamar, July 18, 1918; Reilley to Patterson, September 7, 1918, Corr. CWDW, 13A-A2, Box 512, File 132; Nelson to Patterson, September 7, 1918, Corr. CWDW, 13A-A2, Box 512, File 131.

28. Nelson to Patterson, August 15, 1918, Corr. CWDW, 13A-A2, Box 512, File 131.

29. For details of the incident see Nelson to Patterson, September 3, 1918 (telegram); see also Patterson to Nelson, September 3, 1918, *ibid.*; Patterson to Mrs. Samuel M. Inman, September 3, 1918; Inman to Patterson, September 6, 1918, Corr. CWDW, 13A-A2, Box 494, File 73; Nelson to Patterson, September 7, 1918, Corr. CWDW, 13A-A2, Box 512, File 131.

30. Mrs. Frank Jennings to Patterson, August 20, 1918, Corr. CWDW, 13A-A2, Box 493, File 63.

31. McGehee to Patterson, August 26, 1918, Corr. CWDW, 13A-A2, Box 509, File 123.

32. *Ibid.*

33. Nelson to Patterson, August 19, 1918, Corr. CWDW, 13A-A2, Box 512, File 131.

34. Lamar to Patterson (memorandum), July 23, 1918, Corr. CWDW, 13A-A2, Box 505, File 116.

35. Patterson to Inman, August 15, 1918, Corr. CWDW, 13A-A2, Box 494, File 73.

36. Patterson to Reilley, September 3, 1918, Corr. CWDW, 13A-A2, Box 512, File 132.

37. Patterson to Reilley, September 13, 1918, *ibid.*

38. Patterson to Inman, August 15, 1918, Corr. CWDW, 13A-A2, Box 494, File 73.

39. See for North Carolina example Patterson to Reilley, September 3, 1918, Corr. CWDW, 13A-A2, Box 512, File 132.

40. Patterson to Gifford, July 8, 1918, Corr. CWDW, 13A-A2, Box 496, File 79. In January 1918 the men's State Council Section had suggested that black councils in the southern states be composed of both men and women. The Woman's Committee discussed the matter but decided to leave the exact form and composition of such state and local organizations to be determined at the state level. See WC Minutes, January 29, 1918, p. 278.

41. Patterson to Nelson, August 19, 1918, Corr. CWDW, 13A-A2, Box 512, File 131.

42. See comment in Reilley to Patterson, September 7, 1918, Corr. CWDW, 13A-A2, Box 512, File 132.

43. Nelson to Patterson, September 7, 1918, Corr. CWDW, 13A-A2, Box 512, File 131.

44. Nelson to Patterson, August 30, 1918, *ibid.*

45. "A History of the Activities of the Women of Florida for Service in the World War, 1917–1919. Compiled by the Woman's Committee of Florida, Council of National Defense," signed by Mrs. Frank E. Jennings, state chairman, 11, Reports from State Divisions, State Organization Department, 13L-A1, Box 635; cited hereinafter as Repts. SD with category and box number. Mrs. Frank E. Jennings had succeeded Mrs. William Hocker as state chairman of the Florida Woman's Committee. The Woman's Committee in Florida was infinitely superior to the men's state Council of Defense, which remained a rather lackluster organization.

46. See Patterson to Nelson, August 19, 1918, Corr. CWDW, 13A-A2, Box 512, File 131.

47. McGehee to Patterson, August 12, 1918, Corr. CWDW, 13A-A2, Box 509, File 123.

48. For details on Sally Green see Nelson to Patterson, August 20, 1918, Corr. CWDW, 13A-A2, Box 512, File 131; McGehee to Patterson, August 12, 1918, 13A-A2, Box 509, File 123; McGehee to "My Dear Madam Chairman" (mimeograph), August 26, 1918, Corr. CWDW, 13A-A2, Box 509, File 123.

49. Nelson to Patterson, August 20, 1918, Corr. CWDW, 13A-A2, Box 512, File 131.

50. McGehee to Patterson, August 12, 1918; McGehee to "My Dear Madam Chairman" (mimeograph), August 26, 1918, Corr. CWDW, 13A-A2, Box 509, File 123.

51. McGehee to Patterson, August 26, 1918, *ibid.*

52. McGehee to Patterson, October 12, 1918, *ibid.*

53. Mrs. J. Otey Reid to Patterson, August 20, 1918, Corr. CWDW, 13A-A2, Box 522, File 162. A three-page letter outlining the Sumter County Plan from the secretary of the Sumter County Council of Defense to George F. Porter, chief, Section on Cooperation with States, CND, dated October 10, 1917, was mimeographed and circulated to the state councils and state Woman's Committees by the Washington office in late 1917. Reports of the State Councils, Records of the Field Division, 15-C1, Box 908; cited hereinafter as Repts. SCD with category and box numbers.

54. Nelson to Patterson, September 5, 1918, Corr. CWDW, 13A-A2, Box 512, File 131.

55. Nelson to Patterson, August 14, 1918, *ibid.*

56. Nelson to Patterson, August 19, 1918, *ibid.*

57. Nelson to Patterson, August 15, 1918, *ibid.*

58. Nelson to Patterson, August 17, 1918, *ibid.*

59. *Ibid.*

60. Nelson to Patterson, August 28, 1918, *ibid.*

61. Nelson to Patterson, August 26, 1918, *ibid.*

62. Nelson to Patterson, August 29, 1918, *ibid.* This independent black women's organization paralleled the semi-independent men's organizations, the Negro Patriotic League and the Saturday Service League, that Mrs. Nelson found in Mississippi. See Nelson to Patterson, August 25, 1918, *ibid.*

63. Nelson to Patterson, September 10, 1918, *ibid.*

64. Mrs. Helm Bruce to Patterson, August 20, 1918, Corr. CWDW, 13A-A2, Box 502, File 103.

65. "Minutes of Executive Meeting, North Carolina Woman's Committee, February 14, 1918," Woman's Committee File, Box 39, Records of the North Carolina Council of Defense, Military Collection, World War I Records, Pt. II (North Carolina Division of Archives and History, Raleigh, N. C.). See also Reilley to Lamar, February 20, 1918, Corr. CWDW, 13A-A2, Box 512, File 132.

66. Reilley to Lamar, July 18, 1918, Corr. CWDW, 13A-A2, Box 512, File 132.

67. Reilley to Patterson, September 7, 1918, *ibid.*

68. See footnote 29 above. The failure to develop a genuine black woman's organization in Georgia was attributed to class distinctions among the black women themselves. See "Report on State Organization, January 28, 1918" (Mrs. Joseph R. Lamar), attached to WC Minutes, January 29, 1918, p. 286.

69. Nelson to Patterson, September 3, 1918, Corr. CWDW, 13A-A2, Box 512, File 131. See "Plan of Work, Atlanta Colored Women's War Council" in Gerda Lerner, ed., *Black Women in White America: A Documentary History* (New York, 1972), 498–500.

70. Nelson to Patterson, September 4, 1918, Corr. CWDW, 13A-A2, Box 512, File 131.

71. Nelson to Patterson, August 15, 1918, *ibid.*

72. Nelson to Patterson, August 14, 1918, *ibid.*

73. Nelson to Patterson, September 7, 1918, *ibid.*

74. For references to biographical details on Sally Green see footnote 48 above.

75. Quotation "of unusual ability" is from "A History of the Activities of the Women of Florida," Repts. SD, 13L-A1, Box 635. Information about working for the state labor commissioner in "Report of Florida Division, July 15 to September 15, 1918" (By Mrs. Frank E. Jennings), 8 pp., *ibid.* She is undoubtedly the clubwoman referred to in "Increasing the Patriotic Efforts of the Negroes in the Southern States" (January 7, 1918), 4, Repts. SCD, 15-C1, Box 908.

76. Nelson to Patterson, August 28, 1918, Corr. CWDW, 13A-A2, Box 512, File 131.

77. Excerpt from report of black women of Cobb County, Ga., included in "Bi-monthly Report of the Woman's Committee, Council of National Defense, Georgia Division, March 15–May 15, 1918" (By Mrs. Samuel M. Inman, chairman), 10, Repts. SD, 13L-A1, Box 635.

78. Nelson to Patterson, August 28, 1918, Corr. CWDW, 13A-A2, Box 512, File 131.

79. Nelson to Patterson, August 23, 26, 1918, *ibid.*; see also Dunbar-Nelson, "Negro Women in War Work," 376–77.

80. Nelson to Patterson, August 28, 1918, Corr. CWDW, 13A-A2, Box 512, File 131.

81. Excerpt from report of Negro women of Cobb County, included in "Bi-monthly Report of the Woman's Committee, Council of National Defense, Georgia Division, March 15–May 15, 1918," p. 10, Repts. SD, 13L-A1, Box 635.

82. Reilley to Miss Ida Tarbell, July 24, 1917, Corr. CWDW, 13A-A1, Box 468, File 132.

83. "A History of the Activities of the Women of Florida," 11, Repts. SD, 13L-A1, Box 635.

84. "Report of Florida Division, May 15 to July 15, 1918" (Mrs. William [Elizabeth] Hocker, retiring chairman), 4, *ibid.*

85. "Report of Florida Division, July 15 to September 15, 1918" (Mrs. Frank E. [Minerva P.] Jennings, chairman), 4, *ibid.*

86. Blair, *The Woman's Committee,* 76.

87. Nelson to Patterson, August 22, 1918, Corr. CWDW, 13A-A2, Box 512, File 131; see also Dunbar-Nelson, "Negro Women in War Work," 385. For more details on the social programs of the Woman's Committee see Blair, *The Woman's Committee,* 77–85.

88. Nelson to Patterson, September 5, 1918, Corr. CWDW, 13A-A2, Box 512, File 131.

89. Nelson to Patterson, August 15, 1918, *ibid.*

90. Nelson to Patterson, August 28, 1918, *ibid.*

91. Nelson to Patterson, September 3, 1918, *ibid.*

92. Nelson to Patterson, August 30, 1918, *ibid.*

93. Nelson to Patterson, August 28, 1918, *ibid.*

94. McGehee to Patterson, August 12, 1918, Corr. CWDW, 13A-A2, Box 509, File 123.

95. Nelson to Patterson, August 15, 1918, Corr. CWDW, 13A-A2, Box 512, File 131. A black nurse was already working among the city poor in New Orleans, but she was working independently of the state Woman's Committe, being "hired by a Catholic priest doing settlement work in his parish." Nelson to Patterson, August 15, 1918, *ibid.*

96. "Report of Florida Division, May 15 to July 15, 1918," Repts. SD, 13L-A1, Box 635.

97. "Report of Florida Division, July 15 to September 15, 1918," p. 4, *ibid.*

98. Dunbar-Nelson, "Negro Women in War Work," 384.

99. Nelson to Patterson, August 29, 1918, Corr. CWDW, 13A-A2, Box 512, File 131. The Scheibers argue that the general black community cooperated whole-heartedly in the war effort for reasons of "deeply-felt patriotism" coupled with the hope that this cooperation would help in the battle against discrimination in the postwar period. Scheiber and Scheiber, "The Wilson Administration," 452. My evidence shows that the southern black women, although no less patriotic, hoped to use the wartime cooperation itself to alleviate their position.

100. Emily Newell Blair regarded the organization of black women as "One of the most difficult matters that certain parts of the country had to handle. . . . " Blair, *The Woman's Committee,* 106.

101. McGehee to Patterson, August 12, 1918, Corr. CWDW, 13A-A2, Box 509, File 123.

20 ♀ Women Reformers and American Culture, 1870–1930

Jill Conway

The history of American feminism has an Alice in Wonderland quality. The story of the achievement of legal and institutional liberties for women in America must be accompanied by an account of their loss of psychological autonomy and social segregation. The historian of American feminism must write a double narrative in which something more than the reversals of Looking-Glass Land must be advanced. The historian must relate the outward story of a successful agitation to some causal analysis of why this agitation first for legal rights, then for access to higher education, then for the franchise and for liberation from a traditional Christian view of marriage had so little influence on actual behavior. For there is no escaping the fact that in the very decade of the twenties when the franchise was secured and when a liberal view of marriage ties had finally gained public acceptance that the vast majority of American women began to find social activism unattractive and to return to an ethic of domesticity as romantic and suffocating as any code of the high Victorian era. In fact the stereotype of femininity which became dominant in the popular culture of the thirties differed little from the stereotype of the Victorian lady except that the twentieth-century American woman had physical appetites which dictated that she could only know fulfillment by experiencing maternity and joyfully adapting to the exclusively feminine world of suburbia.[1]

To some historians and social analysts this paradox has seemed so puzzling that nothing short of a plot theory of history can explain this sudden alteration in what appeared to be the direction of social change. Betty Friedan, for instance, feels that the triumph of domesticity can only be accounted for by the recognition by capitalists that women could best serve the economy of abundance as passive consumers.[2] Yet her diagnosis does not take into account the fact that before the thirties women made the role of consumer an important one for social criticism through the organization of the National Consumers' League, a body which pioneered in legal and political campaigns in favor of state and federal welfare legislation. As the history of the League ably demonstrated between 1899, the year of its foundation, and the beginning of the New Deal welfare programs, consumers need not be passive victims of the capitalist system.

More recently historians of feminism have seen an underlying continuity behind the appearance of change in the social position of American women. Both Aileen Kraditor and William O'Neill have concluded that the remarkable stability of the bourgeois family in the twentieth century was the social fact which led to the frustration of all aspirations for change in the role and status of women.[3] Thus the reformers who made divorce and birth control acceptable in the early decades of the twentieth century put emphasis on the need to strengthen the family in a secular society. Both divorce and limitation of family size finally won popular acceptance when they were advocated as reforms which would allow the bourgeois family the flexibility necessary to survive the pressures of an upwardly mobile urban society rather than as reforms which would permit real changes in sexual behavior.[4] In the light of the evidence of historical demography we see the logic working for this kind of reform to preserve the family. Demographic study indicates that the duration of marriage unions was actually lengthening in the twentieth century as compared with earlier centuries such as the seventeenth, customarily regarded as a period of family stability. In fact, increased life expectancy in the twentieth century meant that fewer marriage partnerships were terminated after a short period by death; consequently, the sanctioning of divorce became a social necessity. There is thus no contradiction between the development of liberal attitudes toward the dissolution of marriage and the renewed stress on the value of maternity and domesticity for women. Divorce and birth control, both reforms which could have been advocated in terms opposed to female domesticity, actually won acceptance as measures to preserve the family and along with it female domesticity.

While historians are correct in emphasizing these underlying continuities in the history of American feminism between the Civil War and the 1930s, it is misleading to do so without drawing attention to the fact that women activists of the period represented a real change in feminine behavior. The failure of feminists to understand the significance of the intense social activism of women reformers during these years indicates that new ways of behaving do not necessarily evoke any new view of the female temperament. Though women of the stature of Jane Addams and Lillian Wald were actually wielding national power and influencing the decisions of the White House, neither they nor any of their contemporaries thought about adjusting the image of the female to this position of command. This failure to see women's activism for what it was, a real departure from women's traditional domesticity, indicates the controlling power of the stereotype of the female temperament which continued unaltered from the 1870s to the 1930s. Acquiescence in this control was indeed the major weakness in the ideology of feminism for the stereotype of the female personality was an essentially conservative one although women reformers coupled it with social innovation and occasionally with trenchant social criticism.

We see the controlling power of the stereotype of the female temperament most clearly in the thought of Jane Addams and Lillian Wald.[5] Both women were aggressive public campaigners who relished a good political fight and who hungered after power. Yet they claimed to be reformers in the name of specialized feminine perceptions of social injustice. These specialized perceptions came from women's innate passivity and from women's ability to empathize with the weak and dependent. Like all reformers with a program for action, Jane Addams and Lillian Wald believed they had found a social group who would bring a new, just social order into being, but theirs was a group defined by sex rather than by class. Lacking a clear class consciousness, they expected a sex group to be agents of social change because of the unique qualities with which they believed the feminine temperament was endowed. Because of these qualities women were capable of direct, intuitive awareness of social injustice exactly in the style of the abolitionists who had been fired for the antislavery crusade through direct intuitive perception of social sin. Just what it was in the psyche of a Jane Addams or a Lillian Wald which would permit empathy with the weak and dependent remains shrouded in mystery for the most assiduous biographer. Both women gave evidence from an early age of the capacity to create and dominate large organizations, and they moved naturally into a position of leadership in any area of reform which they took up, whether it be settlement work, child welfare legislation or the international peace movement.

Even though Jane Addams and Lillian Wald could not recognize their drive to power, their adoption of feminine intuition as a style of reform by which to come to grips with the problems of industrial cities is a puzzling choice. One expects tough-minded economic analysis from critics of industrial society. However, middle-class women reformers of their generation needed to find a basis for criticizing an exploitive economic system in which women of their class played no active part. It was for this reason that they were obliged to make such claims for the intuitive social power of the female temperament. They were encouraged in these claims by the dominant biological view of social evolution which did place great emphasis upon the evolutionary significance of biologically determined male and female temperaments. However, to base one's social criticism upon the idea that feminine intuition could both diagnose and direct social change was to tie one's identity as a social critic to acquiescence in the traditional stereotype of women. Further, to the extent that such women succeeded in gaining popular acceptance as reformers they were lending strength to the stereotype and helping to prepare the ground for the acceptance of another view of sexually specialized intellect, the neo-Freudian, romantic and conservative one, which began to gain acceptance in American culture in the twenties and the thirties.

In my study of American women who were both feminists and social critics in the post-Civil War era, two clearly distinct social types have emerged. The first is a borrowing from European culture, the type of the sage or prophetess who claimed access to hidden wisdom by virtue of feminine insights. The second is the type of the professional expert or the scientist, a social identity highly esteemed in American culture but sexually neutral. Jane Addams represents the best example of the Victorian sage to be found in American culture during her active public career from the 1890s to the 1930s. Florence Kelley, the organizer of the National Consumers' League and a kind of composite Sidney and Beatrice Webb for American industrial society, represents one of the best examples of the professional expert who took on the role of the social engineer. What is interesting about the two types is that the sage had great resonance for American popular culture and was celebrated in endless biographies, memoirs and eulogistic sketches.[6] Women who took on that role became great public figures, culture heroines known in households throughout the nation. But the woman as expert did not captivate the popular imagination and did not become a model of feminine excellence beyond a small circle of highly educated women of a single generation. Julia Lathrop, who was the pioneer strategist of the mental health movement, the innovator responsible for the juvenile court movement and the head of the first Federal Child Welfare Bureau which became the model for many New Deal welfare agencies, simply did not excite the faintest ripple of public attention during a lifetime exactly contemporaneous with Jane

Addams. Indeed this remarkable woman remained so anonymous despite a lifetime devoted to public service that Jane Addams wrote a biography of her so that she could serve as a model for future generations of American women.[7] The biography was little read and could not serve its purpose because Jane Addams lost the substance of this consummate political strategist's life in describing the empathetic and unaggressive woman heroine which the stereotype of female excellence required. Similarly Florence Kelley's biographer, Josephine Goldmark, was unable to preserve for future generations any of the fiery personality of this powerhouse of a woman.[8] The surface account of her lifetime devoted to the welfare of the industrial working class was accurately recorded. But the volcanic personality whose rages were so monumental that she could stamp out of a White House conference slamming the door in the face of Theodore Roosevelt is lost. Since women were supposed to be gentle, none of Mrs. Kelley's passion could come through the uncharacteristic calm imposed by her biographer. Thus the achievements of the experts were lost to subsequent generations and the significance of their actual behavior was completely misunderstood.

What survived for popular consumption was the woman reformer as sage and prophetess, the social type of which Jane Addams is the perfect exemplar. This survival led to an unfortunate association of critical perceptions of society with unquestioning acceptance of traditional views of the female psyche. It is the development of this type which we must understand if we want to comprehend how radical discontent could be expended in every social direction except the one which required questioning the stereotype of women.

The path to Jane Addams' identity as a sage lay through the experience of higher education and the recognition that she had access to learning of a scale and quality not available to preceding generations. The Addams family was involved in the abolition movement and important in local Republican politics and through these concerns became committed to equality with men in women's legal rights and educational opportunities. Daughters of the Addams family thus inherited a family tradition of reform without the corresponding obligation to business success which was imposed by such families on their sons. However, the standard curriculum for women's colleges like Rockford Seminary which Jane Addams attended entirely neglected the question of relevance for future vocational or intellectual purposes. Jane Addams was exposed at Rockford to the standard Victorian literary culture together with a high saturation of Protestant Christianity since the seminary's founder hoped to raise up a race of Christian women who could civilize the West.

The result of rigorous training in moral and aesthetic concerns was considerable disorientation when Jane Addams left college and began to try to define some social role in which her education could be put to use. Not only did her education fail to relate her in any significant way to the occupational structure of society, it had also trained her to be a moral agent in a society which expected middle-class women to be passive spectators and consumers. Two possible responses to this situation seem to have attracted the post-Civil War generation of college-educated women. The first was to withdraw to graduate study and acquire a respectable social role through professional training. Graduate school offered both escape from the family and the opportunity to enter a neutral social territory where the traditional rigidity of the American division of labor between men and women had not had time to establish itself. Those of an intellectual bent for graduate work seem to have found this adaptation a satisfactory one. It was the path to the social type of the woman expert. However, for those to whom graduate school was merely a strategy to escape from family discipline, only the second response was possible. Self-deception about an intellectual or professional career culminated in the standard Victorian ailment of emotional prostration. A minor illness took Jane Addams out of the Women's Medical College in Philadelphia in 1882 and kept her an invalid for over twelve months. Travel was of course the major therapy for such persistent nervous and emotional ailments, and it was while visiting London that Jane Addams began to develop the first signs of a nagging social conscience. In England the stereotypes of nativism could not inhibit perception of the sufferings of the London poor. The faces which stared back at the visitor to London's East End were not the faces of degenerate Irish or Poles, but English faces which could arouse the racially selective democratic feelings of young native Americans as no other sight could.[9]

Travel next suggested the idea of expatriation and the refinement of a literary education through involvement in European aristocratic culture. For a woman who had been trained to see herself as an heir to the abolitionist tradition of moral fervor, however, there could be no more than temporary dabbling in the expatriate life. Once she had recognized her common human ties with the urban poor, it was only a matter of time before she put the two styles of life together by visiting an immigrant ghetto in Chicago and espousing the lot of the common man now seen as the logical object of reforming zeal which an earlier generation had directed toward the Negro.

The consequences of the life style which Jane Addams pioneered and other educated women emulated are well known. In New York and Chicago, women were the first founders of settlement houses. They also were preponderant among settlement residents in Philadelphia, Boston and Cleveland. The initial impulse for this kind of feminine migration to the slums was not identification with the working class, as in the European settlement movement, but the recognition that there was a social cure for the neurotic ills of privileged young women in America because their ailments were socially induced. As Jane Addams and Ellen Starr put it when they were looking for a house in an immigrant ward of Chicago in 1889: moving to the ghetto was ". . . more for the benefit of the people who do it than for the other class. . . . Nervous people do not crave rest but activity of a certain kind."[10] By definition "nervous people" in need of releasing activity in American society were not men but women. Men were also discarded as irrelevant in the planning of Hull-House and other women's settlements because they were thought of as "less Christian" in spirit than women and motivated to action entirely by commercial rewards. It was thus as a consequence of an accurate perception of the problems of educated women in American society that middle-class women were brought into contact with the social problems of urban-industrial America. They were on location, settled and ready to become involved in urban problems just before the great depression of 1893–94 struck. Living in an urban slum that winter was the searing, unforgettable confrontation with social injustice which turned all of them into real critics of American society and obliterated their earlier concern with personal adjustment. But in forgetting the reasons for their presence in the urban slums women began to equate their recognition of social problems with special qualities of feminine insight. In *Democracy and Social Ethics* for instance, the work which was the most popular of Jane Addams' early writings on social problems, the culture of poverty is seen through the eyes of a middle-class woman visitor and the perception of the way American society exploited immigrants is made a feminine one. Exploiters are masculine and those who can see the true vision of a democratic society are women.[11]

Quite apart from the process of social selection which took women reformers to the city, there were good intellectual grounds for ascribing special qualities to the female intellect. These were to be found in the current interpretation of the significance of sex differences in the evolution of society. Jane Addams' papers show that she derived her views on this subject from three supposedly unimpeachable sources. She read Herbert Spencer's *Study of Sociology* of 1873 early in her career and accepted from it Spencer's view that the female psyche and mind were of special significance in the evolutionary process because of the innate feminine capacity to empathize with the weak. Once she had met Lester Ward at Hull-House in the decade of the 1890s, she accepted

Ward's assumption that the female was the prototype of the human being and the most highly evolved of the two sexes. In 1900 she met the Scottish biologist and sociologist Patrick Geddes whose *The Evolution of Sex* of 1889 was the major work in English by a biologist of repute on the evolutionary significance of sex differences. Geddes believed that from the smallest single-celled organism to man sex differences were tied to differences in cell metabolism which made female organisms passive and nurturing and male organisms warlike and aggressive. After she met Geddes, she added a natural bent of pacifism to women's special capacity for social insight and played her role as sage with confidence that it conformed to everything current biology and sociology had to say about the place of women in society.[12]

While she held to this traditional picture of women, however, Jane Addams had by 1900 arrived at some fundamental criticisms of American society. She recognized that political institutions which conformed to the classical theory of democracy were incapable of creating the kind of social equality which was central to the American democratic belief. She was convinced that traditional Puritan individualism was no guide to morality in an urban-industrial society. She saw that every social and political institution in America needed radical change if immigrants and workers were to participate in political decisions and receive the benefits of the American industrial economy to the same degree that native Americans did. She thought the family should be modified so that its members could not settle into a private domesticity which made them blind to social suffering outside the family circle; church and charitable institutions needed to be pried loose from adherence to the old Puritan economic ethic and negative morality; business corporations and trade unions needed to be less concerned with productivity and material rewards and more aware of human values; political parties needed to be reformed so that they could become more responsive to the needs and concerns of the urban immigrant. The tendency to violence in American life which she saw as the heritage of the need to coerce a slave population in the South must be eradicated if the divisions in industrial society were not to lead to class warfare. As a diagnosis of American social ills, this was not unimpressive. It was free from the usual Progressive concern with institutionalizing middle-class values. It was future oriented, ready to accept radical change and optimistic about the potential of the American city to become a genuinely creative, pluralistic community.[13]

One can say that important elements of radical discontent are present in this social criticism—an accurate diagnosis of the present and a creative, dynamizing view of the future. Contemporaries certainly thought so. In 1902 when Jane Addams published *Democracy and*

Social Ethics, the work that contained the major themes of her social criticism up to 1900, her mail ranged from appreciative notes from John Dewey and William James calling it "one of the great books of our time" to emotional letters from college students who said they found reading the book a religious experience which liberated them to be moral beings for the first time.[14]

What *Democracy and Social Ethics* lacked was a realistic perception of the social group who would be agents of desirable social change. To Jane Addams and women reformers of her generation, it seemed perfectly clear that women were the only people in America capable of bringing about a new order in which democracy would find social as well as political expression. As an organized force in politics, they would moralize and socialize a state which Jane Addams recognized was at present organized to protect and promote the interests of businessmen. Of even greater importance, women would be able to solve the problems of city government because the efficient management of urban affairs involved generalizing the skills of housekeeping which were exclusively feminine skills.

This celebration of women as makers of the future democratic society was a position from which there was no retreating as the suffrage agitation mounted. Indeed after 1900 the only modification of this feminist creed which Jane Addams made was to celebrate women's unique capacities for internationalism and the mediation of war. The woman as diplomat could settle the problems of world order as well as those of urban government. Such delusions are comic, but they are also very significant when entertained by minds with the range and scope for social analysis which Jane Addams certainly had.

They point to a predicament which was almost universal for middle-class American women of Jane Addams' generation. Intellectually they had to work within the tradition which saw women as civilizing and moralizing forces in society, a tradition given spurious scientific authority in evolutionary social thought. Yet within American society there was no naturally occurring social milieu in which these assumptions about the exclusive attributes of women could be seen for what they were. Women had to create the very institutions which were their vehicle for departure from middle-class feminine life, and in doing so they naturally duplicated existing assumptions about the sexes and their roles. Beatrice Webb remarked after visiting Hull-House that "the residents consist, in the main, of strong-minded energetic women, bustling about their various enterprises and professions, interspersed with earnest-faced self-subordinating and mild-mannered men who slide from room to room apologetically."[15] Since Beatrice Webb knew this model well in herself and Sidney, it is highly probable that the perception was accurate. In settlement houses women could find endless opportunities for social action but no way out of the prevailing romantic stereotypes of men and women as social beings. As social workers struggling to solve the problems of the poor in American cities, women met mostly businessmen—philanthropists and clergymen with wide social concerns. The businessmen could be disregarded as tainted by acquisitiveness and the profits of commercial exploitation. The clergymen were representatives of a religious tradition which had failed to recognize the superior moral qualities of women. Such men could not be accepted as moral or intellectual equals no matter how readily they wrote checks or served on community charities for they were distrusted as agents of a society which subordinated women for economic or religious purposes. Yet without seeing men and women as moral equals, women reformers could find no way out of the traditional stereotype of the female temperament; and they could not see themselves as they really were, notably aggressive, hard-working, independent, pragmatic and rational in every good cause but that of feminism.

The consequence of this failure to question traditional views of femininity meant that the genuine changes in behavior and the impact of women's social criticism were short-lived. On the other hand, the national eminence of the woman reformer as sage merely strengthened sterile romanticism in popular attitudes to women. In this way a generation of women who lived as rebels against middle-class mores was finally imprisoned by them. We see the limitations imposed by this imprisonment in the absence of thought about or concern for sexual liberty in the lives of two women reformers of national eminence always in search of social issues to explore. For them rejection of Victorian bourgeois and economic values was never accompanied by questioning of Victorian sexual stereotypes.

Nothing is more pathetic than the shocked incomprehension of Jane Addams and Lillian Wald when faced with a popularized version of Freudian thought towards the close of their lives. Each in writing the concluding chapters of her memoirs towards the end of the decade of the twenties tried to grapple with the problem of explaining how their intuitive female sage could be distinguished from Freud's irrational woman whose destiny is shaped by her biological nature.[16] They were powerless to deal with the assertion that their long careers as social reformers were merely evidence of failures in sexual adjustment because they had always accepted the romantic view of women as passive and irrational. This acceptance left them with no recourse when they were told their careers of activism represented deviance; for in terms of the stereotype of femininity which they had always accepted, they had been deviant. They had adopted a feminist ideology and a public identity which gave the widest possible currency to a modernized version of the romantic woman. They had acted very differently but had never understood the significance of the difference, much less reflected upon it until it was too late. Quite unwittingly they had helped to prepare a cultural climate ideally suited to the reception of Freudian ideas. Had they ever reflected on the significance of their behavior it is possible that with their superb talents for publicity and popular writing they could have dramatized some other model of feminine excellence besides the gentle, intuitive woman. Certainly they could have brought in question the negative image of the career woman emerging in the mass media of the thirties. As it was they were silent, and the mass media were left free to begin the commercial exploitation of the romantic female without a murmur of dissent from two women who had used the identity of the romantic sage for far more elevated social purposes.

NOTES

1. On this point see Andrew Sinclair, *The Better Half: The Emancipation of American Women* (New York, 1965).

2. Betty Friedan, *The Feminine Mystique* (New York, 1963).

3. See Aileen S. Kraditor, *Up From the Pedestal* (Chicago, 1968), and William L. O'Neill, *Divorce in the Progressive Era* (New Haven, 1967), and *Everyone was Brave: The Rise and Fall of Feminism in America* (Chicago, 1969).

4. See David M. Kennedy, *Birth Control in America: The Career of Margaret Sanger* (New Haven, 1970).

5. Jane Addams' thought on women's role as reformers is most readily available in her *Democracy and Social Ethics* (New York, 1902), *Newer Ideals of Peace* (New York, 1907), *The Long Road of Woman's Memory* (New York, 1916), and *Peace and Bread in Time of War* (New York, 1922). Her two volumes of autobiography are mostly concerned with the question of women's social role. See *Twenty Years at Hull House* (New York, 1910) and *The Second Twenty Years at Hull House* (New York, 1930). Lillian Wald's ideas on women's place in society are only available in print in her two volumes of autobiography, *The House on Henry Street* (New York, 1915), and *Windows on Henry Street* (Boston, 1934). Her speeches and addresses in the Lillian Wald Papers, New York Public Library are a valuable manuscript source for her thought on this question.

6. Winifred E. Wise, *Jane Addams of Hull House: A Biography* (New York, 1935), and R. L. Duffus, *Lillian Wald* (New York, 1953) are examples of the eulogistic biography.

7. Jane Addams, *My Friend Julia Lathrop* (New York, 1935).

8. Josephine Goldmark, *Impatient Crusader,* (University of Illinois Press, Urbana, 1953). See also Dorothy Blumberg, *Florence Kelley: The Making of a Social Pioneer* (New York, 1966).

9. My attention has been drawn to this by Allen F. Davis in his *Spearheads for Reform: The Social Settlements and the Progressive Movement, 1890–1914* (New York, 1967). See also Jane Addams, *Twenty Years at Hull-House,* 66–70.

10. Ellen G. Starr to Sarah A. Haldeman, Chicago, Feb. 23, 1889, Ellen G. Starr Papers, Sophia Smith Collection, Smith College Library.

11. See Jane Addams, *Democracy and Social Ethics,* 13–70, 137–77.

12. Herbert Spencer, *The Study of Sociology* (New York, 1873); Patrick Geddes and J. Arthur Thompson, *The Evolution of Sex* (London, 1889).

13. *Democracy and Social Ethics* was the first systematic statement of her social criticism. It drew on essays and speeches written entirely in the decade of the 1890s.

14. See William James to Jane Addams, New Hampshire, Sept. 17, 1902; Elizabeth D. Stebbins to Jane Addams, New York, July 18, 1909, both letters in the Jane Addams Correspondence, Swarthmore College Peace Collection.

15. *Beatrice Webb's American Diary* (ed. D.A. Shannon, Madison, 1963), 108.

16. See Jane Addams, *Second Twenty Years at Hull House,* 196–99; also Jane Addams, "A Feminist Physician Speaks," a review of *Modern Woman and Sex* by Rachelle S. Yarros, M.D., *Survey,* LXX, 2, (Feb., 1934), 59. See Lillian D. Wald, *Windows on Henry Street,* 5–11, 322.

Suggested Readings for Part III

Barker-Benfield, J.G. " 'Mother Emancipator' The Meaning of Jane Addam's Sickness and Cure." *Journal of Family History* 4 (1979): 395–420.

Bordin, Ruth. *Women and Temperance: The Quest for Power and Liberty, 1873–1900.* Philadelphia: Temple University Press, 1981.

Buhle, Mary Jo. "Women and the Socialist Party, 1901–1914." *Radical America* 4 (1970): 36–55.

Campbell, Barbara K. *The Liberated Woman of 1914: Prominent Women in the Progressive Era.* Ann Arbor: University of Michigan Press, 1978.

Connelly, Mark Thomas. *The Response to Prostitution in the Progressive Era.* Chapel Hill: University of North Carolina Press, 1980.

Curti, Merle. *Social Ideas of American Educators.* Totowa, N.J.: Littlefield Adams, 1959.

Davis, Allan F. "The WTUL Origins and Organization." *Labor History* 5 (1964): 3–17.

——. "Welfare Reform and World War I." *American Quarterly* 19 (1967): 516–553.

——. *Spearheads For Reform: The Social Settlements and the Progressive Movement, 1890–1914.* New York: Oxford University Press, 1967.

——. *American Heroine: The Life and Legend of Jane Addams.* New York: Oxford University Press, 1973.

Degler, Carl. "Charlotte Perkins Gilman on the Theory and Practice of Feminism." *American Quarterly* 8 (1956): 21–39.

——. "What Ought To Be and What Was: Women's Sexuality in the Nineteenth Century." *American Historical Review* 79 (1974): 1467–90.

Drinnon, Richard. *Rebel in Paradise: A Biography of Emma Goldman.* Chicago: University of Chicago Press, 1961.

Feldman, Egal. "Prostitution, the Alien Woman and the Progressive Imagination, 1910–1915." *American Quarterly* 19 (1967): 192–206.

Fetherling, Dale. *Mother Jones: The Miners' Angel.* Carbondale: Southern Illinois Press, 1974.

Garrison, Dee. *Apostles of Culture: Public Librarian and American History.* New York: The Free Press, 1979.

——. "The Tender Technicians: The Feminization of Public Librarianship, 1876–1905." *Journal of Social History* 6 (1972–73): 131–59.

Gordon, Linda. *Woman's Body, Woman's Right: A Social History of Birth Control in America.* New York: Grossman, 1976.

Graham, Patricia Albjerg. "Expansion and Exclusion: A History of Women in American Higher Education." *Signs* 3 (1978): 759–73.

Grimes, Alan P. *The Puritan Ethic and Woman Suffrage.* New York: Oxford University Press, 1967.

Hill, Mary. *Charlotte Perkins Gilman: The Making of a Radical Feminist, 1860–1896.* Philadelphia: Temple University Press, 1980.

Hogelund, Ronald W. "Coeducation of the Sexes at Oberlin: A Study of Social Ideas in Mid-Nineteenth Century America." *Journal of Social History* 6 (1972–73): 160–76.

Jensen, Richard. "Family Career and Reform: Women Leaders of the Progressive Era." In *The American Family in Social-Historical Perspective,* edited by Michael Gordon, pp. 67–80. New York: St. Martin's Press, 1978.

Kenneally, James J. *Women and the Trade Unions.* St. Albans, Vt.: Eden Press, 1978.

_____. "Women and the Trade Unions, 1870–1920: The Quandary of the Reformer." *Labor History* 14 (1973): 42–55.

Kennedy, David. *Birth Control in America: The Career of Margaret Sanger.* New Haven: Yale University Press, 1970.

Kraditor, Aileen S. *The Ideas of the Woman Suffrage Movement, 1890–1920.* New York: Columbia University Press, 1965.

Lubove, Roy. "The Progressives and the Prostitute." *The Historian* 25 (1962): 308–30.

Mann, Arthur. *Yankee Reformers in an Urban Age.* Cambridge: Harvard University Press, 1954.

Marsh, Marsha. *Anarchist Women, 1870–1920.* Philadelphia: Temple University Press, 1980.

May, Elaine T. *Great Expectations: Marriage and Divorce in Post-Victorian America.* Chicago: University of Chicago Press, 1980.

McFarland, C.K. "Crusade for Child Laborers: Mother Jones and the March of the Mill Children." *Pennsylvania History* 38 (1971): 283–96.

McGovern, James. "David Graham Phillips and the Virility Impulse of the Progressives." *New England Quarterly* (1966): 334–55.

_____. "Anna Howard Shaw: New Approaches to Feminism." *Journal of Social History* 3 (1969–70): 135–153.

Newcomer, Mable. *A Century of Higher Education for American Women.* New York: Harper & Row, 1959.

O'Neill, William L. *Divorce in the Progressive Era.* New Haven: Yale University Press, 1967.

_____. "Divorce in the Progressive Era." *American Quarterly* 17 (1965): 205–217.

_____. *The Woman Movement: Feminism in the United States and England.* London: George Allan and Unwin, 1969.

_____. *Everyone Was Brave: A History of Feminism in America.* Chicago: Quadrangle Books, 1971.

Paulson, Ross Evans. *Women's Suffrage and Prohibition: A Comparative Study of Equality and Control.* Glenview, Ill.: Scott, Foresman & Co., 1973.

Rossiter, Margaret W. "Women Scientists in America Before 1920." *American Scientist* 62 (1974): 312–23.

Scott, Anne F. "What, Then, Is the American: This New Woman?" *Journal of American History* 65 (1978): 679–703.

Smith, Daniel Scott. "The Dating of the American Sexual Revolution; Evidence and Interpretation." In *The American Family in Social-Historical Perspective,* edited by Michael Gordon, pp. 321–35. New York: St. Martin's Press, 1978.

Sochen, June. *The New Woman: Feminism in Greenwich Village, 1910–1920.* New York: Quadrangle Books, 1972.

Sugg, Redding S. *Mother Teacher: The Feminization of American Education.* Charlottesville: University of Virginia Press, 1978.

Tentler, Leslie W. *Wage Earning Women: Industrial Work and Family Life, 1900–1930.* New York: Oxford University Press, 1978.

Trattner, Walter I. "Julia Grace Wales and the Wisconsin Plan for Peace." *Wisconsin Magazine of History* 44 (1961): 203–13.

Walsh, Mary Roth. *"Doctors Wanted: No Women Need Apply": Sexual Barriers in the Medical Profession, 1835–1875.* New Haven: Yale University Press, 1976.

4 ⚥ The Illusion of Equality

The paradox of women's position in American society became profoundly evident in the twentieth century. The suffrage victory in 1920, increased numbers of women in the labor force, and women's new sexual freedom enhanced their status. Yet the promise of emancipation has remained largely unfulfilled. As Max Lerner wrote in the 1950s, "In theory, in law, and to a great extent in fact, the American woman has the freedom to compete with men on equal terms: but psychically and socially she is caught in a society still dominated by masculine power and standards." Women found that gaining the vote did not ensure an effective bloc of women voters, armed with the power and determination to promote women's interests. In spite of new job opportunities for women, employers maintained differences in men's and women's salaries. By the mid-1960s, radicals commonly referred to the illusion of equality, and a new generation of feminists boldly attacked what they termed the sexist attitudes that have remained the last barrier to women's emancipation.

The many women's organizations that had been active during the Progressive era continued the struggle for reform during the 1920s. The General Federation of Women's Clubs (GFWC), National Consumers League (NCL), and National Women's Trade Union League (NWTUL) joined with the League of Women Voters (LWV), which carried on the work of the National American Woman Suffrage Association, to bring pressure on the Congress and the state legislatures in relation to a wide range of matters of concern to women. In 1920, they established the Women's Joint Congressional Committee (WJCC) "as a clearing house for the federal legislative efforts of the affiliated organizations." The most conspicuous success of the WJCC was the short-lived Sheppard-Towner bill, designed to ensure protection to mothers and children through federal aid to maternal and health care programs. Both the NCL, under the direction of Florence Kelley, and the NWTUL continued their campaigns in the interest of working women throughout the decade. Little tangible success marked their efforts, however, until the economic crisis of the 1930s generated social legislation on behalf of workers in general. As Clarke A. Chambers makes clear in "The Campaign For Women's Rights," such activity typified the way in which organized women carried on the Progressive spirit in the 1920s, and it kept alive reform issues that became part of the New Deal agenda.

Toward the end of the 1920s, these efforts began to wane. Women's ranks were divided by the issue of an equal rights amendment, which became the sole focus of the Woman's Party. Although the League of Women Voters carried on a widespread effort against discriminatory legislation, its leaders—like those of the NCL and the NWTUL—believed that the amendment would endanger legislation protecting women workers, which they had struggled so vigorously to see implemented. Within the NCL, resources were strained by preoccupation with a constitutional amendment prohibiting child labor. Aside from internal division, women's organizations suffered from the conservative mood of the decade. Membership in the LWV never reached that of the NAWSA, and it began to drop sharply after 1924. The GFWC grew increasingly conservative, and the work of the WJCC succumbed to the charge of Communist influence, something that plagued women's efforts throughout the 1920s.

The focus on women in the 1920s shifted greatly in ways which feminists of the time deplored. The changes in social life and behavior that characterized the decade—the oft-noted revolution in manners and morals—shifted emphasis from a concern for social justice to one glorifying individual gratification. This represented a major shift in the history of women in American life. Trends in illegitimacy and premarital intercourse at the turn of the century had signaled a change in behavior, and by the 1920s the alteration of sexual norms was clearly apparent. The decade witnessed not only a new emphasis upon sexuality, which permeated popular culture, but also the emergence of women's demands for equality of sexual pleasure, both inside and outside of marriage. In "The American Woman's Pre-World War I Freedom in Manners and Morals," James R. McGovern discusses the nature of these changes and presents clear evidence that a radical shift in sexual behavior and attitudes appeared among urban Americans well before the end of the Great War.

The "new woman" who emerged in the 1920s was neither the creation of the prewar feminists nor their successors, who remained active during the decade. She was a product of the new moral climate accentuated by postwar prosperity. The stylish Gibson Girl of the 1890s gave way to the flapper who seemed the very essence of modernity. With her bobbed hair and short skirts, she represented a direct challenge to traditional conceptions of the ideal woman. Relating boyishness to female sexuality, she threatened traditional sex roles. Although lesbianism did assume faddish proportions among bohemians during the 1920s, the androgenous flapper was in fact a monument to heterosexuality.

Most women were neither bohemians nor flappers, but in the 1920s they were enthralled with the technological magic represented by the nation's number-one glamour industry, the motion pictures. The media increasingly created idols for young women, and the movies assumed tremendous importance. The sweet innocents portrayed by Mary Pickford continued to be screened, but increasingly the sexually explicit "vamp" dominated the silver screen. In "Projection of a New Womanhood," Mary P. Ryan shows the ways in which the young movie industry vividly exploited "the flapper's personality complete with her characteristic gestures, energy, and activism." Such films reflected the times and gave role models to young women. They became the most consistent purveyors of the flapper image and the idea of woman as a sexual predator.

The new freedom in morals and manners occurred simultaneously with economic conditions that made it necessary for many women to work. Industrial accidents, sickness and death rates reached extraordinarily high proportions in the first decade of the twentieth century. In addition, cyclical unemployment and low wages made the income of male wage-earners insufficient to meet family needs. It is not surprising that married women's participation in the nonagricultural work force almost doubled between 1890 and 1920. A large number of the women in the working population were immigrants driven by economic necessity and by aspirations toward the American Dream. Native Americans' prejudgment of ethnic characteristics as well as group and family mores shaped immigrant women's attitudes toward work. A woman's ethnic background, as Alice Kessler-Harris noted, "determined her image of herself as a worker and the community's approach to her employment."

Economic necessity and a changing conception of "need" continued to draw women into the labor market during the 1920s. The female labor force grew 26 percent during this time, and consumption patterns changed. These changes profoundly affected the response of middle-income families to the Depression, for, in order to maintain a relatively high standard of living, more members of the family were forced to seek paid employment. According to Winifred D. Wandersee Bolin, "many American families owed their middle-class status not to adequate wages of one person, but to the presence of several wage earners in the family." In the course of the 1930s, the numbers of married homemakers with jobs outside the home increased 50 percent, so that approximately one in every seven married women had entered the labor force. While the increase in the number of working wives had occurred in all social groups, a large majority of white women remained in traditional domestic roles.

In the midst of the Depression, a good deal of pressure was put on women to remain in the home. Most cities refused to hire married women as teachers, and eight states excluded them from civil service jobs; a husband and wife could not both hold federal jobs. Although job segregation was so extreme that few women actually competed against men, those who entered the labor force were blamed for taking jobs from male breadwinners. Such prejudices, combined with the stigma upon a husband's masculinity represented by a working wife, reveal the strength of traditional family values in the midst of economic crisis.

Stripped of its traditional functions, the twentieth-century family became primarily concerned with serving the personalities of its members. Its main function was psychological. According to Rowland Berthoff, "Marriage was in a sense displacing the family itself; a husband and wife now referred colloquially to their 'marriage', implying not so much a fixed social institution as a special arrangement between two people who had 'fallen in love.'" Held together solely by the tenuous bonds of personal relationships, marriages dissolved with increasing rapidity. Divorces, which had reached 100,000 per year in 1914, passed the 200,000 mark by 1929. Many women with a degree of economic independence were unwilling to tolerate unhappy marriages. At the same time, the decline in the birth rate indicated that couples deliberately chose to limit their families in order to maintain their standard of living. Children were no longer an economic asset as they had been in the nineteenth century; they had now become a liability.

The emphasis on personal fulfillment that emerged in the 1920s altered the ideals and aspirations of American women. The hard times of the Great Depression dampened the divorce rate as couples chose security above personal happiness and as a confused society tried to reaffirm traditional sex roles in the face of economic crisis and war. Ruth Schwartz Cowan's study, "Two Washes in the Morning and a Bridge Party at Night," traces the evolution of "the feminine mystique" among middle-class women during the interwar period. The image of the cheerful housewife obsessed with dirt and companionate motherhood was a product of unique economic and demographic conditions. The decline of the servant population and profound technological changes spawned an ideology that Cowan argues was a thinly disguised form of consumerism. The postwar economic developments altered the role of housewives as consumers, but failed to free them from domestic life. The emerging "mystique" idealized the relationship between husbands and wives, encouraged family togetherness and discouraged work outside the home. The home economics movement flourished in the 1920s, and middle-class women were exhorted by advertisers to become more "scientific" homemakers.

In the decade after World War II, prosperity made large families possible, and greater numbers of women accepted the cult of domesticity—"the feminine mystique"—which idealized the affluent suburban housewife devoted to home and family. *The Ideal Marriage,* which appeared in the United States in 1931, charted the course to sexual bliss; the emphasis on home economics and the "scientific" home rationalized domestic drudgery. Yet, personal fulfillment escaped women during these years, just as political power had remained beyond their grasp since the 1920s. The suburban wife was sexually discontented. Her role as housewife expanded in the consumption-oriented society of the 1950s, and the number of hours spent doing housework and related tasks actually increased for unemployed women.

In the late 1950s this picture began to change. Sexual norms became increasingly permissive, and alternative modes of child raising and new forms of marriage gained popularity. In the early 1970s, a best-selling book touted the psychological benefits of "open marriage," which stripped marital relationships of the burdensome responsibilities of the past. The new moral climate of the 1960s not only permitted, but almost demanded, explicit self-analysis and open discussion of sexual matters. This climate led two sociologists to comment: "If there has been a sexual revolution . . . it is in terms of frankness about sex and the freedom to discuss it."

There can be no doubt, however, that behavior was also changing. Due to wide use of oral contraceptives, introduced in 1961, and liberalization of abortion statutes following the Supreme Court decision in the early 1970s, the birth rate plummeted to a point where population growth has stopped. Although marriage has been more popular than ever in American history, there has also been an increasing number of women who remain single. The age of first marriage has risen, and the divorce rate has reached staggering proportions. In the first six months of 1970, more new divorces were granted than in the entire previous decade; in some jurisdictions, such as Marin County, California, they outnumbered legal marriages. At the same time, the sexual activity of women has increased and has become more varied and pleasurable. Studies conducted in the early 1970s indicated that today's teenagers from 15 to 19 are at least twice as likely to have had intercourse as women born during the 1920s. Marital sex has become more satisfying for women, and the traditional gulf between the premarital and extramarital experiences of men and women has closed dramatically.

The changes in attitudes and behavior in recent years have been of immense importance to American women, since they indicate the downfall of the hypocritical double standard and a more equitable distribution of power in sexual and marital relationships. It is easy to overemphasize the "sexual revolution" and place excessive importance on its more bizarre elements, which were in some ways detrimental to the interests of women. The experiences of men and women are converging; however, there has probably been little actual increase in promiscuity. Women clearly no longer value virginity as they once did. Premarital sexual relations in the early teens are associated with the experimental tenor of this era and are followed by a latency period in the mid-teens. The most common postadolescent sexual behavior involves relationships that generally take the form of trial marriages, in which sexual activity is associated with affection and the expectation of marriage.

From 1920 to the present, the most important change in the lives of American women has been in the area of employment, and it has produced widespread social and political consequences. Although the percentage of working women has risen continuously throughout the twentieth century, most women have been segregated in low-paying and routine "women's jobs." New Deal legislation provided further protection for women in the areas of hours and wages, but both the National Industrial Recovery Act and the Fair Labor Standards Act tolerated wage differentials and set minimums for women at lower rates than those for men.

After 1939, wartime production drew thirteen million women into the ranks of labor, and, for the first time, married women exceeded single women in the working population. Although industry dropped one out of every four women employed at the end of the war, the number of working women has grown yearly since 1947. In 1970, women constituted 40 percent of the American labor force. As one might have suspected from the war experience, the greatest postwar increase in employment occurred among married women, and the age distribution of women shifted dramatically.

Even though they have played an increasingly important role in the American economy, women continue to be plagued by unequal pay and job segregation. It was not until the 1960s that they were able to force government action on these problems. Although, by the 1940s competition from women as a cheap labor source generated solid support for equal pay from the union movement, legislation on this subject failed in 1945 and again in 1947. Women's continuing concern with the issue of equal pay led to the Women's Bureau Conference on Equal Pay and to the inclusion of a demand for it in the Republican and Democratic platforms of the early 1950s. However, little was done until President John F. Kennedy appointed the Commission on the Status of Women in 1961. In "A 'New Frontier' for Women," Cynthia E. Harrison analyzes the background and organization of the Commission, illustrating the limitations of male liberals and the complex divisions among feminists.

The Commission's report focused attention on the problem of equal pay and recommended reform in the areas of job discrimination, federal social security insurance, tax law, and federal and state labor laws regulating hours, wages, and night work. The Commission also concerned itself with other differences in the treatment of men and women, and with services provided for women in education counseling, job training, and day-care centers. Although this report led to the passage of the Equal Pay Act in 1963 and the addition of Title VII to the Civil Rights Act of 1964 (prohibiting employment discrimination by the federal government), a careful student of the matter, Carl Degler, could still argue in 1962 that "the sexual division of labor is so nearly complete that it is difficult to find comparable jobs of the two sexes to make a definitive study [of wage discrimination]."

The sexual division of labor remains the crucial economic problem facing women today and accounts for the eagerness with which most women activists have embraced the Equal Right Amendment (ERA). However, in "The Paradox of Progress," William H. Chafe emphasizes the social and political consequences of changes that have taken place in the economic role of American women in the past half-century. Focusing upon the dialectic between behavioral and attitudinal shifts that comprises the process of social change, Chafe argues that World War II proved to be a watershed in the history of American women because it precipitated a rapid increase in the number of married women employed in the economy and a radical upward shift in the average age of employed women. Once established, this pattern affected all of the crucial relationships in women's lives and undermined traditional attitudes toward sex roles. Ironically, the decade of the 1950s created the seedbed for the flowering of feminism in the 1960s. "Perhaps," Chafe writes, "the most important precondition for the revival of feminism. . . was the amount of change which had already occurred in women's lives."

The rebirth of feminism in the 1960s remains the most enduring and ultimately most radical by-product of that much-disturbed decade. Explanation of this phenomenon is at once simple and complex. Few would deny that women are discriminated against in most salient aspects of American life; however, the historian must explain why long-term conditions generated a specific set of responses among certain groups at the precise time when they were able to erect the structual apparatus of a social movement. Even Chafe's explanation seems exceedingly abstract and fails to account for the grievances specific to groups of women who actually constructed the women's liberation movement.

Although it has gained support from women in all segments of the society, the women's liberation movement originated with professional, upper-middle-class women who, during the mid-1960s, found themselves under a form of intense psychological strain that has been termed relative deprivation. Such women perceived their situations relative to those of men of their class whose career patterns they used to evaluate their own lives. The conditions of the 1960s encouraged professional women with long-term political commitments and aspiring professional women in college, who were disillusioned in very special ways by the student civil rights and peace movements, to generate a revival of feminism. Contemporary feminism differs in many ways from its nine-teenth-century predecessor. At times, it seems to lack the necessary coherence to be considered a social movement. But the popularity of traditional women's issues today is immense. Although the majority of American women refuse to accept the direction of the movement, few could be called antifeminist, and a growing majority favor all efforts to enhance women's status in American society.

The feminist movement split asunder on the rock of racial prejudice in the early part of this century, and the relation of black women to the contemporary movement remains a problem. Although they tend to be more favorable than white women to the leading feminist issues, par-ticularly in the economic realm, black women face role conflicts that whites have been able to transcend. Focusing primarily on the struggle for racial dignity, black women have consciously accepted traditional supportive roles in the interest of reversing the history of pathological destruction that white racism has brought to black men. Black women have thus, for the most part, thrown in their lot with efforts to enhance the status of black men, and they have viewed with suspicion feminist efforts that seemed inimical to this goal. To a large degree, black women have remained outside the movement, a fact which Pauli Mur-ray, an Episcopalian priest, civil rights lawyer, successful academician, and one of the founders of the National Organization for Women (NOW), deplores. Murray contends that the issue is one of human rights—women must "transcend the racial barrier" and form an alliance beginning with educated, middle-class women of both races.

In response to International Women's Year and Decade proclaimed by the United Nations, women met in Houston, in November of 1977 to define their most urgent issues and concerns. White and minority women of all classes gathered in a demonstration of feminist solidarity. Black, Hispanic, Chinese and Native American women organized and spoke eloquently of their specific economic grievances, such as teenage unemployment. Conservative women led by Phyllis Schlafly and the members of the Eagle Forum claimed to speak for the majority of American women, but their demonstration failed to disrupt or detract attention from the meeting, which hammered out a consensus on women's issues.

What the women's movement does, however, may have only peri-pheral influence upon the generation of middle-class women born in the fifties who have inherited the benefits won by the movement. Younger women insist that discrimination "doesn't apply to me," despite the facts that the government has failed to enforce laws against sex discrimination in the schools, that only one-fifth of the discrimination complaints are resolved by the United States Commission for Civil Rights, and that child-care centers remain inadequate to aid welfare mothers. The conservative administration of Ronald Reagan has placed a woman on the Supreme Court, but has also cut most of the social programs beneficial to women. The Equal Rights Amendment, stalled three states short of ratification, depends for its survival upon the efforts of moderate organized groups: the National Organization of Women, the Coalition of Labor Union Women, the National Women's Political Caucus, the American Association of University Women, and the Women's Lobby. The generation born in the fifties and reaching maturity in the seventies has yet to learn the paradox of equal rights unequally distributed.

21 &The Campaign for Women's Rights in the 1920's

Clarke A. Chambers

The children of the nation were always the special concern of humanitarian reformers in the 1920's. Especially were the children of the poor the object of programs aimed at liberation from premature and excessive labor, at the enlargement of opportunity through educational, recreational, and welfare measures. If efforts had often been thwarted, the results of reform activity were nevertheless substantial. If the decade had proved uncongenial to statutory regulation, at least the advances in other areas gave cause for authentic satisfaction.

The hope that another disadvantaged group in the population—working women—could win the protection of the state against unreasonable exploitation proved less valid. Two lines of ameliorative action had taken form during the Progressive Era. One pointed toward the organization of women workers into labor unions in order that they might gain, through union, the strength to bargain collectively with employers. It was for this end that the Women's Trade Union League, with the nominal and rhetorical support of the AFL, strove with zeal if not with very large success. The second path led toward legislation, particularly at the state level of government, which would set standards of maximum hours, minimum wages, and decent conditions for women employees. Here notable advances had been won during the culminating

From *Seedtime of Reform: American Social Service and Social Action, 1918–1933*
(Minneapolis: University of Minnesota Press, 1963), pp. 61–83. Copyright © 1963 by the
University of Minnesota. Reprinted by permission.

years of the Progressive Era just before the nation's entrance into the Great War.

The regulation of hours and conditions had come first, the Supreme Court in the classic *Muller* v. *Oregon* case in 1908 upholding such legislation as an entirely reasonable exercise of the state's police power to promote the health, morality, and welfare of the community. Minimum-wage legislation came a bit later, but in the five years before America went to war, eleven states invoked the power to set a floor under wages earned by women. The argument that women, as mothers of the race, required the special protection of the community acting through government presumably applied as logically to the one area, minimum wages, as to the other, maximum hours. The Supreme Court did not see the parallel quite as clearly as the reformers did, but in 1917—as noted earlier—it had sustained by a tie vote an affirmative ruling of the Oregon Supreme Court. Following this *Stettler* v. *O'Hara* decision, three other states, Puerto Rico, and the federal Congress acting for the District of Columbia had established special commissions with the power to set minimum-wage levels in accordance with subjective criteria of health and morality.

Wartime demands had brought tens of thousands of women into the labor force, where they enjoyed relatively high wages and augmented opportunity, if never equal pay for equal work with men, or equal opportunity to enter certain crafts and trades, restricted to men as often by custom and prejudice as by physical requirements. The Woman in Industry Service had proved competent, however, in winning for women special positions of economic influence not previously enjoyed. Women continued, in the postwar decade, to join the labor force, often to supplement the husband's income when it was insufficient to support the family at a decent level, until 1929 over ten million women were gainfully employed where but eight million so labored at the end of the war. The ratio of working women to all women of working age in the nation remained roughly constant—approximately one to five.

With a total labor force pushing fifty million by the end of the decade, women constituted approximately one-fifth of all those employed. Millions of girls and married women worked in the service trades, of course, as waitresses or hotel domestics or telephone operators, as stenographers and as retail clerks; millions more were employed in textile mills, in the garment trades, and on the assembly lines of light industries, many of them, like the household appliance industries, new in the 1920s. The proportion of women working in a particular area of the economy changed but slightly within the decade: about a third of all working women were employed in domestic or personal service, a quarter in manufacturing, a fifth in agriculture, and a tenth in trade and transportation.

Motives for entering the labor force remained much as they had been before the war—to earn at least partial financial independence, to escape from household drudgery, to save up a little extra money before marriage, to find companionship and a more satisfying career than housewifery or spinsterhood offered, and above all necessity. Careful studies of the female working force made during the 1920's indicated that most women sought gainful employment outside the home because they had no alternative—they had to find a job or be thrown onto charity. Many working women were widows or victims of desertion; others were wives of chronically sick or unemployed husbands, or were married to men who could not command wages sufficiently high to supply the family's basic needs. The old notion that women worked for "pin money" was dispelled by studies that proved that most working women earned "the whole or a necessary part of the family income." In any case there was no wage differential between those who worked for the "extras" of life and those who drudged from sheer necessity. A very substantial number were not only wives but mothers of young children as well, driven out of the home into the labor market by the pressures of existence. One analysis, made in mid-decade at the very peak of prosperity, concluded that "the mother works because she has to work, and unless some other method of raising the family income is devised she is in industry to stay."[1] Another study of 728 working mothers in Philadelphia, made by Gwendolyn S. Hughes under the auspices of the Seybert Institution and the graduate department of Bryn Mawr College, indicated that 89 per cent worked from economic necessity—some to meet emergencies, sickness, or unemployment; more to meet regular household expenses.[2]

Although the Women's Trade Union League continued to seek better conditions for women workers through unionization and stepped up these organizational efforts toward the end of the decade, many reformers drew the lesson from long and often humiliating experience that only the rigid enforcement of regulative legislation could be counted on to alleviate the grievances which sprang from the excessive exploitation of the labor of women. Women workers for the most part were lacking in skill; they had few resources to fall back upon other than their availability for cheap labor; the organization of women into trade unions was "a slow and arduous process requiring long periods of time."[3] Frances Perkins added the salient observation, derived from hard factual analysis of female labor in the state of New York, that nearly three-quarters of all women factory workers were employed in plants with fewer than fifty workers; in these small plants the unionization of employees, never easy, was particularly difficult; and management in these small factories could rarely afford the luxury of enlightened or "scientific" policies.[4]

Some studies stressed the objective causes of exploitation and proposed specific remedies; other surveys stressed the subjective costs paid by working women and ultimately by society itself. Those who strained, day after day, month after month, on the assembly line or in sweated industries, before the loom or the sewing machine, could best testify as to what the pace of machine labor involved. Asked by the instructor of a course in remedial English, established by the Women's Trade Union League for immigrant working girls, to write compositions on their factory experience, the class responded with essays later compiled and edited for publication. Complaining of constant fatigue and depression, the girls noted that even the machines on which they toiled were rested and oiled; why, then, could not the same concern be shown for the health and vigor of the workers, whose energies were sapped often beyond repair. From experience they had learned the costs in health and character that excessive hours of labor under conditions of the stretchout and speedup exacted. From their evening classes, apparently, they had picked up a bit of basic economics as well. Maximum-hour legislation, they argued, would spread employment; minimum-wage legislation would increase purchasing power; enlarged leisure and purchasing power would promote sound prosperity throughout the entire economy. Rarely was the pragmatic argument for maximum hours, minimum wages, and full employment put more cogently in that decade.[5]

Confident that their cause was just and that their arguments were irrefutable, encouraged by the sense of organic community which the war had fostered, the reformers set out to consolidate their gains and advance into new frontiers of social action. The immediate goals were the achievement for women workers of an eight-hour day and a forty-eight-hour week, one day of rest in seven, and a prohibition on night work in every state in the Union. Massachusetts led the way with the passage of a forty-eight-hour bill in April 1919. Exemptions there were—of chambermaids, stenographers, and domestic servants—but the Consumers' League and the Women's Trade Union League were generally pleased. Their pleasure was short-lived. The pattern in New York soon proved different.

In New York, the Women's Joint Legislative Conference was able to win a nine-hour day and a fifty-four-hour week for a limited number of women workers in 1919, but subsequent attempts to broaden the coverage and to reduce the maxima were blocked by the Republican-dominated State Assembly. Probably in no other state was there quite such a vigorous proponent of protective labor legislation as Governor Alfred E. Smith, but neither his endorsement nor favorable action by the State Senate was ever sufficient to override the negative of the lower house. Up to Albany from New York City the women went to lobby, only to be rebuffed by arguments of the conservative speaker of the Assembly, Thaddeus Sweet, and others that labor legislation would increase costs and drive industry from the state. Florence Kelley might argue that the "orderly processes of the law" were to be preferred to "clumsy, costly, painful" strikes, but few seemed to fear that the alternative of direct action would be resorted to. "More leisure and more money women must have unless the public health and morals are to suffer irreparably," she protested; but the times seemed prosperous, and to the comfortable and complacent an enlargement of government power appeared not only inappropriate, but downright wicked.[6] Moreover, was not the liberty of employer and employee to bargain and make contracts a sacred freedom? Far from winning new gains, the reform groups had to throw all their resources into a struggle to block repeal of the prohibition on night work in some industries. Distraught and giddy from months of frustrating toil, the WTUL solemnly recorded in the minutes of the executive board, toward the end of the session in 1921, a bit of doggerel which labeled their foes as "tools" and "fools," as "bad" and "mad":

> They're overfed,
> And anti-red,
> And rave around like loons.
> They wave the flag,
> And chew the rag,
> But all of them are prunes,
> Prunes, prunes!
> Yes, all of them are prunes![7]

In 1924, Molly Dewson, formerly of the Consumers' League but now civic secretary of the Women's City Club of New York (whose vice president was Eleanor Roosevelt), carried through a survey of women workers to test their attitudes toward maximum-hour regulations. She reported her findings to bureaus of the state government and to the legislature—a substantial majority of working women desired a forty-eight-hour week, even if a cut in weekly income were involved. A bill put forward in 1926 was set aside and a study of the issue proposed in its place. When the special Industrial Survey Commission reported back, its recommendations included not only a forty-eight-hour week, but minimum wages and equal pay for equal work as well. With these recommendations before it, the state legislature reduced the maximum from fifty-four hours to fifty-one and adjourned.[8]

New York, not Massachusetts, set the pace for the nation. Here and there, partial gains were achieved. As often as not the gains were illusory or temporary as in Minnesota, for example, where a fifty-four-hour law was set aside by the State Supreme Court on a technicality; efforts to amend the bill to make it constitutional were unavailing. Over and over legislative committees and governors, ladies' clubs and associations of social workers were told that "Physical debility follows fatigue. Laxity of moral fibre follows physical debility."[9] But the nation's attention was focused on other issues; the nation's energies were consumed by other affairs. From the end of the war to the election of 1932, only two states added maximum-hour legislation where none existed before; substantial improvements of the regulations were won in twelve of the forty states which had statutes on the books by 1918.

At mid-decade, a special subcommittee of the WTUL, charged with re-evaluating the league's entire legislative program, acknowledged broad and increasing "dissatisfaction with legislation for women as a means to the end for which the Women's Trade Union League" was organized. Political action had become a "slow and painful process" of achieving reform. Perhaps it was time to consolidate forces and place emphasis again on the league's alternative line of action—the organization of women into unions. The board, after prolonged and bitter debate, finally accepted the recommendation to close its Chicago office and invest legislative moneys in one central office in the nation's capital, and acted at the same time to reopen the unionization campaign;[10] this activity will be traced in a later chapter.

If the women's reform associations had been able to hold the line on maximum-hour legislation and win a few slight gains from time to time, no such good fortune attended the parallel movement for minimum-wage statutes. The Consumers' League, the Trade Union League, and the American Association for Labor Legislation had seized the initiative during the years preceding America's entrance in World War I in coordinating the drive for state minimum-wage legislation. They had joined to persuade Massachusetts, in 1912, and eight more states the following year to establish minimum-wage commissions, with permissive rather than mandatory authority. By 1918, eleven states plus the District of Columbia and by 1923 fifteen states in all had regulations of some sort. There the matter rested. That moderate but nonetheless significant benefits had derived from this body of legislation the reform groups knew. The procedures of enforcement were often clumsy and rested as frequently upon the sanction of good will and enlightened public opinion as upon the coercive power of the state; but levels of wages for women had generally been raised, and the minima had not become maxima as some trade union spokesmen had feared. Ten years of experience, it was believed, gave ample evidence that higher wages had a clear bearing on health, moral decency, and industrial efficiency. Furthermore, it was argued, the extension of the principle was justified on the premise that employers properly should bear the costs that society otherwise had to assume in the form of charitable relief to those who broke down from ill health, fatigue, and insufficient income. The minimum wage was a means to prevent the delinquency and disease which, if unprevented, society would have to cure. To the employers it was said that regulations lessened labor turnover, increased worker morale and efficiency; no one, save the marginal, unscrupulous, and unfair producer, had anything to lose.

There was, of course, overt opposition to the extension of minimum-wage regulations. A move in Ohio by the Council of Women and Children in Industry (composed of representatives of the Consumers' League, the Women's Trade Union League, the Urban League, the YWCA, and the WCTU) was successfully blocked by the Ohio Manufacturers' Association. More often, however, the drive for minimum wages was diverted or stopped by apathy and unconcern, and by a widespread feeling that such legislation was of doubtful constitutionality. The Supreme Court of the state of Oregon had upheld minimum-wage legislation in two parallel cases, back in 1914, on the ground that the wages of women workers were a legitimate concern of the state in seeking to improve the health, morals, and general welfare of the community. But the tie vote by which the United States Supreme Court in 1917 sustained the Oregon decision certainly was no ringing mandate to encourage other states to act.

Then, in 1921, the constitutionality of the District of Columbia's minimum-wage act was challenged. The Consumers' League rushed to the defense. Molly Dewson was retained to prepare the factual material for the case, while Felix Frankfurter volunteered his services as counsel. Florence Kelley sensed at once that the crucial battle was at hand. Dropping everything else for the moment, she threw herself into the task of finding the money to underwrite the legal and research costs and to publicize the cause. There is "Merry Hell in general," wrote Mrs. Kelley to Adolf Berle, Jr., describing the office of the Consumers' League as the brief was finally being assembled. "Even Felix up in Cambridge is jumping high jumps twice daily," she added in a postscript.[11] In November 1922 the District Court of Appeals, by a vote of two to one, found the law null and void. The *Adkins* case was taken on appeal at once to the Supreme Court. But Florence Kelley was not hopeful. "There is no short road to Justice and Mercy in this Republic," she wrote dejectedly to an old friend.[12]

Mrs. Kelley's forebodings proved accurate. By five to three (Justice Brandeis again abstaining), the highest tribunal knocked down the District's act, sounding the "death knell" (as Felix Frankfurter said later in life) for all kinds of social legislation and inhibiting the launching of new welfare experiments.[13] Frankfurter had argued that the statute Congress had passed, sitting as the "state legislature" for the District of Columbia, fell well within the boundary of what was reasonable; it was not "arbitrary, wanton, or spoilative." That wages for women workers were considered to have a clear bearing upon health and morality was evidenced by many regulations of several states and by the action of nearly every industrial nation.

To George Sutherland, who had been recently added to the Supreme Court by President Harding, it was not all that clear. Drawing upon the ancient and honorable tenets of nineteenth-century individualism, Sutherland announced for the majority its conviction that minimum-wage legislation constituted arbitrary interference of the state in the private affairs of citizens competent to use their inviolable liberties in such ways as to promote the well-being and progress of society. The freedom of employers and employees to make a contract clearly was covered by the due process clause of the Fifth Amendment. As for the unanimous decision of the court in the Oregon case, the premises on which it rested no longer applied, for women, he argued, had gained a kind of equality with men that rendered special legislative protection for women obsolete. He cited the Nineteenth Amendment as proof that differences in civil status between men and women had reached the "vanishing point." The law was, in light of these historic changes, "a naked, arbitrary exercise of power."

To William Howard Taft, new chief justice, Sutherland's logic was deficient. "The Nineteenth Amendment did not change the physical strength or limitations of women upon which the decision in *Muller* v. *Oregon* rests," he wrote in dissent. Oliver Wendell Holmes, Jr., made a more elaborate attack upon the majority decision. "Freedom of contract" was nowhere to be found in the Constitution. The state had for generations legitimately restricted individual freedom; if legislatures deemed it essential that the government set minimum wages as well as maximum hours, the courts were obliged to accept their judgment as reasonable unless there were overwhelming evidence to the contrary. "It will need more than the Nineteenth Amendment to convince me that there are no differences between men and women or that legislation cannot take those differences into account." Irony and indignation availeth not; Sutherland spoke for the majority of five, and that was that.[14] Mary Dewson, who had labored for months on the case, recalled later in life the bitter conclusion of her legal comrade, Felix Frankfurter: "Molly, you must learn that if the U.S. Supreme Court says a red rose is green, it is green. That's final."[15]

John Kirby, in a cartoon for the *New York World,* depicted a gracious Justice Sutherland handing a scroll to a shabbily-dressed and dejected woman worker and saying: "This decision affirms your constitutional right to starve." Other comments were no more subtle. Even the usually mild-mannered and courtly Mr. Gompers announced that the court had "usurped" authority nowhere granted to it in the Constitution, and concluded that the "brutality of the majority decision can beget nothing but wrath." A more careful critic, Henry R. Seager, noted that five men had overridden three other justices, majorities of two houses of Congress and thirteen state legislatures, thirteen governors, the President of the United States, and many previous courts. It was left to the good gray feminist, Florence Kelley, to comment that not a single woman had participated in the judicial process at any point. Francis Bowes Sayre concluded that the traditional judicial practice of finding in favor of a law in the absence of substantial legal doubt had been violated by the majority. The decision, he said, indicated that the Supreme Court was arrogating to itself a veto power not unlike that exercised by a House of Lords. Governor Louis F. Hart of the state of Washington labeled the decision as infamous as the Dred Scott ruling and stated categorically that any business that could not pay a decent wage was not a desirable business. Governor Walter M. Pierce from Oregon (home of so many pioneer measures of social legislation) was more temperate, but perhaps more to the point: "It is neither humane nor wise socially to allow the untrained to become public charges or worse through lack of a living wage. It is detrimental to the future of individuals as well as the nation to permit child labor under improper conditions. Since the untrained and young cannot hope to stand up under the competition and demands of industry, only government had so far been able to afford them protection." Father John A. Ryan, one of the very first propagandists for the living wage principle, particularly in its application to women workers, blamed the court's ruling upon the persistence of nineteenth-century utilitarianism with its extravagant insistence upon the individual's freedom to do what he wished as long as the freedom of other autonomous individuals was not thereby limited; that such a philosophy was irrelevant in an industrial era, that its capricious application led to inhumane practices, was clear to him as to many others.[16]

Florence Kelley had been through enough battles to know that verbal protest alone was never sufficient to carry the day: the heavier artillery of action would have to be unloosed. Invitations were sent to reform association leaders and to state officials to confer jointly on how best to meet the emergency. On 20 April 1923—Felix Frankfurter and Florence Kelley taking the lead—the delegates gathered in New York City to deliberate upon strategy. Jesse C. Adkins, chairman of the District of Columbia Minimum Wage Board, was there; so were representatives of law-enforcement agencies in this area of social legislation from Wisconsin, Washington, North Dakota, Minnesota, Massachusetts, and New York. Representatives were sent by all the major reform associations—the Consumers' League, of course, the Women's Trade Union League, the League of Women Voters, the National Catholic Welfare Association and the National Council of Catholic Women, the Child Labor Committee, the American Association for Labor Legislation, and the WCTU. The chief of the Women's Bureau, Mary Anderson, arrived; so too did Mary Van Kleeck, now with the Russell Sage Foundation; and Paul Kellogg of the *Survey*.

Felix Frankfurter led the discussion. There was little hope that the court would reverse itself in the near future, he observed. Justice Brandeis' vote could be counted on, of course, in cases on which he would not feel obliged to abstain; but otherwise the lines were drawn rather sharply for the moment. Sutherland was clearly hopeless; and as for Justice Butler, "He is a farmer, and spent from twenty to thirty years of his life in working up a practice [in law]. This is very confining and limited." His major recommendation, therefore, was to revise state minimum-wage legislation along the permissive lines of Massachusetts' law rather than try to incorporate mandatory provisions. In the meantime, he reminded the conference, the court had acted on the District of Columbia statute and nothing else. The "continued aggressive enforcement" of all state laws was absolutely essential. The court had always recognized local differences and until it specifically rejected state laws, the presumption that they were constitutional stood. The analysis and the conclusions were generally shared by the other delegates. F. A. Duxbury, chairman of Minnesota's Industrial Commission, resented, however, what seemed to him slurs on the integrity of Sutherland and Butler; respect for the law and for the courts was called for, even by those who could not agree with the decision. Father Ryan, who had joined Frankfurter in chiding Sutherland and Butler, replied that he had intended no disrespect, that he had merely wished to point out that the five justices were living in the eighteenth century. If any feelings were hurt, he was sorry but he felt it was hardly appropriate for him, above all others, to concur in any notion of judicial infallibility.

Out of the conference came no formal resolution, but only a general agreement. State laws should be enforced with vigor, as always. The suggestion that New York press for a permissive law, on the Massachusetts model, was endorsed. Further study of the economic and legal aspects of the decision would be made, and at once.[17]

Not satisfied with the inconclusive results of the April meeting, the WTUL called one of its own in mid-May, on the eve of the annual Conference of Social Work. Many of the groups represented at the April gathering sent delegates to this one as well. Mary Anderson set a tone of objective analysis, presenting evidence of the disparity in bargaining power that women workers suffered under, of the sub-standard wages that existed in states and in industries not covered by wage minima, and of the obvious relation between decent wages and community health. The presentation was forceful, if objective, but added little to the conclusions stated so cogently, although with so little practical effect, by Frankfurter and Dewson in the Adkins case. Dean Acheson was present to offer advice similar to Frankfurter's several weeks earlier— the states should continue to enforce their own minimum-wage laws; all interested groups should work unceasingly for a redefinition of due process of law along lines that would permit and encourage a reasonable extension of the state's police power. Other delegates were less patient. To wait for the Supreme Court to change its mind on what constituted reasonable regulations and proper procedures was to postpone indefinitely the enforcement of sound measures. Why not amend the Constitution, asked Molly Dewson, to authorize federal regulation of women's wages? Why so delimited a proposal, replied Maud Swartz for the Trade Union League? Why not work for an amendment which would grant broad powers to regulate conditions of labor, of men workers as of women? Elisabeth Christman and Rose Schneiderman, on the other hand, despairing of both judicial self-reform and the amendment procedure, demanded an energetic campaign to organize women into unions as the only valid course. Still others suggested that perhaps the time had come to limit the powers of the high tribunal to review both state and federal legislation.[18]

Divided counsel merely deepened the sense of demoralization. More than two decades of crusading had taught the reformers how to lobby, how to get around recalcitrant employers, how to by-pass stubborn legislative committees, how to stir up public support, how to argue the rule of reason before reasonable courts. It had not taught them how to react to hostile court decisions from which there was no appeal. For the moment they had lost both momentum and equilibrium. John R. Commons, accepting election as president of the Consumers' League in the autumn of 1923, summed it up exactly: "You find yourselves baffled and your work, at least an essential part of it, brought to a standstill by the recent adverse decisions of the Supreme Court" bearing upon child-labor and minimum-wage legislation.[19] Florence Kelley put it more picturesquely: "Truly we are like a semi-paralyzed centipede with its legs all moving at different rates of speed, if at all, and how few legs moving!"[20] In the middle years of the decade, she fell into the closing salutation when writing to intimate friends "Yours, *still* hopefully." But throughout 1923 and 1924, and on into 1925 when the child-labor amendment failed to win ratification, there was little cause for hopefulness. Reporting to the Board of Directors of the Consumers' League in October 1923, Jeanette Rankin, field secretary for the league in Illinois, reported that the "total legislative harvest" for that year was "a law adopting a state flower!"[21] And two years later, with reform still in eclipse, a Seattle lawyer confessed his discouragement to Mrs. Kelley: "the tide is running out now and all we can do is hold fast to our moorings until the tide turns."[22]

Mrs. Kelley was not about to accept the Supreme Court's negative actions as final and irrevocable. Other obstacles had yielded; the court could be circumvented or brought to its senses. The task was clear—to modernize the eighteenth-century Constitution in such ways as to make it possible to meet the new industrial demands of an urban civilization. Until the Constitution was transformed, and until the "court that interprets the Constitution" was modernized, it was "purely academic" to discuss industrial legislation.[23] The goal was clear enough, but not the means. Some advised an amendment authorizing Congress to reenact by a two-thirds majority any federal statute found to be unconstitutional by the court. Others would require a two-thirds majority of the court to rule a state or federal legislative enactment null and void. (At various times the ante was raised to seven and eight judges, until finally a unanimous court was suggested.) A more widely favored proposal was to grant to Congress, by the amendment procedure, broad authority to act in the large arena of social legislation. The legalists tended to prefer persuading the courts, by trying one case after another, to adopt a more permissive attitude toward legislative experiments; judicial self-restraint, not coercive action against the court, was the more efficacious path, they insisted. A few hardy souls suggested enlarging the court to fifteen members, or eighteen; but with Harding and then Coolidge in the White House, what a later generation would know as "packing" the court did not win wide support among reformers who were disrespectful enough of the court as then constituted but were not foolhardy. Whatever means were explored, even Florence Kelley knew they were "far easier to name than to draft."[24]

For a while Mrs. Kelley leaned toward an amendment requiring a seven to two majority to find state and federal legislation unconstitutional, but her closest legal adviser, Felix Frankfurter, would have none of it. "The 7 to 2 proposal will not come off," he advised, "and at the rate at which the Sutherlands and the Butlers are being appointed to the Court, it wouldn't do any good if it did."[25] This proposal might have the backing of Senator Borah and Father Ryan, but it was "utterly hopeless" to expect that either a bill or an amendment so providing could ever be passed. It was unwise, in any case, to seek such a deceptively simple "mechanical remedy" for a complex legal dilemma. The point rather, Frankfurter continued, was to improve the quality of the court itself.[26] Roscoe Pound concurred. The amendment procedure was clumsy; "legislative revision of judicial action" was inadvisable. Ultimately the only proper means of securing the court's approval for social and industrial legislation, without jeopardizing other rights, was to persuade the justices to make a broader and more flexible interpretation of the due process of law provision and the police power. He recommended popular agitation for court reform, however, as one way to bring about "a better judicial frame of mind."[27] Zechariah Chafee added one final caveat—reformers should not forget, in their desire to limit property rights, that legislative bodies often limit personal rights; if a seven to two majority were required to set aside a law, a minority of three could block the unconstitutionality of laws subversive of civil rights.[28]

Agreement upon a single viable course of action was not to be had. The inadvisability of restricting the court's powers came to be abundantly evident. To wait for the court to change its mind seemed futile. In the meantime, as Florence Kelley noted, women and children remained exposed to exploitative actions of unscrupulous employers.[29] A move to win agreement on a strategy of assault upon the court, in July 1924, was abortive.[30] Reformers by that time were focusing their energies upon the child-labor amendment and upon La Follette's crusade for the presidency. The court issue was relevant enough, there was just no way to bring the court to its senses without jeopardizing the equilibrium of government and the security of individual rights. Another battle had been lost, but not before the need for judicial self-restraint had been recognized by this handful of rebels. Almost every legal and political argument of the great court fight in 1937 was anticipated back in 1923 and 1924. Ultimately the issue was resolved as Frankfurter, Pound, Chafee, Freund, and Acheson had recommended—not by statute, not by amendment, but by the addition of new personnel to the court dedicated to a broader interpretation of social welfare and willing to accept legislative action as legitimate unless obviously unconstitutional beyond all reasonable doubt. The frontal assault upon the wisdom—and even, at times, the integrity—of the court may have helped to clarify the issues and thus served to prepare the way for the constitutional revolution that began in 1937.

As for practical and immediate achievements, there were few. The court continued on its path, undeflected by the feeble efforts of the critics. "Don't hurry away from the scene of battle," pleaded Florence Kelley to Molly Dewson in 1924. "So long as there is a *glimmering* chance of usefulness, that's the place to be."[31] Three years later, Mrs. Kelley confided to John R. Commons that their function should be study, research, publicity until the times should change: "Keeping the light on is probably the best contribution that we can make where there is now Stygian darkness."[32]

The candle was kept lit, and was set upon a hill. It was no floodlight or searchlight as long as the mood of normalcy prevailed, but it burned persistently. The motto of the Consumers' League continued to be implemented—"Investigate, Record, Agitate." Throughout the remainder of the decade, the league regularly remained in touch with state officials desirous of enforcing industrial minima. Effective regulation, however, all but collapsed. The voluntary, permissive arrangement in Massachusetts won partial advances for limited numbers of women workers but never more than that. And, at that, Massachusetts led the nation. Arizona's law was struck down by the Supreme Court in 1925, Arkansas' in 1927; local courts followed suit in Kansas and Puerto Rico; in Texas and Nebraska the laws were repealed; in Minnesota the attorney general ruled that its law was no longer enforceable. As late as June 1936, the United States Supreme Court in *Morehead* v. *Tipaldo* ruled that the *Adkins* decision was still controlling, this in negation of a 1933 New York State fair-wage law. Not until 1937 was the *Adkins* rule explicitly overridden.

Just as the Children's Bureau under Julia Lathrop and Grace Abbott was the coordinating agency of federal government in the field of child welfare, so the Women's Bureau under Mary Anderson played a similar role in parallel fields. Its central commitment was to the national community's obligation through government to protect the women of the land for the general good of society. With no regulatory laws to administer, it relied entirely upon "fact finding and fact furnishing" to achieve its ends. "Every movement making for reform needs a reservoir of reliable data upon which to draw and by which to be guided," an official publication of the Women's Bureau declared.[33] Through research and publication, speeches and reports, and sponsorship of conferences, and through cooperation with state labor bureaus and with voluntary associations, its influence was extended to every section of the nation. When the occasion demanded, it could call out a host of allies: the Women's Trade Union League, the Consumers' League, the League of Women Voters, the WCTU, the YWCA, the PTA, the General Federation of Women's Clubs, the American Association of University Women, church and labor union groups. These associations had been formed into a loose alliance in the Women's Joint Congressional Committee, the clearinghouse and coordinating federation which crusaded for maternal and infant health programs, the regulation of child labor, adequate appropriations for the Children's and Women's bureaus, welfare legislation for the District of Columbia, social hygiene, and public health. Mrs. Maud Wood Park, president of the League of Women Voters from 1920 to 1924 and Belle Sherwin, its president from 1924 to 1934, were among the committee's most effective and loyal leaders, but every other member group could also be counted upon to work with Grace Abbott and Mary Anderson within government for common objectives.

Of the making of committees, of course, there was no end; and committee meetings and resolutions can never be taken for effective action. With the best of intentions, women reformers often assembled determined to strike a blow for welfare only to play out a ritualistic role of protest. One woman reformer, long active in the WTUL, once wrote to a friend about the quality of committee work and rhetoric: "I was trying to *show* a dear old Boston lady how a rich man's *do-nothing* son was a worse tramp than the *other* tramps—'Oh Mrs. Faxon, I don't believe you mean that.'—'Yes, I do.'—'O,' she says, 'I've heard people talk on committees like that!'—Now my family says whenever I *get to* talking—'Now don't talk like a committee!' "[34]

There was a good deal of committee talk in the 1920's, particularly when the National Woman's party, a stridently feminist group that had fought for the Nineteenth Amendment, proposed still another amendment to the federal Constitution designed to remove all legal discriminations relating to sex. The proposed amendment took several forms during the decade, but the intent of its original phrasing persisted: "Men and women shall have equal rights throughout the United States and every place subject to its jurisdiction." Put forward by ladies drawn primarily from the wealthy and professional classes, the proposed amendment was viewed at once by a vast majority of women reformers as a measure subversive of all protective and welfare legislation. Florence Kelley, herself a suffragette and feminist, would have nothing to do with a measure that proposed to establish complete "legal equality of the sexes," when it was clear, on the face of it, that because of the special sexual functions of women they could not be afforded absolute equality of treatment without placing in jeopardy their hard-won legal right to special protection.[35] It would be "insanity," she wrote to Newton Baker, to follow the lead of Alice Paul and the Woman's party down a path that would utterly destroy maximum hours and minimum wages, mothers' pensions, and maternity insurance.[36] The proposal, moreover, was legally ambiguous: no one was really against "equal rights," Mary Anderson later recalled of the struggle, but what did "equal" mean and what really constituted "rights"?[37] For a generation women had benefitted from legislation designed to protect them from "untrammeled exploitation," wrote Dean Acheson to Ethel Smith. "All this, to my mind, is now threatened by this sweeping prohibition of unnamed inequalities and disabilities." The courts were likely to rule, he warned, "that this new-won equality guarantees to women all the intolerable and antisocial conditions which their brothers in industry now enjoy."[38] What of the status of laws of desertion and nonsupport, queried Florence Kelley? What of the rules of illegitimacy, seduction, and rape? What of conscription in time of war? "Will husbands need to continue to support their wives?"[39] A special conference of women's groups, in early December 1921, arranged by Florence Kelley, concluded with Alice Paul's announcement that despite the fears of the reformers that, even if the amendment did not pass Congress, its agitation would imperil the whole movement for social legislation, the Woman's party was determined to press for its enactment and ratification.

From this point forward the dispute became increasingly embittered. Alice Hamilton set down her indignation in a draft letter to one of the "equal rights" proponents: "I could not help comparing you as you sat there, sheltered, safe, beautifully guarded against even the ugliness of life, with the women for whom you demand 'freedom of contract.'" Laundry workers, textile workers, "The great army of waitresses and hotel chambermaids, unorganized, utterly ignorant of ways of making their grievances known, working long hours and living wretchedly" would be left unprotected if the amendment carried. A sweeping amendment was not the proper means for removing the discriminations and legal disabilities of sex.[40] The main business of the Women's Industrial Conference, called by the Women's Bureau in January 1923, was interrupted by altercations over the amendment; the conference in January of 1926 was all but broken up by this hotly disputed issue. Sarah Conboy of the AFL fired a parting shot by publicly expressing her wish that the Woman's party ladies might be afforded the opportunity of working in mine and factory so they could learn first hand the problems of working women. Mabel Leslie reported to the Trade Union League that the Woman's party members were "merely theoretical ultra-feminists who [did] not have to work for a living."[41]

The squabble was of no particular significance—the proposed amendment never had a chance of serious consideration—except that it illustrates the kind of irrelevant wrangle which so often engaged the social reformers during the twenties. Their energies were often dissipated in countering charges of radicalism and subversion, and in this instance charges of antifeminism. The thousands of reform-hours consumed in fruitless and rancorous debate with the Woman's party represented time the reformers would have preferred to invest in other pursuits. Year after year, Mary Anderson recorded bitterly in her reminiscences, reform associations "had to lay aside the work they were doing to improve conditions for women and spend their time combating the equal rights amendment."[42]

Less spectacular but of surpassing significance was the workers' educational movement which was so often linked to the reform activities of women's associations in these years. The WTUL had pioneered during the years before the war in training potential trade union leaders in a program that Margaret Dreier Robins inaugurated in Chicago. Arrangements had been made for young working women to enroll as special students at Northwestern University and in the Chicago School of Civics and Philanthropy. Of the forty working girls from seventeen different trades who enjoyed formal course work from 1913 until the program was discontinued in 1926, nearly three-quarters remained active in trade union leadership, a record which the league took as justification of the time and money it had invested in the enterprise. The difficulty of integrating young working women, who were so often of recent immigrant origin and who so rarely had formal educational training, into university classes (even when conducted by such sympathetic professors as Paul Douglas) tended to vitiate the experiment, however, and this particular form of workers' education was never widely adopted.

Established in April of 1921, the Workers' Educational Bureau set out to stimulate and coordinate educational efforts of all sorts. Chaired by James H. Maurer, a functionary of the Socialist party and president of the Pennsylvania Federation of Labor, the bureau drew as well upon the diverse talents of such typical reform leaders as Fannia M. Cohn, of the International Ladies' Garment Workers' Union and the Trade Union League; John Brophy of the United Mine Workers and Abraham Epstein, then secretary of the labor education committee of the Pennsylvania Federation of Labor. Through the Workers' Educational Bureau and through the Brookwood Labor College which it helped to sponsor, the promotion of the ideas of industrial unionism and of political action by labor was achieved. Generally "leftist" in its leanings, the Brookwood Labor College, directed by A. J. Muste, trained a number of young trade union officials who would later contribute substantially to the formation of the CIO.

The major effort for the education of women workers came at the Bryn Mawr summer school, opened first in 1921 on the instigation of Mary Anderson, Hilda Smith, and Dr. M. Carey Thomas, president of the college. Hilda Smith, who later headed up workers' education in the WPA, was named the summer school's director. Raised in a devout Episcopalian household, Hilda Smith turned very early in her life to a career of social service. A graduate of Bryn Mawr in 1910, she had worked summers in settlement camps and had gone on to do casework with the Girls' Friendly Society and to take courses at the New York School of Philanthropy before returning to her alma mater as dean of the college in 1919. Under Miss Smith's direction from 1921 to 1934, the Bryn Mawr School for Working Women drew its students from the trade union movement, from local units of the WTUL and, in the South where trade unionism was unknown, from the YWCA. Here the students received courses in economics, government, the history of the labor movement, remedial social legislation, the causes and cures of unemployment, trade union procedures, public speaking, and composition. That the sessions offered a lively opportunity for curious young women is attested to by the mixture of ethnic and religious groups that composed the student body and by the excellence of its faculty which included outstanding experts like Paul Douglas, Alice Henry, Broadus Mitchell, Carter Goodrich, Colston Warne, Mark Starr, and Stephen Raushenbush. Dedicated to such objectives as widening the influence of the trade union movement, training the students in "clear thinking," stimulating in them "an active and continued interest in the problems of [the] economic order," and promoting "the coming social reconstruction," the Bryn Mawr school made a major contribution to the elaboration of concepts and leadership in the social reform movement.[43] The school had immediate practical consequences as was evidenced by the successful move on the part of the students to organize college employees and to win for them an eight-hour day not only during the summer session but during the regular academic year as well.[44]

The significance of the Bryn Mawr School for Working Women and similar programs conducted at Barnard (1927–1934), the Vineyard Shore School for Women Workers in Industry (1929–1934), and the Brookwood Labor College is difficult to measure. It is fair to suggest, however, that they kept alive a commitment to trade union activity;

they trained many young men and women who were to become union and political leaders of some note during the depression decade; they kindled the aspirations of many young people in times of moral slump; they kept open the path of purposeful social change. Eleanor Roosevelt summed it up at a banquet honoring Dr. M. Carey Thomas, whose initiative had been crucial in the establishment of the Bryn Mawr school: If the New Deal were to win through to higher levels of life, the people must participate intelligently and constructively in social affairs. It was to this end that worker education had been directed, she said, toward giving "people the tools so that they [could] work out their own salvation wisely and well."[45] In so doing the workers' education movement contributed to the larger movement for reform.

Together, proponents of industrial minima, particularly for women and children, enlarged the rationale for legislative action, until by the end of the decade the philosophy of New Deal action in this arena had been elaborated in nearly every detail. Research notes of John R. Commons, made sometime in the mid-1920's, included an observation of Lord Northington's: "Necessitous men are not, truly speaking, free men, but, to answer to present exigency, will submit to any terms that the crafty may impose upon them."[46] The idea could hardly claim originality, but in the United States it did not, until the interwar era, receive much notice or elaboration. It came to be basic to every consideration by liberals whose central commitment was still to the enlargement of individual opportunity and freedom. Necessitous men, insecure men, men made anxious by low wages, uncertain employment, long hours at labor, and arbitrary industrial discipline were truly not free men. The establishment of industrial minima, of measures of social security broadly conceived, it followed, was essential to human liberty. On the heels of this simple conclusion came another axiom—society, through government, had an obligation to force industry to bear its just burden of responsibility for community welfare. If industry paid substandard wages, argued Ethel M. Johnson in 1927, society would somehow in some way have to make up the difference. It might be through "hospitals and dispensaries to care for women who are broken down in health because they did not earn enough to permit them sufficient wholesome food and suitable living arrangements." Or it might be through charitable relief. A minimum wage assessed the burden upon industry where it belonged.[47] If floors under wages could be set by law or administrative ruling as a proper charge against industry, then it could be left to collective bargaining by unions to win living wages above that level.[48] Unless workers, particularly women workers, enjoyed these minimum guarantees, they could not build up reserves for sickness or unemployment. A woman employed at "oppressive" levels, below the minimum, thereby became a "liability rather than an asset to the community," and a burden upon society.[49]

Over and over the point was hammered home—industrial minima were required not alone as humanitarian considerations or as charity but as measures essential to the over-all long-run efficiency of industry, to community health and welfare, and to social stability and orderly progress. The New York Consumers' League offered as its slogan for 1927 "Social Justice Is the Best Safeguard against Social Disorder"; while Florence Kelley, commenting on the violent textile strikes of 1929, insisted that the only alternative to industrial disorder and social strife was "peaceful progress" through legislation.[50]

It was perhaps Newton Baker who best summarized the need for social action to remedy the grievances associated with intense industrialization. Given the growing impersonality of all society, the sanctions of civilization were not as easily applied as once they were. The role of voluntary associations, such as the Consumers' League, was to "investigate, record, agitate" in order that men of good will might act with the knowledge of the consequences of their behavior, while the law coerced the "recalcitrants." The league and its allies could show the way for society to accomplish "on a large and collective scale, in a collective way, that which we so delighted to do as individuals under simpler conditions."[51]

The New Deal drew heavily and specifically upon these concepts, which had grown out of progressivism and had been tempered in the 1920's. The depression afforded the occasion for their implementation, because economic crisis overrode most other considerations in 1933. The National Recovery Administration prohibited child labor, and encouraged codes of labor standards governing hours, wages, and conditions for both women and men workers. When the NRA was broken, the industrial minima were rewritten in the Fair Labor Standards Act of 1938; and this time the Supreme Court concurred. The contribution of liberal reform in the 1920's had been to keep alive the progressive objectives, and then to modify them, extend them, and elaborate a rationale which, under the pressure of emergency, was incorporated as part of the New Deal consensus and program.

NOTES

1. Helen Glenn Tyson, "Mothers Who Earn," *Survey*, 67:5 (1 December 1926), pp. 275–279.

2. Nelle Swartz, review of *Mothers in Industry*, in *Survey*, 67:6 (15 December 1926), pp. 400–401.

3. Resolution in *Proceedings* (1924), pp. 336–337, WTUL, Box 15.

4. Frances Perkins, "Do Women in Industry Need Special Protection? Yes," *Survey*, 55:10 (15 February 1926), pp. 529–531.

5. Monthly Labor Bulletin of Massachusetts WTUL (January 1928), in WTUL Local Bulletins (Radcliffe), Box 1. Box 3, in same collection, contains comments of factory girls to an investigator of the Connecticut Consumers' League.

6. Florence Kelley, "The Inescapable Dilemma," *Survey*, 41:25 (22 March 1919), p. 885.

7. Executive Board of the New York WTUL, Minutes (6 June 1921), in WTUL (Radcliffe), Box 2.

8. The stories in Massachusetts and New York may be traced in WTUL, Box 15; NCL, Box 20; Dewson Papers (F. D. R. Library), Box 17.

9. Dr. George W. Webster quoted in "The Woman's Work Day," *Survey*, 46:4 (23 April 1921), p. 121.

10. Report of Rose Schneiderman, Julia S. O'Connor, and Matilda Lindsay (8 November 1925), WTUL, Box 3.

11. Florence Kelley to Adolf A. Berle, Jr. (31 January 1923), NCL, Box 8.

12. Florence Kelley to Mildred Chadsey (8 March 1923), NCL, Box 11.

13. Felix Frankfurter, *Felix Frankfurter Reminisces* (New York: Reynal, 1960), pp. 101–104.

14. Felix Frankfurter and Mary R. Dewson, *District of Columbia Minimum Wage Cases* (New York: Steinberg, 1923); *Adkins* v. *Children's Hospital,* 261 U.S. 525 (1923).

15. Mary R. Dewson to Isador Lubin (April 1957), Dewson Papers (F. D. R. Library), General Correspondence, Box 18.

16. "The Minimum Wage—What Next?" *Survey*, 50:4 (15 May 1923), pp. 215–222, 256–258, 263; Francis B. Sayres, "The Minimum Wage Decision," *Survey*, 50:3 (1 May 1923), pp. 150–151, 164, 172; Florence Kelley to Mrs. John Blair (1 May 1923), NCL, Box 10.

17. Typescript of Stenographic Report of Minimum Wage Conference (20 April 1923), NCL, Box 10.

18. Mimeographed Report on Conference in Tilton Papers, Box 3; Press Releases, WTUL, Box 25; Correspondence, WTUL, Box 2; Florence Kelley to Edward P. Costigan (31 May 1923), NCL, Box 10.

19. John R. Commons, Notes for Speech (9 November 1923), NCL, Box 8.

20. Florence Kelley to Amy G. Maher (17 March 1923), NCL, Box 11.

21. Jeanette Rankin, Report to Executive Board (25 October 1923), NCL, Box 8.

22. James A. Haight to Florence Kelley (19 December 1925), NCL, Box 11.

23. "Highlights of a Speech Made by Florence Kelley in 1923," in Massachusetts Consumers' League (Radcliffe), Drawer 1.

24. Florence Kelley to Board of Directors (12 June 1923), NCL, Box 11.

25. Felix Frankfurter to Florence Kelley (19 October 1923), NCL, Box 10.

26. Felix Frankfurter to Florence Kelley (25 October 1925), NCL, Box 10.

27. Roscoe Pound to Florence Kelley (22 October 1923), NCL, Box 10.

28. Zechariah Chafee to John R. Commons (1 April 1924), NCL, Box 11. See also Florence Kelley's correspondence, 1923–1924, with Charles Beard, Ernst Freund, Charles Warren, Ethel Smith, Newton D. Baker, Edward P. Costigan, NCL, Boxes 10 and 11.

29. Florence Kelley to Felix Frankfurter (25 June 1924), NCL, Box 11.

30. Correspondence in regard to conference (1 July 1924) that broke up with no agreement having been reached, NCL, Box 11.

31. Florence Kelley to "Dear Sister Dewson" (8 April 1924), NCL, Box 8.

32. Florence Kelley to John R. Commons (13 April 1927), NCL, Box 8.

33. Women's Bureau, *Fact Finding with the Women's Bureau* (Bulletin 84, 1931).

34. Mrs. Peake Faxon[?] to Leonora O'Reilly (no date, c. 1919), O'Reilly Papers (Radcliffe), Box 7.

35. Florence Kelley, "The New Woman's Party," *Survey*, 45:23 (5 March 1921), pp. 827–828.

36. Florence Kelley to Newton D. Baker (3 June 1921), NCL, Box 13.

37. Mary Anderson, *Woman at Work: The Autobiography of Mary Anderson as Told to Mary N. Winslow* (Minneapolis: University of Minnesota Press, 1951), Chapter 16.

38. A carbon copy of Dean Acheson's letter to Ethel M. Smith (8 September 1921) found its way into the files of the NCL, Box 13.

39. Florence Kelley to Mrs. C. J. Evans (16 December 1921), NCL, Box 13.

40. Alice Hamilton, draft of letter to Mrs. Hooker (16 January 1922), Hamilton Papers, Box 1. There is no evidence that the letter was ever sent, but it reflects the feelings of the amendment's opponents.

41. Mabel Leslie to Maud Swartz (4 May 1926), WTUL, Box 3.

42. Mary Anderson, *Woman at Work,* pp. 171–172.

43. Quotation from official statement of the Bryn Mawr School for Working Women (1921 and 1923), in Hilda Smith, *Women Workers at the Bryn Mawr Summer School* (New York: American Association for Adult Education, 1927), p. 7. Papers, bulletins, reports, memoranda of the school, 1921–1933, may be found in Smith Papers, Boxes 2, 3, and 16.

44. Mary Anderson, *Woman at Work,* Chapter 25.

45. Eleanor Roosevelt, Address (24 October 1933), quoted in Hilda Smith, "Autobiography," Smith Papers, Box 16.

46. Research folder on Minimum-Wage Legislation, Commons Papers, Box 9.

47. Ethel M. Johnson, "Fourteen Years of Minimum Wage in Massachusetts" (Typescript, 1927), WTUL (Radcliffe), Box 3.

48. Elizabeth Brandeis to Florence Kelley (20 June 1929), NCL, Box 10.

49. "What Girls Live On and How," *Survey*, 64:6 (15 June 1930), p. 277.

50. Leaflet of New York Consumers' League (1927) in Dewson Papers (Radcliffe), Box 2; Florence Kelley, Report to Board of Directors (27 September 1929), NCL, Box 8.

51. Newton D. Baker, Preface to Maud Nathan, *Story of an Epoch-Making Movement* (Garden City, N.Y.: Doubleday, 1926), pp. xii–xiv.

22 ♀ The American Woman's Pre-World War I Freedom in Manners and Morals

James R. McGovern

The Twenties have been alternately praised or blamed for almost everything and its opposite;[1] but most historians hold, whether to praise or to condemn, that this decade launched the revolution in manners and morals through which we are still moving today. This judgment seems to be part of an even more inclusive one in American historiography to exceptionalize the Twenties. No other decade has invited such titles of historical caricature as *The Jazz Age, This Was Normalcy, Fantastic Interim,* or *The Perils of Prosperity.* Richard Hofstadter's classic, *The Age of Reform,* subtly reinforces this view by seeing the Twenties as "Entr'acte," an interim between two periods of reform, the Progressive era and the New Deal, which themselves display discontinuity.[2]

Revisionism, in the form of a developmental interpretation of the relationship between the Progressive era and the Twenties, has been gaining strong support in recent years. De-emphasizing the disruptive impact of World War I, Henry F. May asked whether the 1920s could be understood fully "without giving more attention to the old regime."[3] He declared that "Immediately prewar America must be newly explored," especially "its inarticulate assumptions—assumptions in such areas as morality, politics, class and race relations, popular art

From the *Journal of American History* 55 (September 1968): 315–33. Reprinted by permission.

and literature, and family life."[4] May pursued his inquiry in *The End of American Innocence* and showed that for the purposes of intellectual history, at least, the Twenties were not as significant as the preceding decade.[5] Political historians have been reassessing the relationship of the Progressive era to the Twenties as well. Arthur Link has demonstrated that progressivism survived World War I,[6] and J. Joseph Huthmacher has established continuity between progressivism and the New Deal in the immigrant's steadfast devotion to the ameliorative powers of the government.[7] Together with May's analysis, their writings suggest that the 1920s are much more the result of earlier intrinsic social changes than either the sudden, supposedly traumatic experiences of the war or unique developments in the Twenties. Since this assertion is certain to encounter the formidable claims that the 1920s, at least in manners and morals, amounted to a revolution, its viability can be tested by questioning if the American woman's "emancipation" in manners and morals occurred even earlier than World War I.

Even a casual exploration of the popular literature of the Progressive era reveals that Americans then described and understood themselves to be undergoing significant changes in morals. "Sex o'clock in America" struck in 1913,[8] about the same time as "The Repeal of Reticence."[9] One contemporary writer saw Americans as liberated from the strictures of "Victorianism," now an epithet deserving criticism, and exulted, "Heaven defend us from a return to the prudery of the Victorian regime!"[10] Conditions were such that another commentator asked self-consciously, "Are We Immoral?"[11] And still another feared that the present "vice not often matched since [the time of] the Protestant Reformation" might invite a return to Puritanism.[12] Yet, historians have not carefully investigated the possibility that the true beginnings of America's "New Freedom" in morals occurred prior to 1920.[13] The most extensive, analytical writing on the subject of changing manners and morals is found in Federick L. Allen's *Only Yesterday* (1931), William Leuchtenburg's *The Perils of Prosperity* (1958), May's *The End of American Innocence* (1959), and George Mowry's *The Urban Nation* (1965).

Allen and Leuchtenburg apply almost identical sharp-break interpretations, respectively entitling chapters "The Revolution in Manners and Morals" and "The Revolution in Morals."[14] Both catalogue the same types of criteria for judgment. The flapper, as the "new woman" was called, was a creature of the 1920s. She smoked, drank, worked, and played side by side with men. She became preoccupied with sex—shocking and simultaneously unshockable. She danced close, became freer with her favors, kept her own latchkey, wore scantier attire which emphasized her boyish, athletic form, just as she used makeup and bobbed and dyed her hair. She and her comradely beau tried to abolish time and succeeded, at least to the extent that the elders asked to join the revelry. Although there were occasional "advance signals" of "rebellion" before the war, it was not until the 1920s that the code of woman's innocence and ignorance crumbled.

May, who comes closest to an understanding of the moral permissiveness before the 1920s, describes in general terms such phenomena of the Progressive era as the "Dance Craze," birth control, the impact of the movies, and the "white-slave panic."[15] He focuses on the intellectuals, however, and therefore overlooks the depth of these and similar social movements. This causes him to view them as mere "Cracks in the Surface" of an essentially conservative society. He quotes approvingly of the distinction made by the *Nation* "between the fluttering tastes of the half-baked intellectuals, attracted by all these things, and the surviving soundness of the great majority."[16] His treatment also ignores one of the most significant areas of changing manners and morals as they affected the American woman: the decided shift in her sex role and identification in the direction of more masculine norms. Again, *The End of American Innocence* does not convincingly relate these changes to the growth of the cities. Perhaps these limitations explain Mowry's preference for a "sharp-break" interpretation, although he wrote seven years after May.

Mowry, who acknowledges especial indebtedness to Leuchtenburg,[17] is emphatic about the "startling" changes in manners and morals in the 1920s.[18] He highlights "the new woman of the twenties"[19] whose "modern feminine morality and attitudes toward the institution of marriage date from the twenties."[20] Mowry concedes to the libidos of progressives only the exceptional goings-on in Greenwich Village society.

These hypotheses, excluding May's, hold that the flapper appeared in the postwar period mainly because American women en masse then first enjoyed considerable social and economic freedom. They also emphasize the effect of World War I on morals.[21] By inference, of course, the Progressive era did not provide a suitable matrix. But an investigation of this period establishes that women had become sufficiently active and socially independent to prefigure the "emancipation" of the 1920s.

A significant deterioration of external controls over morality had occurred before 1920. One of the consequences of working and living conditions in the cities, especially as these affected women, was that Americans of the period 1900–1920 had experienced a vast dissolution of moral authority, which formerly had centered in the family and the small community. The traditional "straight and narrow" could not serve the choices and opportunities of city life.[22] As against primary controls and contacts based on face-to-face association where the norms of family, church, and small community, usually reinforcing each other, could be internalized, the city made for a type of "individualization" through its distant, casual, specialized, and transient clusters of secondary associations.[23] The individual came to determine his own behavioral norms.

The "home is in peril" became a fact of sociological literature as early as 1904.[24] One of the most serious signs of its peril was the increasing inability of parents to influence their children in the delicate areas of propriety and morals.[25] The car, already numerous enough to affect dating and premarital patterns,[26] the phone coming to be used for purposes of romantic accommodation,[27] and the variety of partners at the office or the factory,[28] all together assured unparalleled privacy and permissiveness between the sexes.

Individualization of members served to disrupt confidence between generations of the family, if not to threaten parents with the role of anachronistic irrelevance. Dorothy Dix observed in 1913 that there had been "so many changes in the conditions of life and point of view in the last twenty years that the parent of today is absolutely unfitted to decide the problems of life for the young man and woman of today. This is particularly the case with women because the whole economic and social position of women has been revolutionized since mother was a girl."[29] Magazine articles lamented "The Passing of the Home Daughter" who preferred the blessed anonymity of the city to "dying of asphyxiation at home!"[30] The same phenomenon helps to explain the popularity in this period of such standardized mothers as Dorothy Dix, Beatrice Fairfax, and Emily Post, each of whom was besieged with queries on the respective rights of mothers and daughters.

Woman's individualization resulted mainly because, whether single or married, gainfully employed or not, she spent more time outside her home. Evidence demonstrates that the so-called job and kitchen revolutions were already in advanced stages by 1910. The great leap forward in women's participation in economic life came between 1900 and 1910; the percentage of women who were employed changed only slightly from 1910 to 1930. A comparison of the percentages of gainfully employed women aged 16 to 44 between 1890 and 1930 shows that they comprised 21.7 percent of Americans employed in 1890, 23.5 percent in 1900, 28.1 percent in 1910, 28.3 percent in 1920, and 29.7 percent in 1930.[31] While occupational activity for women appears to stagnate from 1910 to 1920, in reality a considerable restructuring occurred with women leaving roles as domestics and assuming positions affording more personal independence as clerks and stenographers.[32]

Married women, especially those in the upper and middle classes, enjoyed commensurate opportunities. Experts in household management advised women to rid themselves of the maid and turn to appliances as the "maid of all service."[33] Statistics on money expended on those industries which reduced home labor for the wife suggest that women in middle-income families gained considerable leisure after 1914.[34] This idea is also corroborated from other sources,[35] especially from the tone and content of advertising in popular magazines when they are compared with advertising at the turn of the century. Generally speaking, women depicted in advertising in or about 1900 are well rounded, have gentle, motherly expressions, soft billowy hair, and delicate hands. They are either sitting down or standing motionless; their facial expressions are immobile as are their corseted figures.[36] After 1910, they are depicted as more active figures with more of their activity taking place outside their homes.[37] One woman tells another over the phone: "Yes[,] drive over right away—I'll be ready. My housework! Oh, that's all done. How do I do it? I just let electricity do my work nowadays."[38] Vacuum cleaners permitted the housewife to "Push the Button—and Enjoy the Springtime!"[39] Van Camp's "Pork and Beans" promised to save her "100 hours yearly,"[40] and Campbell's soups encouraged, "Get some fun out of life," since it was unnecessary to let the "three-meals-a-day problem tie you down to constant drudgery."[41] Wizard Polish, Minute Tapioca, and Minute Gelatine also offered the same promise. The advertising image of women became more natural, even nonchalant. A lady entertaining a friend remarks: "I don't have to hurry nowadays. I have a Florence Automatic Oil Stove in my kitchen."[42] It had become "so *very* easy" to wax the floors that well-dressed women could manage them.[43] And they enjoyed a round of social activities driving the family car.[44]

It was in this setting that the flapper appeared along with her older married sister who sought to imitate her. No one at the office or in the next block cared much about their morals as long as the one was efficient and the other paid her bills on time. And given the fact that both these women had more leisure and wished "to participate in what men call 'the game of life' " rather than accept "the mere humdrum of household duties,"[45] it is little wonder that contemporaries rightly assessed the danger of the situation for traditional morals by 1910.

The ensuing decade was marked by the development of a revolution in manners and morals; its chief embodiment was the flapper who was urban based and came primarily from the middle and upper classes.

Young—whether in fact or fancy—assertive, and independent, she experimented with intimate dancing, permissive favors, and casual courtships or affairs. She joined men as comrades, and the differences in behavior of the sexes were narrowed. She became in fact in some degree desexualized. She might ask herself, "Am I Not a Boy? Yes, I Am—Not."[46] Her speech, her interest in thrills and excitement, her dress and hair, her more aggressive sexuality, even perhaps her elaborate beautification, which was a statement of intentions, all point to this. Women, whether single or married, became at once more attractive and freer in their morals and paradoxically less feminine. Indeed, the term sexual revolution as applied to the Progressive era means reversal in the traditional role of women just as it describes a pronounced familiarity of the sexes.

The unmarried woman after 1910 was living in the "Day of the Girl."[47] Dorothy Dix described "the type of girl that the modern young man falls for" in 1915 as a "husky young woman who can play golf all day and dance all night, and drive a motor car, and give first aid to the injured if anybody gets hurt, and who is in no more danger of swooning than he is."[48] Little wonder she was celebrated in song as "A Dangerous Girl"; the lyrics of one of the popular songs for 1916 read, "You dare me, you scare me, and still I like you more each day. But you're the kind that will charm; and then do harm; you've got a dangerous way."[49] The "most popular art print . . . ever issued" by *Puck* depicts a made-up young lady puckering her lips and saying "Take It From Me!"[50] The American girl of 1900 was not described in similar terms. The lovely and gracious Gibson Girl was too idealized to be real.[51] And when young lovers trysted in advertising, they met at Horlick's Malted Milk Bar; he with his guitar, and she with her parasol.[52] Beatrice Fairfax could still reply archaically about the need for "maidenly reserve" to such queries as those on the proprieties of men staring at women on the streets.[53] And the *Wellesley College News* in 1902 reported that students were not permitted to have a Junior Prom because it would be an occasion for meeting "promiscuous men," although the college sanctioned "girl dances."[54]

The girls, however, dispensed with "maidenly reserve." In 1910, Margaret Deland, the novelist, could announce a "Change in the Feminine Ideal."

> This young person . . . with surprisingly bad manners—has gone to college, and when she graduates she is going to earn her own living . . . she won't go to church; she has views upon marriage and the birth-rate, and she utters them calmly, while her mother blushes with embarrassment; she occupies herself, passionately, with everything except the things that used to occupy the minds of girls.[55]

Many young women carried their own latchkeys.[56] Meanwhile, as Dorothy Dix noted, it had become "literally true that the average father does not know, by name or sight, the young man who visits his daughter and who takes her out to places of amusement."[57] She was distressed over the widespread use by young people of the car which she called the "devil's wagon."[58] Another writer asked: "Where Is Your Daughter This Afternoon?" "Are you sure that she is not being drawn into the whirling vortex of afternoon 'trots' . . . ?"[59] Polly, Cliff Sterrett's remarkable comic-strip, modern girl from *Polly and Her Pals,* washed dishes under the shower and dried them with an electric fan; and while her mother tried hard to domesticate her, Polly wondered, "Gee Whiz! I wish I knew what made my nose shine!"[60]

Since young women were working side by side with men and recreating more freely and intimately with them, it was inevitable that they behave like men. Older people sometimes carped that growing familiarity meant that romance was dead[61] or that "nowadays brides hardly blush, much less faint."[62] And Beatrice Fairfax asked, "Has Sweet Sixteen Vanished?"[63] But some observers were encouraged to note that as girls' ways approximated men's, the sexes were, at least, more comradely.[64] The modern unmarried woman had become a "Diana, Hunting in the Open."[65] Dorothy Dix reported that "nice girls, good girls, girls in good positions in society—frankly take the initiative in furthering an acquaintance with any man who happens to strike their fancy." The new ideal in feminine figure, dress, and hair styles was all semi-masculine. The "1914 Girl" with her "slim hips and boy-carriage" was a "slim, boylike creature."[66] The "new figure is Amazonian, rather than Miloan. It is boyish rather than womanly. It is strong rather than soft."[67] Her dress styles, meanwhile, de-emphasized both hips and bust while they permitted the large waist. The boyish coiffure began in 1912 when young women began to tuck-under their hair with a ribbon;[68] and by 1913–1914, Newport ladies, actresses like Pauline Frederick, then said to be the prettiest girl in America, and the willowy, popular dancer Irene Castle were wearing short hair.[69] By 1915, the *Ladies Home Journal* featured women with short hair on its covers, and even the pure type of woman who advertised Ivory Soap appeared to be shorn.[70]

The unmarried flapper was a determined pleasure-seeker whom novelist Owen Johnson described collectively as "determined to liberate their lives and claim the same rights of judgment as their brothers."[71] The product of a "feminine revolution startling in the shock of its abruptness," she was living in the city independently of her family. Johnson noted: "She is sure of one life only and that one she passionately desires. She wants to live that life to its fullest. . . . She wants adventure. She wants excitement and mystery. She wants to see, to know, to experience. . . ." She expressed both a "passionate revolt against the commonplace" and a "scorn of conventions." Johnson's heroine in *The Salamander,* Doré Baxter, embodied his views. Her carefree motto is reminiscent of Fitzgerald's flappers of the Twenties: " 'How do I know what I'll do to-morrow?' "[72] Her nightly prayer, the modest " 'O Lord! give me everything I want!' "[73] Love was her "supreme law of conduct,"[74] and she, like the literary flappers of the Twenties, feared "thirty as a sort of sepulcher, an end of all things!" [75] Johnson believed that all young women in all sections of the country had "a little touch of the Salamander," each alike being impelled by "an impetuous frenzy . . . to sample each new excitement," both the "safe and the dangerous."[76] Girls "seemed determined to have their fling like men," the novelist Gertrude Atherton noted in *Current Opinion,* "and some of the stories [about them] made even my sophisticated hair crackle at the roots. . . ."[77] Beatrice Fairfax deplored the trends, especially the fact that "Making love lightly, boldly and promiscuously seems to be part of our social structure."[78] Young men and women kissed though they did not intend to marry.[79] And kissing was shading into spooning (" 'To Spoon' or 'Not to Spoon' Seems to Be the Burning Question with Modern Young America")[80] and even "petting," which was modish among the collegiate set.[81] In fact, excerpts from the diary of a co-ed written before World War I suggest that experimentation was virtually complete within her peer group. She discussed her "adventures" with other college girls. "We were healthy animals and we were demanding our rights to spring's awakening." As for men, she wrote, "I played square with the men. I always told them I was not out to pin them down to marriage, but that this intimacy was pleasant and I wanted it as much as they did. We indulged in sex talk, birth control. . . . We thought too much about it."[82]

One of the most interesting developments in changing sexual behavior which characterized these years was the blurring of age lines between young and middle-aged women in silhouette, dress, and cosmetics.[83] A fashion commentator warned matrons, "This is the day of the figure. . . . The face alone, no matter how pretty, counts for nothing unless the body is as straight and yielding as every young girl's."[84] With only slight variations, the optimum style for women's dress between 1908 and 1918 was a modified sheath, straight up and down and clinging.[85] How different from the styles of the high-busted, broad-hipped mother of the race of 1904 for whom Ella Wheeler Wilcox, the journalist and poet, advised the use of veils because "the slightest approach to masculinity in woman's attire is always unlovely and disappointing."[86]

The sloughing off of numerous undergarments and loosening of others underscored women's quickening activity and increasingly self-reliant morals. Clinging dresses and their "accompanying lack of undergarments" eliminated, according to the president of the New York Cotton Exchange, "at least twelve yards of finished goods for each adult female inhabitant."[87] Corset makers were forced to make adjustments too and use more supple materials.[88] Nevertheless, their sales declined.[89]

The American woman of 1910, in contrast with her sister of 1900, avidly cultivated beauty of face and form. In fact, the first American woman whose photographs and advertising image we can clearly recognize as belonging to our times lived between 1910 and 1920. "Nowadays," the speaker for a woman's club declared in 1916, "only the very poor or the extremely careless are old or ugly. You can go to a beauty shop and choose the kind of beauty you will have."[90] Beautification included the use of powder, rouge, lipstick, eyelash and eyebrow stain. Advertising was now manipulating such images for face powder as "Mother tried it and decided to keep it for herself,"[91] or "You can have beautiful Eyebrows and Eyelashes. . . . Society women and actresses get them by using Lash-Brow-Ine."[92] Nearly every one of the numerous advertisements for cosmetics promised some variation of "How to Become Beautiful, Fascinating, Attractive."[93]

In her dress as well as her use of cosmetics, the American woman gave evidence that she had abandoned passivity. An unprecedented public display of the female figure characterized the period.[94] Limbs now became legs and more of them showed after 1910, although they were less revealing than the promising hosiery advertisements. Rolled down hose first appeared in 1917.[95] Dresses for opera and restaurant were deeply cut in front and back, and not even the rumor that Mrs. John Jacob Astor had suffered a chest cold as a result of wearing deep decolleté[96] deterred their wearers. As for gowns, "Fashion says— Evening gowns must be sleeveless. . . . afternoon gowns are made with semi-transparent yokes and sleeves."[97] Undoubtedly, this vogue for transparent blouses and dresses[98] caused the editor of the *Unpopular Review* to declare: "At no time and place under Christianity, except the most corrupt periods in France. . . . certainly never before in America, has woman's form been so freely displayed in society and on the street."[99]

In addition to following the example of young women in dress and beautification, middle-aged women, especially those from the middle and upper classes, were espousing their permissive manners and morals.[100] Smoking and, to a lesser extent, drinking in public were becoming fashionable for married women of the upper class and were making headway at other class levels.[101]   As early as 1910, a prominent clubwoman stated: "It has become a well-established habit for women to drink cocktails. It is thought the smart thing to do."[102]   Even before Gertrude Atherton described in the novel *Black Oxen* the phenomenon of the middle-aged women who sought to be attractive to younger men, supposedly typifying the 1920s,[103] it was evident in the play "Years of Discretion." Written by Frederic Hatton and Fanny Locke Hatton, and staged by Belasco, the play was "welcomed cordially both in New York and Chicago" in 1912. It featured a widowed mother forty-eight years of age, who announces, "I intend to look under forty—lots under. I have never attracted men, but I know I can."[104]   Again, "I mean to have a wonderful time. To have all sorts and kinds of experience. I intend to love and be loved, to lie and cheat."[105]   Dorothy Dix was dismayed over "the interest that women ... have in what we are pleased to euphoniously term the 'erotic.' " She continued, "I'll bet there are not ten thousand women in the whole United States who couldn't get one hundred in an examination of the life and habits of Evelyn Nesbitt and Harry Thaw...."[106]   Married women among the fashionable set held the great parties, at times scandalous ones which made the 1920s seem staid by comparison.[107]   They hired the Negro orchestras at Newport and performed and sometimes invented the daring dances.[108]   They conscientiously practiced birth control, as did women of other classes.[109]   And they initiated divorce proceedings, secure in the knowledge that many of their best friends had done the same thing.

Perhaps the best insights on the mores and morals of this group are to be found in the writings of the contemporary, realistic novelist, Robert Herrick.[110]   Herrick derived his heroines from "the higher income groups, the wealthy, upper middle, and professional classes among which he preferred to move."[111]   His heroines resemble literary flappers of the 1920s in their repudiation of childbearing. "It takes a year out of a woman's life, of course, no matter how she is situated," they say, or, "Cows do that."[112]   Since their lives were seldom more than a meaningless round of social experiences, relieved principally by romantic literature, many of them either contemplated or consented to infidelity. Thus Margaret Pole confesses to her friend, Conny Wood-yard, " I'd like to lie out on the beach and forget children and servants and husbands, and stop wondering what life is. Yes, I'd like a vacation—in the Windward Islands, with somebody who understood.' 'To wit, a man!' added Conny. 'Yes, a man! But only for the trip.' "[113]   They came finally to live for love in a manner that is startlingly reminiscent of some of the famous literary women of the Twenties.[114]

Insights regarding the attitudes of married women from the urban lower middle class can be found in the diary of Ruth Vail Randall, who lived in Chicago from 1911 to the date of her suicide, March 6, 1920.[115] A document of urban sociology, the diary transcends mere personal experience and becomes a commentary on group behavior of the times. Mrs. Randall was reared in a family that owned a grocery store, was graduated from high school in Chicago, and was married at twenty to Norman B. Randall, then twenty-one. She worked after marriage in a department store and later for a brief period as a model. She looked to marriage, especially its romance, as the supreme fulfillment of her life and was bitterly disappointed with her husband. She began to turn to other men whom she met at work or places of recreation, and her husband left her. Fearing that her lover would leave her eventually as well, she killed him and herself.

The diary focuses on those conditions which made the revolution in morals a reality. The young couple lived anonymously in a highly mobile neighborhood where their morals were of their own making. Mrs. Randall did not want children; she aborted their only child. [116] She was also averse to the reserved "womanly" role, which her husband insisted that she assume.[117] She complained, "Why cannot a woman do all man does?"[118] She wished that men and women were more alike in their social roles.[119] She repudiated involvement in her home, resolved to exploit equally every privilege which her husband assumed, drank, flirted, and lived promiscuously. Telephones and cars made her extramarital liaisons possible. Even before her divorce, she found another companion; flouting convention, she wrote, "He and I have entered a marriage pact according to our own ideas."[120] Throughout her diary she entertained enormous, almost magical, expectations of love. She complained that her lovers no more than her husband provided what she craved—tenderness and companionship. Disillusionment with one of them caused her to cry out, "I am miserable. I have the utmost contempt for myself. But the lake is near and soon it will be warm. Oh, God to rest in your arms. To rest—and to have peace."[121]

That America was experiencing a major upheaval in morals during the Progressive era is nowhere better ascertained than in the comprehensive efforts by civic officials and censorial citizens to control them. Disapproval extended not only to such well-known staples as alcohol, divorce, and prostitution, but also to dancing, woman's dress, cabarets, theaters and movies, and birth control. "Mrs. Warren's Profession" was withdrawn from the New York stage in 1905 after a one night performance, the manager of the theater later being charged with offending public decency.[122] When a grand jury in New York condemned the "turkey trot and kindred dances" as "indecent," the judge who accepted the presentment noted that "Rome's downfall was due to the degenerate nature of its dancers, and I only hope that we will not suffer the same result."[123]   Public dancing was henceforth to be licensed. Mayor John Fitzgerald personally assisted the morals campaign in Boston by ordering the removal from a store of an objectionable picture which portrayed a "show-girl" with her legs crossed.[124]   Meanwhile, the "X-Ray Skirt" was outlawed in Portland, Oregon, and Los Angeles;[125]   and the police chief of Louisville, Kentucky, ordered the arrest of a number of women appearing on the streets with slit skirts.[126]   Witnessing to a general fear that the spreading knowledge of contraception might bring on sexual license, the federal and several state governments enacted sumptuary legislation.[127]   And in two celebrated incidents, the offenders, Van K. Allison (1916) in Boston and Margaret Sanger (1917) in New York, were prosecuted and sent to jail.[128]

Public officials were apprehensive about the sweeping influence of the movies on the masses, "at once their book, their drama, their art. To some it has become society, school, and even church."[129]   They proceeded to set up boards of censorship with powers to review and condemn movies in four states: Pennsylvania (1911), Ohio (1913), Maryland (1916), and Kansas (1917), and in numerous cities beginning with Chicago in 1907.[130]   The Pennsylvania board, for example, prohibited pictures which displayed nudity, prolonged passion, women drinking and smoking, and infidelity. It protected Pennsylvanians from such films produced between 1915 and 1918 as "What Every Girl Should Know," "A Factory Magdalene," and "Damaged Goodness."[131]

Such determination proved unavailing, however, even as the regulatory strictures were being applied. According to one critic the "sex drama" using "plain, blunt language" had become "a commonplace" of the theater after 1910 and gave the "tender passion rather the worst for it in recent years."[132]   Vice films packed them in every night, especially after the smashing success of "Traffic in Souls," which reportedly grossed $450,000.[133]   In Boston the anti-vice campaign itself languished because there was no means of controlling "the kitchenette-apartment section." "In these apartment houses, there are hundreds of women who live as they please and who entertain as they will." [134] Mayor Fitzgerald's "show-girl," evicted from her saucy perch, gained more notoriety when she appeared in a Boston newspaper the following day.[135]   Even Anthony Comstock, that indefatigable guardian of public morals, had probably come to look a bit like a comic character living beyond his times.[136]

When Mrs. Sanger was arrested for propagating birth control information in 1917, she confidently stated, "I have nothing to fear. . . . Regardless of the outcome I shall continue my work, supported by thousands of men and women throughout the country."[137] Her assurance was well founded. Three years earlier her supporters had founded a National Birth Control League; and in 1919, this organization opened its first public clinic.[138] But most encouraging for Mrs. Sanger was the impressive testimony that many Americans were now practicing or interested in birth control.[139] When Paul B. Blanchard, pastor of the Maverick Congregational Church in East Boston, protested the arrest of Van K. Allison, he charged, "If the truth were made public and the laws which prevent the spreading of even oral information about birth control were strictly enforced how very few of the married society leaders, judges, doctors, ministers, and businessmen would be outside the prison dock!"[140]

The foregoing demonstrates that a major shift in American manners and morals occurred in the Progressive era, especially after 1910. Changes at this time, though developing out of still earlier conditions, represented such visible departures from the past and were so commonly practiced as to warrant calling them revolutionary. Too often scholars have emphasized the Twenties as the period of significant transition and World War I as a major cause of the phenomenon. Americans of the 1920s, fresh from the innovative wartime atmosphere, undoubtedly quickened and deepened the revolution. Women from smaller cities and towns contested what was familiar terrain to an already seasoned cadre of urban women and a formidable group of defectors. Both in their rhetoric and their practices, apparent even before the war, the earlier group had provided the shibboleths for the 1920s; they first asked, "What are Patterns for?" The revolution in manners and morals was, of course, but an integral part of numerous, contemporary, political and social movements to free the individual by reordering society. Obviously, the Progressive era, more than the 1920s, represents the substantial beginnings of contemporary American civilization.

The revolution in manners and morals, particularly as it affected women, took the twofold form of more permissive sexuality and diminished femininity. Women from the upper classes participated earlier, as is evidenced by their introductory exhibition of fashions, hair styles, dances, cosmetics, smoking, and drinking. Realistic novels concerned with marriage suggest that they entertained ideas of promiscuity and even infidelity before women of the lower classes. Yet the cardinal condition of change was not sophistication but urban living and the freedom it conferred. As technology and economic progress narrowed the gap between the classes, middle-class women and even those below were free to do many of the same things almost at the same time. Above all, the revolution in manners and morals after 1910 demonstrates that sexual freedom and the twentieth-century American city go together.

NOTES

1. Henry F. May, "Shifting Perspectives on the 1920's," *Mississippi Valley Historical Review,* XLIII (Dec. 1956), 405–27.

2. Richard Hofstadter, *The Age of Reform: From Bryan to F. D. R.* (New York, 1955), 282–301.

3. May, "Shifting Perspectives on the 1920's," 426. See also Henry F. May, "The Rebellion of the Intellectuals, 1912–1917," *American Quarterly,* VIII (Summer 1956), 115, wherein May describes 1912–1917 as a "pre-revolutionary or early revolutionary period."

4. May, "Shifting Perspectives on the 1920's," 427.

5. Henry F. May, *The End of American Innocence: A Study of the First Years of Our Own Time, 1912–1917* (New York, 1959).

6. Arthur S. Link, "What Happened to the Progressive Movement in the 1920's?" *American Historical Review,* LXIV (July 1959), 833–51.

7. J. Joseph Huthmacher, "Urban Liberalism and the Age of Reform," *Mississippi Valley Historical Review,* XLIX (Sept. 1962), 231–41. Other political and economic historians concur on a developmental interpretation. Gerald D. Nash, *State Government and Economic Development: A History of Administrative Policies in California, 1849–1933* (Berkeley, 1964), 250, 291, 326, views the period 1900–1933 as a unit because it was characterized by notable coordination and centralization of authority by agencies of state government in California. Donald C. Swain, *Federal Conservation Policy, 1921–1933* (Berkeley, 1963), 6, sees the national conservation program making continuous advances through the 1920s based upon beginnings in the Progressive period.

8. "Sex O'clock in America," *Current Opinion,* LV (Aug. 1913), 113–14. The anonymous author borrowed the phrase from William M. Reedy, editor of the St. Louis *Mirror.*

9. Agnes Repplier, "The Repeal of Reticence," *Atlantic Monthly,* CXIII (March 1914), 297–304, objected to the "obsession of sex which has set us all a-babbling about matters once excluded from the amenities of conversation" (p. 298). Articles on birth control, prostitution, divorce, and sexual morals between 1910 and 1914 were cumulatively more numerous per thousand among articles indexed in the *Reader's Guide to Periodical Literature* than for either 1919 to 1924 or 1925 to 1928. Hornell Hart, "Changing Social Attitudes and Interests," *Recent Social Trends in the United States: Report of the President's Research Committee on Social Trends* (2 vols., New York, 1933), I, 414.

10. H. W. Boynton, "Ideas, Sex, and the Novel," *Dial,* LX (April 13, 1916), 361. In Robert W. Chambers, *The Restless Sex* (New York, 1918), 143, the heroine remarks, "What was all wrong in our Victorian mothers' days is all right now."

11. Arthur Pollock, "Are We Immoral?" *Forum,* LI (Jan. 1914), 52. Pollock remarks that "in our literature and in our life to-day sex is paramount."

12. "Will Puritanism Return?" *Independent,* 77 (March 23, 1914), 397.

13. Mark Sullivan, *Our Times: The War Begins* (New York, 1932), 165–93, states in colorful and impressionistic terms that significant changes in moral attitudes had taken place in the Progressive era. He attributes much of this to the influence of Freud, Shaw, and Omar Khayyám. Preston William Slosson, *The Great Crusade and After: 1914–1928* (New York, 1930), describes the period 1914–1928 as a unit, but his material dealing with morals centers on the 1920s. For example, there are only five footnotes based on materials written between 1914 and 1919 in his chapter, "The American Woman Wins Equality," 130–61. Samuel Eliot Morison makes brief mention of a "revolution in sexual morals" before 1920 in *The Oxford History of the American People* (New York, 1965), 906–08.

14. Frederick Lewis Allen, *Only Yesterday: An Informal History of the Nineteen-Twenties* (New York, 1931), 88–122; William E. Leuchtenburg, *The Perils of Prosperity: 1914–32* (Chicago, 1958), 158–77.

15. May, *The End of American Innocence,* 334–47, is lightly documented; there are only twelve footnotes to support his discussion of these and similar developments.

16. *Ibid.,* 347. May's view of women's changing attitudes is contradicted by Margaret Deland: "Of course there were women a generation ago, as in all generations, who asserted themselves; but they were practically 'sports.' Now, the simple, honest woman . . . the good wife, the good mother—is evolving ideals which are changing her life, and the lives of those people about her." Margaret Deland, "The Change in the Feminine Ideal," *Atlantic Monthly,* CV (March 1910), 291.

17. George E. Mowry, *The Urban Nation: 1920–1960* (New York, 1965), 250.

18. *Ibid.,* 23.

19. *Ibid.*

20. *Ibid.,* 24.

21. "By 1930 more than ten million women held jobs. Nothing did more to emancipate them." Leuchtenburg, *Perils of Prosperity,* 160. See also Allen, *Only Yesterday,* 95–98. For estimates of the effects of World War I on morals, see Leuchtenburg, *Perils of Prosperity,* 172–73; Allen, *Only Yesterday,* 94; Mowry, *Urban Nation,* 24.

22. Population in urban territory comprised only about 28 percent of the total American population in 1880; but by 1920, approximately 52 percent were living there. Department of Commerce, Bureau of the Census, *Historical Statistics of the United States, Colonial Times to 1957* (Washington, 1960), 14.

23. Scott Nearing and Nellie M. S. Nearing, *Woman and Social Progress* (New York, 1912), 137–41. The Nearings wrote: "The freedom which American Women have gained through recent social changes and the significance of their consequent choice, constitutes one of the profoundest and at the same time one of the most inscrutable problems in American life" (p. 138). William I. Thomas, *The Unadjusted Girl: With Cases and Standpoint for Behavior Analysis* (Boston, 1923), 86. Ernest R. Mowrer, *Family Disorganization* (Chicago, 1927), 6–8. Mowrer attributes "Family Disorganization" to the "conditions of city life" which resulted in a "rebellion against the old ideals of family life. . . ."

24. George Elliott Howard, "Social Control and the Functions of the Family," Howard J. Rogers, ed. *Congress of Arts and Sciences: Universal Exposition, St. Louis, 1904* (8 vols., Boston, 1906), VII, 702.

25. Louise Collier Willcox, "Our Supervised Morals," *North American Review,* CXCVIII (Nov. 1913), 708, observes: "The time is past when parents supervised the morals of their children. . . "

26. There was a surprisingly large number of cars sold and used in America between 1910 and 1920. Approximately 40 percent as many cars were produced each year between 1915 and 1917 as were manufactured between 1925 and 1927. *Facts and Figures of the Automobile Industry* (New York, 1929), 6, 22. There were approximately 7,500,000 cars registered in 1919. "Existing Surfaced Mileage Total" on a scale of 1,000 miles was 204 in 1910, 332 in 1918, 521 in 1925, and 694 in 1930. *Historical Statistics of the United States,* 458. Newspapers reported the impact of the automobile on dating and elopements. For a moralistic reaction to the phenomenon, see Dorothy Dix, Boston *American,* Sept. 5, 1912. For an enthusiast of "mobile privacy" in this period, see F. Scott Fitzgerald, "Echoes of the Jazz Age," *Scribner's Magazine,* XC (Nov. 1931), 460. Fitzgerald wrote: "As far back as 1915 the unchaperoned young people of the smaller cities had discovered the mobile privacy of that automobile given to young Bill at sixteen to make him 'self-reliant.' "

27. Dorothy Dix, "A Modern Diana," Boston *American,* April 7, 1910.

28. Beatrice Fairfax, *ibid.,* May 28, 1908; Dorothy Dix, *ibid.,* Sept. 9, 1912.

29. *Ibid.,* Aug. 21, 1913.

30. Marion Harland, "The Passing of the Home Daughter," *Independent,* LXXI (July 13, 1911), 90.

31. Sophonisba P. Breckinridge, *Women in the Twentieth Century: A Study of Their Political, Social and Economic Activities* (New York, 1933), 112. Overall percentages of women gainfully employed rose from 19 percent of the total work force in 1890 to 20.6 percent in 1900, 24.3 percent in 1910, 24 percent in 1920, and 25.3 percent in 1930. *Ibid.,* 108.

32. While the number of women who worked as domestics declined after 1910, large numbers of women were employed for the first time as clerks and stenographers. In fact, more women were employed in both these occupations between 1910 and 1920 than between 1920 and 1930. *Ibid.,* 129, 177.

33. Martha Bensley Bruere and Robert W. Bruere, *Increasing Home Efficiency* (New York, 1914), 236–41.

34.

Total Amount Expended in Millions of Dollars

Item	1909	1914	1919	1923	1929
(a) canned fruits and vegetables	162	254	575	625	930
(b) cleaning and polishing preparations	6	9	27	35	46
(c) electricity in household operation	83	132	265	389	615.5
(d) mechanical appliances (refrigerators, sewing machines, washers, cooking)	152	175	419	535	804.1

Item	1909	1914	1919	1923	1929
Percentage of expenditures on household equipment to total expenditures	9.9%	9.2%	10.3%	11.6%	13.2%

(a-b) is found in William H. Lough, *High-Level Consumption: Its Behavior; Its Consequences* (New York, 1935), 236, 241. These figures are tabulated in millions of dollars for 1935. Items (c-d) and the percentage of expenditure on household equipment to total expenditures were taken from James Dewhurst, *America's Needs and Resources: A New Survey* (New York, 1955), 702, 704, 180.

35. Realistic novelists note the leisure of the middle-class women. David Graham Phillips, *The Hungry Heart* (New York, 1909) and *Old Wives for New* (New York, 1908); Robert Herrick, *Together* (New York, 1908), especially 515–17.

36. For example, see *Cosmopolitan*, XXXV (May-Oct. 1903); *Ladies Home Journal*, XXI (Dec. 1903–May 1904). A notable exception showing a woman riding a bicycle may be found in *ibid.* (April 1904), 39.

37. *Ladies Home Journal*, XXXIV (May 1917), for example, shows a woman entertaining stylish women friends (34, 89, 92), driving the car or on an automobile trip (36–37, 74), economizing on time spent in housework (42), the object of "outdoor girl" ads (78), beautifying at a social affair or appearing very chic (102, 106). Perhaps the best illustration for woman's activity in advertisements was employed in *Ladies Home Journal* by Williams Talc Powder. It read, "After the game, the ride, the swim, the brisk walk, or a day at the sea-shore, turn for comfort to Williams Talc Powder." *Ibid.*, XXXIV (July 1917), 74.

38. *Collier's*, 56 (Nov. 27, 1915), 4.

39. *Cosmopolitan*, LIX (June 1915), advertising section, 50.

40. *Collier's*, 56 (Sept. 25, 1915), 22.

41. *Ibid.* (Nov. 27, 1915), 25.

42. *Ladies Home Journal*, XXXV (April 1918), 58.

43. *Ibid.*, 57.

44. *Ibid.*, XXXIII (Jan. 1916), 46–47. Women drove their friends and families about in their cars. *Ibid.*, XXXII (July 1915), 34–35; (Aug. 1915), 38–39; (Oct. 1915), 86; XXXIII (Nov. 1916), 71.

45. Susanne Wilcox, "The Unrest of Modern Women," *Independent*, LXVII (July 8, 1909), 63.

46. Nell Brinkley, a nationally syndicated cartoonist and commentator on women's activities, asked this question of one of her young women. Boston *American*, July 14, 1913.

47. Nell Brinkley coined the phrase. *Ibid.*, Nov. 14, 1916.

48. *Ibid.*, May 4, 1915. See also *Ladies Home Journal*, XXXII (July 1915), which depicts a young woman driving a speedboat while her boyfriend sits next to her.

49. Boston *American*, Oct. 1, 1916.

50. *Collier's*, 56 (March 4, 1916), 38.

51. Emma B. Kaufman, "The Education of a Debutante," *Cosmopolitan,* XXXV (Sept. 1903), 499–508.

52. *Cosmopolitan,* XXXIX (Oct. 1905).

53. "Girls, Don't Allow Men to be Familiar," Boston *American,* June 17, 1904; *ibid.,* July 15, 1905.

54. *Wellesley College News,* Feb. 20, 1902. Wellesley relented on "men dances" in 1913.

55. Deland, "The Change in the Feminine Ideal," 291.

56. *Ibid.,* 289.

57. Boston *American,* May 6, 1910.

58. *Ibid.,* Sept. 5, 1912.

59. Ethel Watts Mumford, "Where Is Your Daughter This Afternoon?" *Harper's Weekly,* LVIII (Jan. 17, 1914), 28.

60. Boston *American,* Sept. 5, 1916; *ibid.,* Jan. 4, 1914.

61. Alice Duer Miller. "The New Dances and the Younger Generation," *Harper's Bazaar,* XLVI (May 1912), 250.

62. Deland, "Change in the Feminine Ideal," 293.

63. Boston *American,* March 24, 1916. In a letter to the editor of the New York *Times,* one critic of the "women of New York" complained that they seemed to be part of a "new race" or even a "super-sex." He waxed poetic: "Sweet seventeen is rouge-pot mad, And hobbles to her tasks blase, . . . Where are the girls of yesterday?" New York *Times,* July 20, 1914.

64. Miller, "New Dances and the Younger Generation," 250. According to Helen Rowland, the woman was "no longer Man's plaything, but his playmate. . . ." Helen Rowland, "The Emancipation of 'the Rib,' *Delineator,* LXXVII (March 1911), 233.

65. Boston *American,* April 7, 1910.

66. *Ibid.,* March 20, 1914.

67. *Ibid.,* June 11, 1916.

68. *Ibid.,* Nov. 27, Dec. 8, 1912.

69. On Newport and Boston society women see *ibid.,* July 6, 27, Aug. 10, 24, 1913. Pauline Frederick's picture may be found in *ibid.,* Aug. 2, 1913. For Irene Castle, see Mr. and Mrs. Vernon Castle, *Modern Dancing* (New York, 1914), 98, 105.

70. *Ladies Home Journal,* XXXII (July and Sept. 1915); *ibid.* (Nov. 1915), 8.

71. Owen Johnson, *The Salamander* (Indianapolis, 1914), Foreword, n.p.

72. *Ibid.,* 9.

73. *Ibid.,* 129.

74. *Ibid.,* 66.

75. *Ibid.,* 61.

76. *Ibid.,* Foreword, n.p. Chamber's young heroine Stephanie Cleland in *The Restless Sex,* 191, practiced trial marriage in order to learn by experience. See also Phillips, *Hungry Heart,* 166–80; Terry Ramsaye, *A Million And One Nights: A History of the Motion Picture* (2 vols., New York, 1926), II, 702–04.

77. "Mrs. Atherton Tells of Her 'Perch of the Devil,'" *Current Opinion,* LVII (Nov. 1914), 349.

78. Boston *American,* Feb. 8, 1917.

79. The "kiss of friendship" criticized by Fairfax had become a major issue of her mail by 1913. See, for example, *ibid.*, July 5, 1913. Girls shocked her with inquiries as to whether it was permissible to "soul kiss" on a first date. *Ibid.*, Feb. 13, 1914. An engaged girl asked whether it would be all right to kiss men other than her fiance. *Ibid.*, May 2, 1916.

80. *Ibid.*, Feb. 8, 1917.

81. Fitzgerald, "Echoes of the Jazz Age," 460.

82. Thomas, *Unadjusted Girl*, 95.

83. "Today in the world of fashion, all women are young, and they grow more so all the time." Doeuilet, "When All The World Looks Young," *Delineator*, LXXXIII (Aug. 1913), 20. Advertisements used flattery or played up the value of youth for women and warned that they might age unless certain products were used. *Cosmopolitan*, LIX (Nov. 1915), 112; *ibid.* (July 1915), 81; *Ladies Home Journal*, XXXII (Nov. 1915), 65; *Cosmopolitan*, LIX (Oct. 1915), 57.

84. Eleanor Chalmers, "Facts and Figures," *Delineator*, LXXXIV (April 1914), 38.

85. Boston *American*, March 20, 1910; *Delineator*, LXXXIX (Oct. 1916), 66.

86. Boston *American*, March 28, 1904.

87. New York *Tribune*, April 4, 1912; Eleanor Chalmers, "You and Your Sewing," *Delineator*, LXXXIII (Aug. 1913), 33.

88. Eleanor Chalmers, *Delineator*, LXXIV (April 1914), 38. The sense of relief these changes brought is amusingly described in Dorothy A. Plum, comp., *The Magnificent Enterprise: A Chronicle of Vassar College* (Poughkeepsie, 1961), 43–44.

89. Percival White, "Figuring Us Out," *North American Review*, CCXXVII (Jan. 1929), 69.

90. Boston *American*, Dec. 10, 1916.

91. *Delineator*, LXXXV (July 1914), 55.

92. Boston *American*, Sept. 3, 1916.

93. *Cosmopolitan*, LIX (July 1915).

94. An editorial declared that women's dresses in 1913 had approached "the danger line of indecency about as closely as they could." New York *Times*, July 6, 1914.

95. *Ladies Home Journal*, XXXIV (Oct. 1917), 98.

96. Boston *American*, June 8, 1907. "The conventions of evening dress have changed radically in the last four or five years. Not so very long ago a high-necked gown was considered *au fait* for all evening functions except formal dinners and the opera. Nowadays, well-dressed women wear decolleté dresses even for home dinners, and semi-decolleté gowns for restaurants and theaters." *Delineator*, LXXV (Jan. 1910), 60.

97. *Cosmopolitan*, LIX (July 1915).

98. *Ladies Home Journal*, XXXII (Oct. 1915), 108; *ibid.*, XXXIII (Oct. 1916), 82; *ibid.*, XXXIII (Nov. 1916), 78–79; *ibid.*, XXXIV (Jan. 1917), 53.

99. "The Cult of St. Vitus," *Unpopular Review*, III (Jan.-March 1915), 94.

100. Boston *American*, July 6, 1912. Dix noted "flirtatious" middle-aged women were "aping the airs and graces of the debutante" and "trying to act kittenish" with men.

101. *Ibid.*, Dec. 6, 10, 1912. Anita Stewart, a movie star who wrote "Talks to Girls," though personally opposed to smoking, admitted that "lots of my friends smoke" and "they are nice girls too." *Ibid.*, Dec. 14, 1915. In 1916, the Boston *American* titled a column on a page devoted to women's interests "To Smoke or Not to Smoke." *Ibid.*, April 12, 1916. The *Harvard Lampoon*, LXXI (June 20, 1916), 376, spoofed women smoking: it carried a heading "Roman Society Women Agree to Give Up Smoking" and a commentary below, "Oh, Nero, how times have changed!"

102. Boston *American*, March 7, 1910.

103. Leuchtenburg, *Perils of Prosperity*, 174–75.

104. " 'Years of Discretion'—A Play of Cupid at Fifty," *Current Opinion*, LIV (Feb. 1913), 116.

105. *Ibid.*, 117.

106. Boston *American*, April 10, 1908. Evelyn Nesbitt, the wife of Harry Thaw, was romantically involved with architect Stanford White, whom Thaw shot to death.

107. *Ibid.*, Aug. 25, Sept. 1, 1912.

108. Most of the dances which became very popular after 1910, such as the Turkey Trot, the Bunny Hug, and the Grizzly Bear, afforded a maximum of motion in a minimum of space. The Chicken Flip was invented by a Boston society woman. *Ibid.*, Nov. 11, 1912. See also "New Reflections on The Dancing Mania," *Current Opinion*, LV (Oct. 1913), 262.

109. Louis I. Dublin, "Birth Control," *Social Hygiene*, VI (Jan. 1920), 6.

110. Alfred Kazin, "Three Pioneer Realists," *Saturday Review of Literature*, XX (July 8, 1939), 15. Herrick's biographer, Blake Nevius, declares, "It can be argued that Herrick is the most comprehensive and reliable social historian in American fiction to appear in the interregnum between Howells and the writers of the Twenties. . . ." Blake Nevius, *Robert Herrick: The Development of a Novelist* (Berkeley, 1962), Preface.

111. Nevius, *Robert Herrick*, 177.

112. Herrick, *Together*, 91, 392.

113. *Ibid.*, 263, 250–51, 320–24.

114. Herrick describes the temperament of the modern woman as one of "mistress rather than the wife. . . . 'I shall be a person with a soul of my own. To have me man must win me not once, but daily.' " *Ibid.*, 516. The last sentence above nearly duplicates Rosalind's statement to her beau in *This Side of Paradise*, "I have to be won all over again every time you see me." F. Scott Fitzgerald, *This Side of Paradise* (New York, 1920), 194.

115. Chicago *Herald and Examiner*, March 10–17, 1920.

116. *Ibid.*, March 10, 1920.

117. *Ibid.*, March 11, 1920.

118. *Ibid.*

119. *Ibid.*, March 11, 12, 1920.

120. *Ibid.*, March 13, 14, 1920.

121. *Ibid.*, March 15, 1920.

122. New York *Tribune*, Nov. 1, 1905.

123. New York *Times,* May 28, 1913.

124. *Ibid.,* Dec. 20, 1912.

125. *Ibid.,* Aug. 20, 23, 1913.

126. *Ibid.,* June 29, 1913.

127. Carol Flora Brooks, "The Early History of the Anti-Contraceptive Laws in Massachusetts and Connecticut," *American Quarterly,* XVIII (Spring 1966), 3–23; George E. Worthington, "Statutory Restrictions on Birth Control," *Journal of Social Hygiene,* IX (Nov. 1923), 458–65.

128. Boston *American,* July 14, 21, 1916; New York *Times,* Feb. 6, 1917.

129. *Report of the Pennsylvania Board of Censors,* June 1, 1915 to Dec. 1, 1915 (Harrisburg, 1916), 6.

130. Ellis Paxson Oberholtzer, *The Morals of the Movie* (Philadelphia, 1922), 115–23.

131. *Report of the Pennsylvania State Board of Censors,* 1915, pp. 14–15; *ibid.,* 1916, pp. 24–25; *ibid.,* 1917, pp. 8–9.

132. Boston *American,* Aug. 10, 1913.

133. Ramsaye, *A Million and One Nights,* II, 617.

134. Boston *American,* July 7, 1917.

135. *Ibid.,* Dec. 20, 1912.

136. Heywood Broun, *Anthony Comstock: Roundsman of the Lord* (New York, 1927); Mary Alden Hopkins, "Birth Control and Public Morals: An Interview with Anthony Comstock," *Harper's Weekly,* LX (May 22, 1915), 489–90.

137. Boston *American,* Jan. 4, 1917.

138. Norman E. Himes, "Birth Control in Historical and Clinical Perspective," *Annals of the American Academy of Political and Social Sciences,* 160 (March 1932), 53.

139. Dublin, "Birth Control," 6.

140. Boston *American,* July 16, 1916. According to International News Service, "Mrs. Rose Pastor Stokes was literally mobbed by an eager crowd in Carnegie Hall when she offered, in defiance of the police, to distribute printed slips bearing a formula for birth control." *Ibid.,* May 6, 1916.

23 ♀ The Projection of a New Womanhood: The Movie Moderns in the 1920's

Mary P. Ryan

The ideal of femininity was changing so dramatically around the third decade of the twentieth century that contemporaries began to speak of an entirely "new woman." In 1925 the mothers of Middletown recognized the transformation in their own daughters: "Girls aren't so modest nowadays; they dress differently," "Girls are more aggressive today. They call the boys up to try to make dates with them as they never would have when I was a girl." "When I was a girl, a girl who painted was a bad girl—now look at the daughters of our best families."[1] Historians have called attention to the same transformation of the female image in popular literature, advertising, and the graphic arts, underway even before World War I.[2] Historians have not been as diligent, however, in culling another rich body of imagery regarding the new woman—the moving pictures, which vividly record the full flavor of the flapper's personality, complete with her characteristic gestures, energy, and activism. Although many of these early films have been destroyed, enough remain from which to piece together a schematic moving portrait of the new woman.

Careful analysis of popular movies, furthermore, offers the historian access to the dream-life of past generations, male and female. By the 1920's, movie making had become a smoothly functioning industry, capitalized at over one billion dollars and tooled for the mass production and distribution of fantasies. The output of the major studios (Paramount, Fox, MGM, Universal, Warner Brothers) was manufactured

This article appears by permission of the author.

500

by an army of directors, technicians, writers, and businessmen, all working under the imperative of pleasing an audience that numbered as many as 100 million viewers a week, gathered together in over 18,000 theatres all across America.[3] The understandable result of this collective process was a standardized product that could be simply classified by such formulas as the adventure story, western, comedy, and love story. The success of each popular genre depended upon striking a responsive cord in the mass audience, reaching some common denominator in the experience, hopes, and fears of Americans. This juncture of dream and reality on the silver screen provides the historian a multidimensional cultural document.

Cinema also provides an ideal vantage point from which to observe the making of the new woman. Screen femininity in the twenties was often the creation of woman scenarists, like Bess Meredyth, Anita Loos, Frances Marion, Jeanie MacPherson, and June Mathis,[4] who worked in teams and at a frantic pace to construct captivating images and compelling plots. Their formulaic stories reached an audience which included millions of women often in their formative years. One survey concluded that females between the ages of 8 and nineteen attended the movies an average of 46 times a year[5] in the twenties.

Perhaps the crucial link in this female cultural chain was the star. Well before the studios were willing to identify their actresses by name, the mails were flooded with chatty letters to familiar screen personalities. When Universal revealed the "biograph girl" to be Florence Lawrence, this first starlet was immediately mobbed in St. Louis, hounded by fans begging her autograph and ravaging her clothing.[6] The star was a unique cultural phenomenon, an actress whose personal style enlivened a multiplicity of familiar but fictional roles, blending the real with the imaginary in one glamourous individual. She was, as Stanley Cavell phrases it, an "individuality" that "projects particular ways of inhabiting a social role."[7] By the 1920's national surveys revealed that movie stars had replaced political, business, and artistic leaders as the favorite role models of American youth.[8] In the twenties, the female social role was projected on the screen by such personalities as Madge Bellamy, Clara Bow, Joan Crawford and Gloria Swanson, all vivid embodiments of the new womanhood, known to contemporaries as "the moderns."

By the mid-twenties the sweet heroines of the late Victorian age had been totally banished from the screen by these new women. The cinematic staples of the pre-war era, both the one-reelers that stocked the nickelodeons in working-class neighborhoods and the prestigious features directed by D.W. Griffith, featured actresses like Lillian Gish and Mary Pickford who reveled in motherly sacrifice, sexual purity and shy submission. Another woman who enacted such parts, Linda Arvidson Griffith, described her typical roles as "the peasant, washwoman and tenement lady" staunchly protecting her babes from starvation, and her virginity from despoilment by rich and vulgar villains. When Mrs. Griffith wrote her memoirs in 1925, however, she woefully acknowledged that such true womanhood was regarded as old-fashioned and had been replaced by an antagonistic set of mores: "We were dealing in things vital in our American life and not one bit interested in close-ups of empty-headed little ingenues with adenoids, bedroom windows, manhandling of young girls, fast sets, perfumed bathrooms or nude youths heaving their muscles."[9] Such permissiveness in the display of the female body and the treatment of sexual themes was the most obvious hallmark of the new woman.

Nonetheless, early cinema had not been as asexual as Arvidson liked to remember. One of the first scandals of the screen was the 1896 "Anatomy of a Kiss" which drew out that intimate act to a full 42 frames. As the medium advanced from merely photographing natural phenomena to full-fledged story-telling, sex became a favorite theme, albeit veiled in moralistic condemnations of the villainous roué and the hapless prostitute. It was in the hey day of Griffith, in fact, that female sexuality struck its most aggressive pose in the screen antics of Theda Bara—"The wickedest face in the world, dark, brooding, beautiful and heartless"—luring unfortunate males to self-destruction. Theda Bara made no less than 40 films on the torrid vamp theme in the three years after her first appearance in the 1915 film *A Fool There Was.*[10]

Although the vamp was too extreme a caricature to endure, she had cleared the air of the dangerous vapors of female passion and cleared the way for a more respectable brand of sex appeal. The arrival of the new woman on the screen was clearly apparent by 1919 when she intruded into the wholesomely titled film made by the most Victorian of directors, Griffith's *True Heart Susie.* The heroine, played by Lillian Gish, radiated 19th-century womanhood as she worked, sacrificed, and waited in the blush of innocence for the boy next door. Yet True Heart Susie was a much beleaguered heroine in 1919. In fact she temporarily lost her hero to a member of the fast set, whose city ways included a painted face, short clinging skirts, and a wiggling walk that the camera followed with delight. Even True Heart Susie was momentarily tempted to powder her face with corn starch and hitch up her skirt. The contrived nature of the plot also illustrated the obsolescence of Victorian values. The old virtues did not triumph until Susie's rival had been exposed as a bad cook, sloppy housewife, an unfaithful wife, and then died of pneumonia. The last shot of the film underscored the nostalgia for the old morality and the old code of femininity: as the reunited couple walked into the sunset their images faded into a photograph from their rural childhood.[11]

The backward-looking ethic of *True Heart Susie* becomes even more distinct when the film is compared with the box-office sensation of 1919. It was in that year that Cecil B. De Mille, in collaboration with screenwriter Jeanie MacPherson, transposed the *Admirable Chrichton* into a film entitled *Male and Female.* Under De Mille's direction the play became little more than a sexual display whose centerpiece was the female body. The movie audience was invited to share the hero's fantasy of sexual domination, to gaze upon Gloria Swanson's naked thighs and surging breasts in the frenzy of a shipwreck and watch in amazement as the star gingerly steps into the bath.[12] *Male and Female* grossed the extraordinary amount of one and one-quarter billion dollars, and ensured that sex appeal would become a favorite movie theme. Partial female nudity, excused by the bath or draped only in lingerie became a staple of cinema in the decade to come. De Mille was its undisputed master: "He made of the bathroom a delightful resort . . . a mystic shrine to Venus and sometimes to Apollo. . . . Underclothes became visions of translucent promise."[13] Most every star who came to popularity in the twenties played a lingerie scene, which placed her in a languorous pose with soft, body-hugging silk around her torso. Clara Bow played the familiar lingerie salesgirl in *It* (1927); critics raved about Bebe Daniels' "negligible negligee" in *Stranded in Paris* (1926); *Bertha the Sewing Machine Girl* (1926) was described by William Fox Productions as "A Love and Lingerie Edition of the Great Melodrama"; and Joan Crawford modeled lingerie with matchless sensuality in *Our Blushing Brides* (1930).[14]

The exposure of the star's limbs was but one harbinger of the new woman. The women in lingerie were more than mannequins. They were the personification of the "moderns," females whose whole projected personalities had a new vitality and aura. Whether they played the upper-class flapper as did Gloria Swanson and Norma Talmadge, or the working girls characteristic of Clara Bow and Madge Bellamy, the same spirit surrounded them.[15] The new movie woman exuded above all a sense of physical freedom—unrestrained movement, confident gait, abounding energy—the antithesis of the controlled, quiet, tight-kneed poses of Griffith's heroines. These women moved confidently into a once male world. With a dashing spontaneity they rushed onto dance floors, leapt into swimming pools, and accepted any dare—to drink, to sport, to strip as Bow did in *Saturday Night Kid* (1929). They entered the world of work and college as well as the social circle, dashing down the city streets to offices, shops and classrooms with aplomb and self-assurance. They were an ambitious group, determined to use their bodily charms to make their way in the world.

The Hollywood ingenues enthusiastically embraced the remodeled image of women and imbued their new roles with a spirit of independence. Joan Crawford's scintillating Charleston sequence in *Our Dancing Daughters* (1928) is a case in point. Although the editor cut periodically to lustful male faces, the camera emphasized Crawford's gusto and liveliness, rather than eroticism. When the dancing Crawford ripped off her skirt, it was as if to remove a constricting garment, to facilitate freedom of movement and release of energy, not to entice male admirers. Her Charleston consisted not of bumps and grinds, but of jumps and starts at a frantic pace. Her sheer vitality and self-confidence were at the forefront.[16] In the role of "Dangerous Diana" Crawford upheld the new standard of movie virtue. In contrast, it was the "evil women" of *Our Dancing Daughters* who portrayed shy innocence, a mere ruse to captivate an old-fashioned hero.

The type of sex appeal labeled *It* by Elinor Glyn and presented on film by Clara Bow in 1927 had a similarly wholesome cast. Bow rendered this trait of the new woman as spirited bravado; she seduced her prey at an amusement park and captured her man in the course of a boyish prance through the fun house. The essence of Bow's screen presence was recognized by contemporary critics. Agreeing that Clara Bow had "it," or "good old-fashioned sex appeal," one reviewer described her as "an amusing little person, a slam-bang kid, full of vitality and an easy, none too subtle appeal."[17] The movie moderns did indeed project more of the aura of the slam-bang kid than that of the femme fatale or the vamp. It was her mischievous vivacity that most emphatically eclipsed the old woman.

Yet the stars vitality only embellished a rigidifying set of movie stereotypes; the twenties' films gave precise details on how to become *correctly* modern. Gloria Swanson performed the requisite transformation in *Why Change Your Wife* (1920). In one extravagant gesture she tore off her old garb, draped herself in plumes and lamé, and realigned her shapely form in a stylized seductive posture. The popular stars of the twenties excelled in such movements and poses, the hands placed low on the hip, the jaunt in the walk, the cock of the head that made the new woman a lively reality. The education in the mannerism of the flapper was undertaken with special self-awareness by a shopgirl named Nora (Madge Bellamy) in *Ankles Preferred* (1926). The portion of her anatomy mentioned in the title propelled the plot and mesmerized the camera. Nora regarded the first compliment to her ankles as a lecherous insult. When she retired to her apartment, however, she gazed at her legs with a new interest and pride. Her narcissism reached its fullest development in a situation common to many movies of the era, the heroine's first modeling experience. Goaded on by two lascivious old shopkeepers, Nora tried out a sexy strut, a self-caressing gesture and a heightened hemline. Once this modern style of self-projection had been acquired, Nora's bosses put her to work seducing first the male customers and then a business tycoon from whom they sought financial assistance.[18] This objectification of the female before male admirers was lodged deep in the scenario of the flapper film, and was depicted with entrancing finesse by movie moderns.

These cinematic personalities are more than an historical depository of female images. In the twenties they served as a means of propagating new values and translating popular images into social behavior. As a consequence the movie moderns claim a part in the making of modern womanhood with all the sex roles and sexual stereotyping it entailed. Their initial function was simply didactic and instructional, to train the female audience in fashionable femininity. The movies of the silent era were inherently stereotypical, relying on extravagant images, bold-faced titles and enthralling musical accompaniment. Thus, they were particularly suited to shaping women's aspirations in a uniform direction. Many of the first cinematic lessons were very rudimentary. DeMille's *Why Change Your Wife,* made in 1920, was a simple parable admonishing women to discard the remnants of Victorian womanhood and embrace the flapper model. The audience assimilated this advice through the example of Elizabeth Gordon, played by Gloria Swanson, who at the beginning of the film was a staid, bespectacled wife who reads books on "How to Improve Your Mind" and listens to classical music. The error of her ways was proclaimed by her husband's grimaces at her glasses and chaste attire, and his vulnerability to the wiles of a new woman armed with perfume, short skirts and a panoply of gadgets designed to entrap men. When Robert Gordon divorced his wife to marry this coquette, the first Mrs. Gordon vowed to cling to the old ways, to devote herself to charity, claiming she "hates men and clothes." Upon overhearing a conversation that attributed her divorce to her matronly attire, however, Elizabeth made an abrupt about-face: she exclaimed that she would go the limit to regain her spouse and ordered a "sleeveless, backless, transparent, indecent" wardrobe. The heroine, of course, succeeded in regaining her husband, and their second wedding night found her thoroughly remodeled, dressed in an inanely fashionable gown and dancing a foxtrot.[19] By the midtwenties, this scene of female transformation had been replayed so many times that one reviewer could write of *His Secretary* (1926): "so cliched and worn was it all we finally fell from our seat suffering from some ancient atavistic complaint that the ennui of this theme always rouses in us."[20] The point had been made over and over again: to win husband and happiness, women must join the competition on equal terms with the American flapper.

Such basic lessons were not lost on the movie audience. Studies of female movie-goers, financed by the Payne Fund and conducted between 1929 and 1933 revealed that young women paid close attention to the star's appearance and behavior. Of a Joan Crawford film, one girl said, "I watch every little detail, of how she's dressed, and her make-up, and also her hair." Another surmised, "I'll bet every girl wishes she was the Greta Garbo type. I tried to imitate her walk, she walks so easy as if she had springs on her feet." This young woman's attempt to mimic Garbo succeeded only in provoking laughter, a fate that also befell a black girl enamored of Clara Bow. "After seeing her picture (*It*) I immediately went home to take stock of my personal charms before my vanity mirror and after carefully surveying myself from all angles I turned away with a sigh, thinking that I may as well want to be Mr. Lon Chaney. I would be just as successful." Such an observation suggests the active, often good-humored ways in which young women might interpret the movie message.[21]

Young moviegoers of the twenties were educated in other, more personal matters, as well. One college girl told the Payne Fund interviewers that "movies are a liberal education in the art of making love." She went on to recount such specific benefits of this cinematic education as learning "how two screen lovers manage their arms when they are embracing; there is a definite technique; one arm over, the other under." This young woman was grateful to the movies for providing a remedial education in a subject avoided by her straitlaced parents, while another found cinematic instructions in love-making "more suggestive and effective than I could possibly find in any book by say Elinor Glyn on 'How to Hold Your Man.' " The adolescent girls who flocked to the movies each week were getting their sex education through the prism of the Hollywood clinch, a training which culminated in erotic awareness if not in actual necking parties. The magic of the movies brought one teenager a rich fantasy life: "Buddy Rogers and Rudy Valentino have kissed me oodles of times but they don't know it, God bless 'em!" Whatever the behavioral consequences of this education, its cultural impact cannot be denied. Movies were handmaidens to the modern preoccupation with intimate heterosexual relations. Moving pictures were clearly more effective than static literary images in detailing the active components of flapper sexuality. One sixteen-year-old girl came to these apt historical conclusions: "No wonder girls of older days, before the movies, were so modest and bashful. They never saw Clara Bow and William Haines. . . .if we did not see such examples in the movies, where would we get the idea of being 'hot'? We wouldn't."[22]

It would be very difficult, on the other hand, for a movie-going girl to receive the idea that sexual promiscuity was an approved form of behavior in the nineteen-twenties. The movie heroine was always chaste at heart. Whatever extremes of brash free-living Bow or Crawford might portray, they preserved their virginity until marriage. Likewise, infidelity among the upper classes, so often sanctioned in the films of Cecil B. DeMille, was prescribed only as a means of retrieving a lost spouse or enlivening a spiceless marriage. Sex in the films of the twenties existed as a readiness to display physical attractions, not as a willingness to give in to the yearnings of the flesh; it heightened sexual awareness without promising ultimate gratification.

Sexiness was in fact associated more with apparel, make-up, and perfume than with the body itself. While movie morality kept sexuality within traditional bounds, materialistic desires were given bountiful gratification in the cinema of the twenties. Hollywood fed consumer lusts through its stock of production values—epitomized by the spendthrift DeMille who surrounded his heroines with furs, jewels, modish clothes, and modern household artifacts. Fashion shows and tours of modern homes and apartments became staples of the new woman's movie world. In the 1920's, whole films were devoted to the new joys and pitfalls of consumption with titles like *Charge It, Ladies Must Dress, Gimme.*[23] Thirty-eight films detailed the career of the fashion model, another convenient method of inculcating consumerism. The expansion of the consumer sector of the American economy in the twenties called for an accelerated tempo of shopping and the movies provided incentives and instruction for yet another updated female role.

Movies offered to the women of the twenties, and reveal to historians, something more dynamic than packaged instructions about the new femininity and new female roles. The object of the Hollywood craftsman was to arrange images into engrossing stories. To the movie audience, gathered together in darkness and anonymity, the moving picture offered a vicarious dream life. This cinematic experience has been aptly defined by Raymond Durgnat: "For the masses the cinema is dreams and nightmares, or it is nothing. It is an alternative experience freed from the tyranny of the 'old devil consequences'; from the limitation of having only one life to live. One's favored films are one's unlived lives, one's hopes, fear, libido."[24] Movie fantasies are nonetheless inextricably intertwined with the realities of the age in which they are produced. Films, after all, as Stanley Cavell has pointed out, are composed of photographs, images that reproduce the world outside the theatre. Moreover the basic events presented in contemporary dramas are at least conceivable, perhaps even probable, in the lives of viewers. This evocative mixture of reality and dream, furthermore, is concocted by an industry whose imperative is box office profits. The popular film formula is constructed around the aspirations and anxieties of the contemporary audience. The relation of the world on the screen and American realities has been elegantly described by Barbara Deming. After viewing up to one-fourth of Hollywood's productions between 1942 and 1948, Deming reached this conclusion: "The heros and heroines who are most popular at any particular period are precisely those who, with a certain added style, with a certain distinction, act out the predicament in which we all find ourselves—a predicament from which the movie-dream then cunningly extricates us. But the . . . movie-goer . . . need never admit what that condition really is from which he is being vicariously relieved."[25]

The historian's task, given this interpretation of film culture, is to identify the predicaments which underlie the popular film, to analyze the condition from which the viewer is "being vicariously relieved." In the case of the woman's film, the superficial problem is quite obvious: to win and keep a husband's love, and to secure the social and economic status which accompanies marriage. The Payne Fund survey of movie themes between 1920 and 1933 found the most common plot theme to be winning the loved one. Through six decades of cinema history the problems of the unmarried woman and the neglected wife have been "resolved" in thousands of happy endings, enacted by characters from every walk in life and every social station. One variation on this theme was particularly germane to the twenties, however, and deserves special attention: the predicament of the working girl.

In point of fact the work force had been a familiar environment for young women well before 1920. The rate of female employment skyrocketed in the teens and increased at only a moderate rate, if at all, between 1920 and 1930 when over ten million women were at work outside the home. Most of these women, like their impersonators on the screen, were under thirty years of age and single. The employed women of the twenties were apt to congregate in a relatively new segment of the work force, deserting factories and domestic service to take up white-collar employment. The number of female clerks had increased almost 300 percent between 1910 and 1920; the number of stenographers and typists more than doubled, making women the majority in those occupations.[26] These facts were also reflected in the films of the era. In the twenties the American Film Institute Catalog listed only four films made about factory workers, while only 46 concerned housemaids, most of them in minor roles. On the other hand the catalog lists 49 sales clerks, 28 stenographers, and no less than 114 secretaries who appeared on the screen between 1921 and 1930.[27] On occasion, the films detailed this historical progression in female work roles. For example, *Bertha The Sewing Machine Girl* (1926) carried the heroine from her factory job, to the role of telephone operator, then model, then fashion designer.[28] The movie camera tended to skirt the mundane aspects of white-collar work, preferring to dwell on the glamor of a setting full of consumer goods, entertainment, and eligible men, all of which the young woman could pursue without parental interference. The demand of the economy for women's labor in this job sector, as well as women's responsiveness to this need, was nonetheless very real. By 1925, 34 percent of high school girls in Middletown, for example, aspired to be clerical workers.[29] Fan magazines took pains to associate movie stars with these prosaic roles, pointing out that Joan Crawford was once a shop girl in Kansas City; that Janet Gaynor clerked in a shoe store; and that Frances Marion earned $25 a week as a stenographer before she became a star, then screen writer.[30] Early films no doubt facilitated the transformation of the female work force, reflecting, endorsing, and legitimizing women's assumption of new roles.

By the late twenties, Hollywood seemed to take the work experience of young females for granted. No longer bothering to issue tantalizing invitations to enter the work force, they planted heroines firmly behind desks and counters. At this point, the focus of the film shifted to grappling with the specific complaints of working women. In fact several films began with a sharp critique of the routine and rigid nature of the work situation. The opening shot in *Ankles Preferred* featured Madge Bellamy at a department store counter, annoyed at the customers, bored with her work, and anxiously gazing at the clock. The monotony of woman's work was emphatically underlined by the superimposition of a clock upon Bellamy's forelorn countenance, followed by her jubilation at closing time. The clock motif appeared again in *Our Blushing Brides*. This 1930 film opened with a close-up of the time clock as a long line of workers, mostly female, filed into a department store. Throughout the film the alarm clock stood as the exasperating symbol of work which the women dreamed of throwing out the window forever. The regimentation associated with the conscription of women into the modern work force was presented in other ways as well. The assembly line nature of work in these white-collar occupations was painstakingly delineated in *Our Blushing Brides*. In the opening sequence the camera panned across a massive, dreary locker room as hundreds of women scurried past. They amassed behind the mirror until a clamorous bell sent them rushing to their assigned places at the consumer counter. Once in their stations, the mechanical and impersonal nature of sales work is underscored by the supervisors; one girl was addressed only as number 36, another as number 42.[31] In this department store film and in secretarial films like *Soft Living* (1928), special care was taken to show the working girls laboriously filling out forms and adding up columns of numbers. The movies took cognizance of the discipline imposed by the modern work place, a regimen which the women of the twentieth century rarely escaped by retaining a life-long place in the home.

The work world so bleakly pictured in these films also encroached upon the private lives of the female characters. It established their tedious weekday schedule, composed of a frantic struggle on the subway, hasty meals, and shattered nerves. The homes which these women entered at the end of a work day were a tribute to their meager earnings on the job. The movie set included a carefully constructed working girls' apartment: cramped quarters, shabby furnishings, a tiny table where the roommates took their frugal meals. Silent filmmakers did not hesitate to insert titles expressing the girls' complaints about these conditions, the implicit lot of their sex and class. In fact they frequently used an intertitle to announce the specific wage rate for female labor, usually between twenty-five and thirty-five dollars a week. Once the essential features of woman's work had been established, the thrust of the heroine's dream was obvious—escape.

Impermanence was built into the work situation of these screen heroines. The cheerful camaraderie and spunky optimism characteristic of the working-girl flapper stemmed from the assumption that her job tenure would be brief. The avenue of escape was predictable enough: matrimony. Yet there were a variety of ways to secure a husband while on the job. The bluntest technique was the aggressive use of sexual attractions as employed by the ubiquitous gold digger. No less than 34 films were made on this theme between 1921 and 1930.[32] The most famous movie in this genre, *Gentlemen Prefer Blondes* (1928) written by Anita Loos, approvingly recounted the heavy-handed tactics of Lorelei Lee, who entrapped America's richest bachelor.[33] *Soft Living,* made the same year, traced gold digging directly to the plight of the working girl. The heroine, played by Madge Bellamy, was secretary to an attorney specializing in divorce cases. She embarked upon her hunt for a millionaire after comparing her weekly salary of $35 to the thousands in alimony carted away each week by a deft gold digger. Her original intention was to remain a "kissless bride," file for divorce on trumped-up charges, and retire on her alimony. The typical sexual shyness beneath the flapper exterior was revealed on the heroine's honeymoon when she cowered in the upper berth of the train to avoid viewing a pajama-clad husband. In the end, love triumphed over avarice, and the secretary and millionaire settled into a bone fide love nest. Nonetheless, the fantasy was clear, the secretary had won her millionaire; in the parlance of the day she had "slapped a trap on a sucker's bank roll."[34]

More typically the working girl of the twenties' cinema won her retirement through the promptings of love and trusting submission to her man. Charm, poise, virtue and the advantage of close proximity to eligible men were ingredients in the scenario that captured many a wealthy mate. Secretaries were particularly successful in this regard, placed as they were in close association with their boss. But salesgirls did equally well despite the odds against their meeting millionaires across department store counters. Joan Crawford achieved this success in *Our Blushing Brides,* proving her worth by rejecting the owner's son as an illegitimate lover, later to win him as her spouse. Other working women found rich men in the most unlikely places. The character in the title role of *Five and Ten Cent Annie* (1928) married a street cleaner who conveniently inherited a fortune. A theatre cashier came upon her affluent husband at the box office in *The Girl in the Glass Cage* (1929).[35]

The working girl's fantasy as manufactured by Hollywood was not always this extravagant. In numerous movies of the twenties, heroines found their happy ending in the arms of a man of their own class. A subway guard was the perfect match for both *The Girl From Woolworth's* (1929) and *Sub Way Sadie* (1926).[36] Such alliances were often formed after females had given up their daydreams of independent success, be it as showgirls or department store buyers. The homely solution to this variety of working girl drama was epitomized by *Ankles Preferred.* Madge Bellamy's success in the retail trade took her into the company of many wealthy men, all of whom wanted only the pleasures of her body. Disillusioned by status climbing of this sort Bellamy turned her attention to a more trustworthy young man, who shared her own social world, the lower-class boarding house. Clara Bow illustrated the same sensible solution in *Kid Boots* (1926). She chose as her spouse a humble tailor played by Eddie Cantor, convinced, as a title clearly announced, that unlike many foolish females she craved a man who was "just reliable." The climax of this picture also conveyed the boyish *joie de vivre* with which these marriages were forged. Bow recited her marriage vows to Cantor at the end of a comic chase, attired in disheveled pants and running behind a speeding automobile containing the judge.[37] The role pattern which the movie moderns embraced so ebulliently was mundane reality to millions of American women, the youthful female labor force that retired en masse upon marriage henceforth to rest, however insecurely or impecuniously, on the income of their mates.

The magic of these movies, and their meaning to the historian, lie as much in the anxieties which precede the domestic denouement as in the happy ending itself. Movie fantasies have a double-edged quality, are both "dreams and nightmares" as Raymond Durgnat puts it. At times the nightmares constitute the direct and central themes of the movies; more often, particularly in women's films, fearful visions provide the cutting edge of the romance itself. Imbedded in the images and plots of the movie moderns are a prevalent set of tensions, unfulfilled promises, and unhappy endings for minor characters. These tragic subplots provided the essential dramatic tension in the films of the twenties. Many women lost out in the marriage competition, and not even the most optimistic melodrama tied up every female character in a neat wedding knot. In most working girl stories at least one of the roommates was required to function as a negative example for the audience. In *Our Blushing Brides* the gold digger Frankie was punished for her mercenary sexuality by the discovery that her hard-won husband was a gambler whose expensive gifts were quickly confiscated by the police. A second roommate, a naive and trusting sort named Connie, was deceived into the unsavory position of a kept woman, only to have her concubine marry one of his own class. In this film the odds were two to one against a successful marital alliance. The third roommate, Jerry, played by Joan Crawford, succeeded only because she was painfully cautious in bestowing her love. In fact, the disastrous fate which befell Connie was in many ways the emotional pivot of *Our Blushing Brides*. The forsaken woman happened to turn on the radio to hear an on-the-scene report of her lover's engagement party. Her lost love and lost status were detailed simultaneously in a merciless account of what the fashionable entourage was wearing on this occasion. The finale laced suspense with maudlin sentimentality as the prostrate Connie swallowed poison amid intercuts to her speeding rescuers, while the radio blared cruelly away in the background. This death scene was prolonged to full melodramatic length as the evil male was carted against his will to Connie's bedside, allowing her to die with her romantic illusions intact. This bittersweet story was designed by Bess Meredyth, a woman who created hundreds of such dream portraits. The successful formula, steeped in a pessimistic female consciousness and a cynical view of men, exposed the underside of modern romances. Might not this movie cliché suggest that some women secretly yearned to escape the whole tortuous labyrinth of the sexual marketplace?

Another empathic ploy of these films preyed on the apprehension that marriage itself does not put an end to woman's anxiety. In fact in the twenties almost 300 films were made on the theme of infidelity. [38] In addition to their titillating value these movies harped upon the insecurity of the married woman, inevitably aging and losing her girlish charms within a world constantly replenished by a stream of attractive flappers. Over and over again wives were charged with rejuvenating their appearance in order to retrieve husbands from flirts and gold diggers. One woman's success on the marriage market was all too often another's failure. A dowdy wife was poor competition for the young workers who shared her husband's store or office. The anxieties of upper class wives were endlessly exploited by DeMille, and by the mid-twenties even Theda Bara was placed in the predicament of the shunned wife (*Unchastened Woman*, 1925).[39] Alternately, the older woman was made the object of ridicule. In *Ankles Preferred,* for example, the wives of the shopkeepers were introduced into scenes by their ankles—fleshy, drooping, with sagging stockings—clearly identified as dinosaurs in the modern movie era. On the other hand a few films of the twenties recognized, in a roundabout fashion, that the married woman might be discontented with her role, as well as fearful of losing her husband. One remarkable film, *Dancing Mothers* (1926), ended as the wife defiantly leaves home. Two films of 1922, *The Real Adventure* and *A Woman's Woman,* portrayed older women whose boredom with housework and lack of appreciation from their husbands drove them into business. Although their successful careers culminated either in marital disaster or restoration to the fireside, these themes suggested to at least a few movie-goers the further problems that lay beyond the happy ending.[40]

These dark shadows were further accentuated by the characterization of male-female relations throughout these films. In most movies the male characters were very limply drawn; their chief role was to express, often in a puppylike fashion, the love sickness inspired by the heroines, some of whom overtly manipulated them into marriage. Seen through the woman's eyes, moreover, the movie male was often the object of distrust, even disgust. As Gloria Swanson set out on a second courtship of her ex-husband, her underlying view of the opposite sex was baldly announced in the title: "The more I see of men the better I like dogs." In the course of her uneven courtship in *Our Blushing Brides,* Joan Crawford displayed deep-seated cynicism about men, which she repeatedly pounded home to her roommates. This attitude was expressed to her prospective spouse in the most virulent attacks on his manhood. When she labeled his sweet-talk "ridiculous rubber-stamped lines," he responded: "When it comes to the matter in question I don't trust any modern girl." On their next encounter, when the boss's son intruded upon her in her underwear, she hurled further insults at his masculine ego, saying he wasn't "man enough" to take advantage of the situation, and that it made her "deathly ill" to have him touch her. Crawford's working girl also takes this opportunity to allude to the contradictions of class as well as sex: "I suppose your position entitles you to these little privileges." All in all the animosities in the courtship process cast considerable doubt on the quality of male and female relations after the happy ending.

The relations between female characters were also distorted by the new sexual mores. The sisterly solace associated with Victorian womanhood lingered on in many of these films, as working girls and roommates freely embraced to express sympathy and share joys. Yet the divisions between women were subtly and not so subtly indicated. The fragility of sisterhood was a movie cliché often expressed in a shot of a lonely girl in an empty apartment on evenings when her roommates had dates. The most heart-felt sympathy between women, furthermore, arose to salve the wounds inflicted by males. Female friendship appeared as a supportive by-product of heterosexual relations, not as a primary female bond. The fragmenting effect of the preoccupation with personal attractiveness was symbolized in another recurrent movie image, that of females gathered together before a mirror, obsessed with their own images and oblivious to one another. The conversations that ensued often bordered on the vicious, replete with snide attacks on one another's appearance or reputation. Then, of course, cinema delighted in portraying the most extreme negation of female friendship, the vitriolic "cat fight." This movie cliché was perfected by 1920 when the female rivals in *Why Change Your Wife* scratched, kicked, and threatened to throw acid in each other's faces, par for the course in movie man-hunting.

The melodrama's happy ending could not entirely efface all these peripheral failures and inherent contradictions. As Stanley Cavell observed in another connection, "The walk into the sunset is a dying star; they live happily ever after—as long as they keep walking."[41] The audience that emerged from the darkened theatre in the twenties, to gaze upon mundane reality and perhaps their own quite ordinary mates, might feel a disquieting let-down. The thrills of the film had been built on the activism and gay abandon of the flapper figure, a style that hardly jibes with the unacknowledged denouement into a world of dishes and diapers. At best the female viewer would return to the security of her work-a-day womanhood, content with only a brief relief and catharsis to be renewed in a week or so at the movies. Yet it is unlikely that modern maidens and dancing daughters, the Clara Bow's and Joan Crawford's, could survive unchanged in such a humdrum atmosphere.

As the reality of modern womanhood eclipsed the initial optimism of the flapper éra, these dreams themselves came to seem extravagant, even dangerous, too hedonistic for women returned home and fighting off a depression to boot. Accordingly, the star of the flapper declined precipitiously in the thirties. Its demise was already apparent in *Our Blushing Brides* (1930), the last in a series of Joan Crawford vehicles which included *Our Dancing Daughters* and *Our Modern Maidens*. At the outset of this film, Crawford's effervescence had been reduced to a sparkle in her eye and a spring in her step as she entered the department store. Back home in her sparsely furnished apartment she battered the high hopes of her roommates by calling attention to the chill reality of the working girl's predicament, a stance that she commended because "at least it's real." The stoical Jerry (Crawford) then spent the bulk of the movie ministering to disasters bred by the recklessness of the film's flappers. She became progressively more ridden with cares, looking more like a beaten-down worker than a dashing modern. Jerry's ultimate rescue from work and spinsterhood came suddenly and improbably. Her triumph was rent by contradictions. Her engagement to the boss's son was announced by an act of male possessiveness, her fiancé's genial threat to beat up a male caller. This announcement, furthermore, was made in her lover's hideaway, the scene of his previous seductions and a ferocious argument with the heroine, who is now attired in a costume she once modeled while an employee of her husband-to-be. This is a rather tawdry fantasy—that the working woman can win by marriage the very commodities and privileges that were expropriated from her labor. The screenwriters were making a telling if subtle point about modern womanhood.

Clara Bow exited from the twenties in an equally somber fashion. The thirties found her a box office wash-out attempting a come-back in abysmal roles like that of Nasa in *Call Her Savage*. Although Bow retained her characteristic volatility, it was given a completely different interpretation in this film of 1932. Her devilish pranks lost their gaiety, were judged symptomatic of uncontrollable wildness in her temperament which persisted despite her longing "to be like other girls." The exuberant charms that once won the screen heroine an ideal mate now invited bad matches, broken hearts, alcoholism and loneliness. The flapper had become perverse by 1932, and had to be explained away. Hollywood devised an uncanny solution, tracing Nasa's abnormality to heredity, the fact that she was indeed a savage, descended from an Indian.[42] Such was the ignoble end of the "it girl" as the zesty young actresses of the twenties went the way of the Charleston and the hip flask into a soberer and still unliberated era.

Very few of the stars of the twenties weathered the fashions in womanhood that followed. One sturdy actress fought her way through the Hollywood jungle for forty years only to secure less than savory female roles. She was, of course, Joan Crawford. In 1959 after a series of movies in which she played neurotic, lonely women, Crawford found herself back in the world of the working girl in a film entitled *The Best of Everything*.[43] In many ways the plot of this film replicated the working girl's formula of the twenties. The setting moved to the typing pool and editorial offices of a publishing firm, but the drama was familiar: three young women searching for an honorable escape from the workforce through matrimony. Crawford, however, was too old, too hardened by some 51 years experience of womanhood to have a central role in this plot. As Amanda Farrow she stood on the sidelines, admonishing women against the careerism which made of her a bitter, nasty, carping boss, left only a sterile relationship with a married man. Ironically, however, the very devastation of this woman's life entitled her to some stature and legitimacy in the business world. Crawford made one last-ditch attempt to reform, giving up her lucrative job for marriage in hopes that home life would "soften" her frustrated personality. Yet her marriage was casually allowed to fail. When Amanda returned to her editor's job it was with a new equanimity. In a genuinely warm gesture she extended her businesswoman's hand to the female work force, represented here by the central female character (played by Hope Lange) who we are led to believe will give up her career for marriage and launch another generation on a familiar "happy ending." Yet Joan Crawford's role bespoke another reality of womanhood in the 1950's. Her fans from the twenties had most likely returned to the labor force after a career of homemaking. The typical working woman was no longer an ingenue but a middleaged, married woman—who, unlike Amanda Farrow, could secure only low-paying clerical and retail jobs. The aging of the new woman left at least this fanciful imprint on the screen.[44]

This modern adjustment of woman's roles was insinuated into the minds of millions of movie-goers beginning in the 1920's. But statistics concerning female employment and marriage rates hardly require this kind of confirmation. The fantasies which movies wove around common female experiences contain richer historical meaning. The movie-goer did not merely travel through a remote fantasy land but briefly inhabited a well-contrived make-believe role. In the case of the movie moderns, that role was a glamorous rendition of the social options open to women. Those vicarious lives could channel female expectations in a socially acceptable direction and then reconcile women to their lot, providing both relief and reinforcement in the guise of routine entertainment. The twenties marked the solidification of a new pattern of female roles characterized by a dynamic equilibrium between work, home, and consumer activities. The movies not only fixed these new priorities in the American woman's mind, but simultaneously prepared her for the discontinuities of a woman's life as she traversed the facile transformations of the typical scenario. The movies, particularly in periods like the twenties when female roles were undergoing a major remodeling, constituted a powerful cultural force, shaping individual choices within the boundaries of social and economic possibilities, thus assisting in the creation of a new womanhood. The movie moderns project the historical reality of the American woman's dream.

NOTES

1. Robert S. and Helen Merrell Lynd (New York, 1929) p. 140.

2. Kenneth A. Yellis "Prosperity's Child: Some Thoughts on the Flapper" *American Quarterly,* XXI (Spring, 1969), pp. 44–64; James R. McGovern, "The American Woman's Pre-World War I Freedom in Manners and Moral," *Journal of American History,* LV (September 1968), 315–333.

3. Kenneth MacGowan, *Behind the Screen* (New York, 1965), 256.

4. Lewis Jacobs, *The Rise of the American Film, A Critical History* (New York, 1949), 328–329; MacGowan, 264.

5. Henry James Forman, *Our Movie-Made Children* (New York, 1933), chapter I.

6. Jacobs, 86–87.

7. Stanley Cavell, *The World Viewed: Reflections on the Ontology of Film* (New York, 1971), 33.

8. Fred I. Greenstein, "New Light on Changing American Values: A Forgotten Body of Survey Data," *Social Forces,* XLII (1964), 441–450.

9. Linda Arvidson Griffith, *When the Movies Were Young* (New York, 1969), 198.

10. Marjorie Rosen, *Popcorn Venus, Women, Movies and the American Dream* (New York, 1973), 59–67; Jacobs, 267.

11. *True Heart Susie,* directed by D.W. Griffith, 1919, Film Department, Museum of Modern Art (hereafter MOMA).

12. *Male and Female,* directed by Cecil B. DeMille, 1919, MOMA.

13. Benjamin B. Hampton, *History of the American Film Industry* (New York, 1970), 249; MacGowan, 261–2.

14. Clipping File, MOMA, under *Bertha the Sewing Machine Girl,* title index.

15. Molly Haskell, *From Reverence to Rape: The Treatment of Women in the Movies,* (New York, 1973), 75–82.

16. *Our Dancing Daughters,* MGM, directed by Harry Beaumont, 1928, "The Charleston Episode" MOMA.

17. Clipping file, MOMA, under *It,* title index.

18. *Ankles Preferred,* Fox, directed by J.G. Blystone, 1919, MOMA.

19. *Why Change Your Wife,* directed by Cecil B. DeMille, 1920, MOMA.

20. Clipping File, MOMA, under *His Secretary,* title index.

21. Forman, 141, 145, 225.

22. *Ibid.,* 151, 154, 167.

23. Jacobs, 407.

24. Raymond Durgnat, *Films and Feelings* (Cambridge, Mass., 1967), 135.

25. Barbara Deming, *Running Away from Myself: A Dream Portrait of America Drawn from the Films of the Forties* (New York, 1969), 2.

26. William Chafe, *The American Woman, Her Changing Social, Economic and Political Role 1920–1970* (New York, 1972), 48–50; Joseph A. Hill, *Women in Gainful Occupations, 1870–1920* (Washington, 1929), 42–47.

27. *The American Film Institute Catalog, Feature Films, 1921–1930,* Vol. F2 (New York 1971), 1523, 1545, 1615, 1619, 1631.

28. *AFI Catalog,* 51.

29. Lynd and Lynd, 50.

30. Margaret Thorp, *America at the Movies* (Arno Reprint, 1970 original, New Haven, 1939), 100.

31. *Our Blushing Brides,* MGM directed by Harry Beaumont, 1930, distributed by Films Incorporated.

32. *AFI Indexes,* 1538.

33. *AFI Catalog,* 285.

34. *Soft Living,* Fox, directed by James Tinley, 1928, MOMA.

35. *AFI Catalog,* 249, 292.

36. *Ibid.,* 291, 775.

37. *Kid Boots,* Paramount, directed by Frank Tuttle, 1926, MOMA.

38. *AFI Indexes,* 1549–1551.

39. *AFI Catalog,* 842.

40. *Ibid.,* 636, 992–993.

41. Cavell, 49.

42. *Call Her Savage,* Fox, directed by John Francis Dillon, 1932, MOMA.

43. *The Best of Everything,* Twentieth Century Fox, Directed by Jean Negulesco, 1959, distributed by Films Incorporated.

44. See *Valerie Kincade Oppenheimer,* The Female Labor Force in the United States (Berkeley, 1970).

24 ❧Two Washes in the Morning and a Bridge Party at Night: The American Housewife between the Wars

Ruth Schwartz Cowan

The "feminine mystique" has been part of American cultural life for quite a long while, far longer than Betty Friedan and others have believed; its origins go back to the period after the First World War, not the Second.[1] Political tracts very often idealize the past, and *The Feminine Mystique* was no exception; the norms for American women between the wars were not nearly as bold and adventurous as Betty Friedan would like to think.[2] The cult of true womanhood—that marvelous Victorian combination of Christian sentimentalism and sexual repression[3]—had indeed died by the early 20's, but the ideology that replaced it was, to all intents and purposes, the same "feminine mystique" that Friedan attributes to the 40's and 50's. Whatever it was that trapped educated American women in their kitchens, babbling at babies and worrying about color combinations for the bathroom, the trap was laid during the roaring 20's, not the quiet 50's.

Friedan bases her appraisal of the period between the wars on the fiction that appeared in women's magazines. To some extent her appraisal is correct; those stories often dealt with adventurous, athletic and unconventional women—many of them pursuing a career. But Friedan neglects two aspects of those stories that are just as significant: the career girls were always single and the unconventional ladies were always attended by a truly unconventional number of servants. The housewives who were reading those stories could not possibly have seen themselves mirrored therein; in fact, those stories, with their exotic settings and fanciful plots, were frankly escapist literature. When

From *Women's Studies* 2 (1976): 147-171. Reprinted by permission of Gordon and Breach, Science Publishing, Ltd.

they weren't about strong-minded career girls, they were often about baronnesses, debutantes and Hollywood stars. Why tastes changed after World War II, why—as Friedan accurately noted—postwar fiction tended to be about housewives and not baronnesses, is anyone's guess, but the fact remains that the fiction in the women's magazines in the 20's and 30's is not a reliable indicator of the attitudes and problems of the vast majority of American women. This does not mean, however, that the mass circulation women's magazines are not a reliable source for social history, but it does suggest that we should look at the non-fiction to find a more accurate reflection of what was happening to American women—not in fields of glorious endeavor, but in front of their kitchen sinks, which is where they happened to be. In the advertisements, the informative articles and the advice columns of *The Ladies' Home Journal, McCall's, American Home,* and other similar magazines, a careful reader can watch the feminine mystique descending upon the minds and hearts of American women during the two decades between the wars.

That mystique, like any system of cultural norms, was a complex and subtle affair, continuous with previous ideologies, yet clearly different from them. The mystique makers of the 20's and 30's believed that women were purely domestic creatures, that the goal of each normal woman's life was the acquisition of a husband, a family and a home, that women who worked outside their homes did so only under duress or because they were "odd" (for which read "ugly," "frustrated," "compulsive," or "single") and that this state of affairs was sanctioned by the tenets of religion, biology, psychology and patriotism. Hardly a surprising ideology to be found between the covers of women's magazines, past or present. The feminine mystique differed from previous value systems in its prescriptions about the details—who might reside in that household, how many children that happy family might contain, what the relationship between husband and wife, mother and children, housewife and household ideally might be.

The ideal housewife of the 20's and 30's did not have servants, or to put it another way, the servants she had were electrical, not human. In *The Ladies' Home Journal* for January 1, 1918 "The Householder's Dream of a Happy New Year," had been a cartoon: "Mandy Offers to Stay for Life and Takes Less Wages."[4] Throughout the monthly issues that year, in advertisement after advertisement, Mandy was repeatedly depicted: if you wanted to sell flannel baby's clothes to the readers of *The Ladies' Home Journal* you drew a baby held by a nursemaid; if you wanted to sell fabric, you drew a maid pinning up hems; shampoo—a maid washing her mistress's hair; talcum powder—"Nurse powders baby;" washing soap—a laundress hanging up clothes. All this in a year when, according to the editorial columns of the magazine, domestic help was scarce because of the wartime restrictions on immigration and the attractive salaries offered to women in industry.[5] By the time a decade had passed Mandy had retreated from the advertisements; by 1928 she had almost entirely disappeared into the realms of fiction. In that year if you wanted to sell radiators to the readers of *The Ladies' Home Journal* you drew a housewife playing on the floor with her children; if you wanted to promote supermarkets, women were shown doing their own shopping; cleansing powder—a housewife wiping her own sink; floor wax—an elegant lady polishing her own floor; hand cream—"They'll never know you mopped the floor yourself;" washing machines—"Two washes in the morning and a bridge party at night."

Even before the Depression struck, at a time when prosperity was widespread, American advertisers idealized the woman who was going to buy their product as a housewife, well dressed, to be sure, neatly coiffed and elegantly manicured, but a housewife who cheerfully and resolutely did her housework herself. The only servant in a full-page ad depicting every aspect of housework, an ad for Ivory Soap which appeared in *The Ladies' Home Journal* in 1933, was a confinement nurse.[6] Mandy had not disappeared entirely. She was still an important character in women's magazine fiction. *American Home* still published house plans that included a maid's room,[7] and *Parents' Magazine* still worried about the ways in which servants influence children,[8] but the days when a housewife of moderate means fully expected that she would have at least a maid of all work, and probably a laundress and nursemaid, were clearly over.[9]

On the matter of servants the feminine mystique was a reversal of older attitudes. The servantless household had once been regarded as a trial and tribulation; now it was regarded as a condition dearly to be wished. Adequate household help had always been a problem in America and women's magazines had repeatedly offered advice to housewives who were, for one unfortunate reason or another, coping with their homes singlehandedly. The emphasis in those articles was often on the word, "unfortunate;" the housewife was told, for example, that if help is scarce, it is easiest to serve children the same food that adults are eating, and at the same time—although clearly it would be better for their digestion and your temperament if they ate with a nursemaid in the nursery; hopefully the servant shortage would soon pass.[10] Occasionally a lone voice (often male) would remind the housewife of her patriotic obligations (wouldn't it be more democratic to fire the servants and have the family pitch in and do the work?) or would appeal to the higher reaches of her intellect (think how much chemistry you could learn if you would only do the cooking yourself!)[11] but the housewives apparently managed—somehow—to resist such blandishments. Housework was regarded as a chore, albeit a necessary one, and if it could be palmed off on someone else, so much the better. If one can gauge from the content and tone of advertisements, advice columns and letters to the editor, the American housewife clearly preferred to employ servants whenever economic and demographic conditions permitted her to do so.

This attitude began to change in the years after the First World War. Housework was no longer regarded as a chore, but as an expression of the housewife's personality and of her affection for her family. In past times the housewife had been judged by the way she organized her servants; now she would be judged by the way she organized her kitchen. If she were strong and proud of herself her workroom would be filled with labor-saving devices, meticulously cleaned and color coordinated; if she were insecure, frustrated and lonely, woe to her kitchen—it would be disorderly, dim and uninviting.[12] When the kitchen had been dominated by servants it had been a dreary room, often in the basement of the house. Now that the kitchen had become the housewife's domain it had to be prettied up.

> Time was when kitchens were big and dark, for keeping house was a gloomy business. . . . But now! Gay colors are the order of the day. Red pots and pans! Blue gas stoves! . . . It is a rainbow, in which the cook sings at her work and never thinks of household tasks as drudgery.[13]

Laundering had once been just laundering; now it was an expression of love. The new bride could speak her affection by washing tell-tale gray out of her husband's shirts.[14] Feeding the family had once been just feeding the family; now it was a way to communicate deep seated emotions.

> When the careful housekeeper turns from the preparation of company dinner to the routine of family meals, she will know that prime rib roast, like peach ice cream, *is a wonderful stimulant to family loyalty,* but that it is not absolutely necessary for every day.[15] (Italics mine.)

Diapering was no longer just diapering, but a time to build the baby's sense of security; cleaning the bathroom sink was not just cleaning, but an exercise for the maternal instincts, protecting the family from disease.

Clearly, tasks of this emotional magnitude could not be relegated to servants. The servantless household may have been an economic necessity in the 20's, as the supply of servants declined and their wages rose, but for the first time that necessity was widely regarded as a potential virtue. The servantless housewife was no longer portrayed as "unfortunate;" she was happy, revelling in her modern home and in the opportunities for creative expression that it provided.

> The fact is that the American home was never a more satisfying place than it is today. Science and invention have outfitted it with a great range of conveniences and comforts. . . . All this is, in the main, women's work. For the first time in the world's history it is possible for a nation's women in general to have or to be able to look forward to having homes and the means of furnishing them in keeping with their instinctive longings. The women of America are to be congratulated, not only in the opportunity but because of the manner in which they are responding to it. When the record is finally written this may stand as their greatest contribution.[16]

And what opportunities there were! In earlier years American women had been urged to treat housework as a science; now they were being urged to treat it as a craft, a creative endeavor. The ideal kitchen of the prewar period had been white and metallic—imitating the laboratory. The ideal kitchen of the postwar period was color coordinated—imitating the artist's studio. Each meal prepared in that ideal kitchen was a color composition in and of itself: "Make Meals More Appetizing by Serving Foods that Have Pleasing Contrast of Color."[17] Ready made clothes could be disguised by adding individual hand sewn touches; patterned towels could be chosen to match the decorative scheme in the bathroom; old furniture could be repainted and restyled. The new housewife would be an artist, not a drudge.

The new housewife would also be a consumer, not a producer.

> A woman's virtue and excellence as a housewife do not in these days depend upon her skill in spinning and weaving. An entirely different task presents itself, more difficult and more complex, requiring an infinitely wider range of ability, and for these very reasons more interesting and inspiring.[18]

That task was, of course, buying. The words come from an article about shopping for linens, but they could have been taken from any one of the numerous articles on wise buying—clothes, sheets, rugs, blankets, silverware, appliances—that began to appear regularly in women's magazines through the 20's.[19] In earlier days the young housewife had to be taught to make things well; in the 20's she had to be taught to buy things well. Magazines and manufacturers created new devices to teach her how to be a "professional" buyer: product testing services, gadget buying services, home shopping guides, home demonstrators, new packages, new grading systems. Apparently the devices worked;

scores of sociologists and economists have noted that consumption is now the most important social function still performed by families.[20] Unlike so many familial functions, consumption has been expanding, not contracting; the 20's appear to be the decade in which the expansion began.[21]

In her physical appearance the new housewife looked quite different from her older counterparts. In earlier days the ideal American matron had been plump; corset makers were happy to send her garments that would add inches to her *derrière* if she were unfashionably skinny. After World War I the corset makers changed their tune; the emphasis was on reducing, not increasing. By the end of the 20's advertising campaigns were predicated on the American woman's passion for slenderizing; Sunkist oranges are nutritious, and non-fattening; Fleischman's yeast will aid your digestion and prevent constipation if you are dieting; Postum should be substituted for coffee while dieting because it calms the nerves.[22] By the end of the 20's articles about exercising to keep fit had become a regular feature in *The Ladies' Home Journal*; before the war they had been unknown.[23]

She was thin, this ideal lady, and she was also elegant; her hands were long and well manicured, so were her legs. If she worked hard at her housework during hot weather, she remained "personally irreproachable"—thanks to cream deodorants. She wore a fashionable wool suit with a fur collar to visit her local A & P and applied Pompeian Night Cream to keep from looking tired after an exhausting night of bridge. If life was creating problems for her she knew that one or two dabs of Raquel Orange Blossom Fragrance would guarantee eternal bliss. This particular form of hidden persuasion, the notion that cosmetics can guarantee happiness, seems to have been invented in the 20's.[24] The cosmetics industry must have entered a boom phase after World War I—if the number and size of its advertisements are any gauge of its economic well-being.

Child rearing was the single most important task that this new housewife had to perform. Experts agreed that a child raised by nursemaids was a child to be pitied. The young boy tended by servants would never learn the upright, go-getting resourcefulness of the truly American child, would never become a useful member of the egalitarian republic, and would—horror of horrors—probably fail in the business world.[25] His sister, deprived of the example of her mother, would not know how to manage the myriad appliances of the modern kitchen; she would never learn how to decorate a pineapple salad, or how to wash silk underwear in an electric machine, and consequently— horror of horrors—she would never attract and keep a truly American husband.[26] Even more worrisome was the thought that children raised by nursemaids might never reach adulthood because they would not be tended by persons who were familiar with the latest medical and nutritional information. American mothers, anxious about infant mortality, were advised not to leave their offspring in the care of illiterate, untutored servant girls. In 1918, the editor of *The Ladies' Home Journal* rejoiced in the knowledge that, if present trends continued, the postwar generation of American children would be the first generation to be raised by its mothers; they would be healthy in mind and body and, as a result, they would lift the sagging fortunes of the race.[27] There was very little Freudianism in this new child psychology; mothers were to take over the rearing of their children, not because of the psychological traumas of separation, but because mothers were likely to be better informed and better educated than nursemaids.[28]

Spending time with her children seems to have been as much a moral imperative for the housewife of the 20's as spending time on Christian good works was for her mother. There were no more socks to be knitted for missionaries, or elderly sick relatives to be visited, or Bible classes to attend; instead there were basketball games to watch with her children, card games to play with them, and piano lessons to help them with. Togetherness had become a fact for middle-class Americans long before the editors of *McCall's* coined the term in 1954.[29]

> I accommodate my entire life to my little girl. She takes three music lessons a week and I practice with her forty minutes a day. I help her with her school work and go to dancing school with her . . .
>
> There are now never ten days that go by without my either visiting the children's school or getting in touch with their teacher. I have given up church work and club work since the children came. I always like to be here when they come home from school so that I can keep in touch with their games and their friends . . .
>
> I certainly have a harder job than my mother did; everything tends to weaken the parents' influence. But we do it by spending time with our children. I've always been a pal with my daughter, and my husband spends a lot of time with the boy. We all go to basketball games together and to the State Fair in the summer . . .
>
> We used to belong to the Country Club but resigned from that when the children came, and bought a car instead. That is something we can all enjoy together.[30]

The advent of the Depression apparently accelerated this trend. Magazine editors noted that families were being forced to rely upon their own devices for entertainment; the end of prosperity meant the end of meals in restaurants and parties in hotels. *American Home* published essays on turning basements into playrooms; *The Ladies' Home Journal* discovered the barbecue; *Parents' Magazine* began denoting with an asterisk the articles that would be of interest to progressive fathers (i.e. those who wished to take a hand in rearing their own children).[31]

Life was not always a bed of roses in the model American household, but if the lady of the house had any complaints, she refrained, whenever possible, from discussing them with her husband. "She must never bring her troubles to the table;" dinner time was a moment of sweetness and light in her husband's weary day; he came home from the office to be greeted with a cheering cup of Steero bouillon; his children were scrubbed ("Self respect thrives on soap and water") and anxious to tell him about their day in school (they have done well because they did not forget to have hot cereal for breakfast).[32] Woe unto the housewife who would mar this scene by reminding her husband that he had failed to clean his hair out of the sink that morning— or other such domestic trivia. She was almost always cheerful, this modern housewife; in fact, the constellation of emotions that she was allowed to display in magazines was really rather limited. She could be happy, loving, tender or affectionate; occasionally she was worried, but she was never, never angry. What, after all, did she have to be angry about?

Only one anxious emotion ever creased her brow—guilt; she felt guilty a good deal of the time, and when she wasn't feeling guilty she was feeling embarrassed: guilty if her infant didn't gain enough weight, embarrassed if her friends arrived to find that her sink was clogged, guilty if her children went to school in soiled clothes, guilty if she didn't eradicate all the germs behind the bathroom sink, embarrassed if her nieces and nephews accused her of having body odor, guilty if her son was a laggard in school, guilty if her daughter was not popular with the crowd (her mother having failed to keep her dresses properly ironed).[33] In earlier times a woman could have been made to feel guilty if she had abandoned her children or been too free with her affections. In the years between the wars American women apparently began to feel guilty if their children were seen in public in scuffed shoes. Between the two sources of anxiety there seems a world of difference. Advertisers may have stimulated these guilt feelings, but they could not have created them singlehandedly; the guilt must have been there or advertisers would not have found that they could be successful by playing upon it.

In 1937 Emily Post coined a name for the new American housewife: Mrs. Three-in-One, the lady who is cook, waitress and hostess at her own dinner parties.[34] In almost every essential, Mrs. Three-in-One was no different from the housewives that Betty Friedan described in *The Feminine Mystique.* She was fairly well educated and somewhat sophisticated. Her family was smaller than her mother's, but more attention was lavished upon it. Her infants were weighed every day and their nutritional intake carefully planned. The development of her youngsters was carefully watched and the social affairs of her adolescents carefully—but discreetly—supervised. She drove a car, played bridge and took vacations. She had very few servants, or none at all. In the morning she served her family a light breakfast; lunch was a can of soup for herself. She shopped by telephone, or in a small supermarket, bought most of her clothes ready-made, wore silk stockings, and tied her hair in a neat scarf when doing housework. She could nurse a child through the measles, repair a dripping faucet, decorate a kitchen, discourse on vitamins, give a speech before her ladies' club or entertain her husband's business associates—all with equal facility. She was always cheerful, healthy, up-to-date, and gracious, never angry, frustrated, sick, old-fashioned or—perish the thought—gainfully employed. She was content with her life and had no doubts about her femininity; if she wished for anything it was another appliance or a better rug for the living room. She had the vote, but rarely discussed politics; believed in divorce, but was not herself divorced; practiced birth control but did not discuss sex with her daughter.

No doubt there were more Mrs. Three-in-Ones after World War II than there had been before. The feminine mystique probably became more pervasive after 1945; before that it was a social ideology to which only the middle classes—perhaps only the upper middle classes—could possibly pretend. But the ideologies of the upper middle classes eventually percolate down to everyone else in our society and I would venture to guess that that is precisely what happened to the feminine mystique in the late 40's and early 50's. As families moved up the economic and social ladder the signs of their success were the signs that the mystique had arrived on their doorstep: the wife stops working; the house becomes neater; new rooms are added; the children wear ready-made clothes; they stay in school longer, take piano and ballet lessons; slenderizing becomes a passion; nails must be manicured; choices must be made between muslin and percale sheets, double-oven or single-oven stoves, wool or nylon carpeting. The mother who had once complained about back-breaking toil to make ends meet now has a daughter who complains that despite her appliances she still works 16 hours a day, seven days a week—and doesn't quite know why. This pattern must have been repeated in millions of American homes after World War II, but the underlying ideology that produced it was formed in the decades between the wars.

Social ideologies are responsive to changes in economic and demographic conditions. The advent of the feminine mystique was a major ideological change, and there must have been major social and economic changes that produced it. Friedan believed that the mystique arose after the Second World War and consequently her list of causal conditions—higher education for women, widespread prosperity, domestic disruptions attendant upon the Depression and the war, functionalism and Freudianism in the social sciences, the advent of new marketing and advertising techniques—warrants reexamination. One crucial aspect of the new ideology was its emphasis on the servant-less household; changes in the supply of domestic servants are likely, therefore, to have been an important precondition.

Household labor was generally performed by five different types of workers in the early years of the 20th century: the housewife herself, her children (primarily her daughters), other female relatives (a maiden aunt perhaps, or a grandmother), dayworkers, and servants who lived in. Data on changes in the number of any of those types of labor are rather hard to come by, or are likely to be quite unreliable when we have them. Domestic servants are one of the most difficult categories of workers to enumerate as their labor is often transient, or part-time, or unreported. In the early decades of this century social commentators believed that in every category (except the housewife herself) the supply of labor was declining, and the data that are available tend to support this conclusion. Certainly wages for paid household employees were rising. Lynes estimates that in 1890 a live-in cook received about $4.00 a week in wages (this does not count the expense of room and board); in 1920 this would have increased to $25.[35] The Lynds estimate that in 1924 a single day's work for a day laborer cost the Muncie housewife approximately what a week's labor would have cost her mother.[36] Similarly the Lynds found that the business class housewives in Muncie had roughly half the number of household servants that their mothers had had; according to the Federal Census for Indiana, the number of families per servant increased from 13.5 in 1890 to 30.5 in 1920.[37] Using nationwide statistics as a guide, it appears that most of this increase occurred in the decade from 1910 to 1920; the number of families per servant was roughly 10 in 1900, 10 in 1910 and 16 in 1920.[38] These data do not, of course, tell us anything specific about the *supply* of labor, but they are suggestive; if wages were rising and the proportion of workers to households falling, contemporary social critics may have been right in their assumption that the supply of household servants was declining because of the twin pressures generated by fewer immigrants and more attractive industrial wages.[39] Data on the other two categories of household help, children and female relatives, are, to all intents and purposes, nonexistent, but here again the remarks of social critics may be suggestive. Many observers noted tendencies toward less available labor from those sources as well: grandparents were not as frequently moving in with their married children (in part because houses were smaller); grown daughters seemed inclined to have apartments and jobs of their own before marriage; maiden aunts, like their unmarried nieces, were apparently living alone and liking it more.[40]

The odd thing about these social commentaries is that they are recurrent American themes. Household help has always been a sore point in American life; servants were constantly disappearing from the labor market or otherwise behaving recalcitrantly, and the daughters of the middle classes, if they weren't actually out working at Macy's, were often balking at household labor. Yet none of the other periods in which this scarcity of household labor was proclaimed produced an ideology like the feminine mystique, an ideology which put a premium on the servantless household. Consequently we must assume that the declining supply of servants (paid or unpaid) although it must have been part of the preconditions leading to that ideology, was by no means the whole story.

The story become more complete if we look at what was happening to domestic technology during those years. For the first time in the history of the republic there was, after 1918, a viable alternative to the labor of housewives, domestic servants, maiden aunts and adolescent daughters—the machine. It was a classic American solution: when in doubt, try a machine. For several years before the war, home economists had been pressing for the rationalization of household labor. After the war, as electrification and assembly-line production of consumer goods increased, that rationalization seemed to be at hand.

Almost every aspect of household labor was revolutionized during the 20's; in good part this was due to electrification. In 1907 (the first year for which data are available) only 8% of dwellings in the U.S. had electric service; by the time we entered the war this had risen to 24.3% and by 1925 more than half the homes in America (53.2%) had been wired. If we consider the data for urban and rural non-farm dwellings the figures are even more striking: almost half of those homes had been electrified by 1920 (47.4%) and more than two-thirds by 1925 (69.4%).[41] During this period the price of electricity fell from 9.5 cents per kilowatt hour to 7.68 cents (for an average monthly use of 25 kilowatt hours, which is the order of magnitude then used in homes).[42] The amount of money spent on mechanical appliances grew from $145 millions in 1909 to $667 millions in 1927, an increase of almost 500%, while at the same time expenditure on clothing increased only 250% and on furniture, 300%; similarly the dollar value (in current prices) of electric household appliances produced for domestic consumption soared from $11.8 millions in 1909 to $146.3 millions in 1927.[43]

With the spread of electrification came the spread of electrical appliances: a small motor to power the family sewing machine, a fan, an electric iron (the earliest models had no thermostats, but they were still easier to use than the irons heated on cooking stoves), a percolator, perhaps a toaster, a waffle iron or a portable heater. Automatic refrigerators went on the market in 1916 (at roughly $900); in 1921, 5,000 units were sold, but by 1929 that figure had risen to 890,000 units and the price had fallen to roughly $180.[44] A study of 100 Ford employees living in Detroit in 1929 revealed that 98 families had an electric iron, 80 had electric sewing machines, 49 had electric washing machines, and 21 had electric vacuum cleaners.[45] The benefits of technology were clearly not limited to the upper middle classes.

As household habits were being changed by the advent of electricity, so eating habits were being changed by the advent of the metal can, the refrigerated railroad car and new notions about diet. Before World War I an average American family ate three extraordinarily hefty meals a day.

> Steak, roasts, macaroni, Irish potatoes, sweet potatoes, turnips, cole slaw, fried apples, and stewed tomatoes, with Indian pudding, rice, cake or pie for dessert. This was the winter repertoire of the average family that was not wealthy, and we swapped about from one combination to another, using pickles and chow-chow to make the familiar starchy food relishing. . . . Breakfast, pork chops or steak with fried potatoes, buckwheat cakes, and hot bread; lunch, a hot roast and potatoes; supper, same roast cold.[46]

In 1908 an article appeared in *The Ladies' Home Journal* describing an ordinary family lunch; were that meal to be served today it would be regarded as a state banquet.[47] By the middle of the 20's such meals were no longer the rule: breakfast had been reduced to eggs and/or cereal; lunch was essentially one course, or perhaps soup and a sandwich; dinner was usually no more than three. Commercially canned fruits and vegetables made variations in the classic winter menu possible. Some canned goods (primarily peas and corn) had been on the market since the middle of the 19th century, but by 1918 the American housewife with sufficient means could have purchased almost any fruit or vegetable, and quite a surprising array of ready-made meals, in a can: Campbell's soups, Heinz's spaghetti (already cooked and ready to serve), Libby's corned beef and chili con carne (heated directly in its package), Stokeley's peas, corn, string beans, lima beans, tomatoes, succotash, LaChoy's bean sprouts, Beechnut's chili sauce, vinegar, and mustard, Purity Cross's creamed chicken, welsh rarebit, lobster à la newburg, Van Camp's pork and beans, Libby's olives, sauerkraut and

Vienna sausages, Del Monte's peaches, pineapples, apricots and plums. In the morning the American housewife of the 20's could have offered her family some of the new cold cereals (Kellogg's Corn Flakes, or Krumbles, or Post's Grape Nuts Flakes); if her family wanted pancakes she could have prepared them with Aunt Jemima's pancake mix. Recipes in the women's magazines in the 20's utilized canned goods as a matter of course: canned peaches in peach blancmange; canned peas in creamed finnan haddie. Very often the recipes did not even include the familiar rubric, "canned or fresh," but simply assumed that "canned" would be used. By the middle of the 20's home canning was on its way to becoming a lost art; the business-class wives of Muncie reported that they rarely put up anything, except an occasional jelly or batch of tomatoes, whereas their mothers had once spent the better part of the summer and fall canning.[48] Increased utilization of refrigerated railroad cars also meant that fresh fruits and vegetables were appearing in markets at reasonable prices all through the year.[49] Fewer family meals were being taken at home; restaurants and businessmen's clubs downtown, cafeterias in schools and factories, after-school activities for teenagers—all meant that fewer members of the family were home for meals.[50] Cooking was easier, and there was less of it to be done.

Part of the reason that cooking became easier was that the coal or wood-burning stove began to disappear. After World War I the women's magazines only carried advertisements for stoves that used natural gas, kerosene, gasoline or electricity; in Muncie in 1924 two out of three homes cooked with gas.[51] The burdensome chore of keeping a coal stove lit and regulated—and keeping the kitchen free of the resultant soot—had probably been eliminated from most American homes by the 30's. The change in routine that was predicated on the change from coal stoves to oil or gas stoves (electric stoves were inefficient and rarely used in this period) was profound; aside from the elimination of such chores as loading the coal and removing the ashes, the new stoves were simply much easier to regulate. One writer in *The Ladies' Home Journal* estimated that kitchen cleaning was reduced by one-half when coal stoves were eliminated.[52] As the coal stove disappeared from the kitchen, the coal-fired furnace also started disappearing from the basement. By the late 20's coal furnaces were no longer being advertised in home equipment magazines and homeowners were being urged to convert to oil or gas or electricity, "so that no one has to go into the basement anymore." A good number of American homes were centrally heated by the mid-20's; in Zanesville, Ohio 48% of the roughly 11,000 homes had basement furnaces in 1924.[53]

As the routines of meal preparation became less burdensome in the 20's, so did the routines of personal hygiene. The early 20's was the time of the bathroom mania; more and more bathrooms were installed in older homes and new homes were being built with them as a matter of course. Sixty-one per cent of those 11,000 homes in Zanesville had indoor plumbing and bathroom in 1924.[54] In Muncie in 1890 ninety-five out of every hundred families took baths by lugging a zinc tub into the kitchen and filling it with water that had been pumped by hand and heated on the stove; by 1924 three out of four Muncie homes had running water.[55] The rapid increase in the number of bathrooms after World War I was the result of changes in the production of bathroom fixtures. Before the war those fixtures were not standardized and porcelain tubs were routinely made by hand; after the war industrialization swept over the bathroom industry: cast-iron enamelware went into mass production and fittings were standardized. In 1921 the dollar value of the production of enamelled sanitary fixtures was $2.4 million, the same that it had been in 1915. By 1923 just two years later, that figure had doubled to $4.8 million; it rose again, to $5.1 million, in 1925.[56] The first one-piece, recessed, double-shell cast iron enamelled bathtub was put on the market in the early 20's; by the time a decade had passed the standard American bathroom had achieved its standard American form: a small room, with a recessed tub, tiled floors and walls, brass plumbing, a single-unit toilet, and an enclosed sink.[57] This bathroom was relatively easy to clean, and—needless to say—it helped revolutionize habits of personal cleanliness in America; the body-odor fetish of the 30's can be partly attributed to the bathroom fetish of the 20's.

Similarly, the "tell-tale gray" syndrome of the 30's had its roots in the changing technologies of clothes washing. Soap powders and flakes arrived on the market in the early 20's, which meant that bars of soap no longer had to be scraped and boiled to make soap paste. Electric washing machines took a good part of the drudgery out of the washing process, although they required a considerable amount of time and attention to operate, as they did not go through their cycles automatically and did not spin dry.[58] There was more variation in methods of handling household laundry than in any other domestic chore; the Lynds noted that on the same street in Muncie, families of the same economic class were using quite different washing technologies: hand washing, electric machines, commercial laundries, laundresses who worked "in," and laundresses who worked "out."[59] Advertisements in the women's magazines do not give a uniform picture either: sometimes showing old-fashioned tubs, sometimes depicting machines. Commercial household laundries entered a boom period in the 20's; they began to expand their services (wet wash, rough dry, etc.) and began to do more personal laundry (as opposed to flat work) than they had in past years;[60] nationwide, the number of power laundries doing more than $5,000 business a year rose from 4,881 in 1919 to 6,776 in 1929, and their receipts more than doubled.[61]

While the processes of cooking, heating, cleaning, lighting and washing were revolutionized, other processes—just as much a part of the housewife's daily routine—were changing, but not quite as drastically. The corner grocer, the door-to-door merchant and the curbside market were slowly being replaced by the telephone and the supermarket. In 1918 *The Ladies' Home Journal* referred to supermarkets as "The New Stores Without Clerks;"[62] by 1928 there were 2,600 Piggly Wiggly markets across the country.[63] Telephone shopping had become routine in many households by the end of the 20's. Instead of purchasing whole cases of canned goods or bushels of apples and onions to be stored and used over the months, housewives were now telephoning daily orders and having them hand-delivered: 1 head of lettuce, 1 pat of cream cheese, 1 can of string beans, $\frac{1}{4}$-pound of mushrooms.[64] Hardwood floors were replaced by linoleum; instead of tedious hand polishing, only a mop, soap and water was now required. Heavy cast iron pots and pans were giving way to aluminum and Pyrex. Ready-made clothes were no longer thought "poor-folksy;" by 1928 a good part of each monthly issue of the better women's magazines was devoted to photographs and drawings of clothing that could be bought off the rack. Home sewing, home mending, the once ubiquitous practice of making over dresses—all became vestigial crafts; young women were now being taught how to shop for clothes, not how to make them.[65] Home baking also disappeared; the bakers in Muncie estimated that, depending upon the season, they supplied between 55% and 70% of the city's homes with bread.[66]

Many factors must have contributed to the revolution in household production that occurred during the 20's. On the whole those were prosperous years and prosperity made it possible for many people to buy new equipment for their homes. Vast industrial facilities which were created during the war were converted to the production of consumer goods during peacetime. The apparent shortage of servants and the rise in their wages must have encouraged householders to try the new appliances more readily than they would otherwise have done. The growth of magazines devoted to the interests of modern housewives no doubt encouraged the trend, as did the growth of consumer credit arrangements. Whatever the causes were, the event itself seems indisputable; profound changes in household technology occurred between the end of the First World War and the beginning of the Depression—whether we measure those changes by the number of individual innovations or by the rate of their diffusion. Certain changes did occur after the Second World War: the standard American kitchen achieved its present form, with standardized fixtures and continuous counter space; the automatic washing machine (which could spin and go through its cycles itself) became widespread; the laundromat replaced the commercial laundry; the supermarket replaced the grocery store; frozen foods to some extent replaced canned foods; the dishwasher and the home dryer became more reasonable in price; the ranch home with its open room plan, became more popular. However, all those changes pale to insignificance when compared to the change from oil lamps to electric lamps, coal stoves to gas stoves, coal furnaces to gas and oil furnaces, kitchen heating to central heating, outdoor plumbing to indoor plumbing, not having a bathroom to having one, canning tomatoes to buying canned tomatoes, making dresses to buying them, baking bread to buying it, living with servants and living without them.

Thus, a fundamental productive process was revolutionized by the introduction of new technologies; almost simultaneously an ideology developed which insured that those new technologies would be used in very specific and rather limited ways. In the early days the new technology could have been used to communalize housework. The first vacuum cleaners were large mobile units; they were brought into a home by a team of skilled operators to take over the housewife's cleaning chores.[67] The new washing machines could have been placed in communal laundries where paid employees would take over the housewife's washing chores, and the editors of *The Ladies' Home Journal* advocated that this be done.[68] Those same editors also advocated retention of the wartime communal kitchens, so that the wasteful process of cooking each family's meals separately would be eliminated.[69] Many of the early luxury apartment houses had, along with elevators, communal nurseries on their roofs.[70] Within a very few years, needless to say, those visions of communal housekeeping had died a not very surprising death; this was America, after all, not Soviet Russia. The new domestic technology, communalized or not, could have freed American women to do productive work outside their homes; the growth of the feminine mystique insured that they would not do it.

The advertising industry cooperated in this endeavor, even if it did not invent it. As the size and number of women's magazines increased in the 20's, the amount and the variety of advertising increased also. The American woman was becoming the American consumer *par excellence*; automobile manufacturers, cigarette producers, life insurance companies (not to speak of the advertisers whose wares were of traditional interest to women) all discovered the virtues of the women's magazines. The magazines, of course, found ways to encourage this custom. They used their non-advertising space to advertise in subtler ways: listing new products by their brand names, adopting editorial policies that encouraged women to buy, creating "shop at home" columns for mail-order purchases, sponsoring consumption oriented contests.

> Home building, home decoration and furnishing, *home making,* in fact, is the most outstanding phase of modern civilization. . . . The magazines of today have played an important part in this; they have carried on an intensive sincere campaign for better homes. But an even greater part has been that of the manufacturers. . . . Not only has beauty and convenience and efficiency of home equipment been carefully studied to meet the demand of the modern housewife . . . but back of all this stands the guarantee of the maker of his goods.[71]

Late in the 20's those earnest manufacturers (and their sincere advertising agents) discovered that they could sell more gadgets by appealing to the housewife's fears than by appealing to her strengths; advertisements stopped being informative and started pandering to status-seeking and guilt. An advertisement for soap in 1908 was likely to talk about the clean factory in which the soap was produced and the pure ingredients from which it was made; a similar advertisement in 1928 was likely to talk about the psychological trauma experienced by children who go to school with soiled clothes.[72] It would be difficult to prove that manufacturers and advertising agencies invented the feminine mystique, but it would be equally difficult to deny that they did everything they reasonably could to encourage it.

In a quite different way the proponents of the child health movement also helped to encourage the mystique. The infant mortality rate in the United States in 1915 was 100 for every 1,000 live births, one of the highest in the world. There were very few families who were not touched, in some way, by the spectre of infant death. After the war, with its discouraging reports about the health of young recruits, various public agencies began a concerted effort to improve the health and the physique of America's young people, particularly by disseminating information about proper nutrition and proper care of children during illness. The women's magazines were prime agents in the dissemination of this information; *The Ladies' Home Journal,* for example, started a Babies Registry so that the mothers of registered babies could receive monthly instructional booklets. Professional organizations, such as the Child Study Association (which organized child study groups in cities across the country and began publishing *Parents' Magazine* in 1926), and the federal government were also active in the campaign to improve the health of the young. By the end of the 20's advice to parents on the physical care of their children could be had at every turn: in magazine articles, in thousands of new books, in advertisements, in government pamphlets. The health of children became an overriding, perhaps even a compulsive concern for parents; they were urged to buy GE Mazda Sunlamps to provide Vitamin D for their children, to learn which foods would be most helpful in preventing anemia, to keep Vicks VapoRub on hand in case congestion should develop, to wear masks when they entered a sick child's room, to cleanse their bathrooms with BonAmi because the other (scratchier) cleansers would leave places for germs to breed, to guard against pink toothbrush, to watch for the signs of eczema, to use Castoria for constipation, Listerine for sore throats, and VapoCresoline for whooping cough.[73]

This new concern for the health of children was no doubt necessary, and some of it no doubt worked; the infant mortality rate fell to 65 per 1,000 live births by 1930, before the age of the miracle antibiotics—but the burden that it placed upon the new American housewife was immense. Children had to be kept in bed for weeks at a time; bedpans had to be provided and warmed, "since even the slightest chilling is to be avoided carefully;" in some diseases excrement had to be disinfected before being discarded; food had to be specially prepared; leftovers had to be burned after the sick child's meal; utensils had to be boiled, alcohol baths administered, hands scrupulously washed, mouths carefully masked—and through all this the nursing mother was expected to "get plenty of rest and outdoor recreation," and remain unrelentingly cheerful, "for cheerfulness is needed in a sickroom and the attitude of a mother nursing an ailing child largely influences the speed of recovery."[74] Needless to say, mothers had to remain at home in order for all this nursing to be done; the death of a child whose mother had gone out to work, was a recurrent theme in women's magazine fiction. In this sense, the child health movement was paradoxical; many women made careers out of convincing other women to stay at home and tend their children.

Oddly enough the Depression also served to reinforce the feminine mystique, although many commentators worried about what the economic disaster would do to the family as a social institution. The end of prosperity meant that entertainment outside the home had to be curtailed and it also meant that many families would be unable to pay for domestic servants. The genteel housewife who had formerly kept servants but who had let them go in the early years of the Depression became something of a social stereotype: " . . . a college girl who in recent years has been obliged to live the anxious, circumscribed life of the maid-of-all-work wife of a small-time lawyer with vanishing fees," as Anne O'Hare McCormick described a friend of hers in 1933.[75]

"Doing it yourself these days?" asked the makers of La France Bluing over a stark picture of manicured hands immersed in a laundry tub; indeed, many American housewives were.[76] The need to economize to make ends meet meant that meals had to be planned carefully and cash had to be spent wisely; the editors of *American Home* advised their readers to stop buying over the telephone and go down to the shops in person to make certain they were getting good value for their money.[77] The editors of *The Ladies' Home Journal* were pleased to note that the new emphasis on home entertainment was leading families to remodel their homes—themselves.[78] To save money women learned how to fix electric motors, paint used furniture, sew curtains and—once again—remake last year's clothes. Manufacturers had to keep selling their goods, so prices came down and credit buying arrangements became more flexible. The more goods there were on shelves, the heavier advertising pressure on women became. Cash wasn't available, but time was—women's time—and since the prohibition against women entering the work force was particularly heavy during the Depression (they would, after all, be stealing jobs from unemployed men) the best place to spend that time was at home and the best way to spend it was in all those multitudinous little jobs that make up the daily routine of the housewife who was convinced that the feminine mystique made sense.

The feminine mystique, the social ideology which was formed during the 20's and solidified during the 30's, was quite a functional solution to real economic and demographic conditions. Servants were scarcer and their wages higher. Electricity could save burdensome labor and washday was unquestionably easier to face when the washing was done by machine than when it was done by hand. Infants' lives could be saved if care were taken to sterilize their bottles and balance their diets. In fact the feminine mystique worked; it kept women at home to do jobs that, in one way or another, American society needed to have done. Unfortunately calling the solution functional does not mean that it was wise; it seems tragic that as a society we could not utilize all that new technology without constructing an ideology which oppressed half our citizens.

NOTES

1. Betty Friedan, *The Feminine Mystique* (New York: Norton, 1963). Citations are to be paperback edition (New York: Dell, 1963). For Friedan's argument that the feminine mystique took hold after World War II, see Chapter 8. Other

authors have adopted her chronology. See, for example, Sonya Rudikoff, "Marriage and household," *Commentary*, 55 (June 1973), 61.

2. Friedan, Chapter 2.

3. Barbara Welter, "The cult of true womanhood, 1820–1860," *American Quarterly*, 18 (Summer, 1966), 162.

4. *The Ladies' Home Journal* (January, 1918), 4.

5. "Editorial," *The Ladies' Home Journal* (May, 1918), 4.

6. *The Ladies' Home Journal* (January, 1933), 2.

7. *American Home* regularly published house plans in every issue. About half the plans published between 1928 and 1933 had no maid's room, despite the fact that they were very expensive homes ($9,000 up).

8. Ruth Sapin, "For better or worse, servants influence children," *Parents' Magazine* (January 1929), 20.

9. The prevalence of household servants before World War I, and their disappearance thereafter, is discussed in Russell Lynes, *The Domesticated Americans* (New York: Harper & Row, 1957) Ch. 9. As just one example: an article in *The Ladies' Home Journal* (February, 1908), 44, described a young couple who were struggling along on the husband's meagre salary as a newspaper reporter; they did all the gardening, house painting, and repair work themselves and found various ways to economize on food—but they had a maid-of-all-work.

10. Paraphrased from, *The Ladies' Home Journal* (February, 1918), 49.

11. For an example of the genre see, S. M. Eliot, "The normal American woman," *The Ladies' Home Journal* (January, 1908), 15.

12. "What does your kitchen say about you?" *The Ladies' Home Journal* (March, 1933), 34.

13. "Editorial," *The Ladies' Home Journal* (April, 1928), 36.

14. Advertisement for Fels Naphtha, *American Home* (June, 1937), 64.

15. American Home (April, 1931), 66.

16. "Editorial," *The Ladies' Home Journal* (February, 1928), 32.

17. *Parents' Magazine* (February, 1933), 33.

18. *The Ladies' Home Journal* (March, 1928), 43.

19. For example: "How to buy towels," *The Ladies' Home Journal* (February, 1928), 134, or "When the bride selects bed linens," *The Ladies' Home Journal* (January, 1928), 118.

20. On this point see, for example, John Kenneth Galbraith, *Economics and the Public Purpose* (Boston: Houghton Mifflin, 1973), 29–37.

21. Home economists were very much aware of the change, and of the need to educate women in their responsibilities as consumers. See, for example, Margaret Reid, *The Economics of Household Production* (New York: John Wiley, 1934), Ch. XIII.

22. These advertisements appeared regularly in the monthly editions of *The Ladies' Home Journal* in 1927 and 1928.

23. See, for example, "Keeping in shape," *The Ladies' Home Journal* (April, 1928), 191.

24. See, for example, *The Ladies' Home Journal* (March, 1928), 101.

25. "How we raise our children," *The Ladies' Home Journal* (March, 1928), 193.

26. "Christmas gifts for little girls," *American Home* (December, 1928), 227.

27. "Editorial," *The Ladies' Home Journal* (June, 1918), 4.

28. "Editorial," *Parents' Magazine* (October, 1926), 2.

29. Friedan, 41–42, attributes the concept to the editors of *McCall's*.

30. Remarks made by housewives of the business class in Muncie, Indiana in 1924. Robert S. Lynd and Helen M. Lynd, *Middletown: A Study in Contemporary American Culture* (New York: Harcourt Brace, 1929) 146–147.

31. *American Home* (November, 1931), 81. The idea of converting basements into playrooms was part of the magazine's campaign to encourage home remodelling so that jobs might be created during the Depression. The article on barbecues appeared in *The Ladies' Home Journal* (June, 1937).

32. "She must not bring her troubles to the table," was advice given in an article on Blue Monday, *American Home* (April, 1931), 14. The Steero bouillon ads ran in *The Ladies' Home Journal* in the mid 20's. "Self respect thrives on soap and water," was the motto of the Cleanliness Institute, which placed monthly advertisements in *The Ladies' Home Journal* in 1928.

33. This analysis is paraphrased and abstracted from advertisements in the women's magazines, 1923–1933.

34. Emily Post, *Etiquette,* 5th revised edition (New York, 1937), 823.

35. Lynds, 163 and 171.

36. Lynds, 169.

37. Ibid.

38. *Historic Statistics of the United States, Colonial Times to 1957* (Washington: U.S. Government Printing Office, 1960). These estimates were calculated from Series D 457–463, p. 77, "Private Household Workers Employed," and Series A255, p. 16, "Number of households." As the number of households was overestimated in 1910 and 1920 because of the inclusion of quasi-households in the count (rooming houses, dormitories, etc.) the figures are only a very rough guide.

39. See note 5, Lynes, 156, and Lynds, 170.

40. These phenomena were widely remarked upon. See, Lynds, 25, and 99; Edward Bok, "Editorial," *American Home* (October, 1928), 15 *The Ladies' Home Journal* (March, 1928), 35, an article on buying life insurance: "The old days when the maiden aunt or spinster sister was waiting patiently to take over wiping the noses . . . are rapidly passing. Sister is far too busy paying her own lunch check and insurance policies."

41. *Historical Statistics,* 510.

42. Ibid.

43. *Historical Statistics*, 179.

44. Data from Sigfried Giedion, *Mechanization Takes Command* (New York: Oxford University Press, 1948) 602, *Historical Statistics*, 417 (although the column is headed, "Refrigerators produced," in fact the figures are for refrigerators sold, as is explained on p. 407). The price in 1929 is derived from a Frigidaire advertisement, *The Ladies' Home Journal* (January, 1929), 140.

45. Hazel Kyrk, *Economic Problems of the Family* (New York: Harpers, 1933) 368, reporting a study in *Monthly Labour Review,* 30 (1930), 1209–1252.

46. Lynds, 156–157.

47. *The Ladies' Home Journal* (December, 1908), 46.

48. Lynds, 156. With regard to use of canned goods the Lynds made an interesting observation: "A prejudice lingers among these latter (housewives of the medium and smaller income groups) against feeding one's family out of cans."

49. Lynds, 157.

50. Lynds, 134–135, 153–154.

51. Lynds, 98.

52. *The Ladies' Home Journal* (January, 1908), 44.

53. Lynds, 96, citing a survey in *Zanesville and Thirty-six Other American Cities* (New York: Literary Digest, 1927), 65.

54. Ibid.

55. Lynds, 97.

56. Geidion, 659–703.

57. Helen Sprackling, "The modern bathroom," *Parents' Magazine* (February, 1933), 25.

58. *American Home* (April, 1931), 64, describes, in some detail, how complex a process washing with one of these machines was.

59. Lynds, 174.

60. Ibid.

61. *Historical Statistics,* 526.

62. *The Ladies' Home Journal* (April, 1918), 29.

63. *The Ladies' Home Journal* (February, 1928), 170.

64. See, for example, *American Home* (April, 1931), 48—for a typical shopping list.

65. Lynds, 164–167.

66. Lynds, 155.

67. On the earliest vacuum cleaners see, Geidion, 586.

68. "The after the war woman," *The Ladies' Home Journal* (June, 1918), 13.

69. "Editorial," *The Ladies' Home Journal* (May, 1918), 30; and, "The vanishing servant girl," *The Ladies' Home Journal* (May, 1918), 48.

70. Lynes, 107.

71. Edward Bok, "The American home, the joyous adventure," *American Home* (January, 1929), 287.

72. Compare advertisement for Ivory Soap, *The Ladies' Home Journal* (February, 1908), 5 with Fels Naptha advertisement (January, 1928), 35.

73. These examples were taken from a single issue of *Parents' Magazine* (February, 1933) in which 27 out of 79 advertisements were for drugs or health related items, and two out of the nine featured articles were about diseases.

74. All quotes are from Beulah France, "Home care of contagious diseases," *Parents' Magazine* (March, 1933), 26, 27, 57.

75. *The Ladies' Home Journal* (January, 1933), 13. For a fictionalized version of the same lady, see "Love flies out of the kitchen," *The Ladies' Home Journal* (January, 1933), 42.

76. *The Ladies' Home Journal* (February, 1933), 52.

77. *American Home,* (March, 1933), 50.

78. *The Ladies' Home Journal* (January, 1933), 42.

25 ⚲A "New Frontier" for Women: The Public Policy of the Kennedy Administration

Cynthia E. Harrison

In December 1961, more than four years before the emergence of a vigorous wave of feminism, President John F. Kennedy established the President's Commission on the Status of Women. The creation of the commission, which one newspaper hailed as the launching of a "distaff 'Fair Deal,'" denoted a fundamental shift in federal policy, expressed also in the enactment of equal pay legislation and the prohibition of discrimination against women in the federal civil service.[1] These steps, taken without the impetus of either a widespread feminist movement or a national emergency, marked the federal government's assumption of a new responsibility with regard to equal treatment for women in the labor force. How Kennedy came to appoint such a commission, why the departure in policy took place, and what consequences resulted from the change constitute the subjects of this essay.

Throughout the period 1945 to 1960, government agencies, women's organizations, educators, and journalists expressed concern about proper roles for women. Immediately after the war, those who spoke for working women concentrated on the need to "protect" women in the labor force, including their right to jobs, while providing employment for returning service personnel. Reinstitution of "labor standards" or protective labor laws and the attempt to persuade women to leave their "masculine" jobs for more "feminine" ones in the

From *The Journal of American History* 67 (December, 1980). Copyright Organization of American Historians. Reprinted by permission.

Cynthia E. Harrison is a Ph.D. candidate in history at Columbia University and research fellow in governmental studies at the Brookings Institution. Her research has been supported by the Employment and Training Administration of the United States Department of Labor.

burgeoning clerical and service occupations served both purposes, and both were attempted.[2] A desire to resume "normal" family life and the strong reassertion of traditional sex roles in response to wartime dislocations led many women back to being full-time homemakers.[3]

Later in the 1950s, however, many observers began to voice concern about the educated and talented women who, having taken up careers as full-time homemakers, were denying their talents to their country. Schools and hospitals sorely lacked teachers and nurses. Anxiety over the perceived Soviet threat led many to believe that America needed to harness all its scientific talents, including those of women. These circumstances helped to bring the public's attention to the "under-utilization" of women's abilities.[4]

Although many fields indeed suffered shortages of womanpower, the labor force participation rate of women was actually rising, especially that of married women with children. According to census reports, the proportion of women who worked for wages rose from 31.4 percent in 1950 to 34.8 percent in 1960. Moreover, the proportion of married women, with husbands present, who were employed outside the home increased from 23.8 to 30.5 percent, accelerating a long-term trend. Whereas in 1950, 52.1 percent of women in the labor force were married, by 1960 the percentage had swelled to 59.9. Perhaps most significantly, women who had children under the age of six increased their participation rate by 50 percent (from 12.6 percent in 1950 to almost 19 percent in 1960). The biggest share of this increase occurred early in the decade—by 1955, more than 17 percent of mothers of young children were working.[5]

Despite the mounting numbers of women in paid employment, interest in women's rights and opportunities did not follow a similar pattern of growth. Some, but not all, women's organizations continued to consider women's rights worthy of concern. However, those that did, with the exception of the National Woman's party, viewed it as only one among many worthwhile causes. Attention to equal pay legislation and the Equal Rights Amendment (ERA) declined in the 1950s. No new broad-based women's organization developed to address questions concerning the rights of working women. (In fact, the activist National Women's Trade Union League dissolved in 1950.) Consequently, few of the legal disabilities confronting women were alleviated, employers continued to assign jobs to workers by sex, and pay differentials between male and female workers doing the same work were still a matter of course.[6]

One federal government agency, the Women's Bureau in the Department of Labor, did continue to be concerned with women's status, especially that of women within the labor force. The bureau's active constituency comprised women in labor unions and middle-class women's groups who saw themselves as sympathetic to the needs of working women. Throughout the 1940s and 1950s, the Women's Bureau championed the right of women to work on an equal basis with men and the cause of federal legislation to require equal pay. At the same time, the bureau, which had played a major role in the long struggle to enact protective labor laws for women, was committed to preserving those laws.[7]

This stance of the bureau—advocating equal rights for women without disturbing protective labor legislation—placed it in conflict with women's groups that supported the ERA. The National Federation of Business and Professional Women's Clubs and the National Women's party, both oriented toward middle-class women, provided the nucleus of support for the ERA, while the organizations surrounding the Women's Bureau (for example, the National Women's Trade Union League, the American Association of University Women, the National Consumers League, the National Council of Catholic Women) lobbied in opposition to the amendment. They offered instead the alternative of a national commission on the status of women.

Agitation for a national commission to study the status of women had begun in the 1940s when it appeared that the ERA might be added to the Constitution in gratitude for and in recognition of women's contribution to the war effort. Strong liberal opposition to the ERA developed, however, founded on its apparent threat to hard-won protective labor laws. With the hope of uniting all women's groups behind one proposal, this group of adversaries suggested in 1947 the establishment of a congressional commission on the status of women in lieu of adopting the ERA. They intended to improve women's status without what were perceived to be the damaging consequences of a wide-ranging amendment. Yet they made compromise with ERA advocates virtually impossible by including in the bill to create the commission the statement that "it is the declared policy of the United States that in law and its administration no distinctions on the basis of sex shall be made except such as are reasonably justified by differences in physical structure, biological, or social function." Professional women and those in the better-paying and organized trades viewed protective labor legislation as evidence of a desire to hobble women and handicap their advancement; they supported the ERA and dissented from the philosophy expressed in the new bill. Women who identified with the lowest-paid unorganized women workers deemed protective labor legislation essential and the ERA a meaningless abstraction. They believed that women's wages would decline without minimum wage laws and that women's roles differed from men's in ways that the law should recognize. The fierce dissension among organized women's groups meant that neither the ERA nor a national commission had any reasonable chance of winning the approval of the Congress.[8]

In 1957, however, advocates of a commission received support from a prestigious private source. The National Manpower Council published a report noting the revolution in women's employment and recommending public and private action to enlarge openings for women in the paid labor force and to improve their educational preparation for work. In order to obtain additional necessary information, the council members recommended that the secretary of labor appoint a commission to review federal and state legislation bearing on the employment of women.[9]

The Department of Labor rejected the suggestion. Lack of support from Alice K. Leopold, director of the Women's Bureau, may have been decisive. When the undersecretary of labor asked for her opinion of the National Manpower Council's proposal, she responded that the secretary should "utilize existing facilities, including both Governmental agencies and interested non-governmental organizations" rather than create a commission.[10] Plans to establish a commission on women proceeded no further in the Eisenhower administration, although that administration was not in general unsympathetic toward women's rights. Remarkably, in view of the intense competition to have proposals included in presidential messages, the president endorsed equal pay legislation in the State of the Union Message in 1956 and in annual budget messages and economic reports to the Congress from 1957 through 1961.[11] Still, if the director of the Women's Bureau did not recommend a commission, no internal advisor would plausibly overrule her.

After the election of Kennedy, the new director of the Women's Bureau, Esther Peterson, adopted precisely the opposite position to that of her predecessor. She strongly advocated creation of a commission on women, perhaps because she assumed—correctly—that she would determine the nature and direction of the commission. Kennedy readily assented to her proposal, agreeing even to make it a presidential, rather than a merely departmental, commission. Under Peterson's supervision, the President's Commission on the Status of Women became the centerpiece of the administration's actions on behalf of women, serving to effect specific changes and to heighten public awareness of women's issues.[12]

Kennedy's ready acceptance of Peterson's recommendation to establish a commission on women stemmed at least partially from his political need to "do something for women." Women not only made up more than half the electorate; they were well known to perform most of the less attractive jobs associated with electing Democrats (and Republicans) to office. Moreover, prominent Democratic women from Eleanor Roosevelt on down had assured him that he must recognize this constituency.[13]

Although both Dwight D. Eisenhower and Harry S. Truman were subject to a similar political imperative, they responded mainly by appointing women to highly visible political offices, largely at the entreaty of women party officials. These political women, whose own power derived from their ability to influence patronage, argued that such appointments would inspire appreciation and loyalty from female campaign workers. India Edwards, executive director of the Women's Division of the Democratic National Committee (DNC), who had a close personal relationship with Harry Truman, wielded strong influence, and the President usually acceded to her requests for naming women unless he met opposition from other quarters. Eisenhower was also widely known for his record of choosing women for executive posts, largely at the suggestion of Bertha Adkins, who directed women's activities for the Republican National Committee before she herself accepted a position in the Department of Health, Education, and Welfare.[14]

Because women's issues lacked salience, neither Edwards nor Adkins had any competition for the role of women's spokesperson from any other woman (or man) within the Administration. While it was important to create a "record" with which to impress women voters, it seemingly did not matter if the record were based on appointments or on legislative and executive actions that dealt with discrimination. Neither Truman nor Eisenhower (nor, later, Kennedy) viewed the subject as worthy of his personal attention or the concern of too many advisers. As long as one woman was deemed trustworthy and as long as she did not propose anything that conflicted with the chief executive's policies or philosophy, she enjoyed a relatively free hand. Edwards and Adkins both used their access to foster appointive positions for women.

Margaret Price, chosen by Kennedy to be vice-chairman and director of Women's Activities for the DNC, likewise urged vigorously that Kennedy surpass former administrations in his appointments of women. She prepared a transition document on the records of past administrations in which she included the names and biographies of several potential candidates.[15] Kennedy failed to heed Price's advice, however, and thereby encountered much criticism.

Soon after Kennedy assumed the presidency, Democratic party women began to press him to improve opportunities for women in government. For example, Emma Guffey Miller, a well-known ERA supporter and Democratic national committeewoman from Pennsylvania, protested: "It is a grievous disappointment to the women leaders and ardent workers that so few women have been named to worthwhile positions; that the few who have been named by you are merely replacing other women, while the important posts, formerly filled by women, are now being handed over to men." She concluded with a warning: "As a woman of long political experience, I feel the situation has become serious and I hope whoever is responsible for it may be made to realize that the results may well be disastrous."[16]

In fact, Kennedy's record of appointments did not compare so unfavorably with that of his predecessors. He made only ten Senate-confirmed appointments of women to policy-making executive and judicial posts, but Truman, who won high praise for his record, in a comparable period, had made only fifteen and Eisenhower only fourteen. None of the presidents, Kennedy included, utilized the talents of women significantly. In all three administrations, women held only 2.4 percent of all appointive positions. However, Kennedy's neglect of visible appointments brought reproach. Unlike Eisenhower and Franklin D. Roosevelt, Kennedy failed to appoint a women to a cabinet position. Clayton Fritchey, director of public affairs of the United States Mission to the United Nations and long-time Democratic "pol," pointed out to the president that "*notable* appointments" constituted important symbols to women, and that, as of July 1963, "the present Administration has not done all it could in this respect. . . . Today there are no really famous women serving the Government."[17]

The outcry, therefore, probably resulted from three factors: that expectations were not met, since Kennedy's admirers expected him to exceed the performance of his predecessors; that appointments of women were not so visible as in previous administrations and were not so highlighted by the press; and, most important, that the women party loyalists who expected to control appointments of women lacked access to the chief executive. The Democratic party women, who since the Roosevelt years had been rewarding loyal party supporters with administration posts, suddenly found themselves thwarted and they resented their sudden loss of influence. Edwards remarked that in the Kennedy administration "there was no one at the DNC or in the White House who had any influence with them when it came to women's affairs." Price reportedly never held a private conversation with Kennedy. Emma Guffey Miller voiced the dismay of party women over the exclusion of Price from White House inner circles: "the administration has been lax in recognizing Democratic women. . . . In the Roosevelt and Truman Administrations, the Vice Chairman [and head of women's affairs] was always consulted when women were being named to important posts, but now all Margaret Price knows is what she sees in the newspapers. This is not going to help the Party."[18]

The White House appointments procedure did exclude Price. Kennedy, wrote Theodore Sorensen, "wanted a ministry of talent." To get it, the Kennedy staff broke away from past methods of operation with many of their sensitivities to political "musts" and a well-established role for women, and conducted the search from the White House. Except for minor patronage positions, the President's aides ignored the DNC, figuring that it would not be a source of likely candidates. The Talent Search instituted no compensatory method of including women. Dan Fenn, who ran the recruitment effort, had no sense at all that women represented a pool of ability which should be tapped. Moreover, women were not likely to be found in the places the Kennedy staff did look. The quest centered on elite universities, boards and executive suites of major corporations, and prestigious law firms where women were few in number. The blatant discrimination which kept women out of high-level jobs did not have to come from the Kennedy team; it had already taken place.[19]

Margaret Price could not overcome the consequences of the new Kennedy appointment process. First, Kennedy's association with the DNC differed markedly from that of former presidents. The national committees' power had started to decline in general as primaries and television advertising began to play a greater role in the selection of the candidates. Kennedy's political organization had been largely an independent creation, based on developing contacts in local areas, and run by close personal associates. He did not have a history of working with the DNC and had little reason to turn to its officers for counsel of any kind. Second, Margaret Price was herself very deferential, unwilling to fight to build a power base. When Kennedy initially declined to address the biennial Campaign Conference for Democratic Women, a gathering of more than three thousand, Price accepted the dictum. India Edwards, on the other hand, wrote to the President threatening to cancel the meeting, and Kennedy acquiesced. Third, as a member of the reform wing of the Democratic party in Michigan, Price felt less commitment to the patronage aspect of party politics; she viewed herself less an advocate of women than an advocate among women for the Democratic party, and she did not work as hard for distaff appointments as Edwards had. Calvin Mackenzie observed in his book on the politics of appointments that "the surest way for a group to shut itself out of the appointment process is for it to blunder into a strategy of reticence." That was just what Price unwittingly did. Finally, Price could not claim that Kennedy's failure to appoint more women would bring retaliation at the polls because Esther Peterson, the Director of the

Women's Bureau and Assistant Secretary of Labor, was making sure that Kennedy had plenty of evidence to assert that he had a genuine interest in the status of women.[20]

Kennedy's association with Peterson dated from his earliest days in the Congress when she was a lobbyist for the Amalgamated Clothing Workers and he sat on the House Education and Labor Committee. He had therefore known her for more than a decade, during which she had earned a reputation with the Congress for being a well-prepared and effective advocate of labor's position. She joined Kennedy's campaign before the primaries and worked to build labor support for him, while most other labor leaders supported Hubert Humphrey or Stuart Symington. To reward her efforts during the campaign, Kennedy offered Peterson her choice of administration jobs. When she selected the Women's Bureau, Kennedy chided her, saying, "You don't just want to be director of the Women's Bureau, do you?" and within eight months he elevated her to a new position, assistant secretary of labor, a position she held in addition to being Women's Bureau chief. As assistant secretary, Peterson spoke with far more authority than she could have had merely as director of the Women's Bureau. No previous chief executive had ever recognized the Women's Bureau in this way.[21] Her assertiveness in her dual capacities gave her an added edge of effectiveness, and Emma Guffey Miller, excluded from the inner circles of power, lamented the ascendancy of a woman "of the Esther Peterson type [who] goes out of her way to do the contrary thing." Peterson, she felt, was not one of the "women who are for women."[22]

Peterson may not have shared Emma Guffey Miller's view of what made a woman be "for women," but she did pursue her own plan to elevate women's status. Peterson, coming out of the labor movement, was an advocate of protective labor laws for women and therefore an opponent of the ERA that Emma Guffey Miller and many other party women, themselves middle-class professionals, had championed. Nevertheless, while cognizant of the widespread desire to protect the family, including women's special relationship to it, Peterson believed in women's right to contribute to the society in ways other than as wives and mothers. Furthermore, she had long been involved in working to organize women, in cooperating with the Women's Bureau, and in working with women's organizations such as the National Women's Trade Union League to achieve long-desired reforms—a commission on women, equal pay legislation, inclusion of the lowest-paying occupations (which employed large numbers of women) under minimum wage legislation, and amelioration of some of the conditions working women encountered. As director of the Women's Bureau she aimed to accomplish these goals. The important roles women were playing in the paid labor force and the interest of women's organizations and educators gave potency to her efforts to augment the influence of the Women's Bureau.

Although the Republican Women's Bureau head Leopold refused to endorse a commission (and lacked the attributes to achieve much else), the creation of the President's Commission on the Status of Women cannot be attributed merely to the presence of a Democratic administration. During the Truman years, the status of women aroused more discussion than it did later. Agitation for a national commission was at its peak. Truman took no such step because Edwards provided certain evidence of Truman's regard for women and because no woman came forward with sufficient authority to urge Truman to follow a different course of action. Frieda Miller, the director of the Women's Bureau from 1944 through 1952, whose agenda was virtually identical to Peterson's, had no White House entrée at all. But Kennedy's ties to labor were closer than Truman's, and Peterson, an astute politician with a strong labor background, had access to the highest levels of executive power. Thus, she acted as the catalyst that resulted in the Kennedy administration's unprecedented response to women's changing roles. The Women's Bureau's role as the source of effective policy innovation was new in the Kennedy years. The program that Peterson implemented, in lieu of focusing on executive appointments for women to governmental posts, had two main facets, both long sought by herself and her associates—equal pay legislation and a commission on the status of women.[23]

Peterson proposed that Kennedy appoint a commission on the status of women largely because of her concern about the negative impact of the ERA. Kennedy had unwittingly expressed support for the ERA during the presidential campaign, and Peterson feared the consequences of the endorsement. In a memorandum of June 2, 1961, to Secretary of Labor Arthur Goldberg, Peterson asserted that "such a commission would substitute constructive recommendations for the present troublesome and futile agitation about the 'equal rights amendment.' "[24]

Still, Peterson's aversion to the ERA was not her only motive for establishing the commission. The memorandum went on to suggest that "the commission would help the nation set forth before the world the story of women's progress in a free, democratic society, and to move further towards full partnership, creative use of skills, and genuine equality of opportunity." Peterson did in fact use the commission to educate certain facets of the American public and to help advance programs and policies already initiated by administration and government women.

Kennedy created the President's Commission on the Status of Women on December 14, 1961, just six months after Peterson's memo. Its stated purpose was "to review progress and make recommendations as needed for constructive action" in the areas of private and federal employment policies and practices, federal social insurance and tax laws, federal and state protective labor legislation, treatment of women under the law, and provision of necessary family services.[25]

Membership on the commission and its subsidiary bodies represented many constituencies. Fifteen women served with eleven men on the commission itself, with ten members of the commission coming from the federal government, including the attorney general, the chairman of the Civil Service Commission, and the secretaries of Commerce, Agriculture, Labor, and Health, Education, and Welfare. Eleanor Roosevelt bestowed considerable prestige on the commission by accepting appointment as its "chairman." Peterson, with Goldberg, dominated the selection procedures, choosing from women's organizations, labor unions, educational institutions, and governmental agencies, to supply more than 120 participants for the commission and its seven technical committees. No official of the National Woman's party was invited to join the commission, although Peterson did include two women identified with the pro-ERA National Federation of Business and Professional Women's Clubs. A commission without any ERA supporters would lack credibility, and Peterson cleared the way for the participation by omitting a statement of purpose indicating a preconceived position on the amendment.

Significantly, no women with an exclusively political party background received an invitation to join the commission. Edwards related in her memoir that a newspaperwoman had asked her, "How can it be that a commission on the status of women could be appointed and India Edwards, who has done more for women than any other living woman, is not on the commission?" Edwards herself was not surprised, in view of the diminished role of the DNC with respect to women in the administration: "My being overlooked was understandable to me. How different from the days of President Truman's Administration, when the name of every woman proposed by anyone else for appointment by the President was submitted to me for an OK." Political women wielded little influence regarding appointments to the commission, and Peterson later recalled that she never considered placing a political woman on the commission. She did not view the commission's goals as being relevant to the aims of women who had had careers in political parties. Katherine Ellickson, assistant director of the social security department of the American Federation of Labor-Congress of Industrial Organizations, became executive secretary of the commission and headed the small paid staff; Peterson herself, as executive vice-chairman, held a key place. Clearly, labor union women were "in" and politicos were "out."[26]

The Women's Bureau and Peterson maintained a careful watch on the president's commission. Women's Bureau personnel and sympathizers dominated the commission's secretariat, which implemented all commission and committee requests, planned meetings, answered mail, and communicated with other government agencies between commission meetings. Since the commission met only eight times in the two years of its existence and was robbed of its chairman by the death of Eleanor Roosevelt in 1962 (the administration decided not to replace her), the staff exerted a great deal of influence.

The Women's Bureau, the commission staff, and the commission members viewed the controversy over the ERA as a matter of paramount concern. Improperly handled, the dispute could render the commission nugatory. Hyman Bookbinder, representing the secretary of commerce, broached the issue at the first meeting, feeling, he said, like "the proverbial fool who likes to move in where angels fear to tread." Remarking that the amendment had "divided the country" for years, he asserted that "if this Commission does nothing else [but] get an accommodation of views on this difficult and delicate area, we will have made a substantial contribution." Viola Hymes, president of the National Council of Jewish Women, agreed that the ERA had been "the most divisive . . . issue . . . among women's organizations," which had frozen their positions on it and had not reexamined them for twenty-five years. The commission would, she felt, "enable the women's organizations to take a new look in the light of developments and changes which will be very helpful." "Maybe," she suggested, "the women's groups will get together." To this Peterson declared: "It will be worth the Commission if we do it."[27]

Although the commission claimed to be approaching the subject of the ERA with no preconceived position, there was never a chance that it would endorse the amendment. By design, too many commissioners came from labor or conservative religious groups that opposed it. Nevertheless, the Committee on Civil and Political Rights, the sub-unit of the commission under whose purview the issue fell, worked hard to formulate a position that the commission would accept, short of completely condemning the ERA. At the committee's request, the commission report ultimately stated that, while "equality of rights under the law for all persons, male or female, is so basic to democracy . . . that it must be reflected in the fundamental law of the land," the commissioners believed such equality to be embodied in the Fifth and Fourteenth Amendments. This premise required, however, validation by the Supreme Court, and they urged appropriate test cases. In view of this conviction, the commissioners concluded that "a constitutional amendment need not now be sought in order to establish this principle." The "now" in this last sentence was added at the request of ERA supporter Marguerite Rawalt, a day after the initial wording was adopted.[28]

This carefully constructed position constituted a viable compromise. Partisans of protective laws for women believed that the Supreme Court would continue to uphold such laws as reasonable under the Fourteenth Amendment, even while the justices affirmed women's equality in other areas. For their part, ERA proponents managed to forestall outright rejection of the amendment by the commission—a clear possibility—and, still more, elicited acknowledgement of its potential necessity should the Supreme Court prove reluctant to act. Thus, a breach over the ERA was avoided. Ellickson recalled: "We were all relieved when, under Miss Hickey's skillful chairing, the Commission members, including Rawalt, agreed on this section!"[29]

While the commission discussed the ERA almost gingerly, the members debated the underlying issue of protective labor legislation for women more vehemently than any other. After much discussion, and heavily influenced by Mary Dublin Keyserling (future director of the Women's Bureau), final recommendations endorsed enhancing protective laws for women rather than demanding their application to male workers. Although everyone agreed that extending such labor legislation to men was ultimately desirable, the protectionists obtained a recommendation from the commission for the interim, advocating that laws for women be maintained, strengthened, and expanded.[30] However because the commission did endorse constitutional equality for women, and in a manner acceptable to proponents of protective laws, the subject of the laws themselves lost its power to destroy the cordial working relationship of the members. The commission therefore held together and completed its agenda.

The ERA and protective laws for women aside, most questions elicited general agreement from the start. During its brief life, the commission wholeheartedly lent its prestige to several administration actions on behalf of women. The most significant concerned the Civil Service Commission (CSC).

In preparation for the announcement of the president's commission, Peterson urged administration officials to make the federal government a "showcase" of equal opportunity. A CSC review of requests by agency heads for eligible applicants from the civil service lists showed that only 16 percent of requests to fill places in the lowest grades (one through four) specified men, while an overwhelming 94 percent of those in grades thirteen through fifteen excluded women. The CSC, however, had no power to forbid agency heads from making requests by sex. Except for a brief interlude in the early 1930s, an 1870 law had been interpreted to mean that the president could not prohibit an agency head within the civil service from designating whether he preferred a male or a female for a given position. The president's commission suggested a reexamination of the statute at its first meeting, and on April 9, 1962, it requested a ruling from the attorney general on the long-standing interpretation of the law.[31]

When the attorney general proffered the desired reinterpretation, that the president could indeed stop the discriminatory practice, President Kennedy responded immediately. He directed John Macy, chairman of the CSC, to ensure "that selection for any career position will be made solely on the basis of ability to meet the requirements of the position, and without regard to sex." Macy was to provide "Government-wide leadership" to investigate and eliminate discriminatory practices, even in agencies not subject to civil service jurisdiction.[32] The order itself could hardly guarantee equal opportunities for women in the civil service, but it opened the way for monitoring and enforcement in the future. More important, the policy statement constituted a significant symbol and a standard against which the government's performance could be measured.

Peterson also used the president's commission to advance the cause of the other single most important item on her agenda for women—equal pay legislation. Even before the president's commission was launched, Peterson had concerned herself with the problem of moving an equal pay bill through the Congress. Without detailing a full history of the passage of the Equal Pay Act, it can be stated in sum that the efforts of the Women's Bureau, under Peterson, successfully broke the eighteen-year legislative stalemate by a combination of data-gathering and lobbying. President Kennedy signed the bill on June 10, 1963. An amendment to the Fair Labor Standards Act, the Equal Pay Act stipulated that employers involved in interstate commerce could no longer discriminate among employees on the basis of sex by paying unequal wages for jobs which require "equal skill, effort and responsibility and which are performed under similar working conditions." Compromises resulted in the exclusion from coverage of large numbers of women and the substitution of "equal" work for "comparable" work. Furthermore, "equal pay for equal work" could mean little to the majority of women who were working in sexually segregated occupations. Still, the new law represented the first federal antidiscrimination legislation enacted specifically on behalf of women and directed toward private employers.[33]

Although its focus was narrow, the Equal Pay Act marked the entrance of the federal government into the field of safeguarding the right of women to hold employment on the same basis as men. Traditionally, the business community had justified paying women less by claiming that women worked for "pin money," not to support their families. By making wage discrimination illegal, the federal government undermined this view and implicitly supported the contention that paid employment was consonant with a woman's obligations as wife and mother. The federal government's acceptance of responsibility for ensuring women equitable treatment represented a new commitment.

The combined initiatives of the president's commission and of women in the government, including Peterson, led to innovations in other areas during Kennedy's administration. The Congress enacted legislation in 1962 to assist states in setting up day-care facilities and in May 1963 appropriated $800,000 for that purpose, the first such expenditure since World War II. The president's commission convinced Secretary of Defense Robert McNamara to submit legislation removing statutory restrictions on the number of women officers in the military, a problem the Defense Advisory Council on Women in the Services had hitherto been unable to resolve.[34] Both steps, however small in themselves, indicated a growing recognition on the federal government's part that women's sphere outside the home was expanding.

While advocating enlargement of women's roles, however, the president's commission took care to acknowledge the importance of women's traditional responsibilities. Conflict between the desire and/or need of women to work and the ideal of women at home as wives and mothers resulted in ambivalence, which pervaded the commission's discussions and reports, about a woman's right to define her role. The commission's most frequent justification for promoting opportunities for women in the work force rested on the premise that women needed to work to support their families. All concurred that a woman whose family required her earnings to make ends meet had ample reason to secure employment. Yet, in a burgeoning consumer society, where a college education was soon to be considered the birthright of every child, the concept of "need" broadened to include most working women. By advocating the provision of day-care facilities and rejecting discrimination in favor of male "heads of households," the president's commission certainly appeared to many to be encouraging married women to work. Although the commission attempted to avoid such an implication, it found it difficult to do so.[35]

On October 11, 1963, the commission presented a sixty-page report that concluded its task. After two years of study and occasional meetings, the commission had culled numerous recommendations from its subcommittees. With virtual unanimity, it endorsed improving women's access to education, with benefit of skilled counseling; increasing child care services and aid to working mothers; encouraging equal employment opportunity and availability of part-time employment; securing additional financial benefits for low-income women; supporting equality of rights under the law—preferably under the Fifth and Fourteenth Amendments rather than the ERA; and increasing participation of women in government. It also asked the president to provide for continuing governmental action of behalf of women, and in response, on November 1, 1963, Kennedy established the Interdepartmental Committee on the Status of Women and the Citizens' Advisory Council on the Status of Women. These two groups were to evaluate progress made, provide counsel, and stimulate action.[36] The commission recognized the administration's failure to appoint large numbers of women to high positions, but it did not take an emphatic position on this issue.[37]

While advocating freedom of choice for women, the commission's recommendations proceeded from its view of their special function and characteristics as mothers and homemakers. The report maintained that "widening the choices for women beyond their doorstep does not imply neglect of their education for responsibilities in the home." At another point, the report cautioned that "experience is needed in determining what constitutes unjustified discrimination in the treatment of women workers"—an indication that, because women had special attributes, the commission could envision "justified" discrimination. The commissioners therefore did not endorse adding "sex" to Executive Order 10925, which barred discrimination by federal contractors on the basis of race, creed, color, or national origin. They explained that "discrimination based on sex . . . involves problems sufficiently different from discrimination based on the other factors listed." Their neglect of inequities facing women in the armed services and in the social security system followed from the same belief. Not surprisingly, the commission falied to explore its own assumptions about women, nor did it question the prevailing sex-role structure. It could not, therefore, address root causes of discrimination. In order to effect the moderate change the commissioners had in mind, such an examination was not necessary.[38]

When the commission presented its report to Kennedy, an aide, Myer Feldman, took advantage of the occasion to review the administration's actions in the interest of women. Apart from the commission, Feldman listed the equal pay law; increased coverage under the Fair Labor Standards Act (May 1961) to include retail workers, a large number of whom were women; the Consumer Advisory Council (established July 18, 1962, and headed by Helen G. Conoyer, dean of the School of Home Economics at Cornell University);[39] elimination of the quota system applied to officers in the armed forces; increased provision for day care under welfare statutes; and the new ruling regarding nondiscrimination in the federal civil service.[40] Appointment of women to high governmental and judicial posts was not among the achievements recounted.

The President's Commission on the Status of Women was the brainchild of a labor union woman. Because the labor movement had a history of attempting to achieve goals for women at least partially through federal legislation and executive action, a presidential commission seemed to Peterson and her colleagues to be an appropriate avenue for change. Kennedy, breaking with tradition, heeded the advice of a woman with a labor union background instead of one with political debts to repay by administrative appointment, and in 1961 federal policy toward women veered in a new direction.

The change was significant because the attempt to elevate women's position solely by appointing women to high governmental posts represented perforce a limited strategy. Women appointees in a period in which the status of women was low could not function on behalf of women, even if they wished to maintain their own credibility and to escape being labeled as merely token appointees. To say this is not to denigrate the motives of those interested in appointments for women. They believed that their route did assist women generally by providing female role models, and they also believed that women should have these opportunities in recognition of their own talents. The benefits, however, did not appear to filter down.[41]

The course that Kennedy followed constituted a potentially more fruitful one for advancing the status of women, although the events that ensued were unlikely to have been precisely what the members of the president's commission anticipated. The commission made it clear that it did not regard sexual discrimination to be in the same category as racial bias, and thereby in some respects it retarded effective action toward eradication. Nevertheless, the net effect of the list Feldman described was positive. The Equal Pay Act, civil service reform, and the establishment of the commission constituted early, if minor, successes that helped lead to the quest for more meaningful change.[42] The creation of the president's commission gave a new-found legitimacy to the struggle against discrimination based on sex and initiated a national discussion that continued into the

1980s. As Betty Friedan wrote in 1963, "the very existence of the President's Commission on the Status of Women, under Eleanor Roosevelt's leadership, creates a climate where it is possible to recognize and do something about discrimination against women, in terms not only of pay but of the subtle barriers to opportunity."[43]

Furthermore, as a result of the creation of the national commission, every state instituted similar commissions, which provided vehicles for the participation of many women who had not before been engaged in such issues. The Interdepartmental Committee on the Status of Women and the Citizens' Advisory Council on the Status of Women chose to host annual conventions of the state commissions, creating networks among their women members. The federal bodies sought to contain and direct the agenda, however, and as a consequence in 1966 a group of dissatisfied participants at the Third National Conference of Commissions on the Status of Women were impelled to form the National Organization for Women (NOW).[44]

NOW's founders recognized the intrinsic limitations of governmental bodies "to break through the silken curtain of prejudice and discrimination against women." They acknowledged a debt to the commissions, but indicated that they regarded their recommendations as inadequate and unfulfilled promises. "The excellent reports of the President's Commission on the Status of Women and of the State Commissions have not been fully implemented. . . . They have no power to enforce their recommendations. . . . The reports of these Commissions have, however, created a basis upon which it is now possible to build." The architects of NOW established the organization in order to commence "a civil rights movement for women" that would confront law and custom "to win for women the final right to be fully free and equal human beings." Among the crucial items on the new movement's agenda were "a different concept of marriage, an equitable sharing of the responsibilities of home and children and the economic burdens of their support"—in short, a transformation of sex roles.[45]

Had the women's movement not emerged, enactment of equal pay legislation, prohibition of the most obvious and blatant forms of sex discrimination within the federal government, and creation of federal panels on women's status could all quickly have become dead letters. The president's commission, which endorsed these preliminary reforms, neither predicted nor recommended a feminist indictment of the entire sex-role structure. Nevertheless, the initiators of these early moderate changes, however unwittingly, helped elicit just such a challenge.

NOTES

1. *Christian Science Monitor*, Dec. 15, 1961. The National Organization for Women, the first organized feminist group of the 1960s, was founded in June 1966. The commission also predated the publication of Betty Friedan, *The Feminine Mystique* (New York, 1963), customarily considered one of the earliest harbingers of the women's movement, by more than a year.

2. Protective labor legislation in this context refers to those laws which regulated the conditions under which women worked. Such statutes established the minimum wages women could be paid, the maximum number of hours they could labor, the largest amount of weight they could lift, how late at night they could work, and which occupations they could practice.

3. For a fuller discussion of the experience of the postwar period, see William Henry Chafe, *The American Woman: Her Changing Social, Economic and Political Roles, 1920–1970* (New York, 1972), 192–244; Lois W. Banner, *Women in Modern America: A Brief History* (New York, 1974); National Manpower Council, *Womanpower: A Statement by the National Manpower Council with Chapters by the Council Staff* (New York, 1957); Karen Anderson, "The Impact of World War II in the Puget Sound Area on the Status of Women and the Family" (Ph.D. diss., Duke University, 1976).

4. See the sources cited in 3. For a discussion of women and higher education in this period, see Marian E. Strobel, "Ideology and Women's Higher Education, 1945–1960" (Ph.D. diss., Duke University, 1976).

5. United States, Bureau of the Census, *Statistical Abstract of the United States, 1975* (Washington, 1975), 346–47. For a full examination of this phenomenon, see Valerie Kincade Oppenheimer, *The Female Labor Force in the United States: Demographic and Economic Factors Governing Its Growth and Changing Composition* (Berkeley, 1970).

6. The National Woman's party first proposed an Equal Rights Amendment (ERA) in 1923, which read: "Men and woman shall have equal rights throughout the United States and every place subject to its jurisdiction." The present wording—"Equality of rights under the law shall not be denied or abridged by the United States or by any State on account of sex"—was adopted in 1943. Chafe, *American Woman*, 112; Equal Rights Amendment Project, *The Equal Rights Amendment: A Bibliographic Study* (Westport, 1976), xiii–xiv; *Life and Labor Bulletin*, no. 113 (June 1950), "Miscellany, Congressional Testimony (Special Reports)," box 10, Papers of the Women's Joint Congressional Committee (Library of Congress).

7. See Judith Sealander, "The Women's Bureau, 1920–1950: Federal Reaction to Female Wage Earning" (Ph.D. diss., Duke University, 1977). Upon her retirement as director of the Women's Bureau in 1944, Mary Anderson became chair of the National Committee on Equal Pay, composed of representatives from interested women's groups.

8. Chafe, *American Woman*, 187–88; Minutes, 1947, box 8, Papers of the Women's Joint Congressional Committee; U.S. Congress, House, *A Bill to Establish a Commission on the Legal Status of Women in the United States, to Declare a Policy as to Distinctions Based on Sex, in Law and Administration, and for Other Purposes*, H.R. 2007, 80th Cong., 1st sess., 1947. The House held hearings on the ERA in 1945 and 1948; the Senate, in 1945 and 1956. Although attention to the ERA

waned during the 1950s, the pressure of active party women led both national party platforms to endorse the amendment (with no tangible results) in every presidential election year. See Loretta J. Blahna, "The Rhetoric of the Equal Rights Amendment" (Ph.D. diss., Duke University, 1976).

9. National Manpower Council, *Womanpower*, 6. The National Manpower Council, a group of sixteen, comprising educators, business people, labor union officials, and journalists, was established at Columbia University under a grant from the Ford Foundation in 1951. At the time of the *Womanpower* study, the council included one woman.

10. Alice K. Leopold to the Undersecretary [James T. O'Connell], April 15, 1957, "Women," box 5, Papers of Millard Cass, Records of the Office of the Secretary of Labor, RG 174 (National Archives).

11. "Equal Pay–Administration Support," Jan. 24, 1961, Equal Pay–1961 folder, box 7, Office Files (Women's Bureau, Department of Labor, Washington).

12. Despite common beliefs concerning the lack of effectiveness of presidential commissions in general, a study by Thomas R. Wolanin, *Presidential Advisory Commissions: Truman to Nixon* (Madison, 1975), reaches a different conclusion. Wolanin evaluated all the commissions appointed by the five presidents, and concluded that 58 percent led to substantial government actions. Even this figure is low, however, because of the inclusion of President Richard M. Nixon who departed from tradition by paying much less attention to the commissions he created than had his predecessors. John F. Kennedy's response to his commissions was very supportive. Wolanin's judgment on the President's Commission on the Status of Women, which he claims was less effective than Kennedy's other commissions, fails to take into account actions taken during the life of the commission, looking only at responses to final reports.

13. Joseph P. Lash, *Eleanor: The Years Alone* (New York, 1972), p. 312.

14. India Edwards, *Pulling No Punches: Memoirs of a Woman in Politics* (New York, 1977); Republican National Committee, News Release, July 30, 1953, General Correspondence, 1953–54, box 2, India Edwards Papers (Harry S. Truman Library, Independence, Mo.).

15. Margaret Price to John F. Kennedy, Dec. 8, 1960, "Women–Role in Government," box 1072, Pre-Presidential Papers (John F. Kennedy Library, Waltham, Mass.).

16. Emma Guffey Miller to John F. Kennedy, Feb. 21, 1961, PL9, box 696, White House Central Files, *ibid.* See also Muriel Ferris to Lawrence P. O'Brien et al., May 15, 1961, HU3, box 374, *ibid.*

17. Karen Keesling and Suzanne Cavanagh, "Women Presidential Appointees Serving or Having Served in Full-Time Positions Requiring Senate Confirmation 1912–1977," report no. 78-73G, March 23, 1978, Congressional Research Service (Library of Congress). Oveta Culp Hobby served as secretary of health, education, and welfare from 1953 to 1955, and Frances Perkins held the position of secretary of labor from 1933 to 1945. Clayton Fritchey to John F. Kennedy, July 7, 1963, HU3, box 364, White House Central Files (Kennedy Library); President's Commission on the Status of Women, transcript of the meeting of Oct. 2, 1962, Washington, D.C., 252–53 (Women's Bureau). For 1951–1952, women held 79 of 3,273 appointments; for 1958–1959, 84 of 3,491; and for 1961–1962, 93 of 3,807.

18. Edwards, *Pulling No Punches,* 231–32, 252; Miller to Katie Louchheim, Jan. 26, 1963, Department of State Letters of Congratulations M-Z 1962, box C17, Katie S. Louchheim Papers (Library of Congress).

19. G. Calvin Mackenzie, *The Politics of Presidential Appointments* (New York, 1981), pp. 23–33, 84, 198, 255–59; Telephone interview with Dan Fenn, Jr., May 15, 1981, Boston, Mass.

20. Mackenzie, *The Politics of Presidential Appointments,* pp. 84, 196–97, 209; India Edwards to John F. Kennedy, Apr. 8, 1962, Office of Women's Activities, DNC, box 2, Kenneth O'Donnell to India Edwards, Apr. 10, 1962, 1960 clipping material and correspondence, box 1, India Edwards Papers, (Lyndon Baines Johnson Library, Austin, Tex.); *New York Times,* May 23, 1962; Theodore C. Sorensen, *Kennedy* (New York, 1965), 124–25. Myer Feldman, a Kennedy aide, has asserted that Margaret Price and President Kennedy "enjoyed an excellent relationship," but her influence with respect to women remains obscure. Myer Feldman to Cynthia E. Harrison, Oct. 3, 1979, letter in Harrison's possession. Note also that, by the time Price took over, the Women's Division of the Democratic National Committee had been abolished as a separate entity.

21. Sorensen, *Kennedy,* 123–24; Esther Peterson, telephone interview with Harrison, Oct. 4, 1974; Peterson, interview with Harrison, Washington, D.C., Feb. 27, 1978.

22. Miller to Louchheim, Jan. 20, 1962, Department of State Letters of Congratulations M-Z 1962.

23. Sorenson, *Kennedy,* 439–41. For an argument that the Women's Bureau had been handicapped by the political clumsiness of its directors virtually since its inception, see Sealander, "Women's Bureau."

24. *Washington Post,* Oct. 25, 1960; Peterson to Arthur Goldberg, June 2, 1961, FG 737, box 206, White House Central Files (Kennedy Library). Peterson later became an active supporter of ERA.

25. Executive Order 10980, Dec. 14, 1961, 3 C.F.R. (1959–1963), 500–01.

26. For a complete list of participants, see *American Women: Report of the President's Commission on the Status of Women,* 1963 (Washington, D.C., 1963), 77–85. Edwards, *Pulling No Punches,* 231–32. Mary Hilton, who had served as Chief of the Research Division of the Women's Bureau from 1949 to 1955, was designated Katherine Ellickson's "Special Assistant."

27. President's Commission on the Status of Women, transcript of the meeting of Feb. 12, 1962, Washington, D.C., 51–53 (Women's Bureau).

28. *Ibid.,* 131–32; Minutes of the First Meeting—Feb. 12–13, 1962, President's Commission on the Status of Women (PCSW) Document 18, Papers of the President's Commission on the Status of Women (Women's Bureau); Committee on Civil and Political Rights of the President's Commission on the Status of Women, interim report, April 11, 1963, p. 17, Papers of the President's Commission on the Status of Women, folder 21–22 (Kennedy Library); *American Women,* 44–45; President's Commission on the Status of Women, transcript of the meeting of April 24, 1963, Washington, D.C., 461–62 (Women's Bureau).

29. Katherine Pollack Ellickson, "The President's Commission on the Status of Women: Its Formation, Functioning, and Contribution," Jan. 1976, p. 12 (Walter P. Reuther Library, Wayne State University, Detroit, Mich.).

30. *American Women,* 37.

31. "Employment Policies and Practices of the Federal Government," PCSW Document 17, Papers of the President's Commission on the Status of Women (Women's Bureau). The 1870 law reads: "Women may, in the direction of the head of any department, be appointed to any of the clerkships therein authorized by law, upon the same requisites and conditions, and with the same compensations as are prescribed for men." Executive Departments and Government Officers and Employees, 5 U.S.C. sec. 33 (1958). Interestingly, Herbert Hoover had issued an order prohibiting selection by sex, but his ruling was reversed by Franklin D. Roosevelt at the request of Mary Anderson, director of the Women's Bureau. Anderson feared that, because of the preference given to veterans in the civil service, women would never be hired if agency heads could not specify sex. See Mary Anderson, *Women at Work: The Autobiography of Mary Anderson as Told to Mary N. Winslow* (Minneapolis, 1951), 153. Committee on Federal Employment Policies and Practices of the President's Commission on the Status of Women, "Activities since April 9, 1962," Document 1, Papers of the President's Commission on the Status of Women (Women's Bureau).

32. Robert F. Kennedy to John F. Kennedy, June 14, 1962, John F. Kennedy to Eleanor Roosevelt, June 15, 1962, file 4526, and John W. Macy (form letter), July 24, 1962, file 4644, Eleanor Roosevelt Papers (Franklin D. Roosevelt Library, Hyde Park, N.Y.).

33. Fair Labor Standards Act of 1938, as amended, 29 U.S.C. sec. 206, subsec. d (1964). Judith Hole and Ellen Levine assert that "some activists consider the Equal Pay Act the only law dealing with sex discrimination that is anywhere near properly enforced." Judith Hole and Ellen Levine, *Rebirth of Feminism* (New York, 1971), 29.

34. *New York Times,* May 15, 1963; "Status of Women under Proposed Legislation Regulating from the Bolte Committee Report," May 18, 1962, file 4644, Eleanor Roosevelt Papers; and Robert S. McNamara to Eleanor Roosevelt, July 10, 1962, *ibid.*

35. See, for example, *American Women,* 17, and *Report of the Committee on Home and Community to the President's Commission on the Status of Women* (Washington, 1963), 31.

36. *American Women;* Executive Order 11126, 3 C.F.R. (1959–1963), 791–93.

37. *American Women,* 52.

38. *Ibid.,* 10, 16, 30.

39. *New York Times,* Jan. 19, 1962.

40. Feldman to John F. Kennedy, Oct. 9, 1963, FG 737, box 206, White House Central Files (Kennedy Library).

41. For a discussion of women in appointive positions, see Elsie L. George, "The Women Appointees of the Roosevelt and Truman Administrations: A Study of Their Impact and Effectiveness" (Ph.D. diss., American University, 1972).

42. Thomas J. Morain, "The Emergence of the Women's Movement, 1960–1970" (Ph.D. diss., University of Iowa, 1974), cites Murray Edelman's thesis that "success in achieving a political objective leads to demands for larger amounts of the same benefits" to support his argument that the equal pay law and civil service reform influenced later developments in a positive way. See also Murray Edelman, *The Symbolic Uses of Politics* (Chicago, 1964).

43. Betty Friedan, *The Feminine Mystique* (New York, 1974), 361.

44. The analysis of the impact of the president's commission on the formation of NOW and the rise of the women's movement was developed by Jo Freeman. See Jo Freeman, *The Politics of Women's Liberation* (New York, 1975), 44–70. Freeman focuses on the development of networks, the compilation of data, and the creation of a "climate of expectations." Hole and Levine stated that the "Commission's existence and its report created the political and psychological framework for the growth of the current women's rights movement." Hole and Levine, *Rebirth of Feminism,* 402. NOW, of course, represented only one branch of the women's movement. For a discussion of the genesis of the women's liberation groups arising from the new left, see Freeman, *Politics of Women's Liberation,* 44–70, and Sara Evans, *Personal Politics: The Roots of Women's Liberation in the Civil Rights Movement and the New Left* (New York, 1979).

45. National Organization for Women, "Statement of Purpose (1966)," in *Up From the Pedestal: Selected Writings in the History of American Feminism,* ed. Aileen S. Kraditor (Chicago, 1968), 363–69.

26 ❦ The Paradox of Progress

William H. Chafe

Although historians have largely neglected the role of women in America's past, few groups in the population merit closer study as a barometer of how American society operates. Not only do women comprise a majority of the population, but gender—together with race and class—serves as one of the principal reference points around which American society is organized. The sociologist Peter Berger has observed that "identity is socially bestowed, socially sanctioned and socially transformed," and gender has been one of the enduring foundations on which social identity has rested. It has provided the basis for dividing up the labor of life ("breadwinning" versus "homemaking"), it has been central to the delineation of roles and authority in the family, and it has served as the source for two powerful cultural stereotypes—"masculine" and "feminine." Any change in the nature of male and female roles thus automatically affects the home, the economy, the school, and perhaps above all, the definition of who we are as human beings.[1]

When the nation entered the Depression decade of the 1930s, few people anticipated any major shift in the status of American women. Although the Nineteenth Amendment had enfranchised women in 1920, the ensuing years witnessed none of the revolutionary changes predicted by either proponents or detractors of the suffrage campaign. Many women who were eligible to vote did not register, and those women who did go to the polls generally cast their ballots for the same candidates as their husbands and fathers. The suffragists had optimist-

From *Paths to the Present,* James T. Patterson, ed. (Minneapolis: Burgess Publishing Co., 1975), pp. 8–24. Reprinted by permission.

ically assumed that women would think, act, and vote together as an independent "bloc," but that assumption underestimated the depth and pervasiveness of traditional ideas on woman's "place." Most Americans had grown up believing that within the family fathers and husbands exercised ultimate authority, particularly regarding issues of a "worldly" nature. Thus it seemed perfectly natural that women should follow the lead of men in political or other nondomestic affairs.[2]

Ratification of the suffrage amendment also failed to produce any significant change in the economic opportunities or activities of women. Although the absolute *number* of women in the labor force increased as the population grew, the *proportion* of women at work shifted very little and in 1940 was approximately the same (25 percent) as it had been in 1910. In addition, women made few inroads into the occupational area of greatest interest to feminists—business and the professions. Three out of four new career women in the 1920s and 1930s went into teaching or nursing (already defined as "women's work"), and the percentage of women in male-dominated professions such as law or medicine either remained constant or declined (as late as the 1940s most medical schools had a 5 percent quota on female admissions).[3]

Here too, the principal reason for the absence of change was the persistence of social norms which prescribed separate and segregated spheres of activities for men and women. Since women were expected to make marriage their career, few businessmen showed any interest in training them for management positions. "The highest profession a woman can engage in," one executive wrote, "is that of a charming wife and wise mother." For most people the idea of combining marriage *and* a career was too radical to consider, first because such a notion flew in the face of prevailing beliefs about a woman's primary responsibility, and second because it required a restructuring of the family, with men assuming some of the tasks of cooking, child-care, and homemaking. In light of such a situation, Margaret Mead observed, a woman with career ambitions had to make a choice between irreconcilable alternatives. She could either be "a woman and therefore less an achieving individual, or an achieving individual and therefore less a woman." If she chose the second alternative, she took the risk of losing any opportunity to be "a loved object, the kind of girl whom men will woo and boast of, toast and marry." It was not surprising, then, that most women traveled the prescribed path and decided not to pursue careers, or continue work after marriage.[4]

If anything, the experience of the Depression decade accentuated the difficulty of altering the status of women. Although the Depression encouraged innovations in politics and social welfare policy, it also seemed to have a chastening effect on cultural values, calling people back to the tried and true verities of family, hearth, and home. Nowhere was this better illustrated than in attitudes toward women. Labor, business, and government undertook a concerted campaign to discourage women from taking jobs, especially married women whose employment might deprive an able-bodied man of a job to support his family. At the same time, women's magazines celebrated the virtues of homemaking and lambasted those women who sought careers or employment. "No matter how successful," one article declared, "the office woman. . . . is a transplanted posey. . . . Just as a rose comes to its fullest beauty in its own appropriate soil, so does a home woman come to her fairest blooming when her roots are stuck deep in the daily and hourly affairs of her own most dearly beloved." Perhaps most important, the American people seemed to agree. When the pollster George Gallup asked whether wives should work if their husbands were employed, 82 percent said no, including more than 75 percent of the women.[5]

The eruption of World War II made the first significant dent in this pattern. The national emergency caused new industries to develop and new jobs to open up, providing an opportunity for women, like other excluded groups, to improve their economic position. Almost overnight, the woman munition worker became an accepted part of the labor force. In one California aircraft plant, 13,000 men and no women had been employed in the fall of 1941. A year later there were 13,000 women and 11,000 men. The same story was repeated throughout the nation. The New York Central Railroad doubled the number of its female employees, assigning them to grease and oil locomotives, load baggage, and work on section gangs. Elsewhere, women riveted gun emplacements, welded hatches, took the place of lumberjacks in downing huge redwoods, became precision toolmakers, and ran giant overhead cranes. Hardly a job existed which women did not perform.

The statistics of female employment suggest the dimensions of the change. Between 1941 and 1945 6.5 million women took jobs, increasing the size of the female labor force by 57 percent. At the end of 1940 approximately 25 percent of all women were gainfully employed; four years later the figure had soared to 36 percent—an increase greater than that of the previous forty years combined. Perhaps most important from a social point of view, the largest number of new workers were married and middle-aged. Prior to 1940 young and single women had made up the vast majority of the female labor force. During the war, in contrast, 75 percent of the new workers were married, and within four years the number of wives in the labor force had doubled. Although some of the new labor recruits were newlyweds who might have been expected to work in any event, the majority listed themselves as former housewives and many, including 60 percent of those hired by the War Department, had children of school and preschool age. By the time victory was achieved, it was just as likely that a wife over forty would be employed as a single woman under twenty-five. The urgency of defeating the Axis powers had swept away, temporarily at least, one of America's entrenched customs.[6]

If women took jobs in unprecedented numbers, however, there was little evidence of a parallel shift in attitudes toward equality between the sexes. Women were consistently excluded from top policy-making committees concerned with running the war, and from higher-level management and executive positions. In addition, the war had only a minimal effect on the traditional disparity between men's and women's wages. Although the War Manpower Commission announced a firm policy of equal pay for equal work, enforcement was spotty, and employers continued to pay women less than men simply by changing the description of the job from "heavy" to "light." As a result, a woman inspector in one plant earned 55 cents an hour while her male counterpart was paid $1.20.[7]

The issue of establishing day care centers provided the most revealing example of enduring attitudes. If women were to be equals with men in the labor market, they required some relief from the burden of sole responsibility for homemaking and child-rearing. Government reports showed a direct correlation between female absenteeism and the need to stay at home and care for youngsters, and newspapers were full of stories of children being exiled to neighborhood movie houses while their parents worked. Yet for many Americans, there was no more sacred obligation than that of a woman to rear her children on a full-time basis. "Now, as in peacetime," the Children's Bureau declared, "a mother's primary duty is to her home and children. This duty is one she cannot lay aside, no matter what the emergency." As a result of the profound value conflict over the issue, a federal day care program was at first postponed, then prevented from becoming fully effective.[8]

The staying power of traditional values received vigorous confirmation in the postwar years. Despite effusive expressions of gratitude for women's contribution to the war effort, many Americans believed that women should return to their rightful place in the home as soon as the war had ended. In one of the most popular treatises of the postwar years, Ferdinand Lundberg and Marynia Farnham argued that female employment was a feminist conspiracy to seduce women into betraying their biological destiny. The independent woman, they claimed, was a "contradiction in terms." Women were born to be soft, nurturant, and dependent on men; motherhood represented the true goal of female life. Sounding the same theme, Agnes Meyer wrote in the *Atlantic* that though women had many careers, "they have only one vocation—motherhood." The task of modern women, she concluded, was to "boldly announce that no job is more exacting, more necessary, or more rewarding than that of housewife and mother." Most Americans seemed to agree. A series of public opinion polls taken in the postwar years showed that a large majority of people continued to subscribe to the idea of a sharp division of labor between the sexes, with husbands making the "big" decisions and wives caring for the home.[9]

In fact, the situation was more complicated than either public opinion polls or magazine rhetoric seemed to indicate. It was one thing to focus renewed attention on traditional values, and quite another to eradicate the impact of four years of experience. As observers noted at the time, women had discovered something new about themselves in the course of the war, and many were unwilling to give up that discovery just because the war had ended. Although most of the women workers viewed their employment as temporary when the war began, a Women's Bureau survey disclosed that by war's end, 75 percent wished to remain in the labor force. "War jobs have uncovered unsuspected abilities in American women," one worker commented. "Why lose all these abilities because of a belief that 'a woman's place is in the home'? For some it is, for others not."[10]

The prospect of a job appealed particularly to those women over thirty-five. According to the 1940 Census, the average woman married at age twenty-one and sent her last child off to school when she was thirty-five. With the children out of the house most of the day, many middle-aged women were free to join, or remain in, the labor force. Economic interest in augmenting family income was matched by personal interest in pursuing new activities. Many women workers relished the recognition and sense of accomplishment associated with a job. Work in a factory or office might not seem that much more exciting or fulfilling than washing dishes or cleaning floors, but it had the advantage of providing social companionship, a tangible reward in the form of a paycheck, and contact with the "outside" world.

To a surprising extent, these women succeeded in their desire to remain in the job market. Although the number of women workers declined temporarily in the period immediately after the war, female employment figures showed a sharp upturn beginning in 1947, and by 1950 had once again reached wartime peaks. By 1960 the number of women workers was growing at a rate four times faster than that of men, and 40 percent of all women over sixteen were in the labor force compared to 25 percent in 1940. More important, the women who spearheaded the change were from the same groups that had first gone to work in the war. By 1970, 45 percent of the nation's wives were employed (compared to 11.5 percent in 1930 and 15 percent in 1940), and the 1970 figure included 51 percent of all mothers with children aged six to seventeen. In addition, the economic background of the women workers had shifted significantly. During the 1930s employment of married women had been limited almost exclusively to families with poverty level incomes. By 1970, in contrast, 60 percent of all families with an income of more than $10,000 had wives who worked. In short, the whole pattern of female employment had been reversed. Through legitimizing employment for the average wife and making it a matter of patriotic necessity, the war had initiated a dramatic alteration in the behavior of women and had permanently changed the day-to-day content of their lives.[11]

But if the "objective" conditions of female employment changed so much, why did attitudes toward equality not follow suit? Why, if so many wives and mothers were holding jobs, was there so little protest about continued low pay and discrimination? Why, above all, did the woman's movement not revive in the forties or fifties instead of developing only in the late sixties? Such questions have no easy answers, but to the extent that an explanation is possible, it has to do with the context of the times. The prospect for value changes in any period depends on the frame of reference of the participants, their awareness of the possibility or need for action, and the dominant influences at work in shaping the society. When the appropriate conditions are present, change can be explosive. When they are not present, change can take on the character of an underground fire—important in the long run but for the moment beneath the surface. The latter description fits the situation of women in the forties and fifties and a consideration of the context in which their employment increased during these years is crucial to an understanding of the relationship between behavior and attitudes.

To begin with, most women in the forties and fifties lacked the frame of reference from which to challenge prevailing attitudes on sex roles. Although many women worked, the assumptions about male and female spheres of responsibility were so deeply engrained that to question them amounted to heresy. If social values are to be changed, there must be a critical mass of protestors who can provide an alternative ideology and mobilize opposition toward traditional points of view. In the postwar period, that protest group did not exist. Feminists at the time simply had no popular support and were generally viewed as a group of cranky women who constituted a "lunatic fringe." The Women's Bureau probably represented the views of the majority of the population in 1945 when it described feminists as "a small but militant group of leisure class women [giving vent] to their resentment at not having been born men."[12]

In such a situation, it was not surprising that most women workers exhibited little feminist consciousness. Most had taken jobs because of the benefits associated with employment, not out of a desire to compete with men or prove their equality. When a pattern of discrimination is so pervasive that it is viewed as part of the rules of the game, few individuals will have the wherewithal to protest. It takes time and an appropriate set of social conditions before a basis for ideological protest can develop. With their experience in World War II, women had gone through the first stage of a monumental change. But it would be unrealistic to think that they could move immediately into a posture of feminist rebellion without a series of intervening stages. New perceptions had to evolve; new ideas had to gain currency. And both depended to some extent on the dominant influences at work in the immediate environment.

The second reason for the persistence of traditional attitudes was that women's employment expanded under conditions which emphasized women's role as "helpmates." The continued entry of women into the labor force was directly related to skyrocketing inflation and the pent-up desire of millions of families to achieve a higher living standard. In many instances, husbands and wives could not build new homes, buy new appliances, or purchase new cars on one income alone, and the impulse not to be left behind in the race for affluence offered a convenient rationale for women to remain in the labor force. Men who might oppose in theory the idea of married women holding jobs were willing to have their own wives go to work to help the family achieve its middle-class aspirations. But under such circumstances, the wife who held a job was playing a supportive role, not striking out on her own as an "independent" woman. The distinction was crucial. If women had been taking jobs because of a desire to prove their equality with men, their employment would probably have encountered bitter resistance. In contrast, the fact that they were thought to be only "helping out" made it possible for their efforts to receive social sanction as a fulfillment of their traditional family role.

To say that attitudes did not change, however, did not mean that behavior was without important long-range effects. Indeed, the growing employment of women offers an excellent example of the way in which changes in behavior can pave the way for subsequent changes in attitudes. As more and more wives joined the labor force after 1940, the sexual segregation of roles and responsibilities within the family gradually gave way to greater sharing. Sociological surveys showed that wherever wives held jobs, husbands performed more household tasks, especially in the areas of child care, cleaning, and shopping. In addition, power relationships between men and women underwent some change. Women who worked exercised considerably more influence on "major" economic decisions than wives who did not work. In no instance did the changes result in total equality, nor were they ideologically inspired; but sociologists unanimously concluded that women's employment played a key role in modifying the traditional distribution of tasks and authority within the family.[13]

Similarly, the presence of an employed mother exercised a substantial impact on the socialization patterns of children. Young boys and girls who were raised in households where both parents worked grew up with the expectation that women—as well as men—would play active roles in the outside world. A number of surveys of children in elementary and junior high school showed that daughters of working mothers planned to work themselves after marriage, and the same studies suggested that young girls were more likely to name their mother as the person they most admired if she worked than if she did not work. At the same time, it appeared that these daughters developed a revised idea of what it meant to be born female. On a series of personality tests, daughters of working mothers scored lower on scales of traditional femininity and agreed that both men and women should enjoy a variety of work, household, and recreational experiences. Thus if behavioral change did not itself produce a challenge to traditional attitudes, it set in motion a process which prepared a foundation for such a challenge.[14]

All that was required to complete the process was the development of an appropriate context, and in the early 1960s that context began to emerge. After eight years of consolidation and consensus in national politics during the Eisenhower administration, a new mood of criticism and reform started to surface in the nation. Sparked by the demands of black Americans for full equality, public leaders focused new attention on a whole variety of problems which had been festering for years. Poverty, racial injustice, and sex discrimination had a lengthy history in America, but awareness of them crystallized in a climate which emphasized the need for activism to eradicate the nation's ills. Once the process of protest had begun, it generated a momentum of its own, spreading to groups which previously had been quiescent.

Again, the experience of women dramatized the process of change. Just as World War II had served as a catalyst to behavioral change among women, the ferment of the sixties served as a catalyst to ideological change. The first major sign of the impending drive for women's liberation appeared with the publication in 1963 of Betty Friedan's best-selling *The Feminine Mystique.* Writing with eloquence and passion, Friedan traced the origins of women's oppression to a social system which persistently denied women the opportunity to develop their talents as individual human beings. "The core of the problem of women today," she wrote, "is not sexual but a problem of identity—a stunting or evasion of growth. . . ." Friedan pointed out that while men had abundant opportunities to test their mettle, women saw their entire lives circumscribed by the condition of their birth and were told repeatedly "that they could desire no greater destiny than to glory in their own femininity." If a woman had aspirations for a career, she was urged instead to find a full measure of satisfaction in the role of housewife and mother. Magazines insisted that there was no other route to happiness; consumer industries glorified her life as homemaker; and psychologists warned her that if she left her position in the home, the whole society would be endangered. The result was that she was imprisoned in a "comfortable concentration camp," prevented from discovering who she really *was* by a society which told her only what she *could be*. Although Friedan's assessment contained little that had not been said before by other feminists, her book spoke to millions of women in a fresh way, driving home the message that what had previously been perceived as only a personal problem was in fact a *woman* problem, shared by others and rooted in a set of social attitudes that required change if a better life was to be achieved.[15]

A second—and equally important—influence feeding the woman's movement came from the burgeoning drive for civil rights. Although it was true that blacks and women had strikingly different problems, they suffered from modes of oppression which in some ways were similar. For women as well as blacks, the denial of equality occurred through the assignment of separate and unequal roles. Both were taught to "keep their place," and were excluded from social and economic opportunities on the grounds that assertive behavior was deviant. The principal theme of the civil rights movement was the immorality of treating any human being as less equal than another on the basis of a physical characteristic, and that theme spoke as much to the condition of women as to that of blacks. In its tactics, its message, and its moral fervor, the civil rights movement provided inspiration and an organizational model for the activities of women.

Just as significant, the civil rights movement exposed many women to the direct experience of sex discrimination. Younger activists in particular found that they frequently were treated as servants whose chief function was to be sex partners for male leaders. ("The place of women in the movement," Stokely Carmichael said, "is prone.") Instead of having an equal voice in policy-making, women were relegated to tasks such as making coffee or sweeping floors. Faced with such discrimination, some female activists concluded that they had to free *themselves* before they could work effectively for the freedom of others. The same women became the principal leaders of the younger, more radical segment of women's liberation, taking the organizing skills and ideological fervor which they had learned in the fight for blacks and applying them to the struggle for women.[16]

Perhaps the most important precondition for the revival of feminism, however, was the amount of change which had already occurred in women's lives. As long as the overwhelming majority of women remained in the home, there was no frame of reference from which to question the status quo. Woman's "place" was a fact as well as an idea. With the changes which began in World War II, on the other hand, reality ceased to conform to attitudes. The march of events had already delivered a fatal blow to conventional ideas on woman's place, thereby creating a condition which made feminist arguments both timely and relevant. The experience of *some* change gave millions of women the perspective which allowed them to hear the feminists call for more change. Thus if the women who took jobs during the forties did not themselves mount an ideological assault on the status quo, they prepared a foundation which enabled the subsequent generation to take up the battle for a change in attitudes and ideas.

With the convergence of these forces, the drive for women's liberation surged to national prominence in the late sixties. Like all social movements, the quest for sex equality assumed a variety of political and ideological forms. The more moderate activists found an organizational shelter in the National Organization of Women (NOW), formed in 1966 by Betty Friedan to spearhead the drive for legal and economic reforms. The younger, more radical segment of the movement took root in female cadres of student organizations like SDS and SNCC. Beginning with "consciousness-raising" sessions in which women discussed the common problems they had encountered on the basis of their sex, these more radical activists quickly developed a loose coalition of small cell groups which advocated a revolutionary transformation of society based upon a change in the status of women. Whatever their particular ideological stance, however, all feminists were united in demanding an end to class treatment, to the idea that women—as women—should automatically be expected to take minutes at meetings, get lower pay than men, wash dishes, get up with the baby at night, or place their aspirations behind those of their husbands. Within months, the movement had become a national sensation, its advocates storming professional meetings to demand equal employment opportunities, boycotting the Miss America contest to protest the treatment of women as sex objects, and demonstrating before state legislatures for the repeal of abortion laws. By 1970 the movement was one of the media's biggest news items, rivaling student demonstrations, inflation, and the war in Vietnam for public attention.[17]

The image projected by the mass media told only part of the story, however. While network television and national news magazines focused on splashy demonstrations or the movement's attitude toward lesbianism, women in countless towns and cities were organizing in small groups to consider the reality of discrimination in their own lives and devise a strategy to combat it. Although they never comprised more than a small minority in any community, such women engaged in a remarkable variety of activities and made up in impact what they lacked in numbers. Some joined local NOW chapters and pressured merchants and employers to stop treating women differently from men. Others organized for political action, published children's books which eliminated invidious sexual stereotypes, started abortion and birth control clinics, or established day care centers. Some observers criticized the movement for its lack of focus and organization, but its alleged weaknesses were actually the source of its greatest strength. By not becoming attached to a single issue or piece of legislation, the movement avoided the danger of rising or falling with one victory or defeat. And by emphasizing decentralization and diversity, it gave maximum leeway to the energies and interests of the local women who constituted its lifeblood.

Almost inevitably, the women's movement provoked hostility and controversy. Particularly in its more radical manifestations, it represented an effort to alter the nature of the family, to change the way in which children were raised, and to overthrow conventional attitudes concerning who should hold which jobs. Furthermore, at its foundation the movement was calling for men and women to fashion a new definition of human identity—one which no longer would rely on cultural preconceptions of masculinity and femininity. In the context of such ideas, it was not surprising that a large number of people reacted to the movement with dismay and anger. Many men felt that their authority, their strength, their whole self-image had come under attack. And many women, who had devoted their lives to fulfilling the culturally sanctioned role of homemaker, believed that the movement was judging and indicting them as failures.

The astonishing thing was that in the face of powerful opposition, a considerable change in attitudes did take place. Although opinion surveys in the early seventies showed that many women continued to harbor antagonism toward the movement *per se* ("it's too extreme," "it goes overboard"), the same women in a majority of cases endorsed positive action on feminist issues such as day care centers, repeal of abortion laws, equal career opportunities for women, and a greater sharing of household tasks. Whatever the acceptability of the movement as a movement, its message and ideas seemed to be filtering through. Younger women in particular gave evidence of standing up for their rights. Many women students declared that they were just as committed to careers as men, and announced that they intended to incorporate marriage into their overall work pattern rather than make it the chief end of their existence.[18]

The ultimate test of the movement's impact, of course, was whether the attitudes it espoused had any effect on the behavior of women. Here, the evidence suggested at least some correlation between the campaign to change values and the way in which women conducted their lives. In a survey of women students at a large urban university, two sociologists found that behavior and attitudes toward premarital sex changed significantly in the years after 1965. Prior to that time, rates of premarital intercourse conformed to the pattern established in the 1920s, with engaged women having the highest frequency of premarital sex. After 1965, in contrast, a major increase occurred in the number of women having intercourse while in a "dating" or "going steady" relationship. The same survey showed a sharp drop in guilt feelings related to sexual experience as compared to a similar study done in 1958. Marriage statistics too showed a substantial shift during the 1960s. By 1971 more than half of all women 20 years of age were single in contrast to only one-third in 1960, and the number of unmarried women in the 20–24 age bracket had climbed from 28 percent in 1960 to 37 percent a decade later.[19] If the number of female applicants for graduate study was any indicator, it would seem that some of these single women were postponing marriage in order to pursue a career. Although such developments did not necessarily reflect the overt influence of women's liberation, there seemed to be a common thread uniting the feminists' call for increased autonomy among women, and the growing tendency of younger women to seek professional training and exhibit greater independence in their approach to sex and marriage.

The change in women's roles had perhaps its greatest potential impact in the field of population growth, or demography. Beginning in the 1920s the birth rate went into a gradual decline, reaching a nadir in the midst of the Depression. Although demographers at the time predicted a continued low birth rate, the end of World War II produced a massive upsurge of births which lasted through the late fifties. There then ensued another downturn which in 1967 resulted in a birth rate of 17.9 live births per 1000 persons compared to 27.2 a decade earlier. Some experts believed that the shifts were strictly a function of the economy, with affluence explaining the "Baby Boom" in the fifties. But prosperity had also been cited as a rationale for the *declining* birth rate of the twenties, thereby calling into question its validity as a primary determinant. Others attributed the "Baby Bust" of the sixties to the development of oral contraceptives. But this explanation too had shortcomings. The "pill" had not been available during the low birth period of the thirties, and the decline in birth rate during the sixties had begun three years before the pill was marketed.

A somewhat more persuasive explanation traced the changes in the birth rate to a combination of previous demographic trends and economic developments. According to this analysis, the "Baby Boom" started when young couples began to have families which they had deferred during the war, and continued as the generation born in the twenties and thirties came of age in the midst of an expanding job market. Due to affluence, it was easy for such people to marry early and contemplate large families. By the 1960s, in contrast, a crowded labor market, unsettled social conditions, and the expense of raising families put a damper on the birth rate. Demographers confidently predicted, however, that the "Baby Boom" of the fifties would have an echo effect in the late sixties and seventies, when the children born twenty years earlier began to reproduce. The only problem with this theory was that it failed to anticipate—or explain—the continued decline of the birth rate after 1970. Rather than rising, the birth rate reached an all-time low in 1972 and 1973, achieving the reproduction level required for Zero Population Growth.[20]

Perhaps the best approach to the trends of the sixties and seventies is to see the birth rate as a product of economic and social forces interacting with cultural values. Clearly, it would be a mistake to discount the impact of economic conditions. Concern about the ability to provide for children frequently enters into the decision to limit the size of a family, especially in a time of recession. Similarly, the accessibility of contraceptives provides the means for implementing a decision after it is made. But a crucial variable which demographers have underestimated is the influence of cultural values. Seen in this light, the declining birth rate of the sixties and seventies can be traced to the "multiplier effect" of changing values and economic conditions. During the sixties, women married later, delayed the birth of their first child, and bore their last child at an earlier age. Whether as cause or effect, this trend coincided with many women finding careers and interests outside of the home. The rewards of having a job and extra money tended to emphasize the advantages of a small family and the freedom to travel, entertain, or pursue individual interests. This pattern, in turn, was reinforced during the late sixties by the ideology of feminism and the ecology movement. Two Gallup polls in 1967 and 1971 sharply revealed this shift in values. The earlier survey showed that 34 percent of women in the prime child-bearing years anticipated having four or more children. By 1971, in contrast, the figure had dropped to 15 percent. In the absence of more persuasive explanations, it would appear that female employment and changing attitudes toward the role of women played major parts in confounding the predictions of population experts and producing the low birth rates of the early seventies.[21] The ramifications of these forces—if they continue—promise to have a profound effect not only on the size of the family but, more important, on the roles of men and women within the home.

In the end, of course, the historian's judgment on change depends on the vantage point which he or she adopts. From one point of view, it can be argued that little progress has been made toward sex equality. Great problems remain, particularly in cultural assumptions about woman's "place." Yet, on balance, the trends in employment, marriage patterns, attitudes toward sex and careers, and the birth rate suggest that the world of women has altered greatly since 1930. As the nation entered the mid-seventies, it seemed that for the first time in thirty years, behavior and attitudes were reinforcing each other; and the direction of events indicated that changes in the family, the economy, and women's definition of themselves would continue to be dominant themes in the social history of modern America.

NOTES

1. Peter Berger, "Social Roles: Society in Man," in Dennis H. Wrong and Harry L. Grace, eds. *Readings in Introductory Sociology* (New York, 1967). For a much more detailed discussion of the material covered in this section, see William H. Chafe, *The American Woman: Her Changing Social, Economic and Political Roles, 1920–1970* (New York, 1972).

2. Emily Newell Blair, "Are Women a Failure in Politics?" *Harpers* CLI (October 1925), pp. 513–22; Stuart H. Rice and Malcolm Willey, "American Women's Ineffective Use of the Vote," *Current History* XX (July 1924), pp. 641–47; Seymour M. Lipset, *Political Man* (New York, 1963), pp. 209–11, 217, 221–23.

3. Janet Hooks, "Women's Occupations Through Seven Decades," *Women's Bureau Bulletin* No. 232 (Washington, D.C., 1951), p. 34; Willystine Goodsell, "The Educational Opportunities of American Women, Theoretical and Actual," *Annals* of the American Academy of Political and Social Science CXLIII (May 1929); Florence Lowther and Helen Downes, "Women in Medicine," *Journal of the American Medical Association*, October 13, 1945.

4. *Independent Woman* VI (October 1922); Mabel Lee, "The Dilemma of the Educated Woman," *Atlantic Monthly* CXLVI (November 1930), pp. 590–95; Margaret Mead, "Sex and Achievement," *Forum* XCIV (November 1935), pp. 301–3.

5. Claire Wallas Callahan, "A Woman With Two Jobs," *Ladies Home Journal* XLVII (October 1930), p. 114; "America Speaks, The National Weekly Poll of Public Opinion," November 15, 1936.

6. Katherine Glover, *Women at Work in Wartime* (Washington, D.C., 1943); "Women in Steel," *Life*, August 9, 1943; Eva Lapin, *Mothers in Overalls* (New York, 1943); "Changes in Women's Employment During the War," *Women's Bureau Bulletin* No. 20 (Washington, 1944); International Labor Organization, *The War and Women's Employment* (Montreal, 1946). See also Chafe, *American Woman*, pp. 135–50.

7. Florence Cadman, "Womanpower 4 F," *Independent Woman* XXII (September 1943); Women's Advisory Committee Archives, National Archives, Boxes 133–135; International Labor Organization, *The War and Women's Employment*, p. 221; Women's Bureau memorandum, October 9, 1945, folder entitled "Equal Pay—General," Women's Bureau Archives, Federal Record Center, Suitland, Maryland.

8. Helen Baker, *Women in War Industries* (Princeton, 1942); "Women Drop Out," *Business Week*, August 21, 1943; "More Child Care," *Business Week*, August 26, 1944; G. T. Allen, "Eight Hour Orphans," *Saturday Evening Post*, October 10, 1942; Katherine Lemoof, "The Children's Bureau Program for the Care of Children of Working Mothers," in Women's Bureau Archives.

9. Ferdinand Lundberg and Marynia Farnham, *Modern Woman, The Lost Sex* (New York, 1947); Agnes Meyer, "Women Aren't Men," *Atlantic* CLXXXVI (August 1950); Hadley Cantril, *Public Opinion, 1935–1946* (Princeton, 1951), p. 1047, The *Fortune* Survey, *Fortune* XXXIV (August and September 1946).

10. "Women Workers in Ten Production Areas and Their Postwar Employment Plans," *Women's Bureau Bulletin* No. 209 (Washington, D.C., 1946), p. 5; "Give Back Their Jobs," *Woman's Home Companion* LXX (October 1943), pp. 5–7.

11. National Manpower Council, *Womanpower* (New York, 1955); Elizabeth Baker, *Technology and Women's Work* (New York, 1964), vii; National Manpower Council, *Work in the Lives of Married Women* (New York, 1957), pp. 17, 72; *New York Times*, October 10, 1970; Elizabeth Waldman, "Changes in the Labor Force Activity of Women," *Monthly Labor Review* XCIII (June 1970).

12. Women's Bureau Memorandum, August 22, 1945, Women's Bureau Archives.

13. Mildred Weil, "An Analysis of the Factors Influencing Married Women's Actual or Planned Work Participation," *American Sociological Review* XVI (January 1951), pp. 91–96; Lois Hoffman, "Parental Power Relations and the Division of Household Tasks," in F. Ivan Nye and Lois Wladis Hoffman, eds. *The Employed Mother in America* (Chicago, 1963), pp. 215–30; Robert Blood, "The Husband-Wife Relationship," in Nye and Hoffman, pp. 282–305; Robert Hamblin and Robert Blood, "The Effect of the Wife's Employment on the Family Power Structure," *Social Forces* XXXVI (May 1958), pp. 347–52; David Heer, "Dominance and the Working Wife," *Social Forces* XXXVI (May 1958), pp. 341–47.

14. Ruth E. Hartley, "Children's Concepts of Male and Female Roles," *Merrill-Palmer Quarterly* VI (January 1959–60), pp. 83–91; Selma M. Matthews, "The Effect of Mothers' Out-of-Home Employment Upon Children's Ideas and Atti-

tudes," *Journal of Applied Psychology* XVIII (February 1954), pp. 116–36; Elizabeth Douvan, "Employment and the Adolescent," in Nye and Hoffman, pp. 142–64; Lois Hoffman, "Effects on Children: Summary and Discussion," in Nye and Hoffman, pp. 196–202.

15. Betty Friedan, *The Feminine Mystique* (New York, 1963), especially pp. 11, 69, 271–98.

16. Susan Brownmiller, "Sisterhood Is Powerful," *New York Times Magazine,* March 15, 1970; Allan Matusow, "From Civil Rights to Black Power: The Case of SNCC, 1960–1966," in Barton Bernstein and Allan Matusow, eds. *Twentieth Century America* (New York, 1969); Richard Gillam, "White Racism in the Civil Rights Movement," *Yale Review* LXII (Summer 1973), pp. 520–43.

17. Susan Brownmiller, "Sisterhood Is Powerful"; "Women's Lib: The War on Sexism," *Newsweek,* March 23, 1970; Robin Morgan, ed. *Sisterhood Is Powerful* (New York, 1970); *Notes From the Second Year* (New York, 1970).

18. *The Gallup Opinion Index,* September 1970, Report No. 63; Louis Harris and Associates, "The 1972 Virginia Slims American Woman's Opinion Poll: A Survey of the Attitudes of Women on Their Roles in Politics and the Economy"; Amy Hogue, "Women at Duke: Their Attitudes and Aspirations," unpublished honors paper, 1973; Adeline Levine and Janice Crumrine, "Women and the Fear of Success: A Problem in Replication," paper presented at the American Sociological Association Meeting, August 1973; *New York Times,* March 24, 1972.

19. Robert K. Bell and Jay B. Clarke, "Pre-marital Sexual Experience Among Coeds, 1958 and 1968," *Journal of Marriage and the Family* XXXII (February 1970), pp. 81–84; *New York Times,* November 5, 1971; "Birth Dearth," *Christian Century,* November 24, 1971.

20. Paul Woodring, "There'll Be Fewer Little Noses," *Saturday Review,* March 18, 1967; "End of Baby Boom," *Science Digest,* September 1967; "Falling Birthrate," *Scientific American,* April 1968; "Z.P.G.," *Scientific American,* April 1971; Lawrence A. Mayer, "Why the U.S. Population Isn't Exploding," *Fortune,* April 1967; "Levelling Off," *Scientific American,* February 1973; "The Surprising Decline in the Birth Rate," *Business Week,* June 3, 1972; Herman Miller, *Rich Man Poor Man,* p. 236; Conrad Taueber, "Population Trends and Characteristics," in Sheldon and Moore, pp. 27–76.

21. *New York Times,* February 21, 1972.

27 ♀ The Liberation of Black Women

Pauli Murray

Black women, historically, have been doubly victimized by the twin immoralities of Jim Crow and Jane Crow. Jane Crow refers to the entire range of assumptions, attitudes, stereotypes, customs, and arrangements which have robbed women of a positive self-concept and prevented them from participating fully in society as equals with men. Traditionally, racism and sexism in the United States have shared some common origins, displayed similar manifestations, reinforced one another, and are so deeply intertwined in the country's institutions that the successful outcome of the struggle against racism will depend in large part upon the simultaneous elimination of all discrimination based upon sex. Black women, faced with these dual barriers, have often found that sex bias is more formidable than racial bias. If anyone should ask a Negro woman in America what has been her greatest achievement, her honest answer would be, "I survived!"

Negro women have endured their double burden with remarkable strength and fortitude. With dignity they have shared with black men a partnership as members of am embattled group excluded from the normal protections of the society and engaged in a struggle for survival during nearly four centuries of a barbarous slave trade, two centuries of chattel slavery, and a century or more of illusive citizenship. Throughout this struggle, into which has been poured most of the resources and much of the genius of successive generations of American Negroes, these women have often carried a disproportionate share of responsi-

From *Voice of the New Feminism,* Mary Lou Thompson, ed. (Boston: Beacon Press, 1970), pp. 88–102. Reprinted by permission of the author. Copyright © 1970 by Pauli Murray.

bility for the black family as they strove to keep its integrity intact against a host of indignities to which it has been subjected. Black women have not only stood shoulder to shoulder with black men in every phase of the struggle, but they have often continued to stand firmly when their men were destroyed by it. Few Blacks are unfamiliar with that heroic, if formidable, figure exhorting her children and grandchildren to overcome every obstacle and humiliation and to "Be somebody!"

In the battle for survival, Negro women developed a tradition of independence and self-reliance, characteristics which according to the late Dr. E. Franklin Frazier, Negro sociologist, have "provided generally a pattern of equalitarian relationship between men and women in America." The historical factors which have fostered the black women's feeling of independence have been the economic necessity to earn a living to help support their families—if indeed they were not the sole breadwinners—and the need for the black community to draw heavily upon the resources of all of its members in order to survive.

Yet these survival values have often been distorted, and the qualities of strength and independence observable in many Negro women have been stereotyped as "female dominance" attributed to the "matri-archal" character of the Negro family developed during slavery and its aftermath. The popular conception is that because society has emascu-lated the black male, he has been unable to assume his economic role as head of the household and the black woman's earning power has placed her in a dominant position. The black militant's cry for the retrieval of black manhood suggests an acceptance of this stereotype, an association of masculinity with male dominance and a tendency to treat the values of self-reliance and independence as purely masculine traits. Thus, while Blacks generally have recognized the fusion of white supremacy and male dominance (note the popular expressions "The Man" and "Mr. Charlie"), male spokesmen for Negro rights have sometimes pandered to sexism in their fight against racism. When nationally known civil rights leader James Farmer ran for Congress against Mrs. Shirley Chis-holm in 1968, his campaign literature stressed the need for a "strong male image" and a "man's voice" in Washington.

If idealized values of masculinity and femininity are used as criteria, it would be hard to say whether the experience of slavery subjected the black male to any greater loss of his manhood than the black female of her womanhood. The chasm between the slave woman and her white counterpart (whose own enslavement was masked by her position as a symbol of high virtue and an object of chivalry) was as impassable as the gulf between the male slave and his arrogant white master. If black males suffered from real and psychological castration, black females bore the burden of real or psychological rape. Both situations involved the negation of the individual's personal integrity and attacked the foundations of one's sense of personal worth.

The history of slavery suggests that black men and women shared a rough equality of hardship and degradation. While the black woman's position as sex object and breeder may have given her temporarily greater leverage in dealing with her white master than the black male enjoyed, in the long run it denied her a positive image of herself. On the other hand, the very nature of slavery foreclosed certain conditions experienced by white women. The black woman had few expectations of economic dependence upon the male or of derivative status through marriage. She emerged from slavery without the illusions of a specially protected position as a woman or the possibilities of a parasitic existence as a woman. As Dr. Frazier observed, "Neither economic necessity nor tradition has instilled in her the spirit of subordination to masculine authority. Emancipation only tended to confirm in many cases the spirit of self-sufficiency which slavery had taught."

Throughout the history of Black America, its women have been in the forefront of the struggle for human rights. A century ago Harriet Tubman and Sojourner Truth were titans of the Abolitionist movement. In the 1890's Ida B. Wells-Barnett carried on a one-woman crusade against lynching. Mary McLeod Bethune and Mary Church Terrell symbolize the stalwart woman leaders of the first half of the twentieth century. At the age of ninety, Mrs. Terrell successfully challenged segregation in public places in the nation's capital through a Supreme Court decision in 1953.

In contemporary times we have Rosa Parks setting off the mass struggle for civil rights in the South by refusing to move to the back of the bus in Montgomery in 1955; Daisy Bates guiding the Little Rock Nine through a series of school desegregation crises in 1957–59; Gloria Richardson facing down the National Guard in Cambridge, Maryland, in the early sixties; or Coretta Scott King picking up the fallen standard of her slain husband to continue the fight. Not only these and many other women whose names are well known have given this great human effort its peculiar vitality, but also women in many communities whose names will never be known have revealed the courage and strength of the black woman in America. They are the mothers who stood in schoolyards of the South with their children, many times alone. One cannot help asking: "Would the black struggle have come this far without the indomitable determination of its women?"

Now that some attention is finally given to the place of the Negro in American history, how much do we hear of the role of the Negro woman? Of the many books published on the Negro experience and the

Black Revolution in recent times, to date not one has concerned itself with the struggles of black women and their contributions to history. Of approximately 800 full-length articles published in the *Journal of Negro History* since its inception in 1916, only six have dealt directly with the Negro woman. Only two have considered Negro women as a group: Carter G. Woodson's "The Negro Washerwoman: A Vanishing Figure" (14 *JNH*, 1930) and Jessie W. Pankhurst's "The Role of the Black Mammy in the Plantation Household" (28 *JNH*, 1938).

This historical neglect continues into the present. A significant feature of the civil rights revolution of the 1950's and 1960's was its inclusiveness born of the broad participation of men, women, and children without regard to age and sex. As indicated, school children often led by their mothers in the 1950's won world-wide acclaim for their courage in desegregating the schools. A black child can have no finer heritage to give a sense of "somebodiness" than the knowledge of having personally been part of the great sweep of history. (An older generation, for example, takes pride in the use of the term "Negro," having been part of a seventy-five-year effort to dignify the term by capitalizing it. Now some black militants with a woeful lack of historical perspective have allied themselves symbolically with white racists by downgrading the term to lower case again.) Yet, despite the crucial role which Negro women have played in the struggle, in the great mass of magazine and newspaper print expended on the racial crisis, the aspirations of the black community have been articulated almost exclusively by black males. There has been very little public discussion of the problems, objectives, or concerns of black women.

Reading through much of the current literature on the Black Revolution, one is left with the impression that for all the rhetoric about self-determination, the main thrust of black militancy is a bid of black males to share power with white males in a continuing patriarchal society in which both black and white females are relegated to a secondary status. For example, *Ebony* magazine published a special issue on the Negro woman in 1966. Some of the articles attempted to delineate the contributions of Negro women as heroines in the civil rights battle in Dixie, in the building of the New South, in the arts and professions, and as intellectuals. The editors, however, felt it necessary to include a full-page editorial to counter the possible effect of the articles by women contributors. After paying tribute to the Negro woman's contributions in the past, the editorial reminded *Ebony*'s readers that "the past is behind us," that "the immediate goal of the Negro woman today should be the establishment of a strong family unit in which the father is the dominant person," and that the Negro woman would do well to follow the example of the Jewish mother "who pushed her husband to success, educated her male children first and engineered good marriages for her daughters." The editors also declared that the career woman "should be willing to postpone her aspirations until her children, too, are old enough to be on their own," and, as if the point had not been made clear enough, suggested that if "the woman should, by any chance, make more money than her husband, the marriage could be in real trouble."

While not as blatantly Victorian as *Ebony,* other writers on black militancy have shown only slightly less myopia. In *Black Power and Urban Crisis,* Dr. Nathan Wright, Chairman of the 1967 National Black Power Conference, made only three brief references to women: "the employment of female skills," "the beauty of black women," and housewives. His constant reference to Black Power was in terms of black males and black manhood. He appeared to be wholly unaware of the parallel struggles of women and youth for inclusion in decision-making, for when he dealt with the reallocation of power, he noted that "the churches and housewives of America" are the most readily influential groups which can aid in this process.

In *Black Rage,* psychiatrists Greer and Cobbs devote a chapter to achieving womanhood. While they sympathetically describe the traumatic experience of self-deprecation which a black woman undergoes in a society in which the dominant standard of beauty is "the blond, blue-eyed, white-skinned girl with regular features," and make a telling point about the burden of the stereotype that Negro women are available to white men, they do not get beyond a framework in which the Negro woman is seen as a sex object. Emphasizing her concern with "feminine narcissism" and the need to be "lovable" and "attractive," they conclude: "Under the sign of discouragement and rejection which governs so much of her physical operation, she is inclined to organize her personal ambitions in terms of her achievements serving to compensate for other losses and hurts." Nowhere do the authors suggest that Negro women, like women generally, might be motivated to achieve as *persons.* Implied throughout the discussion is the sexuality of Negro females.

The ultimate expression of this bias is the statement attributed to a black militant male leader: "The position of the black woman should be prone." Thus, there appears to be a distinctly conservative and backward-looking view in much of what black males write today about black women, and many black women have been led to believe that the restoration of the black male to his lost manhood must take precedence over the claims of black women to egalitarian status. Consequently, there has been a tendency to acquiesce without vigorous protest to policies which emphasize the "underemployment" of the black male in relation to the black female and which encourage the upgrading and education of black male youth while all but ignoring the educational and training needs of black female youth, although the highest rates of unemployment today are among black female teenagers. A parallel tendency to concentrate on career and training opportunities primarily for black males is evident in government and industry.

As this article goes to press, further confirmation of a patriarchal view on the part of organizations dominated by black males is found in the BLACK DECLARATION OF INDEPENDENCE published as a full-page advertisement in *The New York Times* on July 3, 1970. Signed by members of the National Committee of Black Churchmen and presuming to speak "By Order and on Behalf of Black People," this document ignores both the personhood and the contributions of black women to the cause of human rights. The drafters show a shocking insensitivity to the revitalized women's rights/women's liberation movement which is beginning to capture the front pages of national newspapers and the mass media. It evidences a parochialism which has hardly moved beyond the eighteenth century in its thinking about women. Not only does it paraphrase the 1776 Declaration about the equality of "all Men" with a noticeable lack of imagination, but it also declares itself "in the Name of our good People and our own Black Heroes." Then follows a list of black males prominent in the historical struggle for liberation. The names of Harriet Tubman, Sojourner Truth, Mary McLeod Bethune, or Daisy Bates, or any other black women are conspicuous by their absence. If black male leaders of the Christian faith—who concededly have suffered much through denigration of their personhood and who are committed to the equality of all in the eyes of God—are callous to the indivisibility of human rights, who is to remember?

In the larger society, of course, black and white women share the common burden of discrimination based upon sex. The parallels between racism and sexism have been distinctive features of American society, and the movements to eliminate these two evils have often been allied and sometimes had interchangeable leadership. The beginnings of a women's rights movement in this country is linked with the Abolitionist movement. In 1840, William Lloyd Garrison and Charles Remond, the latter a Negro, refused to be seated as delegates to the World Anti-Slavery Convention in London when they learned that women members of the American delegation had been excluded because of their sex and could sit only in the balcony and observe the proceedings. The seed of the Seneca Falls Convention of 1848, which marked the formal beginning of the women's rights struggle in the United States, was planted at that London conference. Frederick Douglass attended the Seneca Falls Convention and rigorously supported Elizabeth Cady Stanton's daring resolution on woman's suffrage. Except for a temporary defection during the controversy over adding "sex" to the Fifteenth Amendment, Douglass remained a staunch advocate of women's rights until his death in 1895. Sojourner Truth and other black women were also active in the movement for women's rights, as indicated earlier.

Despite the common interests of black and white women, however, the dichotomy of a racially segregated society which has become increasingly polarized has prevented them from cementing a natural alliance. Communication and the cooperation have been hesitant, limited, and formal. In the past Negro women have tended to identify discrimination against them as primarily racial and have accorded high priority to the struggle for Negro rights. They have had little time or energy for consideration of women's rights. And, until recent years, their egalitarian position in the struggle seemed to justify such preoccupation.

As the drive for black empowerment continues, however, black women are becoming increasingly aware of a new development which creates for them a dilemma of competing identities and priorities. On the one hand, as Dr. Jeanne Noble has observed, "establishing 'black manhood' became a prime goal of black revolution," and black women began to realize "that black men wanted to determine the policy and progress of black people without female participation in decisionmaking and leadership positions." On the other hand, a rising movement for women's liberation is challenging the concept of male dominance which the Black Revolution appears to have embraced. Confronted with the multiple barriers of poverty, race, and sex, the quandary of black women is how best to distribute their energies among these issues and what strategies to pursue which will minimize conflicting interests and objectives.

Cognizant of the similarities between paternalism and racial arrogance, black women are nevertheless handicapped by the continuing stereotype of the black "matriarchy" and the demand that black women now step back and push black men into positions of leadership. They are made to feel disloyal to racial interests if they insist upon women's rights. Moreover, to the extent that racial polarization often accompanies the thrust for Black Power, black women find it increasingly difficult to make common cause with white women. These developments raise several questions. Are black women gaining or losing in the drive toward human rights? As the movement for women's liberation becomes increasingly a force to be reckoned with, are black women to take a backward step and sacrifice their egalitarian tradition?

What are the alternatives to matriarchal dominance on the one hand or male supremacy on the other?

Much has been written in the past about the matriarchal character of Negro family life, the relatively favored position of Negro women, and the tensions and difficulties growing out of the assumptions that they are better educated and more able to obtain employment than Negro males. These assumptions require closer examination. It is true that according to reports of the Bureau of the Census, in March 1968 an estimated 278,000 nonwhite women had completed four or more years of college—86,000 more than male college graduates in the nonwhite population (Negro women constitute 93 per cent of all nonwhite women), and that in March 1966 the median years of school completed by Negro females (10.1) was slightly higher than that for Negro males (9.4). It should be borne in mind that this is not unique to the black community. In the white population as well, females exceed males in median years of school completed (12.2 to 12.0) and do not begin to lag behind males until the college years. The significant fact is that the percentage of both sexes in the Negro population eighteen years of age and over in 1966 who had completed four years of college was roughly equivalent (males: 2.2 per cent; females: 2.3 per cent). When graduate training is taken into account, the proportion of Negro males with five or more years of college training (3.3 per cent) moved ahead of the Negro females (3.2 per cent). Moreover, 1966 figures show that a larger proportion of Negro males (63 per cent) than Negro females (57 per cent) was enrolled in school and that this superiority continued into college enrollments (males: 5 per cent; females 4 per cent). These 1966 figures reflect a concerted effort to broaden educational opportunities for Negro males manifested in recruitment policies and scholarship programs made available primarily to Negro male students. Though later statistics are not now available, this trend appears to have accelerated each year.

The assumption that Negro women have more education than Negro men also overlooks the possibility that the greater number of college-trained Negro women may correspond to the larger number of Negro women in the population. Of enormous importance to a consideration of Negro family life and the relation between the sexes is the startling fact of the excess of females over males. The Bureau of the Census estimated that in July 1968 there were 688,000 more Negro females than Negro males. Although census officials attribute this disparity to errors in counting a "floating" Negro male population, this excess has appeared in steadily increasing numbers in every census since 1860, but has received little analysis beyond periodic comment. Over the past century the reported ratio of black males to black females has decreased. In 1966, there were less than 94 black males to every 100 females.

The numerical imbalance between the sexes in the black population is more dramatic than in any other group in the United States. Within the white population the excess of women shows up in the middle or later years. In the black population, however, the sex imbalance is present in every age group over fourteen and is greatest during the age when most marriages occur. In the twenty-five to forty-four age group, the percentage of males within the black population drops to 86.9 as compared to 96.9 for white males.

It is now generally known that females tend to be constitutionally stronger than males, that male babies are more fragile than female babies, that boys are harder to rear than girls, that the male death rate is slightly higher and life expectancy for males is shorter than that of females. Add to these general factors the special hardships to which the Negro minority is exposed—poverty, crowded living conditions, poor health, marginal jobs, and minimum protection against hazards of accident and illness—and it becomes apparent that there is much in the American environment that is particularly hostile to the survival of the black male. But even if we discount these factors and accept the theory that the sex ratio is the result of errors in census counting, it is difficult to avoid the conclusion that a large number of black males have so few stable ties that they are not included as functioning units of the society. In either case formidable pressures are created for black women.

The explosive social implications of an excess of more than half a million black girls and women over fourteen years of age are obvious in a society in which the mass media intensify notions of glamour and expectations of romantic love and marriage, while at the same time there are many barriers against interracial marriages. When such marriages do take place they are more likely to involve black males and white females, which tends to aggravate the issue. (No value judgment about interracial marriages is implied here. I am merely trying to describe a social dilemma.) The problem of an excess female population is a familiar one in countries which have experienced heavy male casualties during wars, but an excess female ethnic minority as an enclave within a larger population raises important social issues. To what extent are the tensions and conflicts traditionally associated with the matriarchal framework of Negro family life in reality due to this imbalance and the pressures it generates? Does this excess explain the active competition between Negro professional men and women seeking employment in markets which have limited or excluded Negroes? And does this competition intensify the stereotype of the matriarchal society and female dominance? What relationship is there between the high rate of illegitimacy among black women and the population figures we have described?

These figures suggest that the Negro woman's fate in the United States, while inextricably bound with that of the Negro male in one sense, transcends the issue of Negro rights. Equal opportunity for her must mean equal opportunity to compete for jobs and to find a mate in the total society. For as long as she is confined to an area in which she must compete fiercely for a mate, she will remain the object of sexual exploitation and the victim of all the social evils which such exploitation involves.

When we compare the position of the black woman to that of the white woman, we find that she remains single more often, bears more children, is in the labor market longer and in greater proportion, has less education, earns less, is widowed earlier, and carries a relatively heavier economic responsibility as family head than her white counterpart.

In 1966, black women represented one of every seven women workers, although Negroes generally constitute only 11 per cent of the total population in the United States. Of the 3,105,000 black women eighteen years of age and over who were in the labor force, however, nearly half (48.2 per cent) were either single, widowed, divorced, separated from their husbands, or their husbands were absent for other reasons, as compared with 31.8 per cent of white women in similar circumstances. Moreover, six of every ten black women were in household employment or other service jobs. Conversely, while 58.8 per cent of all women workers held white collar positions, only 23.2 per cent of black women held such jobs.

As working wives, black women contribute a higher proportion to family income than do white women. Among nonwhite wives in 1965, 58 per cent contributed to 20 per cent or more of the total family income, 43 per cent contributed 30 per cent or more and 27 per cent contributed 40 per cent or more. The comparable percentages for white wives were 56 per cent, 40 per cent, and 24 per cent respectively.

Black working mothers are more heavily represented in the labor force than white mothers. In March 1966, nonwhite working mothers with children under eighteen years of age represented 48 per cent of all nonwhite mothers with children this age as compared with 35 per cent of white working mothers. Nonwhite working mothers also represented four of every ten of all nonwhite mothers of children under six years of age. Of the 12,300,000 children under fourteen years of age in February 1965 whose mothers worked, only 2 per cent were provided group care in day-care centers. Adequate child care is an urgent need for working mothers generally, but it has particular significance for the high proportion of black working mothers of young children.

Black women also carry heavy responsibilities as family heads. In 1966, one-fourth of all black families were headed by a woman as compared with less than one-tenth of all white families. The economic disabilities of women generally are aggravated in the case of black women. Moreover, while all families headed by women are more vulnerable to poverty than husband—wife families, the black woman family head is doubly victimized. For example, the median wage or salary income of all women workers who were employed full time the year round in 1967 was only 58 per cent of that of all male workers, and the median earnings of white females was less than that of black males. The median wage of nonwhite women workers, however, was $3,268, or only 71 per cent of the median income of white women workers. In 1965, one-third of all families headed by women lived in poverty, but 62 per cent of the 1,132,000 nonwhite families with a female head were poor.

A significant factor in the low economic and social status of black women is their concentration at the bottom rung of the employment ladder. More than one-third of all nonwhite working women are employed as private household workers. The median wages of women private household workers who were employed full time the year round in 1968 was only $1,701. Furthermore, these workers are not covered by the Federal minimum wage and hours law and are generally excluded from state wage and hours laws, unemployment compensation, and workmen's compensation.

The black woman is triply handicapped. She is heavily represented in nonunion employment and thus has few of the benefits to be derived from labor organization or social legislation. She is further victimized by discrimination because of race and sex. Although she has made great strides in recent decades in closing the educational gap, she still suffers from inadequate education and training. In 1966, only 71.1 per cent of all Negro women had completed eight grades of elementary school compared to 88 per cent of all white women. Only one-third (33.2 per cent) of all Negro women had completed high school as compared with more than one-half of all white women (56.3). More than twice as many white women, proportionally, have completed college (7.2 per cent) as black women (3.2 per cent).

The notion of the favored economic position of the black female in relation to the black male is a myth. The 1966, median earnings of full-time year-round nonwhite female workers was only 65 per cent of that of nonwhite males. The unemployment rate for adult nonwhite women (6.6) was higher than for their male counterparts (4.9). Among nonwhite teenagers, the unemployment rate for girls was 31.1 as compared with 21.2 for boys.

In the face of their multiple disadvantages, it seems clear that black women can neither postpone nor subordinate the fight against sex discrimination to the Black Revolution. Many of them must expect to be self-supporting and perhaps to support others for a considerable period or for life. In these circumstances, while efforts to raise educational and employment levels for black males will ease some of the economic and social burdens now carried by many black women, for a large and apparently growing minority these burdens will continue. As a matter of sheer survival black women have no alternative but to insist upon equal opportunities without regard to sex in training, education, and employment. Given their heavy family responsibilities, the outlook for their children will be bleak indeed unless they are encouraged in every way to develop their potential skills and earning power.

Because black women have an equal stake in women's liberation and black liberation, they are key figures at the juncture of these two movements. White women feminists are their natural allies in both causes. Their own liberation is linked with the issues which are stirring women today: adequate income maintenance and the elimination of poverty, repeal or reform of abortion laws, a national system of child-care centers, extension of labor standards to workers now excluded, cash maternity benefits as part of a system of social insurance, and the removal of all sex barriers to educational and employment opportunities at all levels. Black women have a special stake in the revolt against the treatment of women primarily as sex objects, for their own history has left them with the scars of the most brutal and degrading aspects of sexual exploitation.

The middle-class Negro woman is strategically placed by virtue of her tradition of independence and her long experience in civil rights and can play a creative role in strengthening the alliance between the Black Revolution and Women's Liberation. Her advantages of training and her values make it possible for her to communicate with her white counterparts, interpret the deepest feelings within the black community, and cooperate with white women on the basis of mutual concerns as women. The possibility of productive interchange between black and white women is greatly facilitated by the absence of power relationships which separate black and white males as antagonists. By asserting a leadership role in the growing feminist movement, the black woman can help to keep it allied to the objectives of black liberation while simultaneously advancing the interests of all women.

The lesson of history that all human rights are indivisible and that the failure to adhere to this principle jeopardizes the rights of all is particularly applicable here. A built-in hazard of an aggressive ethnocentric movement which disregards the interests of other disadvantaged groups is that it will become parochial and ultimately self-defeating in the face of hostile reactions, dwindling allies, and mounting frustrations. As Dr. Caroline F. Ware has pointed out, perhaps the most essential instrument for combating the divisive effects of a black-only movement is the voice of black women insisting upon the unity of civil rights of women and Negroes as well as other minorities and excluded groups. Only a broad movement for human rights can prevent the Black Revolution from becoming isolated and can insure its ultimate success.

Beyond all the present conflict lies the important task of reconciliation of the races in America on the basis of genuine equality and human dignity. A powerful force in bringing about this result can be generated through the process of black and white women working together to achieve their common humanity.

ᕬSuggested Readings for Part IV

Bennett, Sheila K. and Elder, Glen, Jr. "Women's Work in the Family Economy: A Study of Depression Hardship." *Journal of Family History* 4 (1974): 153–72.

Bernard, Jesse. *Women, Wives and Mothers: Values and Opinions.* Chicago: Aldine Publishing Co., 1975.

Bird, Caroline. *The Invisible Scar.* New York: David McKay Co., 1966.

_____. *Born Female: The High Cost of Keeping Women Down.* New York: David McKay Co., 1968.

Blackwelder, Julia Kirk. "Women in the Work Force: Atlanta, New Orleans, and San Antonio, 1930–1940." *Journal of Urban History* 4 (1978): 331–58.

Blood, Robert O. "Long Range Causes and Consequences of the Employment of Married Women." *Journal of Marriage and the Family* 27 (1965): 43–47.

Bolin, Winifred D. Wandersee. *Women's Work and Family Values, 1920–1940.* Cambridge: Harvard University Press, 1980.

_____. "The Economics of Middle Income Family Life: Working Women During the Great Depression." *Journal of American History* 65 (1978): 60–74.

Chafe, William H. *The American Woman: Her Changing Social, Economic and Political Role.* New York: Oxford University Press, 1972.

_____. *Women and Equality: Changing Patterns in American Culture.* New York: Oxford University Press, 1977.

Clive, Alan. "Women Workers in World War II: The Case of Michigan." *Labor History* 20 (1979): 44–72.

Cowan, Ruth Schwartz. "From Virginia Dare to Virginia Slims." *Technology and Culture* 20 (1979): 51–63.

Degler, Carl. "Revolution Without Ideology: The Changing Place of Women in America." *Daedalus* 93 (1964); 653–670.

Evans, Sara. *Personal Politics: The Roots of Women's Liberation in the Civil Rights Movement and the New Left.* New York: Alfred A. Knopf, 1978.

Fass, Paula. *The Beautiful and the Damned: American Youth in the 1920s.* New York: Oxford University Press, 1977.

Filene, Peter Gabriel. *Him/Her/Self: Sex Roles in Modern America.* New York: Harcourt Brace Jovanovich, 1975.

Firestone, Shulamith. *The Dialectic of Sex.* New York: Bantam Books, 1970.

Freeman, Jo. *The Politics of Women's Liberation.* New York: David McKay Co., 1975.

Friedan, Betty. *The Feminine Mystique.* New York: W.W. Norton, 1963.

Goode, William J. *World Revolution and Family Patterns.* Glencoe, Ill.: The Free Press, 1963.

Gross, Edward. "Plus Ca Change...The Sexual Structure of Occupations Over Time." *Social Problems* 16 (1968): 198–208.

Hammer, Patricia. *Decade of Elusive Promise: Professional Women in the United States 1920–30.* Ann Arbor: University of Michigan Press, 1978.

Haskell, Molly. *From Reverence to Rape: The Treatment of Women in the Movies.* New York: Holt, Rinehart & Winston, 1973.

Hole, Judith and Levine, Ellen. *The Rebirth of Feminism.* New York: Quadrangle Books, 1971.

Hurt, Morton. *Sexual Behavior in the 1970s*. New York: Playboy Press, 1974.

Johnson, Dorothy E. "Organized Women as Lobbyists in the 1920s." *Capitol Studies* 1 (1972): 41–58.

Klaczynska, Barbara. "Why Women Work: A Comparison of Various Groups—Philadelphia, 1910–1930." *Labor History* 17 (1976): 73–87.

Lasch, Christopher. *The Culture of Narcissism; American Life in an Age of Diminishing Expectations*. New York: W.W. Norton, 1979.

_____. *Haven in a Heartless World: The Family Besieged*. New York: Basic Books, 1977.

Lemons, J. Stanley. *The Woman Citizen: Social Feminism in the 1920s*. Urbana: University of Illinois Press, 1973.

Lerner, Max. *America As A Civilization*. New York: Simon & Schuster, 1957.

Mandle, Joan. *Women and Social Change in America*. Princeton: Princeton Book Co., 1979.

Reiss, Ira. *The Social Context of Premarital Sexual Permissiveness*. New York: Holt, Rinehart & Winston, 1967.

_____. *Heterosexual Relationships: Inside and Outside Marriage*. Morristown, N.J.: General Learning Press, 1973.

Robinson, Paul A. *The Modernization of Sex: Havelock Ellis, Alfred Kinsey, William Masters, and Virginia Johnson*. New York: Harper & Row, 1976.

Rubin, Lillian Breslow. *Worlds of Pain: Life in the Working-Class Family*. New York: Basic Books, 1976.

Sherfy, Mary Jane. *The Nature and Evolution of Female Sexuality*. New York: Vintage Books, 1973.

Shorter, Edward. *The Making of the Modern Family*. New York: Basic Books, 1976.

Smigel, Edward O. and Seiden, Rita. "The Decline and Fall of the Double Standard." *Annals* 376 (1968): 7–17.

Smuts, Robert W. *Women and Work in America*. New York: Columbia University Press, 1959.

Steere, Geoffrey H. "Freudianism and Childrearing in the Twenties." *American Quarterly* 20 (1968): 759–65.

Stricker, Frank. "Cookbooks and Law Books: The Hidden History of Career Women in Twentieth Century America." *Journal of Social History* 10 (1976): 1–19.

Vanek, Joann. "Time Spent in Housework." *Scientific American* 231 (1974): 116–21.

Vinoskis, Maris A. "An Epidemic of Adolescent Pregnancy? Some Historical Considerations." *Journal of Family History* 6 (1981): 205–30.

Ware, Cellestine. *Woman Power: The Movement For Women's Liberation*. New York: Tower Publications, 1970.

Ware, Susan. *Beyond Suffrage: Women in the New Deal*. Cambridge: Harvard University Press, 1970.

Yellis, Kenneth A. "Prosperity's Child: Some Thoughts on the Flapper." *American Quarterly* 21 (1969): 44–64.

Zaretsky, Eli. *Capitalism, The Family and Personal Life*. New York: Harper & Row, 1976.

2 3 4 5 6 7 8 9 0